CHOICE REVIEW

The Dynamics of Aging

Other Titles of Interest

Aging from Birth to Death: Interdisciplinary Perspectives, edited by Matilda White Riley

Life Course: Integrative Theories and Exemplary Populations, edited by Kurt W. Back

Death and Decision, edited by Ernan McMullin

The Family in Post-Industrial America: Some Fundamental Perceptions for Public Policy Development, edited by David P. Snyder

Health for the Whole Person: The Complete Guide to Holistic Medicine, edited by Arthur C. Hastings, James Fadiman, and James S. Gordon

Medicaid Eligibility: Problems and Solutions, Marilyn P. Rymer, Conchita Gene Oksman, Lawrence N. Bailis, and David J. Ellwood

Health Goals and Health Indicators: Policy, Planning, and Evaluation, edited by Jack Elinson, Anne Mooney, and Athilia E. Siegmann

Systems of Health Care, Douglas R. Mackintosh

Assuring Quality Ambulatory Health Care: The Martin Luther King Jr. Health Center, edited by Donald Angehr Smith and Gitanjali Mukerjee

Impacts of Program Evaluation on Mental Health Care, edited by Emil J. Posavac

Valuing Life: Public Policy Dilemmas, edited by Steven E. Rhoads

About the Book and Authors

THE DYNAMICS OF AGING
Original Essays on the
Processes and Experiences of Growing Old

Forrest J. Berghorn, Donna E. Schafer, and Associates

As the proportion of elderly people in the population continues to increase, concern about the complex processes of aging has grown apace, in both social and personal terms. In these original essays by scholars and service professionals, a much-needed interdisciplinary approach to gerontology is taken. The authors probe such diverse phenomena as biological changes, mental capabilities, social expectations, public policy, and interactions between person and environment. They also address the pragmatic realities of service techniques and delivery systems for exercise, health care, transportation, and leisure programs, all of direct relevance to the elderly. A bibliography is provided in the companion volume, *Aging and the Aged: An Annotated Bibliography and Research Guide* (Linna Funk Place, Linda Parker, and Forrest J. Berghorn).

Forrest J. Berghorn is assistant director of the Gerontology Center and associate professor of American studies at the University of Kansas. **Donna E. Schafer** is the administrative assistant and a research associate in the Gerontology Center and currently a doctoral candidate in American studies at the University of Kansas. **The contributing authors** represent the disciplines of physiology, psychology and human development, anthropology, American studies, sociology, political science, geography, and social welfare.

The Dynamics of Aging

Original
Essays on the Processes
and Experiences
of Growing Old

Westview Press
Boulder, Colorado

Forrest J. Berghorn,
Donna E. Schafer,
and Associates

Copyright © 1981 by Westview Press, Inc.

Published in 1981 in the United States of America by
   Westview Press, Inc.
   5500 Central Avenue
   Boulder, Colorado 80301
   Frederick A. Praeger, Publisher

Library of Congress Cataloging in Publication Data
Berghorn, Forrest J.   1932–
   The dynamics of aging.
   Bibliography: p.
   Includes index.
   1. Gerontology – United States – Addresses, essays, lectures. 2. Aging – Addresses, essays, lectures. 3. Geriatrics – Addresses, essays, lectures. 4. Aged – Services for – United States. I. Schafer, Donna E., joint author. II. Title.
HQ1064.U5B374   305.2'6   80-36687
ISBN 0-89158-781-0
ISBN 0-89158-782-9 (pbk.)

Printed and bound in the United States of America

Contents

Figures and Tables

Tables

Preface

Americans, on the average, live longer today than they ever have before, and their life expectancy is continuing to rise. For this and other reasons, the process of aging and the experiences associated with the later years of life are becoming increasingly important subjects to young and old alike. This book is intended to provide the reader with a comprehensive exploration into the subject of aging. The chapters assembled here have been written specifically for this volume. The authors are either scholars representing a number of academic disciplines or service professionals whose work is concerned with meeting the everyday needs of older people. While the book draws upon the knowledge of different disciplines, it attempts to view the experience of aging as a consequence of interrelated processes.

Our overall objective has been to produce a general volume that is interesting and accessible to students and lay readers as well as useful to gerontologists. Since much of the content in the following chapters derives from research findings, the nonprofessional reader is likely to encounter some unfamiliar concepts and specialized terms. However, we have made every effort to explain such concepts clearly and to adequately define special terms. The selections in which programs for the elderly are examined provide descriptions of the work of service organizations and present the authors' observations concerning the major issues and problems of service delivery.

The book is composed of an introduction and seven parts. The introductory chapter presents an overview of important concepts and themes related to aging processes that are discussed in later essays. Part 1 examines physical and mental changes associated with growing old and the manner in which individuals come to terms with their mortality. Part 2 considers examples of programs that have been successful in providing for the physical and mental health needs of older Americans. Part 3 examines the social context in which Americans grow old. The subject of Part 4 is a network of governmental agencies, federal and local, that serve the elderly. Part 5 explores the personal relationships of older people and how such relationships affect the quality of life. The possibility of living creatively in the later years is examined in Part 6. Finally, Part 7 explores the relationship between the aging individual and the environment.

We would like to express our appreciation for the encouragement and valuable suggestions that many people gave us as the book was taking shape. In particular, we extend our special thanks to Patty Hodgins and Ben Zimmerman for their thoughtful reading of the manuscript. However, any deficiencies that remain in the conception and composition of this volume are, of course, the responsibility of the authors.

F.J.B. and D.E.S.

The Contributors

Forrest J. Berghorn is assistant director of the Gerontology Center and associate professor of American studies at the University of Kansas.

Donna E. Schafer is the administrative assistant and a research associate in the Gerontology Center at the University of Kansas.

Part 1

Mary Jane Moore is associate professor of anthropology at San Diego State University.

Wayne H. Osness is professor and chairman, Department of Health, Physical Education and Recreation, University of Kansas, and is president of the National Association for Physical Education and Sport.

Nancy Wadsworth Denney is associate professor of psychology at the University of Kansas.

Shirley L. Patterson is associate professor of social welfare at the University of Kansas.

Part 2

Lynn J. Young was recreation supervisor for the Johnson County Park and Recreation District, Kansas.

W. Kay Kent is administrator and health officer for the Lawrence–Douglas County Health Department, Lawrence, Kansas.

Virginia Schmitt is coordinator of services to older adults, Community Mental Health Center–South, Lee's Summit, Missouri.

Cynthia J. Arnold is a nurse clinician, services to older adults, Community Mental Health Center–South, Lee's Summit, Missouri.

Linda J. Redford is instructor in nursing at the University of Kansas Medical Center.

Part 3

Jill S. Quadagno is assistant professor of sociology and assistant director of the Gerontology Center at the University of Kansas.

David A. Hardcastle is professor and dean, School of Social Welfare, University of Kansas.

Allan J. Cigler is associate professor of political science at the University of Kansas.

Cheryl Swanson is assistant professor of political science at the University of Kansas.

Linna Funk Place is instructor of history at the University of Missouri–Kansas City and is a member of the Humanities Advisory Board, National Council on Aging.

Part 4

Jacob U. Gordon is associate professor and chairman, Department of African Studies, University of Kansas, and president of the Kansas Regional Chapter of the National Caucus/Center on the Black Aged.

Anita Renee Favors is executive director of the Wyandotte/Leavenworth Area Agency on Aging and serves on the Board of Directors of the Mid-America Congress on Aging.

George R. Peters is director of the Kansas State University Center for Aging, and is associate professor of sociology and social work at Kansas State University.

Calvin D. Broughton was executive director of the Planning Council on Services for Aging, Lawrence, Kansas.

Constance B. Wiseman is transportation manager for Independence, Inc., Lawrence, Kansas.

Marjorie Jantz is assistant director of the Johnson County–Greater Kansas City Retired Senior Volunteer Program.

Part 5

Walter H. Crockett is professor of psychology and speech communication and human relations at the University of Kansas.

Allan N. Press is associate professor of social welfare at the University of Kansas.

Geoffrey H. Steere is associate professor of American studies at the University of Kansas.

Dennis M. Dailey is associate professor of social welfare and is a certified sex therapist and educator, American Association of Sex Educators, Counselors and Therapists.

Part 6

Elbert C. Cole is executive director of The Shepherd's Center and executive director of the Mid-America Resource and Training Center on Aging, Kansas City, Missouri.

Beulah Duncan is senior scholar coordinator, Adult Life Resource Center, Division of Continuing Education, University of Kansas.

Mary Laning Neil is director of the Civic Health Foundation of Greater Kansas City, Missouri.

Edeen Martin is museum services and special projects coordinator for the Mid-America Arts Alliance, Kansas City, Missouri.

Part 7

Robert F. Wiseman is associate professor of geography at the University of Kansas and senior reseach analyst for the Department of Housing and Urban Development, Division of Policy Development and Research.

Charles F. Longino, Jr., is associate professor of sociology at the University of Miami.

David E. Campbell is assistant professor of psychology at the University of Kansas.

K. Anthony Edwards is assistant professor of human services at Northern Kentucky University.

1

An Interdisciplinary Perspective on Aging

Forrest J. Berghorn and Donna E. Schafer

The subject of aging is almost as inclusive as the subject of life itself. In this volume, aging is discussed in a broad range of contexts, including biological changes, social expectations, public policy, and interactions between the person and the environment. Even the term *aging* has several meanings, depending on who is using it and in what context. In one sense, it refers to physical developments over the entire life course. The "body grows and then declines in a trajectory which figuratively resembles a bell-shaped curve. The declining part of the curve is characterized by losses in bodily functions which cause a body to age."[1] In another sense, the term refers to the ways in which an individual's personality changes with age and how he or she lives through the later years of the life course. Moreover, the directions that a person's aging takes will be strongly influenced by the social, cultural, and environmental settings in which aging occurs. In short, *aging* as it is used here includes both the process of growing old and the experience of being old. Some people reading this are already sharing with their contemporaries the experience of late adulthood. For readers who are still young, old age may seem little more than a distant event, a vague premonition of their future. But in fact, all are steadily approaching it, and most will someday be counted among the elderly.

Young and old alike form expectations about the way older people will think and act that are based on general impressions about the effect of chronological age. However, the number of years since birth is only one of several ways of defining how "old" a person is and, therefore, these expectations are sometimes misleading. Consider for a moment the first thing you notice about any person you encounter for the first time. Aside from perceiving the person's sex and race, you are most likely to immediately form an impression of that person's age based on how he or she looks. We all have fairly fixed expectations about the way a person should look at a certain age, which suggests that there is a similarity in the biological changes that take place as people grow older. Still, our first impression of a person's age has been wrong on enough occasions to further suggest that there are important individual variations in the process of biological aging. Beyond this problem of inferring chronological age from someone's appearance, we may also be confused because some people who otherwise appear quite old are able to function better than some people who appear younger. So, we can see that there is more than one way of thinking about age, even in strictly biological terms.

If you spend a bit more time with this hypothetical person, you probably will soon form another impression; that is, what this person's thoughts and attitudes are and how he or she expresses them. Again, there are certain mental sets that we are inclined to associate with particular chronological ages. When these expectations are not met, we express our surprise, albeit to ourselves, with such phrases as "that kid seems mature for his age," or "she seems to be so young at heart." As is true for biological aging, people tend to share some changes in mental functioning as they grow older. In addition, contemporaries at any age will have shared, to some extent, in the experience of particular historical events that will predispose them to certain attitudes and ways of looking at the world. For example, the generation that grew up during the Great Depression will have formed somewhat different attitudes about money from the generation that grew up during the more affluent 1950s. At the same time, there is also a great deal of individual variation in attitudes and mental abilities, even among members of the same generation. Such variation is in part related to physiological processes and to social opportunities that allow one to develop and exercise his or her mental capacities, opportunities such as education and occupation.

There are, of course, many things you would learn fairly quickly about your new acquaintance. For example, it usually does not take Americans long to inquire: "What do you do?" So it would probably not take you long to learn the person's occupation, or that he or she is retired. You might also tell each other where you live, and perhaps what your neighborhood or apartment complex is like. And the more you talk with your acquaintance, the more his or her physical, or sexual, attractiveness may intrude on your consciousness. These are just a few examples of those characteristics that, taken together, define one's social age, as distinguished from one's chronological, functional, or mental age. Up to a certain age, young people are expected to be in school. Beyond that point and through the middle years, they are for the most part expected to be engaged in an occupation; men particularly are supposed to be "breadwinners" during these years. Later, it is anticipated that people will retire. These expectations, however, are not always confirmed, since one's social age is not necessarily synchronized with one's chronological age. There are, for instance, middle-aged people who are in school, and who are labelled "nontraditional" students. In the same sense, one person may still be working at age 75 while another is retired at 50. You would probably be surprised to learn that any of these nontraditional circumstances applied to your acquaintance.

Similarly, living arrangements to some extent conform to stages of the life cycle, and thus you would have some expectations about where your acquaintance lives. If she were a 65-year-old woman and said she lived in an apartment, you would probably assume that it was in a complex for senior citizens, not one for "swinging singles." In general, older people tend to reside in disproportionate numbers in the older sections of cities, in small towns, and in rural areas. Conversely, they are underrepresented in newer suburban areas. Of course, the type of housing any person lives in will depend in large measure on his or her economic status and social background. But the living arrangements of some older people are limited by their physical or mental capabilities.

The chances are that your acquaintance will not be sexually attractive to you unless his or her age is relatively close to your own. While it is not completely acceptable for a couple to vary widely in age, the age range considered "close enough" is greatest during the middle years. It is more acceptable if it is the man who is much older, although even in this case he runs the risk of being labelled a "dirty old man." There is a well-established relationship between age and expectations regarding sexual behavior in American society. Individuals of advanced age are generally assumed to be completely asexual, and many people are incredulous at behavior that violates this assumption. There is little doubt that one's choice of partner is strongly influenced by such age-related, social prescriptions.

If, after your hypothetical conversation, a third party should happen to ask how old your acquaintance is, you might have to take a few moments to gather your various impressions together before answering—for as we have seen, there are many dimensions of aging.

Thus far aging has been presented as a series of separate but related components. However, we must not overlook the fact that these components are in constant interaction and exist only in the context of individual lives. It is, after all, a *person* who ages, and no one is simply a biological or economic or intellectual being. No one reacts to others or to events in an exclusively political way, or in any other isolated fashion. While this idea may appear obvious, we tend to lose sight of it when thinking, writing, or talking about later life. Too often we oversimplify and make sweeping generalizations about the problems associated with old age. In casual conversation, maga-

zine and newspaper articles, books, and on television, we frequently encounter assertions such as: "The problem for old people is their fixed
income"; "The worst thing about old age is loneliness"; or "The major problem facing old people today is poor health." All these statements may be true
in part, or true for some people; but as definitive conclusions about late
adulthood, they are wholly inadequate.

There are a variety of reasons why people tend to oversimplify complex
problems such as those associated with growing old. Although a detailed examination of these reasons is beyond the scope of this chapter, one can see
intuitively that it is much easier to be satisfied with broad, though incom-
pletely founded, generalizations than to expend thought on more complex
explanations. But oversimplification occurs not just because it is the path of
least resistance. No one can possibly find meaning in the myriad events and
countless interactions that constitute the world we live in without classifying, generalizing, and simplifying to some extent. "Since the situations we
are in seldom repeat themselves exactly and since change seems to be the
rule of nature and of life, our perception is largely a matter of weighing prob-
abilities, of guessing, of hunches concerning the probable significance or
meaning of 'what is out there' and of what our reaction should be toward it,
in order to protect or preserve ourselves and our satisfactions."[2]

Thus, a person's perceptions and the generalizations built from them are
formed in encounters with the outside world. The collective perceptions of
many generations of people compose an important part of that world, the
part we call culture. Because each culture contains a particular, though
mutable, set of values, beliefs, and behavioral prescriptions, it in turn in-
clines the perceptions of its individual members in certain common directions. As Hallowell observes, "It is rapidly becoming a psychological com-
monplace that human beings groomed under different conditions may be
expected to vary in perceptual experience, functionally related to needs,
which, in turn, are in part defined by a culturally constituted order of reality."[3]

In literally countless ways, society reinforces our perception of what is
"normal." Some years ago, for instance, it was pointed out that virtually all
our primary school textbooks presented a picture of the "normal" American
family as a white, middle-class mother and father with two children, living
in a pleasant ranch-style home in the suburbs. By implication, then, children living in inner-city slum areas, many of whom had but one parent,
learned that they were "abnormal." The "normal" family having thus been
separated from the "abnormal" family, it was a short step to the faulty conclusion that people who lived in these "abnormal" circumstances had "abnormal" personalities. That is, they lived in slums because they liked living that
way and, indeed, they were not capable of living any other way.[4]

In terms of age, our society constantly reinforces the feeling that to be "normal" is to be youthful, vigorous, and productive. All one has to do is spend a few hours in front of a television set to feel the full impact of this emphasis on youth. Again, by implication, those who are no longer young are consigned to an "abnormal" status. And since old age is rarely portrayed as a normal part of the life cycle, it is not surprising that people avoid thinking about it as a natural part of their own lives. Consequently, it is easy for people to substitute stereotypes and simplistic generalizations for a more complex but accurate picture of old age.

One such generalization is that older people constitute a homogeneous group and experience later life more or less uniformly. In recent years there have been a number of studies, many based on interviews with older people, that refute this generalization. It is apparent that "old people have at their disposal differing amounts of money or other economic resources, have different feelings of self-worth, interact with friends and neighbors with varying degrees of frequency and closeness, belong to differing social classes, and live in diverse housing conditions."[5] Why then should this perception of uniformity be maintained in the face of so much evidence to the contrary? Obviously, it satisfies some underlying need; if one is convinced that the experience of old age is uniform, it follows that all older people have an equal opportunity to live successful lives. Failure to do so, then, can be blamed on personality deficiencies rather than on a system that harbors unequal conditions.

Having accepted the idea that all old people are pretty much alike, it is easy to attribute characteristics to old age that are markedly distinct from middle age. A reasonable extension of this attribution is that old age happens suddenly, like getting married. Again, recent studies have indicated that, while many changes do occur as people grow older, on the average they occur gradually rather than precipitously, at least until advanced old age. Although people must adjust to changing circumstances as the years go by, in many ways they remain "themselves." By and large, they maintain rather consistent goals and strategies for attaining them throughout their lives; they do not become senior citizens overnight. As Mandelbaum observes, the "great shock of the future, as it creeps up upon us in simple tomorrows, is likely to be how much it manages to resemble yesterday."[6]

The idea that one becomes old suddenly tends to reinforce the notion that chronological age is the significant determinant of behavior in later life. As we have seen, there are several ways of defining a person's age and, of these, chronology is perhaps the least important in determining individual behavior. Certainly, older people do share with each other their chronological age, along with some conditions that are clearly age-related. Still, if one were to select randomly a small group of, say, 70-year-olds, it might well be discovered that there are many differences among them despite their common chronological age.

There appear to be two contradictory sets of beliefs about the aging experience that are widely held in American society. Both sets represent overgeneralizations about this experience and, therefore, they both distort it. One set places undue emphasis on the negative aspects of aging and describes old age in pejorative terms. The other set romanticizes old age by emphasizing, and oversimplifying, its potentially desirable characteristics. Later, we will attempt to explain how it is possible for these contradictory views to exist side by side in the United States.

The pejorative characterization embodies ideas concerning the physical, social, and psychological conditions that are presumed to accompany old age. Much of what we hear, watch, and read, emphasizes the sick, socially isolated, abandoned, and thoroughly miserable condition of the elderly. Physically, old people are depicted disproportionately as shriveled, impotent, constipated, disabled, and disheveled. And these unattractive conditions of course stand in marked contrast to the glowing health, physical vitality, and strength of youth. With ironic force, Grandma, a character in Edward Albee's play *The American Dream*, instructs us about the physical qualities of old age: "My sacks are empty, the fluid in my eyeballs is all caked on the inside edges, my spine is made of sugar candy, I breathe ice; but you don't hear me complain. Nobody hears old people complain because people think that's all old people do. And that's because old people are gnarled and sagged and twisted into the shape of a complaint."[7]

Similarly, the mental functioning of older people is often denigrated, while we associate creativity, alertness, flexibility, and problem-solving ability with younger people. All too often the mental qualities of older people are stereotyped as rigid, forgetful, garrulous, and reactionary. It is a rare person in our society who has not heard the adage, "You can't teach an old dog new tricks." Another idea equates being old with being poor and alone. The purveyors of this idea frequently refer to old people as being abandoned, which implies a relationship between old age and helplessness. In other words, if the elderly are not supported by their families they will be unable to cope with life's demands. One often reads newspaper and magazine accounts of the aged living in dire poverty, unable to pay utility bills and reduced to eating dog food in order to survive. Some older people, of course, do live in extreme conditions similar to these.

However, before we accept this grim picture as being representative of old age in the United States, we should examine these ideas more closely. When it comes to the health of older people, the public image seems to be worse than the apparent reality. According to Harris, a comparatively small proportion of old people (21 percent) report that poor health is a very serious personal problem for them, while more than half of the general public (51 percent) thinks that it is a very serious problem for the elderly. Also, the public assumes that the level of health care for the elderly is a much more serious problem than do older people themselves.[8]

The widespread belief that old people as a group are poor, and that their poverty is more oppressive than it is for poor people who are younger, can also be questioned. There is no doubt that retirement reduces one's income substantially while inflation erodes it still further. For Harris's sample, the median household income of those under 65 was approximately $12,000, and of those 65 and older, about $4,800.[9] But these figures are deceptive. The elderly support fewer dependents and generally have fewer obligations and/or expectations. As a case in point, about 70 percent of people 65 and older own their own homes. Nevertheless, while only 15 percent of the elderly feel that inadequate funds is a very serious problem for them, 62 percent of the public assumes that it is a very serious problem.[10] The impact of poverty should not be underestimated, but it is inaccurate to assume that the older population as a whole can be viewed as miserably poor.

There is a wide gap, moreover, between the public's perceptions and the self-reported experience of older people in regard to loneliness. Sixty percent of the public believes that loneliness is a very serious problem for most of the aged. Of those 65 and older, only 12 percent said that loneliness was a very serious personal problem.[11] Apparently older people do not view their fate in any more adverse a light than younger people view theirs.

The perceptions of both young and old about the conditions of old age include a rather remarkable inconsistency. Young people may readily accept the proposition that most families are willing to abandon their elderly members, and yet insist that they would never do such a thing themselves. Even the elderly are susceptible to inconsistent thinking about old age. Harris finds that older people view the condition of their contemporaries in a more unfavorable light than they do their own. He notes that they apparently assume that life is really tough for most people over 65 and that their own experience is merely an exception to the rule. This inconsistency results in the striking finding that people 18 to 64 and people 65 and older are in essential agreement about the conditions of later life even though these views run counter to the self-reported experience of both age groups.[12] Such is the strength of the pejorative set of beliefs.

Certainly, advancing age brings with it the decline of some faculties. However, everyday observation and research findings indicate that many characteristics need not decline or, at least, do not decline uniformly among the aged population. Indeed, some faculties may be enhanced by the experience of growing old. Clearly, then, the pejorative view of old age is highly selective, the selection being influenced by cultural values that can override even personal experience. On the whole, Americans seem preoccupied with such attributes as independence, economic productivity, health, and physical strength. These qualities are more susceptible to decline in old age than less valued personal traits such as serenity, folk wisdom, and altruism. There-fore, growing old represents a threat to the value system inculcated in Amer-icans, and we tend to exaggerate those consequences of the aging process that undermine the qualities we learn to value most in early life.

> For younger people the [pejorative] view can only serve to make them fear the future, feel needless pity and guilt over the often exaggerated misery of the old, and to imagine unrealistically that youthful experience is a world apart from that experienced by older people. The [pejorative] view directs attention away from the abilities and contributions of the elderly and toward old people as a problem. Younger people may shun the old as harbingers of assumed unhap-piness to come, thus both avoiding potentially corrective experiences and avoiding also the pleasure and profit that comes from being with and learning from older people. Such are the prices Americans pay for their value orienta-tion.[13]

Considering the strength and pervasiveness of the pejorative view, it is surprising to find a competing view of old age that is prevalent in American society. But there is one, and this competitor distorts the experience of aging in an entirely different way—by romanticizing it. Gubrium calls it "the myth of the golden years" and suggests a number of its central ideas.[14] One of these is that the social environment of old people is stable and undemand-ing, and that the ideal relationship is that of the mutually enriching elderly couple. It follows, then, that older people who are in tune with their stage of life should have nothing about which to complain. If they do, their com-plaints can be attributed to their personalities rather than to their circum-stances. Many couples, of course, derive great satisfaction from their rela-tionships, finding in the other person a source of comfort and support. What the romantic view ignores, however, is the high incidence of widow-hood in the later years. A closely related idea is that aging represents a pro-cess of diminishing needs and desires. As mentioned previously, it is a com-mon belief that older people lose their sexual desires. In fact, it is widely believed that with advanced age one loses the need for most things that lend excitement to the earlier years. These romantic ideas about old age are anal-ogous to Mark Twain's characterization of heaven, wherein reside all man-ner of things we find terribly tedious in life and nothing that occupies our interest on earth.[15]

According to the romantic view, older people are highly altruistic, espe-cially in their relationships with the young. This is a convenient belief, for it suggests that older people are eager to do things for their children, such as caring for the grandchildren. Further, good health is viewed as an outcome of voluntarily remaining spry and living a healthy life. Again, the burden is placed on the older person to remain healthy during a time of life when health problems become more common. It is interesting to note that as a compliment the word *spry* is reserved for the elderly.

While the pejorative set of beliefs exaggerates the decline of those characteristics that are highly valued in American society, the romantic set exaggerates the importance to later life of characteristics that are tangential to America's value orientation. In other words, we reserve for the later years those attributes that are not significant qualities of American life in general. And, of course, the actual conditions of old age do not conform to romantic notions. Old age is no more static than other stages of the life cycle. To remain physically and socially functional, not to mention remaining satisfied with life, there are a great many common experiences and contingencies to which the older person must adapt. Successful adaptation may be difficult, however, because there are comparatively few socially prescribed roles, or ways of behaving, to guide the older person through his or her later years.[16] Far from being undemanding, the relative normlessness of old age forces the individual to more or less chart his or her own course. Considering its simplistic conclusions, one must wonder at the persistence of the romantic view of old age.

What is more, the ideas that make up the romantic view are polar to those constituting the pejorative view. This contradiction, however, is not without its utility. As Gubrium points out, "the myth [of the golden years] allows the devaluation of old age to occur without remorse."[17] This set of often trivial notions, then, serves as a rationale for conveniently ignoring the unfortunate conditions in which some older people are forced to live. As such, it provides a basis for dismissing old age rather than a basis for challenging Americans to demand and carry out remedial social action where it is needed.

There also exists in American society a perception of our history that influences our thinking about old age. We imagine a time when Americans lived harmoniously in extended-family households, each family providing for its members' well-being. Within such families, elderly members held a position of respect; they ministered to the needs of younger members and in return were sustained until the end of their lives. No abandoned elderly here. This view of our past, evocative of the sentimental magic captured in Currier and Ives prints, has been discounted by Goode as "the classical family of Western nostalgia."

> When we penetrate the confusing mists of recent history we find few examples of this "classical" family. Grandma's farm was not economically self-sufficient.

Few families stayed together as large aggregations of kinfolk. Most houses were small, not large. We now *see* more large old houses than small ones; they survived longer because they were likely to have been better constructed. The one-room cabins rotted away. True enough, divorce was rare, but we have no evidence that families were generally happy. Indeed, we find, as in so many other pictures of the glowing past, that in each past generation people write of a period *still* more remote, *their* grandparents' generation, when things really were much better.[18]

The consequence of viewing past family relations nostalgically is that we may tend to judge the present as being worse than it is because we imagine the past to have been better than it was.

Historical research has demonstrated that families of the past exhibited essentially the same structure they do today.[19] American households from colonial times to the present generally have been nuclear rather than extended. Young American families have always tended to establish their own separate households, although both present and past nuclear families have existed in the wider context of kin networks. What has changed over time is the dynamics of family interaction. This does not mean, however, that at one time family interactions were uniformly harmonious. For example, Greven provides us with a picture of a family life in eighteenth-century Massachusetts. At that time, fathers presided over the disposition of property and, at their pleasure, could pass it on to their sons either through "deeds of gift" or in their wills. At least early in the century, there appears to have been some reluctance on their part to transfer property during their lifetimes. It does not seem unreasonable to assume that Greven's data imply that fathers were unwilling to trust the well-being of their later years to filial devotion. Whether this is actually the case or not, Greven does suggest that later generations of sons were intent on seeking their independence.

> During the early decades of the century especially, the late marriages of men, the delays in the transferences of many estates from fathers to sons, and the frequent prolongation of paternal controls over lands conveyed to sons indicate the strength of paternal authority and the acceptance of filial dependence and obedience. The third generation, however, also proved to be distinctive insofar as many sons began to seek ways of limiting their fathers' control over their inheritances and found practical ways of establishing their independence, although not too often as young men.[20]

In the nineteenth century, Bridges points out, the family was often the focal point of conflicting values and social prescriptions resulting from the underlying pressures of industrialization. It faced the impossible task of accommodating the needs of fathers, who sought in the home a retreat from the demands of the marketplace, and of the children, who needed to be prepared by that same home to compete for positions in the marketplace.[21]

Only recently have historians turned their attention to the history of age relations, and therefore our understanding of the subject is far from complete. The histories of aging that do exist, particularly by Fischer and Achenbaum, have been evocative, and the broad outlines of age relations in America's past already have begun to take shape. At the same time, the social history of aging is a complex subject and historians disagree fundamentally about even these broad outlines, Fischer and Achenbaum being no exception. So, it is necessary to include conflicting interpretations as well as points of agreement in summarizing the historical perspective on aging in America. To begin, Achenbaum concurs with other historians that age relations, like so many other aspects of human experience, have been distorted by wishful thinking about the "good old days." "I agree that there never was a 'golden epoch' in the history of old age. The elderly once upon a time were *not* automatically granted positions of authority or invariable adoration in western civilization. The situation of aged men and women in early America, while different in some respects from other past (and present) preindustrial societies, was not exceptional in this regard."[22]

Fischer, too, takes the position that there was never a utopia for old people in American society, although he emphasizes the veneration of old age in colonial America. Puritans were instructed to treat their elders with deference and respect, but veneration meant more than this. In Puritan society, old age was seen as a gift from God, and longevity as a sign of virtue. "Veneration was an emotion of great austerity, closer to awe than affection. It had nothing to do with love. A man could be venerated without . . . even being liked very much."[23] Veneration was not simply preached, it was also practiced. It was reflected in the whole concept of "eldership." Older men were accorded positions of authority in church and state affairs, for it was generally argued that wisdom accompanied old age. They were also honored in their churches by being seated in pews close to the pulpit, which mirrored their position in society.

However, veneration had its darker side. For one thing, it tended to isolate the old person from younger people. "If open hostility between the generations was not allowed, affection was not encouraged either. Veneration, after all, is a cold emotion. The elderly often complained that they had lived to become strangers in their own society, aliens in their own time. And so they were, in a psychic sense—strangers in the hearts of their own posterity, aliens from the affection of their own kin."[24] Secondly, because veneration was integrally tied to authority, honor was generally for the well-to-do, and the elderly poor were often scorned. It should not come as a surprise to find that for old slaves life was not enviable. While some were treated with consideration, many were worked until their deaths, and others were even left to starve (if they could not be sold) once their laboring days were over.

By the nineteenth century, the veneration of old age was no longer a dominant social force, nor was the Puritan cosmology that spawned it. The prevailing orientation toward the elderly, according to Achenbaum, was at this time related to the general perception of social roles. While old age was not exalted above other ages, old people were assigned socially useful roles in accordance with their past experience and their present capability. Since relatively few people lived to a ripe old age, those who did were thought to be exemplars of correct living and moral virtue. As such, the elderly were accepted as role models and "trustworthy counselors on moral matters."[25] Not limited to these more passive roles, they also were expected to continue performing useful tasks as long as they were able to do so. This may have meant continuing in lifelong occupations or it may have meant carrying out domestic duties. No system of retirement yet existed, and the elderly were expected to work along with other members of society.

Although it was accompanied by positive perceptions and useful roles, old age in early America was not necessarily a pleasant stage of life. The medical arts were primitive compared to our own time and little could be done to alleviate the physical suffering that accompanied advanced age. "To be old in early America was to be wracked by illness. It was to live in physical misery, with pain as a constant companion. A protracted life, wrote one clergyman, 'is not so properly called living, as dying a lingering death.'"[26] To make matters worse, since they were models of virtuous living, the elderly were expected to bear their physical burdens stoically, without complaint or self-pity.

Both authors agree that a dramatic change in age relations occurred over time in American society. However, they disagree about the underlying sources of that change and when specifically it occurred. In part, at least, the reasons for their disagreements are: the subject with which they are both dealing is indeed complicated; to some extent they are looking at different evidence; and they are examining this evidence on the basis of somewhat different models of social change. A major division of evidence that applies to the work of both is a distinction between (1) changes in the perceptions of old age and old people and (2) changes in social roles and in the cultural conditions in which the elderly lived.

Using such evidence as seating arrangements in meeting houses, words used to describe the elderly, clothing styles, and inheritance patterns, Fischer concludes that the perceptions of old age and the elderly changed radically at the end of the eighteenth and beginning of the nineteenth century. For example, privileged seating in meeting houses came to be based on criteria other than age, clothing styles increasingly flattered the young not the old, and derogatory words in reference to the elderly were introduced into the vocabulary. This change, signaling an end to veneration and casting the elderly in a new and negative light, was brought about by the revolutionary spirit of the times, which introduced the ideas of equality and liberty into Western culture. Thus, age relations were revolutionized along with the wider social order.[27]

On the other hand, Achenbaum, emphasizing labor force participation and other social roles, finds no revolutionary periods in the history of age relations. Instead he traces a series of more or less evolutionary developments associated with the more fundamental processes of industrialization, urbanization, and bureaucratization. As America shifted from an agrarian to an industrial and urban society, the basis of the older person's authority, vested in land ownership, was eroded. Further, entrepreneurial and bureaucratic economic organization stressed efficiency and productivity in the labor force, which placed older people at a disadvantage. While early generations had perceptually separated the later years from the rest of the life cycle, it was only with the modernizing processes of the latter half of the nineteenth century that derogatory attitudes toward the elderly became dominant. At the same time, the actual conditions under which old people lived did not change in a way that was distinct from other age groups during this period.[28]

Ameliorative action during the early decades of the twentieth century, both authors agree, effectively differentiated the condition of old people from younger members of society. Pension plans, Social Security, and the retirement system as we know it all emerged in those early years. Although many elderly people remained self-sufficient, the general effect of this ameliorative activity was to create a subgroup of older, nonworking Americans who were, by and large, dependent on the federal government primarily and, to a lesser extent, on private organizations and family for their support. However, it did nothing to enhance the decidedly negative perceptions of the aged at the time. It has only been in recent years that a corrective portrait of old age has begun to emerge, with the help of organizations such as the Gerontological Society, retirement associations, and political action groups such as the Gray Panthers.

Such are the broad outlines of the history of America's age relations. Before leaving the subject it should be noted that the dependent condition of the elderly that has developed in the twentieth century is largely an economic dependency; and the same social policies that have made them economically dependent have in a sense liberated them. No longer is it necessary for the older person to continue laboring until he or she is physically incapacitated. At least for those who are reasonably healthy and have an adequate income, retirement makes possible the pursuit of alternative lifestyles in the later years.

So we might ask, is life for the elderly today better or worse than it was in the past? Again, we can see that the answer to such a sweeping question is not a simple one. We must be more specific about the period in the past and the aspects of life to which we are referring. In colonial America, old people were treated with respect, or more exactly with awe, but they also suffered terribly from the infirmities that often accompanied advanced age. In the early republic, they were able to fulfill meaningful social roles, particularly in regard to work, but then they had no choice but to continue working throughout their lives. The end of the nineteenth and beginning of the twentieth centuries appears to have been a period in which working and living conditions for older people were at their lowest ebb. This was a time when the consequences of industrialism weighed most heavily on working people in general and also exacerbated negative attitudes toward old age. But on the other hand, advances in health care and early stirrings of social reform are likely to have brought some relief to those who were ill and/or disabled. Today, many older people are dependent on the state for their survival and, for all elderly, there are few clearly defined social roles. Yet, while the pejorative myth of old age is still widespread, social attitudes toward old people are improving. And the advent of the retirement system has meant that many Americans are now free to pursue rewarding leisure-time activities throughout their later years.

An integral part of this discussion on the history of age relations is the type of evidence on which generalizations are based and the models of social change that help organize that evidence. In any research endeavor, the meaning that is extracted from data is not necessarily self-evident, but depends on the investigator's system of values, concepts, and procedures. The procedures, or methods, employed in an investigation establish the "ground rules" on which the data are interpreted and conclusions drawn. To illustrate, consider a soccer match with its set of rules that define the limits of the field of play, the type of activities in which each player can engage, and the ultimate purpose of these activities. If you remove a player from the context defined by the rules and accepted procedures of the game, his activities lose their meaning. What was once understandable behavior is now little more than a man kicking a ball. Indeed, for a novice spectator who is not familiar with the complex structure of the game, this is how it appears. Similarly, activities of scholars will appear mystifying unless the observer has some notion of the "rules" governing a given investigation.

Aging can be studied through a variety of research methods. However, the studies reported in the chapters of this book characteristically employ one of three procedures: interview surveys, experiments, or cohort designs. These procedures represent particular ways of collecting and organizing data, and much of the available information on aging is dependent on them. Therefore, it should be helpful to consider each procedure briefly at this point.

One way to find out about the experience of aging is to ask people who are going through it what it is like. The interview survey has done much, for example, to dispel the many misconceptions about aging that have existed in our society. There are a number of essential elements in the design of this research technique, but only a few of the more important ones can be considered here. First of all, one must determine who will be interviewed from among the entire population of people in which one is interested. For example, if you are interested in the characteristics of older people residing in a particular city, it would not be possible to interview every member of that population. There are several schemes for selecting a sample of such people, but they are all based on one general principle—randomness. The random, or probability, sample always meets two basic requirements: (1) the researcher must be able to identify all members of the population to be sampled; and (2) he or she must ensure that each member of the population has an equal chance of being selected for the sample. Some information will often be available about certain fundamental characteristics of the population, such as sex ratio, racial composition, and age distribution. By comparing the sample with the population from which it was drawn in terms of these characteristics, the researcher will be able to further assess the sample's representativeness.

A common set of questions, asked exactly the same way insofar as possible, should be used for each interview. This will ensure that the information gathered will be consistent and comparable. Therefore, it is necessary to design an interview schedule, or questionnaire, for the interviewer to follow. Essentially two types of questions with some variation may be contained in the schedule. The focused question includes a predetermined set of alternative responses. The advantage of this type of question is that the researcher retains a high degree of control over the information that will result from the interview. A second type of question is nondirective, or openended. The response to such a question is not predetermined and, as a result, the researcher may gain unanticipated insight into the subject he or she is investigating. The problem with nondirective questions is that a portion of any given response may be irrelevant to the researcher's purposes.[29]

Research based on interviews frequently makes use of scales or indices constructed from responses to combinations of focused questions. Presumably each question included in the scale is an indication of some dimension of the phenomenon that the entire scale measures. For example, Palmore and Kivett measured the "organizational activity" of older adults by combining several questions such as the number of religious services, the number of club meetings, and the number of union meetings they attended.[30] Combining questions in this way exacerbates the problem of validity, which is implicit in individual questions as well. That is, do responses to a question on a scale actually measure what the researcher is intending to measure? Closely associated with this problem is that of reliability. If a question or scale is reliable, responses to it will remain consistent over time, assuming that the phenomenon being measured should theoretically remain unchanged throughout that time period.[31]

The principal advantage of the interview survey is that the researcher is able to study the attitudes and behavior of people in a natural setting. At the same time, it is extremely difficult to account for the multitude of extraneous factors that are present in such a setting and that may influence the outcome of the investigation in unknown ways. In short, the investigator gains environmental validity but sacrifices a degree of control. Experimental research designs allow a researcher to exclude nonessential factors by one of two techniques. "They may be eliminated through control of the environment (as in the laboratory), or they may be neutralized through random assignment of research participants to independent variable conditions."[32] The only differences, then, between different experimental conditions are those created by the manipulation of the independent variables.

Experimental designs can become extremely complicated, but this discussion will be restricted to a relatively simple illustration. In a classical experiment, "one observes the relationship between two variables by deliberately producing a change in one (the independent variable) and looking to see whether this alteration produces a change in the other (the dependent variable)."[33] In conducting such experiments, subjects are randomly assigned to one of two groups (a control group or an experimental group). Subjects in the experimental group receive some specific treatment by the experimenter, while those in the control group do not. The two groups are then measured in terms of the dependent variable. If the measurements vary significantly, then the difference may be attributed to the effect of the experimental treatment, or independent variable. In the following example, the researchers add a pretest to the study design.

> An actual example of a classical experiment can be seen in a research study conducted by Edsel Erickson et al. (1969). The experiment involved "disadvantaged" young children from the inner city. Part of the research consisted of an experiment in adding special verbal-skill training to a regular kindergarten situation. The experiment focused on any changes in measured intelligence that might occur during the kindergarten experience. Some children were assigned to a regular kindergarten and some were assigned to kindergartens in which special verbal skills were taught. In other words, the teaching of verbal skills was the experimental or independent variable. Measured intelligence,

determined at the pretest and post-test by use of the Stanford Binet intelligence test, was the dependent variable. The experimental group consisted of all the children who were given special verbal skills training, and the control group were those children who received no special training.[34]

A variation of this classical design is what is called the "natural experiment." It is not considered a true experiment because of the lack of random assignment. In this case, no special treatment is administered by the experimenter; rather, a change under consideration is allowed to occur naturally. For instance, suppose you are interested in whether a specific television program has a positive effect on the self-image of older people. In a classical experiment, you would ask two groups of older people to view several hours of television programming, and include the specific program only in the hours of television viewed by the experimental group. In the natural experiment, you would have to search out a group of older people who watched television, but not the specific program, and another comparable group that watched approximately the same amount of television including that program. In both cases you would then measure the self-esteem of each group. While the difference between the two approaches may seem slight, it is actually quite important. "Variables which can be made to produce large effects in the laboratory are sometimes relatively unimportant in nature because their effects are swamped by variables which were controlled in the laboratory setting. Conversely, variables which cannot be made to produce large effects in the laboratory are sometimes of considerable importance in nature."[35] If the results of an experiment are to be considered representative of a larger population, then the rules of sampling discussed in connection with the interview survey must be applied to the experimental design.

The two methods of collecting and organizing data that have just been discussed can form the basis of another analytic procedure, cohort analysis. The term *cohort* has several meanings. It originally denoted a division within the Roman legion. In recent times it has acquired a more general meaning: in common usage it refers to a group of companions or comrades. It also has a more specialized meaning. For researchers it refers to "those people within a geographically or otherwise delineated population who experienced the same significant life event within a given period of time."[36] For those interested in studying human development over the life course, a cohort is determined by the date of birth. That is, individuals born in the same month, or year, or decade, for examples, could be considered members of a cohort. The concept of cohorts has been employed primarily by developmental psychologists and political scientists and increasingly by gerontologists. Two requirements for any cohort analysis are longitudinal data (i.e., data collected on more than one occasion) and an age distribution within that data.

To illustrate the purpose of cohort analysis, let us look at the activity levels of a sample of elderly urban residents.[37] Figure 1.1 is constructed on the basis of cross-sectional data; that is, it records the levels of activity for a group of people 61 to 81-plus years of age, measured at one point in time (1973). It can be seen that activity levels increase until age 65, then decline until age 70, and increase again until approximately age 75, at which point they decline steadily. Three underlying explanations for this rather interesting configuration are possible. It could be associated with the aging process; it could be associated with differences in the historical experiences of people at different ages; or, of course, it could be a combination of the two. Could one expect to find a similar decline in activity among presently younger individuals as they reach age 66 (aging effects), or will members of the cohort aged 66 to 71 continue as they grow older to reflect similarly low levels of activity (cohort effects)?

One can think of reasons for accepting the former explanation. Most people have retired by age 66, with a corresponding decline in activities related to their previous occupation; and, after age 75, people's activities may be limited somewhat by physical disabilities that are common at an advanced age. On the other hand, it is also possible that the relatively low levels of activity between 68 and 72 represent a cohort effect. That is, people in this cohort, who were born between 1897 and 1901, were likely to have been engaged in work and rearing children through the worst years of the Great Depression. Given the particular demands on young families at this time of economic stress, it would be exceedingly difficult for most people to engage in additional activities. This shared historical experience may have influenced the activity patterns of the cohort's members for the rest of their lives. Which of these explanations is more compelling? Using only the cross-

Figure 1.1: Levels of Activity for a Group of
People Sixty-one to Eighty-one Plus
Years Old in 1973.

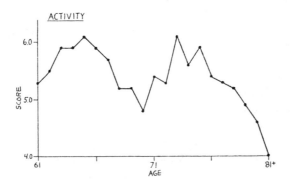

sectional data in Figure 1.1, it is impossible to tell.

To decide which explanation is correct, one would need to add longitudinal data to the analysis. This could be done by measuring the activity levels of this same sample at another point (or points) in time. If, for instance, the sample had been tested again in 1978, each individual would have grown 5 years older. Correspondingly, each cohort would have advanced 5 years in age, as shown in Table 1.1. With this expanded data base, a researcher could begin to answer the questions posed above. For example, one could determine the degree to which the cohort exhibiting relatively low levels of activity in 1973 continued to do so in 1978 (cohort effects), or the extent to which members of that cohort increased their activity levels as they grew 5 years older (aging effects). To undertake a cohort analysis, one need not retest the same individuals that were tested initially. It is acceptable to test different individuals at subsequent times as long as they are randomly selected from the subpopulations constituting the various cohorts.

The methodological issue of the relative importance of cohort effects as opposed to aging effects has philosophical implications for the field of gerontology. In essence, it is the reflection of a larger question: Is human development in later life primarily a matter of continuity with one's earlier years (cohort effects), or is it better explained as a process through which individuals, because of aging effects, acquire a status unique to elderly people? Indeed, the interplay between those forces that tend to sustain continuity throughout life and those forces leading toward a special status in later life is an underlying theme running through the chapters of this book.

Each individual develops certain distinctive personality characteristics during his or her earlier years that to some extent determine how he or she will respond to the events of later life.[38] Consequently, researchers find considerable variation among older people, even within the same cohort. At the same time, they find patterns of behavior that are related to specific periods in the life cycle. Many changes that affect the functioning and well-being of the individual are more characteristic of one time of life than of other times. As just a few examples: adjusting to parenthood is a principal concern during young adulthood; a person is more likely to be widowed in old age; and,

Table 1.1: Age Groupings for Four Cohorts at Two Times of Measurement

Time of Testing	AGE GROUP				
	61-66	67-72	73-78	79-84	85-90
1973	Cohort 1	Cohort 2	Cohort 3	Cohort 4	-
1978	-	Cohort 1	Cohort 2	Cohort 3	Cohort 4

of course, adjustment to retirement is associated with the seventh decade of life. Thus, most people will experience significant life changes at approximately the same age. Some people are lucky enough to avoid many of the difficulties that occur most often in later life. For others, however, the problems of old age are cumulative. The trauma of losing a spouse, for example, may be added to the difficulty of dealing with several chronic health problems, and these problems may be compounded by reduced financial resources.

To the extent that the rest of society treats its older members differentially on the basis of age alone, it can be said that people acquire a special status as they grow old. Some scholars suggest that in America the elderly actually constitute a "quasi-minority group."[39] Others foresee the emergence of a subculture of older Americans.[40] Older people, then, are likely to face both the problems that come with advanced age and the differential treatment that comes with special status.

At the same time, it is possible for the aging individual to preserve a degree of continuity with his or her earlier years. As Atchley observes, "Lifelong experience . . . creates certain predispositions that individuals will maintain if at all possible."[41] Declining physical capacity and the loss of some social roles may make it difficult to continue preferred activities, but people frequently cope with such losses "by consolidating their activities and redistributing their commitments among those activities that remain."[42] As just one example, a woman who in her earlier years was primarily committed to rearing her children may, once her children have grown, redirect her energies into community service. While the latter activity does not substitute for the previous one, it does maintain her predisposition to respond to the needs of others. Thus, she continues to live in a way that is consistent with her value orientation.

As scholars have frequently observed, older people in our society have come to be thought of as "a social problem." The public tends to conceive of them as passively awaiting rather than actively shaping their own destinies; if their lives are to be improved, it must be through the intervention of others. These conceptions are only partially accurate. It is true that many people must rely on financial, medical, and other forms of assistance for survival in their later years. But what is too often ignored is that most older people will have developed inner resources for dealing with life's problems, and that in a variety of ways they actively influence the course their lives will take. Some recent research has indicated that the elderly can, and do, develop their own viable coping strategies.[43] Indeed, without this problem-solving capacity, many would not have survived to old age. Through coping with problems over many years, people acquire a sophistication about life than can be instructive to those who are younger. So by studying the subject of later life, we can not only learn about older people, we can learn from them.

Notes

1. Andrea Fontana, *The Last Frontier: The Social Meaning of Growing Old* (Beverly Hills, Calif.: Sage Publications, 1977), p. 25.

2. Hadley Cantril, "Perception and Interpersonal Relations," in E. P. Hollander and R. G. Hunt (eds.), *Current Perspectives in Social Psychology* (New York: Oxford University Press, 1967), p. 284.

3. A. Irving Hallowell, "Culture and Personality," in P. B. Hammond (ed.), *Cultural and Social Anthropology* (New York: The Macmillan Company, 1965), pp. 458–459.

4. See, for example, William Ryan, *Blaming the Victim* (New York: Random House, 1971), pp. 112–135.

5. Forrest J. Berghorn et al., *The Urban Elderly* (Montclair, N.J.: Allanheld, Osmun, and Co./Universe Books, 1978), p. 8.

6. Seymour J. Mandelbaum, *Community and Communications* (New York: W. W. Norton & Co., 1972), p. 19.

7. Edward Albee, *The American Dream* (New York: Signet Books, 1961), pp. 82–83.

8. Louis Harris and Associates, Inc., *The Myth and Reality of Aging in America* (Washington, D.C.: National Council on Aging, Inc., 1975), p. 30.

9. Ibid., p. 142.

10. Ibid., p. 30.

11. Ibid., p. 30.

12. Ibid., p. 142.

13. Berghorn et al., op. cit., pp. 11–12. For a related discussion of the effect of values on the aging process, see Margaret Clark and Barbara G. Anderson, *Culture and Aging: An Anthropological Study of Older Americans* (Springfield, Ill.: Charles C. Thomas, 1967).

14. Jaber F. Gubrium, *The Myth of the Golden Years* (Springfield, Ill.: Charles C. Thomas, 1973), p. 200.

15. Mark Twain, *Letters from the Earth* (Greenwich, Conn.: Fawcett Publications, 1962), pp. 15–20.

16. For more detailed discussions of social roles in later life, see Bernard S. Phillips, "A Role Theory Approach to Adjustment in Old Age," *American Sociological Review* 22 (1957), pp. 212–217, and Arnold M. Rose, "Mental Health of Normal Older Persons," in A. M. Rose and W. A. Peterson (eds.), *Older People and Their Social World: The Sub-Culture of the Aging* (Philadelphia: F. A. Davis Co., 1965), pp. 193–199.

17. Gubrium, op. cit., p. 184.

18. William J. Goode, *World Revolution and Family Patterns* (New York: The Free Press, 1970), p. 7.

19. Edmund Morgan, *The Puritan Family* (New York: Harper & Row, 1966); Kenneth A. Lockridge, *A New England Town: The First Hundred Years* (New York: W. W. Norton & Co., 1970); Bernard Farber, *Guardians of Virtue* (New York: Basic Books,

1972); John Demos, *A Little Commonwealth* (New York: Oxford University Press, 1970).

20. Philip J. Greven, Jr., *Four Generations: Population, Land, and Family in Colonial Andover, Massachusetts* (Ithaca, N.Y.: Cornell University Press, 1970), p. 272.

21. William E. Bridges, "Family Patterns and Social Values in America, 1825–1875," *American Quarterly* (Spring 1965), pp. 3–11.

22. W. Andrew Achenbaum, *Old Age in the New Land: The American Experience Since 1790* (Baltimore: The Johns Hopkins University Press, 1978), pp. 4–5.

23. David Hackett Fischer, *Growing Old in America* (New York: Oxford University Press, 1977), p. 30.

24. Ibid., p. 72.

25. Achenbaum, op. cit., p. 17.

26. Fischer, op. cit., p. 67.

27. Ibid., pp. 77–112.

28. Achenbaum, op. cit., pp. 39–86.

29. For introductory, but more detailed, discussions of interview techniques, see John Madge, *The Tools of Social Science* (Garden City, N.Y.: Doubleday and Co. [Anchor Books], 1965), pp. 154–289, and Michael H. Walizer and Paul Wienir, *Research Methods and Analysis: Searching for Relationships* (New York: Harper & Row, 1978), pp. 263–294.

30. Erdman Palmore and Vira Kivett, "Change in Life Satisfaction: A Longitudinal Study of Persons Aged 46–70," *Journal of Gerontology* 32, no. 3 (May 1977), pp. 311–316.

31. An especially clear introduction to the concepts of validity and reliability can be found in Walizer and Wienir, op. cit., pp. 401–421. For a more advanced discussion, see P. B. Baltes, H. W. Reese, and J. R. Nesselroade, *Life-Span Developmental Psychology: Introduction to Research Methods* (Monterey, Calif.: Brooks/Cole Publishing Co., 1977).

32. C. Daniel Batson, "Experimentation in Psychology of Religion: An Impossible Dream," *Journal for the Scientific Study of Religion* 16, no. 4 (1977), p. 414.

33. Barry F. Anderson, *The Psychology Experiment* (Belmont, Calif.: Brooks/Cole Publishing Co., 1966), p. 21. For a more advanced treatment of experimental designs, see D. T. Campbell and J. C. Stanley, *Experimental and Quasi-Experimental Designs for Research* (Chicago: Rand McNally, 1963).

34. Walizer and Wienir, op. cit., p. 238.

35. Anderson, op. cit., p. 26.

36. Norval D. Glenn, *Cohort Analysis* (Beverly Hills, Calif.: Sage Publications, 1977), p. 8.

37. These data derive from a study reported in Berghorn et al., op. cit.

38. For more detailed treatments of the relationship between personality and later life, see Bernice Neugarten (ed.), *Middle Age and Aging* (Chicago: University of Chicago Press, 1968).

39. E.g., Milton L. Barron, "The Aged as a Quasi-Minority Group," in E. Sagarin, ed., *The Other Minorities* (Waltham, Mass.: Xerox College Publishing, 1971).

40. Arnold M. Rose, "The Subculture of the Aging: A Framework for Research in Social Gerontology," in A. M. Rose and W. A. Peterson (eds.), *Older People and Their*

Social World (Philadelphia: F. A. Davis Company, 1965).

41. Robert C. Atchley, *The Social Forces in Later Life* (Belmont, Calif.: Wadsworth, 1980), p. 27.

42. Ibid.

43. See Berghorn et al., op. cit., Ch. 6.

PART ONE
Imperatives of Aging

The processes considered in this section represent those aspects of growing old about which young people are generally most fearful. It is not unreasonable, after, all, to recoil at the prospect of facing physical deterioration, loss of mental acuity, the deaths of close friends and relatives, and ultimately, the inevitability of one's own mortality. However, is growing old as foreboding as it might at first seem? The answer to this question should be important to everyone, since the physiological changes that accompany advancing age are, to some extent, unavoidable and mark the elderly as a distinct subgroup in the population. At the same time, the consequences of these changes are not experienced uniformly by old people. As the chapters in this section point out, it is possible for people, by their actions and attitudes, to retain some continuity with their middle years and to influence the quality and duration of their later years.

Just as individuals vary in respect to biological aging, whole cultural groups mature and age at varying rates. Moore compares the rates at which selected populations on the average mature and age and considers why some groups have higher life expectancies than others. She suggests that while genetic factors clearly are important in determining life expectancy, the average longevity of a population is not entirely a matter of biological determinism. Some of the more long-lived cultural groups also are those in which individuals tend to lead vigorous lives and continue to have meaningful social roles into advanced age. Their diets may also promote long life. Osness describes the major biological changes occurring in body systems as people age, and reviews prominent theories offering explanations for these changes. In so doing, he suggests that a lifestyle that includes good nutritional habits and physical activity helps delay the debilitating effects of biological aging. Whether or not diet and exercise actually extend a person's life, it is quite likely that they will enable the person to enjoy the later years more fully.

Physical health and mental functioning are, of course, integrally related, and Denney examines the way aging affects a person's mental performance. The research she describes indicates that older people perform less well than younger adults on most tests of problem-solving ability. On the other hand, age differences are reduced on tests involving mental abilities that older people generally continue to exercise in their everyday lives. Moreover, some differences in the performance of younger and older people may be attributable to cohort effects. That is, education may affect levels of performance, and older cohorts have had fewer years of formal schooling than younger cohorts.

Although a person may die at any age, death as an abstraction has come to be associated primarily with old age. Indeed, this may be a major reason why we tend to fear growing old and avoid thinking about it. However, as Patterson notes, older people themselves appear to be better able to cope with the idea of death than younger adults. Furthermore, she suggests that the attitudes of Americans toward death may be changing. And, throughout her chapter, we can see that individual attitudes toward death will modify the context in which that inevitable event occurs. Thus, while these chapters underscore universal physiological processes, they also demonstrate that the individual's actions, attitudes, and social milieu all influence the ways in which the imperatives of aging are experienced.

2

Physical Aging:
A Cross-Cultural Perspective

Mary Jane Moore

Introduction

The topic of aging has not been studied extensively in the discipline of an-thropology. Although anthropologists study the full life cycle of people in a culture, they spend very little time on old age. Both Clark and Myerhoff sug-gest reasons for this; for example, Clark suggests that American an-thropologists ignore this stage of life because of their own negative feelings about growing old.[1] There are exceptions to this generalization, however, such as Hart and Pilling's description of the gerontocratic Tiwi of Melville and Bathhurst Islands of Australia and Kleemeier's study of aging and leisure in many diverse cultures.[2]

Perhaps the most well known and earliest systematic study of the aged is Simmons' work involving comparison of 109 cultures.[3] He gathered ethnographic data from the Yale Human Relations Area Files in order to find any observable universal trends in how old people adjust to senescence (growing older) and how people in each culture interact with their elders. In this and later work, he came to the conclusion that people who are the most successful in aging remain active in their society and achieve fulfillment through participation as long as possible.[4]

Recently two excellent treatments of aging and culture have been pub-lished: Myerhoff's *Number Our Days*, and Myerhoff and Simić's *Life's Career – Aging*.[5] The former is a study of very old Jewish-Americans from Eastern Europe living in Venice, a southern California beach town. The lat-ter is an edited volume of essays on old age and aging in five different cultures: the Chagga of Tanzania, Yugoslavians, Mexicans near Mexico City, Mexican-Americans in East Los Angeles, and Jewish-Americans in

Venice, California. In the introduction to this book, Simić comments on the late entrance of anthropology into the field of gerontology.

If cultural anthropology has been slow to study aging cross-culturally, biological anthropology has been even slower. Biological anthropologists have long been interested in growth and development that includes an element of aging. For example, there are certain structures—even in the fetus and embryo—that deteriorate and must disappear before the next stage of development can appear. However, senescence as a distinct developmental period has not been a traditional area of inquiry. Because growth and maturation end after adolescence, human beings spend only about one-quarter of their lives maturing and the remaining three-quarters growing old.

Growth and Maturation

If we can look at senescence as the last stage of the human life cycle, then those factors that influence the first quarter of the cycle will be helpful in understanding the aging process. There is abundant evidence that both individuals and populations differ in growth and maturation rates. For example, adult average stature attained in world populations ranges from 140 cm. (4 feet, 7 inches) in the Ituri pygmies to a tall 185 cm. (6 feet, 1 inch) found in the Nuer of Africa. The rate at which individuals approach their adult height can differ significantly. Figure 2.1 shows the mean height velocities of five different boys from a British longitudinal growth study. These maximum height velocities illustrate how individuals can enter their adolescent growth periods at different chronological ages. Those boys who experience their maximum height velocity before the average velocity peak of the population are considered early maturers, and with the late maturers, the peak is after that of the average maximum velocity.

Maturation rate in females is determined, in addition to height velocities, by noting the age when menstruation begins (menarche). This is a convenient method by which a population's average maturation rate can be measured. The variation of the average age at menarche in different populations is shown in Table 2.1. Quite a range is evident—from the menarchal age of 12.5 years in rural Naples, Italy, to age 18 in the Bundi of New Guinea.

Much work has been undertaken in trying to explain the variation in growth and maturation.[6] Growth and development is the result of complex interaction between heredity and environment. Studies of monozygotic (identical) and dizygotic (fraternal) twins show that there is a greater difference in height between dizygotic twins than between monozygotic twins. Table 2.2 shows the difference through age 4. At birth the monozygotic pairs are less similar than the dizygotic because monozygotic twins often

Figure 2.1: Maximum Height Velocity Curves of Five Boys of
           the Harpenden Growth Study. The relation between
           individual and mean velocities during the adolescent
           spurt is shown by solid lines (——) for the individuals
           and dashed line (- - -) for the average curve constructed
           by averaging their values at each age.

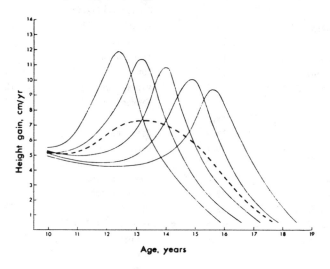

Source: J. M. Tanner at al., "Standards from Birth to
          Maturity for Height, Weight, Height Velocity,
          and Weight Velocity; British Children, 1965,"
          Archives of Disease in Childhood (41:1966),
          pp. 454-471, 613-635. Reprinted by permission.

receive unequal nutrients during development in the uterus. Correspondingly, the correlation coefficients of the MZ pair increase after uterine effects
diminish.

Another method of illustrating the role of genetic factors is to compare the
variation of adult height within families with the variation within a population. The range of variation in adult height is about 25 cm. (~10 inches) for
the males of most populations, 16 cm. (~6 inches) between brothers, and 1.6
cm. (0.6 inch) between monozygotic twins brought up together.[7] The influence of heredity in maturation rate is demonstrated by the contrast between female twins and women of different degrees of relatedness. As seen in
Table 2.3, there is marked contrast in difference in age of menarche between
monozygotic twins and between that of more distantly related women.

Perhaps one of the most important environmental factors affecting growth
and development is nutrition. Malnutrition delays growth. This has been

Table 2.1: Mean Ages of Menarche by Population Group

Population Group	Age	Population Group	Age
Europe		Near East and India	
Oslo	13.2	Bagdad (well-off)	13.6
Stockholm	13.1	Istanbul (well-off)	12.3
Helsinki	13.2	Tel Aviv	13.2
Copenhagen	13.2	Iran (urban)	13.3
Netherlands	13.4	Tunis (well-off)	13.4
North-east England	13.4	Madras (urban)	12.8
London	13.0	Madras (rural)	14.2
Belgium	13.0		
Paris	13.2	Asiatics	
Zurich	13.1	Burma	13.2
Moscow	13.0	Singapore (average)	12.7
Warsaw	13.0	Hong Kong (well-off)	12.5
Budapest	12.8	Japan (urban)	12.9
Romania (urban)	13.3	Mexico	12.8
Carrara, Italy	12.6	Yucatan (well-off)	12.5
Naples (rural)	12.5	Eskimo	13.8
European-descended		Africans	
Montreal	13.1	Uganda (well-off)	13.4
Sydney	13.0	Nigeria, Ibadan (university-educated parents)	13.3
USA, all areas	12.8		
New Zealand	13.0	South Africa (urban)	14.9
Pacific		African-descended	
New Zealand (Maori)	12.7	USA, all areas	12.5
New Guinea (Bundi)	18.0	Cuba, all areas	13.0
New Guinea (Megiar)	15.5	Martinique	14.0

Source: J. M. Tanner, Fetus Into Man (Cambridge, Mass.:
          Harvard University Press, 1978); data for period between
          1960 and 1975. Reprinted by permission.

seen in the effects of famine associated with war. During both world wars
where records were kept, heights of different age groups dropped as the food
intake of the children became restricted. If the period of malnutrition is not
too severe or does not last too long, children recover completely by the
phenomenon called "catch-up growth." This spurt in height velocity after
onset of normal nutrition gives the individual a buffer against adverse effects
of periodic starvation. These regulatory powers would have been adaptive in
early times when small tribal populations were dependent on uncertain food
supply. In well-nourished children, major diseases may slow down growth,

Table 2.2: Mean differences between lengths of monozygotic twin pairs (~140 pairs) and same-sexed dizygotic twin pairs (~90 pairs) from birth to 4 years, and within pair correlation coefficients.

	Mean difference in length (cm.)		Correlation coefficient	
	MZ pairs	DZ pairs	MZ pairs	DZ pairs
Birth	1.8	1.6	0.58	0.82
3 months	1.4	1.6	0.75	0.72
6 months	1.3	1.9	0.78	0.65
1 year	1.3	1.8	0.85	0.69
2 years	1.1	2.4	0.89	0.58
3 years	1.1	2.9	0.92	0.55
4 years	1.1	3.2	0.94	0.60

From R. S. Wilson, "Concordance in Physical Growth for Monozygotic and Dizygotic Twins," Annals of Human Biology 3 (1976):1. Reprinted by permission.

Table 2.3: Mean Difference in Age at Menarche between Women of Decreasing Degree of Relationship

Relationship	Difference (months)
Identical twins	2.8
Fraternal twins	12.0
Sisters	12.9
Unrelated women	18.6

Source: J. M. Tanner, Growth at Adolescence (Oxford, Blackwell, 1962). Reprinted by permission.

but the effects are seldom permanent. In chronically undernourished children, though, the combination of inadequate nutrition and disease can cause them to be smaller than average adults.

Other environmental influences on growth and maturation include socioeconomic status, number in the family, urbanization, and psychosocial stress. Children from different socioeconomic classes differ in size and maturation rate—the lower the socioeconomic status, the smaller the child and slower the rate of development. These same effects are seen as the size of the family increases. Large families tend to produce smaller children. In many European countries, boys living in towns are between 2 and 5 cm. taller than children in the villages.[8] Psychosocial stress can inhibit the secretion of growth hormone. This has been documented in clinical cases of severe stress. How much stress affects the growth rate of the average child is difficult to say. Most children when adequately nourished continue to grow under stressful circumstances. However, studies in England have shown that boys grow more slowly while in boarding schools than during their holidays at home.[9]

A phenomenon that is related to the above environmental factors in growth and development is "secular trend." During the last 100 years in industrialized countries, and in some developing ones, the average height of adults has been increasing, with individuals maturing at an earlier age. Since 1880 there has been about 1 cm. increase per decade in adult height and a 0.3 year decrease per decade in age at menarche.[10] Most investigators attribute this secular trend to better nutrition (more protein and calories in early infancy, in particular) and better medical care and sanitation.

Even when all the environmental factors are taken into consideration, there remain population differences in growth and development rate. Asiatic children from high socioeconomic groups are distinctly shorter than European and African children from comparably favorable environments. Well-off Nigerians are not as tall as blacks in the United States, for instance.[11] Here we have the interaction of genetic and environmental factors mentioned earlier.

Because populations do differ in maturation rate, it is not surprising that there are different patterns of aging in various populations. Some of the genetic and environmental factors involved in growth and development are also important in the rate of aging.

Genetics of Human Longevity

Most biologists believe there is a "genetic program" that is responsible for the different maximum life spans for mammals and other animal classes. The theory holds that, in effect, the fertilized egg includes a timetable for embryonic development, birth, and all the other developmental stages including senescence. How this program operates is the subject of much basic research in biological gerontology. There is evidence that environment, particularly nutrition and temperature, influences the way it works. Insects and rodents reared under cool or cold conditions, or slightly underfed, live longer than those in control groups. In a classic study, McCay and Crowell were able to extend the life span of rats by as much as one-third by restricting the calories in their diet when they were young.[12]

The species-specific maximum life span in humans is around 100 years; different authors will cite from 95 to 110 years as the maximum life span. There have been reports of very long-lived individuals from many different countries.[13] We will discuss several populations that have been known for their extreme longevity later. Although maximum life span has essentially been the same in recent human history, the *average* life span has not. Due to the development of more complex culture and reduction of environmental hazards, the average human life span has increased from 29.4 years (70,000 years ago) to 72.5 years (United States in 1970). Table 2.4 shows the general progression. For example, the introduction of antibiotics in industrialized countries after World War II has played an important part in the U.S. increase from 61.5 years in 1900 to 72.5 years in 1970.

Longevity is clearly a multifaceted phenomenon. Besides the important sociocultural aspects, we need to examine genetic factors. By simple observation, one sees that longevity "runs in families." Do studies support this observation? As early as 1934, Pearl and Pearl published results of a study in

Table 2.4: Average Life Span of Human Populations in the Past and Present

Time period	Average chrono-age at 50% survival (years)	Maximum life span potential (years)
Wurm (about 70,000-30,000 years ago)	29.4	69-77
Upper Paleolithic (about 30,000-12,000 years ago)	32.4	95
Mesolithic (about 12,000-10,000 years ago)	31.5	95
Neolithic Anatolian (about 10,000-8000 years ago)	38.2	95
Classic Greece (1100 B.C.-1 A.D.)	35	95
Classic Rome (753 B.C.-476 A.D.)	32	95
England (1276 A.D.)	48	95
England (1376-1400)	38	95
U.S.A. (1900-1902)	61.5	95
U.S.A. (1950)	70.0	95
U.S.A. (1970)	72.5	95

Source: R. G. Cutler, "Evolution of Human Longevity: A Critical Overview," Mechanisms of Ageing and Development 9 (1979): 337. Reprinted by permission.

which they attempted to look for a familial component in longevity by comparing the ages at death of the parents and grandparents of long-lived individuals (ninety or over) with ages at death of persons bearing the same relationships to control subjects. Recently Abbott and colleagues conducted a follow-up analysis of the descendents of the Pearls' study.[14] They found with a sample of 9,205 progeny a small positive correlation between the average age at death of the descendents and the original subjects. Two interesting aspects of their study were that parents who died at an age of 81 or more had offspring who lived on the average some 5 to 7 years longer than offspring of parents who died at 60 or younger. In the correlation between parent and offspring, the relationship between mother and child was closer than that between father and child.

Perhaps the best evidence for genetic factors that influence human longevity is Kallman and Sander's work in 1948. They compared over 900 pairs of monozygotic and dizygotic twins and found that the mean difference in longevity between the dizygotic pairs (78.3 months) was twice that between monozygotic pairs (36.9 months). Kallman and Sander noted in their paper that in cases where adult identical twins lived apart in different environments, many of them aged identically. They stated, "The similarities often included the degree of general enfeeblement or its absence, the graying and thinning of hair, the configuration of baldness and senile wrinkle formation and the types and extent of eye, ear, and tooth deficiencies."[15]

While it is widely recognized that there are probably genetic components in longevity, the mechanism through which these factors work still eludes investigators. Certainly there are many examples of single-gene traits that cause early death, but so far there is no single gene known in humans that prolongs life. It may be that the genetic component of longevity operates not through nonspecific genes for longevity but through an absence of deleterious genes leading to premature death.[16] But recent research in heart disease and immunology has brought promising findings that suggest some single genes that may be operating in longevity after adulthood. A growing body of research suggests that high-density lipoproteins (HDL) protect against heart attacks. Glueck and his colleagues have identified two groups of people who are genetically endowed either with high HDL or low LDL (low-density lipoproteins) concentrations. High concentrations of LDL have been linked to an increased risk of heart attack or stroke.[17] These people with the high HDL or low LDL levels rarely have arteriosclerosis and have life spans as much as 5 to 12 years longer than average. The other area of interest, the immune system, is becoming one of the most promising systems being investigated in both basic and applied aging research.[18] It is involved with many of the diseases of the aged and offers potential in minimizing the deteriorative processes of aging.

Long-Lived Human Populations

The most well known long-lived populations with a high percentage of older persons have been described by Leaf.[19] They are the Hunzakut of the Karakoram mountain range in Pakistan, the Vilcabambans in Ecuador, and the Abkhasians in Georgia, U.S.S.R. Reports of people being 115, 120, and even 130 years old are common among all three groups. To illustrate the degree of longevity present in these populations, we can compare the number of individuals aged 90 and over in Abkhasia with other populations. Of the ethnic Abkhasians, 2.6 percent are over 90. The overall figure for the U.S.S.R. is 0.1 percent, and for the United States it is 0.4 percent.[20]

Are there common denominators found in all three populations that can explain these accounts of longevity? If one does a quick comparison, it is apparent that certain factors are common among the three groups.[21] Each of the populations is situated in a moderately mountainous terrain, with the altitude averaging between 1,500 to 5,000 feet. The Vilcabambans and Hunzakut farm at a bare subsistence level, while Abkhasians keep herds of sheep and goats in addition to limited horticulture.

One striking factor is the low-fat, low-calorie diet of these long-lived populations. The older Abkhasians consume 1,700 to 1,900 calories a day with 73 grams of protein, 47 grams of fat, and 381 grams of carbohydrates. Milk is a main source of protein; sour milk and low-fat cheese are used at all meals in all seasons. Elderly Vilcabambans' daily diet averages 1,200 calories: 35 to 38 grams of protein; 12 to 19 grams of fat, and 200 to 250 grams of carbohydrate. The contribution of animal protein and animal fat to the diet is very low. The average daily intake of the Hunzakut is 1,923 calories: 50 grams of protein, 36 grams of fat, and 354 grams of carbohydrate. Meat and dairy products account for only 1 percent of the total. In the United States the average daily intake for Americans of all ages is 3,300 calories, with a high fat consumption of 157 grams. Table 2.5 summarizes the average caloric intake and the different percentages of protein, fat, and carbohydrates in the

Table 2.5: Content of the Diets of Three Long-Lived Groups and of the U.S. Population

	Abkhasians	Vilcabambans	Hunzakut	U.S.
Daily calories	1900	1200	1923	3300
% protein	15	13	11	16
% fat	9	6	8	24
% carbohydrate	76	81	81	60

diets of the three groups and the United States.

The use of alcohol and tobacco is moderate in Abkhasia except for feast time, when there are many rounds of wine toasting. The Vilcabambans smoke and drink heavily; however, there is disagreement among visiting physicians as to how many inhale while smoking. There is no data available for Hunza. In all three locations the aged work regularly and are physically active. There is no retirement age. Leaf feels they maintain their fitness simply by the high level of physical activity demanded by their mountainous terrain.[22] It is possible that genetic isolation may have played a part in the longevity of the Vilcabambans and Hunzakut. Hunza is one of the most inaccessible places on earth, and the isolation of the small interrelated community of Vilcabamba could have harbored a pocket of centenarians that had very few "bad" genes—those that increase the risk of fatal disease. Because Abkhasia has been a crossroads for travel for centuries, its population can scarcely have maintained any significant degree of genetic isolation. It is possible, though, that remote mountain villages could have escaped contact.

Perhaps one of the more important factors present in these long-lived populations is the status of the old people in their culture. They enjoy a high self-esteem made possible by the respect and value placed upon them by their families and society. Benet, a cultural anthropologist, has visited the Abkhasians and other long-lived populations in the Caucasus at least six times. She maintains that the most important factors that promote their good health and longevity are continuity in daily routines and diet and the fact that the aged are "surrounded by numerous respectful progeny of several generations [and] retain a feeling of individual worth and importance that prolongs useful life."[23]

Certainly all the factors discussed above are important. But is there a genetic mechanism such as differential fertility that favors longevity in a particular population? It is obvious that there are many populations around the world that share some of the characteristics of the Hunzakut, Vilcabambans, and Abkhasians—low caloric intake, mountainous terrain, esteem for the elderly, etc. And yet these populations are not known for their longevity. There is a possibility, then, that genetic factors could play a part. Populations could differ in "longevity gene" frequencies as they differ in gene frequencies for blood groups, enzymes, and other genetic traits. More probably, populations could differ in the amount of deleterious genes (the genetic component of heart disease, cancer, autoimmune diseases, etc.) and thus show variation in the number of older healthy people living in each population. The extremely old in Abkhasia often have long-lived relatives, and clans of long-living people are known in other Caucasus populations.[24] Both Leaf and Benet report that women who are long-lived have more children.

According to data from the Institute of Gerontology in Kiev, women now in the 80 to 104 age group had twice as many children as women in the 60 to 79 age group.[25] Men in the long-lived populations are known for their interest in sex and for fathering children well into their later years. The significant relationship between fertility and longevity has also been demonstrated in Wyshak's study of genealogical records of the Mormon Church at Salt Lake City.[26] Thus, after many generations there could be an increase in individuals who either have "longevity genes" or lack the deleterious genes that shorten life.

Recent and Future Research

Recently two anthropologists, Mazess and Forman, have reported that exaggerations of ages have occurred in Vilcabamba and that the people are not as long-lived as they claim.[27] They undertook a household census and examined birth, marriage, death, and other records at three different times. After careful study of the records and genealogies constructed from the village households, they concluded that the oldest individual was 96 when he died. Systematic age exaggeration began at about 70 years and amounted to as much as 20 to 40 years. These data tend to cast suspicion on the claims of longevity in Hunza and Abkhasia. Leaf is convinced that there is a high probability that ages have been exaggerated in those two regions also (personal communication with Leaf, 1979).

A relatively new dating technique, called amino acid racemization, may help in sorting out claims of exaggerated old age from legitimate cases of extreme longevity. Helfman and Bada of the Scripps Institution of Oceanography have refined the technique so that a tooth can be used to tell the age of an individual within 10 percent of the actual age.[28] In the spring of 1979, while a group of Russian gerontologists were visiting Johns Hopkins University, a tooth from a Georgian woman from the Caucasus area was analyzed by the amino acid racemization method to be 99 years old. The woman was documented to be 96 years old. The difference of 3 years is well within the experimental error of the method. The Soviet scientists plan to send more samples of teeth, when they are available, from the Caucasus area.[29]

Most of the studies of long-lived populations are primarily concerned with sociocultural factors or with physiological medical parameters. Few researchers design investigations so that data can be used to support or disprove the possibility of genetic factors in longevity. Recently a joint United States–U.S.S.R. research program has been planned by gerontologists and anthropologists in Moscow and Tiblisi (Soviet Georgia) and the universities of Kansas and Kentucky. This project hopes to use a holistic and comparative approach that will pinpoint some of the genetic and environmental factors involved in longevity and aging.

The Kansas group, which includes anthropologists, sociologists, psychologists, physiologists, and medical doctors, will be working in Alexanderwohl, a Mennonite community in south-central Kansas. This community was chosen for a number of reasons. The church records provide a genealogical depth of six to seven generations. Despite the migration of the community from Prussia to Russia to Kansas, accurate church records go back to 1625. These records will provide documentation of trends in longevity during the last three centuries. The people of Alexanderwohl share a common religion, history, and agrarian subsistence that provide cohesiveness and cultural continuity. Families with varying degrees of inbreeding and families with no known consanguinity (blood relations) live side by side within the same community. This permits the investigation of the role of consanguinity in aging and longevity. It is hoped that this comprehensive approach will clarify the relative roles of nutrition, pace of life, stress, and genetics in the process of aging and longevity.

Summary

There are similarities between the factors affecting growth and maturation rates and those that may affect the rate of aging and longevity. Genetics, nutrition, disease, and psychosocial stress are among those that are important in both areas of investigation. Much more is known about the sociocultural aspects of aging than the biological. But research like the joint Russia–United States project may begin to fill in the gaps. For example, one of the topics the Kansas group will be studying is menarche, menopause, and reproduction, in order to see if the rates of these developmental stages are related to longevity. (Abkhasian women experience menarche at age 16 or 17 and many continue to bear children until their late 50s and early 60s.)

The three long-lived populations of Abkhasia, Vilcabamba, and Hunza all live in a rural mountainous environment. Certainly the rural nature of these living environments is a positive factor. There is the slower pace, a regular rhythm of daily activities, the sense of community in the village, and continuity of life's stages from birth to old age with one's friends and relatives. Although there are common denominators in cultural ways of aging, anthropologists who have studied different groups comment on the variability of the aging process.[30]

This chapter has attempted to look at biological aspects of aging but not to the exclusion of sociocultural factors. Perhaps the importance of the two are best seen as an interaction in which biological factors emerge first in importance, and then sociocultural conditions emerge that permit the individual to live to his or her full potential life span. For example, if one has a family history of an unusual amount of heart disease and cancer, he or she will have a low probability of reaching an advanced age. Yet another individual, whose family history lacks the predisposition for these diseases, may need the positive effects of high social status and the sense of continuity to reach his or her full life span. Thus, a sort of genetic bottleneck may be operating in the long-lived populations that has screened out those individuals who had genetic tendencies for fatal adult diseases. This screening, plus the increased fertility of the very old, provide the background for sociocultural factors to maximize life span.

The recent research from Vilcabamba does shed doubt on the claims for extreme longevity. Even if the amino acid racemization method does prove that the Abkhasians and other Caucasus populations are not that long-lived, the unusual vigor and healthy active lives of these older people are reasons enough for our interest and research.

Notes

1. M. Clark, "The Anthropology of Aging: A New Area for Studies of Culture and Personality," *Gerontologist* 7 (1967), p. 55, and B. Myerhoff, "Aging and the Aged in Other Cultures: An Anthropological Perspective," in E. E. Bauwens (ed.), *The Anthropology of Health* (St. Louis: C. V. Mosby, 1978).

2. C.W.M. Hart and A. R. Pilling, *The Tiwi of North Australia* (New York: Holt, Rinehart and Winston, 1960), and R. W. Kleemeier (ed.), *Aging and Leisure* (New York: Oxford University Press, 1961).

3. L. W. Simmons, *The Role of the Aged in Primitive Society* (New Haven, Conn.: Yale University Press, 1945).

4. L. W. Simmons, "Aging in Preindustrial Societies," in C. Tibbits (ed.), *Handbook of Social Gerontology* (Chicago: University of Chicago Press, 1960).

5. B. Myerhoff, *Number Our Days* (New York: E. P. Dutton, 1978), and B. Myerhoff and A. Simić, *Life's Career – Aging* (Beverly Hills, Calif.: Sage Publications, 1978).

6. P. B. Eveleth and J. M. Tanner, *Worldwide Variation in Human Growth*, Vol. 8 (International Biological Programme, New York: Cambridge University Press, 1976).

7. J. M. Tanner, *Fetus Into Man* (Cambridge, Mass.: Harvard University Press, 1978).

8. Eveleth and Tanner, op. cit.

9. Tanner, op. cit.

10. Ibid.

11. Eveleth and Tanner, op. cit.

12. C. M. McCay and M. F. Crowell, "Prolonging the Lifespan," *Science Monthly* 39, (1934), p. 405.

13. For a detailed account, see A. Comfort, *The Biology of Senescence* (New York: Elsevier, 1979).

14. M. H. Abbot, E. A. Murphy, D. R. Bolling, and H. Abbey, "The Familial Component in Longevity: A Study of Offspring of Nonagenarians: II, Preliminary Analysis of the Completed Study," *Johns Hopkins Medical Journal* 134 (1974), p. 1; and M. H. Abbott, H. Abbey, D. R. Bolling, and E. A. Murphy, "The Familial Component in Longevity—A Study of Offspring of Nonagenarians: III, Intrafamilial Studies," *American Journal of Medical Genetics* 2 (1978), p. 105.

15. F. J. Kallman and G. Sander, "Twin Studies on Aging and Longevity," *Journal of Heredity* 39 (1948), p. 349.

16. M. H. Abbott, H. Abbey, D. R. Bolling, and E. A. Murphy, "The Familial Component in Longevity—A Study of Offspring of Nonagenarians: III, Intrafamilial Studies," *American Journal of Medical Genetics* 2 (1978), p. 105.

17. C. J. Glueck, P. S. Gartside, R. W. Fallat, J. Sielski, and P. M. Steiner, "Longevity Syndromes: Familial Hypobeta and Familial Hyperalphalipoproteinemia," *Journal of Laboratory Clinical Medicine* 99 (1976), p. 941, and C. J. Glueck et al., "Hyperalphalipoproteinemia and Hypobetalipoproteinemia in Octogenarian Kindreds," *Atherosclerosis* 27 (1977), p. 387.

18. T. Makinodan, "Immunity and Aging," in C. D. Finch and L. Hayflick (eds.), *Handbook of the Biology of Aging* (New York: Van Nostrand Reinhold, 1977). There is an increasing amount of data demonstrating an association between the histocompatibility complex (HLA) and a variety of disease states. The HLA system (human leukocyte antigens) is a genetic system in which antigen groups in white blood cells are inherited. The HLA-A1-B8-Dw3 linkage group has been associated with decreased immune cell function and decreased survival in women. See L. J. Greenberg and E. J. Yunis, "Histocompatibility Determinants, Immune Responsiveness and Aging in Man," *Federation Proceedings* 37 (1978), p. 1258.

19. Alexander Leaf, "Every Day is a Gift When You are Over 100," *National Geographic* 143 (1973), p. 93, and "Getting Old," *Scientific American* 229 (1973), p. 45.

20. S. Benet, *Abkhasians: The Long-Lived People of the Caucasus* (New York: Holt, Rinehart & Winston, 1974).

21. Ibid.; S. Benet, *How to Live To Be 100* (New York: Dial Press, 1976); D. Davies, *The Centenarians of the Andes* (London: Barne and Jenkins, 1975); and Leaf, "Getting Old."

22. Leaf, "Getting Old."

23. Benet, *How to Live.*

24. Leaf, "Getting Old," and Benet, *How to Live.*

25. Benet, *How to Live.*

26. G. Wyshak, "Fertility and Longevity in Twins, Sibs and Parents of Twins," *Social Biology* 25 (1979), p. 315.

27. R. B. Mazess and S. H. Forman, "Longevity and Age Exaggeration in Vilcabamba, Ecuador," *Journal of Gerontology* 34 (1979), p. 94.

28. P. Helfman and J. Bada, "Aspartic Acid Racemization in Dentine as a Measure of Aging," *Nature* 262 (1976), p. 279.

29. T. H. Maugh, "Any Horse Trader Could Have Told You," *Science* 205 (1979), p. 574, and personal communication with Masters.

30. Myerhoff and Simić, op. cit.

3

Biological Aspects of the Aging Process

Wayne H. Osness

The Nature of Biological Aging

Although the aging process is a well-accepted biological phenomenon, civilizations since the beginning of time have sought ways to retard this process, with the ultimate goal of immortality. It has only been in our relatively recent past that a systematic effort has been made to more clearly understand the scientific implications of the biological process. As life has a beginning, so does it have an end, and with the passage of time the cumulative biological changes that occur in all species ultimately result in a decreased ability to function. The length of time it takes for the biological changes to occur varies greatly from one individual to another, regardless of the absence or presence of complicated pathological conditions. Although the average life expectancy in ancient Greece was approximately 35 years, Sophocles wrote some of his best works and achieved great success at the age of 85. Moreover, his death at age 90 clearly illustrates that the maximum life span has not been extended very much since that time. Those who reach a similarly advanced age today probably experience the same type of biological insufficiency that Sophocles did, even though we have the advantage of a much greater degree of medical sophistication.

The fact that the average life expectancy in our present society has reached approximately 70 years of age simply means that a greater number of our contemporaries live to their 80s and 90s as compared with the people of ancient Greece. This added longevity has been attributed to better nutrition and more effective treatment of disease. However, it appears that the real key to longevity lies in a more complete understanding of the biological aging process itself. Such understanding would provide us with the knowledge necessary not only to extend life but also to improve the quality of life during advanced years. It is doubtful that individuals of any species actually attain their full physical potential, either in longevity or capacity. Continued study is important so that the aging process can be carefully observed under controlled conditions and a greater proportion of individuals eventually helped to come closer to that potential. The efforts of many of our best biological scientists have provided the bases for several theories attempting to explain the biological aging process. It appears certain that continued research generating a greater amount of supporting information will help us to utilize these theories, which can then be used as a guide to further study and the acquisition of more sophisticated understanding of the aging process. Some scientists project that more thorough knowledge of the aging process may make it possible to extend human life to 150 or possibly 200 years. Needless to say, this is an optimistic prediction, but one that appears to be well within the realm of possiblity.

This chapter explores the nature of the aging process by providing an overview of the available research evidence relating to the body systems that are most critical to biological function. Each system is treated separately, in order to more clearly describe various aspects of the aging process, and is then integrated into a discussion of the theories of biological aging. It is important to note that, while all of these theories have been developed on the basis of research evidence related to aging, some have more documented support than others. The descriptions of both the body systems and the theories involve some technical concepts that may be unfamiliar to the lay reader. However, I have attempted to present such concepts so they may be understood without a thorough knowledge of biological and chemical terminology, and a glossary of technical terms has been supplied at the end of the chapter. The final section addresses the issue of lifestyle intervention in the aging process and includes an examination of those components that have been shown to affect physiological aging.

The Skeletomuscular System

In most cases, as the aging process continues, a decrease in the intensity and duration of physical activity occurs. That is, physical activity becomes slower and less efficient. Rubinstein speculates that these changes are largely due to disease and nutritional deficiencies.[1] Motor disorders and dysfunction were first thought to be associated with bones, ligaments, and joints rather than muscle tissue.[2] However, it is well known that muscle disuse causes muscle atrophy and a reduction in bone diameter. Since both of these phenomena occur with aging, it is difficult to determine whether slowness and decreased efficiency are due to the aging process or to disuse. It is probably a combination of both: activity levels decrease with age, and the aging process makes it more difficult to maintain a sufficient level of physical activity.

From a structural standpoint, the older individual experiences a greater number of long-bone fractures, greater vertebral atrophy, and a greater number of compression fractures of the bone. It has been observed that the bone mass decreases with age in women but not in men.[3] The density of bone also decreases with age in all races and in both sexes.[4] This decrease in both mass and density of bone tends to explain the greater susceptibility of bone to fractures and dysfunction among the aged. Further research indicates that an increased reabsorption of calcium from bone into the bloodstream occurs with age.[5] The reabsorption is most noticeable in those bones that do not experience tension and stress. It has also been noted that a reduced ash content occurs as density decreases, and the bones so affected are much more susceptible to injury.

The most common type of structural illness today is rheumatoid arthritis, typically a problem of older age groups. It has been estimated that 40 million people in the United States are afflicted with this disease, which is an inflammation of the joint and deterioration of the bone in those locations. In many cases a very serious decrease in function occurs. The joints are simply not capable of handling the tension and stress of physical activity without considerable pain and discomfort. The lack of function elicits disuse, and disuse causes continued atrophy of the associated muscle tissue. The cause of the affliction is unknown and the treatment is very often ineffective.

Motor efficiency and function changes occurring during the aging process are very complex. One the one hand, the nervous pathways and receptors could be the cause of this decrease in functionality and, on the other hand, the cause could lie in the reduction of the integrity of muscle tissue itself. The solution to the problem is hindered by the intervention of motivational factors in the measurement process. With older individuals it is very possible that the data generated are measuring the motivation of the subject to accomplish the task and not the motor efficiency or muscular function at all. This problem will have to be solved before current researchers will be able to deal effectively with interventions designed to improve efficiency and function from a biological standpoint. It is generally agreed that training programs using physical exercise will improve both of these conditions, but we still do not understand why this is so.

A considerable amount of work has been done relative to muscle tissue change during the aging process. It has been observed that muscle weight decreases as a fraction of total body weight with age.[6] An increase in extracellular water has been found to occur, with an increase in sodium and chloride ion concentrations.[7] However, potassium concentrations have been found to decrease in the extracellular water space,[8] while collagen and fat concentrations associated with muscle tissue increase with age. All of these factors most certainly affect both muscular efficiency and function.

The decrease in mass of muscle tissue appears to be due to a decrease in the number of fibers[9] as well as the diameter of these fibers.[10] Muscle fibers, or muscle cells, do not undergo cell division. When a fiber is destroyed it is not replaced. The change in diameter would mean that protein substances are released from the fiber, leaving less contractile (protein) substance available for muscular function. It is important to note that changes are not uniform in muscles of different functions. Types of motor units, given muscle groups, and individual muscle fibers vary a great deal in their response to the aging process. Therefore, it appears that opportunity exists for the retardation of cell deterioration through intervention programs. As an example, the physically active diaphragm deteriorates very little compared to a 39 percent decrease in the fibers of a soleus muscle that is restricted in activity.[11] White muscle fibers decrease in both number and volume with age. The decrease in volume can be attributed to a decrease in the number of myofibrils within the fiber. The red muscle fibers (endurance-related) decrease in number only, leaving the possibility that the number of myofibrils in the fiber remains the same. The white fibers (related to short-term activity) do not appear to decrease in number as rapidly as red fibers. This could create a condition seriously affecting the endurance of the aged tissue. Normal fibers, both red and white, tend to be very consistent in size in the young adult. A much greater variation in size occurs in fibers found within the aged muscle tissue. Another interesting fact is that the number of muscle spindles does not change with the decrease in size of given fibers. The number of spindles present in fibers of different parts of the body varies greatly, but this number appears to stay the same regardless of the change in fiber diameter with age. The effectiveness of these spindles to provide sensory feedback as the aging process continues has not been studied.

The strength of a muscle group depends on the size and number of fibers within that muscle group. As we increase the size and number of fibers we increase strength, and as we decrease size and number we reduce strength. It could be the aging process that causes decrease, or it could be the lack of muscle activity in later years. Another factor that may be important to muscular strength is anabolic hormone concentrations. These concentrations decrease with age and could cause a decrease in protein retention within the fibers. If we increase the concentration of hormone, we could then increase protein synthesis, which would elicit a greater muscle size and strength. This procedure has been used successfully in drug therapy for older individuals who have been confined for a long period of time and unable to do normal daily chores. The administration of these hormones tends to elicit greater strength, but only when the muscle tissue is challenged with an activity overload.

The change in physical function of the older individual is usually caused by a decrease in both strength and endurance. Most of our discussion thus far has related to the strength factor; we now turn to the endurance factor. In normal muscle tissue, endurance is related to the ability of the cardiovascular system to deliver oxygen that allows for adequate energy production. However, the oxygen supply does not appear to be a limiting factor for the aged performer, nor does the decreased mobilization of glucose to produce energy. If the muscle tissue is sufficiently developed to provide a given level of function, it appears that the endurance factor will not be limiting to that function. This is somewhat surprising, in that we recognize a very definite decline in the function of the cardiovascular system in its ability to pump and distribute blood.

Although the skeletomuscular system is susceptible to the aging process after a plateau between the ages of 25 and 30, it is well documented that the functionality of individuals can be considerably above or below the expected capacity. A training program that involves muscle overload will increase oxygen uptake by muscle tissue, increase the muscle mass, increase the functional capacity of muscle tissue, and increase the cellular activity that allows for both muscular strength and energy production. These changes will increase both strength and endurance of almost any muscle group regardless of its efficiency and functionality prior to the intervention program. The maximal effect of training decreases with age but it does not seem to be limited to a given age or functionality. Whether one is young or old, it is harder to improve strength and endurance if the individual is in good functional condition prior to the intervention. It is unfortunate that so many older individuals suffer from hypokinetic (poor physical condition) disease when it can be avoided without serious risk or high incidence of injury.[12] This is true not only of humans but also in the animal kingdom, where the aging process has been observed as considerably slower among wild animals than domesticated animals living in a more sedentary environment.[13] Very definite differences between the two have been noted in the effectiveness and viability of muscle tissue, which in turn determines the effectiveness and viability of physical function.

The Neurosensory System

Less is known about the aging of the neurosensory system than most other biological systems within the human body. Much of the research data are conflicting and provide little basis for an accurate understanding of what occurs, much less for the cause of such occurrences. However, it is well known that nerve cells decrease in number after the age of 25. There is a decreased capacity to send impulses from the brain, but this decrease is not uniform to all parts of the body and from all areas of the brain. As in the case of the skeletomuscular system, those areas that are most active appear to age less rapidly. Conduction velocity also decreases with age and varies considerably among individuals of a given age and functionality.[14] The decrease in the effectiveness of the neurosensory system appears to be more of a concern for the control and function of the skeletomuscular system than it does for recall and reasoning processes that are specific to the neurosensory system itself.[15]

Along with the reduced motor control, it has also been found that sensory input to the central nervous system is impaired with age. It is entirely possible that these two are related because of the importance of sensory input to motor control. Some evidence would indicate that the problem occurs at the synapse, where a greater concentration of inhibitor substance is produced as opposed to a decreased concentration of transmitting substance. Some researchers also have noted a decrease in the myelination of the peripheral nerves. There appears to be a definite increase in lipofuscin (age pigment), which is well known as a factor in the aging process. However, it is not known whether the increase in lipofuscin concentration is a result of the aging process or one of the causes of it. Efforts to reduce the concentration of this substance in tissue have not been successful in reducing the effects of the aging process.

A change in sensory feedback from muscle spindles also affects motor control.[16] It has been noted that the number of intrafusal fibers in the spindle has decreased but there does not appear to be a decrease in extrafusal fibers surrounding the spindle. If this is true, it would lead one to believe that the spindle would not be as effective in resetting itself in a new position for feedback after the muscle has begun to contract or relax. Finite motor movement would be less possible under these circumstances. This could be a possible reason for the slowness and less efficient motor movement patterns observed in the elderly.

There are still other factors associated with sensory input. Studies involving vision in the elderly have indicated the existence of a less flexible lens which tends to yellow with time. This causes distortion in the image on the retina and also less color discrimination. The loss of sensitivity to high frequencies appears to be the first change occurring in audio sensitivity. The range of frequencies begins to diminish along with conductivity of auditory bone structures. It has also been noted that a loss of sensory cells in the organ of Corti occurs that would effect the sensitivity and transmission of the auditory response to the brain. Not as much is known about the propriocerebellar function, which provides tissue stretch and information to the brain about the position of body segments, such as the lower arm. Decreases in nerve conduction velocity would make a difference in coordination, but there is speculation that a decrease in the number of receptors or the effectiveness of these receptors also occurs. Most of the factors associated with sensory input to the brain could be related to a decreased blood supply in the area of the nerve cells or receptors. This is particularly true in the case of vision and hearing.

The Connective Tissues

The connective tissues are made up of large molecules that form a very well organized framework of collagen, elastin, and several other large molecules. The interaction of these molecular structures varies with function and degrees of organization. Research on the aging process has been difficult because of the inability to get tissue samples over a period of time. We have only scratched the surface in our quest to understand the function and change of connective tissues. Only collagen and elastin have been studied to the extent that generalizations can be made.

The physical properties of connective tissue change greatly with time.[17] A great deal of change occurs in the first 5 years of life, with moderate change occuring between the ages of 10 and 30. After 40, a slow degeneration begins that decreases the diameter of the tissue cells.[18] The decrease in the volume of cartilage begins between the ages of 20 and 30 in both weight-bearing and non-weight-bearing body segments. The color of the tissue changes from translucent bluish to opaque yellow. Changes on the surface of cartilage include cracking, fraying, and shredding. In addition to this anatomical change, progressive cell death occurs[19] and irregular bodies are formed, causing a mild dysfunction that continues to become more critical. The depth and diameter of tissue continues to decrease, and the percent of water decreases about 40 percent with advanced age.[20]

Collagen, one of the most abundant substances in connective tissues, tends to hold it together. It becomes much more stable and less elastic with age, and therefore less responsive to mechanical stress. This may be due to chemical activity in the protein which results in the cross-linking of large molecules.[21] This cross-linking tends to bind the protein strands together, and the greater the maturation the more stable the cross-links tend to be. This process, which seriously limits tissue flexibility, has been related to diet.[22] Studies have also indicated that physical activity levels affect the condition of this tissue. Among young individuals the activity will provide for periodic muscle overload, increase the strength, and maintain the viability of the connective tissues. This overload is often not experienced by the aged.

Elastin also undergoes a predictable chemical modification with age.

Chemical cross-links appear to form, similar to those in collagen.[23] This causes a similar decrease in flexibility of the tissue, and therefore a reduced range of motion at the joint as well as greater susceptibility to injury.

One of the most abundant connective tissues is the skin. The tension of the skin increases with maturation and reaches an all-time high at puberty. Then a slight decrease in this tension occurs, followed by a slow increase with age. An increase in collagen concentration in the skin occurs, decreasing the elasticity and flexibility of the tissue. It has also been noted that a decrease in microcirculation occurs, along with a decrease in fat concentrations. It appears that more of the tissues of the skin are replaced with collagen during the aging process and the collagen then becomes cross-linked,[24] causing reduced flexibility. An increase in the incidence of skin infection is related to the decrease in immune system activity of the aged. A concomitant loss of sweat gland and lubrication gland activity occurs which increases the rigidity of the tissue.

The tissues of heart valves react in a similar way to the aging process, with the increased collagen concentration and a decreased number of cells. Little information is available on function as it relates to this change, but it is well known that the pumping action of the heart decreases with age.

Cells produce the large molecules found in intracellular space that form the organized framework of connective tissue. It is important for us to determine if the cell is responsible for producing poor-quality molecular substances with age or if it continues to produce the same type of molecule and the structural matrix then changes as a functioning substance. At present, we have little information to help us resolve this mystery. It is, however, important to realize that connective tissue responds to its environment. Both volume and strength will change as conditions change. This provides an excellent opportunity for prevention, since we can change the environment externally to create the desired response. This response may be counter to the aging process and therefore retard the rate of change.

The Cardiopulmonary System

The failure of the cardiovascular system to function effectively accounts for more than one-half of the deaths in our society today. The aging process that occurs in the system is progressive and physiologically irreversible. The components of this aging process are varied, but fortunately are understood to a greater degree than most other physiologic systems.

As in other tissues, the concentration of lipofuscin or "age pigment" increases in the tissues of the heart.[25] This increase occurs at a rate of 0.3 percent to 0.6 percent per decade of life. The effect of this concentration continues to be a mystery, but the changes in concentration are well documented. The heart also experiences a replacement of muscle tissue with connective tissue.[26] The rate at which this occurs has not been quantitatively established, but the loss of muscle tissue has been considered responsible for loss of forceful contraction of the muscle tissue in the heart. The loss of cells has not been related to the decrease of muscle tissue in the heart with age. Some hearts actually get bigger, and some get smaller. This is quite predictable in that the hearts that lose muscle tissue tend to decrease in size, but when the connective tissue becomes fatigued and hypertension occurs within the system, the heart begins to increase in size due to the great pressure. This causes a decrease in the force of contraction and eventually in the pumping action of the heart.

It has also been noted that a loss of nervous tissue occurs in the heart. The nodal system that controls the electrical activity of the heart, and therefore the rate of contraction, decreases with a concomitant increase in collagen. The decrease in nervous tissue appears to occur with the loss of cells in the nodal areas.

A reduction in cardiac output of the heart with age has been observed. This change occurs at the rate of approximately 1 percent per year after 20 years of age. The heart rate decreases per unit of time and the stroke volume also decreases.[27] This condition eventually reduces the profusion of tissues within the body of blood and therefore reduces the supply of oxygen for energy production in cells. Among those tissues affected is the heart muscle itself. This decreases the ability of the heart to produce energy and, therefore, to maintain effective contractility. This problem is often complicated with a decrease in the size of the coronary arteries due to arterial problems.

The end result of decreased cardiac output is a decrease in the ability of the heart to function as a pump. The force of contraction is reduced along with the velocity of blood flow, creating a less responsive flow of blood to critical tissues.[28] The heart also becomes less responsive to hormones in the blood, which under normal conditions will increase the force of contraction and thereby the cardiac output. However, this lack of responsiveness to hormonal agents means that the heart does not speed up under physical and emotional stress as much as it would normally; therefore it may conserve badly needed oxygen and energy reserves. The system would experience fatigue at a faster rate under these sets of circumstances but would also conserve oxygen and possibly reduce the risk of a heart attack.

It is very encouraging to note that the changes described thus far do not occur as intensely in people who have achieved a reasonable or high degree of physical fitness.[29] Individuals who have maintained a relatively active life have continually challenged the heart in such a way that tissue reduction is minimized. It is also encouraging to note that those individuals who are recovering from a cardiovascular incident may improve cardiovascular function through rehabilitative exercise programs.[30] These programs may not be appropriate for all cardiovascular patients and certainly should be carried out within the confines of a well-supervised program. A complete evaluation of cardiac condition and pathology is necessary prior to starting such a program. The resulting cardiovascular changes tend to improve the function of the heart as a pump and reduce the effect of the aging process. Most epidemiological studies indicate that sedentary individuals run a risk of a cardiovascular problem two or three times greater than that of physically active individuals. These studies have been conducted using subjects of all ages, including those in their 60s and 70s.

The condition of the arterial delivery system is also critical to cardiovascular function. It has already been noted that increased resistance in the arteries increases the pressure within the heart. This increase in resistance is due largely to more rigid and smaller arterials.[31] The replacement of smooth muscle by connective tissue in the arterials causes a loss of elasticity and an increase in rigidity. This condition, called arteriosclerosis, is one of the critical factors associated with high blood pressue. Elevated blood pressure (hypertension) is observed in most aged individuals and is considered one of the major health problems associated with age.[32]

Another condition of the arteries, atherosclerosis, is due to a plaquing process that occurs within the layers of the arterial wall. As lipid (fat) substances move through the arterial wall they sometimes become lodged within the tissues and begin to create a softening condition within these tissues. Later this softened material becomes hard, and a plaque is formed that reduces the size of the interior space of the vessel. This reduces the blood supply and also the ability to transport oxygen to tissue farther from the heart.[33] When the heart is less effective as a pump, and less efficient, it needs more oxygen to do the same amount of work. At the same time, the blood, and therefore oxygen, supply to the heart muscle is decreased. When the energy supply is less than the energy needed to keep the heart going, the "usual" kind of heart attack—a myocardial infarction—occurs. Although this condition represents our greatest health hazard today for older individuals, the projection of future problems is even greater. Most elderly individuals of today were not observed to have the plaquing condition as young adults. Now, this irreversible condition is observed in most of our young adults as well.

An added problem is that advancing age produces a decreased response to pressure changes within the arterial system. As the arteries become less flexible and the pressure increases, the body does not respond normally to reduce the pressure. In most cases, the pressure continues to increase as the aging process continues.

Rather encouraging results have been observed from the use of physical exercise as a means of reducing the incidence of arterial rigidity and plaquing. The evidence is not as complete and conclusive as that of the heart response to exercise, but most researchers would agree that very positive changes can occur with regular and appropriate physical activity. Although the condition is not reversible, it seems that it can be retarded through physical exercise and certain types of dietary intervention.

The Immune System

The function of the immune system is to protect the body and maintain the integrity of its tissues. The components of this system are the thymus, the spleen, and the lymph nodes. The immune system consists largely of the reticular endothelial structures, which are made up of two kinds of cells, the T cells and the A and B cells.[34] The T cells go through the thymus prior to biological activity. The thymus is located above the heart and is quite susceptible to steroids and stress, which will reduce its size and function, possibly affecting this process. The A and B cells do not go through the thymus but act directly within the bloodstream.

If foreign bacteria (antigen) enter the body through the intestinal area, A cells (white cells) engulf the bacteria and digest them. The waste is encapsulized in the white cell, which goes back to the lymph node. At the node, the white cell stimulates B cell production specific to the given foreign substance, and the A cell goes out into the blood to destroy more antigens. The A cell also leaves memory cells in the lymph node for a secondary defense. This is how immunizations work. The A cells pick up the bacteria and take them to the lymph node where specific B cells are ready and waiting to attack the specific invader. The T cells act as helpers or suppressors of the defense process,[35] and the A and B cells are largely responsible for the actual defense against foreign bodies.

It has been well documented that the immune system is not as effective in the aged.[36] Young adults have little problem in producing new A and B cells and can therefore ward off most invading substances. However, with age the ability to produce new cells that attack bacteria and other foreign substances is reduced by approximately 50 percent. The problem is magnified by the fact that the A and B cells that are produced are not as effective in function. This degradation process begins shortly after sexual maturity when the thymus gets smaller and less active. As a result, the substances secreted by T cells that help or suppress A and B cell activity do not enhance the fight against foreign bodies.[37] The suppressants appear to be more prevalent in older age, hindering the ability of the A and B cells to respond quickly.[38] It does not appear that these cells wear out, but rather that the activity and regeneration process is suppressed. The older individual then is much more susceptible to invasion by bacteria and much less able to cope with foreign bodies that previously were quickly neutralized.

The immune system may also attack substances produced by the body itself, a phenomenon called autoimmunity. The immune system indiscriminately attacks and destroys the body's own molecular substances to the point that it is difficult for the tissues to survive. The suppression that normally comes from the T cells appears to be lost, and the aggressive A and B cells attack substances throughout the body that are necessary for normal functioning. The older person is more susceptible to this danger than the younger individual.

Theories of Cellular Aging

It has been said that there are as many theories associated with the biological aging process as there are researchers studying the phenomenon. The literature supports this position to some extent, but if the theories are reviewed carefully they can be classified into groups that share critical concepts and observations. Most of these theories will fit within two basic categories—"unprogrammed" theories and "programmed" theories. Unprogrammed theories posit a random series of events that contribute to the aging process as time passes. The programmed theories hypothesize genetic factors and events that are programmed before birth and implemented through the central nervous system and the endocrine system.

Unprogrammed Theories

One of the most popular theories of the aging process is that of somatic mutation. This theory takes the position that aging is an accumulation of defects occurring within the genes (chromosomes), resulting in a loss of information at a particular spot on the molecule. Radiation is known to be one of the greatest causes of this problem. If the cell divides, as the cells of some tissues do, the daughter cells will not be the same as the parent cell and therefore will not function effectively in their predetermined role. If a cell does not divide but continues to renew its intercellular substances, the loss of the message on the chromosome will tend to bring in and produce ineffective materials, which also causes the production of poor-quality cells and a loss of cellular function. The more poor-quality cells or materials within cells, the greater the dysfunction of the resulting organism.

This theory is supported by the fact that it is possible for chemical substances, called free radicals, to be present within the cell that will chemically react with the chromosome to cause the same problem as described above, resulting in aging phenomena. Many chemical substances have been administered in attempts to bind up the free radicals that tend to cause this illicit chemical activity, but this process has been found to be ineffective. Some gerontologists feel that this chemical activity occurs through a cross-linking of chromosomal substances and not through free radicals at all. This too may cause an inactivation of the genetic material that produces new substances within the cell and thereby result in a reduction of functionality.

The error-catastrophe theory is similar to the somatic mutation theory in that it also addresses itself to alterations in the molecular biology of the cell as the materials within the cell turn over and new substances are formed to continue the cellular activity. The message indicating what kind of materials to bring in to the cell comes from the chromosome, which is located in the cell's nucleus. The genetic material sends out another substance that carries this message to the other parts of the cell and is responsible for bringing in the right kind of protein substances to produce the appropriate type of protein within the cell. The error-catastrophe theory states that the message carrying the substance becomes contaminated, or the message becomes confused, and the wrong proteins are brought into the cell, thus producing materials that are ineffective in conducting the cellular activities. After maturity, this process occurs until a large number of cells have become incapacitated and therefore hinder the functionality of the total individual.

The protein–cross-linking theory is similar to the others but has some very distinct differences. This theory takes the position that collagen cross-links with the protein of the cell and this process continues with age. The original cellular protein production occurs uninterrupted, but once the protein is formed, the chemical cross-linking occurs in such a way that the molecule becomes stronger but less flexible. If this happens in a muscle cell, the contractibility of the cell is impaired considerably. It also affects the chemical activity of the protein substance within the cell. The elasticity of the tissue, particularly in tendons and arteries, decreases significantly, even to the point where viable muscle tissue is replaced with scar tissue. An example of this loss of flexibility can be seen in the skin pinch test. In the young individual the pinched fold of skin quickly disappears, but in the older individual the fold remains longer because the flexibility of the tissue has decreased. For many years, scientists have been trying to find an enzyme to break the cross-linking bonds that tend to increase with age and decrease human functionality. These efforts have so far been unsuccessful.

Another theory quite different from these, yet still of the "unprogrammed" school of thought, is the hypothesis that autoimmunity is a key process in aging. In autoimmunity the antibodies making up the immune system attack the body's own protein in addition to foreign protein substances that might enter the body from different sources. In other words, the immune system reacts against its own tissue and, in a sense, rejects itself. This activity is con-

sidered random and inceases with age, but it must be realized that this condition might also be programmed to the point that it is nature's way of completing the life cycle. This theory relates to the others in that antibodies are
also proteins and, if the molecular substances within the proteins are
malformed due to a poor-quality messenger substance, the malformed antibodies do not function as they should and erroneously attack the tissues
that are needed for total body function rather than the invading antigens.

One of the oldest theories of aging is the lipofuscin pigment theory. It has
been known for years that lipofuscin, also called "age pigment," increases
with age. This occurs mainly in the heart and brain. The substance is made
up chiefly of protein and lipid (fat) substances, but the specific chemistry is
unknown. The function of the lipofuscin pigment within the cell is also
unknown, but certain chemical substances tend to decrease the concentration. Some researchers think that an accumulation of the pigment causes
the aging process to occur. However, it must be noted that this substance
could also be a *result* of the aging process, since as aging continues the concentration increases. It could also be an expression of the cell's failure to
metabolize to form energy. Some researchers have also related this process to
free radical activity because it appears to be related to intercellular oxida-
tion, which is part of the metabolic process.

Another, and very old, theory is that of calcium shift, which has been
postulated by those scientists who have related stress to the aging process. It
is well known that aging occurs as a result of, or along with, a change in soft
to harder and less flexible tissues. At the same time, bones get weaker and
decrease in both density and mass. This circumstance makes it easy to
speculate that calcium, which is largely responsible for healthy bone, moves
from the bone tissues to soft body tissues, making the bone weaker and the
soft tissues more rigid. The aging process, then, is here considered to be the
cumulative effect of this shift over a period of time. There is some evidence
that such shifting tends to occur at a greater rate as stress and body tension
increases. However, no attempt has been made to support this theory with
data from controlled experimentation.

Intervention in the aging process, if the process is unprogrammed, would
come through the reduction of "accidents" that have detrimental effects on
biological function. These accidents must be more clearly defined and we
must have more data in support of one or the other of these theories before
effective intervention can occur. It is interesting to note, however, that the
theories have all been postulated since World War II, although civilizations
have been concerned about the aging process for thousands of years. It is
quite easy for even the nonresearcher to see that one or two breakthroughs
in research on the aging process could effect a rather significant change in
the longevity of human beings as well as improve functioning of the
physical organism during the first 70 or 80 years.

Programmed Theories

Cell division is programmed to a very specific degree during the developmental stages of the human life span. The mitotic-exhaustion theory states that this specificity continues through the aging process and that cells can only divide a certain number of times. When the cell gets close to the end of its capacity to divide, many things begin to happen that result in illnesses and incapacities. If the organism is able to survive these challenges, then the final stage of life is ended through the inability of the cells to divide and maintain life. This theory relates to all cells except nerve and muscle cells. It is strongly suggested that this process is preprogrammed and that it is as much a part of the life cycle as the developmental stage. The mechanism through which the process occurs has not been described, but it is thought to be triggered in some way when the reproductive phase of life has reached its plateau.

Another of the programmed theories of the aging process is the rate-of-living theory. According to this theory, there is a finite amount of energy available to the living being, and just so many heartbeats available during a lifetime. We simply run out of energy and therefore the heart and vital organs stop functioning. Smaller organisms have a higher heart rate and a reduced life span. Larger animals, like the elephant, have a low heart rate and a very long life span. Little research has been done to test this theory on humans who have either a very low or a very high resting heart rate. It is, however, interesting to note that individuals who are in good physical condition have a relatively low resting heart rate, and there is some indication that they have greater longevity. Those who support the theory also make note of the fact that brain weight is related to body size and that this relationship is a good measure of longevity. As the brain weight per unit of body weight increases, so does longevity within species of the animal kingdom. Therefore, the combination of lifetime energy, brain complexity, and body weight may be a factor in the longevity of the human.

The programmed theory that has the most support at present and appears to be gaining support among researchers is the central nervous system–endocrine theory. This theory states that aging is just another stage of development and that the same process that turns on certain activities during development turns them off after sexual maturity. This means that there is a regulated control of the phases of life and that the aging process is not a series of accidents or unprogrammed incidents. This does not mean that we cannot do something about the aging process. We know a great deal about hormonal control and what triggers the onset of maturity, which means that we may also be able to learn about those events that trigger maturation and aging. Once we know the process and the mechanism for control, we can then begin to alter it positively. It is understood that other factors are superimposed on this programmed aging process. Stress, nutrition, and exercise, among others, affect the rate and the mechanism associated with programmed aging.

We can learn a great deal about programmed aging from lower forms of animal life. There we see the same possible hormonal control affecting the rate of change from one developmental stage to another. This process of metamorphosis starts in the brain and affects changes within the genetic makeup of the cell. We see the insect evolve from the egg to the larval stage, then to the pupa (cocoon stage), and finally to the adult insect stage. Specific genes are engaged at given times, and aging occurs in a programmed way because of the cell environment that turns on a certain portion of the genetic substance. We may be able to turn on and turn off this genetic message to the cell in such a way that the aging process can be altered to maintain integrity of tissues and thereby affect longevity and functionality. The fact that we do not understand these mechanisms completely at this time means that more research on this process will be necessary before we can develop intervention strategies.

Intervention in the Aging Process

Although some scholars still feel that the aging process is finite and predictable, it is obvious from our review of the theories of aging that, despite what we have learned in the past 20 years, we are still not able to predict the process. If the explosion of knowledge continues, we can expect, in the not too distant future, additional breakthroughs and support for certain of the theories presented above. Although we have a long way to go, we now understand the nature of the biological aging process much better than we did only a few years ago. It appears reasonable that an even greater knowledge of the nature of the process could lead to an improvement in the human condition and possibly to increased longevity. Regardless of how we feel about intervening in the aging process through hormonal control mechanisms, it is also possible to affect the process through more natural intervention tactics. Changing a person's lifestyle to include better nutritional and activity habits may be a more widely acceptable strategy for promoting better health. It appears probable that interventions such as these could improve longevity, but it is almost certain that such practices can delay the effects of aging and improve the quality of life during the later years.

Intervening in the aging process has taken many forms through the years. Until only a few years ago, interventions were highly mystical and in many cases profit-motivated. More recently, aging and the biological theories that describe it have been carefully studied to determine the feasibility of intervention techniques that are scientifically based.

Interventions with drugs have not been demonstrated to be an effective solution except in disease conditions. Nutrition and exercise appear to be the most acceptable and effective interventions. If the nutrition of an individual is inappropriate, the effect of aging is magnified. A good diet will help the body resist disease and avoid abnormally rapid aging, but it will not necessarily improve the function of the various systems that have been discussed in this chapter. Physical activity, on the other hand, has been shown to improve physical condition and make it possible for the older person to live a more complete and satisfying life. The most important issue is the intensity and duration of the activity, the objective being to maximize development and minimize injury. This is why an older person must consult a physician prior to changing his or her level of activity. The physician will be able to diagnose the existence of possible pathology that may be affected by this change in lifestyle. Before changing one's level of activity, one should have a work-capacity evaluation and receive a prescription for an exercise program. If this is not done, the person may undertake a level of activity that is not sufficient to elicit the type of change that will improve physical condition. Conversely, the person may undergo a too-aggressive exercise program that is actually harmful and possibly lethal.

Organized exercise programs conducted by trained professionals will help to eliminate the possibility of too little or too much exercise. These programs usually include warm-up, flexibility, relaxation, and aerobic activities designed to stimulate and improve the cardiopulmonary system. Aerobic activities are total body activities such as walking, running, cycling, and swimming. Not only do they add more oxygen to the tissue, but they also improve the efficiency of oxygen utilization. Greater oxygen supply provides more energy production, and increased energy production reduces fatigue. This is particularly important to the heart, which needs a great deal of energy to withstand both physical and emotional stress. In addition to cardiopulmonary conditioning, appropriate physical exercise can also enhance an older person's strength, hand-eye coordination, reaction time, and muscle tone.

Glossary

Anabolic hormone. A hormone associated with protein retention, sometimes used to improve muscular strength.

Atherosclerosis. A condition occurring in the arteries, characterized by fat deposition in the tissues and causing a decreased interior space.

Collagen. A substance made of protein and associated with muscle tissue; it is noncontracting and has the function of holding the tissues together.

Elastin. The principal constituent of yellow elastic tissue.

Extrafusal. Those muscle fibers that are responsible for contraction leading to body movement.

Intrafusal. Muscle tissue within the muscle spindle that resets the spindle for continued activity.

Muscle spindle. A sensory unit within muscle tissue that sends signals to the brain indicating stretch and body segment position (e.g., the position of the lower arm).

Myelination. The lipid covering of portions of the axon of certain nerve cells that helps to increase the velocity of an impulse.

Myofibril. A tiny fiber found in muscle tissue inside the cell and responsible for contraction.

Nodal. Refers to the nodes made of nervous tissue controlling the activity of the normal heart.

Organ of Corti. A hearing organ located in the inner ear.

Reticular endothelial system. A network of cells that make up the immune system, having the power to ingest foreign particulate matter.

Notes

1. L. J. Rubinstein, "Aging Changes in Muscle," *Structure and Function of Muscle,* Vol. 2 (New York: Academic Press, 1960), pp. 226–298.

2. F. McKeown, *Pathology of the Aged* (London: Butterworth Co., 1965).

3. J. Degueker, J. Remans, P. Franssen, and J. Waes, "Aging Patterns of Trabecular and Cortical Bone and Their Relationships," *Calcium Tissue Research* 7 (1971), pp. 23–30.

4. M. Trotter, G. E. Broman, and R. R. Peterson, "Densities of Bones of White and Negro Skeletons," *Journal Bone Joint Surgery* 42A (1960), pp. 50–58.

5. F. D. Sedlin, A. R. Villanaeva, and H. M. Frost, "Age Variations in the Specific Surface of Howship's Lacunae as an Index of Human Bone Resorption," *Anatomy Record* 146 (1963), pp. 201–207.

6. M. Rockstein and K. Brandt, "Changes in Phosphorous Metabolism of the Gastroenemius Muscle in Aging White Rats," *Proceedings of the Society of Experimental Medicine* 107 (1961), pp. 377–380.

7. C. H. Lowry, A. B. Hastings, T. Z. Hull, and A. N. Brown, "Histochemical Changes Associated with Aging," *Biological Chemistry* 143 (1942), pp. 271–280.

8. H. Dubois, "Water and Electrolyte Content of Human Skeletal Muscle: Variation with Age," *Review of French Studies of Clinical Biology* 17 (1972), pp. 503–513.

9. E. Guttman and V. Hanzlikova, "Motor Unit in Old Age," *Nature* 209 (1966), pp. 921–922.

10. S. I. Frubel-Osipora, "The Neuromuscular System," *The Basis of Gerontology,* D. F. Chebotarev and N. V. Malkovskij, eds. (Moscow: Meditsina, 1969), pp. 128–129.

11. S. Tucek and E. Gutmann, "Choline Acetyltransferase Activity in Muscles of Old Rats," *Experimental Neurology* 38 (1973), pp. 349–360.

12. B. Kraus and W. Raab, *Hypokinetic Disease* (Springfield, Ill.: Charles C. Thomas, 1961).

13. Z. Hruza, "Aging of Cells and Molecules," *Handbook of the Pathology of Allergies* 6, 4 (1972), pp. 83–108.

14. I. Wagman and H. Leese, "Conduction Velocity of Ulnar Nerves in Human Subjects of Different Ages and Sizes," *Journal of Neurophysiology* 15 (1952), pp. 235–244.

15. H. Brody, "Organization of the Cerebral Cortex. III. A Study of Aging in the Human Cerebral Cortex," *Journal of Comparative Neurology* 102 (1955), pp. 511–556.

16. M. Swash and K. P. Fox, "The Effect of Age on Human Skeletal Muscle. Studies of the Morphology and Innervation of Muscle Spindles," *Journal of Neurological Science* 16 (1972), pp. 417–432.

17. M. Schubert and D. Hamerman, "Aging and Osteoarthritis," *A Primer on Connective Tissue Biochemistry* (Philadelphia: Lea and Febiger, 1968), pp. 247–268.

18. D. S. Jackson, "Temporal Changes in Collagen-Aging or Essential Maturation," *Aging, Advances in Biology of Skin*, Vol. 6, W. Montagua, ed. (New York: Pergamon Press, 1965), pp. 219–228.

19. R. Silberberg and M. Silberberg, "Male Sex Hormones and Osteoarthrosis in Mice," *Journal Bone Joint Surgery* 43A (1961) pp. 243–248.

20. E. H. Jebens and M. E. Monk-Jones, "On the Viscosity and pH of Synovial Fluid and the pH of Blood," *Journal Bone Joint Surgery* 41B (1959), pp. 388–400.

21. S. P. Robins, M. Shimokomaki, and A. J. Bailey, "The Chemistry of the Collagen Cross-links. Age-Related Changes in the Reducible Components of Intact Bovine Collagen Fibers," *Biochemistry Journal* 131 (1973), pp. 771–780.

22. A. V. Everitt, "Food Intake, Growth and the Aging of Collagen in Rat Tail Tendon," *Gerontologia* 17 (1972), pp. 98–104.

23. P. M. Gallop, M. A. Paz, B. Pereyera, and O. O. Blumenfeld, "The Maturation of Connective Tissue Proteins," *Israel Journal of Chemistry* 12 (1974), pp. 305–317.

24. D. A. Hall, "The Aging of Connective Tissue," *Aspects of the Biology of Aging*, Symposium No. 21 of the Society for Experimental Biology (New York: Academic Press, 1967), pp. 101–126.

25. R. R. Kohn, "Heart and Cardiovascular System," *Handbook of the Biology of Aging*, C. E. Finch and L. Hayflick, eds. (New York: Van Nostrand Reinhold Co., 1977), Ch. 12.

26. M. Brandfonbrener, M. Landowne, and N. W. Shock, "Changes in Cardiac Output with Age," *Circulation* 12 (1955), pp. 557–566.

27. Ibid.

28. L. T. Heller and W. V. Whitehorn, "Age-Associated Alterations in Myocardial Contractile Properties," *American Journal of Physiology* 222 (1972), pp. 1613–1619.

29. W. H. Osness, "Aging Now and in the Future: A Physiological Perspective," *Journal of Social Welfare* 5, 1 (1978), pp. 15–23.

30. W. H. Osness, "Cardiac Rehabilitation through Exercise for Older Americans," *Gerontology Review* 1, 5 (1978), pp. 1–2.

31. A. D. Bender, "The Effect of Increasing Age on the Distribution of Peripheral Blood Flow in Man," *Journal of the American Geriatric Society* 13 (1965), pp. 192–198.

32. M. Landowne, M. Brandfonbrener, and N. W. Shock, "The Relation of Age to

Certain Measures of Performance of the Heart and Circulation," *Circulation* 12 (1955), pp. 567–576, and D. J. Mozersky, D. S. Sumner, D. E. Hokanson, and D. E. Strandness, "Transcutaneous Measurement of the Elastic Properties of the Human Femoral Artery," *Circulation* 46 (1972), pp. 948–955.

33. C.T.M. Davies, "The Oxygen Transport System in Relation to Age," *Clinical Science* 42 (1972), pp. 1–13.

34. K. Shortman and J. Palmer, "The Requirement for Macrophages in the In Vitro Immune Response," *Cell Immunology* 2 (1971), pp. 399–410.

35. H. S. Lawrence and M. Landy, *Mediators of Cellular Immunology* (New York: Academic Press, 1969).

36. W. Andrew, *Cellular Changes With Age* (Springfield, Ill.: Charles C. Thomas, 1952).

37. E. Friedberger, G. Brock, and A. Fürstenheim, "Zur Normalantikörperkurve des Menschen Durch die Verschiedenen Lebensalter und Ihre Bedeutung für die Erklärung der Hautteste," *Z. Immunitätforschung* 64 (1929), pp. 294–319.

38. T. Futuhata and M. Eguchi, "The Change of the Agglutinin Titer with Age," *Proceedings of the Japanese Academy* 31 (1955), pp. 555–557.

4

Aging and Mental Processes

Nancy Wadsworth Denney

In recent years there has been a growing interest in the area of cognitive development during the adult years, especially the later years. Cognitive development involves the development of the ability to think, reason, and solve problems. Early work in the field focused predominantly on the time from birth to adolescence, since it was often assumed that no major changes in cognition took place beyond the adolescent years.[1] However, recent research indicates that there may be a number of changes in cognition after adolescence. These findings have resulted in an increase in the volume of research in cognitive development during the adult years. The research in this area can be classified according to three main theoretical orientations: psychometric research; Piagetian research; and problem-solving research. The results of the research in each of these three areas will be reviewed in this chapter and implications will be examined. However, before such research can be discussed, it is necessary to explore some of the methodological issues that are so important for accurately understanding and interpreting the research results.

The methodological issues that are critically important in developmental research can best be illustrated with examples from research in psychometric intelligence. This research is based upon individuals' performances on standard intelligence tests, which tend to measure a variety of different cognitive abilities such as vocabulary, perceptual-motor abilities, basic mathematical computation, spatial abilities, memory, and so forth. Because research on adult age differences in performance on standard intelligence tests has been conducted with a variety of research designs, it is possible to illustrate that different results are sometimes obtained with different designs.

Two basic research designs have traditionally been used with developmental research, the cross-sectional design and the longitudinal design.

With the cross-sectional design, individuals of a variety of different ages are selected to be tested during one testing period. For example, 30-year-olds, 50-year-olds, and 70-year-olds might all be tested in the same year. With the longitudinal design, on the other hand, individuals serve as test subjects on several occasions, at all the age levels under investigation: for example, at age 30, in 1950; again at age 50, in 1970; and yet again at age 70, in 1990. The use of these two research designs has often given somewhat different perspectives on age differences in adult intelligence. Most of the cross-sectional studies have yielded results indicating that intelligence increases until the early adult years and decreases thereafter.[2] Longitudinal studies, on the other hand, have tended to show stability or slight increases in intelligence from early adulthood through most of the adult years, with declines only during the very late adult years.[3]

This discrepancy in the results obtained from the two designs is at least partially a result of the fact that age and cohort are confounded in the cross-sectional design, while they are not confounded in the longitudinal design. That is, in the cross-sectional design age and cohort cannot be studied independently of each other, while in the longitudinal design they can. *Age* refers to the number of years an individual has been living; *cohort* refers to a group of individuals born at the same time. It is important to make the distinction between age and cohort. Individuals of the same age might have characteristics in common simply because they are the same age; likewise, members of the same cohort might have common traits as a result of living through the same time.

In the cross-sectional design, for example, comparing 50-year-olds and 70-year-olds in 1970, the 50-year-olds belong to a cohort born in 1920, whereas the 70-year-old belong to a cohort born in 1900. Thus, age and cohort are confounded; you cannot determine whether differences between the two groups are a result of age changes or differences in the characteristics of the two cohorts. In a longitudinal design, on the other hand, testing the same individuals when they are 50 and again when they are 70, their year of birth is constant; thus, the test groups differ with respect to age but not with respect to cohort. Any differences that are found can then be attributed to age rather than to cohort. The results of cross-sectional studies, therefore, reflect both cohort and age differences. The results of longitudinal studies reflect age changes independent of cohort differences.

Since the results of the cross-sectional studies of standard intelligence test performance tend to indicate a decline in intelligence after early adulthood whereas the results of the longitudinal studies tend to indicate a decline starting much later, the cross-sectional results may mean that there are cohort differences in intelligence, with older cohorts performing less well than younger cohorts. There could be a number of reasons for this—for example, it may be that the older cohorts perform less well because they have less education than the younger cohorts. As can be seen in Table 4.1, elderly individuals have, on the average, completed fewer years of school than younger adults. On the other hand, it may be that the older cohorts perform less well because they are not used to taking tests. Not only have elderly individuals had fewer years of school in which they might be exposed to testing, but during those years there was much less standardized testing than there is today. Yet another possibility is that the older cohorts have not had to meet as many cognitive demands as younger cohorts. Because of the increasing complexity of all aspects of life in recent years, the cognitive demands that each succeeding generation has had to deal with may have increased. That is, life today may require more thinking, reasoning, and problem solving than was required in the past. Such increases in cognitive demands might stimulate better cognitive performance.

While the longitudinal design is somewhat better than the cross-sectional design in that age and cohort are not confounded, there are difficulties associated with longitudinal studies as well. The developmental changes exhibited by one cohort in a longitudinal study cannot be generalized to other cohorts; other cohorts could change in different ways. In the longitudinal study age and time of measurement are confounded. If events occuring at the time of measurement affect performance, then that effect will be confounded with changes due to aging. Consider a hypothetical example of a longitudinal study of activity level conducted with adults from the age of 50 to the age of 70. Suppose that the results indicated a decline in activity from age 50 to age 68 followed by an increase in activity from age 68 to age 70. Suppose also that the year the individuals in the study turned 68, a bus program for the elderly was instituted in the city where the study was conducted. The program provided a bus that would pick people up at their door and take them wherever they wanted to go within the city at any time. If the

Table 4.1: Years of Education Completed (1970 Figures) by Age Group

Years of Education Completed	Age= 25-64	Age= 65+
No School (0)	0.7%	3.1%
Elementary (1-8)	21.3%	56.7%
High School (9-12)	55.4%	28.3%
College (13 or more)	22.6%	11.9%

researcher were not aware of the bus program he or she might conclude on the basis of the study results that activity level decreases in individuals up to the age of about 68 and increases thereafter. The researcher might assume that this is a natural developmental function. However, if the researcher became aware of the fact that the increase in activity level coincided with the institution of the bus program, he or she would no doubt suggest that the results could have been influenced by the program. Thus, the developmental function obtained in this hypothetical longitudinal study would be affected both by actual age changes and by a time-of-measurement effect. For this reason, one should not generalize from the developmental function obtained with one cohort to other cohorts. If the bus program actually was the cause of the increase in activity level, one would not expect to find a similar increase at age 68 in another cohort.

Two developmental psychologists, Schaie[4] and Baltes,[5] have proposed research designs that at least partially remedy some of the difficulties associated with cross-sectional and longitudinal designs. Schaie suggested that the analysis of developmental change should take into account three sources of variation—age, cohort, and time of measurement. These three components are always confounded in developmental research. In cross-sectional designs age and cohort are confounded, as was discussed earlier; time of measurement is not confounded because only one time of measurement is involved. Thus, with the cross-sectional design no estimate of the importance of time of measurement is obtained. In longitudinal designs, age and time of measurement are confounded, as was discussed above, but no estimate of the importance of cohort is obtained because only one cohort is measured.

Schaie proposed three experimental designs that would each separate the effects of two of the three components in his developmental model. The cross-sequential design involves the measurement of two or more cohorts at two or more times of measurement. For example, individuals born in 1920, 1930, and 1940 might all be tested in 1960, 1970, and 1980. Age would clearly be confounded in this design. Once year of birth and time of measurement are established, age is also determined. If individuals were born in 1930 and tested in 1960, they would have to be 30 years old. This is true for all three of the components in Schaie's model. Any two of the components can be independently varied in any research design, but then the third component is always determined and, therefore, confounded with the other two components. In the cohort-sequential design, two or more cohorts are measured at two or more age levels. For example, individuals who were born in 1920, 1930, and 1940 might be tested when they were 40, 50, and 60. Time of testing would, of course, be confounded in this design. In the time-sequential design, two or more ages are tested at two or more times of measurement. For example, 40-, 50-, and 60-year-olds might be tested in 1970, 1980, and 1990. Cohort is the confounded variable in this design.

By using one of the designs proposed by Schaie it is possible to separate the effects of two of the three components. In many ways these designs provide more informative results than the traditional cross-sectional and longitudinal designs. The latter two designs, however, have been the bases of most of the studies conducted to date. One reason that Schaie's designs have not been used more often is that they are very difficult to conduct. For example, if you wanted to conduct a cohort-sequential study testing individuals from three different cohorts when they were 50, 60, and 70 years old, and if the cohorts were separated by 10 years, as can be seen from Figure 4.1, it would take 40 years to complete the study. Not many researchers are willing to take on a 40-year study. In spite of the fact that the more informative designs such as those devised by Schaie are seldom used, it is still important to understand some of the points Schaie made regarding the cross-sectional and longitudinal designs. With the cross-sectional design it must be kept in mind that any differences between age groups do not necessarily represent age-related changes; the differences could reflect cohort differences as well. Further, it is important to remember that the age-change effect obtained in a longitudinal study might not represent a general age-change function. Because time-of-measurement effects are confounded with age in longitudinal designs, any developmental functions obtained with such designs might reflect time-of-measurement effects rather than age-change effects. These considerations must be taken into account when interpreting the results of developmental research. Keeping them in mind, we can proceed to a discussion of research in adult cognitive development.

Figure 4.1: Examples of a Cohort Sequential Design

Cohort	1940	1950	1960	1970	1980
1890	50*	60	70		
1900		50	60	70	
1910			50	60	70

Year of Testing

*Age

Psychometric Research

One of the major approaches to understanding cognition is the psycho-metric intelligence approach, in which a number of the different abilities thought to make up intelligence are measured. The main psychometric theorists with a strong developmental orientation are Cattell[6] and Horn.[7] They made a distinction between two very general types of abilities. What they called "fluid" intelligence includes abilities such as inductive reasoning, figural relations, and associative memory. These abilities are nonverbal—for example, determining which figure should go next in a series of figures or eliminating a figure that does not belong in a series. Some representative problems of this type are shown in Figure 4.2. Fluid intelligence is purported to be closely associated with the neurophysiological state of the individual. What Cattell and Horn called "crystallized" intelligence, on the other hand, includes such abilities as vocabulary, verbal comprehension, and semantic relations. These are predominantly verbal abilities and are purported to be largely determined by learning and acculturation. Some examples of the kinds of questions that measure crystallized intelligence are presented in Figure 4.3. Horn and Cattell[8] have found that performance on measures of fluid intelligence begins to decline following adolescence, while performance on measures of crystallized intelligence increases throughout most of the life span.

Other researchers have also found that different intellectual abilities follow different developmental patterns over the life span. Nonverbal abilities such as abstract reasoning, perceptual-motor speed, spatial percep-tion, and the like have been found by a number of investigators to decline from early adulthood through old age.[9] Verbal abilities, on the other hand, have been found to increase throughout most of the life span,[10] with the excep-tion of a possible decline after the age of about 60.[11] Thus, it appears that there are eventual declines in almost all the abilities tested on standard in-telligence tests. However, the research also clearly indicates that the age at which abilities begin to decline many vary considerably depending upon the type of ability tested. Nonverbal intellectual abilities seem to begin declining much earlier than verbal, experience-related abilities.

These conclusions regarding the development of intellectual abilities across the life span are based not only on cross-sectional and longitudinal research, but also on research with some of the designs suggested by Schaie[12] and Baltes.[13] It is therefore possible that there are some actual age-related changes in intellectual functioning. However, it is important to note that research on intellectual functioning also indicates that there are substantial cohort differences as well as actual age-related changes.[14]

Figure 4.2: Examples of Problems that Measure Fluid Intelligence

1. Choose the Correct Figure to Complete the Series:

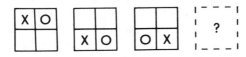

Alternatives:

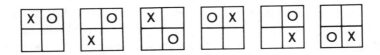

2. Choose the Odd Member of the Group:

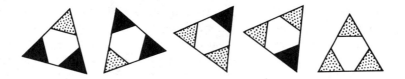

Figure 4.3: Examples of Problems that Measure Crystallized Intelligence

Vocabulary tests in which the subject is asked to define a list of
    vocabulary words.

Verbal analogies in which the subject is to select the word from a list of
    alternatives that best completes analogies such as the following:
    bird is to air as fish is to

Verbal comprehension question in which the subject is presented with a
    problem situation and is asked what he would do in the situation.
    For example, the subject might be asked "What would you do if you
    were in a shopping center and found a little child who was lost?"

Verbal fluency problems in which the subject might be shown a picture of a
    little boy carrying something and asked to name all of the things
    that he or she can think of that the little boy could be carrying
    as fast as possible.

Piagetian Research

A second major approach to understanding cognition is based on Piagetian theory.[15] Piaget, a biologist by training, developed a very comprehensive "stage" theory of cognitive development that encompasses birth through adolescence. The different stages result from changes in the cognitive structures of the child as he or she matures and interacts with the environment. Piaget used a wide variety of different tasks to assess cognitive functioning. Recent research on adult age differences in performance on such tasks indicates that elderly adults tend to perform less well than middle-aged adults. For example, the elderly have been found to perform relatively poorly on tasks that measure their ability to classify similar objects together,[16] to distinguish between animate and inanimate objects,[17] and to imagine what things would look like from another person's perspective,[18] as well as their level of moral reasoning[19] and their level of scientific thinking.[20]

While the results of these studies indicate a lower level of performance by elderly adults than by middle-aged individuals on Piagetian tasks, the results of studies of conservation abilities are less clear. In tests of conservation, the subject is presented with two quantities of something that are equivalent with respect to a relevant dimension. Then the experimenter alters one of the two quantities in some way that does not change it with respect to the relevant dimension, and asks the subject whether the two quantities are the same or different. For example, the experimenter might present the subject with two beakers of water that are the same shape and contain the same amount of water, as illustrated in Figure 4.4. The experimenter then might pour the water from one of the two beakers into a third beaker of a different shape, asking the subject which of the two beakers now has more water. Of course, the correct answer is that the two beakers have the same amount of water, even though the water level in the two beakers is different because the beakers are shaped differently.

In several cross-sectional studies, elderly individuals have been found to understand the principles of conservation less well than younger adults.[21] However, in other studies, such age-related differences have not been found.[22] It appears that, while age-related differences are rather consistently found on most of the other Piagetian abilities, conservation may be an exception. Perhaps the reason is that while most of the other abilities are not exercised much by elderly individuals, conservation abilities are used by virtually all elderly people on a daily basis. For example, in order to cook one has to understand conservation; one has to realize that one cup of sugar is still one cup of sugar whether it is in the measuring cup or in a pan or bowl. Likewise one has to realize that 10 pennies are worth 10 cents whether they are stacked in a pile or spread out on the table if he or she is to use money ef-

Figure 4.4: A Conservation Problem

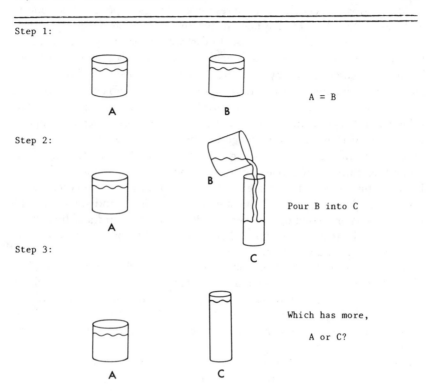

Step 1:

A = B

Step 2:

Pour B into C

Step 3:

Which has more,

A or C?

fectively. Thus, it may be that frequently used abilities do not decline as much in old age as abilities that are not used often.

In summary, it appears that performance on most of the Piagetian abilities may decline with age. However, it is important to keep in mind that all of the Piagetian studies to date have been cross-sectional and, as a result, it is not possible to determine whether the age differences reflect age-related changes, cohort differences, or both.

To illustrate what the research on age differences in abilities measured by Piagetian tasks is like, some of the research on classification abilities will be presented in greater detail. Inhelder and Piaget[23] studied the free classification of geometric stimuli as well as the free classification of small toy objects. In a study with geometric stimuli, Inhelder and Piaget presented children with objects that varied in dimensions such as color, shape, and size and asked them to group the objects that were alike or that went together. Three developmental stages were reportedly obtained with the geometric stimuli. In the first stage, "graphic collections," Inhelder and Piaget reported that children are unable to overlook the spatial configuration of the stimuli. This stage included two general types of responses. In one type, children tend to make representations of objects with the stimuli, such as putting a triangle over a square and calling it a house. In the other type of response, children form lines of two- or three-dimensional figures in which each item is added because of some similarity it shares with the previously added item. However, in this stage, the criterion for adding items often changes from one addition to the next. Although similarity influences grouping in this stage, Inhelder and Piaget state that the main criterion for adding elements appears to be that of forming a unified figure. These two types of responses were observed in children between the ages of 2.5 and 5. Inhelder and Piaget's second stage, "non-graphic collections," was thought to begin at about 5 or 5.5. During this stage, objects are grouped according to similarity alone. Sometimes, however, not all the stimuli are grouped, and sometimes different groups are based upon different criteria. In the third and final stage, all the stimuli are grouped, and they are all grouped according to two dimensions (e.g., size and shape) simultaneously.

Using toy stimuli, Inhelder and Piaget reported that younger children placed together objects that shared some interrelationship, such as a baby in a crib, while older children placed together similar items, such as all the furniture or all the people. So, with both geometric and toy stimuli, children appear to change as they grow older from categorizing items that share complementary relationships to categorizing items that resemble each other in some way. Similar developmental changes in classification styles have been reported by a number of other researchers.[24]

Research on classification abilities during middle and old age suggests that the elderly may tend to revert to categorizing according to the types of criteria used by young children. Denney and Lennon[25] compared a group of middle-aged adults with a group of elderly adults on a task involving classification of geometric stimuli and found that the elderly individuals grouped them much as young children do. The vast majority of elderly individuals made designs with the stimuli. The middle-aged group put similar objects (e.g., objects that were the same shape, color, or size) together in piles.

Research indicates, however, that both young children[26] and elderly adults[27] are capable of classifying according to the same criteria used by older children and younger adults. In both the Denney and Acito[28] study with young children and the Denney and Denney[29] study with elderly adults, the subjects observed an adult model classifying similar stimuli together. Both the young children and the elderly adults, after observing the model, tended to classify the stimuli according to the similarity criterion.

This research indicates that although many elderly adults do not choose to classify according to similarity on their own, they have the ability to do so. Thus the classification criterion one uses may depend on environmental factors.[30] Both young children and elderly adults are capable of sorting according to similarity; they simply prefer to use complementary criteria. Why? Denney suggests the possibility that neither group experiences much pressure for categorizing in any particular way. She further suggests that under such circumstances categorizing according to complementary criteria might be the most natural response because complementary items are grouped naturally in time and space. One often sees complementary things together, such as cars in garages and baseballs with bats. Therefore, the relationship between such items is readily apparent for all individuals and may predominate unless the individuals are confronted with external pressures for organizing their experience in another way. The transition seems to start in the young child at about age 6, when the child's formal education begins, with its attendant emphasis on similarity relationships and more abstract forms of thought. This emphasis continues throughout one's education and into many occupations. In fact, it is only after retirement that many individuals are freed from demands to catergorize according to similarity, and this is the time when there appears to be a return to the use of complementary criteria for categorization. Denney[31] found that occupation is, in fact, highly related to one's preference for classification criteria. Middle-aged individuals whose occupation involved fewer cognitive demands tended to classify more like young children and elderly adults than individuals whose occupations were more cognitively demanding. Thus, elderly adults' preference for complementary criteria may reflect an isolation from educational and occupational pressures to use more abstract criteria. Denney suggests that individuals may simply learn from experience with the environment which categorization criteria are most relevant to their own lifestyles. And, at least in our culture, the most relevant criteria seem to depend upon the age of the individual.

In summary, it appears that there are eventual declines in most of the Piagetian abilities. However, it may be that the greatest declines are in those abilities that the elderly are least often called upon to use. Frequently used abilities, such as conservation, may exhibit very little decline. Further, research indicates that elderly adults are, at least in some cases, capable of performing in the same way as younger adults even though they might not tend to do so on their own. It is not clear why they do not perform like younger adults if they have the ability, but it has been suggested that they might perform in the way that is most adaptive given their particular life situation.

Problem-Solving Research

A third major way of understanding cognition is through the problem-solving approach. With few exceptions,[32] most of the studies involving performance on traditional problem-solving tasks have yielded age differences, with elderly adults exhibiting poorer performance than young adults. Such differences have been obtained with cross-sectional studies of performance on traditional concept-learning problems. With these problems the individual is presented, one at a time, with stimuli that vary on a number of dimensions such as shape, color, and size, and is told, with each presentation, whether the stimulus is a positive or negative instance of the concept. For example, if the concept were "red square," all stimuli that were both red and square would be positive examples of the concept, while all stimuli that were not red and square would be negative examples. The individual's task is to determine what the concept is. In general, elderly adults perform less well than younger adults on such tasks.[33]

Similar age differences have also been found with cross-sectional studies of performance on a variety of "search" tasks, in which the individual is supposed to find the correct stimulus or stimulus arrangement from a variety of alternatives. In these tasks the subject is presented with a number of stimulus alternatives and is told that he or she is to figure out what the correct stimulus or stimulus arrangement is. In order to solve the problem the subject selects alternatives and, with each selection, is told whether the correct stimulus or stimulus arrangement is included in the selected sample. The object is to find the correct solution in as few sample selections as possible. Elderly adults have been found to be less efficient on both nonverbal problems in which the subject selects stimuli with, and receives feedback from, a mechanical apparatus,[34] and verbal problems in which the subject asks questions and receives verbal feedback from the experimenter.[35]

Elderly adults also seem to do more poorly than younger adults on tasks that require a change in the concept or strategy they are using during the experimental session. In this type of task the subject learns to solve a problem or set of problems with a certain strategy. Then the problem or problems are changed such that the original strategy is either no longer useful at all or no longer the most efficient strategy. Both Heglin[36] and Wetherick[37] found that elderly individuals had more difficulty changing the concepts they were using than younger adults did.

Cross-sectional age differences in verbal reasoning have also been found. Bromley[38] reported that elderly adults perform less well on proverb interpretation tasks than younger adults. Friend and Zubek[39] reported similar age differences in "critical thinking" on a test composed of a number of practical problems. And, on a test of logical reasoning, Morgan[40] also obtained age differences, with elderly adults performing at a lower level than younger adults.

Arenberg[41] conducted a longitudinal study of the more traditional type of problem solving. He tested individuals between the ages of 24 and 87 on logical problem solving and then retested the same individuals 6 years later. His cross-sectional comparison showed an increase in errors with increasing age; the largest difference occurred between the groups under 60 and over 60. On the other hand, his longitudinal trends revealed the decline only in individuals over the age of 70.

Although the research in problem solving among adults indicates that elderly adults tend to perform more poorly than young adults, it is not clear why such age differences are obtained. To illustrate how one might go about determining why elderly adults often perform in a way different from younger adults, a line of research with one type of problem-solving task, the Twenty Questions task, is quite useful. In the Twenty Questions task the subject is presented with a picture of a number of common objects such as a lamp, a house, a cow, an airplane, a shoe, and so forth. The subject is told to try to figure out which object the experimenter is thinking of by asking as few questions as possible. The questions have to be the type that can be answered either "Yes" or "No." The subject's queries can be classified as either "constraint-seeking" questions, which eliminate a whole class of items at a time (e.g., "Is it a living thing?"), or "hypothesis-testing" questions, which elminate only one item at a time (e.g., "Is it the bicycle?").

Using the Twenty Questions task with children, Mosher and Hornsby[42] found that the percentage of constraint-seeking questions increased while the percentage of hypothesis-testing questions decreased with increasing age. Denney and Denney[43] found a reversal of this early developmental trend among the elderly. They compared a group of elderly women with a group of middle-aged women and found that the latter asked significantly more constraint-seeking questions than the former. Similar results were obtained with both men and women in a study by Kesler, Denney, and Whitely.[44]

Denney and Denney[45] were interested in whether elderly individuals who do not use constraint-seeking questions on their own are capable of using such questions. They conducted a study with elderly individuals who asked no constraint-seeking questions on a pretest. Half these individuals were asked to take turns playing the Twenty Questions game with the experimenter. When it was the experimenter's turn, he or she asked constraint-seeking questions. The other half of the subjects were just asked to continue playing the Twenty Questions game with the experimenter—that is, the experimenter and subject did not take turns; the subject always asked the questions. All the individuals were then given a posttest. The results indicated that the subjects who had observed the experimenter asking constraint-seeking questions had learned to ask those types of questions; the individuals who did not observe the experimenter asking constraint-seeking questions did not ask such questions on the posttest.

Since elderly individuals are able to use the constraint-seeking strategy after they are given training, one might wonder what other conditions would result in the use of this strategy by the elderly. Some investigators have suggested that elderly people may not use some of the more sophisticated cognitive strategies they are capable of using for a variety of non-cognitive reasons, such as lack of motivation, lack of good feelings about their own abilities, and lack of practice. In a recent study, Denney[46] examined some of the possible reasons for the use of rather inefficient cognitive strategies by elderly adults. A series of three experiments was undertaken. In the first, the effects of both motivation and practice were investigated. Motivation was manipulated by giving money for efficient performance. The subjects were given 20 tokens at the beginning of a Twenty Questions game. They were told that one of the tokens would be taken each time they asked a question. They were also told that they would be given a quarter for each token they had left after they found the correct solution. Thus, the fewer the questions they needed to solve the problem, the more money they received. In the practice condition subjects were given the same number of problems as the subjects in the motivation condition, but no mention was made of either tokens or money. Neither motivation nor practice had any effect on problem-solving performance. In the second experiment, the effect of imposing a delay between the administration of the instructions and the beginning of the problem-solving task was investigated. It was assumed that elderly individuals might not use efficient strategies because they do not take time to plan their approach to the problem. If this is the case, then providing them with more time to plan might facilitate their performance. However, there was no difference between the performance of the individuals who were delayed and those who were not. In the third experiment, the effect of prior success on another cognitive task was studied. This experiment was based on the assumption that elderly individuals might not perform very well on cognitive tasks because they do not have much confidence in their cognitive abilities. Half the individuals in this study were given another cognitive task immediately preceding the Twenty Questions game and were told that they had done very well on this task, regardless of how good their performance actually was. The other half of the subjects were exposed to the same task but were given no feedback on their performance. Individuals who received positive feedback on the previous task did no better on the Twenty Questions task than individuals who did not receive feedback. The results of these three experiments indicate that it is easier to change the performance of older people on cognitive tasks through direct training than by altering noncognitive factors such as motivation or confidence.

It is also possible that the performance of older people is more directly related to the demands of the task at hand than to factors such as those examined above. To test this possibility, Denney[47] compared the performance of elderly individuals on the standard Twenty Questions problems with their performance on similar but much more difficult problems. On the more difficult problems the experimenter told the subject that she was thinking of "animals" on some problems and of "something" on other problems; on these problems the subject was to guess what the experimenter was thinking of without being given an array of alternatives. Denney reasoned that if the problems were so difficult as to be virtually insoluble without the use of an efficient strategy, the elderly individual would use an efficient strategy if it existed in his or her repertoire. Both middle-aged and elderly individuals were included in this study. The results indicated that whereas the middle-aged adults used the constraint-seeking strategy on both the standard and difficult problems, the elderly adults used the constraint-seeking strategy only on the difficult problems.

Denney also compared the performance of middle-aged and elderly individuals on both the standard Twenty Questions task and a task that might be more conducive to the use of the constraint-seeking strategy. The stimuli for the second task were a set of standard playing cards, which were used for two reasons: First, playing cards are composed of easily classified elements (e.g., color, suit, and number). Second, it was assumed that many people play cards, and therefore use such classifications rather frequently. In the study, middle-aged individuals used the constraint-seeking strategy with both types of problems, while the elderly subjects tended to use the strategy only with the playing cards.

The results of the two studies in which task variables were manipulated indicate that under certain conditions elderly adults use the constraint-seeking strategy nearly as frequently as middle-aged adults. Since the adults in this study were not given training, the results indicate that elderly adults have a constraint-seeking strategy in their repertoires and use it when it is either necessary or very obvious. However, it is not clear why middle-aged adults are more likely than the elderly to use efficient strategies on the standard Twenty Questions task. Elderly adults may be unlikely to use the constraint-seeking strategy because they are not frequently called upon to use it in their daily lives and, therefore, do not readily think of it. Another possibility is that the elderly lack energy for both physical and mental activities, and tend to take the easiest, although sometimes less efficient, way of approaching a problem. It may be that the standard Twenty Questions game is easiest to solve with a hypothesis-testing strategy. However, when the subjects are not presented with a finite set of alternatives, the constraint-seeking strategy might be easier because the problem would be almost insoluble without such a strategy. Likewise, the dimensions (e.g., color, suit, and number) in a deck of playing cards might be so obvious that the use of constraint-seeking strategy would be very easy and, in fact, much easier than naming each individual card. These are a few possible explanations, but there are a number of others and there is no evidence to support any of them as yet.

Additional analyses by Denney and her associates[48] indicated that the variable most strongly related to the use of constraint-seeking questions in older adults was their level of education. People with more education tended to ask more constraint-seeking questions. The fact that education significantly affects performance on the Twenty Questions task suggests that elderly adults may perform more poorly on the task at least in part because they have had less education than younger adults. Thus, the age differences that have been found in performance on the Twenty Questions task may be, at least partially, a result of cohort differences. More research is needed to determine if this is in fact the case.

The research with the Twenty Questions task indicates that elderly adults tend to use less efficient problem-solving strategies than younger adults. The results also indicate that elderly adults are capable of using more efficient strategies than they sometimes tend to use on their own. The use of more efficient strategies can be facilitated both by direct training on the problem-solving task in question and by using tasks that lend themselves to the use of more efficient strategies. Such results indicate that the manipulation of cognitive factors rather than noncognitive factors seems to have most effect on the problem-solving performance of elderly adults. Research also suggests that education is highly related to performance on the Twenty Questions task. This suggests that the rather poor performance on the Twenty Questions task by elderly individuals may be, at least partially, a result of cohort differences.

Although the results of these studies indicate that the performance of elderly individuals on the Twenty Questions task can be facilitated, they do not indicate why elderly individuals are less likely than middle-aged adults to use the constraint-seeking strategy in the first place. It may be that the elderly individuals have never used strategies like the constraint-seeking strategy before, but that they are able to learn to use the strategy when the situation demands it. On the other hand, it may be that elderly adults have used the strategy before but they have not been using it recently and, therefore, tend not to think of it as readily as younger individuals, who are more likely to use such strategies in their everyday lives. Or it may be that although they are capable of using such strategies they do not use them unless it is necessary because such strategies require more mental energy than less efficient ones. These are only a few of the possible explanations for the obtained age difference.

Since the cognitive strategies of elderly individuals can be changed, it is important to reflect on whether cognitive retraining is a good thing. The helpfulness of such intervention would depend on why the elderly use the strategies they do in the first place. Denney[49] has suggested that, with respect to classification for example, elderly individuals may actually use the most adaptive means for their particular life situation. If this were the case, it would not be beneficial, and might even be detrimental, to attempt to change their classification styles. Thus it is important not to assume that it would be best to change the cognitive functioning of elderly adults to be more similar to that of middle-aged adults until research indicates that it would be beneficial.

Overview

The results of studies on cognitive abilities indicate that there are age differences among adults in most of the cognitive abilities, with elderly adults performing less well than younger adults. The abilities in which there are the greatest age differences appear to be those that elderly adults are least likely to use in their daily living. Smaller differences are obtained in abilities that are frequently used by elderly adults. There is some evidence that some of these age differences could be a result of actual age changes, i.e., of individuals actually performing more poorly as they get older. For example, age changes have been obtained in the longitudinal research on performance on both intelligence tests and traditional problem-solving tasks. There is, however, also evidence that some of these age differences in cognitive abilities may be the result of cohort effects, i.e., of differences in the performance of different generations. For example, cross-sectional research designs often yield larger age differences than longitudinal designs, suggesting that there are cohort differences in addition to age changes. The fact that education is significantly related to performance on the Twenty Questions task also suggests that there may be cohort differences in performance on the Twenty Questions task. The most reasonable conclusion is that there are probably both age-related differences and cohort differences in most cognitive abilities.

As was illustrated with the training research conducted with the classification and Twenty Questions tasks, elderly individuals are often capable of better performance than they exhibit on their own. The research presented indicates ways in which the cognitive abilities of elderly individuals can be facilitated. Direct training on the cognitive ability in question typically facilitates performance; so does arranging the task to lend itself to the use of efficient strategies. Thus, cognitive performance can be improved by manipulating cognitive factors. However, the manipulation of noncognitive variables such as motivation, time to plan, and self-confidence may not be successful in facilitating the performance of elderly individuals. Noncognitive factors such as lack of self-confidence, anxiety, low motivation, and so forth, do not seem to affect cognitive performance. Of course, it may be that there are other noncognitive variables that would have more of an effect on performance. However, the research to date indicates that performance may be facilitated much more readily by cognitive than by noncognitive types of intervention.

Notes

1. See, for example, J. H. Flavell, "Cognitive Changes in Adulthood," in L. B. Goulet and P. B. Baltes (eds.), *Life Span Developmental Psychology: Research and Theory* (New York: Academic Press, 1970).

2. See, for example, K. W. Schaie and C. R. Strother, "A Cross-Sectional Study of Age Changes in Cognitive Behavior," *Psychological Bulletin* 70 (1968), pp. 671–680; K. F. Reigel, "Ergebnisse und Probleme der Psychologischen Alternsforschung," Teil 1 and 2, *Vita Humana* 1 (1958), pp. 52–64, 204–243; J. E. Droppelt and W. L. Wallace, "Standardization of the Wechsler Adult Intelligence Scale for Older Persons," *Journal of Abnormal and Social Psychology* 55 (1955), pp. 312–330; D. Wechsler, *The Measurement and Appraisal of Adult Intelligence* (Baltimore: Williams and Wilkins, 1958).

3. See, for example, Schaie and Strother, ibid; W. A. Owens, "Age and Mental Abilities: A Longitudinal Study," *Genetic Psychological Monographs* 48 (1953), pp. 3–54; W. A. Owens, "Age and Mental Ability: A Second Follow-up," *Journal of Educational Psychology* 57 (1966), pp. 311–325; N. Bayley and M. H. Oden, "The Maintenance of Intellectual Ability in Gifted Adults," *Journal of Gerontology* 10 (1955), pp. 91–107; R. B. Burns, "Age and Mental Ability: Re-testing with Thirty-Three Year Intervals," *British Journal of Educational Psychology* 36 (1966), p. 116.

4. K. W. Schaie, "A General Mode for the Study of Developmental Problems," *Psychological Bulletin* 64 (1965), pp. 92–107.

5. P. B. Baltes, "Longitudinal and Cross-Sectional Sequences in the Study of Age and Generation Effects," *Human Development* 11 (1968), pp. 145–171.

6. R. B. Cattell, *Abilities: Their Structure, Growth, and Action* (Boston: Houghton Mifflin, 1971).

7. J. L. Horn, "Organization of Data on Life Span Development of Human Abilities," in L. B. Goulet and P. B. Baltes (eds.), *Life Span Developmental Psychology: Research and Theory* (New York: Academic Press, 1970).

8. J. L. Horn and R. B. Cattell, "Age Differences in Fluid and Crystallized Intelligence," *Acta Psychologica* 26 (1967), pp. 107–129.

9. See, for example, J. E. Birren and D. F. Morrison, "Analysis of the WAIS

Subtests in Relation to Age and Education," *Journal of Gerontology* 29 (1974), pp. 182–189; C. Eisdorfer, E. W. Busse, and L. D. Cohen, "The WAIS Performance of an Aged Sample: The Relationship Between Verbal and Performance I.Q.'s," *Journal of Gerontology* 14 (1959), pp. 197–201; C. Eisdorfer and F. Wilkie, "Intellectual Changes with Advancing Age," in L. F. Garvik, C. Eisdorfer, and J. E. Blum (eds.), *Intellectual Functioning in Adults* (New York: Springer Publishing Company, 1973); G. A. Foulds and J. C. Raven, "Neural Changes in Mental Abilities of Adults as Age Advances," *Journal of Mental Science* 94 (1948), pp. 133–142.

10. See, for example, J. E. Birren and D. F. Morrison, "Analysis of the WAIS Subtests in Relation to Age and Education," *Journal of Gerontology* 16 (1961), pp. 363–369; P. J. Rhudick and C. Gordon, "The Age Center of New England Study," in L. F. Jarvik, C. Eisdorfer, and J. E. Blum (eds.), *Intellectual Functioning in Adults* (New York: Springer Publishing Company, 1973); Schaie and Strother, op. cit., pp. 671–680; C. R. Strother, K. W. Schaie, and P. Horst, "The Relationship Between Advanced Age and Mental Abilities," *Journal of Abnormal and Social Psychology* 55 (1957), pp. 166–1760.

11. See, for example, J. E. Birren, "Increments and Decrements in the Intellectual Status of the Aged," *Psychiatric Research Reports* 23 (1968), pp. 207–214; L. F. Jarvik and J. E. Blum, "Cognitive Declines as Predictors of Mortality in Twin Pairs: A Twenty-year Longitudinal Study of Aging," in E. Palmore and F. Jeffers (eds.), *Prediction of Lifespan* (Lexington, Mass: Heath, 1971); K. F. Riegal and R. M. Riegal, "Development, Drop, and Death," *Developmental Psychology* 6 (1972), pp. 306–319; K. W. Schaie and G. Labouvie-Vief, "Generational versus Ontogenetic Components of Change in Adult Cognitive Behavior: A Fourteen-Year Cross-Sequential Study," *Developmental Psychology* 10 (1974), pp. 305–320.

12. Schaie, op. cit.

13. Baltes, op. cit.

14. See, for example, Schaie and Labouvie-Vief, op. cit.; J. R. Nesselroade, K. W. Schaie, and P. B. Baltes, "Ontogenetic and Generational Components of Structural and Quantitative Change in Adult Behavior," *Journal of Gerontology* 27 (1972), pp. 222–228; K. W. Schaie, G. F. Labouvie-Vief, and B. V. Buech, "Generational and Cohort-Specific Differences in Adult Cognitive Functioning: A Fourteen-Year Study of Independent Samples," *Developmental Psychology* 9 (1973), pp. 151–166; Schaie and Strother, op. cit.

15. J. H. Flavell, *The Developmental Psychology of Jean Piaget* (New York: Van Nostrand Co., 1963).

16. M. Annett, "The Classification of Instances of Four Common Class Concepts by Children and Adults," *British Journal of Educational Psychology* 29 (1959), pp. 223–236; N. W. Denney, "Classification Abilities in the Elderly," *Journal of Gerontology* 29 (1974), pp. 309–314; N. W. Denney and J. Cornelius, "Class Inclusion and Multiple Classification in Middle and Old Age," *Developmental Psychology* 11 (1975), pp. 521–522; N. W. Denney and M. L. Lennon, "Classification: A Comparison of Middle and Old Age," *Developmental Psychology* 7 (1972), pp. 210–213.

17. N. W. Denney and B. Mallinger, "Animism and Related Tendencies in Senescence," *Journal of Gerontology* 4 (1949), pp. 218–221.

18. D. D. Bielby and D. E. Papalia, "Moral Development and Egocentrism: Their

Development and Interrelationship across the Life-Span," *International Journal of Aging and Human Development* 6 (1975), pp. 293–308; P. E. Comalli, S. Wapner, and H. Werner, "Perception of Verticality in Middle and Old Age," *Journal of Psychology* 47 (1959), pp. 259–266; W. R. Looft and D. C. Charles, "Egocentrism and Social Interaction in Young and Old Adults," *International Journal of Aging and Human Development* 2 (1971), pp. 21–28; K. Rubin, "The Relationship Between Spatial and Communicative Egocentrism in Children and Young and Old Adults," *Journal of Genetic Psychology* 125 (1974), pp. 295–301; K. H. Rubin, P. Attewell, M. Tierney, and P. Tumolo, "The Development of Spatial Egocentrism and Conservation Across the Life-Span," *Developmental Psychology* 9 (1973),   p. 432.

19. Bielby and Papalia, ibid.

20. V. Clayton, "The Role of Formal Operational Thought in the Aging Process" (unpublished manuscript, State University of New York at Buffalo, 1972); C. Tomlinson-Keasey, "Formal Operations in Females from Eleven to Fifty-Six Years of Age," *Developmental Psychology* 6 (1972), p. 364.

21. D. E. Papalia, "The Status of Several Conservation Abilities Across the Life-Span," *Human Development* 15 (1972), pp. 229–243; Rubin, Attewell, Tierney, and Tumolo, op. cit.; S. Sanders, M. Laurendeau, and J. Bergeron, "Aging and the Concept of Space: The Conservation of Surfaces," *Journal of Gerontology* 21 (1966), pp. 281–285.

22. See, for example, K. Rubin, "Extinction of Conservation: A Life-Span Investigation," *Developmental Psychology* 12 (1976), pp. 51–56; S. C. Selzer and N. W. Denney, "Conservation Abilities Among Middle Aged and Elderly Adults" (paper presented at the biennial meeting of the Society for Research in Child Development, March 1977, New Orleans).

23. B. Inhelder and J. Piaget, *The Early Growth of Logic in the Child* (New York: Harper and Row, 1964).

24. See, for example, Annett, op. cit.; J. Kagan, H. Moss, and I. Sigel, "Psychological Significance of Styles of Conceptualization," *Monograph of the Society for Research in Child Development* 28 (1963), pp. 73–112; Denney, op cit.; N. W. Denney, "Classification Criteria in Middle and Old Age," *Developmental Psychology* 10 (1974), pp. 901–906; N. W. Denney, "Evidence for Developmental Change in Categorization Criteria for Children and Adults," *Human Development* 17 (1974), pp. 41–53.

25. Denney and Lennon, op. cit.

26. N. W. Denney and M. Acito, "Classification Training in Two- and Three-Year-Old Children," *Journal of Experimental Child Psychology* 17 (1974), pp. 37–48.

27. D. R. Denney and N. W. Denney, "The Use of Classification for Problem Solving: A Comparison of Middle and Old Age," *Developmental Psychology* 9 (1973), pp. 275–278.

28. Denney and Acito, op. cit.

29. Denney and Denney, op. cit.

30. Denney, "Evidence for Developmental Change."

31. Denney, "Classification Criteria."

32. See, for example, D. K. Smith, "The Einstellung Effect in Relation to The Variables of Age and Training," in *Dissertation Abstracts* 27B (New Brunswick, N.J.: Rutgers—The State University, 1967), p. 4115; N. E. Wetherick, "A Comparison of

the Problem-Solving Ability of Young, Middle-Aged and Older Subjects," *Gerontologia* 9 (1964), pp. 164–178.

33. D. Arenberg, "Concept Problem Solving in Young and Old Adults," *Journal of Gerontology* 23 (1968), pp. 279–282; J. F. Brinley, T. J. Javick, and L. M. McLaughlin, "Age, Reasoning, and Memory in Adults," *Journal of Gerontology* 29 (1974), pp. 182–189; W. L. Carpenter, "The Relationship Between Age and Information Processing Capacity of Adults," *Industrial Gerontology* 8 (1971), p. 55–57.

34. See, for example, D. Arenberg, "A Longitudinal Study of Problem-Solving in Adults," *Journal of Gerontology* 29 (1974), pp. 650–658; E. A. Jerome, "Decay of Heuristic Processes in the Aged," in C. Tibbetts and W. Donahue (eds.), *Social and Psychological Aspects of Aging* (New York: Columbia University Press, 1962); M. L. Young, "Problem-Solving Performances in Two Age Groups," *Journal of Gerontology* 21 (1966), pp. 505–509; M. L. Young, "Age and Sex Differences in Problem Solving," *Journal of Gerontology* 26 (1971), pp. 330–336.

35. See, for example, D. R. Denney and N. W. Denney, "The Use of Classification for Problem Solving: A Comparison of Middle and Old Age," *Developmental Psychology* 9 (1973), pp. 275–278; H.G.A. Rimoldi and K.W.V. Woude, "Aging and Problem Solving," *Industrial Gerontology* 8 (1971), pp. 68–69.

36. H. J. Heglin, "Problem Solving Set in Different Age Groups," *Journal of Gerontology* 11 (1956), pp. 310–317.

37. Wetherick, op. cit.

38. D. B. Bromley, "Some Effects of Age on the Quality of Intellectual Output,"

39. C. M. Friend and J. P. Zubek, "The Effects of Age on Critical Thinking Ability," *Journal of Gerontology* 13 (1958), pp. 407–413.

40. A. B. Morgan, "Differences in Logical Reasoning Associated with Age and Higher Education," *Psychological Reports* 2 (1956), pp. 235–240.

41. Arenberg, op. cit.

42. F. A. Mosher and J. R. Hornsby, "On Asking Questions," in J. S. Bruner, R. R. Olver, and P. M. Greenfield et al. (eds.), *Studies in Cognitive Growth* (New York: Wiley, 1966).

43. Denney and Denney, "The Use of Classification for Problem Solving."

44. M. S. Kesler, N. W. Denney, and S. E. Whitely, "Factors Influencing Problem Solving in Middle-Aged and Elderly Adults," *Human Development* 19 (1976), pp. 319–320.

45. N. W. Denney and D. R. Denney, "Modeling Effects on the Questioning Strategies of the Elderly," *Developmental Psychology* 10 (1974), pp. 400–404.

46. N. W. Denney, "The Effect of the Manipulation of Peripheral, Noncognitive Variables on Problem-Solving Performance Among the Elderly," *Human Development* 4(1980), pp. 268–277.

47. N. W. Denney, "The Effect of Task Variables on Problem-Solving Performance Among Adults" (unpublished manuscript, University of Kansas, 1979).

48. N. W. Denney and D. M. Thissen, "Determinants of Cognitive Ability in the Elderly" (unpublished manuscript, University of Kansas, 1979); M. S. Kesler, N. W. Denney, and S. E. Whitely, op. cit.

49. Denney, "Classification Abilities."

5

On Death and Dying

Shirley L. Patterson

A recent survey[1] of nationally and internationally known books on aging revealed interesting information on material related to death and dying. A content analysis of forty-eight books published between 1956 and 1976 indicated that over 90 percent of them devote less than 5 percent of their space to discussions of death and dying. Moreover, approximately 65 percent of these books devote less than 1 percent of their space to this issue. On the other hand, the proliferation of recent research on death, emanating from a wide range of professions and disciplines, indicates that the subject is being explored more extensively by scholars. Yet taboos associated with dying and aging appear to retain some power, even for experts in the field of aging. A noted gerontologist has observed:

> Old age in America is often a tragedy. Few of us like to consider it because it reminds us of our own mortality. It demands our energy and resources, it frightens us with illness and deformity, it is an affront to a culture with a passion for youth and productive capacity. We are so preoccupied with defending ourselves from the reality of death that we ignore the fact that human beings are alive until they are actually dead. At best, the living old are treated as if they were already half dead.[2]

Indeed, the closeness in time of the elderly to death is likely to account for some of the discomfort with this issue experienced by nonelderly persons. If this is true, then as Kalish points out, "the individual and social issues relating to death are in many ways individual and social issues of aging. We may certainly hypothesize that one of the significant reasons that the old in this society are avoided and isolated is their proximity to death."[3]

What is death? The nature and meaning of death has been studied by scientists, dramatized by poets, argued by lawyers, struggled with by physicians, and questioned by human beings of every description. Death has many meanings, depending on how you have been socialized, your ethnic background, your age, and the social context in which you live. Over the life span, an individual's understanding of death may change gradually, as a function of growth and development, or abruptly, as a function of the intrusion of a tragic event. There is little doubt that death has different meanings to people at different periods in their lives.

Definitions of Death

There are at least several distinct ways death can be defined: biologically, psychologically, and socially. Although biological, or physical, determinants of death continue to rest on the presence or absence of respiration and heartbeat, major advancements in medical technology tend to complicate the issue. Sophisticated devices can not only detect the slightest indicator of the presence or absence of life, but can support and maintain vital systems through such life-sustaining equipment as respirators and kidney and heart-lung machines. Even though these advances have provided many individuals with a "second chance," technology also has served to blur the line between life and death. Richard Schultz has identified and outlined current thinking on physical death:

1. *Clinical death* is said to occur when spontaneous respiration and heartbeat cease. Resuscitation may be attempted and in some cases will revive the individual. An example of the latter case is an individual who suffers a major heart attack and is promptly given emergency treatment to resuscitate her or him.
2. *Brain death* is a second type of death. If deprived of oxygen (anoxia), brain cells begin to die within four to six minutes if the person is not resuscitated immediately. The most highly evolved part of the brain, the cortex, dies first. This part of the brain is involved in controlling voluntary action, thought, and memory. The midbrain dies next, followed by the death of the oldest part of the brain, the brainstem. If the cortex and midbrain are destroyed, the person lapses into an irreversible coma and only the vegetative functions remain. Thus an individual could be in a deep coma and still be able to breathe unaided, and, with the aid of intravenous feeding, he or she could remain alive almost indefinitely.
3. *Biological or cellular death*, the physical death of the various organ systems, occurs last. Different organs die at different rates and an organ is defined as dead when it has degenerated to a point where any type of intervention would not bring it back to a functional state again.[4]

In everyday life, people experience or perceive "deaths" that are not related to physical or biological death. According to Kalish, psychological death is a condition that occurs when "an individual ceases to maintain awareness of himself or his environment. He is totally and, presumably, permanently comatose."[5] This kind of a situation is graphically illustrated by the highly publicized Karen Ann Quinlan case. In 1975, medical experts determined that Karen, probably as a result of ingesting a combination of alcohol and drugs, was in a deep irreversible coma. Insofar as could be known, she no longer had knowledge or awareness of herself, others, or her immediate social milieu. At this writing Karen Ann Quinlan remains alive in a coma and is breathing without the support of a respirator.

On another level, one might speculate that psychological death could be perceived as an inability to relate meaningfully to other human beings. If this is so, then individuals who experience grave difficulty in developing and maintaining consistent, in-depth relationships with others may be viewed, at least temporarily, as psychologically dead. Certainly, mental health professionals are repeatedly called upon to deal with long-term dysfunctional-relationship problems.

Social death, on the other hand, may be attributed primarily to behaviors external to the individual. That is, the individual may be viewed and treated by others as dead although he or she remains physically alive. Kalish points out that a person may be treated as socially dead by one or many people.[6] Indeed, that individual also may have a similar perception of his or her status. To put it another way, social aliveness is the recognition and acknowledgment that one is a person by the self and by others.

There are numerous circumstances under which social death can be observed as a function of others' behavior. For example, a parent of a severely retarded child may respond to the physical but not the social or emotional needs of that child. Institutionalization is another circumstance that is fertile ground for the occurrence of social death. When an older person enters a nursing home, it is not uncommon for that person to be treated as socially dead. Finally, such behavior may also be noted when an individual has received a diagnosis of terminal illness. In some sense, this person ceases to exist for others and is treated accordingly. Moreover, significant others in the lives of handicapped, the old, and the terminally ill may go through a process of anticipatory grief at the time social death occurs.[7] Thus, mourners may carry out their grief in advance of the actual physical death.

The impact of this behavior may have serious consequences for the individual under sentence of social death, especially if he or she is cognizant of a change in status. An older person in an extended care facility, for example, may become isolated from close friends and relatives. Somehow the guilt that results from avoiding such a person is easier to deal with than confronting the person. As a result, decisions may be made about the person's future, possessions, or living arrangement without consultation. After all, it is assumed that he or she is in no condition to deal effectively with such matters. It is not difficult to understand how the socially dead might experience a sense of helplessness in relationships and a lack of control over their lives. Indeed, social death may be a precipitating factor in physical death, particularly for the old.

The Meaning of Death

For the young in this society, death assumes the shape of some distant future event that has no immediate personal relevance. For the old, however, death has an immediacy and a reality shaped, in part, by the meaning of time. In a study of middle-aged men and women, Neugarten concludes that people in this age range have developed not only an awareness of the finiteness of time, but also a different perception of time. "Life is restructured in terms of time-left-to-life rather than time-since-birth."[8] Therefore, the distance from death becomes a more salient concept than distance from birth. For instance, it is not uncommon for the middle-aged person to reflect on how he or she will use time during the latter half of life. Kalish observes that, for the old, an awareness of the birth-to-death time parameter alters and influences both the meaning and use of time. To the elderly, personal futurity is limited by the boundary of death, and meaningful ways to use time left to live may or may not exist.[9] This sense or perception of time is graphically captured in a poem by Harvey Hostetter, a midwestern octogenarian considering his own death.

My Funeral

Most any man who lives a span
    Of fourscore, has to know
That pretty soon at night or noon,
    He sure will have to go.

Some day a neighbor or physician
    Will say it's time for a mortician
To get me into right condition
    To be put on exhibition:
What's left of me, where all can see,
    Admission free, no charge or fee.
And some folks, not meaning jokes,
    Are sure to say—as well they may
On that delightful burial day,
    "How natural he looked that way.
As there he lay, till moved away!"

When I am in bed or sack,
  I never do sleep on my back.
But now in my Sunday clothes,
  When I am entirely dead,
And cannot speak nor turn my head,
  For purpose of this last display, `
The undertaker has his way,
  As is old custom, I suppose.

When my old body is worn out,
  And can't eat nor cavort about,
Please put it back into the soil
  From whence it came to live and toil.

With brief delay, put it away.
  But don't allow yourself to say
"That is the last of him!"
  But read my rhymes at lonely times,
With eyes that are not dim;
  And believe, as you surely can,
There is no death to soul of man!

The poem, of course, reflects more than a sensitivity to time left to live. It is a statement about the meaning of life; a melding of the humor, sadness, and hope of human existence.

The meaning of death is frequently related to the concept of loss in our society.[10] For older people, as well as other age groups, the imminence of death has the potential to trigger recognition of all that will be lost through this event: the self, including the body; the ability to see, touch, hear, taste, and smell; important roles; significant others; opportunities for further life experience; and the achievement of goals.

In addition to its relationship with the event of death, the concept of loss has an especially powerful meaning when associated with the aging process. For the old and the aging, loss and adaptation to loss is a predictable theme of everyday life. Butler and Lewis succinctly describe the little deaths that accrue with age:

> Losses in every aspect of life compel the elderly to expend enormous amounts of physical and emotional energy in grieving and resolving grief, adapting to the changes that result from loss, and recovering from the stresses inherent in these processes. The elderly are confronted by multiple losses, which may occur simultaneously: death of a marital partner, older friends, colleagues, relatives; decline of physical health and coming to personal terms with death; loss of status, prestige, and participation in society; and, for large numbers of the older population, additional burdens of marginal living standards. In-

evitable losses of aging and death are compounded by potentially ameliorable cultural devaluation and neglect.[11]

Indeed, in another book, Butler suggests that it is easier for the old to adapt to the single loss of physical death than the multiple losses that occur through daily living.[12]

In a sense, the experience of intensive and successive losses provides the older person with an opportunity to rehearse for his or her own death.[13] These "rehearsals," then, add substance to ways of thinking, feeling, and behaving when confronted with the death of the physical self. Although reactions to one's own death may be unpredictable until that crisis is precipitated, it is possible that such reactions may be tempered by "practice" and a sense of perspective. To put it another way, the aging individual may deal more constructively with death precisely because she or he has had to deal with the accumulated losses of a lifetime.

The Dying Process

The process individuals go through when facing imminent death is a source of some debate. Investigators have variously labeled this process in terms of stages, phases, preterminal orientations, and emotional reactions. Comparison of the work of several investigators reveals not only some differences but some striking similarities as well. In an attempt to achieve a measure of clarity on this issue, the work of various researchers is reviewed here.

The most widely known investigation into the process of dying is the work of Elisabeth Kübler-Ross.[14] The Swiss-born psychiatrist began a systematic study of death and dying at the University of Chicago (which operates a teaching-research hospital) when, in 1965, a group of theology students approached her for assistance with a paper on terminally ill patients. From interviews with more than two hundred dying patients, Kübler-Ross identified five stages in the dying process: (1) denial and isolation; (2) anger; (3) bargaining; (4) depression; and (5) acceptance.

1. *Denial and isolation.* The most common first response made by the patients she interviewed was, "No, not me, it cannot be true." Characteristic of this stage are feelings of shock, numbness, and disbelief. Patients who wish to maintain the facade of denial, if only temporarily, might seek a second opinion or go to a faith healer. Kübler-Ross views denial as a healthy defense for dealing with a painful situation in the short run. It serves as a buffer or a brief respite, allowing the patient an opportunity to begin to face the reality of dying and to mobilize other less radical defenses.[15]

2. *Anger.* Once the first reaction to impending death passes and partial acceptance occurs, the patient responds with, "Why me?" Feelings of anger, rage, and resentment well up at the unfairness of life interrupted so prematurely. This anger may be displaced on anyone in the immediate environment: family, friends, or hospital personnel. Those surrounding the patient may view this rage as a personal attack. In actuality, it is a furious cry of anguish at the untimeliness of death, an envy of people who enjoy good health, and rage about all that will be left undone and unfulfilled.[16]

3. *Bargaining.* The typical response at this stage is, "Yes, me, but . . .". A terminally ill person knows from past experience that rewards follow good behavior. The patient's thinking may go something like this: "If God has decided to take me from this earth, and He did not respond to my angry pleas, He may be more favorable if I ask nicely." This is similar to a child first demanding, then asking nicely for something. If the parents continue to say no, the child may promise to do certain household tasks if the response will change from a no to a yes. For the patient, the bargain is often a wish for an extension of life, followed by a wish for a few days without pain. It is an attempt to postpone, to delay death's inevitability.[17]

4. *Depression.* The fourth stage in the dying process is characterized by a great sense of loss. Kübler-Ross differentiates two types of depression: reactive depression, which results from past losses and may be accompanied by guilt or shame (e.g., shame at the disfiguring loss of a breast from cancer); and preparatory depression, which takes into account impending losses, a giving up of all the patient has ever known and loved. In contrast to the reactive depression, preparatory depression is often silent. The former may call for active, verbal intervention, but the latter may require only the presence of one who can give reassurance on a nonverbal feeling level.[18]

5. *Acceptance.* The final stage in the Kübler-Ross framework represents a working through of prior emotional reactions, if enough time is available to confront the death event. In this stage, the patient is frequently withdrawn and weak, and demonstrates very little response to others. Acceptance is not resignation. It is a period of time when the dying individual may contemplate the end of life with a certain degree of equanimity and quiet expectation.[19] This time, as one patient aptly phrased it, is "the final rest before the long journey."[20]

Kübler-Ross points to the importance of hope in the life of the dying individual. In her view, the meaning of hope changes over time. In the early stages, the patient's hope may be that a mistake has been made and the diagnosis is incorrect. After the diagnosis has been confirmed, hope may take the form of a wish for the discovery of a cure. Toward the end of life, the patient simply may have hope for a peaceful, painless death. According to Kübler-Ross, the maintenance of some form of hope provides the nourishment and energy a patient may need through endless weeks or months of suffering. The presence of hope mitigates the fear of rejection or abandonment by the physician, hospital staff, family, friends and others.[21]

The work of Kübler-Ross represents an insightful, humane perspective on the dying process, yet she has had her detractors. A major criticism revolves around her description of the sequential nature of the stages. However, if her earliest work is carefully read, one may note Kübler-Ross' awareness of the nonsequential, and sometimes repetitive, aspects of this process. For example, she states, "Denial, at least partial denial, is used by almost all patients, not only during the first stages of illness or following the confrontation, but also later on from time to time."[22] In her latest work, Kübler-Ross makes it clear that the stages in the dying process are not necessarily sequential or mutually exclusive. People may skip stages, regress to an earlier stage, or not achieve the final stage.[23] Shneidman expresses the dynamics of the dying process by pointing out, "The emotional stages seem to include a constant interplay between disbelief and hope and, against these as a background, a waxing and waning of anguish, terror, acquiescence and surrender, rage and envy, disinterest and ennui, pretense, taunting and daring and even yearning for death—all these in the context of bewilderment and pain."[24]

A somewhat different perspective on the dying process is presented by psychiatrist E. Mansell Pattison.[25] The framework he suggests is divided into three phases: (1) the acute phase; (2) the chronic living-dying phase; and (3) the terminal phase. In each phase, the dying individual confronts certain emotions, fears, and issues. However, Pattison states unequivocally that the entire living-dying process is characterized not only by a continual interplay between denial and acceptance, but by different levels of awareness of denial and acceptance.

1. *The acute phase.* The key word in this part of the schema is crisis. Knowledge of impending death triggers anxiety in the acute crisis period. To counter anxiety before it goes beyond a level of tolerance, the dying individual will use whatever defense mechanisms are available. Responses in this phase may range from immobilization and disbelief to overwhelming feelings of inadequacy, bewilderment, confusion, indefinable anxiety, and unspecified fear.

2. *The chronic living-dying phase.* In the middle phase, earlier unspecified fears become clearer and more focused, including: fears of the unknown, of loneliness, of sorrow, of loss of family and friends, of loss of body, of loss of self-control, of suffering and pain, of loss of identity, and of regression to a primordial state. A constructive resolution of the death event is dependent

on specification of and working through the various fears that impinge on the life space of the dying individual.

3. *The terminal phase.* Both physical and psychological withdrawal appear to signal the beginning of the terminal phase of the dying process. This period may be marked by conservation of energy, lessened anxiety, emotional disorganization, and apathy. Hope remains an important ingredient for facilitating living until death occurs. Pattison differentiates between expectational hope and desirable hope. In the early phases, for example, the patient may have a set of expectations that center around a remission or cure. In the terminal phase, however, the patient may hope that death will not come, which is a desirable wish but no longer expectable as a hope.

As a part of a larger study on dying and death, the "psychological autopsy" (a psychosocial instrument) was modified for use in a geriatric hospital.[26] The purpose of this procedure was to collect and analyze all relevant psychological and social information around an individual patient's death with the aim of improving and humanizing the care of terminal patients. After analysis of 120 psychological autopsies, it became obvious that there are a number of different orientations to death. The investigators classified most of the preterminal orientations as acceptance, apathy, apprehension, or anticipation: "Acceptance refers to patients who spoke about death in a dispassionate and realistic way; apathy describes patients who seemed indifferent to almost any event, including death; apprehension refers to patients who openly voiced fear and alarm about death; and anticipation applies to patients who showed acceptance plus an explicit wish for death."[27] Kastenbaum and Weisman[28] later analyzed 35 of the 120 well-documented psychosocial situations of their elderly patients. Two distinct types of dying individuals emerged: (1) those who were withdrawn and inactive, yet appeared aware and accepting of imminent death; and (2) those who were fully aware of the prospect of death and yet remained active participants in projects and experiences until they were interrupted by death.

Although Kübler-Ross, Pattison, Kastenbaum, and Weisman differ in the way they view the dying process, they also agree in several crucial areas. These areas might be characterized as common emotional reactions to dying and transient states of being in the dying process. In particular, Kübler-Ross and Pattison would concur that such emotional reactions as fear, denial or disbelief, anxiety, loneliness, and depression may be commonly associated with dying. All four investigators appear to agree that such transient states of being as isolation, withdrawal, inactivity, activity, and acceptance may accompany the dying process.

Attitudes Toward Death

A most common human reaction to death of the self is fear. Fear or anxiety about death may take many psychological or physical forms such as fear of pain or physical suffering, of loss of competence, of isolation and abandonment, and of the unknown.[29] How people of various ages react to the fearfulness of death has been the source of some investigation. Puner suggests that the fear of death is not basic or elemental, especially in animals or small children.[30] The very young child may be afraid of the dark, thunder, or dragons but has difficulty in perceiving death as permanent. In a well-known study of death anxiety in children, Nagy interviewed 378 children, 3 to 10 years old.[31] The results of her study yielded three relatively circumscribed developmental phases: (1) for ages 3 to 5, death is seen as a temporary departure or sleep, not as a finality; (2) for ages 5 to 9, death is seen as final and is personified as either a separate person or a dead person, but is still distant from the self; and (3) for ages 9 and above, death is recognized as not only final but inevitable, even for the self. The data from this study suggest that the relationship between death and anxiety is established as early as 3 years of age, when death is viewed as separation.

Throughout young adulthood, the fear of death, or death anxiety, is relatively low.[32] It is difficult for young people to consciously imagine that death will ever mar the vital, robust physicalness of the body. If there is a period when one has a strong belief in immortality, it is, perhaps, during this stage of life. It is in the middle years that the fear of death seems to peak. The awareness of time left to life is heightened in the middle-aged adult, according to the Neugarten study referred to earlier. Puner graphically describes this awareness by pointing out: "It is in the middle years, somewhere between 40 and 55, that the fear of death is strongest. It is a newly developed fear made worse by every intimation of mortality, greying hair, loss of physical stamina, the advent of wrinkles, aches, and ailments that most likely will never go away. The fear is often combined with anger or a sense of outrage that what a man or woman has spent a lifetime building will some day collapse, that all is wasted in the inevitability of death."[33]

In older age groups the fear of death, itself, appears to be relatively low. Kalish reports that comparative studies of the elderly and other age groups indicate that death is not only less frightening to older people, but is much more a topic of conversation and contemplation for this population.[34] Two recent studies provide supportive data for lower death anxiety among older people than their younger counterparts. Bascue and Lawrence explored the relationship between death anxiety and future-time orientation in a sample of eighty-eight institutionalized Caucasian women, 62 years of age and older.[35] They found that older women who were future oriented or who exhibited anxious, possessive, or submissive attitudes about time characteristically were more anxious about death than those who did not exhibit these attitudes. This study appears to support the limited futurity orientation held by many older people in this society. Certainly, this notion comes through clearly in Harvey Hostetter's poem when he asserts that death may be expected soon by anyone who has lived more than 80 years.

In another study, survey and ethnographic data were used to examine attitudes toward death across contrasting social categories.[36] The survey included 1,269 blacks, Chicanos, and whites ranging in age from 45 to 74. The study focused on the relationship between death attitudes and race, age, sex, and social class. The results of the study indicated that the four social stratum variables taken together accounted for very little variation in death attitudes. Of all the variables, age alone was significant in predicting attitudes toward death. Moreover, it was the middle-aged respondents (45 to 54) who expressed the greatest fear of death and the older respondents (65 to 74) who expressed the least. The investigators summarized some important themes that are pertinent to the discussion in this chapter, mentioning "the crisis experienced by many middle-aged people in suddenly confronting death and the resolution exhibited by older individuals toward death, [and] age as a leveler of prior social distinctions, as aging individuals of various walks of life deal with the common biological imperatives of dying."[37] These data, then, provide additional evidence in support of the differences in death attitudes among age groups.

Coping with Death and Dying

How do older people in this society cope with the process of dying and the fact of death? Based on data reviewed earlier, it appears older people are less fearful and thus more accepting of death than younger people. Kalish proposes three major reasons for lower death anxiety in the elderly: (1) the older person tends to place less value on his or her own life, and that evaluation is often shared by others in society; (2) the normal life expectancy, of between 65 and 75 years, may have become such a given that it is easily incorporated into the thinking of the elderly; and (3) losses incurred throughout the life span tend to socialize people to their own deaths.[38]

There is little doubt that with advancing age people become progressively more devalued by society through exclusion from much that is valued by the culture: meaningful work; useful contributions; adequate social and financial resources. Social devaluation fosters lowered self-esteem among the elderly and, thus, reinforces continued devaluation by the nonelderly public. The consequences of this process have an impact, for example, on the quality of medical care received by the aged dying patient. One study revealed that hospital personnel, in a wide range of medical facilities, viewed the death of younger age groups as representing "high social loss" and the death of older people as "low social loss." Moreover, this affected the quality and type of care the older individual received.[39] It is not surprising, therefore, to hear an older person comment, "I've lived a full, long life and now I'm ready to go." It is also not surprising to hear a younger person attribute such an attitude to an older person.

Being prepared for death through loss experiences in life is indeed probable for those individuals who have had enough birthdays. The intensive and successive losses that accompany the aging process frequently result in the kind of pain and anguish associated with the death of a loved one. The gerontological literature abounds in such examples: loss of work, loss of health, loss of the right to choose, loss of status, loss of potency, and sensory loss.[40] Socialization for dying is furthered by the loss of significant relationships through the death of a friend, a relative, or a spouse. For those who are widowed late in life, death may be welcomed or, at least, viewed as a relatively positive alternative to living. In Bermant's *Diary of an Old Man*, the main character, Cyril, poignantly describes the circumstances surrounding the death of a widowed friend.

> They buried old Harry this morning. I don't know why I call him old Harry, but old Harry it's been for as long as I've known him. He was 74—tried to make out he was only 73, but he was 74 if a day, and a nice old soul, but he did not wear well. Some men don't begin to straighten out till they get widowed—as if the wife kept them from the sun; others fall apart. Harry was a faller-apart. He used to say: "It's all right for you, Cyril. You lost your wife Elsie when you were still a young man. You had time to get used to your own company. But Deirdre and me have been together thirty-eight years. It's a bit late at my age to get used to myself." He went up to his bed straight after her funeral and never came down, at least not on his own legs.[41]

Major advances in medical technology, improved medical care, and the eradication of many diseases have increased the possibility of longer, healthier lives in old age, and the probability of maintaining human life via sophisticated equipment. Therefore, the potential of supporting biological life beyond competency to make informed medical decisions is of significant concern to older citizens. One attempt to deal with this issue may be found in the efforts of euthanasia groups encouraging people to sign Living Wills or other similar documents.

The Living Will[42]

To my family, my physician, my lawyer, my clergyman

To any medical facility in whose care I happen to be

To any individual who may become responsible for my health, welfare or affairs

Death is as much a reality as birth, growth, maturity and old age—it is the one certainty of life. If the time comes when I, _____

_____, can no longer take part in decisions for my own future, let this statement stand as an expression of my wishes while I am still of sound mind.

If the situation should arise in which there is no reasonable expectation of my recovery from physical or mental disability, I request that I be allowed to die and not be kept alive by artifical means or "heroic measures." I do not fear death itself as much as the indignities of deterioration, dependence, and hopeless pain. I therefore ask that medication be mercifully administered to me to alleviate suffering even though this may hasten the moment of death.

This request is made after careful consideration. I hope you who care for me will feel morally bound to follow its mandate. I recognize that this appears to place a heavy responsibility upon you, but it is with the intention of relieving you of such responsibility and of placing it upon myself in accordance with my strong convictions that this statement is made.

                                        Signed _____
Date _____
Witness _____ Witness _____
Copies of this request have been given to _____

                                        _____

The Living Will, then, is an attempt by potentially powerless individuals to influence medical decisions in advance, while they are still in good health. The document is legally binding only in states that have passed "Death with Dignity" legislation. In effect, the Living Will is a plea to be allowed to die naturally without intervention by artifical or heroic measures. Some older people have opted to exercise even greater choice over the death event. In the moving pictorial essay *Gramp*, Mark and Dan Jury present a portrait of the life and death of their grandfather, who had been deteriorating physically over time.[43] At age 81 he removed his false teeth and announced that he was no longer going to eat or drink. Three weeks later, he died. The grandfather consciously decided not only when he was going to die, but how he was going to die—with his dignity intact.

Other means of coping with death may be related to the inner experience of the elderly. For instance, Erikson's last stage of human development, Ego Integrity versus Despair, is the culmination of all prior stages and involves "the acceptance of one's one and only life cycle as something that had to be and that, by necessity, permitted of no substitutions."[44] Although this stage is the least well defined, it seems to suggest a relationship between death and resolution of life. It is as though a basic acceptance of one's life as having been appropriate, inevitable, and meaningful somehow provides mastery over the fear of death.

Similarly, Butler's concept of the life review posits a series of psychological tasks preceding death.[45] The life review is considered a universal phenomenon affecting persons of any age who are near death. This process gives the opportunity to put one's life in a positive perspective, but may also lead to such negative effects as depression or guilt about past events. Butler views reminiscence in the aged as "part of a normal life review process brought about by the realization of approaching dissolution and death. It is characterized by the progressive return to consciousness of past experiences and particularly the resurgence of unresolved conflicts which can be looked at again and reintegrated. If the reintegration is successful, it can give new significance and meaning to one's life and prepare one for death, by mitigating fear and anxiety."[46] Although both Erikson's and Butler's theories appear to have salience for older people in coping with death, they await further substantiation through additional empirical study.

One final note on coping with death: Even though most people still die within a hospital or nursing home setting, there are exciting new movements in this country related to care of the dying that recall old customs. These movements might be described as family and community alternatives for coping with the death of loved ones. One such alternative is the hospice system of care for the terminally ill.

The hospice movement, which has its roots in Europe, is a humane approach to coping with death. A hospice is a place where people go when they are on a journey. It is a place of transition. The goal is "to keep the patient pain-free, comfortable, and fully alert during the final phases of his illness and his life. This goal is achieved through a highly sophisticated—although basic—scientific and artistic system of palliative care."[47] The major components of the hospice system include the alleviation and control of physical, psychological, social, and spiritual pain, or any combination of these four. To provide a coordinated approach to the patient and the family, interdisciplinary teams are utilized in both the planning and care phases of the processs of dying. Moreover, medical and nursing services are available on a round-the-clock, 7-day-a-week basis. A viable hospice program also provides home care services in collaboration with inpatient facilities. To foster continued meaningful interaction, the family together with the patient is regarded as the unit of care in the hospice system. The program involves follow-up with the family after the death of the patient to lend emotional support. To provide concrete aid (e.g., transportation) and friendship to the dying and the family, volunteers are used extensively as an integral part of the hospice care team.[48] A hospice is a place with an emphasis on living—truly living until death comes.

Another alternative, which increasing numbers of people are beginning to select, involves returning to or remaining at home to die, surrounded by the care and concern of family. Professional home care services (e.g., medical procedures by visiting nurses) may be performed to assist the family, but the major emphasis is on members participating supportively in the dying process. Home care has the potential of lifting the fearful veil of death and drawing families together to share a common grief. Thus, death again has the possibility of being viewed as a natural part of the life cycle.

Summary

The last decade has witnessed the beginning of a gradual breakdown of taboos related to death and dying. On the one hand, people remain under the influence of cultural attitudes focusing on the deviancy of death and the immortality of youth. On the other hand, people are beginning to come under the influence of attitudes emphasizing the inevitability and normality of death that occurs at an advanced age. This ambivalence is clearly reflected in the diverse ways that individuals still view and react to death and the process of dying. For the aged who have suffered from accrued losses, death may seem a welcome release. Indeed, the years of "rehearsal" for death, coupled with contemplation of the meaning of one's life, uniquely prepare older people for their confrontation with death. The movement away from denial and toward an acceptance of death also has precipitated the initiation of more humane measures of coping with death, which include Living Wills, hospice care, and dying at home within the circle of the family. As change continues in our society, it is likely that people will become more concerned about quality-of-life issues rather than about dying, which, after all, occurs only once in each lifetime.

Notes

1. Hannelore Wass and Martha Scott, "Aging Without Death?? " *The Gerontologist* 17, 4 (August 1977), pp. 377–380.

2. Robert N. Butler, *Why Survive? Being Old in America* (New York: Harper & Row, 1975), p. xi.

3. Richard A. Kalish, "Death and Dying in a Social Context," in Robert H. Binstock and Ethel Shanas (eds.), *Handbook of Aging and the Social Sciences* (New York: Van Nostrand Reinhold Company, 1976), pp. 484–485.

4. Richard Schulz, *The Psychology of Death, Dying, and Bereavement* (Reading, Mass.: Addison-Wesley Publishing Company, 1978), p. 91.

5. Richard A. Kalish, "A Continuum of Subjectively Perceived Death," *The Gerontologist* 6, 2 (June 1966), p. 74.

6. Ibid., p. 73.

7. For a discussion of the meaning of anticipatory grief, see C. Knight Aldrich, "Some Dynamics of Anticipatory Grief," in Bernard Schoenberg et al. (eds.), *Anticipatory Grief* (New York: Columbia University Press, 1974), pp. 3–9.

8. Bernice L. Neugarten, "The Awareness of Middle Age," in Bernice L. Neugarten (ed.), *Middle Age and Aging* (Chicago: The University of Chicago Press, 1968), p. 97.

9. Kalish, 1976, op. cit., pp. 486–487.

10. Ibid., pp. 487–488.

11. Robert N. Butler and Myrna I. Lewis, *Aging and Mental Health*, 2d ed. (Saint Louis: The C. V. Mosby Company, 1977), p. 34.

12. Butler, op. cit., p. 1.

13. Kalish, 1976, op. cit., p. 490.

14. Elisabeth Kübler-Ross, *On Death and Dying* (New York: Macmillan Publishing Company, 1969).

15. Ibid., pp. 38–42.

16. Ibid., pp. 50–52.

17. Ibid., pp. 82–84.

18. Ibid., pp. 83–87.

19. Ibid., pp. 112–114.

20. Ibid., p. 113.

21. Ibid., pp. 138–141.

22. Ibid., p. 39.

23. Elisabeth Kübler-Ross and Mal Warshaw, *To Live Until We Say Good-bye* (Englewood Cliffs, N.J.: Prentice-Hall, 1978), pp. 24–25.

24. Edwin S. Shneidman, *Deaths of Man* (Baltimore: Penguin Books, 1974), p. 7.

25. E. Mansell Pattison, "The Living-Dying Process," in Charles A. Garfield (ed.), *Psychosocial Care of the Dying Patient* (New York: McGraw-Hill Book Company, 1978), pp. 145–153.

26. Robert J. Kastenbaum, *Death, Society, and Human Experience* (Saint Louis: The C. V. Mosby Company, 1977), pp. 173–177.

27. Avery D. Weisman and Robert Kastenbaum, *The Psychological Autopsy: A Study of The Terminal Phase of Life*, Community Mental Health Monograph No. 4 (New York: Behavioral Publications, 1968), p. 22.

28. Robert Kastenbaum and Avery D. Weisman, "The Psychological Autopsy as a Research Procedure in Gerontology," in Donald P. Kent, Robert Kastenbaum, and Sylvia Sherwood (eds.), *Research Planning and Action for the Elderly: The Power and Potential of Social Science* (New York: Behavioral Publications, 1972), pp. 214–216.

29. Shneidman, op. cit., p. 5.

30. Morton Puner, *To the Good Long Life: What We Know About Growing Old* (New York: Universe Books, 1974), p. 230.

31. Maria H. Nagy, "The Child's View of Death," in Herman Feifel (ed.), *The Meaning of Death* (New York: McGraw-Hill Book Company, 1959), pp. 79-98.

32. Schulz, op. cit., p. 29.

33. Puner, op. cit.

34. Kalish, 1976, op. cit.

35. L. O. Bascue and R. E. Lawrence, "A Study of Subjective Time and Death Anxiety in the Eldery," *Omega* 8, 1 (1977), pp. 81-90.

36. Vern L. Bengtson, Jose B. Cuellar, and Pauline K. Ragan, "Stratum Contrasts and Similarities in Attitudes Toward Death," *Journal of Gerontology* 12, 1 (January, 1977), pp. 76-88.

37. Ibid., p. 87.

38. Kalish, 1976, op. cit.

39. Barney A. Glaser, "The Social Loss of Aged Dying Patients," *The Gerontologist* 6, 2 (June 1966), pp. 77-80.

40. Butler, op. cit., pp. 1-21. See also Robert C. Atchley, *The Sociology of Retirement* (New York: Halsted Press, 1976), and Ewald W. Busse and Eric Pfeiffer (eds.), *Behavior and Adaptation in Late Life*, 2d ed. (Boston: Little, Brown and Company, 1977).

41. Chaim Bermant, *Diary of an Old Man* (New York: Holt, Rinehart and Winston, 1966), p. 9.

42. Kastenbaum, op. cit., p. 221.

43. Mark Jury and Dan Jury, *Gramp* (New York: Grossman Publishers, 1976).

44. Erik H. Erikson, *Childhood and Society*, 2d ed. (New York: W. W. Norton and Company), 1963, p. 268.

45. Butler and Lewis, op. cit., pp. 49-50.

46. Ibid., p. 49.

47. Robert Woodson, "Hospice Care in Terminal Illness," in Charles A. Garfield (ed.), *Stress and Survival: The Emotional Realities of Life-threatening Illness* (Saint Louis: The C. V. Mosby Company, 1979), p. 325.

48. Ibid., pp. 325-336.

PART TWO
Meeting the Health Needs of Older People

The delivery of health care is currently receiving widespread evaluation in this country. Increasingly, alternatives to traditional health care systems are being considered and, at times, implemented. These national trends are reflected in approaches to health care for the elderly, which is not surprising, since the elderly need and use health services disproportionately to their numbers. Add to this the fact that the proportion of older people in the population is increasing, and it becomes clear that alternative approaches will be necessary to relieve the strain on primary health care institutions. A major objective of alternative services is the development of a delivery system that is both economical and humane. Toward these ends, considerable emphasis is being placed on developing preventative strategies that can help the older person maintain an optimum level of functioning, at least until more intensive medical care is required.

The chapters in this section describe programs that illustrate alternative approaches to health care for older people. While the section of course does not include all of the innovative programs that have been undertaken, these selections do provide a view of several that have been effective in meeting the health needs of the elderly. The authors are service professionals who have been instrumental in developing and implementing the programs they describe. They provide us with their informed perspective on the problems, benefits, and future prospects of programs such as theirs. Young focuses on the procedures necessary for developing a comprehensive community physical fitness program for older adults. Kent reviews the efforts of one county health department to bring a range of services, from preventative health screening to nursing home monitoring, to the senior citizens of the county. In their chapter, Schmitt and Arnold discuss the manner in which a mental health center responds to the mental health needs of the elderly by providing a wide range of basic human services. Finally, Redford describes an experimental program undertaken by the students at one school of nursing to provide preventative medical services to residents of an age-segregated high rise.

In general, these selections demonstrate ways in which health services can be designed to enlist the active participation of those people who are receiving the services. Through such participation, the health needs of the elderly can be met without rendering them more dependent on the service provider than is absolutely necessary.

6

Physical Fitness in Later Life: A Community Model

Lynn J. Young

Today many Americans are discovering the benefits of regular exercise. The President's Council on Fitness and Sports has determined that regular exercise may deter the onset of degenerative disease, improve the ability to survive a heart attack, and increase independence through improved health and mobility.[1] While most people have participated in planned exercise programs as part of their elementary and secondary school experience, very few have continued organized fitness programs into later life. One reason for this is that communities have only recently begun to provide older people with opportunities for pursuing organized fitness activities. Another reason is that many older people, after years of relative inactivity, are reluctant to resume physical exercise. If they do, however, the result may well be an improvement in their circulation, heartwork capacity, strength, flexibility, and general feelings of well-being.

As explained in Chapter 3, growing old is accompanied by a number of fundamental physiological changes (e.g., greater inflexibility of tendons and ligaments, bone calcification, increased heart rate, decreased circulation, loss of strength, and loss of skin tone). However, such changes can be mitigated by participation in a systematic program of physical fitness. Fitness programs may consist of several types of exercise. Whether the older person engages in individualized exercise regimens, group exercise activities, or competitive sports, it is important that such programs be based on sound physiological principles. Certain specific precautions such as a doctor's approval, an individually paced program, and a knowledge of self-testing measures should be taken to promote safe and constructive results. Although such precautions are necessary, the older person should realize that the real danger lies in a sedentary life. Those who have experienced a satisfactory fitness program may be excellent examples to their peers, and they can encourage those who are hesitant to begin an appropriate program leading to optimum physical functioning. Specifically, a fitness-oriented older adult can advise practitioners on the special exercise needs of their peer group, disseminate promotional material on established fitness programs, or serve as leaders or assistants in community fitness programs.

Practitioners overseeing organized recreational programs must understand that the elderly will have special needs. Programs for older adults that simply adapt approaches to fitness designed for the young are not sufficient. Therefore, schools of education need to broaden their physical fitness emphases to include the later stages of the life cycle, if they have not already done so. Practitioners should keep in mind that many predilections of older people regarding exercise will have been conditioned by earlier experiences. For example, they may prefer age-segregated, and even sex-segregated, activities, and they may feel more comfortable in a group setting. Recreation professionals might well capitalize on this group preference in order to encourage a personal commitment to exercise on the part of older people. Participants are likely to enjoy a program much more if there is an emphasis on group interaction and socializing. Moreover, programs for the elderly should not be overly regimented nor oversimplified. It is all too easy to underestimate the abilities and resources of such people. As is true at all ages, the older adult's sense of independence, intelligence, and personal integrity must be respected. Hitherto fitness specialists have witnessed a rather large dropout rate among older participants in their programs. This is not hard to understand since many programs do not suit the needs of this age group.

A generalized program of fitness for the elderly may be conceived as a continuum of fitness preparedness. The individual then may become involved in the program at an appropriate point and, in effect, move along the continuum at an individualized rate. At one extreme is the individual who is simply seeking information about fitness. The next step is taking an initial fitness course, followed by an expanded exercise regimen. The final step on the continuum is the challenge of competitive sports. Of course, a person may elect to remain at any point along the continuum.

A Model for a Community Fitness Program

The development of a community fitness program for the elderly should begin with a review of existing area organizations that could provide opportunities for physical activities for older citizens. Representatives of relevant organizations should meet to develop goals and assess resources that are available. Goals appropriate to such a program include the development of: (1) physiological capacities such as strength, flexibility, endurance, and cardiovascular functioning; (2) a social setting that makes exercise more enjoyable; and (3) an individual (psychological) commitment to exercise as an avenue to life enrichment. The course of action a given community will take to achieve these goals will of course depend in large measure on the particular services already available in that community. However, the following recommended activities (which correspond to the steps of the fitness continuum) represent a comprehensive, model program of physical fitness.

Educational Programs

Two distinct informational strategies should be developed to meet the objectives of this first step on the fitness continuum. First, an attempt should be made to reach as large a portion of the older population in the community as possible with information about the benefits of fitness and the opportunities available in the community. Such information may be dispersed through the mass media, direct mailings, and through concerned professionals in the community such as physicians, public officials, and business leaders. A major emphasis should be an attempt to eliminate the fear that older people might have about starting a fitness regimen.

Second, and concurrent with the dissemination of educational materials to older people, is the development of training materials for potential leaders of fitness programs. An excellent way of developing competent fitness practitioners for this age group is to prepare a manual explicating the following components of a fitness-oriented program:

1. a review of physiological issues associated with older adult exercise
2. an outline of a suitable exercise session format
3. a description of warm-up exercises along with the purpose of such exercises
4. a description of flexibility exercises, including a discussion of limitations imposed by age
5. an explanation of the various procedures for improving physical strength and cardiovascular functioning
6. a review of methods for achieving conscious relaxation and better posture
7. a discussion of exercises related to special physical problems such as postural and muscular weakness, auditory and visual handicaps, and cardiovascular problems

A Structured Fitness Program

The cornerstone of a community approach to fitness for senior adults is a comprehensive, structured fitness program consisting of exercise classes and designed to encourage the development of a participant's commitment to fitness. Classes should focus on individual fitness objectives that may be mastered by participants at their own pace. At the same time, participants should be strongly motivated to continue exercises outside of the class setting. Such motivation may be achieved through four strategies not often emphasized in current programs: (1) educating people about the benefits of continued exercise; (2) providing home assignments that, in effect, extend the classroom program; (3) employing a "station" method for self-learning; and (4) referring participants to other ongoing fitness programs.

A generalized format for a structured fitness class consists of several segments, each lasting from five to twenty minutes. The first segment, five to ten minutes long, consists of direct instruction by the fitness leader or guest speakers, but may also include discussions and handouts of printed exercises. A five- to ten-minute period of warm-up exercises follows this instructional segment. Warm-up is followed by a period of conditioning lasting between fifteen and twenty minutes. This segment begins with group conditioning (e.g., flexibility, strength, and endurance exercises), but as participants gain competence, the "station" method of conditioning may be introduced. In this method, the instructor divides the exercise room into four or more special exercise areas. Each area, or station, emphasizes a certain portion of the exercise program such as flexibility exercises, strength builders, walking and running, posture development, balance, or other aspects of fitness that may be indicated for the class. Individuals may proceed from station to station on a rotating basis and do the exercises prescribed by the instructor. The use of stations increases an individual's competence in a personal exercise program by deemphasizing the need for the instructor in all phases of the program. The instructor then becomes a guide and monitor during this portion of the class session. The final segment, five to ten minutes in length, is a relaxation session involving deep breathing, conscious tensing and relaxing of muscles, and mental concentration. Senior adult participants may share responsibility for conducting this last segment, which also helps to develop skills that may be used at home. Recordings are available that narrate techniques of conscious relaxation and aid in mental concentration. Use of these recordings will help people reduce tension, sleep better, and feel more energetic.

Regardless of whether specific fitness classes exactly follow this prescribed format, there are several basic requirements that will ensure the success and effectiveness of such classes. The main requirement is that classes be conducted by leaders who are well trained in geriatric fitness as well as in the interpersonal skills that are essential in developing individual commitments to fitness. A second requirement is that classes emphasize the importance of continuing exercise regimens at home. To this end, classes should utilize exercise equipment that is generally available at home (e.g., chairs, books, ropes, and balls). Furthermore, the class leader should provide explicit "homework" assignments and instructions for maintaining records of fitness progress. Third, the intensity of class exercises should match the physical capacities of the participants. However, it is generally accepted that classes should meet at least twice a week, and preferably three times. The length of exercise sessions should increase from twenty-five minutes to fifty-five minutes as individuals develop endurance. Finally, classes should provide for the development of aerobic power through exercises that decrease the heart rate at work. By personally monitoring their own heart rates in class, participants can easily learn to judge the appropriate intensity of exercise for them. Table 6.1 shows the desired heart rate after exercise for those people who are fit and for those who are not.[2] The rates are derived by subtracting one's age from 200 if one is physically fit, or from 170 if one is not fit.

Group Activities and Sports

For senior adults who have attained a satisfactory level of fitness, it is imperative that the community provide abundant opportunities for further physical activity. Unfortunately, communities tend to disregard the benefits obtained from offering this advanced level of activity to older people. A comprehensive community program of fitness for older citizens would provide basic instruction in games and sports. Classes need not be segregated

Table 6.1:   Desired Heart Rates After Exercise[2]

Age	For Novice	For Physically Fit
30	140	170
40	130	160
50	120	150
60	110	140
70	100	130
80	90	120

according to age, but might well be separated according to ability. City leagues should be open to senior adults who can benefit by participating in competitive sports such as tennis, golf, volleyball, bowling, badminton, and the like. For these activities, age-segregated groupings are more advisable in order to maintain a reasonable level of competition. Finally, older people should be able to compete in Masters Individualized Sports.[3] The value of intensive involvement in competitive sports long has been recognized. According to one Masters swimmer, "Participation [in Masters swimming] provides competition, a great motivational device which can induce men and women to continue a training program."[4] He further contends that an older person in training for competitive sports is comparable in fitness to a much younger sedentary person. Through proper implementation of this trilevel fitness program, communities may aid older Americans in developing and/or continuing the fitness they once enjoyed at an earlier age, thus enhancing their enjoyment of life.

Notes

1. Richard Davis, ed., *Aging: Prospects and Issues* (Los Angeles: University of Southern California Gerontology Center, 1976), p. 243.

2. *Fit Kit: Canadian Home Fitness Test.* Published in Canada by the Rousseau Publishing Co. By permission of the Minister of Supply and Services, Canada.

3. Masters Individualized Sports is a national sanctioning and record-keeping organization that coordinates and publicizes age-graded sports competition.

4. Paul Hutinger, "Delaying the Aging Process" (report given at a Masters Swim Clinic, Western Illinois University, 1973), p. 1.

7

A Multi-Service County Health Department

W. Kay Kent

County health departments, or their equivalents, are designed to provide many health services to people of all ages. Some health department programs, such as health education or immunization, may be equally important to all age groups, while others may be designed specifically for individuals in a certain stage of the life cycle. The county health department discussed here provides a range of services specifically for older people. For those who are not restricted to their homes or to an institutional setting, the department conducts a health education program at congregate meal sites and a health screening clinic. In addition, it monitors the quality of health care in nursing homes. Let us take a closer look at the objectives and implementation of each of these services.

Health Education

The major objective of the health education program is to provide information on health issues to help the older person improve his health and learn to recognize early signs and symptoms of disease. A nurse from the health department holds monthly discussions at all congregate meal sites in the county, an effective means of reaching large numbers of older people. The health discussions are usually held just before or after the midday meal, and the topics covered are actually determined by the immediate concerns of the participants. The health problems that have been of most concern to older people thus far are arthritis, hypertension, heart disease, stroke, bowel and bladder problems, special diets, and hearing loss.

Discussion is stimulated by the use of audiovisual materials and handouts.

The nurse encourages questions and answers them in a simple, nontechnical manner. Two factors contribute to the success of this program: (1) over time the nurse has established a relationship with the groups; and (2) the participants have had an active part in determining discussion topics.

A Health Screening Unit

One of the major rationales for developing a health screening clinic in a community is that many people have a tendency to avoid visits to the doctor. There are many reasons for their reluctance. For example, some feel as though they are imposing on the doctor's time when all they have is a "minor" complaint. Others anticipate an unpleasant experience, and still others cannot afford the fee. This is not to suggest that a clinic can substitute for regular contact with a physician, but it can represent a first step toward medical care for those people who, for whatever reason, have not sought help from a doctor.

The health department sponsors semiweekly screening clinics in the county's largest community and monthly clinics in three smaller outlying communities. The main clinic is located in an apartment complex for the elderly, but serves the community's entire older population. In the past year, 59 percent of the visits to the clinics were by individuals who live outside the complex. Screening does not involve diagnosis, but instead identifies those who need more comprehensive attention. Individuals identified as needing further examination are referred to their physicians. The activities of the clinics can be divided into three broad areas of concern. First, through health promotion and education, individuals can be assisted in improving their health habits in order to achieve the highest possible level of health. For instance, a clinic can help patients on salt-restricted diets to find ways of making meals more palatable and therefore the diets easier to follow. It can also encourage better nutritional habits and provide flu immunizations, among other things. Second, the clinic is able to detect predisease conditions of elderly patients, such as obesity and poor nutrition, and to detect instances of disease in its earlier stages—for example, anemia, diabetes, and glaucoma. Through the early detection of disease, individuals can be helped to get treatment before problems progress to such a degree that they require hospitalization or nursing home care. Finally, the clinic can monitor patients with disease conditions.

At present, there are sixteen hours of nursing service and two hours of nutritionist service per week at the main clinic, and twelve hours of nursing service per month at the other sites. The number of clinic visits per year has increased in 4 years from 1,174 to 4,960. In the past year, 15 percent of the people in the county who were 60 and older received service from the clinic.

Approximately 11 percent of all visits to the clinic result in referrals to private physicians, mental health centers, or audiologists. The rapidly increasing use of the clinic and the fair number of referrals indicate the value of screening clinics.

Home Health Care

The visiting nurse service, which is separate from the county health department, provides a broad range of health-related services for individuals who are restricted to their homes. Physical, speech, and occupational therapy, nutrition services, nursing services, and homemaker services are included—important resources for the elderly because they provide alternatives to hospital and nursing home care. Reimbursements for home health services to the elderly are usually through Medicare, Medicaid, or direct fee for services. Medicare and Medicaid provide coverage for a limited number of diagnostic and treatment services and for rehabilitative services. Since Medicare will pay only for services that help a patient reach his maximum rehabilitation potential, those that maintain an individual at a particular level are not reimbursable. The exclusion of payment for maintenance care is a significant problem, since the chronic conditions of the elderly often require only maintenance care in order to prevent unnecessary deterioration. Hopefully, this regulation can be changed in the future so that no one who needs home health care will be denied services because of inability to pay. Until such time, however, the United Fund and county appropriations may be alternative means of assisting individuals who cannot pay for health services that enable them to remain in their homes.

Nursing Home Inspections

Each adult care home, or nursing home, is monitored approximately once each month by the health department's "nurse surveyor." During these unannounced visits the nurse inspects the physical condition of the home, as well as the quality of health care provided the residents. The findings of each inspection are discussed with the home's administrators. A report of the inspection is sent to the home and to the state health department, and a record also is kept at the county health department. The nursing home files at the health department may be reviewed by the public on request. In addition to these periodic inspections, the health deparment monitors the homes through complaints received from family and friends, patients and employees, and other concerned citizens. These complaints are investigated and the resulting reports filed with those emanating from the regular inspections. If a home consistently fails to correct observed problems, its license to operate may be withdrawn by the state department of health.

As desirable as it might be for people to live out their lives in relative independence, there always will be a portion of the elderly population who must spend their last years in an institutional setting. These people are entitled to the best health care possible, but there are many problems involved in institutional care today that prevent the realization of this goal. One of the major problems involves the cost of quality care, a second is the lack of status in nursing home employment, and a third involves the consequences of government regulations. Let us first examine the problem of costs.

An important factor in the cost of operating a nursing home is high staff turnover, which has been well documented and is hardly surprising for a field that pays minimum wages with few fringe benefits. Moreover, the work is often frustrating and at times depressing. The turnover problem is at the heart of a controversy surrounding the training of nursing home aides. Until recently, aides were limited to on-the-job training, which usually meant simply observing another aide for a few days. Today, some state nursing home regulations require that aides be certified by attending an approved training program or successfully completing a standard examination. The nursing home industry contends that this requirement for certification is too costly to be continued (one of the reasons being the high rate of staff turnover) and is seeking its elimination. Since more rigorous training for aides is an obvious step toward a desirable level of health care, adequate compensation for nursing home aides (if it reduces staff turnover) may prove a less costly approach in the long run; but the question remains of who should bear the immediate financial burden of a large-scale effort to increase compensation. A systematic investigation of the ability of nursing homes to assume this burden should be undertaken, and potential sources of support for aide training programs should be explored.

Another aspect of the problem of nursing home costs is the maintenance of round-the-clock professional nursing service. Homes that are licensed as intermediate care facilities are required to maintain licensed nursing personnel on duty only during the day shift. However, satisfactory health care can only be achieved when appropriately trained staff are available at all times. Although this increases the cost of operating such institutions, it is a step that must be taken, since heart attacks, strokes, and other medical emergencies do not occur only on the day shift.

A second impediment to proper nursing home care is the low status of professional positions in nursing homes. This low status is particularly evident in the nursing profession, and therefore it has been difficult for homes to recruit competent professionals. Besides the fact that it is less appealing for those in the medical profession to work with patients whose conditions are chronic, rather than with those who are likely to be cured, there has traditionally been little emphasis placed on careers in geriatric nursing in schools of nursing and in the nursing literature. However, this latter circumstance is beginning to change.

Finally, government regulations that are intended to protect patients from harm sometimes have the unintended consequence of creating an atmosphere that is more institutional than homelike. Regulations have the tendency to produce uniformity in the handling of patients and their belongings rather than allowing for individuality, which is so important to the well-being of the older patient. In the implementation of regulations needed to protect patients, care must be taken to maintain an environment in which the older person can feel at home. In the final analysis, a nursing home is not only a place in which to receive care but also a place in which to live.

8

A Community Mental Health Center: Toward a Program of Service for the Elderly

Virginia Schmitt and Cynthia J. Arnold

There are several reasons why a relatively small proportion of older people tend to use mental health facilities. Many of the elderly are not informed about the services provided at mental health centers. Also, few mental health professionals have been trained to treat older people and, in general, their training has been predicated on a model of treatment in which clients must take the initiative in seeking assistance. The mental health center discussed here has attempted to expand services for older people by seeking out those individuals in need and by developing programs that address not only specific mental health problems but also social and economic problems that contribute to emotional stress.

The expansion of the center's services for older people began with a door-to-door survey designed to locate isolated elderly residents of a low-income area having a highly concentrated older population. This survey identified 209 elderly people with a variety of needs, some of which were severe enough to require immediate intervention. The procedure used in this initial outreach effort was to secure from ministers in the target area a list of older adults who seemed to be in need of assistance. While this procedure served the center's immediate purposes, more systematic survey procedures might produce a more comprehensive result. A team of volunteers made home visits to each of the individuals on the list, and these individuals in turn were invited to suggest others who might be in need of help.

On the first visit, the volunteers undertook a needs assessment and also observed, among other things, the subjects' physical condition, attitudes toward their circumstances, and the condition of their homes. Moreover, they gave each subject a booklet containing phone numbers of various agencies and sources of help, as well as the number of the mental health center. The volunteer's name was also printed in each booklet. A return visit three months later and a third visit six months after that enabled the mental health center's staff to determine whether this information was actually being used and, if so, to what extent it helped lessen the elderly person's degree of isolation. During these return visits, the volunteers also updated the subject's needs assessment. If the subject was in need at that time, he or she was referred to an appropriate source of help.

This outreach project was assisted by an advisory board consisting of ministers from various churches, older adults from the target area, and staff members from agencies in service to the elderly. The board met on a monthly basis. An attempt was made to increase public awareness of the project through newspapers and television. This effort was successful; for example, many inquiries about the project were stimulated by a feature article in a local newspaper. Also, one local television station covered a home visit and presented highlights on its evening news program. Finally, mental health center staff spoke to church groups and at nutrition sites.

Several conclusions can be drawn from information obtained through the home visits. For the most part, these older adults were, in effect, stranded in their own homes and were unable to take advantage of existing facilities from which they potentially could benefit. The most significant cause of this isolation was the lack of adequate transportation. Most of the subjects expressed a desire, or at least a willingness, to attend a life enrichment program and a congregate meal program but were unable to do so because they did not have the necessary transportation. Also, they were struggling to keep their homes in satisfactory condition, principally because they lacked the money and functional capacity to successfully maintain them. Seventy-eight individuals stated they needed help right away with minor home repairs. An additional ninety-three declared a need for help in yard work and heavy-duty cleaning, and seventy-four needed help with light housecleaning. Only fourty-seven indicated they were able to pay for even a part of the costs of these services. Observations by interviewers substantiated the fact that many people interviewed were simply not able to maintain their homes beyond minimal standards. Yet many of these same individuals exhibited the ability to remain independent, self-sufficient, and out of a nursing home. Finally, loneliness was identified as a major problem for many of these older adults. When new avenues for social interaction were proposed to them, their response was quite positive.

This is not to say that older people are uniformly eager to embark upon new, ameliorative programs. Expressions of reluctance to take advantage of available services generally relate to a fear of being uprooted and of losing independence. The importance of independence is suggested by the fact that several individuals insisted on cooking their own meals even though using a stove presented a possible physical danger to them. Moreover, some individuals actually would refuse meals delivered to their homes if they felt there would be too much prying into their personal affairs. The fear of being uprooted might also help explain some negative reactions to the term *mental health center*, which perhaps was associated in some people's minds with *mental hospital*.

It should be pointed out that lack of money is not always the major difficulty confronting older people. There are financially secure people existing at a minimal level of subsistence. "Saving for a rainy day" is a primary objective for many people. Also, some older people feel vulnerable to exploitation by unethical and unfeeling schemers. Some subjects, for instance, thought they had contracted to have their yards raked and cut only, but were charged a large amount of money for "full service yard treatment." Other subjects felt they had been exploited by firms rendering a variety of home repair services. Another pervasive difficulty facing these older subjects was inflexible organizational structures. Many widows reported long-drawn-out efforts to obtain Social Security. One widow reported a wait of nine months for clarification of her Social Security status. Organizations dispensing meals delivered to the home had fairly strict geographical boundaries, excluding some who needed this service. Congregate meal programs were being operated on specific ratios, and when ratios were overextended, potential clients were placed on waiting lists. One particular woman contacted the mental health center because she was about to lose her home. She was referred to an agency considered appropriate for dealing with her problem. After seven other stops along the way the woman's problem found its way back to the center again. With the help of local churches, money was obtained for her.

The mental health center's goal has not been just to determine the needs of elderly citizens, but to respond to them as quickly and thoroughly as possible. Thus, a follow-up program of service delivery was begun. Its purpose was to attack the three major areas of need determined by the survey: loneliness, lack of transportation, and need for home repairs. There were four basic objectives identified for this program:

1. to link the existing resources of health, social welfare, and human service agencies to the specific case management plan for each older adult found to be in need;

2. to identify volunteer resources in the community through active contact with clubs, service organizations, and businesses;
3. to establish a "senior companion" program to occasionally relieve
   families of their responsibilities for the elderly member; and
4. to develop a pool of volunteers who would provide a wide assortment
   of home repair and home maintenance services.

In a survey of available services to older adults it was determined that
many organizations are geared to meeting only the social needs of the older
adult. However, there are basically two categories of needs. Type 1 needs
may be met with social activities, while Type 2 needs may be met by providing assistance with deeper emotional problems such as coping with losses
and adjusting to the more debilitating consequences of growing old. It would
be a mistake to impose Type 1 solutions on Type 2 problems and vice versa.

At the heart of the follow-up program is the ongoing activity of our older
adult support groups. These groups meet Mondays through Thursdays for
five hours each day. During the sessions, members enjoy contact with other
older adults from the community, share their problems and concerns, and
learn additional communications skills. The groups are goal-oriented and
are intent upon meeting the basic human needs of the whole person as
outlined by Abraham Maslow[1].

At the bottom of Maslow's hierarchy are bodily needs. One cannot advance to the next level, safety and security, until bodily needs have been
adequately met. The psychological needs, which make up the next two
levels, must in turn be met in order for the individual to develop a positive
self-concept. The final goal for each individual is self-actualization, a continuous, life-long process. It is not uncommon to find elderly people rooted
at the bottom of the hierarchy of needs. The very existence of such people is
threatened, primarily because of fixed incomes and the fear of exploitation.
The family is the principal unit in which basic needs are usually met, but
many older people live alone and have no family or very weak family ties.

The essential fact that members of the support groups develop a caring attitude toward each other provides participants with the strength to overcome many of their problems. Furthermore, there is evidence that work
with these same people on an individual basis had only a limited effect on
improving their level of functioning, while the informal group setting provides the sense of security and concerted action necessary to enhance
problem-solving skills.

Each group session begins with a problem-solving period during which
each person discusses whatever problems have occurred since the last group
meeting. This is an important part of the session, since members are able to
share information and render emotional support. Every group session also

includes an educational component. Assertiveness training and some transactional analysis techniques are used to help members gain a better understanding of their own feelings and how to handle them. Role playing is also used to help people express their feelings.

Sessions are structured so that the entire group meets together at several times during the day. The problem-solving session that begins the day is attended by all members, after which the group breaks up into smaller units. The activities of these units vary. One group may play table games, while another (consisting of newer members or members with a relatively low level of functioning) may engage in simple crafts, which help coordination and build self-confidence. Still others may sing, celebrate birthdays, or take field trips. Lunch is a second time in which the whole group is together. Members bring brown-bag lunches, and mealtime becomes a vehicle for building social skills. The final half-hour of the day, which is spent in relaxation exercises, is the third time that the group is together.

The group sessions are led by a registered nurse with a master's degree in counseling and guidance. She is assisted by a commmunity worker having extensive experience dealing with people, and by some trained volunteers. The size of the groups varies from eight to twenty or more members, depending upon the length of time the particular groups have been organized. Most participants attend only one group session per week; however, some come to two or more and a few come to all four, depending upon their individual needs. One important outgrowth of the weekly meetings is a telephone reassurance service. Members exchange telephone numbers and call each other just to chat or when specific problems arise. Members also get together informally during the week to share a meal, play cards, and the like.

The two major obstacles in maintaining these group meetings are the above-mentioned lack of transportation and the responsibility that some older people feel to remain at home with relatives who are also elderly and who are physically disabled. By working closely with the Voluntary Action Center of Kansas City, staff members of Community Mental Health Center–South have recruited a number of capable volunteers who provide transportation or serve as friendly visitors to invalid persons, thus enabling more people to take advantage of the groups. However, there is a need for more volunteers to serve in these capacities as well as to help with minor home repair and home maintenance. Area churches and service groups represent potential sources for meeting these volunteer needs. Two groups presently being approached are newly retired persons and high school and college students. It is hoped that the efforts of these two age groups can be coordinated, thus allowing the young people to benefit from the know-how and experience of the retirees and the retirees to benefit from the energy and agility of the students. An additional goal of the center is to better coordinate its Older Adult Program with those of other agencies having similar objectives, thereby maximizing the effectiveness of existing services and avoiding duplication.

Notes

1. Abraham Maslow, *Motivation and Personality* (New York: Harper & Row, 1970).

9

Health Care and Health Promotion for Older Americans: Problems and Approaches

Linda J. Redford

The growing proportion of elderly in our population has significant ramifications for the existing health care delivery system in this country. Individuals over 60 years of age are more apt to suffer some form of chronic impairment than those in the younger age groups. They thus require more frequent and intensive health services. With an increasing proportion of the population in need of such services and rapidly escalating costs for such services, a critical situation is developing for provider and consumer alike. It is likely that our current episodic, disease-oriented approach to health care delivery for older people cannot continue as a dominant model.

The age-segregated, congregate living setting provides an excellent opportunity for examining health care practices and testing new models of health care delivery. While it may be argued that such living arrangements are anomalies in our society, it is evident that they are increasing in number and popularity.[1] Considering this trend, such living settings would seem to be one logical focal point for providing efficient and economical health care to large segments of the older population in the future.

This chapter examines some of the common health care alternatives available to older individuals living in age-segregated, high-rise apartments in a large midwestern city. It discusses an attempt to provide more comprehensive and cost-effective approaches to the health care of the elderly living in such congregate settings. Also, lay health care systems are discussed, and strategies for better integration of lay and formal health care systems are explored. The data presented here are based on interviews with residents of two age-segregated, high-rise apartment complexes. One of the high rises is located in an inner-city area, the other in a suburb. The resident population of the inner-city high rise is predominantly black, while all residents of the suburban high rise are white. For purposes of this chapter, findings from the two high rises are presented together and in a descriptive fashion.

Traditional Approaches to Health Care Services

The high rises discussed here have few direct health services provided to the residents. The services that are provided are generally limited to basic screening procedures, i.e., blood pressure checks, urine tests for sugar and protein, blood tests for determining hemoglobin levels, and occasionally tests for glaucoma. County health departments, visiting nurse associations, and other agencies that have received federal money for community screening projects have provided such services in high rises for the last one to two years. Recently, these agencies have been forced to curtail screening activities in many of the high rises due to decreases or complete withdrawal of federal and state funding.

Another service occasionally provided to residents of the high rise is some form of home health service. Such services may include professional nursing services or custodial types of services provided by home health aides or homemakers. The duration of these services is limited by Medicare regulations and/or personal finances. A further limitation is the residence requirement in high rises that inhabitants must be self-sufficient. Should a resident become incapacitated to the point of requiring home health services for an extended period, he or she will most likely be asked to move out.

More stable sources of health care are local private physicians, clinics, and hospitals, although they are less accessible. Most of the high-rise residents have a regular source of medical care. For residents of the inner-city high rise, that source of care will generally be a community- or hospital-based clinic and occasionally a private physician or a combination of all the above. Residents of the suburban high rise typically use private physicians unless they have been referred to hospital-based clinics for specialized care. No community medical clinics or hospital-based clinics were located in the particular suburban community studied.

Hospitals are utilized primarily for acute care. The emergency room is used in evenings and on weekends when physicians' offices and clinics are not open and the problem is sufficiently severe and/or incapacitating to require immediate attention. However, the elderly do not consider the emergency room a resource for treatment of more routine problems that they think can wait until regular office hours. In fact, reluctance to use the emergency room results at times in critical delays in the treatment of life-threatening problems.

The elderly generally perceive hospitalization as an undesirable alternative, but acquiesce to it when circumstances dictate. Those who place high value on their self-sufficiency feel distressed by the dependent role forced upon the patient by the structure of the hospital environment. However, when an illness forces the older person to become dependent, he or she often welcomes the hospital as an alternative to dependence on family and friends. Since residents in the high rises are covered by Medicare, financing of hospital care does not present a serious barrier to this form of care.

Health Care Services in a Congregate Living Setting

In the fall of 1978, graduate student nurses at the University of Kansas were assigned to the two high rises. As a part of their clinical requirements in a series of gerontological nursing courses, the nurses were to provide a comprehensive range of health services and health promotion activities to the residents. Since blood pressure screening sessions provided by other nurses were well accepted and attracted a large proportion of the residents, it was decided that this might be an effective entrée. Sessions were scheduled at both locations for the one day of the week the nurses would be available throughout the semester. The intention was to introduce residents to the nurses and acquaint them with the times nurses would be available in the high rise. The screening sessions were to be limited to two or three times in order to avoid duplication of existing services. However, soon after the graduate student nurses arrived, the other agencies experienced a funding cut and curtailed their screening activities in both high rises. The residents were quite vocal in their views of the necessity for continuing this screening; therefore, it became a biweekly activity within the current program.

Gradually, the nurses expanded their roles beyond basic screening activities. Residents who were identified as having had no recent health assessment were advised of the availability of such a service. Many of these residents welcomed the opportunity to have a health assessment by the nurses. The health assessment consisted of an in-depth medical, social, and psychological history and a thorough physical examination. During the health assessment the nurse generally instructed the client about the purpose of each portion of the physical examination. She discussed findings and explained their implications with the client. As this tended to be a time-consuming activity, only a small number of residents received the complete assessment. In addition to providing direct health services, the nurses polled residents regarding their interest in health education classes. Several topics of interest were defined by residents of the high rises and a number of group classes were held during the semester.

On the whole, the elderly residents accepted the services provided by the nurses. Serious problems with the program did not become readily apparent until services were discontinued for the summer. At this time, satisfaction of the residents turned to dismay and dissatisfaction, particularly as a result of the discontinuation of blood pressure screening for three months. Although phone numbers were provided for consultation with nurses during this period of disrupted service, the residents did not ask for assistance by telephone. However, resident managers did call to inform faculty of the nursing program about the residents' concern over disruption of services.

A review of health charts and data collected during the program indicated further problems. While the services provided may have improved the episodic care for a few residents, they made few real advances in improving the health status or health practices of residents. The utilization of blood pressure screening as an entrée appears to have begun a scenario of traditional, episodic health care approaches. Although the residents viewed this as a very necessary service and became quite dependent on the service and/or the people providing the service, the data collected in the high rises indicate that the program was far from effective as a method for identifying health problems and was an inefficient use of resources from the standpoint of time and finances.

Over a nine-month period, 124 of the 190 residents in the suburban high rise had blood pressure checks on one to twenty-eight different occasions. Of the new residents screened, 54 were currently under treatment for hypertension. No new nor untreated cases were detected. Blood pressures were taken a total of 975 times. On only five of those occasions were abnormal fluctuations in blood pressure found. Three such fluctuations proved temporary and the blood pressures were within normal limits one week later. The other two required a change in the medical treatment. On three other occasions, residents complained of difficulties attributable to their blood pressure medications; however, their blood pressures were well controlled. Seventeen problems unrelated to blood pressure were detected. In all of these cases, the resident complained of the problem and probably would have consulted the nurse, if available, regardless of the screening program.

Over eighty nursing hours were assigned to the blood pressure screening program in the nine-month period. Had the nurses' time been reimbursed at the standard screening rate per blood pressure, the cost would have been over $1,900. This is a high cost for the detection of less than twenty-five problems that required professional nursing judgment and/or management. Nursing time could be much better utilized for more sophisticated detection activities, for health education, and for health promotion activities. While it can be argued that the screening program gives consumers the opportunity to voice other concerns, the experience in high rise apartment buildings for the elderly indicates that screening is an inadequate means for providing such a forum. Rarely is adequate time or privacy available for such interaction between nurse and consumer.

The Informal System of Health Care

On the basis of the experiences in the high rises, it appears that traditional approaches to health screening and health services may do little to promote the health of large numbers of elderly consumers, prevent health problems, or provide a better coordination of health care. The development of an effective health program, and its evaluation, depends in part on understanding several factors not accounted for in traditional approaches. In addition to the actual health status of the people being served, one needs to understand their beliefs about health and their health practices.[2] Another factor of importance is the extent of the resources available in the immediate environment that can be integrated into the health care program. Furthermore, for any health program to be effective from both a health benefit and a financial viewpoint, the consumer must become an active and involved participant in the program.

Through interviews with samples of residents in the two high rises described earlier, informal discussions with managers, and direct observations, I examined the informal health network in these congregate living sites. Social networks in the high rises influenced general health practices among the residents. One aspect in which this influence is particularly pronounced is that of physical exercise. Exercise was generally acknowledged by residents to be an important factor in maintaining good health. Neither complex offered a routine exercise program, but residents formed small groups to walk in areas near the high rises or in shopping areas where they could enjoy the safety and comfort of an enclosed mall. Walking was the most accepted and popular form of physical activity, but the complexes offered little space for exercise other than the hallways. The likelihood of a given individual participating in an activity such as routine daily walks largely depended on whether others in that person's social network also participated in the activity. Often an individual expressed the desire to become more physically active but noted that none of his or her friends would or could undertake such activities. People expressed reluctance to walk unaccompanied outside the complex for fear of physical assault. Occasionally they would walk alone in the hallways of the complex, but few did so on a regular basis. In essence, routine physical activity among the elderly in the high rises is a social activity. A consistent exercise program depends upon the willingness of residents to participate with others in specific physical activities.

Interaction within social networks also influences eating habits. Most individuals interviewed displayed a sound knowledge of good nutritional practices, but many admitted "not eating like I should" because it is not enjoyable to prepare and eat meals alone. While residents frequently prepare their own meals, they rarely share them with others. Their reason for not sharing meals may be largely economic, but this area needs further study. Congregate meals, when available, tend to be popular with residents. A federally funded congregate meal program near one of the high rises provides such an opportunity for these residents. Those who take advantage of the program indicate that visiting with friends is their primary reason for going. Many admit not caring a great deal for the food.

Another form of combining social interaction and good nutrition habits is eating in restaurants. It is common practice for some high-rise dwellers to eat at restaurants with friends on Sundays after church. In addition, social activities in the high rises usually involve food. Covered-dish dinners provide the opportunity for residents to eat in a congenial social setting at minimal individual cost. Refreshments are available at most large gatherings in the high rises. This, however, poses a problem for individuals who want to control weight or who require special diets, since most refreshments are high in calories and/or salt.

The process of lay diagnosis evident among the elderly in these high rises is no less complex than that undertaken by the physician. An individual, on perceiving a symptom, attempts to make sense of the symptom by comparing it to past experiences with similar symptoms. This classification process is, in part, a matter of placing the symptom in a context in which beliefs about its relevant properties (such as causation, consequences, and appropriate therapies) can be predicted. Once a symptom is classified, the individual is able to plan a therapeutic strategy based on predictive alternatives derived from past experiences or knowledge.

If an individual fails in personal attempts to place the symptom in a context on which remedial action can be used, the tendency is to broaden the context by consulting with others. He or she will then make use either of a physician (or other medical provider) or of support from the informal network of fellow residents, depending on the degree of disability incurred from the symptom and the consequences perceived to derive from it. The informal lay network tends to be the initial or sole resource in a majority of illnesses among the elderly.

Therapy among residents of the high rises tends to incorporate a broad spectrum of activities and remedies, such as the utilization of home remedies, over-the-counter drugs, and prescribed medications. These various forms of therapy may be used alone or in combinations. Sharing home remedies, over-the-counter products, and even prescribed medications is common practice.

Advice about appropriate medication or about therapeutic techniques tends to occur in interactions among acquaintances and friends in the high rises. No specific individuals in either high rise appear to be idenitified as lay therapists or healers. However, certain individuals tend to be consulted more than others during illness or crisis situations. These people do appear to play supportive and, possibly, advisory roles. Some of the residents are regarded as good sources of medical information because of their past experience in the formal health care system. Further study of such relationships is needed if lay therapy networks are to be well understood.

Evaluations of both the diagnosis, or classification, of the problem and the effectiveness of selected therapies and therapists occur repeatedly throughout an illness. If symptoms are not resolved or alleviated within the time deemed appropriate, the opinions of fellow residents, friends, family, and/or health providers are often solicited. If it is determined that the diagnosis is inaccurate, the entire diagnostic process may be repeated and a new diagnostic label adopted. The therapy alone may be judged ineffective and another therapy instituted. The evaluation of specific therapies is usually quite succinct: either it works or it doesn't work, and if it doesn't work, it needs to be changed.

The evaluation of any health provider, say, a physician, is based on a broader spectrum of criteria. The effectiveness of the therapy recommended by the doctor is an important aspect in the evaluation process, but so is the length of time one must wait to see him, his attitude toward the patient, the cost, and a number of more peripheral factors. Not only is there a sharing of the criteria for evaluation of therapists among the high-rise residents, some interesting commonalities in the ranking of criteria for evaluation are evident. This suggests some formalization of the process within the social network of the high rise.

The referral system in the high rises reflects results of this evaluation process. New residents entering the high rise, or residents seeking a different health care provider, are readily steered toward certain providers and away from others by fellow residents. Since neither the evaluation nor the referral procedures in the high rises are well organized or formalized, the recommended referrals may be overlapping or contradictory. However, such advice appears to have a significant influence on the choice of health care providers. In many cases, the referral process includes more direct assistance. Information is shared about procedures for entering specific health care agencies, including how to get an appointment, how to get to the agency, how to avoid long waits, and how to pay the bill. In a number of instances, other residents provide transportation for those who do not have it.

A number of resources exist in the high rises for providing many health and health support services currently provided by individuals, groups, and agencies from outside the high rise. Several individuals with past experience in formal health-care-provider roles live in the complexes. Many of these individuals have health assessment skills, particularly basic ones such as taking blood pressure, temperature, pulse, and respiration. A few are licensed nurses who practiced their professions until retirement. Others are experienced in domestic services and, in a number of cases, still work in private homes providing services similar to those provided by home health aides and homemakers in formal service agencies. However, none of them presently provides such services to other residents of their high rise. Transportation is occasionally provided by residents to those in need, but a more systematic approach to transportation needs is called for and could be provided, in many instances, by those living in the complexes.

Strategies for Future Health Care Approaches

The health programs discussed in this chapter, and most formal health programs for the elderly in this country, focus on what the health provider can do for the elderly rather than exploring ways the elderly can be assisted in taking a more active role in their own health care and that of others. Current health care approaches tend to foster a dependency on the provider, rather than developing an interdependent working relationship between provider and consumer. As this chapter suggests, there exists a lay health care network that operates simultaneously with, but on a different level from, formal health services. However, decisions and actions taken on either level may profoundly affect actions taken on the other level.

For health care services ever to approach maximum effectiveness and efficiency, both providers and consumers must better understand the beliefs and values that shape the decision-making processes of the other. Health providers must recognize and understand the diagnostic, therapeutic, and referral processes existing within the informal networks of the population they serve. The beliefs and values shaping the decision-making process and the alternate choices for actions will vary among population groups. Factors such as ethnicity, socioeconomic level, and generational membership may influence health decisions and choices of therapies. It is beyond the scope of this chapter to explore the nature of these influences, but it should be noted that this is an area deserving further study.

An understanding of the lay diagnostic and therapeutic process enables the provider to appreciate the relevance of folk therapies and how they might best be incorporated into the medical therapy regimen. This may be one of the most effective methods for increasing compliance with medical requirements, a vexing problem to most medical providers. An understanding of the lay system will also enable the provider to be alert for folk therapies that may prove detrimental or interact adversely with medically prescribed therapies. It then becomes the role of the health provider to inform the consumer of the danger as well as why the danger exists.

Consumers also need to have a better understanding of the criteria relevant in the decision-making process of health providers. Health providers tend to closely guard the knowledge on which they base their decisions about the treatment of others. This knowledge is vital to the consumer if he or she is ever to be able to make educated decisions and act as a partner in his or her own health care. It is the responsibility of health care providers to impart this information to consumers as part of the process of delivering health services. To many providers this might seem to border on an act of heresy, but ethics and the cost of health care dictate that the consumer must become a more informed participant in the process. Health providers are often guilty of discouraging folk therapies without knowledge of their potential benefits, whether they be physiological or psychological. The consumer, on the other hand, may alter the therapy regimen prescribed by a health provider because he or she is unaware of the action, effects, and/or anticipated benefits of the regimen.

The referral process is another area in which consumers and health providers would do well to learn from each other. Much of what the provider labels an abuse of services is the result of (1) lack of knowledge about the most effective use of alternative services, (2) the inaccessibility or unavailability of more appropriate services, and (3) the result of a diagnostic decision based on criteria different from those used by the health provider. The most effective use of the formal health system, and the rationale for referrals within the system, should be basic components of health education given by professionals. Health providers can, on the other hand, learn much from consumers about gaps and barriers within the formal system that result in what appears to be less than efficient use of services. Consumers can also educate providers about the informal support systems, which if understood and appreciated by the health provider could be used as a valuable adjunct to formal health services.

Efforts to identify and make use of the experience and knowledge of older Americans in the provision of health services will require attitudinal changes among both health providers and the elderly. Changing attitudes takes time and strong incentives, but the time for intitiating changes is now. Models for developing informal health services that provide financial reimbursement to older individuals willing and able to provide services will do much to speed the process. Whatever the incentives, the participation of elderly people in the planning and implementation of health services not only makes use of important human resources, but is also therapeutic. It allows older people to demonstrate to themselves and others that they can influence the course of their own lives.

Notes

1. "The Status of Federally Assisted Housing in the Kansas City Metropolitan Region," Mid-America Regional Council Housing Policy Committee, January 1976.

2. Madeleine Leininger, *Nursing and Anthropology: Two Worlds to Blend* (New York: John Wiley & Sons, 1970), pp. 83–110.

PART THREE
Social Parameters of Aging

Up to this point, we have been examining the physical consequences of aging that must be confronted in one way or another by all people in all societies. Although it is these biological changes that determine the maturation and aging processes, it is the social context that largely defines the meaning of growing old. Thus, people in different societies may experience similar physiological changes as they grow old, but the manner in which such changes are perceived and the impact they have on the behavior of the aging individual will vary from one society to another. We turn now to an exploration of the social context within which Americans grow old.

In essence, the remainder of this book is devoted to the study of the social environments in which elderly Americans live. This particular section considers several large-scale forces—demographic trends, economics, politics, and ethnicity—over which any given individual has very little control. (Part 5 deals with the personal relations of older Americans, and Part 7 examines the interaction between the older person and the environment.) One of the factors influencing the conditions under which the elderly live is the relative size of the older population, as well as the composition of that population. Quadagno discusses the demographic trends, particularly the relationship between fertility and mortality rates, that determine the proportion of older people in a society. She describes the characteristics of America's older population, including its male/female composition and residential patterns. She also discusses the implications of population trends for the future of our society. Hardcastle focuses on the economic consequences of demographic trends. He examines in detail the implications of retirement for both the older individual and the economy in general. A major issue he addresses is the viability of the Social Security system as a predominant source of income for retired people.

The transfer of funds from the younger working members of society to older retired members has political as well as economic implications. Cigler and Swanson examine the political orientations of older people in comparison with younger adults. They further discuss the impact of political participation by the elderly on the political system, emphasizing the struggle of various interest groups (including those representing the elderly) for federally appropriated resources. To be an effective political force in the coming years, the elderly will have to make a more concerted effort than has been the case thus far. Nevertheless, Cigler and Swanon suggest that age-related issues will become increasingy prominent on the political agenda in the future.

The cultural heritage into which one is born will exert an influence on one's world view that lasts throughout life. It also will determine to some degree the kinds of experiences a person will have as he or she ages. Place examines the influence of this cultural heritage as it varies among ethnic groups in the United States. She outlines the distinctive histories of several ethnic groups and considers how each history affects the way old age is perceived and old people treated. She emphasizes how this ethnic factor shapes the social roles and family relationships of those elderly who have retained strong ethnic ties.

10

Who Are the Elderly?
A Demographic Inquiry

Jill S. Quadagno

Introduction

Although dramatic events pique our interest and capture headlines in newspapers, it is the more prosaic circumstances that reflect the true dimensions of human society and set limits on human lives. Figures reflecting changes in birth and death rates are not likely to inspire awe or despair. Unless attention is drawn to their meaning, most people are unaware of the impact these measures have on the quantity and quality of life.

At the same time, it is important to recognize that the figures themselves are the creations of people making day-to-day decisions. Masses of data that are presented as qualities of populations appear to be imposing scientific calculations beyond the control of individual people. However, these figures arise from human actions that are social products, mirroring whatever people do. This chapter will focus on the changes in fundamental population characteristics that have brought about rising demands for attention to the presence of growing numbers of older men and women.

Several purposes can be achieved by examining the statistical dimensions of aging. Past and present trends in age composition can be identified, and these trends can then be used as a basis for making population projections into the future. Changes in the characteristics of the older population can also be identified, and once identified can serve as a resource for locating potential problem areas where the need for services to specific categories of people can be evaluated. In general, demographic figures are useful ways of analyzing the social and economic impact of a changing population.

Before introducing these topics, a word of caution is necessary. Demographic analysis, in the long run, relies on the availability and accuracy of the most recent census counts taken by public or private agencies. In the United States, the Bureau of the Census acts as the central clearinghouse for all national population data. Despite careful efforts to assure accuracy, the Bureau of the Census recognizes that miscounts and miscalculations sometimes occur due to a variety of factors. Age, in particular, appears to be one of the most difficult variables to pin down precisely; it has been estimated that population reports of age may be inaccurate by as much as 5 percent.[1] Thus, the student should always be aware of the possibility that hidden errors may detract from the overall accuracy of the figures presented.

The Aging of Societies

Two or three centuries ago, the experience of growing old was reserved for only a small percent of the population. In 1790 when the first federal census was taken in America, less than 20 percent of the people survived from birth to the age of 70. Now more than 80 percent of the population can expect to do so.[2] Table 10.1 documents the growing visibility of older people.

This increase is also significant in terms of raw numbers. In 1900 there were 3,080,000 people over age 65 in the United States. By 1975 this figure had risen to 22,400,000, and it is estimated that there will be over 30.6 million aged by the year 2000. This trend is visually represented in Figure 10.1.

This transformation can be most simply explained by examining changes in life expectancy. Life expectancy is calculated from the average age at death for a given cohort—a group of people who were born during the same time period. Although an individual can obviously die before or after this calculated age, the figure refers to the statistical average for that group of people. It is a measure of the number of years the "average" person can expect to live, given his or her date of birth.

A gradual increase in life expectancy has occurred in the United States over the past century. A child born in 1900 could expect to live an average of 47 years; by 1977 life expectancy was nearly 80 years. While these gains in life expectancy are typical of most modern, industrial societies, they do not apply to all people in every nation. As shown in Table 10.2, in Afghanistan or Senegal life expectancy is only about 40 years, due to extremely high infant mortality in these countries which greatly reduces life expectancy at birth.

Life expectancy must be distinguished from life span, which refers to the greatest number of years any member of a species has been known to survive. As shown in Table 10.3, the life span of humans appears to be somewhere between 110 and 120 years. Life span varies by species and is longer than life expectancy. It is likely that no member of any species has yet lived as long as it may be possible for a member of that species to live. The life expectancy of human beings has been drawing closer to the current human life span over the past century.

Table 10.1: The Changing Age Composition
of the American Population:
Percent Age 65+ as a Proportion of Total Population

Year	%65+
1870	3.0
1880	3.4
1890	4.2
1900	4.4
1910	4.5
1920	4.7
1930	5.6
1940	6.8
1950	8.2
1960	9.2
1970	9.8
1975	10.5

Source: data from Census of Population,
1960 and 1970, PC(1)-1B and
Current Population Reports,
Series P-25, Nos. 519 and 601.

Figure 10.1: Growth of the Older Population in the
Twentieth Century

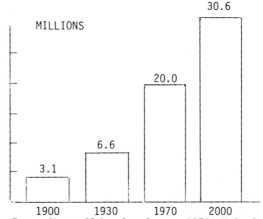

Source: Facts About Older Americans, 1976. U.S., Dept.
of Health, Education and Welfare, Office of
Human Development, Administration on Aging,
DHEW Publication No. (OHD) 77-20006.

Jill S. Quadagno

Table 10.2: Life Expectancy at Birth for Selected Nations, by Sex

Nation	Years Involved	Male	Female
Norway	1972-1973	71.32	77.60
Sweden	1970-1974	72.11	77.51
Netherlands	1973	71.2	77.2
France	1972	68.6	76.4
Canada	1970-1972	69.34	76.36
Puerto Rico	1971-1973	68.92	76.05
U.S.A.	1974	68.2	75.9
United Kingdom	1970-1972	68.9	75.1
Hong Kong	1971	67.36	75.01
Spain	1970	69.69	74.96
Italy	1970-1972	68.97	74.88
New Zealand	1970-1972	68.55	74.60
Australia	1965-1967	67.63	74.15
USSR	1971-1972	64	74
Israel	1974	70.13	73.27
Portugal	1974	65.29	72.03
Fiji	1970-1975	68.5	71.7
Argentina	1970-1975	65.16	71.38
Singapore	1970	65.1	70.0
Mexico	1965-1970	61.03	63.73
Paraguay	1970-1975	60.3	63.6
China	1970-1975	59.9	63.3
Korea	1970-1975	58.8	62.5
Brazil	1960-1970	57.61	61.10
Philippines	1970-1975	56.9	60.0
Morocco	1970-1975	51.4	54.5
Egypt	1970-1975	51.6	53.8
South Africa	1970-1975	49.8	53.3
Burma	1970-1975	48.6	51.5
Papua-New Guinea	1970-1975	47.7	47.6
Senegal	1970-1975	38.5	41.6
Afghanistan	1970-1975	39.9	40.7
India	1951-1960	41.89	40.55
Ethiopia	1970-1975	36.5	39.6
Bangladesh	1970-1975	35.8	35.8

Source: Demographic Yearbook, 1975, 27th ed. (New York:
         United Nations, 1976). Reproduced by permission.

Furthermore, we must be careful to separate quantity of life from quality of life. One writer has suggested that, given a human life span of over 100 years, society's goal might be that all persons should live healthy and active lives until their hundredth birthday and then die peacefully in their sleep as they begin their hundred and first year.[3]

Individuals can only grow older. However, the concept of aging can refer to either individual aging or the "aging" of a population. An aggregation of individuals, a population, may grow younger as well as older, depending on the interaction of fertility, mortality, and migration.[4] Fertility is a measure of

Table 10.3: Variations in Life Span and Life Expectancy by Species

Common Name	Life Span In Years	Life Expectancy In Years
Man or Woman	110-120	70-80
Chimpanzee	30	15-20
Lion	40	20-25
Dog	34	10-12
Cow	30	20-25
Sheep	20	10-15
Goat	19	12-15
Camel	50	25-45
Horse	62	40-50
Elephant	98	70

Source: Adapted from Albert I. Lansing, "General Biology of Senescence," Handbook of Aging and the Individual, James E. Birren, ed. (Chicago: University of Chicago Press, 1959), p. 121. Reprinted by permission of the University of Chicago Press.

birth rates and is an indicator of the entry of new lives into a given population. Mortality refers to death rates, the exit of people from society. Migration figures also depict entry and exit, not in the biological sense, but in terms of the movement of individuals from one area or region to another.

The Demographic Transition

The demographic transition refers to a long-term and presumably permanent change in the birth and death rates of societies.[5] Before the transition begins, both birth and death rates are high. Mortality rates begin to decline first, in response to changes in public health and education resulting from industrialization. The initial effect of reduced mortality is to make the population increase in size and also grow "younger," because declining death rates are most likely to affect infants and young children, increasing their survival. In the latter part of the transition, birth rates decline as well and the population "ages," i.e., an increase in the proportion of older people occurs.

Demographers have found it useful to classify societies according to their degree of "agedness." Populations with less than 4 percent age 65 and over are called young, those with 4 to 6.9 percent are described as youthful, those with 7 to 9.9 percent are mature, while those with 10 percent or more are called aged. Table 10.4 shows that with the exception of Greenland, all of the young and youthful populations are found in Africa, Asia, and Latin America, while the mature and aged populations that have passed through

Table 10.4: Classification of Countries by Degree of Agedness

Country	Percent 65 and Over	Country	Percent 65 and Over
YOUNG POPULATIONS		**MATURE POPULATIONS**	
New Guinea	1.1	Japan	7.0
Kuwait	1.6	Uruguay	7.5
Nigeria	2.0	Yugoslavia	7.5
Zambia	2.1	Canada	7.9
Greenland	2.3	Australia	8.3
W. Samoa	2.7	New Zealand	8.4
Guatemala	2.7	Poland	8.4
Nicaragua	2.9	Romania	8.5
Colombia	2.9	Finland	8.6
Haiti	3.0	Gibraltar	8.6
Costa Rica	3.1	Iceland	8.8
Ecuador	3.2	Bulgaria	9.5
Korea	3.2	United States	9.9
Bahamas	3.4		
Kenya	3.5		
Afghanistan	3.5	**AGED POPULATIONS**	
Sri Lanka	3.5		
Tunisia	3.5		
Mexico	3.7	Netherlands	10.1
Paraguay	3.8	Italy	10.4
Uganda	3.8	N. Ireland	10.5
Iran	3.8	Czechoslovakia	10.6
Liberia	3.9	Ireland	11.1
Turkey	3.9	Switzerland	11.3
		Hungary	11.5
YOUTHFUL POPULATIONS		Denmark	12.0
		Scotland	12.1
		England & Wales	12.4
Swaziland	4.1	Luxembourg	12.6
Algeria	4.4	W. Germany	12.6
Botswana	4.6	Norway	12.9
Surinam	4.6	France	13.4
Guadaloupe	4.7	Sweden	13.7
Iraq	5.1	Austria	14.1
Martinique	5.1	E. Germany	15.5
French Guiana	5.3	Monaco	22.1
Tanzania	5.5		
Lesotho	6.4		

Source: Data computed from <u>Demographic Yearbook 1971</u> (New York: United Nations, 1972), Table 7. Effective dates vary from country to country ranging from 1962 to 1971. See original source for actual dates. Copyright, United Nations (1972). Reproduced by permission.

the demographic transition are found in Europe, Japan, and North America.

These population characteristics can be represented by a population pyramid, a visual device that subdivides societies into male and female and their respective age categories. A young society is pyramidal or triangular in form, since the fertility rate is high and most people are therefore quite young. The older countries present a square profile, since fewer children are born. Figure 10.2 verifies this predicted profile for the United States by comparing the year 1910, when the country was relatively young, with 1970, when the population had aged.

One additional way of assessing the age composition of a society is to calculate the dependency ratio. This measure is calculated as the ratio of persons under age 20 and over age 65 to those who are between the ages of 21 to 64. The dependency ratio has been used as a substitute for the actual figures regarding the number of persons in the work force compared to those not in the work force, which are often not available in developing countries.[6] In a young society, the expected dependency ratio is sixty-four (comprising fifty-nine young and five old dependents) for every hundred persons of working age. In the transitional phase of development, when declining mortality affects infants and children particularly, the dependency ratio rises to a peak of ninety-two, of which eighty-seven are young and five are old. Finally, in a modern society, total dependency declines to sixty. The drop in the birth rate reduces the proportion of young dependents to forty-four, while the proportion of old dependents triples to sixteen.

Figure 10.2: Population Pyramids for the United States, 1910 and 1970

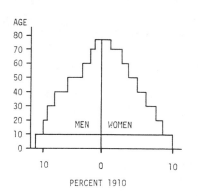 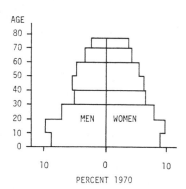

Source: U.S. Bureau of the Census, General Population Characteristics, Final Report PC(1)-B1 United States Summary (U.S. Government Printing Office, 1972), p. 1-276.

Changes in the Characteristics of the Aged

As the proportion of older people in American society has changed over the past centuries, the characteristics of older people have also changed. The population varies from generation to generation in terms of such factors as sex, race, education, ethnic origin, and place of residence. As these factors change, the needs of the people change, and society cannot handle the problems of the aged without first knowing who they are.

For every 106 male babies born, only 100 female babies are born, so the number of male births always exceeds the number of female births in the population. However, from birth on, male death rates are higher at every age level, a difference that becomes increasingly apparent with advancing age.

Progress has been made in the past decades in the reduction of mortality, particularly for those in the older age groups. However, males and females have not shared equally in these advantages. In 1900, females had only a small advantage (2.9 years) over males in life expectation at birth. Between 1900 and 1974, life expectancy at birth increased by 20 years for males and 25 years for females. As Table 10.5 indicates, by 1977 a male infant could expect to live to be about 72 years of age, while female life expectancy was 81, a gap of 9 years. As yet, no satisfactory explanation for the continued widening of this gap has been forthcoming.

The reason women tend to live longer than men is difficult to pinpoint precisely because of the complexity of assessing the relative importance of heredity as opposed to environmental factors. The differences may result largely from differences in the lifestyles, roles, and environments of men and women. Traditionally, men have engaged in more stressful, demanding, and dangerous occupations.[7] Further, women are more likely to secure earlier diagnosis and appropriate treatment for health problems of all kinds.[8] Additionally, fewer women today die in childbirth. On the other hand, there is evidence supporting a biological basis for the difference between the death

Table 10.5: Life Expectancy at Birth, Males and Females, USA Population, 1960 to 1977

	1960	1965	1970	1973	1974	1977
Males	66.6	66.8	67.1	67.6	68.2	72
Females	73.1	73.7	74.8	75.3	75.9	81

Source: Statistical Abstracts of the United States, 1976, 97th Annual Edition, Washington, D.C.: U.S. Department of Commerce, Bureau of the Census, July, 1976, pp. xiii-xiv, and January, 1978, Release of the Bureau of Census.

rates of the sexes. For example, male fetal and infant mortality is greater than female fetal and infant mortality. As the lifestyles of men and women become more similar, it may be possible to more clearly distinguish between genetic and environmental factors.

The net effect of this life expectancy differential is that it produces a preponderance of older women in later life. This is a relatively recent phenomenon, which first appeared sometime in the 1940s. Table 10.6 indicates the ratio of males to females at all ages and for those 65 and over from 1910 to 1975. In 1910 there were 106 males to every 100 females of all ages and 101.1 males for every 100 females over age 65. By 1975 the sex ratio had dropped to 94.9 for all ages and 69.3 for those over 65. Thus, for every 100 elderly women, there are only 69 elderly men. Regardless of the cause, it is clear that the number of older women exceeds that of older men in the population and that social policy in the future should take this differential into account.

Blacks are a relatively small segment of the elderly population. In 1970 they made up over 11 percent of the total population of the United States but only 8 percent of the elderly population. The main reason for this differential in later life is the high death rate among blacks, although fertility also plays some role. However, although the black population has always experienced higher mortality rates than the white population, these differences have been declining in recent years. After age 65 this trend is reversed, and death rates are considerably lower for blacks than they are for whites of both sexes.

At least some, if not most, of the differences between death rates for whites and blacks can be explained by differences in socioeconomic status, which research has clearly associated with mortality. The higher the level of income, occupation, and education, the lower the death rates.[9] In addition to socioeconomic status, other social and cultural factors less readily identifiable also contribute to differences in the death rates between blacks and whites. Genetic factors may also play a significant part. Recent investigations have revealed that specific gene-linked diseases have an affinity for certain ethnic and racial groups. The relatively favorable mortality position

Table 10.6: Sex Ratio of Males to Females, USA Population, 1910-1975

	1910	1920	1930	1940	1950	1960	1970	1975
All Ages	106	104.1	102.5	100.7	98.6	97.1	94.8	94.9
65 years and older	101.1	101.3	100.5	95.5	89.6	82.8	72.1	69.3

Source: Statistical Abstracts of the United States, 1976, 97th Annual
         Edition, Washington, D.C.: U.S. Department of Commerce, Bureau
         of the Census, July, 1976, p. 25.

above age 65 of blacks as compared with whites suggests that socioeconomic differences do not operate at the older ages in the same way they do among those younger than 65. One possible explanation is that those blacks who have survived the excessive environmental stresses of their younger years may be genetically stronger.[10]

Over the past century, there has been a changing flow of immigrants to the United States, and this has affected the ethnic composition of the older population at different times. Most obvious has been the dramatic downward trend in the proportion of foreign-born among the aged.[11] Until 1950, from one-third to one-fourth of the older population was foreign-born. However, the decline in the rate of immigration between 1920 and 1940, and the additional effects of quotas in restricting immigration after World War II, have reduced this figure to less than 10 percent. The decline in foreign-born aged is illustrated in Table 10.7.

There are several reasons why it is relevant to consider the proportion of the aged who are foreign-born. One problem is that adjustment to a strange culture is a major difficulty in and of itself, regardless of concerns associated with aging. The following excerpt illustrates the conflicts of immigrants in their first contact with American culture: "Largely peasants, they had not the background or skills to make their way in the economy. . . . they found places for themselves only with difficulty. Bringing with them cultures markedly different from that of the United States, it was long before they could create for themselves the forms of expression that would give satisfaction."[12]

A second problem concerns relationships with children. The first-generation immigrant's desire to maintain old world customs often conflicted with

Table 10.7:   Percentage of White Population Aged 60-64 that is Foreign Born, USA, 1900-1980

Year	Percent Foreign Born
1900	33.63
1910	30.33
1920	25.83
1930	26.84
1940	24.20
1950	23.26
1960	16.27
1970	9.56
1980*	5.74

Source: U.S. Censuses of Population: 1950, Vol. 11, Table 39; 1960, PC(1)-1D, Table 161; 1970, PC(2)-1A, Table 1; and Current Population Report, Series P-23, No. 59 (May, 1976).

*Estimated from projections in Current Population Report, Series P-23, No. 59 (May), 1976.

those of their children, who had begun to adopt the ways of their new society. For example, among Polish immigrants there was expressed bitterness revolving around the economic obligations of second-generation adult children to their aged parents. Complaining about their children, the parents stated, "After they finished school, they got married, and they are no help for the parents at all. They leave home and forget their poor old parents."[13] The older Poles were not psychologically or financially prepared to maintain themselves independently of their adult children, who would have had clear-cut familial obligations in the old country. The adult children adopted the American perspective, which prescribes that one's primary obligation is to one's own children, aged parents being secondary.[14]

The problems of adjustment to old age that are experienced to a greater or lesser extent by all people are accentuated for the foreign-born, who have different experiences and expectations about old age. For the remainder of this century, over 90 percent of those entering old age will have been born and reared in the United States.[15] Problems associated with acculturation will not continue to affect most older people, but within a complex and diverse society such as ours there will always be subgroups in the population who approach the experience of aging from a unique perspective (see Chapter 13 in this volume).

Over the past century, American society has been transformed from a predominantly rural society to one in which most of the population resides in urban areas. This change has, of course, affected all age groups, but it has had a particularly intense impact upon the aged, not only for those who migrated to cities but for those left behind as well. The process of urbanization is illustrated in Table 10.8. In 1910 over 50 percent of the older population lived on farms or in small towns. By 1970 more than 71 percent of all aged people lived in urban areas.

In spite of the general trend toward urbanization, the aged still tend to be more heavily concentrated in the countryside than the young who have migrated toward cities in search of better employment opportunities. This out-migration of young adults has caused problems for the older people left behind, for it jeopardizes the economic stability of the area. In general, the rural aged are among the most impoverished members of society, living in the poorest housing, having poorer health and more disabilities, and having less access to needed services. They are also at "a special disadvantage because of the scarcity of younger family members to assist financially and physically."[16]

The extent of deprivation suffered by many older people in rural areas cannot be minimized. However, it has also been argued that the quality of life is higher in small towns and the social adjustment to aging less difficult, due to a more intimate environment that enhances an individual's ability to maintain control over his or her life situation. For example, farmers have

Table 10.8:   Rural-Urban Distribution of the White Population Aged 60-64,
              USA, 1910-1970

Year	Urban	Rural nonfarm	Rural Farm
1910	48.7	25.2	26.1
1920	52.6	20.6	26.7
1930	57.8	19.9	22.3
1940	59.0	19.4	21.5
1950	66.8	18.7	14.4
1960	71.2	20.0	8.9
1970	71.7	22.4	5.9

Sources: U.S. Censuses of Population: 1930, Vol. 11, Ch. 10, Table 16;
           1940 Vol. IV, Part 1, Table 6; 1950, PC(1)-1D, Table 158; 1970,
           PC(1)-1D, Table 189.

the option of choosing partial rather than full retirement and can move from the farm into town when necessary.[17] This pattern is evident in Table 10.8, which shows a decrease in the number of older people on farms but an increase, since 1930, in the number living in nonfarm areas or small towns.

The urban aged, a category that includes over 70 percent of the older population, have advantages denied to older people residing in rural areas but face problems of a different nature. Services are more readily available and mass communication makes knowledge about these services easier to obtain.[18] However, the anonymous, impersonal urban environment makes life lonely and isolated for many older people, and fear of crime further reduces the life space of inner-city residents.[19]

It would be a difficult task to prove that either urban or rural living provides a lifestyle that is inherently more suited to the aging process. What is important to recognize is that a major shift in population has occurred, making urban living the mode. While we cannot, as a society, afford to ignore the rural aged, at the same time we must recognize that most older people presently reside in cities and that this pattern is likely to persist for some time.

One of the concomitants of modernization has been mass education, an innovation that initially benefited the young more than the old. Traditionally, the informal knowledge about customs, skills, and community history possessed by older people provided them authority and prestige. With the onset of mass education, this type of knowledge was quickly outdated as younger people obtained a formal education they could apply to the new occupations created by modern technology.[20] As more highly educated people reach old age, the educational inequities between age groups have begun to disappear. Among those entering old age early in the century, only about 10 percent had completed high school. Nearly 45 percent had less than an eighth-grade education. By the year 2000, it is predicted that over 70 percent of all those over age 65 will have attained this level, and over 30 percent will have had some college training as well.[21]

The potential impact of a group of well-educated older citizens cannot be underestimated. They will have an increasing awareness of options available to them and will have a greater ability to function competently and effectively in a complex bureaucratic system. This, in turn, should lead to an improved ability to mobilize resources on their own behalf and to organize effectively to promote their own welfare. Certainly, the problems associated with growing old will not disappear, but they will be increasingly less likely to be associated with the more basic problems of a permanent underclass of poorly educated individuals.

Internal migration, the movement of people from one part of the country to another, has had a tremendous effect on the distribution of the aged population in the United States in a variety of ways. In terms of actual numbers, older people tend to be most numerous in the largest states, New York and California, each of which have nearly two million people over age 65. In all states the number of older people increased between 1970 and 1975. However, proportionally these increases have not been evenly distributed. Some states have, for a variety of reasons, attracted or maintained a larger proportion of older people. These trends are visually represented in Figure 10.3.

In 1975 nine states had an unusually high proportion of older persons in

Figure 10.3: Proportion of Population Aged 65+, 1975

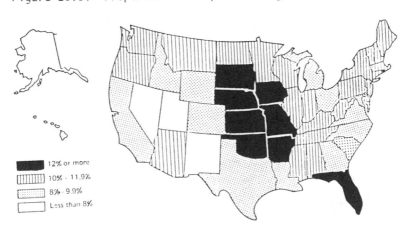

Source: <u>Facts about Older Americans</u>, 1976. U.S., Department of Health, Education, and Welfare, Office of Human Development, Administration on Aging, National Clearinghouse of Aging, DHEW Publ. No. (OHD) 77-20006.

Table 10.9: Estimated Population Aged 65+, by State, 1975

State	Number (000's)	Percent of Total Population	Rank[1]	Percent Increase, 1970-1975
Total	22,613	10.4	--	12.2
Excluding Puerto Rico and outlying areas	22,400	10.5	--	12.2
Alabama	378	10.5	23[t]	16.6
Alaska	9	2.6	54[t]	32.4
Arizona	223	10.0	29[t]	38.6
Arkansas	271	12.8	2	14.5
California	2,056	9.7	34[t]	14.8
Colorado	210	8.3	44[t]	12.3
Connecticut	321	10.4	26	11.6
Delaware	50	8.6	42[t]	14.6
District of Columbia	71	9.9	32[t]	1.0
Florida	1,347	16.1	1	36.7
Georgia	430	8.7	41[t]	17.7
Hawaii	57	6.6	50[t]	29.6
Idaho	79	9.6	35[t]	17.2
Illinois	1,153	10.3	27[t]	5.9
Indiana	531	10.0	29[t]	8.0
Iowa	364	12.7	3	4.2
Kansas	285	12.6	4	7.4
Kentucky	368	10.8	20[t]	9.6
Louisiana	346	9.1	37	13.4
Maine	125	11.8	10[t]	9.5
Maryland	340	8.3	44[t]	14.0
Massachusetts	672	11.5	13[t]	6.1
Michigan	815	8.9	39[t]	8.8
Minnesota	440	11.2	16[t]	8.0
Mississippi	253	10.8	20[t]	14.4
Missouri	601	12.6	4[t]	7.6
Montana	75	10.0	29[t]	9.5
Nebraska	194	12.5	6	6.2
Nevada	44	7.4	49	42.9
New Hampshire	87	10.6	22[t]	11.4
New Jersey	767	10.5	23[t]	10.6
New Mexico	90	7.8	47[t]	28.2

their total population. Florida, which has the highest proportion of older people (16.1 percent), draws retirees to its favorable climate. In contrast, the central midwestern farm belt states, Kansas, Missouri, Nebraska, and South Dakota, as well as Oklahoma, Arkansas, and Rhode Island, had disproportional numbers of older people due to the out-migration of young adults to urban areas. Table 10.9 shows both the number and proportion of older people by state, as well as the percent increase in the 5-year period between 1970 and 1975. Some states that do not have a disproportionate number of older people in the population, such as Arizona and Nevada, still experienced a substantial increase in the total number of older people. However, younger people have also been migrating to these areas, so that the population of these states has not "aged."

Table 10.9 (cont.)

State	Number (000's)	Percent of Total Population	Rank[1]	Percent Increase, 1970-1975
New York	2,030	11.2	16	4.0
North Carolina	492	9.0	38[t]	19.5
North Dakota	73	11.5	13[t]	10.3
Ohio	1,066	9.9	32[t]	7.3
Oklahoma	334	12.3	8	11.8
Oregon	259	11.3	15	14.7
Pennsylvania	1,377	11.6	12	8.7
Rhode Island	113	12.2	9	8.8
South Carolina	229	8.1	46	20.6
South Dakota	85	12.4	7[t]	5.9
Tennessee	441	10.5	23[t]	15.4
Texas	1,158	9.5	36	17.3
Utah	91	7.5	48	18.1
Vermont	52	11.0	19	9.9
Virginia	424	8.5	43[t]	16.4
Washington	365	10.3	27[t]	13.9
West Virginia	211	11.7	11	8.9
Wisconsin	512	11.1	18	8.8
Wyoming	33	8.8	40	9.7
American Samoa	1	2.4	55	4.8
Guam	2	1.8	56[t]	21.6
Puerto Rico	203	6.6	50[t]	14.6
Trust Territories	4	3.5	53	27.9
Virgin Islands	4	3.8	52	52.8

[1] States are ranked in order of decreasing percentages (highest percentage is rank 1, lowest is 54).

[t] Tied in ranking. States with identical percentages receive identical rank number with following rank number(s) skipped.

Source: <u>Facts about Older Americans,</u> 1976. U.S. Department of Health, Education and Welfare, Office of Human Development, Administration on Aging, National Clearinghouse on Aging, DHEW Publ. No. (OHD) 77-20006.

Conclusion

It is possible to look at the characteristics of each generation of people presently living and make estimates about what their future years will be like when they grow old. We know that by the year 2000 the aged will be better educated, increasingly composed of females, and less likely to be foreign-born. The vast increase in the proportion of aged we have seen in the past century may level off, at least in the United States, so that the problems we will have to face in the future will be different from those of past years. Instead of concerns about greater numbers of elderly people, we will be concerned about a better lifestyle and environment for the aged. As a social problem, aging is quite different from any other, for one day we will all grow old.

This chapter has examined both societal aging and individual aging in terms of patterns that can be identified by numerical calculations. Both aspects are important in identifying trends in the demography of aging. Societies age because individuals make decisions about how many children to have, because modern technology improves health care, and because of a variety of subtle interactions between people and their environment. The cultural beliefs and values of the people can never be separated from the larger statistical trends, for it is this very culture which shapes these trends. Demography is more than the study of fertility, mortality, and migration; it is also the study of social change. Understanding the processes of change can help us to control the direction of change. If we use this knowledge wisely, we can all look forward to a more comfortable and secure old age.

Notes

1. Bureau of the Census, *Statistical Abstract of the United States*, 97th Annual Edition (Washington, D.C.: Department of Commerce, 1976).

2. David Hackett Fisher, *Growing Old In America* (Oxford: Oxford University Press, 1978), p. 3.

3. Leonard Hayflick, "The Strategy of Senescence," *Gerontologist* 14 (1974), pp. 37–45.

4. Phillip M. Hauser, "Aging and World-wide Population Change," in Robert H. Binstock and Ethel Shanas (eds.), *Handbook of Aging and the Social Sciences* (New York: Van Nostrand Reinhold, 1976).

5. Donald Cowgill, "Aging and Modernization: A Revision of the Theory," in Jaber F. Gubrium (ed.), *Late Life, Communities and Environmental Policy* (Springfield, Ill.: Charles C. Thomas, 1974).

6. Hauser, op. cit.

7. Erdman Palmore and Frances C. Jeffers, *Prediction of the Life Span* (Lexington, Mass.: D. C. Heath and Co., 1971).

8. Bureau of the Census, op. cit., p. 30.

9. Evelyn M. Kitagawa and Phillip Hauser, *Differential Mortality in the United States: A Study in Socioeconomic Epidemiology* (Cambridge, Mass.: Harvard University Press, 1973).

10. Bureau of the Census, op. cit., p. 32.

11. Ibid.

12. Oscar Handlin, *Immigration as a Factor in American History* (Englewood Cliffs, N.J.: Prentice-Hall, 1958).

13. Arthur Wood, *Hamtramck: Then and Now* (New York: Bookman Associates, 1955).

14. Helena Z. Lopata, "The Polish American Family," in Charles H. Mendel and Robert W. Habenstein (eds.), *Ethnic Families in America* (New York: Elsevier, 1976).

15. Peter Uhlenberg, "Changing Structure of the Older Population of the USA

During the Twentieth Century," *Gerontologist* 17 (1977), pp. 197–202.

16. Francis Carp, "Housing and Living Environments of Older People," in Robert H. Binstock and Ethel Shanas (eds.), *Handbook of Aging in the Social Sciences* (New York: Van Nostrand Reinhold, 1976).

17. Ward W. Bauder and Jon A. Doerflinger, "Work Roles Among the Rural Aged," in E. Grant Youmans (ed.), *Older Rural Americans* (Lexington: University of Kentucky Press, 1967).

18. Philip Taietz, "Community Complexity and Knowledge of Facilities," *Journal of Gerontology* 30 (1975), pp. 357–362.

19. Richard A. Sundeen and James T. Mathieu, "The Fear of Crime and Its Consequences Among Elderly in Three Urban Communities," *Gerontologist* 16 (1976), pp. 211–219.

20. Cowgill, op. cit.

21. Uhlenberg, op. cit., pp. 197–202.

11

Getting Along
After Retirement:
An Economic Inquiry

David A. Hardcastle

The most probable economic consequence of retirement is a reduction in the level of one's income and standard of living. A reduced standard of living has accompanied retirement for the majority of people in the past and, in all likelihood, this will continue to be the case in the future. In this chapter we will examine what retirement is; the demographic features of the retired; the factors affecting the economic well-being of the elderly; the consumption patterns of the retired; and inferences about the economic welfare of the elderly and retired in the future based on demographic trends.

Retirement can be defined operationally as the cessation of work. Full retirement is the complete cessation of income-producing work and partial retirement is the reduction of such activity. People other than the elderly can be retired, but this discussion will be limited to the implications of retirement for the elderly. The elderly are defined for our purposes as persons 65 and older, unless otherwise indicated. So, operationally, we are concerned with the economic well-being or welfare of persons 65 and older whose primary source of income is not work.

Demography: The Increasing Elderly

Currently, the elderly constitute a significant proportion of the American population. They represent approximatey 11 percent of the population nationally, with regional variations to as low as 8.9 percent in the intermountain west and more than 12 percent in the heartland states of Iowa,

Nebraska, Kansas, and Missouri (see Table 11.1).[1] Both the elderly population and the median age of the population of the United States are increasing. The median age is rapidly approaching 30. This rise, and the proportional rise in the numbers of elderly, has been accompanied by declining birth rates (about a 38 percent decline since 1960; see Table 11.2). The intrinsic rate of natural increase (i.e., the rate of population increase that would eventually prevail if the birth and death rates remained unchanged over a long period of time) indicates that the United States will undergo a population decrease. However, the notion of an intrinsic rate of natural increase is difficult to interpret for the United States since 1970. If the birth

Table 11.1: Population by Ages for Sections of the Country in Percentages, 1976

	Under 5 yrs	5-17 yrs	18-64 yrs	65 yrs+
United States	7.1	23.2	59.0	10.7
New England	6.2	23.1	59.2	11.5
Middle Atlantic States	6.3	22.5	59.7	11.4
East North Central	7.2	23.9	58.7	10.2
West North Central	6.9	23.3	57.6	12.2
South Atlantic	7.2	22.8	59.1	10.9
East South Central	7.8	23.8	57.6	10.8
West South Central	8.2	23.9	57.7	10.2
Mountain West	8.6	24.3	58.2	8.9
Pacific	7.0	22.5	60.6	9.9

Source: Statistical Abstracts of the United States, 1977 (98th Annual Edition), Bureau of the Census, U.S. Department of Commerce, 1977, p. 29.

Table 11.2: Birth Rates
             in Percentages, 1960-1975

Year	Birth Rates/1000 Population
1960	23.7
1965	19.4
1970	18.4
1975	14.8

Source: Statistical Abstracts of the United States, 1977 (98th Annual Edition), Bureau of the Census, U.S., Department of Commerce, 1977, p. 55.

and death rates for the period 1970 to 1974 remain constant over a long period of time, the population of the United States will decline by 0.4 percent. On the other hand, if the intrinsic rate for 1975 remains constant, the United States will suffer a population decline of 6 percent.[2]

Coupled with the declining birth and death rates are increasing life expectancies. The average lifetime in 1970 was 70.75 years, with males averaging 67.01 years and females 74.64 years. However, for persons born in 1975, the average life expectancy is 72.5 years, with the prediction for white females over 7.0 years longer than that for white males, and minority females expecting 8.7 years more of life than minority males.[3] For people who have reached age 65, the average life expectancy has increased from 12.1 more years for males and 13.6 years for females in 1941 to 13.7 more years for males and 18.1 years for females in 1975.[4] This trend toward longer lives, and the increased proportion of elderly in the total population, is projected to continue into the next century (see Table 11.3). The implications for retirement of such age shifts will be explored in greater detail in a later section of this chapter.

Not only are the numbers and proportion of elderly increasing but, logically, so are the numbers and proportion of the retired through the turn of this century (Table 11.4). The actual rates of retirement in the future, given recent changes in Social Security and federal laws on mandatory retirement, cannot be exactly predicted. But it is probably safe to say that while the proportion and absolute numbers of elderly will increase, fewer will be workers and a greater absolute and proportionate number will be retired.

Income Levels of the Retired

To be old and retired is generally to be poorer than other members of society. The per capita income over a lifetime rises steadily, peaking at the 55-to-64 age level (see Table 11.5). Family income peaks at the 45-to-54 age level, declining thereafter. Families headed by persons age 65 or older have only 69 percent of the mean income for all families, and 55 percent of the income of families headed by people at the peak income age level of 45 to 54. The income of families headed by the elderly is lower than all family income except for families headed by persons age 14 to 24.[5]

Authorities such as Palmore have predicted that the income gap will close and the United States will eventually become an age-irrelevant society so far as socioeconomic status is concerned. By the year 2000, Palmore projects, men over age 65 will have 73 percent of the income of the working male under 65, and women over 65 will have 90 percent of the income of younger working women.[6] Other authorities, such as Havighurst, predict that dire poverty among the elderly is likely to be abolished, although relative poverty

Table 11.3: Population Age 65 Years and Older to Year 2020 (in 000)

Year	Age 65 and Older Population (% of Total)	Age 65-74	Age 75-84	Age 85 and Older
1976	22,924 (10.7%)	14,174	6,775	1,966
1980	24,927 (11.2%)	15,493	7,140	2,294
1990	29,824 (12.2%)	17,804	9,140	2,881
2000	31,822 (12.2%)	17,436	10,630	3,756
2020	45,102 (15.5%)	28,127	12,199	4,776

Source: Statistical Abstracts of the United States, 1977 (98th Annual Edition), Bureau of the Census, U.S. Department of Commerce, 1977, p. 327.

Table 11.4: Labor Force Participation Rates by Sex 1960-1990, Age 65 and Over (in Percents)

	1960	1965	1970	1975	1980	1990
Male	32.2	26.9	25.8	20.8	19.1	16.1
Female	10.5	9.5	9.2	7.8	7.6	7.2

Source: Statistical Abstracts of the United States, 1977 (98th Annual Edition), Bureau of the Census, U.S. Department of Commerce, 1977, p. 387.

Table 11.5: Money Income of Families by Age of Family Head and Per Capita Income for Age Band, 1976

Age of Head	Mean Family Income	Per Capita Income
	$16,870	$5,051
14-24	$10,150	$3,799
25-34	15,531	4,495
35-44	19,081	4,395
45-54	21,119	5,701
55-64	18,635	6,605
65+	11,635	4,891

Source: U.S., Department of Commerce, Bureau of the Census, Statistical Abstracts of the United States, 1977, p. 447.

for the aged will remain. The elderly will become an economic force similar to the teenagers of the 1960s and 1970s, representing a large income base in the aggregate but with small individual amounts of marginal income.[7] In the past, however, the income gap between the elderly and the rest of society has been reduced only to expand again. For example, in 1962 families headed by persons 65 and older had 50.6 percent of the income of families headed by persons 14 to 64. In 1966 the gap had widened, with families headed by the elderly having only 46 percent of the income of other families. Per capita income follows a similar pattern. In 1961, the per capita income of persons 65 years and older was 47.7 percent of that of the 14-to-64-year-old population. It then declined to a low of 40.5 percent in 1967 and did not exceed the 1961 figure again until 1972.[8]

In 1975, approximately 12.3 percent of people of all ages were poor, compared to 15.3 percent of the elderly. This represented an increase from the 1974 figures (11.2 percent and 14.6 percent, respectively), contrary to the trends predicted by Palmore. The proportion of poor minority elderly was even higher: 36.3 percent for blacks and 32.7 percent for Spanish-Americans, compared with 13.4 percent for whites. Furthermore, for the total population, almost 18 percent fall within the "near-poor" income range, but one-quarter of the elderly are "near poor."[9] Some authorities, such as those of the Institute for Socioeconomic Studies, are even more pessimistic in their estimates of the proportion of elderly who live in poverty. The institute estimates that 32 percent of the population 65 and older are poor.[10]

Sources of Income in Retirement

The elderly, especially the retired, have relatively little money because their income is derived primarily from nonwork sources. Income is always derived from productivity of either labor, land, or capital. In other words, it is based on the productivity created by or contributed by the utilization of labor (work, land, or capital) beyond the cost of the labor and land. In American society, the generally preferred source of income is work, which is central to other sources of income, especially retirement-related income. Retirement-related income derives from work, capital, land, and/or transfer income. An understanding of work is central to understanding retirement and reduced retirement income. Heilbroner states there are two basic functions that societies must perform "to bring human nature into social harness:

1. A society must organize a system for producing the goods and services it needs for its own perpetuation.
2. It must arrange a distribution of the fruits of its production among its own members, so that more production can take place."[11]

In other words, every society must develop (1) a means of producing sufficient goods and services for itself and for the next generation until that generation is ready to produce for itself, and (2) a means of equitably distributing that production. The most common form of social production and distribution is through work or activity that produces something of value for other people.

As noted, work is the generally perferred source of income in American society. Capital income, on the other hand, is income from savings, investments, capital production, and other proprietary sources. Income produced by the ownership of land, or what is produced on that land, can be distinguished from capital income, but its effects on retirement are similar. The third and major form of retirement income is transfer income, taken from the earning part of society and transferred to the nonearning part through public (taxation) or private (donation and family) means. For the elderly and retired, the transfers are intergenerational. Intergenerational transfers might be made on a private and personal level by the passing of income from parents to children, or from children to parents. On a governmental level, transfers are made through such programs for the elderly as Supplemental Security Income; Old Age, Survivors, and Health Insurance (Social Security); and the transfer of goods and services or in-kind income, such as Medicaid, recreational services, food stamps, Meals on Wheels, and so forth.

The problem the retired elderly pose for society relates largely to their shift from work to transfer income and how such transfer income is viewed. Transfer income does not fit within the wage or income theory based on marginal productivity of labor, land, or capital. The rationales for the use of transfer income are that (1) it is short term, and (2) its duration results from the assumption that the recipient is temporarily not part of the work force. Circumstances prohibiting participation in the labor force may include age (either too young or too old to participate); disability; unemployment due to technological advances; and "mothering."

The social definitions of who is legitimately not in the labor force form a precarious foundation upon which to base transfer income. Over the past half-century, the conceptions of who belongs in the labor force have tended to change. At the time of the Social Security Act's inception in 1936, mothers without spouses were defined as out of the labor market and entitled to transfer benefits through the Aid to Families with Dependent Children (AFDC) titles of the Social Security Act. Changes in the act over the past 20 years have redefined mothers into the employment market. Economic self-support and self-sufficiency is now a major goal for AFDC recipients. As Kreps points out, the 1967 amendments to the Social Security Act that require mothers of dependent children to work or undergo job training is evidence of the belief that income claims should accrue only to persons who cannot legitimately acquire earnings. Once mothers have been socially defined as capable of working, any assumption of entitlement to transfers based on sex, "mothering," or the absence of a male breadwinner are no longer socially valid.[12] The elderly may go through the same redefinitions.

The proportion of one's life that is devoted to work, as opposed to leisure, apparently depends more on the nation's economic development than on the individual's work efforts. The more economically productive societies can afford greater periods of leisure and a retirement of longer duration for their populations than the less productive societies. Kreps indicates that labor force activity rates for males are highest in agriculturally based and lowest in industrially based countries. Industrially or economically advanced countries can delay their citizens' entry into the labor force until they reach full maturity, 20 to 22 years of age, and can allow retirement or withdrawal from the labor force at age 65 or below. For agriculturally based economies, entry into the work force occurs at earlier ages, and withdrawal later.[13] Since the numbers of employed elderly and labor force participation rates are both projected to decline, major economic and social concerns will continue to involve the questions of whether sufficient intergenerational transfer income will be available for retirement, whether the responsibility for retirement resides in the public or private sectors, and what the appropriate relationship is between work and retirement. The public-versus-private sector controversy is centered on the proper division of responsibility between the public sector and the private sector (the individual, his or her employer, and family). A related concern is whether retirement income should be tied to the individual's personal history of productivity or based more broadly on a concept of social responsibilities and social good. This social approach would tie retirement benefits to society's conception of a desirable standard of living for retirement. That standard might vary in accordance with society's ability to support the elderly. This approach is more likely to be attached to the public sector and be associated with guaranteed annual incomes for the elderly, as contrasted with social insurances or other wage-related retirement schemes.

The private or individualized approach to retirement income is generally based on investments, savings, and other "set asides" for retirement. Given the trend toward higher future income based on real gains in marginal productivity or income, Americans have not developed a pattern of savings and investments for retirement. In fact, the expectation of higher future incomes and inflation has induced Americans to spend more heavily at the present time (often exceeding current income), to borrow against future earnings for current consumption, and not to save. This is the basis for the heavy-credit economy and deficit spending of both government and individuals. This condition contributes to inflation because the demands for goods and services are not underwritten by productivity. Inflation discourages saving since one's money will be worth less in the future. If a dollar saved today is to be worth only ninety cents next year in terms of real purchasing power, and fifty cents 5 years from now, it is better to spend the dollar today. It is also better to borrow and spend the borrowed dollars because the future repayment will be lower in real terms.

A second reason for the reluctance to save for retirement is the demands made on families and individuals during their working lives. During the early stages of the working life, the primary concern is for the establishment of a family and household. Economic demands tend to exceed income and the family borrows for durable goods, such as appliances, and to purchase housing. When a worker reaches his or her late 30s and 40s, the family must face the expenses of education for the children. As Kreps points out, at no time during their work lives do families tend to save significantly or set aside discretionary income for retirement. This is true even though during the middle years, ages 35 to 64, when the wage curve is at its peak, income may exceed expenses for most occupational categories. Savings generally occur only when there are mandatory savings for retirement or forced capital investments, such as the retirement plans offered by employers and the taxes of the Social Security program.[14]

The Social Security Progam

The single most important source of income for the retired elderly is Social Security, the mandatory Old Age and Survivors Insurance (OASI) program of the federal government. As Table 11.6 indicates, in 1971 90 percent of the retired population received retirement benefits, and of those people 87 percent received Social Security. However, among people 62 and over, 31 percent of all units (married couples and single individuals) and 49 percent of married couples had to continue working. Public assistance, with the liberalization of Social Security benefits, was received by only 10 percent of all single individuals and married couples combined. Personal contributions from families and friends accounted for less than 1 percent of the benefits of all units. For the approximately 87 percent who are Social Security beneficiaries, Social Security was the primary source of income. In 1971, only 27 percent of Social Security beneficiaries had income from earnings, as compared to 45 percent of the nonbeneficiaries. With the exception of personal assets, Social Security income was generally not supplemented by other forms of income.[15]

Earnings are a slightly greater source of retirement income for minorities, especially blacks, than they are for whites—approximately one-third of blacks and 30 percent of whites listed earnings as a source of income. This

Table 11.6
Percent of People Age 65 and Older by Specific Income Sources, 1971

Income Source	All Units	Married Couples	Nonmarried Persons
Number (in thousands)	15,637	6,300	9,336
Percent of Units with--			
Earnings	31	49	18
Wages	24	38	14
Self-Employed	9	16	5
Retirement Benefits	90	92	88
Social Security	87	89	85
Government Employment Pensions	6	8	5
Private Pensions and Annuities	17	23	12
Veterans Benefits	8	8	8
Unemployment Insurances	1	2	1
Public Assistance	10	6	13
Income from Assets	49	58	43
Personal Contributions	1	0.5	2

Source: Susan Grad, Income of the Population Aged 60 and Older, 1971 (Washington, DC: U.S. Department of Health, Education and Welfare, Social Security Administration, Office of Research and Statistics, 1977), p. 25.

difference corresponds to the greater dependence by blacks on public assistance (35 percent compared to 8 percent for whites), less use of Social Security benefits (77 percent compared to 88 percent for whites), and less income from assets (12 percent compared to 53 percent for whites).[16] Except for work, blacks are by and large dependent on public means for retirement income.

Since Social Security is the primary source of retirement income, two questions require attention: is the income provided by Social Security adequate, and why, if it is an "insurance" program, is it classified as a transfer and not an investment? Although the benefits are improving, they have generally been considered less than adequate. Former Social Security Administration Commissioner Robert M. Ball has indicated that the federal government's perspective on support for retirement is to provide the elderly with income that falls between two extremes: (1) a lower extreme of minimum subsistence as defined by the government's own definition of poverty, and (2) an upper level not exceeding the level attained while working. To make certain that at least the minimum standard is met, cost-of-living escalators have been built into OASI benefits. It is because of the upper limit that the poor are consigned to poverty in retirement. Ball has indicated that a person will need between two-thirds and three-fourths of his or her work income to retire at a satisfactory level.[17] As Table 11.5 indicates, income for families whose heads are 65 and older is 69 percent of the income of all families, or at the lower end of this two-thirds-to-three-fourths standard. Brotman's data indicate that the median incomes of families whose heads are 65 and older was only 55 percent of the median income of the working-age families.[18]

In regard to the second question, the reason that many retired people receiving Social Security benefits do not receive between two-thirds to three-fourths of their work income is the "social insurance" aspect of Social Security. Another former commissioner of Social Security, Robert J. Altman, stated during the 1963 Curtis Hearings on Social Insurances that the bases of the OASI system were the "principles of individual equity and social adequacy."[19] However, these principles are both ambiguous and contradictory. Individual equity relates to benefits received relative to contributions, while social adequacy refers to a socially defined standard of living. In OASI's attempt to partially satisfy the two contradictory criteria, it has satisfied neither.

Social Security is a transfer because benefits are only loosely linked to the Federal Insurance Corporation of America (FICA) tax, a work tax that forms the basis of the worker's and employer's contribution. There is no statutory assurance or explicit contract that the taxes paid by a worker will, in fact, lead to future benefits for him or her. No direct or accrual relationship exists between contributions and benefits. The contract is implied, at best, and is dependent on the continuing good will of Congress and the administration.

The Social Security program, as evidenced by recent publicity, is in fiscal difficulties. The major difficulty rests in the relationship of the size of the benefit pool, or OASI trust fund, and the demands made on it. Currently, the benefit pool represents an intergenerational transfer rather than an "over life" enforced savings program. In any given year, as much money is withdrawn from the benefit pool as is contributed. In fact, the demands on the pool are greater than the contributions, leading to the constant increase in the FICA tax. For the working class, it is the single largest tax paid. If there is a significant downturn in the taxes being paid because of increased unemployment, the pool would essentially be bankrupt within a year. This problem is being addressed by increasing the work tax. The current version of the Social Security Act projects that by the year 2011 the employer and employee will each pay a tax of 7.45 percent on the employee's wages, or approximatley a 15 percent combined tax.[20] According to some projections, the tax for both the employee and employer will be above 10 percent each, or 20 percent combined, by the turn of the century. However, there is some possibility that coupled with the projections of increasing tax rates there will be a reduction or elimination of the postretirement ceiling on work income. If the earnings ceilings are eliminated a person can receive benefits and work simultaneously without significant reduction of benefits. The intent is to encourage the elderly to continue working and hence continue paying the FICA tax.

If these projections prove correct, the concept of retirement will be altered. The ability of retired people to continue working without a reduction in their OASI benefits blurs the line between the concepts of retirement and work. The recipient is allowed to produce income that is subject to the Social Security tax, hence replenishing the benefit pool, although not replenishing it as fast as the benefits are withdrawn. The viability of this approach (given the trend for the elderly to work less) has yet to be tested. One reason the elderly cut back their work effort is that working reduces their Social Security benefits. Social Security benefits have a work test. The test is whether the recipient does work, not whether he or she can work. If the recipient does work, benefits are reduced according to a formula. By changing the formula for benefit reduction to allow the elderly to keep more of their work income, a greater work incentive is provided and older people will be more likely to continue working. This is compatible with the demographic trends indicated above. Population shifts will produce a decline in the ability of society to offer intergenerational transfers to the elderly. The trend argues against early retirement and for keeping the elderly working.

Consumption Patterns of the Retired

Horror stories abound concerning the low levels of consumption and extreme poverty of the retired. Newspapers have carried reports of the elderly living on dog food. While some of the stories are probably true, there is a dearth of reliable information on the consumption patterns of the retired. Most of the information is anecdotal and concerns only a limited part of the retired population.[21] For example, *U.S. News and World Report*, in a 1975 article entitled "Life for the Elderly in 1975—Many Are Hungry and Afraid," cited many cases of persons over 65 who had been relegated to dilapidated housing in "gray ghettoes" and were subsisting on only one meal a day. Unfortunately for purposes of determining the prevalence of such inadequate consumption patterns, the report was based on few case studies.[22]

One might hypothesize that people relying solely on Social Security benefits will be forced to live with an inadequate consumption level. Some authorities, such as Borzilleri, argue that the Consumer Price Index (CPI), the measurement used to adjust Social Security benefits, is biased away from the consumption needs of the elderly. The particular components of the index are more representative of the consumption patterns of persons other than the retired. Borzilleri argues that, if an index were constructed around the presumed buying patterns of older people, the price increases for items most often consumed by them would be in excess of the CPI for 1970–77 by 4 percent. Additionally, the greater need of the elderly for medical care subjects them more often to its rapidly inflating costs.[23]

On the other hand, it can be correctly argued that the retired do not face certain costs associated with the expenses of the working population. They do not pay any FICA tax on their retirement benefits. Their income tax is also reduced, as are property taxes in many states. They have no, or fewer, work-related expenses such as insurances, special clothing, and transportation costs. The mortgages on their homes are often paid. The retired, in general, also face fewer "dependent-related" costs such as support and education of children. These reductions mean the retired can maintain a higher standard of living on lower income, since their spending is focused more directly on their own needs.

Basically, then, the retired exist on lower incomes than do the working population. Some of their needs, especially work-related needs, are less. However, they do have needs for food, clothing, housing, and transportation. These basic needs are often exacerbated by the very condition of growing older. Food costs per person may increase as the number of people in the household decreases and because of special diets. Medical care costs, even with Medicare and Medicaid, are increasing. The elderly average $1,745 a year in health care costs, with $576 coming from their own incomes. While yearly hospital costs average $769, other costs are significant, with physicians' services averaging $302 a year and various other services $674 a year. The $1,745 average is some 589 percent higher than the health care costs of the young and 163 percent of the health care costs of working-age people in the 20-to-65 age group. Even with the large subsidies of Medicare and Medicaid, the elderly pay more "out of pocket," on the average, for health care than do the young and the working population.[24]

A major area of expenditures for the retired aside from food, clothing, shelter, and medical care relates to their new-found leisure time. The first fact of retirement is that the person has more free time to fill, and the second is that there is less income to use in filling it. The major task of retirement may be the adjustment to the second fact, the reduction of income, rather than the first, the loss of the work role and the greater leisure time. Studies of life satisfaction of the elderly indicate that the level of available income, especially in relation to prior income levels, is the most important factor; it is more important than the loss of the work role.[25]

The retired cannot readily utilize commercial recreation and travel as leisure pursuits because of their lower incomes. Less than two-thirds own their own vehicle, compared to 83.8 percent of households headed by people under 65. Television ownership, a major form of entertainment for the elderly, is essentially the same for heads of households over 65 as for those under 65. However, color TV ownership for the elderly is significantly lower, with 49.8 percent owning color TV compared to 61 percent of all households. Ownership of other "creature comforts," some of them bordering on necessities, is also less common for the elderly. For example, heads of households 65 years and older own proportionately fewer room and central air-conditioning units, refrigerators, freezers, and washing machines than do heads of households under 65.[26]

Intergenerational Transfers, Birth Rates, and Longevity: Implications for the Future

Greater longevity and the general decline of fertility rates have profound implications for Social Security intergenerational transfers. Will the country be able to afford a retired elderly population? A fertility rate per family of about 2.11 children is needed for a stable population. This is the replacement rate. However, given the erratic changes in birth rate, even a 2.11 birth rate will not lead to short-run stability. As indicated by earlier cited data on birth rates per 1,000 population, longevity, and the intrinsic rate of natural increase, there will be an increasing and disproportionate number of elderly compared to the working-age population. For example, in 1974, some 36 percent of the population was generally considered to be of prework age, or below 20 years of age. Some 54 percent were of work age, or between 20 and 64 years old, with another 10 percent at retirement age, or above 64 years old. The Duke Center for the Study of Aging and Human Development projected that by the year 2000 only 30 percent of the population will be of prework age, with 58 percent of working age. Of the remaining population 12 percent will be retired. Kreps estimates that the current intergenerational transfer from the average younger worker to the retired is approximately 12 percent. Over the next quarter-century this will increase to 18 percent in OASI taxes if a stable population and economy are maintained. However, if retirement age is lowered to 55, there will be a three-fold increase in the OASI tax rate.[27]

The demographic data presented earlier indicating inceases in the elderly population can be coupled with a decline in general labor force participation for the elderly during the last quarter-century. In the 1950s, about half the population over 65, males and females, was in the labor force; by the 1990s it is projected that only 16.1 percent of the males and 7.2 percent of the females over 65 will be in the labor force. Numbers of persons not in the labor force have gone from approximately 5.5 million males in 1967 to over

6.7 million males in 1975—an approximate gain of 25 percent. While their rate of participation in the labor force has gone up, the absolute numbers of females over 65 *not* in the labor force has also gone up, from approximately 9.25 million in 1967 to almost 11.5 million in 1975. The gain, therefore, of females age 65 and above not in the labor force is approximately 24 percent.[28]

The implications of these shifts are dramatic in their potential impact on Social Security and other intergenerational transfers. As Sheppard and Rix state, "Under the current retirement-age policy, an increase in the number of aged means an increase in the number of retired, who, as nonproducers, must be supported by the working population. They constitute, therefore, a dependency burden. How great a burden depends on the number of workers and on increases in disposable income available to support these dependents."[29] The decreased participation of the elderly in the work force and their dependency will be reflected in either lower benefits or increased efforts to move the elderly from retirement back into the work force. This will probably negate or reverse the current trend of earlier retirements.[30]

From the point of view of the marginal productivity of labor, intergenerational transfer (whether through the taxation and transfer of the Social Security system, or through family means) essentially involves taking income from the work force and transferring it to the nonworking population. The private (family) transfers are generally made from adults during their working years to their offspring up to 20 years of age or so. The offspring, in turn, transfer their income through private means during their work years to their children (see Figure 11.1).

Private transfers of parental support to children are relatively simply handled. The parents support the children until the children attain maturity and are able to support themselves. Since childbirth usually occurs between the ages of 20 and 40, the offspring reach work age when the parents are between 40 and 60 years old, or before their retirement age. Intergenerational

Figure 11.1:   Intergenerational Transfer Pattern from Generation 1 (Parents) to Generation 2 (Children) Based on 45 Years of Work Life. Transfers go from parents to children.

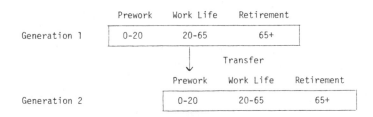

transfers through the public system work in the same way except that there is no family or personal relationship between the generations. Workers in general are taxed, and the government transfers the income to prework-age individuals and the retired. In American society, families generally handle the basic transfer to the prework population while the government, because of the decline of familial responsibility, handles the transfer to the elderly. Therefore, we have a situation in which transfer is occurring from the working population to two sets of nonworkers: the prework force and the retired (see Figure 11.2).

As the age of entering the work force increases (beyond age 20 for college students), and as the age of retirement is lowered and longevity increases for the elderly, greater strain is placed on the working population. This strain will be especially severe when the current "baby boom" workers, born between 1945 and 1960, enter retirement. Workers will be responsible for three generations: themselves, their offspring, and the retired. If, as in Figure 11.3, offspring do not enter the work force until age 22, and retirement begins at 62 with a life expectancy of 72, the work force is responsible for three generations for a minimum of 32 of its 40 working years. While the actual situation will be complicated by the age of workers when their children are born and the size of the elderly population at retirement, the principle is the same. If currently defined terms of the work force, work age, and retirement prevail, a smaller work force will support a growing nonworking population.

Figure 11.2: Intergenerational Transfers from Working Population to Retired Population and to Pre-Work Population or Children. The intergenerational transfer to pre-work population is through private means. The transfer to retired is through the FICA tax.

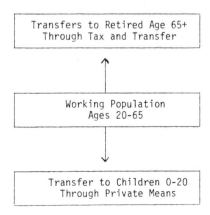

Figure 11.3:   Intergenerational Transfers from Work Force to Nonworking Population and Impact on Ability of Work Population to Save for Their Retirement. The work force is responsible for three generations for 32 of its 40 working years.

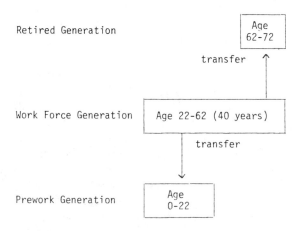

Although we cannot predict the future with certainty, we can anticipate it and react both to the conditions that may lie ahead and to the underlying values of our society. Marmor has reported that the elderly make up approximately 10 percent of the population, yet receive about 25 percent of the federal budget for all special assistance programs. In contrast, children, who compose approximately 38 percent of the population, receive only 9 percent of the federal outlay.[31] This is indicative of the increasing influence of the elderly as a constituency. As they become more politically active and their constituency grows, they will make a greater claim on the resources of society. The elderly have made a prior work contribution and therefore should be able to demand benefit from society. The question of how much of society's goods and services should be received by the nonworking and the retired in the future will be one of our major sociopolitical issues.

Notes

1. *Statistical Abstracts of the United States, 1977; 98th Annual Edition* (Washington, D.C.: Bureau of the Census, U.S. Department of Commerce, 1977), p. 25.

2. Ibid., p. 56.

3. Ibid., pp. 67, 66.

4. Ibid., p. 65.

5. Herman B. Brotman, "Income and Poverty in the Older Population in 1975,"

The Gerontologist 16, no. 1 (February 1976), p. 23.

6. Erdman Palmore, "The Future Status of the Aged," *The Gerontologist* 17, no. 1 (February 1977), p. 23.

7. Robert J. Havighurst, "The Future Aged: The Use of Time and Money," *The Gerontologist* 15, no. 1, (February 1975), pp. 10–14.

8. Brotman, op. cit.

9. Ibid., pp. 24–25. The income of the "near poor" is 125 percent of the poverty level. Poverty is defined as $3,257 annual income in 1965 dollars for a two-person family with a head 65 or older. "Near poor" is $4,040 annual income in 1965 dollars. For unrelated individuals 65 or older, poverty is $2,592 and "near poor" is $3,215 annual income, again in 1965 dollars.

10. *The Socioeconomic Newsletter* 11, no. 10 (October 1977), p. 2.

11. Robert L. Heilbroner, *The Making of Economic Society* (Englewood Cliffs, N.J.: Prentice-Hall, 1972), p. 5.

12. Juanita M. Kreps, *Lifetime Allocation of Work and Income: Essays in the Economics of Aging* (Durham, N.C.: Duke University Press, 1971), pp. 33–35.

13. Ibid., p. 64.

14. Ibid., pp. 86–95.

15. Susan Grad, *Income of the Population Age 60 and Older, 1971* (Washington, D.C.: Department of Health, Education and Welfare, Social Security Administration, Office of Research and Statistics, 1977), p. 28, Table 10.

16. Ibid., p. 29.

17. Robert M. Ball, "Income Security After Retirement," *Social Policy, Social Ethics, and the Aging Society* (Chicago: Committee on Human Development, University of Chicago, 1976), pp. 33–35.

18. Brotman, op. cit.

19. Robert B. Stevens, ed., *Statutory History of the United States: Income Security* (New York: Chelsea House Publishers, 1970), p. 454.

20. See A. Haeworth Robertson, "OASDI: Fiscal Basis and Long Range Cost Projections," *Social Security Bulletin* 40, no. 1. (January 1977), pp. 20–21, and "Issues in the 1978 Budget," *Brookings, The Brookings Bulletin* 14, no. 1–2 (Spring–Summer 1977), p. 3.

21. For examples of such research, see Robert M. Gibson, Marjorie S. Mueller, and Charles R. Fisher, "Age Differences in Health Care Spending: Fiscal Year 1976," *Social Security Bulletin* 40, no. 8 (August 1977), pp. 3–14, on health care costs; J. Barry Mason and William D. Bearden, "Profiling the Shopping Behavior of the Elderly Consumers," *The Gerontologist* 18, no. 5 (October 1978), pp. 454–461, on shopping patterns; Janet Murray, "Activities and Expenditures of Preretirees," *Social Security Bulletin* 38, no. 8 (August 1975), pp. 5–21, on expenditure patterns of preretirees (ages 58–63); and Martha A. Plonk and Mary Ann Pulley, "Financial Management Practices of Retired Couples," *The Gerontologist* 17, no. 3 (June 1977), pp. 256–261.

22. "Life for the Elderly in 1975—Many Are Hungry and Afraid," *U.S. News and World Report* 78 (February 10, 1975), pp. 48–51.

23. Thomas C. Borzilleri, "The Need for a Separate Consumer Price Index for Older Persons," *The Gerontologist* 18, no. 3 (June 1978), pp. 230–236. Also see "Living Standard Declines for New York City's Elderly," *Aging* (November–December 1975), p. 5.

24. Gibson et al., op. cit.

25. For example, see Walter F. Chatfield, "Economic and Sociological Factors Influencing Life Satisfaction of the Aged," *Journal of Gerontology* 32, no. 5 (September 1977), pp. 593–599, and Anne H. Rosenfeld, *New Views on Older Lives, A Sample of NIMH-Sponsored Research and Service Programs* (Rockville, Md.: National Institute of Mental Health, 1978), pp. 20–28.

26. *Statistical Abstracts*, op. cit., p. 462.

27. Juanita M. Kreps et al., *The Economic Implications for Older Americans of a Stable Population* (Durham, N.C.: Duke Center for the Study of Aging and Human Development, December 1976), pp. 4–5.

28. Data from U.S. Bureau of the Census, *Current Population Reports*, Series P-25, no. 614 and 601 (Washington, D.C.: Department of Commerce), and U.S. Bureau of Labor Statistics, *Special Labor Force Report* 156 (Washington, D.C.: Department of Labor).

29. Harold L. Sheppard and Sara E. Rix, *The Graying of Working America: The Coming Crisis in Retirement Age Policy* (New York: The Free Press, 1977), p. 13.

30. See H.R. 5383 modifying compulsory retirement.

31. Committee on Human Development, University of Chicago, *Social Policy, Social Ethics, and the Aging Society* (Chicago: University of Chicago, 1976), p. 24.

12

Politics and Older Americans

Allan J. Cigler and Cheryl Swanson

Students of American politics have become increasingly interested in studying the political behavior of older Americans. Two related developments underlie this recent interest. The steady rise in the number and cost of social programs for the elderly, coupled with the increasing public concern over government spending and taxation, are likely to make generational issues highly controversial items on the political agenda in the near future. In addition, the rising number and proportion of older citizens in the population creates the possibility of a new, potent political force in American politics. The impact of the elderly on politics and public policy may be felt in the electoral arena and the formal governmental decision-making process. But the specific nature of the political role that will be played by older Americans is a matter of considerable debate.

Older Americans, as participants in the nomination and election process, can influence the selection of candidates sympathetic to their interests. There is some question, however, whether the aged are or can ever be sufficiently homogenous in their political orientations and identifications to respond cohesively as a group. The elderly may also have an important influence on the political process through membership in age-based interest groups. But the question of how influential these groups are and whether they are likely to grow in political stature in the future is open to conjecture.

This chapter will address these issues by examining the levels of both individual and collective political activity that characterize older people, and by exploring the possibility of older Americans becoming more politically homogeneous and cohesive in the future. Its central thesis is that while age-related political consciousness is likely to grow, and may be particularly evident on specific political issues, the possibility of older Americans acting as a permanent electoral bloc or with a high degree of cohesion in interest group politics is unlikely.

The Potential for Age Cleavage

The American political system has been under great stress during the past 15 years and is in the process of transition.[1] From the Depression until the mid-1960s, the major issues on the domestic political agenda concerned questions of economic welfare, the role of government in the regulation of economic life, and the relationship between the states and the federal government. Generally speaking, socioeconomic status divisions dominated politics. Those less well off tended to support government provisions for social and economic security and the regulation of private enterprise. Those better off economically tended to take the opposite positions. The Democratic coalition, by and large, represented the less well off. Its supporters tended to be concentrated among the urban ethnic working class in the East, with Catholics, Jews, Italians, Irish, Eastern Europeans, and blacks being major constituents. On a variety of issues southerners joined in the coalition. The Republican coalition was concentrated in the rural and suburban areas outside the South, was made up of more established ethnic groups, businessmen, and farmers, and was largely Protestant in religious affiliation.

Divisions on the basis of age had little influence during the New Deal era. One's ethnic or socioeconomic status was of paramount concern. Although the radical Townsend Movement, based on age grievances, received much media attention in California during the 1930s, organized political activity focused on age-based concerns had virtually no influence in national politics. Social Security legislation was passed without the involvement of age-based interest groups. On issues affecting the elderly, the electorate was divided less on the basis of age than on the conflict between the working and upper classes.

On the other hand, the economic, ethnic, and ideological positions that developed during the New Deal and provided structure to parties, elections, and voter preferences seem less relevant now. New issues have been added to the political agenda, and opinions on these issues seem unrelated to traditional political divisions. Dawson has suggested that the opinions and attitudes of the American electorate are in "disarray," and that "politics as usual" reflected in New Deal political arrangements and coalitions cannot structure current politics.[2]

The issues that predominate in American politics at present appear to be of two types. "Valence" issues—general evaluations of the "goodness" or "badness" of the times—seem to be particularly important, especially concerns about the cost of living. Yet such issues do not divide us politically. Every one is against rising costs. Another set of important issues in contemporary politics is characterized by a cultural-moral dimension. Issues like abortion, ratification of the Equal Rights Amendment, capital punishment, penalties for marijuana use, and the like divide the electorate; but individual positions on these issues are unrelated to the traditional New Deal groups and identifications. Neither the valence nor the cultural-moral issues appear to have the capacity to realign political groups into stable coalitions of interests.[3] As a result, what we are witnessing in American politics is a proliferation of interest groups concerned with single-issue politics. Some are age-based interest groups, ranging from those concerned with lowering property taxes at the local level to protecting retirement benefits for the elderly at the national level.

The irrelevance of previous political arrangements to contemporary politics, and the focus on narrow interest concerns, raises the possibility that politics in the future will be structured far differently. The breakdown of traditional political identifications and the spread of single-issue politics may mean that future orientations toward politics will be dictated by the immediate circumstances of individuals.

Although age has not been the basis for an important cleavage in American politics in the past, there is a good deal of evidence to indicate that age consciousness will increase in the political arena. Older citizens are generally viewed as culturally and morally conservative, so that the rapid change in moral standards in the last two decades has heightened intergenerational conflict. The increasing number of cultural-moral issues on the political agenda may also act as a stimulus to trigger age group and generation consciousness. But more importantly, the role of government in the lives of older Americans appears likely to lead to political conflict in the future. The elderly are highly dependent upon the government and will become more so. In 1978, for example, $112 billion (or 24 percent of federal expenditures) went to the elderly; and it is projected that in 50 years the outlay will be 40 percent of the total budget (or $635 billion).[4]

This so-called "greying of the budget" is causing deep concern among some policy makers, especially now that inflation is rising rapidly and growth rates are sluggish. Some perceive older Americans as active contenders for political benefits and think they are demanding too much. A key factor is that Social Security payroll deductions are now widely viewed as added taxes rather than as premium payments into an old age insurance program.[5] And Social Security benefits are increasingly being viewed as transfer payments. For example, in 1978 Joseph Califano, Jr., Secretary of Health, Education and Welfare, noted that federal payments to the elderly constitute "the largest income redistribution in the history of this country."[6] Although one-quarter of the elderly are considered poor by government standards, a member of the Carter administration is on record as saying that the elderly are "demanding a selfish share" of special concessions and services, and that such demands "could create resentments" on the part of employed taxpayers.[7] Clearly, old age benefits are being viewed by many as subsidies rather than earned benefits. As a result, such benefits are becoming increasingly controversial.

A key factor in the increasing public debate over age benefits and its potential for spawning age group and generational conflict is the change in the ratio between those in the work force and those who are economically dependent. Cutler has studied the past and projected dependency ratios in the United States, covering the period 1930 to 2050. His findings are presented in Table 12.1. These data are conservative, since old age was defined as 65 and older. Trends toward early retirement and longevity changes were not considered. If 60-plus were used to define old age, the 1970 ratio would increase from .177 to .273.[8] The table indicates that the dependency ratio has jumped markedly since the start of the New Deal and appears to be leveling off. A major rise is not predicted until the postwar "baby boom" generation reaches retirement age, around the year 2020 and thereafter.

In addition to changes in the dependency ratio, the aggregate growth of expenditures for older Americans may foster generational conflict. Social Security benefits, for example, climb automatically each July if the Consumer Price Index for the first three months of the year is 3 percent or more above the figure for the same period in the previous year. Although many of the elderly argue that persons on fixed incomes suffer the most during inflationary times (since many pensions do not have inflationary clauses), many of the elderly are the beneficiaries of government cost-of-living increases, while few others in society are so protected. And as the Social Security system moves from a pay-as-you-go, deferred-wages program to a program financed out of general revenue funds, the tax burden on the younger, active labor pool will increase.[9]

There seem to be few easy political answers to paying for benefits for the elderly. Raising the mandatory retirement age provides a good example. Even with the option of working beyond 65, few people in that age group

Table 12.1: Old Age Dependency Ratios, 1930-2050

1930	1940	1950	1960	1970	2000	2020	2050
0.97	0.118	0.133	0.167	0.177	0.177	0.213	0.257

Source: N. Cutler, "A Foundation for Research in 'Political Gerontology,'" *The American Political Science Review* 80 (September 1977): 1013. Reprinted with permission.

continue to remain fully employed. The Senate Committee on Human Resources has estimated that only two-tenths of 1 percent will choose to work beyond the age of 65.[10] Only 2 percent of the General Motors work force work until 68, which is their mandatory retirement age.[11] Among federal employees, about 1 out of every 2,100 elects to work until age 70.[12] Clearly, early retirement is the rule, and the proportion of early retirees is likely to increase. The pressure for old age benefits is likely to be even greater than the current demographic projections, based on age 65, imply. In this period of unstructured politics, then, age has the potential for becoming a major political cleavage in society. While the elderly are highly dependent upon government, old age benefits are likely to become more controversial.

The Political Orientation of Older Americans: Public Opinion and Electoral Behavior

Much of the discussion of the impact of old age on future politics is predicated on the assumptions that various age groups respond to politics differently, have different political interests, and will act cohesively in electoral and interest group politics. But will they? The notion that there is a strong relationship between age and political behavior is part of conventional wisdom, a wisdom that has become popularized in recent years. Older Americans are viewed as being more conservative, more Republican, and much less likely to participate in politics than their younger counterparts. But conventional wisdom is often misleading and sometimes incorrect.

In reality, the relationship between age and political behavior is very complex. The complexity of the relationship derives from the fact that an individual's age connotes two different aspects of his or her life that may be important politically. First of all, age determines one's position in the life cycle. Second, the historical generation to which a person belongs is also the result of age. The distinction is crucial, yet the two implications of age are often confused in the explanation of the impact of age on political attitudes and behavior.[13]

The notion that older Americans are politically conservative is based on a life cycle interpretation, which is supported by strong theoretical and experimental evidence that conservatism increases during the middle and later stages of life. The cycle is usually conceptualized as a number of stages in an individual's life demarcated by role-changing events such as entering school, completing a formal education, entering the labor force, marriage, birth of the first child, exit of the last child from the home, and retirement.[14] Both biological and social aspects of aging may operate during the life cycle to predispose individuals to be conservative. In this context, conservatism may be defined as inflexibility and resistance to change, or it may be defined in more political terms as opposition to liberalism-egalitarianism.[15]

Three general factors associated with the aging process may make individuals less flexible with age, and hence potentially politically reactive against the forces of change. Particularly in the later stages of the life cycle, aging brings about losses in personal status and, although new statuses may be acquired, "those statuses which provided a lifetime of gratification can never be replaced."[16] In a youth-oriented culture, an individual's biological losses may lead to psychologically felt threats and frustrations.[17] Finally, the stability of one's lifestyle, occupation or career, and family may decrease in later life, and the older person may experience a loss of personal freedom. These conditions may predispose older people to "respond to threatening situations through the application of their own personally-validated stereotypes."[18]

Glenn has suggested that biological factors, in and of themselves, may be related to the tendency to become less flexible with age.[19] For example, the decline in energy and the loss of brain tissues could be linked to increasing rigidity and resistance to change in later years. Experiments in attitude change and flexibility have shown that older individuals exhibit much more rigidity than young individuals.[20]

There are other related aspects of the process of growing old that may predispose the oldest citizens in the population to be the most conservative. Some conservatives, including ex-president Richard Nixon and former governor of California Ronald Reagan, have argued that they became conservative due to their experience with the growing welfare state. The accumulated wisdom of experience, especially a growing cynicism about human nature, may predispose some people to become conservative in one area in particular: they may place a high priority on law and order due to a belief that people are by nature evil and that restraint is needed to ensure social stability.[21] However, an argument can also be made that the later stages of the life cycle can lead people in a liberal direction. Aging individuals may experience losses in income and status, making them more sympathetic to policies and programs emphasizing a more equitable distribution of resources.[22]

Are the older members of the population more conservative than younger members? Comparing age groups in the literature on public opinion is difficult because different, arbitrary distinctions of age groups are used and, to some degree, the findings are a function of the particular question asked. In general, opinions on most issues vary somewhat with age, but usually not by wide margins and occasionally not even in the predicted direction. Using Gallup polls, Ippolito et al. found that older people were less likely to support busing, abortion, and the ERA, but were more likely to oppose capital punishment and reductions in social spending than younger voters.[23] Riley and Foner found that existing research indicates that age is positively related to such things as opposition to school integration and interracial marriage and to support for more restrictive standards of sexual behavior and harsher treatment of criminals.[24] Concerning international relations, the big distinction between old and young is along isolation-nonisolation lines, rather than traditional liberal-conservative lines. For example, in the late 1960s the polls showed that older Americans were more against admitting Red China to the United Nations and against involvement in Vietnam than younger Americans.[25] However, the isolationism of older Americans is probably a generational effect, since many of them formed their political orientations during a period when noninvolvement in foreign affairs was the political norm. While the older group was probably more against the Vietnam war for generational reasons, conservatism due to age may better explain the fact that older Americans were less sympathetic to war protest.[26] Overall, older Americans seem to be somewhat more culturally and morally conservative than younger Americans.

Yet one has to be impressed with how little age cleavage seems to be a part of American public opinion, at least up to now. A case can be made that on important political questions there is more intra-age variation than inter-age differences. For example, analyses of the 1972 election have found that the major division in the election was over a set of issues that reflected cultural permissiveness versus cultural conservatism (issues such as abortion and the relaxation of marijuana laws).[27] Although people were divided along these lines, the division was largely unrelated to age, at least when ballots were cast. And George Wallace, perhaps the leading proponent of cultural conservatism in the late 1960s, received the bulk of his votes not from older Americans but from persons under 35.[28] Intragenerational variation has been more important politically than intergenerational conflict. Age groups, including the elderly, have been anything but monolithic with respect to public opinion and voting behavior.

A case can be made that most differences between older and younger Americans are due to generational effects. For example, studies of electoral behavior as well as the monthly polls presented in newspapers consistently indicate that the older members of the electorate are, as a group, proportionately more Republican than any other age group. However, one must not necessarily interpret this to mean that the older one gets, the more appealing the Republican Party becomes (a life cycle interpretation). Party identification has strong historical roots, and members of the electorate tend to retain their initial partisan identification throughout their lives. The realignment of party attachments in the late 1920s and through the 1930s is largely the reason most older Americans identify with the Republican Party today.[29] Before the New Deal, people entering the electorate identified with the Republican Party to a disproportionate extent. They have voted Republican ever since, and compose the bulk of the over-65 segment of the population today. During the 1930s, however, the bulk of new voters identified with the Democratic Party, and in the next decade Democrats will be disproportionately represented among older people. The New Deal generation will then be senior citizens. The aging process itself appears to have little to do with party identification.

A key point is that much of political behavior is habit, particularly for the older members of the electorate. Party identification was and still is a key factor in voting behavior, particularly for the pre–New Deal and New Deal generations. As much as anything, it was probably party identification that prevented older Americans from supporting Wallace in 1968. And party identification has been important in structuring political attitudes as well. It probably suppresses the influence of aging and conservatism on political behavior.[30]

There is a good deal of research on how people acquire their political orientations and identifications. Much of it suggests that people retain the opinions they formed when young, and rarely change.[31] Holloway and George have argued that such a tendency means that older people change less in response to events than younger people; and in a period "when change itself seems to be the only constant, such relatively fixed opinions would be a conserving and conservative influence, regardless of their original ideological content."[32] As a result, the age differences that do exist are less a matter of older people becoming conservative than a matter of their remaining the same while successive generations enter the electorate somewhat more liberal. Today's older voters have probably changed somewhat in a liberal direction, but comparatively less than the change toward liberalism represented in successive generations.[33]

In discussing the future role of age as a political cleavage, one must keep in mind that many of the factors that structured politics through most of the New Deal and postwar years are not as important today. Age cleavages may not be strong in the near future because party identification still influences older Americans' political behavior and, to some degree, this reduces age conflict. In the long run, however, age may be strongly related to political behavior. There is much evidence that the traditional political socialization process is breaking down in American politics.[34] It is evident that the family as an agent in passing on political values and identifications is weakening, and over the past 15 years many young voters have entered the electorate without party identification.[35] For generations born after the early 1960s, politics may be based less on historical experience and more on response to circumstances of the moment. One implication is that future generations of the elderly may be less anchored in their political values and identifications and more politically volatile.

This potential political activity of the aged may be gauged by examining the relationship between age and political alienation. There is a good deal of evidence that older age is associated with political cynicism and alienation.[36] One study conducted during the height of the Vietnam war found that in spite of the widespread perception that it was the nation's youth who were alienated, those over 65 far outstripped other age groups in terms of alienation.[37]

Even though today's elderly are more alienated and less trusting about politics than younger members of the electorate, they are not more likely to withdraw from politics.[38] When education is taken into account, the elderly participate at levels comparable to other age groups in the population.[39] Indeed, lower voting rates for people over 65 are usually due to the generational factor of lower educational levels among the elderly. As the better-educated middle-aged reach old age, the participation levels among the elderly should increase. Thus, if old age benefits are threatened in the future, it cannot be assumed that the elderly will be politically passive.

Yet there are major barriers to older Americans acting as an electoral bloc, in spite of what appear to be common interests and circumstances. Although age consciousness may grow in the future, particularly if old age benefits are challenged, the elderly are still a rather heterogeneous group in society, both in terms of needs and background identifications. Status differences among the elderly are apparent. Families headed by older persons have a greater diversity in income than younger families. Older citizens are also divided ethnically and racially. Furthermore, it should be remembered that "old age" spans many years. For example, people can be classified into the "young old," aged 55 to 75, and the "old old," those older than 75.[40] The "old old" will make up 44 percent of those over 65 in the year 2000, if projections are accurate.[41] The needs of these two groups differ. Many people over 75 are particularly in need of medical and nursing assistance. The "young old" are particularly concerned with income maintenance and retirement opportunities in areas such as recreation and life-enriching activities. The "young old" and the "old old" may view the political process quite differently and may even be major competitors for governmental funds.

Overall, we must be extremely cautious in making inferences about the future possibility of age being a major cleavage in mass politics. The forces that structured politics in the past and that suppressed potential cleavages based on age will not be a large part of future politics. At the same time, age-related issues are likely to be major items on the political agenda in the future. On some issues, like defending levels of government assistance to the elderly against the claims of other interests, older Americans may be expected to act with a great deal of unity. But the barriers to electoral cohesion among the aged, particularly the diversity of socioeconomic and physical circumstances, will probably prevent older Americans from being electorally unified on many other issues.

Aging Interest Groups

Very few studies have directly examined the influence of age-based interest groups on the allocation of resources in American society.[42] Instead, inferences are often made about the probable influence of these groups based on the characteristics of their potential membership (e.g., number of aged, political participation, political efficacy) and the characteristics of the groups themselves (e.g., resources, cohesion). Like the literature on public opinion and electoral politics, these studies suggest two competing views about the impact of elderly groups, but in this case on public policy. One view forecasts a great deal of political conflict in the future between age-based groups and other interests in society. Some foresee a gerontocracy in the late twentieth and early twenty-first centuries, when age-based groups will exert enough political power to influence policies along redistributive lines, with major shifts in government resources from the young to the old. Another prediction is that senior citizens groups will become involved in a whole host of policy issues beyond those that confer direct benefits to the elderly. Senior citizens groups at the local level may lobby against bond issues that are perceived to benefit only the nonelderly while costing older citizens. Others predict that age-based groups will act as conservative watchdogs on government spending, blocking all but the most incremental change.

The data on age-based groups suggest altogether different conclusions to other observers. The elderly and the groups that represent them are not considered to be a very potent political force. Some gerontologists suggest that most political gains for older Americans can be attributed to presidential leadership, political parties, or other more powerful interest groups such as unions.[43] One political scientist sees most government policy for the aged as a product of social change in which the younger generation prefers to transfer responsibility for care of the elderly from their shoulders to the government's.[44] Gray power's Achilles heel supposedly lies in the propensity of the elderly to withdraw from political life (although this view has been discredited by some research), a lack of group consciousness, and characteristics of mass-based groups that block effective political action.

These two viewpoints are too broad and imprecise to yield a realistic appraisal of the future impact of age-based groups on public policy. While new data on senior power is scarce, it is possible to examine age-based groups more systematically on the basis of the information that does exist. The power of organizations for the elderly is examined on the basis of the following considerations:

1. The strengths and weaknesses of age-based groups from an organizational perspective
2. The nature of age-based group demands and their potential impact on public policy
3. The role of such groups in various stages of the policy-making process
4. Political system characteristics that influence the nature and behavior of interest groups

Much of the discussion on the potential power of senior citizens groups is based on the notion that the increasingly greater number of older people in our society can be expected to join pressure groups that represent their interests. This belief rests on several assumptions: first, that the older generation perceives common needs and shares a group identity or consciousness; second, that the perception of shared needs and common interests is a sufficient condition for effective organization; and third, that a large group membership is a sufficient condition for effective political action.

As mentioned earlier, the elderly are an extremely diverse group, with different backgrounds, social classes, and occupations. However, this important fact does not rule out the possibility that certain subgroups of the elderly may coalesce around specific issues. For example, Rose[45] and Anderson and Anderson[46] have identified a subculture of the aging that rests on shared values such as serenity, sociability, and independence. These shared values are politically salient for older Americans who favor housing developments segregated on the basis of age. The activity of ad hoc pressure groups organized solely for the purpose of age-group separation has been linked to the passage of legislation upholding the right to exclude the nonelderly from certain residential areas in Arizona. Thus, it is possible to identify a set of shared values that leads to interest group activity among the elderly, in this case relatively affluent retired persons living in the Sunbelt. However, the impact of these kinds of groups on the overall distribution of public resources is probably slight. They organize to support or oppose a specific piece of legislation, not to continually intervene in the political process on behalf of issues affecting the elderly. Furthermore, groups that are primarily organized for the purpose of passing a single piece of legislation will usually not survive long enough to ensure that their goals are realized in the policy implementation process. Shared interests on bread-and-butter issues such as retirement benefits are also an inducement for the elderly to organize, and groups organized around them have tended to be influential in the political process.

While the perception of common needs is necessary for organization, economists question whether it is sufficient for effective organization. The "rational actor" model, which guides much economic theory, suggests that even individuals who share common problems are not inclined to join organizations that attempt to influence public policy.[47] The major drawback to group participation is the "free rider" problem, stemming from the tendency of most "rational" individuals to decide not to bear the costs of group participation (time, membership dues) because they can enjoy the benefits of the group's efforts (favorable legislation) whether they join the group or not. This problem is most serious for large groups because: (1) the larger the group the less likely an individual will be to perceive his or her voluntary contribution as having any impact on the outcome; and (2) social incentives (benefits) such as status and fraternity are likely to be more effective in small groups.[48] Economists hypothesize that large organizations that persist over time are those which can offer potential members selective benefits. These are benefits that can be withheld from nonmembers, such as reduced rates on insurance policies and travel. Organizations likely to be in the best position to offer such benefits are those which were formed for some purpose other than a purely political one[49] and are in the business of providing material benefits to their clientele (labor unions, professional societies) on a fee-for-service basis.[50]

Mass membership organizations representing the aged, which have experienced the largest sustained growth, tend to embody the assumptions of the rational actor model. The three largest organizations are the National Retired Teachers Association–American Association of Retired Persons (NRTA-AARP), the National Council of Senior Citizens (NCSC), and the National Association of Retired Federal Employees (NARFE). NRTA-AARP was originally formed to improve the material needs of the elderly through the private sector by securing insurance plans for its membership. While the organization participates in the political process, political functions have always been subordinate to its insurance-related activities. In addition to insurance coverage, NRTA-AARP offers other selective benefits including reduced prices on travel and drugs. This organization, whose membership mainly consists of retired professionals, has grown the fastest of any of the elderly groups and is one of the largest voluntary associations represented in Washington.[51]

NSCS was formed for a political purpose—the passage of Medicare. However, this highly successful group (250,000 members and a 250 percent growth rate from 1971 to 1974) has very close financial ties with organized labor, the primary function of which is economic as opposed to political. Most members of NSCS are former blue-collar workers who receive a host of selective benefits as a result of their membership. NARFE was also formed for a political reason—to support the passage of the Federal Employees Pension Act in the 1920s. Its major activity is lobbying the Congress for benefits for federal retirees. However, this seemingly political function is analogous to the primarily economic one assumed by unions in the private sector. The group has concentrated almost solely on bread-and-butter issues affecting the federal employee (labor-management relations) as opposed to broader political issues affecting the elderly. NARFE offers some selective benefits, but they are more modest than those available through NRTA-AARP and NCSC. This may account, in part, for the fact that while NARFE is among the top three age-based mass membership oranizations in terms of group size, it has the smallest membership of the three (150,000) and a much smaller growth rate (17 percent, 1971 to 1974).

All three of these age-based groups have characteristics that are crucial to organizing large numbers of senior citizens.[52] However, while some people see large organized groups of the elderly as a potent political force, we must be circumspect in translating group size into group power. There are a number of intervening variables such as resources, political skills, and group cohesion that influence a group's effectiveness.

Large groups can certainly gain the attention of elected political officials by referring to their numbers and their potential to influence electoral outcomes. However, the size and diversity of the group itself limits the kinds of demands that can be made and may also limit the proportion of total resources that can be devoted to purely political activities. Because NRTA-AARP and NCSC are such diverse groups, the range of political issues that can be addressed without damaging group support is limited to relatively noncontroversial ones. For example, in the early 1960s NRTA-AARP did not lobby for Medicare. In over 50 years of its existence NARFE has rarely, if ever, taken a stand on any issue other than incremental changes in retired employee benefits. NCSC has been active in a broader range of issues and has taken some positions that generate greater political conflict, such as support for Medicare and income tax reform. Support for these two issues is not surprising, given the values this group shares with organized labor. However, NCSC has never supported the radical kinds of policies that would be necessary to bring the 3.3 million poor aged above the poverty line. Nor has this group strongly embraced the special needs of the black poor, a group that by some estimates experiences twice the incidence of poverty of the white elderly.

A second consideration is the proportion of resources age-based mass-membership groups can devote to political activities. It may be hypothesized that mass-membership groups are handicapped by the need to channel resources away from political activity and toward organization maintenance, particularly the provision of selective benefits alluded to earlier. As previously stated, it is more rational for individuals to voluntarily join small rather than large organizations, because in small organization individuals are more likely to see a relationship between their individual contribution and their individual benefit. Furthermore, small groups can more effectively provide social incentives to participate in lieu of material ones. It is much harder to give and withhold nontangible rewards (prestige, respect, friendship, sense of belonging) in a mass-membership group.[53]

At the national level there are four trade associations, one professional society, and a confederation of social welfare agencies that are concerned with aging issues.[54] One of the newest national aging organizations consists of a group of professionals concerned with the special problems of the black aged. The trade associations include: the American Association of Homes for the Aged (about 1,000 affiliates), the American Nursing Home Association, the National Council of Health Care Services (consisting of commercial enterprises in the long-term care business), and the National Association of State Units on Aging (NASUA), which consists of administrators of agencies for the aging in each state. The professional society, the Gerontological Society, is composed of individuals, many in education, who are primarily interested in research and training. The National Council on Aging (NCOA) has 1,400 affiliates, the majority of which consist of public and private health, social work, and community action agencies. Its primary role is that of technical consultant to organizations that deal with problems of the elderly. Finally, the National Caucus on the Black Aged includes about 150 black and white professionals who are concerned with giving greater priority to the minority elderly. This organization has lobbied for some fairly far-reaching changes that include replacing or correcting the deteriorated housing in which a majority of aged blacks live.[55]

Except for the National Caucus on the Black Aged, these organizations support distributive policies,[56] which involve some sort of subsidy or remedial action directed toward the needs or problems of a particular group. This type of policy is likely to be relatively noncontroversial. Political competition and conflict are low because: (1) the subsidy involves limited change; (2) the policy is designed to reduce the seriousness of a problem rather than eliminate it; and (3) due to the conditions described in 1 and 2, one group's gain is not perceived as another group's loss.

Groups like NCOA, NASUA, and the Gerontological Society focus on a particular type of distributive policy—middleman programs.[57] These organizational middlemen are primarily concerned with their status as vendors for the elderly. The trade associations, for example, are interested in the conditions surrounding the payment of funds to the aged, as these conditions may enhance or impede the effectiveness of their organizations. Similarly, a major concern of the Gerontological Society is obtaining its fair share of the appropriations available for research on aging problems. Middleman organizations do not tend to evaluate policies according to their impacts on the aged;

what is most important is the relationship between the nature of a program and the well-being of the organization. While the aforementioned groups engage in political activities, with the exception of the National Caucus on the Black Aged political functions are secondary to their purposes. Like the mass-based groups, these organizations offer their membership a wide range of selective benefits.

Aging Organizations and the Policy Process

The policy process approach, which has received a great deal of emphasis in the general analysis of public policy,[58] is particularly useful in analyzing the influence of aging organizations on public policy. The process approach defines policy making as a series of discrete activities, all of which contribute to the overall direction and content of public policy. These policy activities include agenda setting (getting problems to government), policy formulation (developing policy alternatives), policy adoption (selecting a particular course of action), and implementation (carrying a particular course of action into effect). The role of aging organizations will be explored in each stage of the policy process, on the assumption that their degree and character of influence varies according to the type of activity being considered.

Agenda Setting

Group influence in agenda setting is highly dependent on access. Decision makers who act as gatekeepers to the formal government agenda are strongly influenced by the degree of legitimacy accorded various social groupings.[59] Since the New Deal, there has been a common perception that the government should legitimately be involved in some matters related to the aged. Perhaps more importantly, the group itself is accorded a certain degree of status and respect. While older Americans have suffered from discriminatory practices, as a group they have received considerably more deference than those that are poor, female, or nonwhite. Access for the aged has been institutionalized with the establishment of the Administration on Aging (AOA); the creation of several subcommittees in Congress to deal with problems of the aging, particularly the Senate Special Committee on Aging; and the designation of a counsellor to the president on aging during the last several administrations. Similar types of committees and agencies also have been created in state governments.

Policy Formulation

It is difficult to determine the influence of organizations for the elderly at the national level relative to the design of policy proposals. NCSC and NRTA-AARP produce position papers and policy statements on matters related to the aging. NARFE focuses only on recommendations related to sub-committee activity on retirement benefits. The kinds of proposals recommended by the national groups discussed thus far are likely to involve small changes within the existing policy framework, that is, distributive policies.

> The mass membership organizations—NCSC, NRTA-AARP, and NARFE —adopt policy positions and present testimony on income transfer programs favoring increases in the size of benefits; extension of eligibility for benefits to a greater number of persons; extension of the conditions and time periods for which benefits are due; and relaxation or elimination of the conditions that can make one eligible for benefits. Their attention is directed especially toward Social Security and Medicare, programs that ideologically are nurtured by the "social insurance" mythology. Comparatively little attention is given to Old Age Assistance and Medicaid, programs that transfer stigmata as well as purchasing power. And virtually no attention is given to portions of these programs—such as Title IV of the Social Security Act, making federal grant-in-aid funds available to state welfare agencies for social services to the aged—that do not concern direct income transfer.[60]

Mass membership groups have been slow to formulate the more controversial redistributive policies. Redistributive policies represent a conscious attempt by government to redirect the allocation of resources from one group in society to another.[61] For example, such policies may consciously attempt to shift resources from the young to the old or from the upper and middle classes to the elderly poor. Along these lines, the NCSC has been the most supportive of policies with a redistributive orientation (e.g., income tax reform).

There is a middle-range policy type on the continuum from small change and low conflict to large change and high controversy. It is regulatory in nature and designed to redirect or change behavior. Compared to proposals of a more distributive nature, regulatory proposals have received considerably less attention from national mass-based groups. The one proposal of a regulatory nature that has received a great deal of attention from NCSC and NRTA-AARP is mandatory retirement. It is unclear how active national organizations have been in the regulation of the nursing home industry, which primarily falls within the jurisdiction of state governments.[62]

The three policy types mentioned in connection with the activities of the age-based groups are outlined in Table 12.2 according to the amount of change the policy represents from the status quo and the amount of political controversy likely to be generated by each policy type. Examples of age-related policies are given for each category.[63]

It should also be noted that much of the initiative for policy formulation in general originates in the White House. In the Carter administration, for

Table 12.2: Policy Categories Applied to Policies Affecting the Elderly

Policy Category	Change from Status Quo	Extent of Political Conflict	Policy Examples
Distributive	Low	Low	Increase in Social Security benefits
			Research grants on aging
Regulative	Moderate	Moderate	Prohibition of job discrimination by age
			Nursing home regulation
Redistributive	High	High	Medicaid*
			Old Age Assistance

*Medicaid is considered to be more redistributive than Medicare, which was formulated explicitly for the elderly, because Medicaid is not tied conceptually to the notion of contributing to the cost of health care (self help) through the purchase of insurance. Medicaid, of course, benefits those among the elderly whom the law designates as poor or destitute.

example, the former president of NCSC was appointed as counsellor to the president on aging. However, there has been a great deal of skepticism as to how much input he would have in policy design. In the 1976 Carter campaign for the presidency, the seniors desk had the lowest budget and the smallest staff of any of the eleven desks established by the Democratic Presidential Campaign Committee.[64]

Policy Adoption

Separating policy formulation activities from those related to policy adoption is somewhat artificial since policies are often formulated with an eye toward what will pass the legislature. The diverse constituency of mass-membership groups often discourages lobbying for more controversial regulatory and redistributive policies. Also, since the primary function of many of these groups is providing special services to members, rather than engaging in political activity, they could not be expected to lobby for policies that would drastically reorder government priorities with respect to the aged.

Still another consideration is the formal and informal processes through which we adopt policies. Political analysts describe the process as one of multiple-majority building. Proposals must travel through a veritable obstacle course (particularly in the legislature) before they are adopted and become binding on the rest of society. Under these rules of the game, policies that represent low change and are relatively uncontroversial have the greatest chance of succeeding. Policies that represent more moderate change may have a greater acceptance rate if groups with common interests can present a united front.

Prospects for coalition building among the mass-membership aging groups are uncertain since these groups, particularly NCSC and NRTA-AARP, represent very different constituencies. Among all aging groups, NCSC stood alone in the fight for Medicare, and it has not received enthusiastic backing from groups like NRTA-AARP on the issue of tax reform. Still, in 1978 the senior citizens groups overcame their differences and successfully lobbied for the passage of an amendment to the Age Discrimination in Employment Act that limited mandatory retirement. Cooperation among the aging groups is also credited for extending the Older Americans Act, which in 1978 offered over $1 billion a year in services to the poor, more than double the amount allocated in 1974.[65] The perception of a politics of scarcity may forge a closer relationship among the senior citizens organizations. The same perception may also foster more organized opposition to the interests of elderly Americans. However, the probability of organized opposition is still highly dependent on the nature of the policy proposed. Distributive policies are likely to generate less opposition since one group's gain is not seen as meaning a loss to other groups.

Implementation

Aging groups exert an incredible amount of energy in influencing how money authorized by Congress will be spent by government agencies. The subgovernment phenomenon—so prevalent in American politics—characterizes the politics of aging in this regard. A subgovernment consists of a group of policy specialists who tend to dominate all phases of policy making in a particular policy area. Its members usually include officials from a government agency or bureau and representatives from one or more interest groups. Members of a congressional subcommittee may also be included in a subgovernment.[66]

Trade associations, professional groups, and even mass-membership groups lobby administrators in their role as middlemen for their share of appropriations. NASUA has traditionally had close ties with the Administration on Aging, while NCSC, NRTA-AARP, and NCOA have been the chief beneficiaries of aging programs administered by the Office of Economic Opportunity and the Department of Labor. The Gerontological Society's administrative allies are at the National Institutes of Health.[67] Therefore, rather than mounting a concerted effort toward developing a coordinated national program to benefit the elderly, many organizations prefer to create and maintain strong organizational ties with agencies responsible for approximately 134 programs for the elderly. Aging organizations and government agencies have a vested interest in maintaining the presently fragmented service programs for the aged. In the transportation area alone, eight federal agencies finance 31 programs for the elderly. One by-product of this complex system is that many of the programs are vastly underutilized by the intended recipients.[68] Also, it is extremely difficult to determine if a combination of the services available is adequate to meet the needs of older Americans, particularly the elderly poor.

The existence of numerous subgovernments, organized around specialized aging interests, promotes a policy cycle that continues to formulate distributive policies of an incremental and fragmented nature. Subgovernment participants are able to monopolize policy making in a given area, and they therefore have little incentive to propose policies that might prove controversial. Controversy would invite the attention of outside interests and disturb mutually rewarding relationships that have been established over time.[69]

Conclusions

The impact of older people on public policy can manifest itself in two spheres, the electoral arena and the formal governmental decision-making process. It has been argued that, although age has not proven to be a major cleavage in American politics in the past, the potential for more cohesive electoral behavior on the part of older Americans in the future may create greater cleavage. The rise of moral-cultural issues on the political agenda and the increasing proportion of governmental expenditures earmarked for the elderly may also stimulate age-related conflict. The demise of the traditional factors that have structured politics, such as party identification, may mean that future voters will respond to politics in a manner strongly related to immediate circumstances. Previous research on the relationship between aging and political behavior may need major modification in this new political context.

The major argument against age-related conflict is the political diversity of the nation's elderly. Campbell, for example, notes that "age groups will continue to remain as heterogeneous in economic, social, and geographical characteristics as they are now, and this heterogeneity will frustrate attempts to make common cause among people who resemble each other only in age."[70] And in spite of the growth of the older population, the elderly compose only 15 percent of the general electorate.

Threats to retirement incomes and benefits may be the crucial stimulating force necessary to override this social heterogeneity. Although "senior power" has been limited in our youth-oriented culture, another strategy for the aged would be to find pride and dignity in old age. For example, the increasing use of the term *senior citizen* is an overt attempt to create a positive self-image among older Americans. This process is not unlike that used by black groups in the 1960s. Perhaps the trend toward early retirement may lead to the "development of an aging identity that takes on meaning through the reinforcement of time and experience."[71]

While the future of older Americans in relation to the electoral process is highly unpredictable, the involvement of age-based interest groups in the policy-making process has become increasingly routinized in the past decade and will become more so in the future. There are a number of interest groups that have been successful in securing a share of public benefits. However, the difficulty of effective group organization, as well as a fragmented and decentralized policy-making process, limits the nature of demands that are likely to be made. Both mass-based groups and other age-related groups, such as trade associations and professional societies, see it in their best interest to limit conflict by pressing for small incremental changes within the existing policy framework that has been established for the aged. While it is possible for senior citizens organizations to form a powerful coalition with each other or with other groups, the set of motives, needs, and political constraints identified in this chapter render close cooperation on a continuing basis unlikely.

The portion of the federal budget devoted to the elderly has certainly increased over the years. However, these increases cannot be attributed solely to pressure group activity. Much of the increase in federal outlays has been caused by incremental changes in policies established years ago. Some of these increases are a result of Congress trying to make previously established policies viable in the face of rising inflation. While elderly organizations no doubt played a role in pressing for these changes, the changes do not reflect a move to bring about a radical redistribution of resources.

But as we enter the 1980s it is clear that it is an already established policy of American government to undertake responsibility for meeting the needs of older citizens. Though these needs are growing, and funding to service such needs is rapidly increasing, such a responsibility is unlikely to be abrogated or seriously modified in the future. In spite of periodic protestations that federal spending must be cut and that government redistribution of private resources must cease, government's involvement in the lives of older citizens is likely to further increase. Yet there is a good possibility that generational political conflict will never reach a level of high intensity even if age consciousness grows.

Historically, the American political system has demonstrated a remarkable ability to defuse questions that threaten to cause severe conflict. In spite of the great amount of change that has characterized American politics since the early 1960s, formal governmental institutions have changed little, and still "reward moderation and marginal change, and discourage deviant policies and comprehensive changes."[72] Programs that aid the elderly are unlikely to be eliminated or benefits greatly decreased. What is more likely is that many potentially controversial programs that benefit the aged will be altered legislatively in form to make them more politically acceptable. For example, Social Security tax increases during periods of high inflation are unlikely to be viewed with enthusiasm by the bulk of the electorate, and we think it quite likely that politicians will seek other methods to pay for Social Security benefits (since decreasing benefits would be dangerous politically as well). In the immediate future we are likely to see Social Security benefits at least partially funded from Treasury revenues rather than from direct contributions. Such action would greatly lessen potential generational conflict.

We have already pointed out how policy specialists, including age-related interest groups that influence decision making, are motivated by needs that have a conservative influence on the policy process. In addition, governmental institutions operate by rules (such as majority rule in both houses of Congress) that have a conserving effect on the context of public policy. Proponents of a particular course of action must anticipate the needs and priorities of large numbers of individuals whose support is necessary to win approval of a policy. The policy result is more likely to include something for everyone rather than a radical change that provides noticeable benefits for one group at the expense of others. In the next decade, for example, we are likely to see the adoption of a comprehensive national health insurance program in the United States. Current health programs aiding older Americans are likely to be integrated into this program. But the program will offer benefits to all Americans, and funding is likely to come largely from general tax revenues. Again we will find a situation in which a federal progam is redistributive in character but this character is largely obscured. And most Americans seem to be less concerned that they get the most benefits than that they get some benefits.

There will continue, of course, to be certain issues that bring generational conflicts to the forefront of politics. But over the long term the commitment to older Americans by American society is likely only to grow stronger.

Notes

1. See, for example, E. C. Ladd, Jr., and C. D. Hadley, *Transformations of the American Party System* (New York: Norton, 1975).

2. R. E. Dawson, *Public Opinion and Contemporary Disarray* (New York: Harper and Row, 1973).

3. For a discussion concerning the properties of issues amenable to realignment, see J. Sundquist, *Dynamics of the Party System* (Washington, D.C.: The Brookings Institution, 1973), pp. 279–298.

4. S. Roberts, "Greying of the Budget Puts U.S. in Bind," *Kansas City Times*, December 30, 1978.

5. R. H. Binstock, "Aging and the Future of American Politics," *The Annals of the American Academy of Political and Social Science* 415 (September 1974), p. 205.

6. Roberts, op. cit.

7. Ibid.

8. N. Cutler, "A Foundation for Research in 'Political Gerontology'," *The American Political Science Review* 80 (September 1977), p. 1013.

9. Ibid.

10. "Now the Revolt of the Old," *Time*, October 10, 1977, p. 18.

11. C. Pati and R. C. Jacobs, "Mandatory Retirement at 70: Separating Substance from Politics," *The Personnel Administrator* 24 (February 1979), p. 21.

12. Ibid.

13. N. Cutler, "Aging and Generations in Politics: The Conflict of Explanations and Inference," in A. R. Wilcox, ed., *Public Opinion and Political Attitudes* (New York: Wiley, 1974), p. 540.

14. N. D. Glenn, "Aging and Conservatism," *The Annals of the American Academy of Political and Social Science* 415 (September 1974), p. 178.

15. Good general sources on the subject include ibid., pp. 176–186, and Cutler, "A Foundaton for Research," particularly pp. 1018–1020.

16. Cutler, op. cit., p. 1019.

17. Ibid.

18. Ibid.

19. Glenn, op. cit., p. 180.

20. See, for example, L. Z. Breen, "The Aging Individual," in C. Tibbitts, ed., *Handbook of Social Gerontology* (Chicago: University of Chicago Press, 1960), pp. 145–162, and H. J. Heglin, "Problem Solving Set in Different Age Groups," *Journal of Gerontology* 11 (July 1956), pp. 310–316.

21. Glenn, op. cit. 181.

22. Ibid.

23. D. Ippolito, T. Walker, and K. Kolson, *Public Opinion and Responsible Democracy* (Englewood Cliffs, N.J.: Prentice-Hall., 1976), pp. 95–96.

24. M. W. Riley and A. Foner, *Aging and Society: An Inventory of Research Findings* 1 (New York: Russell Sage Foundation, 1968).

25. See, for example, R. Erikson and N. Luttbeg, *American Public Opinion: Its Origins, Content and Impact* (New York: Wiley, 1973), pp. 188–190, and Dawson, op. cit., pp. 126–127.

26. Dawson, op. cit.

27. S. M. Lipset and E. Raab, "The Election and the National Mood," *Commentary* 55 (January 1973), pp. 43–50.

28. P. E. Converse et al., "Continuity and Change in American Politics: Parties and Issues in the 1968 Election," *American Political Science Review* 73 (December 1969), pp. 1101–1105.

29. See, for example, N. Nie et al., *The Changing American Voter* (Cambridge, Mass.: Harvard University Press, 1976).

30. V. O. Key, Jr., *Public Opinion and American Democracy* (New York: Knopf, 1961), pp. 449–453, suggests that party identification is so powerful that identifiers change political attitudes and perceptions to fall in line with their chosen party. Other researchers have found that party identification and issue orientation were so clearly related that perhaps they should not be viewed as separate concepts. See William Shaffer, "Partisan Loyalty and the Perceptions of Party, Candidates, and Issues," *Western Political Quarterly* 25 (September 1972), pp. 424–434.

31. D. Jaros, *Socialization to Politics* (New York: Praeger, 1973), p. 43.

32. H. Holloway and J. George, *Public Opinion: Coalitions, Elites, and Masses* (New York: St. Martin's Press, 1979), p. 84.

33. The attitude change in all age groups also seems to be a function of demographic group affiliation. For example, Nie et al., op. cit., pp. 263–269, find that young Jews entering the electorate after 1960 were more conservative than their elders.

34. See, for example, L. Seagull, *Youth and Change in American Politics* (New York: New Viewpoints, 1977), pp. 71–93.

35. N. Nie et al., op. cit., pp. 47–73. See also P. Abramson, "Generational Change and the Decline of Party Identification in America: 1952–1974," *American Political Science Review* 70 (June 1976), pp. 469–478.

36. See, for example, R. Agger, M. Goldstein, and S. Pearl, "Political Cynicism: Measurement and Meaning," *Journal of Politics* 23 (August 1961), pp. 477–506, and R. Gilmour and R. Lamb, *Political Alienation in Contemporary America* (New York: St. Martin's Press, 1975), pp. 63–68. Other researchers have not found alienation to be a function of either life cycle or generation effects. See N. Cutler and V. Bengtson, "Age and Political Alienation: Maturation, Generation, and Period Effects," *The Annals of the American Academy of Political and Social Science* 415 (September 1974), pp. 160–175.

37. Gilmour and Lamb, op. cit., p. 64. Using data collected by the Survey Research Center at the University of Michigan in 1968, for example, the authors find over double the percentage of "extreme alienated" among those over 65 as those in the 18-to-34 age group (29 percent to 13 percent).

38. M. Hout and D. Knoke, "Change in Voting Turnout, 1952–1972," *Public Opinion Quarterly* 39 (Spring 1975), pp. 52–68.

39. L. W. Milbrath and M. L. Goel, *Political Participation*, 2d ed. (Chicago: Rand McNally, 1967), p. 114. According to the authors, age makes the biggest difference among the least educated persons; the best educated are likely to vote at all ages.

40. B. Neugarten, "Age Groups in American Society and the Rise of the Young-Old," *The Annals of the American Academy of Political and Social Science* 415 (1974), p. 197.

41. P. Ragan and W. J. Davis, "The Diversity of Older Voters," *Society* 15 (1978), p. 50.

42. See A. Holtzman, "Analysis of Old Age Politics in the United States," in C. B. Vedder, ed., *Gerontology: A Book of Readings* (Springfield, Ill.: Charles C. Thomas, 1963).

43. M. K. Carlie, "The Politics of Age: Interest Group or Social Movement?" *Gerontologist* 9 (1969), pp. 259–263.

44. R. H. Binstock, "Interest Group Liberalism and the Politics of Aging," *Gerontologist* 12 (1972), pp. 265–280.

45. A. M. Rose, "The Subculture of the Aging: A Framework for Research in Social Gerontology," in A. M. Rose and W. A. Peterson, eds., *Older People and Their Social World* (Philadelphia: F. A. Davis, 1965).

46. W. A. Anderson and N. Anderson, "The Politics of Age Exclusion: The Adults Only Movement in Arizona," *Gerontologist* 18 (1978), pp. 6–12.

47. M. Olson, Jr., *The Logic of Collective Action* (Cambridge, Mass.: Harvard University Press, 1965), Chapter 6.

48. Ibid., p. 63.

49. Ibid., Chapters 1 and 6.

50. To be most effective, some organizations must rely on coercion—for example, unions and the closed shop.

51. NRTA-AARP grew from one million members in 1969 to six million members in 1973. H. J. Pratt, "Old Age Associations in National Politics," *The Annals of the American Academy of Political and Social Science* 415 (1974), p. 112.

52. While the media has given quite a bit of attention to the Gray Panthers, it is a comparatively small group that is highly decentralized and locally based. It consists of both the elderly and younger persons who want to work together at the local level on issues they choose. The Gray Panthers was organized to perform purely political functions, and of all the aging groups, it is considered to be the most radical. While the group's consciousness-raising activities may be influential in getting aging issues on the agenda, it is not considered by most observers to be very influential in other stages of the policy process at the national level.

53. Olson, *The Logic of Collective Action*, Chapter 2.

54. Binstock, op. cit., pp. 268–271.

55. H. Jackson, "National Caucus on the Black Aged," *Aging and Human Development* 3 (1978), pp. 228–229.

56. T. J. Lowi, "American Business, Public Policy, Case-Studies, and Political Theory," *World Politics* 16 (1964), pp. 677–715.

57. Binstock, op. cit., pp. 268–271.

58. C. O. Jones, *An Introduction to the Study of Public Policy*, 2d ed., (North Scituate, Mass.: Duxbury, 1977), and J. E. Anderson, *Public Policy-Making* (New York: Praeger, 1975).

59. R. W. Cobb and C. D. Elder, *Participation in American Politics* (Baltimore, Md.: Johns Hopkins, 1975), pp. 92–93.

60. Binstock, op. cit., p. 272.

61. Lowi, op. cit., pp. 677–715.

62. The Gray Panthers have been very active in this policy area.

63. It should be noted that in practice it is often difficult to categorize policies using this typology. A policy may contain elements of one or more types. Or, as in the case of the federal income tax, the intent of the policy may be redistributive but the policy may be implemented in such a fashion as to be more distributive in nature (tax loopholes).

64. R. H. Binstock, "Federal Policy Toward the Aging—Its Inadequacies and Its Politics," *National Journal Reports* 10 (1978), pp. 1838-1845. For a discussion of attempts to formulate national policy at the grass roots level, see T. Hickey and C. T. Davies, "The White House Conference on Aging: An Exercise in Policy Formulation," *Aging and Human Development* 3 (1972), pp. 233-238.

65. L. E. Demkovich, "Senior Citizens Groups Put Past Differences Aside in the Hope of Improving the Plight of the Elderly," *National Journal Reports* 10 (1978), pp. 1726-1727.

66. For a more detailed description of the concept of subgovernment see J. L. Freeman, *The Political Process: Executive Bureau–Legislative Committee Relations* (Garden City, N.Y.: Doubleday, 1955).

67. Binstock, op. cit., pp. 273-277.

68. R. L. Stanford, "Services for the Elderly: A Catch-22," *National Journal Reports* 10 (October 1978), pp. 1718-1721.

69. S. Redford, *Democracy in the Administrative State* (New York: Oxford University Press, 1969), Chapter 4.

70. Angus Campbell, "Politics Through the Life Cycle," *The Gerontologist* 2 (1971), p. 117.

71. Binstock, "Aging and the Future of American Politics," p. 204.

72. R. Dahl, *Pluralist Democracy in the United States* (Chicago: Rand McNally and Co., 1967), p. 326.

13

The Ethnic Factor

Linna Funk Place

As the study of aging has progressed, scholars and service workers have increasingly acknowledged the diversity that characterizes the group of people termed "old." Since the 1960s considerable effort has been made to identify and examine various subgroups within the elderly population. Students being introduced to the field of gerontology are reminded that greater diversity exists within the group of people over 65 than between that group and the rest of the population. Some writers speak of the "young old" and the "old old"; and recently there has been considerable discussion of the differences between the "normal" elderly and the "frail" or "vulnerable" elderly. Other categorizations are based on residential-geographic location and the often dramatic differences in needs and service delivery for each type of setting. Socioeconomic differences among the aged serve to create another set of subgroups with markedly different ways of meeting needs—many older people are very poor, but at the other end of the continuum is a smaller group of elderly that can well afford a comfortable and sun-drenched retirement. Thus the attempt to disaggregate the elderly population has resulted in a number of schemes, each of which sheds further light on some aspect of the aging process. Obviously these categories are not mutually exclusive—an old person may be urban, poor, and frail. There is still another way of differentiating among the elderly, and that is on the basis of racial/ethnic identity.

Ethnicity and Aging: An Overview

A number of observers have insisted for many years that the way an individual ages is as much influenced by cultural heritage and tradition as it is by the more universal physiological processes. This is particularly significant in a pluralistic society such as ours. Eleven million Americans are foreign-born; of these, approximately one-third still prefer their native language.[1] As an early scholar of ethnic gerontology observed: "In America subcultures abound. And the corollary is that there is a variety of patterns of aging."[2] Social workers have long been aware of the difficulty that foreign birth can mean to an old person in this country, and the literature is filled with poignant—and occasionally humorous—examples of the clash of cultures. Yet culture is more pervasive and more profound an influence than diet, language, and clothing styles. Our cultural heritage shapes our expectations about life, about being old, about relationships with our family and friends. It guides our responses to pain and death; it provides content and purpose to our days. Thus, Bengtson argues:

> It should be obvious that any attempt to develop social policy for the aged which ignores the great range of cultural and social variation in the human experience runs the risk of mistakenly inferring universal and causal connections between the biological events of aging and the consequences of growing older in a pluralistic society such as America. Certainly there are biological imperatives in growing older. But what is truly remarkable to me is that these imperatives are handled in quite different ways by various cultural, socioeconomic and ethnic groups.[3]

In recognizing the importance of ethnic background to the aging experience, gerontologists join researchers and practitioners in a number of fields in which the "ethnic factor" has become an important one. While some speak of a "new ethnicity" and others simply acknowledge the ethnic pluralism that has always existed in American society, there has been renewed attention to the role that ethnic origin plays in such social phenomena as political behavior, residential patterns, health practices, and growing old. Earlier in this century, when interest in immigrant groups was high, many scholars sought to demonstrate that the process of assimilation to a common culture occurred with all groups within the society. Later evidence, however, suggested that the process was neither simple nor inevitable. Many groups seemed to maintain some degree of cohesion and cultural identity as expressed by certain traditions, folkways, and institutions. In some instances this has been the consequence of discrimination and prejudice, with the result that a group was isolated or held at a distance from mainstream society; in others, it was more of a deliberate decision to maintain at least some of the old ways; and in still others it was perhaps a combination of both factors. The result has been that members of ethnic groups have often experienced ethnicity both as a source of pride and identity and as a badge of minority status.[4]

Nonethnic observers have also been sensitive to both views. Thus, some stress the minority status of ethnic elderly and, in fact, refer to all such individuals as "minority elderly."[5] This approach tends to emphasize the poverty and exclusion from services (that is, economic issues) that are especially burdensome to some members of these groups. Other researchers, while still acknowledging the problems of ethnicity, point out that the ethnic community can provide solace and security for its elderly members. Both aspects of ethnicity have figured prominently in the literature and will be dealt with more fully later.

Before proceeding further, however, it is important to consider what the terms *ethnicity* and *ethnic group* mean and how they are currently being used, particularly in the study of aging. Glazer and Moynihan note that "ethnicity seems to be a new term,"[6] and Bell adds, "the term ethnicity is clearly a confusing one."[7] Despite the confusion, there is general agreement about certain key characteristics: a shared history, a sense of belonging or fellow-feeling on the part of members, and some distinctive customs, transmitted from older to younger generations, which provide a focus for group activity and identity. A number of writers have pointed out that although an individual is born into an ethnic group, there is, in modern life, some degree of choice as to how fully one will maintain membership.[8] The fact that ethnic groups survive in the modern world and, indeed, flourish suggests that they do serve important functions for their members. Ethnicity is first of all a source of personal identity and history for the individual. A man who considers himself an ethnic American summarizes these feelings eloquently:

> What is an ethnic group? It is a group with historical memory, real or imaginary. One belongs to an ethnic group in part involuntarily, part by choice. Given a grandparent or two, one chooses to shape one's consciousness by one history rather than another. Ethnic memory is not a set of events remembered, but rather a set of instincts, feelings, intimacies, expectations, patterns of emotion and behavior; a sense of reality; a set of stories for individuals—and for the people as a whole—to live out.[9]

Ethnic groups can serve another function within society—they can become the highly visible bases for organization and action toward specific goals. A group can often act more effectively than an individual in making claims upon government and service agencies. As such, the ethnic group will be especially important to its members, like the elderly, who have special need of the services and support of the larger society.[10]

A common theme throughout the writings on aging and ethnicity is the urgent need for more data and systematic research in the field. The lack of information and low level of comparability among studies that do exist is repeatedly stressed by authors who are in general agreement with the observation that "the relationship between age and ethnicity has, until recently, been neglected in gerontological research."[11] Gradually, as interest in demographic research developed in the late 1960s and early 1970s, scholars began to consider particular subgroups within the aging population, initially showing special interest in black and Spanish-American elderly, and later in Jews, Asian-Americans, and other ethnic communities.[12] In this respect, the development of ethnic gerontology reflects broader movements within American society at the time, as do similar trends in other academic disciplines.

Jackson, one of the best-known writers on black aging, has stressed throughout her work that not only lack of information but also incorrect views and stereotypes of the minority aged prevent real understanding of the relationship between ethnicity and aging, and hinder the development of humane social policy.[13] In recent years the body of information relevant to aging and ethnicity has increased considerably. What is still needed, however, is the analysis of a wide range of variables in order to determine when ethnic identity is significant, when age is significant, and what relationship exists between the two.

The significance of ethnicity has been considered from several perspectives. Much of the literature that is important to the study of aging and ethnicity has been influenced by two methodological traditions, one anthropological and the other sociological. Both focus considerable attention on the organization and behavior of groups of people, but the questions asked and the procedures employed are often quite different. Anthropological writings typically examine a group—for example, a total society, an ethnic enclave, or a subpopulation such as the elderly—in the context of the environment in which that group lives. Anthropological research considers the total range of activities and relationships in which an individual participates. This holistic perspective, argue anthropologists, ensures against the pitfalls of regarding the aged as somehow unconnected to the rest of society.[14] Sociological studies also acknowledge the importance of a wide variety of influences upon a person or group, but they assess the nature of such influences by identifying, measuring, and controlling for variables that are thought to explain a particular relationship or situation. Sociologists have developed increasingly rigorous and sophisticated techniques of analysis that make it possible to compare findings from a number of studies, to measure change over time, and to determine trends and generalizations. Thus, much of the research that is rooted in the sociological tradition falls under the heading of "ethnicity as variable." Rather than focusing on the ethnic group, these studies examine some other category of social stratification such as age, marital status, or residential location. Ethnicity then becomes one of a number of hypothesized variables; that is, the researcher will test to see what, if any, impact ethnicity has on the problem in question. By way of an introducton to the field, then, let us consider some relevant discussions in light of these two perspectives, and then turn to an examination of specific ethnic groups.

Anthropological and Sociological Perspectives

Two themes of particular importance to the study of aging emerge from the anthropological literature. Interestingly, both are expressed in terms of conflict: the first, the conflict between the established and the new, often stated as tradition versus modernization; and the second, the clash of differing value systems. The first is especially evident in cross-cultural studies, where comparisons, implied or stated directly, are made either between two or more societies in terms of their relative modernity, or between earlier and later stages of the same modernizing society. The second theme has provided a focus for examining ethnic groups within American society. In recent years, American anthropologists have evinced considerably more interest in the aged as a subject of inquiry and, at the same time, have turned their attention to American society and culture.

Much of the early anthropological literature documented remote and often preindustrial people, and the data on the aged was somewhat peripheral to the real purpose of the studies. Perhaps the best-known work of this type is Leo Simmons' *The Role of the Aged in Primitive Society*. Although dated and somewhat flawed methodologically, it remains a widely used work. It is a study of the status and treatment of the aged in seventy-one tribes located throughout the world. Attitudes toward and treatment of the aged were largely inferred from ethnographic reports, rather than determined from direct inquiry or observation. Simmons categorized the tribes in a hierarchy of increasing complexity. He produced five general conclusions that have had considerable influence on theoretical development in ethnic gerontology:

1. Attitudes toward old people vary widely, but in most traditional societies they are treated with respect as long as they perform some kind of needed function.
2. This function contributes to the ongoing activity of the society and is perceived by all age groups to be important.
3. Old people tend to fare worse in more complex societies.
4. Old women especially decline in status and function in more complex societies.
5. Most traditional societies make a distinction between useful old age and decrepitude; a person reaching this final stage is, in some way, often rejected by the society.[15]

Perhaps the greatest significance of Simmons' work was the support it seemed to give the view that modernization displaced and devalued the aged. Although he was dealing with premodern societies, Simmons' evidence clearly indicated that increasing complexity of social organization re-

sulted in lower status for the elderly. It is a theme that has recurred throughout the literature of aging and has had a special appeal for those interested in
the impact of ethnicity, for older ethnics are often perceived as being more
"traditional" than the larger American society of which they are a part.

Later research, employing participant-observer techniques, focused specifically on the elderly. Some, in the Simmons tradition, examined preindustrial and transitional peoples.[16] Generally, these works support Simmons'
conclusions, although later writers challenged as too simplistic the image of
all traditional societies being an ideal setting for the aged.[17] These studies
provide a basis for comparison between the Old World and immigrant ethnic groups in the United States. However, one must keep in mind that the
circumstances in a country today may be very different from those of the
period when large numbers of people were leaving for the United States.
The traditions that endured in the immigrant group may be changed from
those that survived in the "old country," and comparisons between the two
would thus be misleading. The cross-cultural studies tend to be quite general
and descriptive, with little historical perspective, and give an impression of a
homogeneous Irish, Russian, etc., elderly population. Cowgill and Holmes
organized a number of these studies of both traditional and modern societies
and sought to demonstrate the impact of modernization on the aged. Their
conclusions are that the status of old people generally declines with increasing modernity. They made a number of perceptive observations, and their
work marks an early effort at theoretical development in the study of culture
and aging, but it is limited by inadequate data and adherence to a Western
model of modernization that stresses rapid industrialization and urbanization.[18]

The particular values dominant within a society will influence how the old
are perceived by younger generations as well as how the aged view themselves. How is success defined? What are the approved attitudes toward
work, leisure, and family? There is, of course, enormous variety in the responses to these questions. In this country, as noted elsewhere in this volume, success is frequently defined in economic terms and a heavy emphasis
placed on competitiveness, achievement, and independence. What are the
implications of such a value system for those who are usually removed from
mainstream economic activity—namely the elderly? Clark and Anderson
considered the impact of dominant American values in their study of 1,200
men and women over age 60 who were divided into two groups representing
mentally well and psychiatrically hospitalized individuals. They examined
the ways these individuals adapted to growing old in terms of two measures
—morale and self-esteem. They concluded that in order to age successfully,
an individual actually had to make a value shift from the active, goal-
directed orientation of younger years to a more passive set of values charac-

terized by cooperation and harmoniousness with others and present-mindedness. The explanation for this imposed value shift lies in the fact that our society, unlike traditional societies, defines age in formal (i.e., reaching a specific age) rather than functional terms. There is, in other words, an abrupt and institutionalized break between society and the old person, and, since the aging individual is no longer able to participate directly in the productive life of earlier years, values appropriate to that life must be discarded.

> Those who survive best in their later years are simply those who have been able to . . . pick up, as workable substitutes, the alternative values which have been around all along: conservation instead of acquisition and exploitation; self-acceptance instead of continuous struggles for self-advancement; being rather than doing; congeniality, cooperation, love, and concern for others instead of control of others. These are the values the aged of this society have been forced to embrace.[19]

Such an adaptation is at best difficult and can be the cause of much stress in the individual. It is, suggested Anderson, actually a process of deculturation. "Within our society, the majority of the aged are in an anthropological sense 'cultureless.' Their lives are lived outside and apart from the viable body of tradition that constitutes the daily pattern of younger Americans."[20] The value clash that occurs, then, is both personal and generational.

In a more optimistic vein, Clark suggested that the ability of most old people to make the value shift successfully refutes earlier theories of personality development that stated that personality was fixed relatively early in life. On the contrary, it would appear that human beings continue to grow, change, and adapt throughout the life cycle and, that being the case, old age should be viewed as another stage of development, a time for further creative expression.[21] We might speculate further that most older Americans make the adaptation with relative ease because they expect and anticipate at least some of the changes.

A consideration of cultural values has several implications for understanding the relationship between aging and ethnicity. Clearly, the values that are dominant within a particular society will have direct bearing on attitudes held by and about the elderly. Value systems vary greatly across cultures, and there is strong evidence that the experience of growing old will vary accordingly. Clark and Anderson's findings tend to demonstrate support for the argument that modernization has negative consequences for the aged. Yet, there is evidence that in a country such as Japan—where modernization has also been rapid and all-encompassing, characterized by massive urbanization and industrialization—the changes affecting the elderly have been less shattering. To be sure, there have been strains and readjustments, but the values of Japanese society regarding the family, as well as the appropriate means of achieving success, have apparently been compatible with both the process of modernization and the maintenance of traditional attitudes toward the aged.[22] Although modernization represents an overwhelming social transformation, it nevertheless can be shaped by cultural variation.

The value clash that occurs as people grow old in this country in effect symbolizes the clash that often occurs between ethnic Americans and mainstream society. The transition to old age can be even more stressful for those who have altogether different expectations for the final years, based on their own cultural background. In an important study of work habits among industrial laborers, Gutman observed that most workers, both foreign- and native-born, came from premodern, preindustrial settings prior to World War I. These people had to be trained to certain work habits necessary to a smoothly efficient industrial economy—punctuality, regularity, and discipline. Although the inculcation of these new patterns was often disruptive to traditional practices, which flowed to very different rhythms, it did not completely destroy them. The relationship between traditional and modern ways was a dynamic one; traditional practices and customs continued to shape industrial developments.[23] What then do we mean by *traditional*? Usually the word is used to describe a setting that is a rural or tightly knit homogeneous community, one in which people share values and world views and have a strong sense of group cohesion. Members of such a community are not necessarily illiterate (the Jews of the East European shtetls prized learning and scholarship), but most communication is by word of mouth. Human relationships are organized according to one's age and sex and social position at birth rather than personal achievement. The schedules of life are determined more by the seasons and the agricultural cycle than by the clock. Technology is not advanced and there is not the specialization of labor as we know it; people tend to work in trade or agriculture, with some assuming the role of religious leader. Many of today's elderly were born during the period 1893 to 1919, the last era of massive infusion of people from premodern backgrounds into the American industrial economy. As such, they are products of a traditional world quite different from the one we know today.

Gerontologists have paid considerable attention to how the aged in general meet the changes and crises that confront them. Ethnic elderly also retire, are widowed, and suffer declines in health. How do they differ in their responses to these circumstances from nonethnic elderly? Research has demonstrated the variety of patterns of aging based on ethnic differences, and there is now a growing interest in interpreting the established questions and issues in gerontology in light of these differences. To date, the number of writings in the ethnicity-as-variable category that are directly relevant to ethnic gerontology is actually rather small.

An example of the kind of ethnic differences that occur is the considerable variation in the circumstances of widowhood. These differences stem from culturally influenced family organization and attitudes toward friendship and neighboring, as well as residence, economic status, and level of education. Generally, widowed ethnic elderly are more likely to live with adult offspring than are nonethnic elderly, and widowed females somewhat more likely to do so than widowed males. There are distinctions between ethnic groups as well. Individuals from strongly Catholic backgrounds are less likely to live alone than are Protestants and Jews, and Chevan and Korson concluded that "a traditional Catholic, [i.e., ethnic] background is thus protection against living alone during widowhood because familistic orientations appear strongest among these groups."[24]

Widowed mothers' involvement with their children also varies by ethnic group. Irish, Italian, and Polish widows are more likely than German and English women to rank the role of mother as the most important in their lives—a pattern that is consistent with a Catholic-Protestant breakdown. Lopata found a correlation between women who ranked the role of mother first and relatively frequent visits from children.[25] Even within an ethnic group, relations with children may vary according to which parent is involved. Irish men, for example, traditionally seek an egalitarian friendship with adult children, rather than the patriarchal relationship common to such groups as the Italians and the Poles.[26]

The isolation of widowhood may also be relieved by friendship, and again, cultural variation is evident. Blacks, Irish, and Scandinavians all place a special priority on friendships. Woehrer suggested this could be accounted for in part by the fact that Irish and black families tend to stress collateral relationships, in which a brother-sister type of friendship is the ideal, rather than the more usual "lineal" relationship in which authority and guidance flow from parent to child.[27] Catholic widows are less likely to have high levels of friendship than their Protestant counterparts, and Jewish women have a very low level of friendship activity, perhaps due to a "cultural orientation minimizing friendship."[28] As a woman grows older, she is increasingly likely to have only friends from the same nationality and religion.[29]

Change—much of it related to the forces of modernization and value conflicts discussed earlier—has affected the lives of the widowed. The ethnic aged tend to be concentrated in urban areas and the disintegration of the old ethnic neighborhoods has left the elderly in an especially vulnerable position. Younger generations have moved away, and cultural resources such as grocery stores, churches, and clubs have disappeared. As ethnic offspring move into higher social and economic levels, they are somewhat less inclined to maintain older relatives in the home and show greater willingness to use nonethnic alternatives for old age care.[30] There is some indication that improved socioeconomic status also means widowed women define their life roles in different ways than do women of lower classes for whom traditional ethnic and religious orientations remain significant.[31] The widowed (both men and women) born in this country of foreign-born parents are more likely to live alone than their foreign-born peers,[32] a trend that suggests a possible change in values associated with life in the new country. Widowhood, then, illustrates the great diversity caused by ethnic influences in the experience of growing old.

Gerontologists have only recently turned their attention to the study of ethnic aging, and the body of theory and research produced within the discipline is relatively small. Scholars have been aware of the importance of considering the full cultural context in which an individual grows old as well as the need to examine specific widely experienced aspects of aging in terms of ethnic identity. The differing emphases of these two approaches reflect the debate underlying most discussion in ethnic gerontology. Stated in simplest terms, the question is: Which has the greatest bearing on growing old— ethnic origins or the physiological imperatives of aging? There are those who argue that the consequences of growing old are so great that they obscure other kinds of status, such as ethnicity, class, socioeconomic status, and education, that have been important throughout life: "these other variables lose their normal relevance, swamped by the single factor of advanced age."[33] But the evidence seems to support a somewhat more balanced view. Certainly there are myriad influences affecting the life of an old person and ethnicity may be confounded with, for example, social class. Some physiological processes are universal and probably unaffected by ethnicity, but as one observer noted, "the larger the role played by learning and environmental factors, the greater the likelihood that ethnicity is a meaningful variable."[34] Several studies of multiethnic housing for the aged show that ethnic cohesion remains important in the formation of friendships and social activities. At the same time, residents are willing to cross ethnic boundaries to form mutual help networks and to participate in formally organized activities such as bus trips and a hot lunch program.[35] It would seem, then, that people are inclined to maintain the patterns of a lifetime, but also show great flexibility in meeting the demands of old age.

A variation of the ethnicity-or-old-age debate has come to be known as the double jeopardy hypothesis. The term, which dates from the mid-1960s, was originally used to describe the situation of elderly blacks but is now used in reference to all minority groups within the society. The question of the minority status of the ethnic elderly underlies much of the discussion, which revolves around two opposing views of ethnicity and aging: "The first perspective suggests that the minority aged suffer from a situation of double jeopardy, that is, the experience of both race *and* age discrimination combine to make their relative status more problematic than that of either the aged or racial minorities considered separately. The second perspective views *advancing age as a leveler* of racial inequalities that existed in mid-life."[36] Using data collected from black, Mexican-American, and Anglo residents of Los Angeles, Dowd and Bengtson proceeded to test the double jeopardy hypothesis in terms of income, self-assessed health, social interaction, and two measures of life satisfaction. Their findings were mixed, and did not completely support the concept of double jeopardy. Double jeopardy did exist for elderly blacks and Mexican-Americans on the variables of income and self-assessed health, but it was not proved with regard to social interaction, or, for black elderly, with regard to life satisfaction. The data seemed to give some support to the age-as-leveler view, for variation between ethnic groups on some measures declined with age.[37]

This overview of the present state of ethnic gerontology suggests that it is still in the early stages of development. Gerontologists continue to struggle with questions of methodology and theory. To date, the evidence has clearly demonstrated that there are differences in the way people grow old, and at least some of these differences can be associated with ethnic origins. What remain are the considerably more difficult tasks of determining under what circumstances ethnic heritage will be significant and attempting to account for reasons why differences occur. The first question is perhaps best answered by comparing different ethnic groups on important gerontological topics, while the second demands an understanding of the full cultural setting in which people grow old.

Some of the variation seems to be explainable in terms of a value clash, both generational and cultural. At other times the answer appears to be associated with the degree of modernization a society has achieved, but, as has been suggested, this conclusion can be oversimplified. Ours is an advanced, highly modernized society, but within it flourish a variety of groups of people who have responded in different ways, and with varying levels of success, to the demands of American life. By studying the aged in their cultural settings, we may arrive at insights not only into the aging process, but also into how cultural diversity continues. Hopefully, we will come to a better understanding of the circumstances that contribute to a successful and enjoyable old age—keeping in mind always that there will not be a single answer. Sensitivity to cultural differences can contribute to a broader understanding of aging in general, and will perhaps dictate a social policy that responds to diversity. Keeping in mind the importance of understanding the cultural context as well as the need to focus on specific, age-related issues, we turn to a consideration of the elderly in ethnic groups.

Ethnic Groups in American Society

A number of questions particularly relevant to an understanding of the ethnic elderly should guide our discussion. An important consideration is the values and consequent expectations and aspirations the group has espoused. Have these values been in conflict with dominant American values? If so, what changes have occurred and what adaptations have been made by the ethnic group, especially regarding family structure and attitudes toward the elderly? The role of the family is another vitally important criterion for assessing the circumstances of the aged. In an excellent review of ethnic families and the elderly, Woehrer suggested that ethnic family relationships should be considered in terms of the structure of the nuclear family; the interdependence between the related families of different generations as measured by proximity, visiting patterns, and mutual assistance; and finally, the family's relationship to the larger society.[38] We need also to be aware of any special institutions, besides the family itself, that are characteristic of the ethnic group, both those transplanted from the old country and those developed here as ethnic responses to the New World experience. Some of these institutions, such as the black church and the Jewish voluntary association, might be considered coping mechanisms that enable ethnic groups to deal with minority status.[39] These clubs, associations, and churches may have a special significance to the ethnic elderly and can help us understand their relationship both to their own group and to the larger society. Finally, we need to keep in mind those characteristics of social organization and behavior that were previously discussed, which contribute to the maintenance of the traditional ways that ethnic peoples brought with them.

Native Americans

Very little is known about the present circumstances of Native American elderly. The issues are extremely complex, for the Indian population is diversified by tribal affiliation, geographic location, and degree of assimilation into Anglo culture. The most traditional in values and family structure are generally those in the rural areas and on reservations. At the other end of the spectrum are highly acculturated urban individuals who maintain few of the old ways. Many Native Americans live well below the poverty level and experience chronic unemployment. Poor health and malnutrition are widespread and persistent, and American Indians have the lowest life expectancy —44 years—in this country.[40] The lives of many, especially those on the reservations, are further complicated by a maze of government regulations that often seem to inhibit rather than facilitate the development and use of services. The history of the American Indian in the past 100 years has been a disrupted and tragic one, as white society systematically attempted to stamp out tribal culture, at the same time keeping Indians at arm's length. Many of today's older Native Americans went through the government boarding schools—often spending years at a time away from their families.[41] One of these children was Jim Whitewolf, a Kiowa Apache born at the end of the nineteenth century. His life, unlike nearly any Indian's today, spanned both eras—the frontier and the reservation—and in that respect the culture conflict was perhaps even more severe. His experiences demonstrate how disruptive the boarding school years were. School undermined the old ways, but Jim never really understood or accepted the white world either—Santa Claus and scientific farming seemed equally meaningless. Jim spent much of his life culturally adrift, but found comfort in family and later in the Native American Church. Despite a strong sense of family obligation, Jim steadfastly refused to be a burden to his relatives in old age.[42]

Kinship obligations and respect for elders as embodiments of wisdom and special knowledge were important features of most tribes. They continue to be significant values, especially in those tribes that had relatively late contact with Europeans, such as the Eskimos, or that are geographically isolated, as is the case with the Pueblo Indians of the Southwest. Physical isolation does not necessarily prevent change, but it can make it possible to shape change according to cultural precept. Some tribes still designate special roles for the elderly, such as midwifery. Migration to the cities has meant that some reservations are occupied mainly by the old people left behind, but there is apparently still a high level of return visits.[43] Some observers report that older relatives continue to be included in the homes of adult children.[44] Although it is difficult to generalize, the impression is that many Native Americans still adhere to traditional kinship norms. What are desperately needed are the medical, dental, and legal services that will assist families in the care of their aged.

Native Americans have participated in the ethnic resurgence of the past 15 years, and the consequences may be positive for the elderly. There have been two dimensions to the movement, exhibiting both traditional and modern approaches to the solution of the problems. One is a revival of certain traditional tribal institutions and customs in which the elderly have often played a significant role; the other is a broadly based Indian activism including many tribes which, in its most political expression, is referred to as the "Red Power" movement. The latter has voiced many goals, not the least of which is an improved quality of life for all ages.

Black Americans

The black aged were the first to receive serious attention from gerontologists interested in cultural differences, but the information is still sparse. Much of the discussion has been clouded by controversy over the nature of black family life, the role of religion, and the impact of a life of poverty and discrimination. Recent studies have begun to dispel the myths and stereotypes that have prevailed, and in so doing have demonstrated the enormous variety that exists within the black population. There is often greater similarity between blacks and whites of the same socioeconomic status than between people of the same race who differ widely in socioeconomic background.[45] When looking at other ethnic groups, we must often make comparisons between the old country and life here in order to understand the shift from premodern to modern ways. Black people have a long history in this country, and while it is important to identify sources of African culture when speaking of black Americans, it is also necessary to consider another kind of immigration that occurred here—the move from rural to urban locales.

According to the 1970 Census, 65 percent of the black elderly lived in the South, although not all these were necessarily in rural areas. The black aged are generally poorer, die younger, and are more likely to be widowed than their white counterparts.[46] In keeping with the national trend, there are more older black women than men. Black women have often been in the work force at least part of their lives and are somewhat more likely than black men still to be working after age 65. The vast majority of blacks are Protestants. Both rural and urban blacks usually have a lower educational level than whites. Although black people have a shorter life expectancy than whites, an interesting phenomenon occurs in the mortality rates—those who live past age 68 are more likely than whites to live to a very old age.[47]

Much of the discussion of the black elderly has focused on the nature of the family and the role of women. Some have suggested that the disruptions of slavery and later urban poverty were so overwhelming that the traditional family was destroyed, to be replaced by an absent-male, female-dominated household. Other evidence, however, indicates that there is relatively little difference in marital status between older blacks and whites, although current marital patterns among younger blacks could result in racial differences in the future.[48] Those who challenge the image of a black matriarchy argue that the black woman became strong out of necessity, but the culture did not develop into a matriarchy.[49] Some of the differences that do exist are possibly due more to socioeconomic status than cultural tradition. A survey of Chicago widows, for example, uncovered resentment and bitterness toward men and marriage on the part of older black women. They tended to rank the role of wife lower, and shared fewer activities with their husbands, than white women. The black women were poor and all had been born in the South. Their origins left them unprepared either socially or culturally to meet the demands of urban life, and, like lower-class women generally, they tended to have marital relationships based on shared duties and reciprocal obligations rather than warm emotional attachments.[50]

Whatever the structural organization of the family, most observers agree that kinship obligations and extended-family relationships have been extremely important to black people. This is sometimes accounted for in terms of survival – the family has often been the only buffer between the individual and a harsh environment. Blacks are also inclined to include nonrelatives in a kin-like relationship that entails mutual support and assistance. The degree to which this occurs is in some question. A study in Los Angeles found that blacks had high levels of family interaction and relied less on friends and neighbors than did whites,[51] while a Kansas City survey found that blacks were consistently more likely to depend on friends and neighbors than were whites.[52] The Kansas City researchers concluded that their findings were possibly related to the effects of segregation and urban neighborhood cohesion.

The extended family has been especially important to the black elderly. Assistance between young and old flows in both directions. There is a long tradition of taking relatives into the household, although the pattern may be the reverse of other ethnic groups. Older black women frequently take minor relatives into their own homes.[53] Older people are often the center of family respect and care, and younger generations have been willing to make considerable sacrifices in order to ensure the well-being of older relatives.[54] Elderly black parents provide assistance to their children such as babysitting, and adult children in turn give financial aid, run errands, and help in times of crisis. While more rural than urban blacks may own their own homes, most black aged, like other ethnic elderly, apparently desire independent living arrangements, while at the same time hoping that some relatives will live close by.[55] The continuing segregation of urban life has meant that many black families maintain geographical proximity even when living in separate households. As with other groups, the number of older people living alone seems to be rising. In the past, older blacks often had an integral economic function in the family, but this has declined in recent years, a trend that may have a negative effect on attitudes toward the aged.[56]

The family has been the principal source of support to aged blacks, but other institutions have been important as well. The role of the church in the lives of black people has long been debated, some arguing that blacks are more religious than whites, others saying there is little difference in religiosity. Perhaps the real issue is not the level of spiritual commitment, but the importance of the church as a social institution. Understood in this way, the high level of participation by blacks in church and church-related activities can be viewed as a means of socializing and of coping with the white world. Particularly in rural areas, the church has often been the only social organization available to blacks.[57] In both rural and urban areas it has been a source of unity and group pride. Black people have vigorously organized themselves in recent years, and the elderly have also begun to make a claim on society. The Black Caucus is one result of those efforts and is described elsewhere.

Black elderly often express a higher level of morale than whites, a finding that puzzled observers who expected the hardships of discrimination and poverty to take their toll. Blacks have also shown themselves more willing to acknowledge their ages. Perhaps, speculated one writer, this is because older blacks "may well think of themselves as having lived through the worst of it and thereby enjoy an increased measure of personal satisfaction. Old age may be perceived as a kind of reward in itself."[58] Both the Kansas City and Los Angeles studies found little difference between blacks and whites in terms of morale, and both suggested that the commonly experienced problems of old age served to level differences between the two groups.[59] Perhaps a lifetime of struggle has indeed enabled the black person to meet old age with toughness and strength of character.

Spanish-Americans

Like the black aged, the Spanish-American population is diverse, not only in terms of socioeconomic status and residential location, but also on the basis of national origin. Thus, the Spanish-Americans in New York are predominantly Puerto Rican, while people of Mexican birth or ancestry are most heavily concentrated in the West and Southwest.* Nevertheless, the common ties of language, family structure, and Roman Catholicism allow some generalizations when speaking of Spanish-Americans.

Gerontologists have been particularly interested in Spanish-American family structure and the degree to which the family provides support to its aged members. Alvirez and Bean identified three characteristics of traditional Mexican-American family life that apply to other Spanish-Americans as well: the profound loyalties felt toward all family members, including those beyond the nuclear unit; the dominance of the male members; and the subordination of younger to older members, expressed in terms of respect and obligation.[60] An old man in rural New Mexico put the matter succinctly: "My wife says it will be a sad day when children don't hold up their fathers and grandfathers as the ones who have the last word."[61] These ideals have undergone modification, especially with migration to the cities, but there is still considerable support for the widely held assumption that the

---

*Differences in national origin, as well as ideology, are reflected in controversies over terminology. The terms *Chicano, Latino, Latin-American, Hispanic-American,* and *Spanish-American* have all been used in recent years. For purposes of this discussion, the term *Spanish-American* will be employed in a general sense to include all persons with a Spanish-speaking heritage.

family continues to play a vital role in the lives of elderly Spanish-Americans.

Traditional patterns of family organization and obligation remain stronger in the rural areas and the position of the elders is more clearly defined. Aged family members are often accorded special privileges and appear to have a high sense of self-worth as advisors and tradition-bearers to the young.[62]

> My stories: they are memories that I have accumulated, memories of a long life, and now I have use for them. The children listen so eagerly, and often I find that my son or my daughter-in-law will put aside whatever they are doing and sit with the children. It is a temptation: I carry on like a talkative priest. But later I say to myself: we are all here for God's purposes, and through me younger people can learn about what it was like in the past, and they can find out about their family. No one should want to look only to the future. If there are some people who don't care about the past, they are lost souls.[63]

The importance of the family to the Spanish-American is not limited to rural people, however; there is considerable evidence suggesting that levels of emotional support, visiting, and material assistance remain high even in urban areas. In both New York and Los Angeles, Spanish-American elderly have the highest frequency of contact with children in comparison with black and white aged. Cantor found that Spanish-American elderly in New York were somewhat less likely to continue to maintain their own homes and more likely to move in with family members. The New York survey also showed Spanish-Americans to have the highest level of mutual assistance between elderly parents and their children. Parents were actively and directly involved in their adult children's lives, giving advice, babysitting, and helping in times of crisis. Spanish-American parents were the least likely to give and the most likely to receive gifts of money from their children, a fact that may reflect their relatively greater poverty. Both Spanish-American and black children were more likely than their white counterparts to assist their parents in a variety of ways, including daily chores. Cantor concluded that this greater level of involvement between parents and children was due to the cultural tradition of family obligations and to the physical closeness and accessibility of Spanish-American and black parents to their children.[64] Urban geographic patterns thus serve to reinforce existing kin network systems.

Even in so modern a situation as big city transportation, a vital concern of the elderly, traditional roles continue to be significant. One study of transportation patterns among Los Angeles Mexican-American elderly found clear differences between men and women, which were explained in terms of culturally defined sex roles. Men proved to be considerably more self-reliant and independent than women, either driving themselves or taking the bus. When it was necessary to depend on others, men were more likely to seek nonfamilial assistance than were the women. Women also had poorer health and a greater fear of crime than did the men, and they were somewhat less likely to speak English.[65] A Mexican-American woman who remains at the center of an attentive family circle may experience little difficulty in moving about, but for a woman whose family support has weakened or vanished the situation may be one of double jeopardy. The problems of an older woman in an urban area are compounded by language handicaps and a set of culturally imposed expectations that are no longer valid.

We have already considered the effect that attitudes toward independence and dependence will have on the lives of the elderly. The issue has been closely linked to dominant American values, but it is important to other cultures as well. At the heart of the matter seems to be the question of who the culture decrees should assume the independent and dependent roles. Is there always some degree of tension between the two positions? Coles' portrait of traditional, rural New Mexicans, while acknowledging some changes, depicts a relatively serene ordering of the generations, with old age yielding gracefully to those younger: "we all stand on the shoulders of others."[66] But when traditional patterns are relocated to urban areas, stress often results and readjustments are needed. Mexican-American men who lose their independence because of poor health or loss of a driver's license may suffer greater social and psychological consequences than the traditionally more dependent women.[67] In this situation, individuals are acting according to traditionally prescribed patterns—for example, the dominant, self-reliant male—but the exigencies of modern life may dramatically alter those patterns. Clark and Mendelson also examined the Mexican-American community in Los Angeles, as personified by Señora Chavez, a woman who maintained a fairly traditional matriarchal relationship with her adult children. Señora Chavez did seem to have greater feelings of self-esteem and independence than the typical older Anglo, but her "pride, power and freedom" had unhealthy psychological consequences for her children, who remained in a rather dependent position.[68]

The predominant trends in Spanish-American family life seem to be in a different direction from those exemplified by Señora Chavez and her family. The strains imposed by many changes in lifestyle and family structure have left their mark on the elderly. The Spanish-American respondents in New York were much more likely to show symptoms of mental stress than white or black aged; the source of their concern was children and family. They also showed a lower level of life satisfaction than either white or black elderly.[69] Poverty, poor health, and changing family patterns all weigh heavily on the aged Spanish-American. It is difficult to predict what the long-range effect of improved socioeconomic status and lifestyle will be. Clearly the more visible trappings of ethnic life will give way over time. Yet, the Spanish-American family has proved to be an enormously vital and adaptive institution, and it is obvious that mutual assistance and support continue. Perhaps an interdependent relationship, rewarding to all parties, will become the ideal. The nature of the assistance may change, particularly as it becomes easier for adult children to pay for services rather than render them directly. But the sense of loyalty and obligation that motivates such assistance will probably continue to be a feature of Spanish-American life for some time to come.

Attitudes about independence and dependence have institutional as well as personal consequences. A number of researchers have observed that both rural and urban Spanish-American elderly feel that it is the responsibility of government to provide assistance to the aged. Spanish elderly in New York used Old Age Assistance and Medicare to a much greater degree than either the black or white informants; the differences were tied to culturally defined attitudes about charity and self-reliance.[70] Rural Mexican-Americans in the Southwest, although not well-informed about the types of government programs available to them, still feel that the government should provide extensive assistance.[71] These attitudes may in part be explained by an ancient Spanish custom, which dictated a clear set of obligations to the poor.[72] They may also be a consequence of absorbing American attitudes about "not being a bother" to family members, and a desire to continue to live independently.[73] Thus, traditional and modern values have converged to create a set of expectations about the right to receive assistance.

Mexican-Americans have expressed a basically negative view of the aging process. One analysis of responses to opinion items regarding characteristics of old age, both positive and negative, found considerable agreement among ethnic groups regarding negative aspects of aging but diversity concerning the positive potential of older individuals measured by questions such as "Older people can learn new things just as well as younger people can." Mexican-Americans were the least positive in their responses.[74] Some group differences were also revealed in response to the query, "What are the three things you like most about being the age you are?" Blacks and Mexican-Americans both mentioned good health and leisure time, while whites responded with good health, "travel and hobbies," a difference in language that probably reflects economic resources. Blacks mentioned independence and relationships with friends and neighbors, while Mexican-Americans' responses listed children and a good home life.[75]

Asked when a person is old, both rural and urban Spanish-Americans tend to set a relatively low age,[76] a response that may reflect a certain realism, since Spanish-Americans often retire relatively early and also die younger than blacks or whites. The tendency toward early retirement has been accounted for in both cultural and socioeconomic terms, revealing once again the often compounding effect of ethnicity and other factors in the life of an old person. Many Spanish-American men are engaged in lower-class manual labor, and physical decline means the end of employment.[77] At the same time, work has not traditionally had the same value in Spanish cultures that it has in those influenced by the Protestant ethic, and, at least in the more rural areas, one's worth as a person is not necessarily linked to productivity.[78]

The changes in family patterns have left some older Spanish-Americans isolated. Neither family nor government has fully met the needs of many Spanish-American elderly. Like other groups, such as the Italians and Poles, who place a high priority on family relationships, Spanish-Americans have a relatively low level of non-kin friendships and contact.[79] But older Spanish-Americans are demonstrating a willingness to organize and develop their own resources. In Los Angeles, for example, older Mexican-Americans are forming senior citizens clubs. These organizations are not traditional to Mexican-American society, and appear to be a modern response to urban life—a conscious effort on the part of members to meet their social and psychological needs.[80]

Asian-Americans

Asian-Americans are also a heterogeneous group, diversified by national origin as well as immigration history. There are substantial numbers of Chinese, Japanese, and Korean aged, and some Filipino and, more recently, Vietnamese aged residing in the United States. Oriental immigration continues; in addition to the Vietnamese, other national groups have come steadily to this country. The Chinese populaton alone increased from 237,000 in 1960 to 435,000 in 1970.[81] Like Spanish-Americans, Asians are probably undercounted in the U.S. Census. And, as with most ethnic elderly, there is relatively little research to draw upon. A considerable amount of the work that has been done, however, is by Oriental Americans who are able to apply special understanding and insight to their findings.

Differing immigration patterns have influenced the circumstances of the Asian elderly. There are, for example, more elderly Chinese males than females, in direct contrast to the national trend. This is due to the practice, beginning in the nineteenth century, of Chinese men coming alone to the New World with the often unfulfilled intention of either sending for a wife or returning to China. Japanese immigrants, on the other hand, tended to come in family groups or to send for Japanese brides, and traditional values of filial responsibility and loyalty had a somewhat better chance to take hold.[82] Both Chinese and Japanese Americans have stressed educational attainment and shown great willingness to sacrifice for younger generations. Since World War II especially, both groups have experienced marked upward mobility, with increasing numbers represented in the professions.

Many elderly Asian-Americans do not speak English and have maintained distinctive religious and dietary practices. They reside predominantly in urban areas, and the Chinese in particular have clustered in highly visible enclaves or "Chinatowns." The Japanese are located primarily on the West Coast. Their experiences in this country have not always been benign, for racial prejudice and discrimination have been a fact of life. Many Japanese, some of whom had been in this country for generations, underwent the shattering upheaval of the relocation camps during World War II, an experience that undermined long-held attitudes of respect toward elders.[83]

Respect for elders was central to the ancient value system of Oriental society and was institutionalized in elaborate rules of conduct governing virtually every aspect of life. Orientals have traditionally placed great emphasis on an authoritative family structure and obligations of young to old, child to parent. Independence from one's family and the search for self-fulfillment had no place in such a world. It was a system that was seriously challenged by life in the United States, where achievement and individualism were so important.[84] The changes were slow at first, for Asians maintained tightly knit groups for several generations—both from choice and because of hostile outside pressure. But as younger people attended universities, improved their economic status, and adopted American ways, the old patterns began to change.

It would appear, however, that change has been considerably slower than with some other ethnic groups. Predictably, people living in areas of ethnic concentration, such as Chinatown, remain the most traditional. Although there are examples of the aged suffering isolation and neglect, adult children for the most part still feel an enormous sense of responsibility—sometimes reinforced by guilt and group pressures—toward the elderly. Few are institutionalized. The reports vary on living arrangements. Some suggest that younger Asian-Americans generally prefer that their parents do not live with them, and sometimes the feeling is mutual, as documented in a recent study of Mandarin Chinese in Los Angeles.[85] Other reports argue that grandparents still routinely live with adult children, particularly if the older relative is widowed or "helpless."[86] The use of the word *helpless* is reminiscent of Leo Simmons and suggests again that societies continue to distinguish between competent and dependent old age. Still other observers suggest that respect and assistance are still given to elderly parents, but that traditional forms have changed in keeping with American patterns. So, for example, an aged Japanese parent is now more likely to reside with a daughter than with the first-born son, although the son will continue to give financial assistance.[87] The advantage of such live-in arrangements is that traditional Oriental patterns of age mixing can continue, with older family members helping in some child-rearing tasks.

Those older Asian-Americans who do live alone may remain in ethnic neighborhoods, residing in special quarters such as those provided by Chinese benevolent associations. In some cases they will benefit from community customs of charity and assistance to the elderly, such as free meals in an ethnic restaurant.[88] There is no question, however, that some older Asian-Americans are very poor and without family or friends. For them, the stereotype of "the Chinese (or Japanese, etc.) take care of their own" has been particularly onerous, for there is a decided lack of services and facilities designed with the elderly Oriental American in mind.[89] This has become an issue of importance with Asian-Americans who are trying to focus attention on the special needs of their older population. At the same time, however, there is some evidence that Asian-Americans, like the Spanish, are beginning to build on the sense of community that already exists in order to provide for old age. The Chinese have a long history of benevolent associations and clubs. In addition to these traditional organizations, which have not been fully successful in helping the elderly, some modern variants have appeared. The Chinese Retirement Association of America, organized by professionals, is one such effort that, although presently limited, may be an indication of increased efforts at self-organization on the part of the older Chinese.

White Ethnic Groups

Next to the Native Americans, perhaps the least studied group in ethnic gerontology is the "white ethnic." These are usually people of Southern and Eastern European origin: Poles, Slavs, Italians, Greeks, Spanish and Portuguese, and Russian Jews. Some scholars include the Irish as well. White ethnics are predominantly Roman Catholic, Eastern Orthodox, or Jewish in faith. Greeley estimated in the mid-1960s that half of American Catholic adults were first or second generation immigrants.[90] In general, white ethnics are part of the "new immigration" that began in the late nineteenth and early twentieth century. Although this immigration tapered off by the 1920s, there have been occasional new waves of immigrants throughout this century, such as the displaced persons of World War II.

In many respects, these are the hidden ethnics, and the question of how many individuals may properly be included is troublesome. At issue is not only the problem of identifying who is "ethnic," but also how many generations to include in the count. Is a fourth-generation Croatian still ethnic? Nine million Europeans have entered this country since World War II.[91]

The 1960 Census defined "foreign white stock" as immigrant or child of at least one immigrant and counted 33 million Americans in that category. Krikus, who does not include Northern and Western Europeans, suggests the number is close to 40 million, but he is apparently including third and fourth generation as well. Part of the answer is linked to people's self-perception. Thus, 75 million Americans "identified themselves" as ethnic: German (20 million), English (19.1), Irish (13.3), Spanish (9.2), Italian (7.2), Polish (4.0), or Russian (2.2)—mostly Jews.[92] Of course, the way such identification actually does or does not influence behavior is not revealed by such figures.

It is somewhat misleading to treat the white ethnics as a single group, but there are certain common threads of origin. The ancestors of today's white ethnic population were often rural and peasant people who placed a high value on family integrity and duty. Generally, the families were organized in a "lineal" structure—authority and direction descending from the father and mother to the offspring, a relationship that continued through adulthood.[93] The immigrants tended to settle in urban areas where they could find employment in the industries, and many of their descendants today are still employed in blue-collar jobs, although a large number have also moved into upper-middle-class and upper-class status. The harsh changes that accompanied immigration were often disruptive to family life, an experience that has been documented by sociologists and novelists alike. The strains between old ways and new—and consequently between generations—began early. The problems varied depending on the traditions involved. The Poles, for example, found it hard to enforce economic customs that dictated that wage-earning children should give their incomes to their parents for the general use of the family.[94] Yet many of the immigrant groups, bolstered by strong religious and social institutions, managed to establish close-knit enclaves where at least some of the traditions endured.

Ironically, some of those aspects of urban life most often deplored by social critics—high population density, lack of privacy—served to enhance certain traditional practices and to tighten the bonds between generations. But as younger people began to move out, and urban renewal challenged the old neighborhoods, many older ethnics found themselves isolated in the inner city, forming a substantial percentage of the often-mentioned urban elderly. When considering the problems these people face, it is sometimes difficult to determine what may be attributed to specifically ethnic needs and expectations. Lawton, for example, in his study of Jewish residents in a slum area, did not explain his findings in terms of ethnicity, but nevertheless acknowledged that the scarcity of specifically Jewish resources in the environment (synagogues, physicians) undoubtedly contributed to the low level of well-being experienced by the residents.[95]

Attitudes toward family living arrangements reveal some of the same ambivalence, on the part of both young and old, expressed by other ethnic
groups. A survey of working-class Polish and Italian families, groups that
have traditionally maintained close-knit, intense family relationships, indicated both adherence to ethnic ties and certain breaks with tradition.
Nearly half the group of adult offspring said they preferred keeping an elderly widowed relative in a family home, whatever the physical condition of
the older person. Respondents accepted the fact that institutionalization
might be necessary, but ethnic affiliation was an important factor. A large
majority of the respondents indicated a preference for an old age home that
was staffed by people of the same ethnic group, and said that they would
want the institutional sponsor to be either the Catholic church or an ethnic
organization, rather than state or national government or a private agency.
There were some interesting parallels between Spanish- and Asian-American
families in terms of socioeconomic differences. Respondents with high incomes and more education preferred independent living for elderly relatives,
while those with less education and income preferred residence with a family
member. Generation of immigration was also a factor, sometimes in surprising ways. Predictably, first-generation Americans were most likely to prefer
living arrangements with the family, second generation less so, and third
generation the least. However, the pattern was reversed for the case of a bed-
ridden relative. The survey also showed that first-generation Americans
were more willing to resort to "outside" (nonethnic) resources and facilities
than were the second and third generation, a finding also comparable to
studies of Chinese and Mexican elderly.[96] Polish old people, undoubtedly
expressing sentiments felt by other ethnic elderly, were both distressed by
lack of attention from their children and pleased by the opportunity to
demonstrate independence and self-sufficiency in old age.[97]

Certain cultural values and expectations persist, sometimes causing problems to white ethnic families. Social service agencies have found that the
Eastern European Jews' norm of an emotionally aloof father and a warmer,
more expressive mother still prevails, and may be the basis for unhappy relations within a family.[98] On the other hand, the stereotyped image of the
"Jewish mother" is not fully supported; several studies suggest that Jewish
women tend to give first priority to their relationships with their husbands,
and at the same time do not have a wide circle of friends. Thus, widowhood
for these women, especially those in the inner city, may bring isolation and
loneliness.

Retirement is difficult for many older people, but it can bring special problems to ethnic men who have never been truly integrated into the community. Ethnicity was at least partially a factor, in this case a negative one, in

the lives of Polish and Hungarian steelworkers who experienced isolation and a loss of self-worth upon retirement. These men had continued to speak their native languages through their working lives, and their sense of manhood had been intimately linked to the hard physical labor of the mills—a perception that is in part culturally influenced. Language difficulties, compounded by poor health, took a heavy toll in their later years.[99]

Some white ethnic elderly have been especially active in voluntary associations, an involvement that may be related to a lower level of family interaction. A study of Nebraska white ethnics found that older people were more likely than younger informants to state that their ethnic origins were very important. Those individuals who stated that ethnic identity was important to them also had the highest rate of voluntary-association membership.[100] Organizations such as these bring together people of like background who seek the opportunity to express themselves in familiar ways in the company of others who know and understand. For some it is the last expression of a life no longer shared by younger generations. That is the case with a group of elderly Jews on the West Coast who participate in their senior citizens community center with a determination born of long struggle. These people are survivors—survivors of the persecutions in Eastern Europe and of an often difficult life in the big cities of this country. In their later years they sought the warmer climate of the seashore. Now, in isolation from their families, they have reestablished the rich traditions they knew in childhood, traditions that provide a sanctuary and have become a means of adapting to the contingencies of old age. They flourish in part because of the isolation from family and friends, and in part, ironically, because the circumstances of old age are not altogether dissimilar from the demanding life in the European villages long ago.[101] For these people, as for the club members in Nebraska, ethnicity is a rich resource, a link to an identity that can never be completely discarded.

Conclusions

"She wears old age like a bunch of fresh-cut flowers."[102] With these words an old man in the mountains of New Mexico lovingly described his wife. For them, old age was an achievement, the suitable reward for long and well-lived years. But, we can argue, that's in the mountains; in the cities of modern America old age presents a very different picture. Yet, when we consider the lives of the ethnic elderly we can see, without indulging in romanticism, that old age is not necessarily disconnected from family and past experience. The bonds of cultural continuity endure through generations and across oceans.

There is something paradoxical about seeking uniformities among the experiences of the ethnic elderly, for to recognize ethnicity as an important factor is to recognize diversity. Indeed, the rhetoric of the various groups is strikingly similar in their insistence that diversity *within* the group be acknowledged as well. And they further remind us that the elderly will be helped
only when outsiders abandon old stereotypes, particularly ones that assert
that the Chinese, or Mexicans, or Italians, or whoever "take care of their
own."

In spite of that caution, however, it is clear that the family remains the primary source of support and assistance for many ethnic elderly. As with the
ethnic group itself, so with the ethnic family; it has proved to be a remark-
ably adaptable, resilient structure, able to make the changes and modifications necessary to survival. There has been a dynamic and flexible relationship between young and old. The aged have not generally been rigid an-
tiquarians encrusted with outmoded ways, nor have their offspring been
uniformly rejecting and self-serving. We have noted several cases in which
older parents seemed more willing to live alone than their children were to
have them remain apart. There is some indication that improved socioeconomic status results in a somewhat different kind of relationship between
parents and adult children, but this does not necessarily mean isolation and
loneliness for the aged.

As discussions elsewhere in this book have indicated, the bleak predictions
that modernization inevitably leads to the demise of the family have proved
unfounded. In fact, there is increasing evidence that the nuclear family as we
know it has been the norm in many societies for generations. Modernization
is often discussed in terms of economics and production, and viewed from this
perspective, it would appear that the role of the aged has declined. But modernization has been a considerably broader phenomenon than merely an accelerated economy. As societies modernized, the function of the family unit
changed, but the structure remained much the same. Thus, in traditional
societies the family performed a wide variety of functions—educational,
religious, and economic. Today, those functions have been assigned to other
institutions in the society, and the family now is principally a source of affection and emotional support—a refuge. Old people do not now perform
specialized economic roles as in premodern societies, but the family is no
longer a full-scale economic unit encompassing all levels of production. As the
functions of the family changed, so did the kinds of rewards it could offer.

Modernization did change one of the principal features of traditional societies—physical proximity. If relatives did not necessarily live together in
their native villages, they often lived close by. To some extent, the urban ethnic
neighborhoods of the late nineteenth and early twentieth centuries in this

country reconstructed village life and enabled the ethnic group as well as individual families to remain cohesive. Those neighborhoods are changing rapidly, often with distressing consequences to the elderly; but in their place, something of an "electronic neighborhood" appears to form—one in which family relationships are maintained through telephone and rapid transit. In many of the ethnic groups we considered, the level of contact between generations remains high, but the nature of those contacts has changed. Perhaps certain customs and traditions will fade as a result; others might be intensified. Meals, for example, have always been a way to gather families together, and certain traditional holidays and festivals along with special foods might become increasingly important.

Immigration is primarily an experience of the young; grandparents do not often accompany the travellers. New arrivals to this country had to reconstruct the traditions of the homeland without older role models present. The immigration experience itself was an adventure, a positive decision about one's future, and one of the values that became nearly universal to all ethnic groups was that of independence. Even when family obligations remained strong, so too did the desire to be independent and self-reliant. Thus, in every group we considered, old people expressed their desires not to be a burden, to be independent. And in every group, that independence was given up only when frailty or incompetence took over.

Ethnic identity apparently becomes more important with increasing age. Whether that is a cohort effect or genuinely an aspect of social aging is yet to be resolved. Human beings seek order, meaning, and definition in their lives, and companions to share those meanings. Some of the more obvious signs of ethnicity—the ways of the immigrant—have vanished, but the endurance of the ethnic group itself suggests strongly that certain traditions and structures continue to provide support and assurance to its members. Within that structure old people may or may not have culturally defined roles as the tradition-bearers to the young, but they will continue to seek shared understandings with those their own age. The ethnic groups all have old age associations. These are generally social in nature, their purpose being to enrich the lives of members and provide the kind of support perhaps otherwise lacking. While some have traditional origins, such organizations are in many ways distinctly modern phenomena—the consequence of a society in which people tend to associate primarily with those of the same age. But what is also significant is the fact that they are organizing along ethnic lines. Thus it is the Chinese Retirement Association, the Mexican Senior Citizens Club, the Jewish Community Center. The most successful seem to be those in which traditional practices are still relevant—where ethnicity becomes a resource for the aged.

Notes

1. Donald V. Fandetti and Donald E. Gelfand, "Care of the Aged: Attitudes of White Ethnic Families," *The Gerontologist* 16 (1976), p. 544.

2. Donald P. Kent, "The Elderly in Minority Groups: Variant Patterns of Aging," *The Gerontologist* 11 (1971), p. 26.

3. Vern L. Bengtson, "Ethnicity and Aging: Problems and Issues in Current Social Science Inquiry," in *Ethnicity and Aging*, edited by Donald E. Gelfand and A. J. Kutzik (New York: Springer, 1979).

4. Michael Novak, "Probing the New Ethnicity," in *White Ethnics: Their Life in Working Class America*, edited by Joseph Ryan (Englewood Cliffs, N.J.: Prentice-Hall, 1974), pp. 158–167; Nathan Glazer and Daniel P. Moynihan, *Beyond the Melting Pot* (Cambridge, Mass.: MIT Press, 1970); Nathan Glazer and Daniel P. Moynihan, editors, "Introduction," *Ethnicity: Theory and Experience* (Cambridge, Mass.: Harvard University Press, 1975), pp. 1–26; Milton Gordon, *Assimilation in American Life: The Role of Race, Religion and National Origins* (New York: Oxford University Press, 1964); R. A. Schermerhorn, *Comparative Ethnic Relations: A Framework for Theory and Research* (New York: Random House, 1970).

5. See, for example, *The Gerontologist* 11 (1971), a special issue devoted to the elderly in minority groups.

6. Glazer and Moynihan, *Ethnicity*, p. 1.

7. Daniel Bell, "Ethnicity and Social Change," in Glazer and Moynihan, *Ethnicity*, p. 156.

8. Ibid., p. 153; Talcott Parsons, "Some Theoretical Considerations on the Nature and Trends of Change of Ethnicity," in Glazer and Moynihan, *Ethnicity*, p. 57.

9. Michael Novak, *The Rise of the Unmeltable Ethnics* (New York: Macmillan, 1971–1972), pp. 47–48.

10. Bell, pp. 169–171.

11. Danny R. Hoyt and Nicholas Babchuk, "Ethnicity and the Voluntary Associations of the Aged" (paper presented at the Society for the Study of Social Problems meetings, September 1978), p. 1.

12. Bill Bell, "The Minority Elderly," in *Contemporary Social Gerontology: Significant Developments in the Field of Aging*, edited by Bill Bell (Springfield, Ill.: Charles C. Thomas, 1976), p. 316.

13. Jacquelyne Johnson Jackson, "Aged Negroes: Their Cultural Departures From Statistical Stereotypes and Rural-Urban Differences," *The Gerontologist* 10 (1970), pp. 140–145.

14. Jennie Keith, "The Ethnography of Old Age," *Anthropological Quarterly* 52 (1979), p. 1.

15. Leo Simmons, *The Role of the Aged in Primitive Society* (New Haven, Conn.: Yale University Press, 1945).

16. Irwin Press and Mike McCool, "Social Structure and Status of the Aged: Toward Some Valid Cross-Cultural Generalizations," *Aging and Human Development* 3 (1972), pp. 297–306; Nina Nahemow and Bert N. Adams, "Old Age Among the Baganda: Continuity and Change," in *Late Life: Communities and Environmental Policy*, edited by Jaber F. Gubrium (Springfield, Ill.: Charles Thomas, 1974), pp. 147–

166; Austin J. Shelton, "The Aged and Eldership Among the Igbo," in *Aging and Modernization*, edited by Donald O. Cowgill and Lowell D. Holmes (New York: Appleton-Century-Crofts, 1972), pp. 31–49; Donald O. Cowgill, "The Social Life of the Aging in Thailand," *The Gerontologist* 8 (1968), pp. 159–163; Charles Edward Fuller, "Aging Among South African Bantu," in Cowgill and Holmes, *Aging and Modernization*, pp. 51–72.

17. See, for example, Malcolm Arth, "Ideals and Behavior: A Comment on Ibo Respect Patterns," *The Gerontologist* 8 (1968), pp. 242–244.

18. Cowgill and Holmes, *Aging and Modernization*.

19. Margaret Clark and Barbara G. Anderson, *Culture and Aging: An Anthropological Study of Older Americans* (Springfield, Ill.: Charles C. Thomas, 1967), p. 429; see also Margaret Clark, "The Anthropology of Aging: A New Area for Studies of Culture and Personality," *The Gerontologist* 7 (1967), pp. 55–64, and "Cultural Values and Dependency in Later Life," in Cowgill and Holmes, *Aging and Modernization*, pp. 263–274.

20. Barbara G. Anderson, "The Process of Deculturation—Its Dynamics Among United States Aged," *Anthropological Quarterly* 45 (1972), p. 211.

21. Clark, "The Anthropology of Aging."

22. Erdman Palmore, *The Honorable Elders* (Durham, N.C.: Duke University Press, 1975); S. N. Eisenstadt, "Transformation of Social, Political, and Cultural Orders in Modernization," in *Comparative Perspectives on Social Change*, edited by S. N. Eisenstadt (Boston: Little, Brown, 1968), pp. 264–269. See also Lowell D. Holmes, "The Role and Status of the Aged in a Changing Samoa," in Cowgill and Holmes, *Aging and Modernization*, pp. 73–101, and Andrei Simić, "Aging in the United States and Yugoslavia: Contrasting Models of Intergenerational Relationships," *Anthropological Quarterly* 50 (1977), pp. 53–64.

23. Herbert Gutman, "Work, Culture and Society in Industrializing America," *American Historical Review* 78 (1973), pp. 531–587.

24. Albert Chevan and J. Henry Korson, "The Widowed Who Live Alone: An Examination of Social and Demographic Factors," *Social Forces* 51 (1972), p. 50; see also Charles H. Mindel and Robert W. Habenstein, editors, *Ethnic Families in America: Patterns and Variations* (New York: Elsevier, 1976).

25. Helena Z. Lopata, *Widowhood in an American City* (Cambridge, Mass.: Schenkman Publishing, 1973), pp. 143, 135.

26. Carol Woehrer, "Cultural Pluralism in American Families: The Influence of Ethnicity on Social Aspects of Aging," *The Family Coordinator* 27 (1978), pp. 331, 334.

27. Ibid., p. 331.

28. Lopata, p. 209.

29. Ibid., p. 186.

30. Fandetti and Gelfand, p. 546.

31. Lopata, pp. 79–80.

32. Chevan and Korson, p. 50.

33. Anderson, p. 213.

34. Richard A. Kalish, "A Gerontological Look at Ethnicity, Human Capacities, and Individual Adjustment," *The Gerontologist* 11 (1971), p. 82.

35. Edward Wellin and Eunice Boyer, "Adjustments of Black and White Elderly to

the Same Adaptive Niche," pp. 39–48, and Randy Frances Kandel and Marion Heider, "Friendship and Factionalism in a Tri-Ethnic Housing Complex for the Elderly in North Miami," pp. 49–60, both in *Anthropological Quarterly* 52 (1979).

36. James J. Dowd and Vern L. Bengtson, "Aging in Minority Populations: An Examination of the Double Jeopardy Hypothesis," *Journal of Gerontology* 33 (1978), p. 427.

37. Ibid., pp. 430–434.

38. Woehrer, p. 330.

39. Joan Moore, "Situational Factors Affecting Minority Aging," *The Gerontologist* 11 (1971), p. 89.

40. Willie R. Jeffries, "Our Aged Indians," in *Triple Jeopardy: Myth or Reality?* (Washington, D.C.: National Council on Aging, 1972), p. 9.

41. Ibid., p. 8.

42. Charles S. Brant, editor, *Jim Whitewolf: The Life of a Kiowa Apache Indian* (New York: Dover, 1969).

43. John A. Price, "North American Indian Families," in Mindel and Habenstein, *Ethnic Families*, pp. 256, 268.

44. Jeffries, p. 10.

45. Jackson, p. 141; Jacquelyne J. Jackson and Bertram E. Walls, "Myths and Realities About Aged Blacks," in *Readings in Gerontology*, edited by Mollie K. Brown (St. Louis: C. V. Mosby, 1978), pp. 95–113, and Gordon F. Streib, "Social Stratification and Aging," in *Handbook of Aging and the Social Sciences*, edited by Robert H. Binstock and Ethel Shanas (New York: Van Nostrand Reinhold, 1976), p. 175. (In 1970, 50.2 percent of black elderly were poor, in contrast to the overall national average of 17.9 percent; 41.6 percent of black households headed by an individual over age 65 were poor, in contrast to the national figure of 16.4 percent. Philip M. Hauser, "Aging and World-Wide Population Change," in Binstock and Shanas, *Handbook of Aging*, p. 83.)

46. Streib, p. 174.

47. Jackson, "Aged Negroes," p. 141.

48. Ibid.

49. Lopata, pp. 80–87.

50. Robert Staples, "The Black American Family," in Mindel and Habenstein, *Ethnic Families*, p. 229.

51. Dowd and Bengtson, pp. 432–433.

52. Donna E. Schafer and Robert Wiseman, "Racial Differences in the Support Networks of Older People" (paper presented at the thirty-first annual meeting of the Gerontological Society, Dallas, 1978).

53. Staples, p. 228.

54. Marvin B. Sussman, "The Family Life of Old People," in Binstock and Shanas, *Handbook of Aging*, p. 226. For a description of an older black who functioned as tradition-bearer and role model to her family, see Kathryn L. Morgan, "Caddy Buffers: Legends of a Middle-Class Negro Family in Philadelphia," *Keystone Folklore Quarterly* 11 (1966), pp. 67–88.

55. Jacquelyne J. Jackson, "Aged Blacks: A Potpourri in the Direction of the Reduction of Inequities," in *Growing Old in America*, edited by Beth B. Hess (New Brunswick, N.J.: Transaction Books, 1976), p. 403.

56. Jackson, "Aged Negroes," p. 141.

57. Stanley H. Smith, "The Older Rural Negro," in *Older Rural Americans*, edited by E. Grant Youmans (Lexington: University of Kentucky Press, 1978), p. 279.

58. Mark Messer, "Race Differences in Selected Attitudinal Dimensions of the Elderly," *The Gerontologist* 8 (1978), p. 248.

59. Forrest J. Berghorn et al., *The Urban Elderly: A Study of Life Satisfaction* (Montclair, N.J.: Allanheld, Osmun, 1978), p. 128; Dowd and Bengtson, p. 431; see also Marjorie Cantor, "Effect of Ethnicity on Life Styles of the Inner-City Elderly," in *Community Planning for an Aging Society*, edited by M. Powell Lawton, Robert J. Newcomer, and Thomas O. Byerts (Stroudsburg, Pa.: Dowden, Hutchinson and Ross, 1976), pp. 56–57.

60. David Alvirez and Frank Bean, "The Mexican-American Family," in Mindel and Habenstein, *Ethnic Families*, p. 276.

61. Robert Coles, *The Old Ones of New Mexico* (Garden City, N.Y.: Anchor Press/ Doubleday, 1976), p. 68.

62. Ibid.; Olen E. Leonard, "The Older Rural Spanish-Speaking People of the Southwest," in Youmans, *Older Rural Americans*, pp. 239–261; Ben Crouch, "Age and Institutional Support: Perceptions of Older Mexican-Americans," *Journal of Gerontology* 27 (1972), pp. 524–529; Robert Staples, "The Mexican-American Family: Its Modification Over Time and Space," *Phylon* (1971), pp. 179–192.

63. Coles, p. 69.

64. Cantor, pp. 51–55; Dowd and Bengtson, p. 432.

65. Deborah Newquist and Fernando Torres-Gil, "Transportation and the Older Mexican-American: Sex Differences in Mobility Patterns and Problems," Report of the University of Southern California Social and Cultural Contexts of Aging Research Project, Andrus Gerontology Center, n.d. (late 1970s), pp. 7, 9.

66. Coles, p. 75.

67. Newquist and Torres-Gil, p. 12.

68. Margaret Clark and Monique Mendelson, "Mexican-American Aged in San Francisco: A Case Description," *The Gerontologist* 9 (1969), p. 94.

69. Dowd and Bengtson, p. 431.

70. Cantor, p. 49.

71. Crouch, p. 339.

72. Leonard, p. 247.

73. José Cuellar, "El Senior Citizens Club: The Older Mexican-American in the Voluntary Association," in Barbara Myerhoff and Andrei Simić, editors, *Life's Career —Aging: Cultural Variations on Growing Old* (Beverly Hills, Calif.: Sage, 1978), p. 213.

74. Bengtson, pp. 31–32.

75. Andrus Gerontology Center, "Social and Cultural Contexts of Aging," (University of Southern California: Community Survey Report, 1977), p. 6.

76. Crouch, pp. 525–526; Bengtson, p. 27.

77. Crouch, p. 525; Cantor, p. 48.

78. Leonard, p. 249. For a general discussion of culture and retirement, see Margaret Clark, "An Anthropological View of Retirement," in *Retirement*, edited by Frances M. Carp (New York: Behavioral Publications, 1972), pp. 117–156.

79. Dowd and Bengtson, 433–434.

80. Cuellar, p. 229.

81. Lucy Jen Huang, "The Chinese American Family," in Mindel and Habenstein, *Ethnic Families*, p. 145.

82. Richard Kalish and Sam Yuen, "Americans of East Asian Ancestry: Aging and the Aged," *The Gerontologist* 12 (1972), pp. 38–40.

83. Christie Kiefer, "Lessons from the Issei," in Gubrium, *Late Life*, p. 175; Richard Kalish and Sharon Moriwaki, "The World of the Elderly Asian American," *Journal of Social Forces* 29 (1973), p. 192; Sylvia Junko Yanagisako, "Two Processes of Change in Japanese-American Kinship," *Journal of Anthropological Research* 31 (1975), pp. 201–202.

84. Francis L. K. Hsu, "American Core Value and National Character," in *Psychological Anthropology: Approaches to Culture and Personality*, edited by F.L.K. Hsu (Homewod, Ill.: Dorsey, 1961).

85. Frances Wu, "Mandarin-Speaking Aged Chinese in the Los Angeles Area," *The Gerontologist* 15 (1975), p. 274.

86. Huang, p. 141.

87. Yanagisako, p. 209–210.

88. Huang, p. 140.

89. Kalish and Yuen, p. 37; Kalish and Moriwaki, p. 188.

90. Andrew Greeley, "An Alternative Perspective for Studying American Ethnicity," in *Ethnicity in the United States: A Preliminary Reconnaissance* (New York: John Wiley & Sons, 1974), p. 298.

91. Fandetti and Gelfand, p. 544.

92. Perry L. Weed, *The White Ethnic Movement and Ethnic Politics* (New York: Praeger Publishers, 1973), p. 4.

93. Woehrer, p. 331.

94. Helena Z. Lopata, "The Polish American Family," in Mindel and Habenstein, *Ethnic Families*, p. 26, and Lopata, *Polish Americans: Status Competition in an Ethnic Community* (Englewood Cliffs, N.J.: Prentice-Hall, 1976), pp. 100–101.

95. M. Powell Lawton, Morton H. Kleban, and Maurice Singer, "The Aged Jewish Person and the Slum Environment," *Journal of Gerontology* 26 (1971), pp. 231–239.

96. Fandetti and Gelfand, p. 548.

97. Lopata, "The Polish American Family," p. 26.

98. Bertha G. Simos, "Relations of Adults with Aging Parents," *The Gerontologist* 10 (1970), p. 138.

99. David L. Ellison, "Alienation and the Will to Live," *Journal of Gerontology* 24 (1969), pp. 361–367.

100. Hoyt and Babchuk, p. 11.

101. Barbara G. Myerhoff, "A Symbol Perfected in Death: Continuity and Ritual in the Life of an Elderly Jew," in Myerhoff and Simić, editors, *Life's Career—Aging*, pp. 163–206.

102. Coles, p. 51.

PART FOUR
A Service Delivery Network

During the past 40 years, the federal government has invested an increasing proportion of its resources to finance programs that provide services for older Americans. Concurrently, state and local governments have been devoting greater portions of their tax revenues to provide services for their elderly constituents. Over a period of time, therefore, there has developed a fairly complex array of administrative agencies, service delivery organizations, and advocacy groups that derive at least a portion of their funding from tax dollars. As a result, publicly funded programs for the aged, or "formal support" programs as they are sometimes called, can currently be found under the auspices of many government agencies.

With the passage of the Older Americans Act in 1965, and through subsequent amendments, Congress committed itself both to funding specific services for older people and to developing a comprehensive organization for providing those services. The organization of agencies to administer Older Americans Act programs, sometimes called "the aging network," operates at the national level (Administration on Aging), at the regional, state, and substate levels (Area Agencies on Aging), and at the local level. The chapters in Part 4 present examples of "formal support" programs that share in common the fact that they are largely, and in some cases exclusively, publicly funded. Moreover, in different ways they constitute responses to the federal initiatives represented by the Older Americans Act and the organizational structure it engendered.

In his essay, Gordon discusses the efforts of the Black Caucus to achieve greater representation for minority elderly in federally supported programs. In particular, he focuses on the efforts of the Black Caucus to promote the training of educators and service professionals to improve the quality of services provided for the nation's minority elderly. In so doing, he traces the history of both the Black Caucus and gerontology in higher education. The selections by Favors, Peters, and Broughton and Wiseman describe agencies that are part of "the aging network." Favors describes the Area Agencies on Aging, a significant organizational outcome of the 1973 amendments to the Older Americans Act. As she explains, these agencies were created to identify the needs of older people in their jurisdictions and to subcontract with local organizations to provide services that meet those needs. Peters further explores the activities of the Area Agencies on Aging and evaluates their performance to date. He comments on prospects for Area Agencies and on their future role in the aging network.

A local service delivery organization, which represents the final link in the aging network, is presented by Broughton and Wiseman. While this and similar organizations provide a wide range of services, the chapter concentrates on the provision of transportation to the elderly. Transportation is especially crucial since, beyond its intrinsic usefulness, it permits access to many other services as well. Finally, Jantz provides an overview of the Retired Senior Volunteer Program (RSVP). Although RSVP is currently under different federal auspices, it emerged as a national program through funding from the Administration on Aging. Many organizations rely heavily on volunteers, and many of those volunteers are older people, but RSVP is distinct in that it specifically emphasizes the role that older people can play in providing services to others. Although federal and local governments are not likely to lessen their support of services for older citizens in the foreseeable future, there is a growing recognition among researchers and policy makers that governmental resources are limited and can affect the quality of life in only so many ways. Thus, it seems likely that future initiatives in program development will increasingly rely on the skills of the elderly themselves and take into account their informal support networks of assistance from family, friends, and neighbors.

14

The Black Caucus and Gerontology in Higher Education

Jacob U. Gordon

The fundamental precept of the National Caucus on the Black Aged (NCBA) is that the black elderly in the United States often experience multiple jeopardy from racial discrimination, ageism, and poverty. Blacks are faced with certain crucial problems that differentiate them from other aged persons in the United States.[1] However, the problems of the black aged and indeed the political and historical development of the NCBA cannot be fully understood without a knowledge of the birth and growth of gerontological studies in the United States.

The History of Gerontological Studies

The field of gerontology as an area of graduate study did not gain widespread recognition until the mid-1950s. However, the impetus and foundation of social gerontology was established during the 1940s through the efforts of professional groups and other private organizations concerned about the implications of an unprecedented increase in the number of older persons in the population.

The first organized attempt to define the sociological aspects of aging was made in 1943, when a subcommittee of the Social Science Research Council's Committee on Social Adjustment was appointed by the committee's chairman, Ernest W. Burgess, to study old age.[2] The committee's research planning report[3] and the subsequent monograph by Pollack[4] served as a definitive guide to the major social issues and a basis for sociological research on aging. Clark Tibbitts, a prominent member of the committee, developed the following generally accepted concept of social gerontology:

> Social gerontology is concerned with changes in the social characteristics, circumstances, status and roles of individuals over the second half of the life span; with the nature and processes of adjustment, personality development and mental health of the aging individual and with the biological and psychological processes of aging insofar as they influence social capacity and performance in later life. Secondly, social gerontology seeks to discover the role of the environment, culture and social change as determinants of aging and of the behavior and position of older people in society; the behavior of older people as groups and in the aggregate; and their impact on social values and institutions and on economic, political and social organization, structure and function.[5]

In 1945, two other significant events occurred, the first being the publication of a pioneering study of aging in more than seventy preliterate societies by Leo Simmons.[6] Also in 1945, what was to become the most influential of the organized groups, the Gerontological Society, was founded by a group of biologists.[7] The organization's membership soon expanded to include social scientists and practitioners of clinical medicine and social welfare. A major goal of the society has been to promote training for careers in research and teaching in the area of gerontology.

In 1957, with the assistance of a grant from the National Institute of Mental Health, the Gerontological Society's Psychology and Social Science Section sponsored two summer training institutes in social gerontology[8] attended by representatives from sixteen universities throughout the United States. The participants formed the Inter-University Training Institute in Social Gerontology for the specific purpose of carrying out a project designed to shape the scientific field of social gerontology, to prepare additional college faculty for teaching about aging, and ultimately to increase the number of social scientists trained to teach, carry on research, and offer services in aging.[9] Their efforts were enhanced through the publication of three volumes that compiled the existing scientific knowledge on the psychological and social aspects of aging: *Handbook of Social Gerontology*, by Tibbits;[10] *Handbook of Aging and the Individual: Psychological and Biological Aspects*, by Birren,[11] and *Aging in Western Societies*, by Burgess.[12] These works became the standard social science reference works on gerontology and have been used as textbooks in gerontology courses. During the summer institutes held at the University of Michigan in 1959, teaching syllabuses for four courses in aging in the fields of economics, psychology, sociology, and social welfare,[13] and for one interdisciplinary course in social gerontology,[14] were prepared and published. This project had a significant impact on the amount of gerontological training offered on university campuses, because the majority of the institute participants subsequently introduced courses and/or directed research in gerontology for the first time in their respective institutions.

Another early accomplishment in gerontology was the addition of a new division, Maturity and Old Age, to the American Psychological Association in 1946. In the same year, the *Journal of Gerontology* began publication. The first International Gerontological Congress was held in Belgium in 1948. In 1950, the Carnegie and Rockefeller foundations began supporting research in gerontology, and 1955 marked the beginning of some government support of research in gerontology.[15]

From the 1960s to the present, there has been increased governmental activity making the public more fully aware of the needs of the aged. The White House Conference on Aging, held in 1961 and again in 1971, focused on some of the needs and problems of the aged populaton in the United States and brought about significant legislation. The President's Council on Aging was established in 1962, and the Older Americans Act of 1965 provided for the establishment of the Administration on Aging in the Department of Health, Education and Welfare. The Medicare plan under Social Security was also passed in 1965.

Title V of the Older Americans Act provided for support of teaching costs, trainee stipends, short courses, and curriculum development in gerontology. Grants were made to help initiate, expand, or strengthen research and instructional programs with a primary focus on social, economic, and professional services. Support of training in areas of need, which lay largely outside the support areas of other programs, was the primary responsibility of the Title V grant program.

In March 1966, the first grant under Title V was made to the University of Georgia, followed by grants to sixteen other universities.[16] The new programs in aging ranged from specialized research to broad fields such as planning and administration. It is important to note here that these early efforts in the development of gerontological studies, training, and research excluded black Americans and ethnic minorities in general. Hobart Jackson observed that available evidence indicated that professional education in aging for blacks was woefully inadequate, and that racism was still rampant in a number of existing aging programs in higher education and in federal agencies responsible for underwriting these programs.[17] It was not until 1971 that any black students (and then only three) were recipients of grants under the Title V stipend program. Before 1971, no training programs in aging were federally funded at the more than one hundred black institutions of higher education in the United States.[18]

That year, the Administration on Aging, under Title V, made available approximately $200,000 for aging programs at six black institutions of higher education. Only one of these institutions, Fisk University, received a grant for graduate training. The other five received limited support for undergraduate training. The inadequacy of this appropriation was noted by Jacquelyne J. Jackson:

> In my judgment, none of these programs are satisfactory, due principally to the paucity of resources made available to them, a lack of qualified personnel to man them, and the great likelihood that they were not designed to contribute significantly to an incease in black professionals in gerontology. Current black and white trainees in federally funded aging programs differ in a number of important ways. Most important may be the disproportionate number of blacks involved as trainees in undergraduate programs geared principally towards social service for lower-level professional occupations. The problem involves the far greater constriction of blacks to very few educational and occupational outlets, and almost none primarily concerned with developing academic professors, researchers, and top-level administrators. Relatively little attention has been given to establishing priorities in training blacks as aging professionals, and, above all, much more attention should be given first to those who, in turn, can serve as trainers.[19]

It was apparent to many black educators and practitioners interested in the well-being of the elderly that the interests of older black Americans were not sufficiently addressed in these general gerontological programs, nor did it appear that the 1971 White House Conference on Aging was likely to correct this situation.

Thus the National Caucus on the Black Aged, Inc. (NCBA), was founded in Philadelphia in November 1970 by the late Hobart C. Jackson, former executive vice-president and director of the Stephen Smith Geriatric Center in Philadelphia. One major impetus for founding NCBA was to ensure that the 1971 White House Conference on Aging would include information on the critical and special needs of elderly blacks.[20] Hobart Jackson charged the conference organizers with failing to give adequate attention to the problems of the black aged and those who were endeavoring to represent their interests. The NCBA threatened to boycott the conference and commenced preparations for a possible "Black House Conference on Aging."

General discontent among several groups involved with the conference precipitated a series of changes in the conference that were intended as a response to the complaints of these groups. NCBA was given a planning role, and a session on aging and aging blacks was added to the agenda. Moreover, the conference program was expanded to include seventeen sessions on topics of special concern to NCBA as well as other organizations. NCBA was able to make recommendations at a "special concerns" session for dealing with several problems seen as particularly critical, among them the disproportionate number of elderly blacks living in poverty and the lack of sufficient data on the black aged. The absence of such data, NCBA leaders argued, made it impossible to formulate realistic policy.

The recently established gerontology programs in predominantly black institutions of higher learning were seriously affected by President Nixon's failure to include in his budget request for fiscal year 1974 any provision to continue training for work with the aged under the Older Americans Act and other existing sources of funding within the Department of Health, Education and Welfare. In response to the Senate Special Committee on Aging (Hearings on Training Needs in Gerontology, June 19, 1973), Hobart Jackson wrote,

> While the impact of this curtailment of training will be felt by the overall population, it will be particularly devastating to blacks and other minorities where efforts have just recently been undertaken to involve them in these training programs. The training of blacks and other minorities in the field of gerontology already lags tremendously behind that for others and the effect of these cutbacks will be to make an already bad situation much worse. The indications are very strong that the removal of this funding source will automatically mean discontinuing this training. Instead of discouraging these efforts as will obviously be the effect of the cutbacks, the Federal Government should be encouraging this training by increasing the funding available.[21]

While minority aging programs would have been seriously impeded by the lack of support for students, the 1973 Nixon administration policy to reduce faculty support on a commensurate basis with the reduction of student support posed a serious dilemma for all gerontology training programs. The Association for Gerontology in Higher Education, which included educators from twenty-six universities, petitioned against the impending legislation. It became apparent that the administration intended to terminate all training support by June 30, 1974, and a later directive noted that there would be a 50 percent reduction of support for faculty under the Administration on Aging (AoA) training programs effective June 30, 1973.[22]

The immediacy of these decisions allowed no time for universities to respond with alternative means of maintaining their programs. Therefore, during the ensuing year, representatives of the Association for Gerontology in Higher Education met repeatedly with AoA and other Washington officials to support the continuation of federal assistance for gerontology training. Arguments in favor of expansion of Title V funding were succinctly stated by Wayne Vasey, codirector of the University of Michigan Institute of Gerontology:[23]

1. There is a need for trained persons to work with the aged who remain in the community, instead of institutions.
2. There is a need for trained manpower to cope with new congressional and presidential initiatives to help the aged.
3. There is a need to provide training assistance on a national level for emerging state programs: federal-state-local cooperation in assistance to the aged.

After continuous debate, negotiations, and pressure from the Senate Special Committee on Aging, a federal decision was made in April 1974 to extend long-term training support for faculty. Support for institutional training grants was also extended, but for the academic year 1974–75 only. The Department of Health, Education and Welfare appropriations for 1974 included an allocation of $9.5 million, $4 million of which was reserved for funding short-term training activities at state and local levels. Appropriations for aging have increased substantially since 1974.

The Position of NCBA

NCBA occupies the middle ground between old age and black rights groups, and spends time in both camps championing the cause of the black elderly. For example, NCBA reminds organizations and policy makers involved with aging issues that among the 8.1 percent of the elderly who are black, the poverty rate is more than twice that of whites over 65. The Black Caucus also has an advocacy role to play with respect to groups such as the National Association for the Advancement of Colored People (NAACP) and the National Urban League, which tend to be oriented toward the problems of black families and teenagers rather than those at the other end of the age spectrum. For example, when several minority organizations criticized Congress for approving the mandatory retirement proscription (contending that most black males leave the work force before reaching retirement age and the main effect of the law would be to prevent minority young people from obtaining jobs), NCBA brought to their attention the beneficial impact the legislation would have on employment opportunities for the many elderly black women who need to keep working beyond age 65 out of economic necessity.

Lacking a mass membership base and substantial staff resources, NCBA restricts its focus to the subgroup of poor, black aged and to a relatively narrow span of issues. Generally, income policy is of greatest importance to the Black Caucus, including Social Security and employment programs. Health care is ranked second in priority, although the organization has not actively entered the national health insurance debate. Housing is another NCBA concern. The group has also called for reinstatement of a rehabilitation grants program that would make it possible for elderly couples to repair their homes, providing them with more postretirement options.

NCBA thus tends to concentrate upon programs and policies that provide the basic necessities of life. While many other national organizations worry about financing the Social Security system in the twenty-first century, NCBA focuses upon a socioeconomic group in which some individuals are not now covered by Social Security benefits (e.g., domestic workers). Therefore, many of the black aged must rely upon antipoverty programs for assistance. Gaining access to the programs may be difficult for an individual due to ignorance of eligibility, inability to deal with application forms, transportation problems, and racial discrimination. For NCBA, making it possible for elderly blacks to take advantage of government benefits and services already on the books is as important as winning new legislative victories. Accordingly, the Black Caucus calls for enrolling more middle-aged and elderly persons in programs such as the Comprehensive Employment Training Act, and claims credit for bringing about the 1978 Civil Rights Commission report that found evidence of age discrimination in federal assistance programs.

The outlook of its membership and the dependency of black aged on government programs generally makes NCBA liberal in its policy orientation. In response to a question about its place on the political spectrum in relation to other old age organizations, a staff member said, "More liberal than . . . any other national organization!" The prominence of staff members in the NCBA is apparent from the activities of its National Center for the Black Aged, established in 1973, which emphasizes service development and provides technical assistance. (See Figure 14.1 for NCBA's general structure.) The caucus and the center are inseparable, but they perform different functions. The caucus operates the political advocacy activities of the NCBA, and the center operates the educational programs and grant projects. Recent center programs have included a two-day conference titled "Careers in the Field of Aging," a two-day conference for black colleges on writing proposals for federal research grants, and a symposium, "Health and the Black Aged."

Among NCBA's major accomplishments are a $6.9 million housing project for the elderly in Washington, D.C., and a $5 million development project in Houston, Texas. It also sponsors a Rural Senior Employment Program (RSEP) that provides part-time employment in community service for low-income persons 55 and over. Additional activities include a national antivictimization project for the elderly; the training of minority faculty and professionals in the field of aging; publication and dissemination of research results; and a job bank where employers and minority professionals are matched.

Figure 14.1:   NCBA Governmental Structure

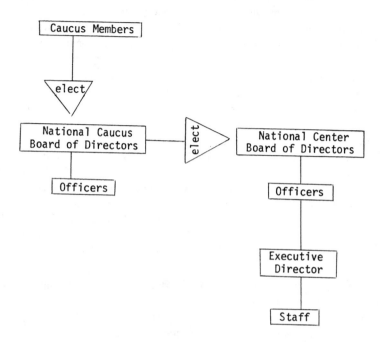

The Black Caucus's publication *Golden Age* contains a calendar listing forthcoming events of the Gerontological Society, the Western Gerontological Society, the Association of Gerontology in Higher Education, and similar organizations.[24] The annual NCBA conference is an occasion for hearing from federal officials and discussing issues, but it plays no direct role in developing or approving public policy positions. Positions on political issues are defined by the caucus's board of directors, who are advised by a public policy committee appointed by the chairman. The current committee has thirteen members, six of whom are caucus directors. Since NCBA does not function with the resources or formality of the large old age organizations, it does not prepare lengthy, detailed explications of issues and recommended policy approaches such as those promulgated by other groups.

The center's budget is less than $3 million, of which $1.3 million is a Title V employment program contract. NCBA also has a Labor Department contract to operate a transportation service for elderly residents living in and around a public housing project in Springfield, Massachusetts, and receives research grants from other federal and state government sources. While federal funds are 95 percent of the center's present income, the staff has not been satisfied with the total amount of funds at its disposal. The only other income is from dues, which total about $10,000 annually.

The future of NCBA depends on many factors, the most important of which is its ability to continue to mobilize other black organizations, such as the black church and the NAACP, and other aging organizations. The NCBA's future also depends on the sensitivity and nature of our government's response to the needs of the elderly, and particularly on its willingness to provide adequate funding to organizations such as the Black Caucus.

Notes

1. Hobart Jackson, "Origin of the National Caucus on the Black Aged" (address to the National Caucus on the Black Aged, Indianapolis, Indiana, June 17, 1972).

2. R. E. Kushner and M. E. Bunch, *Graduate Education in Aging within the Social Sciences* (Ann Arbor: The University of Michigan, Division of Gerontology, 1967), p. 77.

3. E. W. Burgess, C. Tibbitts, R. J. Havighurst, and R. W. Cavan, *Social Adjustment in Old Age: A Planning Report* (New York: Social Sciences Research Council, 1946).

4. O. Pollack, *Social Adjustment in Old Age* (New York: Social Sciences Research Council, 1948).

5. Clark Tibbitts, *Handbook of Social Gerontology: Societal Aspects of Aging* (Chicago: University of Chicago Press, 1960).

6. Leo Simmons, *The Role of the Aged in Primitive Society* (London: Oxford University Press, 1945).

7. M. Adler, "History of the Gerontological Society," *Journal of Gerontology* 13 (1958), pp. 94–100.

8. Robert W. Kleemeier, *Aging and Leisure: A Research Perspective into the Meaningful Use of Time* (New York: Oxford University Press, 1961).

9. W. Donahue, "Training in Social Gerontology," *Geriatrics* 15 (1960), pp. 801–809.

10. Tibbitts, op. cit.

11. James Birren, ed., *Handbook of Aging and the Individual: Psychological and Biological Aspects* (Chicago: University of Chicago Press, 1959).

12. Ernest W. Burgess, *Aging in Western Societies* (Chicago: University of Chicago Press, 1960).

13. H. W. Franke and R. C. Wilcox, *A Syllabus and Annotated Bibliography on the Economics of an Aging Population* (Ann Arbor: The University of Michigan, Division of Gerontology, 1959).

14. R. G. Kuhlen and W. W. Morris, *A Syllabus and Annotated Bibliography on the Psychological Aspects of Aging and the Aged* (Ann Arbor: The University of Michigan, Division of Gerontology, 1959).

15. M. R. Koller, *Social Gerontology* (New York: Random House, 1958), p. 9.

16. W. Donahue, "Development and Current Status of University Instruction in

Social Gerontology," in R. E. Kushner and M. E. Bunch, eds., *Graduate Education in Aging Within the Social Sciences*. Division of Gerontology, University of Michigan, Ann Arbor, 1967.

17. Hobart Jackson, "National Caucus on the Black Aged: A Progress Report," *Aging and Human Development* (August 1971).

18. Dolores Davis, "Guide for Minority Aging Program at the Institute of Gerontology, University of Michigan: Student Perception Approach" (Ph.D. dissertation, School of Education, University of Michigan, 1974), pp. 18–25.

19. J. J. Jackson, "Present Training Programs" (address to the Gerontological Society Twenty-Fifth Annual Scientific Meeting, San Juan, Puerto Rico, December 21, 1972).

20. Hobart Jackson, "Origin of the National Caucus."

21. Quoted in Davis, op. cit. (1974).

22. U.S. Department of Health, Education and Welfare, *Aging* (Sept.–Oct. 1973), p. 8.

23. U. S. Congress, Senate, Special Committee on Aging Hearings, Part 1, *Training Needs in Gerontology*, letter from Wayne Vasey, 93rd Cong., 1st sess., June 19, 1973.

24. NCBA, *Golden Age*, vols. 1–3, no. 2 (1979).

15

What Are Area Agencies on Aging?

Anita Renee Favors

In 1965, Congress passed the Older Americans Act, which heralded an alternative approach to providing social services for the elderly. For one thing, it did not withhold services from people whose income and assets rendered them ineligible for services from other public welfare agencies. For another, it adhered to the principle that the elderly have special needs and, in regard to services, should be considered separately from the general public. It was comprehensive legislation, for it responded to a broad range of needs. The original act of 1965 and its subsequent amendments committed the federal government to assisting older people in obtaining an adequate retirement income, the best possible physical and mental health care, suitable housing, and opportunities for individual initiative in planning and managing their own lives.

One provision of the Older Americans Act, as amended in 1972, established permanent nutrition programs for the elderly. Congress recognized that many older people may not eat adequately because they cannot afford to do so, because they may be unable to prepare meals for themselves or to shop, and/or because incentive may be lacking to prepare a meal if it is to be eaten alone. Thus, the act authorizes funds for low-cost, nutritionally sound meals to be served at centrally located facilities such as schools, churches, and community centers.

Another section of the act authorizes funds for establishing multipurpose senior centers. These centers are intended to be a focal point in communities for the development and delivery of social services. The act also authorizes funds for research in aging and for training professionals to deal more effectively with the elderly. One portion of the act, as amended in 1975, is intended to promote useful, part-time community service activity for low-income older persons who are not employed.

In order to implement these and other provisions, the Older Americans Act established an organizational and funding structure for providing services. As part of the 1973 amendments to the act, the Area Agencies on Aging were created. They were established as private, nonprofit organizations, with each agency serving a specific geographical area. There is an average of ten area agencies per state, and they receive funds for implementing their services from their respective state agencies on aging. The state departments on aging, in turn, receive an appropriation from the Administration on Aging, which is under the Department of Health, Education and Welfare. Each area agency has the responsibility of identifying the needs of older people. (For an example of such an organization, see Chapter priority of these needs. The agency must subcontract funds to community organizations that can provide the appropriate services for responding to the needs of older people. (For an example of such an organization, see chapter 17 in this volume.) In addition, it is mandated to oversee the development of specific support services, such as information and referral and legal services. By assisting in the coordination of programs, the agency can help improve the existing service network. It also can locate additional community resources with which to inaugurate new programs.

In essence, then, the Administration on Aging and the Area Agencies on Aging, along with their subcontracted organizations, represent the major formal network supporting the elderly population of the United States. The design of this network provides the opportunity for local community planning of service programs with input from older citizens. In order to obtain the desired level of citizen input, each agency creates an advisory council consisting of representatives from the elderly population and the general public. Since conditions affecting the needs of elderly people will vary from one locality to another, it is appropriate that priorities for meeting such needs be established by the local agencies. For example, planning for social services must take into account the number of people with low incomes who reside within a given area.

In a survey of the nation's Area Agencies on Aging, two-thirds of which responded (there were a total of 555 at the time), it was found that the highest-priority needs identified at the local level were:

1. transportation (listed as the number one priority by 48 percent of the agencies)
2. income assistance (15 percent of the agencies)
3. information and referral (9 percent of the agencies)
4. nutrition services (7 percent of the agencies)

5. health services and treatment (6 percent of the agencies)
6. homemaker services (5 percent of the agencies)

Transportation is cited as a major need so frequently because it is an "access" service. In other words, if transportation is not available, it is then not possible to take care of other pressing needs such as getting to a congregate meal site, grocery store, or health clinic.

Area Agencies on Aging have readily responded to the need for nutrition services. Presently, the congregate meal program in the state of Kansas alone services over 7,500 meals per day to persons over 60 years of age. Additionally, the 1978 amendments to the Older Americans Act provide for a program of home-delivered meals to assist persons unable to leave their homes. In the past, home services have not been designated as priority areas. However, the 1978 amendments mandate that a certain percent of funding go toward in-home services to the elderly. This emphasis on in-home services goes hand in hand with the new amendment's concentration on serving the "frail and vulnerable" elderly.

16

Area Agencies on Aging and the Service Delivery Network

George R. Peters

Today, 599 Area Agencies on Aging (AAAs) are in existence. They employ more than 4,000 paid staff and utilize the services of more than 20,000 volunteers. It is estimated that 90 percent of all persons 60 years of age or older live in areas that are within an AAA planning and service area. The goal in the near future is for 100 percent coverage. This will be accomplished in part by increasing the number of AAAs and redrawing area boundaries in some states to provide coverage to all areas outside existing boundaries. It is clear that they now represent an important component of the network of services and support systems that are emerging in both the public and private sectors to respond to the needs of older Americans. This essay will attempt to answer several questions about Area Agencies on Aging: What is their place in the service delivery network? Why were they created? What do they do? How successful have they been? What are their future prospects?

It is important to understand AAAs as a manifestation of public policy on the one hand and as a part of an integrated service structure for the aged on the other. The original Older Americans Act (OAA) was signed into law in 1965. The passage of the act culminated a long struggle to develop a national service program that would focus on the needs and wants of older Americans. Movement toward such a program began during the 1950s and reached a peak in arousing public consciousness in a White House Conference on Aging in 1961. Two legislative proposals were introduced between 1961 and 1965 in regard to these issues, but action was not taken until passage of the Older Americans Act in 1965. The deprivations and degradations of growing old in American society were repeated frequently and forcefully by advocates of the aged.

In the final analysis three broad issues emerged as matters of public concern and eased somewhat the passage of the Older Americans Act. (1) The increasing visibility of the aged both in absolute numbers and as a proportion of the American population was recognized. It was apparent that the shift from a younger to an older society would continue and that the problems of the aged would worsen unless action to redress them were taken. (2) The aged, as a group, constituted a significant proportion of those in American society who were poor, destitute, and lacking adequate means to ameliorate their condition. (3) It was doubtful that existing service systems could or would be capable of responding adequately to the multiple needs of older Americans.

The passage of the Older Americans Act, in addition to recognizing the needs of older people and providing an alternative approach to providing services to the elderly, reflected two emerging trends in federal grant programs. First, because it isolates a particular clientele to be served rather than a function to be performed, the act cuts across the functional lines (e.g., health, transportation, housing) along which social grant programs are typically organized. Second, whether called Great Society, New Federalism, or Special Revenue Sharing, the act is an example of a trend in federal government programs to devolve responsibility to state and substate levels for planning, resource allocation, and accountability.

As a statement of public policy the Older Americans Act is clear in its intent to officially recognize the rights of older Americans to live out their lives with dignity, self-respect, and a maximum of independence. The act mandates the creation of a service and support system to achieve these ends. It sets forth as objectives in behalf of older persons adequate income; physical and mental health; suitable housing; health care and therapy designed to return those needing institutional care to as high a level of functioning as possible; employment opportunities; retirement in health, honor, and dignity; the pursuit of meaningful activity; efficient community services; benefit from research; and freedom in planning their own lives.

To implement the objectives of the act required the development of an organizational and funding structure, which has been described in the previous chapter. At issue during the entire formation of the service system was whether "comprehensive planning" for aging within the vertical domain of the Older Americans Act provides the most effective and economic alternative for meeting the needs of older people. That question remains an issue, and is one to which we shall return below. The more central point is, however, that a choice has been made to move toward a vertical structure for service delivery to the aging. Emphasis has been and continues to be placed on developing and strengthening this structure.

It is impossible to provide a single description that adequately characterizes each AAA. There is great diversity in planning and service areas, which affects planning and delivery of services to the elderly. This diversity is also seen among AAAs. Thus, AAAs vary in size of staff and geographic area served, auspices, funding levels and sources, range of projects funded, and in their relationships with State Units on Aging (SUAs). The SUAs are expected to administer federal funds allocated to AAAs, provide oversight on fiscal and program activities, give technical assistance to AAAs, and assure that AAA program plans are consistent with state and federal program priorities. To carry out such functions requires that SUAs establish both formal and informal working relationships with AAAs. Some reasons for variation in these relationships are discussed below.

The need for diversity among AAAs was recognized early, when the Administration on Aging (AoA) granted waivers to sparsely populated states such as Alaska, North Dakota, and South Dakota, thus allowing state-wide planning and service areas with the functions of an AAA retained at the level of state government. In an attempt to limit diversity, Title III regulations of the Older Americans Act suggested a minimum of 50,000 elderly persons in a planning and service area in order for an AAA to be formed. Nonetheless, two-thirds of the AAAs deal with populations below that minimum.

The number of counties served by AAAs ranges from one to as many as twenty-eight. Typically, AAAs with small numbers of counties in their planning and service areas are located in urban settings. It is in such settings that larger numbers of older people reside. On the other hand, larger proportions of older people reside in the rural areas and smaller communities. The size of staff is also highly variable among AAAs. A study completed in 1976 showed that staff size ranged from one to twenty-three nonclerical workers. The most common number of professional staff members at that time was three. Currently, the number of professional staff is typically four or five. All AAAs make use of volunteers, but the number employed and their activities are variable.

While the 1973 amendments were still pending in Congress there was considerable controversy over whether AAAs should be administratively lodged in governmental auspices. Ultimately, AoA regulations permitted this decision to be made by states. A few states standardized the auspice statewide in county governments, in councils of government (COGs), or in economic devlopment district agencies (EDAs). Most states, however, designated AAA auspices on the basis of one-at-a-time assessments of the organizational and political resources and histories of their planning and service areas. Thus, across and within states one finds AAAs variously located in county governments, COGs, and EDAs. At least one-fifth of the AAAs are nonprofit private corporations and still others are administratively housed in agencies such as community mental health centers or community colleges.

AAAs also vary in their funding levels and sources. All AAAs receive funding from the AoA, funding that is first allocated to SUAs on a formula basis and then distributed through them to planning and service areas. The federal allocation formula is based on the number of persons 60 years of age and older residing in a state and weighted by the number of minority and poor aged. States must use this formula in the allocation of funds to planning and service areas, but may add other weighting components such as size of area, commitments to aging program grants from previous years, or staff performance. As a result, states may differ greatly in amounts of AoA moneys received, as may planning and service areas within states. Additionally, AAAs vary in the extent to which the AoA is their sole or major source of funding. Finally, states vary in the amounts of money they provide to support aging programs under the Older Americans Act. It is estimated that less than one-half of the states provide such funding beyond the matching dollars required by the federal government.

The AAAs differ in the range of projects funded. Agencies that receive multiple funding, that have a larger number and more diverse concentration of older people and of established agencies and organizations who serve them—more typical in urban settings—and that have been in existence for a longer period of time will often fund and coordinate a larger and more diverse set of programs and projects.

Finally, AAAs vary in their relationships with the SUAs. In some states SUAs are administratively located at the very top levels of state government, and are established as autonomous departments within the governmental structure. In other states the SUAs are located as divisions or sometimes offices of established state bureaucracies such as departments of social and rehabilitation services. Still other states have formed commissions on aging. While some states have concentrated all aging services into a single unit of state government, others have spread them over a number of state agencies. The location of the SUA within state government frequently has significant implications for the activities, credibility, and political clout of AAAs and Older Americans Act programs. It clearly influences the extent to which AAAs can look to the SUA for support and assistance. Relations between AAAs and SUAs have their informal as well as formal dimensions. There are rather unfortunate differences among AAAs in terms of establishing good working relationships with SUAs.

The diversity among AAAs was not totally without design. Indeed, in some respects allowing for diversity was the only way the AAAs could be established. The underlying justification for diversity was that it provided states and AAAs the opportunity of developing structures tailor-made to local situations. Such diversity, however, was not without problems and cost. Thus, establishing the AAA network was in some cases a slow and painful process. It is likely that programs in some areas suffered. For some AAAs meeting their mandated duties was extremely difficult. Some of the problems resulting from diversity remain today.

Why Were the AAAs Created?

Prior to the 1973 amendments the activities and projects of the Older Americans Act were largely the responsibility of federal and state personnel. They were expected to plan for the elderly, ensure the delivery of services, conduct research on the aging, involve them in projects, and gather information on their needs and aspirations. In advance of such activities states were expected to designate units on aging, create state plans for aging, and develop regulations for community grantees. These activities, while mandated, were to be carried on with a minimum allocation of resources. The amounts appropriated for the purposes in 1966 were $7.5 million and in 1967 $10.25 million. Amounts increased to $23 million in 1969 and $33 million in 1971. These allocations were hardly adequate to accomplish the multiple tasks of implementing activities and are minuscule when compared to the estimated $543.1 million allocated under the Older Americans Act for 1979.

Additional problems were created in 1967 as a result of a reorganization within HEW that placed the AoA in a more broadly defined Social and Rehabilitation Service, where it remained until the 1973 amendments to the Older Americans Act were implemented. This action, some maintained, decreased the effectiveness of AoA and reduced the "visibility" of aging as a high priority in public policy and administration. Many felt that the Social and Rehabilitation Service, which in their view was completely welfare oriented, was a totally inappropriate place to situate an agency concerned with the dignity of older Americans. Before 1967 and after 1973, AoA was located in the office of the secretary of HEW under the direction of a commissioner on aging.

The early history of OAA programs was plagued by problems. Programs were inadequately funded, were provided with only broad and ambiguously defined state service priorities, and were so numerous and small that it was generally agreed that the basic needs of most older people were not being met through them. For their part, SUAs did little more than get themselves established and disburse funds as best they could. The SUAs operated under severe constraints. Most states had had only minimal state-wide programming efforts before the passage of the Older Americans Act and little had been accomplished to establish viable state-level administrative units on aging. Typically, states were dependent upon funding from the AoA since only a few states had allocated state funds to aging services. In effect SUAs were given heavy responsibilities, little direction, and few resources. The outcome was considerable confusion and frustration even though most states took their responsibilities quite seriously.

Attempts to strengthen the position of the AoA and particularly the SUAs and to clarify their tasks were made in the 1969 amendments to the Older Americans Act. Despite these amendments, concern continued to grow over the future of OAA programs and the model developed to implement them. That concern culminated in the 1971 White House Conference on Aging, where older people and advocates for the aged expressed their dissatisfaction with the existing structure and reaffirmed the pressing need for effective service programs for the aged. The White House conference laid the foundation for the 1973 amendments. These amendments called for a total restructuring of the manner in which federal grant funds were allocated to and distributed within the states. For the first time, a relatively unambiguous statement of priorities would serve as a guide in the development of services for the aging. The AAAs were created.

Three underlying reasons may be offered for the creation of the AAAs. First, it was decided, with opposition, to create a separate and integrated service structure for the aging as the most effective means of responding to their needs. Second, dissatisfaction was expressed with the system for planning and coordinating aging services through only federal and state aging units. Third, strong sentiment existed for increasing local input into decision making and for moving planning, coordinating, and administrative functions closer to the local level, where it was felt problems were more intimately and fully understood.

The AAA concept was not without its critics. Grave concern was expressed over the creation of another layer of bureaucracy by forming the AAAs. Doubt was expressed about whether AAAs would in fact serve as coordinators of social services by linking up with other already existing social service agencies as mandated in the Older Americans Act. It was feared that AAAs would become even more dependent upon the federal bureaucracy because they relied on the AoA for the major portion of their funding. Further, it was predicted by some that AAAs, rather than coordinate with other agencies, would jealously guard and try to expand their policy space in the field of aging. Finally, some critics were acutely aware of the massive costs that could potentially be incurred under the AAA system. We will return to some of these issues in a later section.

What Do AAAs Do?

The AAAs serve as a major focal point for advocacy for older Americans. Within that role they are expected to perform multiple functions. Simultaneously, AAAs are to serve as catalysts for change, planners, needs assessors, resource inventory takers, services coordinators, resource mobilizers, program evaluators, managers of services, grant writers, information brokers, and providers of assistance to service providers. Such activities are intended to make existing services more effective and accessible to the elderly and to expand existing resources on behalf of the elderly. As pointed out elsewhere, AAAs are not intended to be direct service providers and may do so only when such services are needed but are not available from other agencies or community groups. Rather, they exist to plan for and facilitate the creation of needed services, to reorient existing service systems, and to generate resources for needed services.

The multiple roles assumed by AAAs have, on the one hand, enhanced their position as major components within the aging network and established their credibility within planning and service areas. On the other hand, the broad spectrum of functions assigned AAAs has made their task difficult. With multiple roles come multiple demands that may conflict with one another or create overload, which may be related to the relatively high turnover rates observed in AAAs as staff members experience "burnout." Such difficulties are also relevant to the questions of how successful AAAs have been in carrying out their functions.

How Successful Are the AAAs?

It is not possible to provide a final answer to this question, in part because the AAAs are yet relatively new components of the aging network. Indeed, the aging network itself is relatively new, and thus continues to experience change and redefinition. Furthermore, the issue of "success" may be measured in several ways.

If the success of AAAs is measured by numbers of older people participating in meals programs, senior center activities, health services, transportation programs, and other programs funded under the Older Americans Act, then the agencies have had a significant impact on the life conditions of millions of older people. Or, if success refers to the number of programs made possible by agency activities, then the AAAs clearly have a good track record. If, however, success means reaching all old people in need or responding to the full range of needs and wants of older people effectively, the answer may be different. The AAAs themselves recognize that their activities and programs may not be reaching all who need them. Concern is often expressed among AAA staff about identifying and making available services to the "hidden aged"—i.e., persons whose lifestyles and life experiences make them unlikely to readily seek out help from formal service systems even if it is badly needed. Like it or not, AAAs are also bound to some extent by program priorities set by the federal AoA and SUAs. Thus, the "sweet smell of success" is often tainted when one hears of local program needs that cannot be met because they fall outside the parameters of established priority areas.

In fact, the different AAAs vary in terms of how successful their programming has been. A number of reasons have been offered for this variation. For example, the states were at different stages of development in their ability to deliver services to older people when the AAAs were created. States having a history of established programs for the aging and administrative units to run them had a definite advantage over states lacking such a history. It has also been noted that urban AAAs have experienced somewhat less difficulty in establishing ongoing comprehensive programs than their rural counterparts. In part, at least, this reflects the richer and more concentrated resource base typically present in urban as opposed to rural settings. The AAAs have also experienced varying degrees of difficulty in establishing a rapport and credibility with local communities and counties within their planning and service areas and in attracting and holding highly skilled staff to conduct program activities. Thus, just as it was impossible to provide a single description of AAAs, given their variability, it is also impossible to appropriately apply a single measure of success.

It appears that some of the concerns of the critics of the AAA concept have emerged as realities. As was predicted by some, the agencies have become more, rather than less, dependent upon the AoA vertical system. In an important way, that dependency is reflected in the fact that the major funding source for most AAAs continues to be the AoA. This dependency is likely to continue as long as funding for aging services at the federal level increases. Further, there is some evidence that AAAs, because of their dependence upon the AoA vertical system, have not expended full effort to create linkages with other existing service networks. Rather, concern has often been given to "carving out a policy space" for AAAs and then increasing control over the programs and services offered. Such actions have given credibility to the fear that the formation of AAAs would result in an additional layer of bureaucracy. Precisely how such issues relate to the effectiveness of AAAs is unclear and may never be known.

Despite the complexity of the issue of AAA effectiveness, the fact is that increasing numbers of older people have access to and are participating in programs funded under the Older Americans Act. Success at a given moment is different from success over time. Perhaps the safest conclusion is that the final determination of AAA effectiveness will be made by the next two generations of older Americans and by the policy makers who must evaluate and judge the outcomes of current public policy.

What Future Prospects Exist for AAAs?

The AAAs have survived the turmoil and difficulties of becoming established. They are now a recognized part of the network of services provided for older Americans. They have achieved visibility, credibility, and legitimacy—both in the eyes of the older people they serve and the general public. To be sure, they continue to confront serious and pressing problems. These, however, are now more the problems of service delivery and program development than of fledgling agencies struggling to justify their very existence. What then does the future hold for the AAAs? We turn briefly to this issue, cautioning the reader that prediction in the areas of politics, public policy, and social programming is hazardous.

Having achieved a level of maturity, the AAAs are now in the process of building, strengthening, and broadening programs mandated under the Older Americans Act. The prospects for the near future are that such activities will continue, barring drastic changes in public policy or decreases in funding levels. Increasing effort will be given to upgrading skill levels of staff as an important means of increasing program effectiveness. The numbers of AAAs are unlikely to increase greatly, although states may redraw the boundaries of planning and service areas to bring them more into line with program needs and the needs of the aging population. It is likely that strides will be made to reach an even broader spectrum of the aged population than is currently reached, by targeting special populations for service. The AAAs are also likely to expend energy consolidating the gains they have already made, thereby securing a significant portion of the "policy space" regarding aging services. At the same time, the homeymoon period is over for AAAs and they will experience increasing demands for accountability.

At one time, it was proposed that all programs relating to the aged be consolidated under the jurisdiction of the AoA. This will probably not happen, given the vested interests that other agencies have in retaining programs perceived as belonging to them. In all likelihood, programs mandated for the SUAs and AAAs will be restricted to those currently provided by the Older Americans Act. A second recent proposal would greatly increase the size of AAA staffs, to as many as 60 or more people, while cutting back on the number of AAAs. This proposal would create "super AAAs" with a larger funding base but also larger planning and service areas and populations to be served. This too seems unlikely to occur, given the strong local support for AAAs. While a certain amount of tinkering with the system is likely to occur through changing rules and regulations, the basic structure of the AAAs and the AoA vertical system is unlikely to change.

In the long run, the large majority of older persons targeted for programs will have been reached. That does not mean that all older people will choose to participate even if they need services. It does mean that, at that point, the number of new programs will decline sharply. AAA activities will then concentrate more on program maintenance than program growth. The AAAs will not disappear. Rather they will become an even more highly institutionalized segment of American society.

The foregoing is, of course, based upon the assumption that the status quo in public policy regarding older Americans will be maintained. This assumption may prove false. Indeed, there is now some discussion that suggests that singling older people out for special attention may have been a mistake. Perhaps, it is argued, we should abolish the AoA and create a new system. While such action seems unlikely at present, the winds of politics and social issues have been known to shift.

Summary

This essay has reviewed the emergence and growth of AAAs. As was seen, AAAs are the creatures of public policy and legislation. They make up a key component of the aging network and are charged with the important responsibilities of planning and coordinating comprehensive systems of services for the elderly. They were created as a means of more effectively responding to the pervasive problems of older Americans. While the AAAs have experienced many problems in their early developmental stages and have had varying degrees of success in building programs, they have also become established and recognized as viable agencies both at the local and federal levels. Given time and barring significant changes in public policy, the AAAs will significantly increase the likelihood that older Americans can live out their lives in dignity and with a maximum of independence.

References

The following works were used as reference materials for this chapter. Since they are not cited throughout the text I wish to acknowledge here their contribution to the ideas developed in this selection.

Center for Public Management. *Curriculum Research Findings and Training Intervention Strategies for Strengthening the Capacities of Area Agencies on Aging.* Final report submitted to the AoA, 1976.

Hudson, Robert B. "Client Politics and Federalism: The Case of the Older Americans

Act." Paper presented at the 1973 meetings of the American Political Science Association.

———. "Rational Planning and Organizational Imperatives: Prospects for Area Planning in Aging." *Annals of the American Academy of Political and Social Sciences* 415:41–54.

Peters, George R. "Interagency Relations and the Aging Network: A Study of the State Unit on Aging and the Area Agencies on Aging in Kansas." Paper presented at the 1976 meeting of the Gerontological Society.

Rones, Phillip L. "Jobs With Agencies On Aging." *Occupational Outlook Quarterly*, Fall 1976, pp. 31–33.

Steinberg, Raymond M. *A Study of Funding Regulations, Program Agreements, and Monitoring Procedures Affecting the Implementation of Title III of the Older Americans Act.* Final report submitted to the AoA, 1976.

U.S. Department of Health, Education and Welfare. *AoA Occasional Papers in Gerontology, No. 3, Employment Issues in Agencies on Aging,* 1979 (DHEW Public. No. [OHD] 79-20079).

U.S. Department of Health, Education and Welfare. *Older Americans Act as Amended,* March 1976.

17

Delivering Services to the Elderly: Transportation as a Case Example

Calvin D. Broughton and Constance B. Wiseman

This chapter describes a community organization, the Douglas County Council on Aging, which delivers a variety of services to the elderly. It represents the last link in the formal support network described in Chapters 15 and 16. The organizational structure of the agency consists of a board of directors responsible for setting policy and an executive director responsible for policy implementation. The agency has been incorporated as a nonprofit organization and is funded by the local Area Agency on Aging as well as by city and county governments and private donations.

The well-documented increase in the proportion of older people in the populations of many communities has created a correspondingly greater demand for social services of varying kinds. At the outset, communities will have to choose between two basic alternatives for their planning and growth patterns. Many agencies, as did the Council on Aging, will begin with an incremental approach; that is, providing just one or two services, with the prospect of adding services as resources become available. Such planned growth can be frustrating for the agency's staff, since the existence of the agency is likely to stimulate consumer demand for as yet nonexistent services. Other communities may choose to provide a comprehensive program of service delivery from the beginning. However, this may result in a fragmented delivery of services because the agency is overextended. Lack of planning, in either case, will most likely result in consumer alienation and public distrust of the agency due to its disjointed approach.

It is almost axiomatic that the type of service to be planned should be based upon the type of needs present in the given community. A comprehensive needs assessment is necessary to determine accurately the needs of each community's population. People's needs vary according to their sex, race, and income. The assessment must consider the size of the elderly population in the community, the general state of that community's economy, and the services already available to the general public. Whatever the needs of a particular community, the services designed to meet these needs should be rendered in such a way that the individual feels that he or she is part of a dignified transaction.

As shown in Chapter 15, the service most often identified in the Administration on Aging needs survey was transportation. The importance attributed to this service is not surprising, since it not only is a need in its own right but also enables people to take advantage of other community services. Because of its importance, the transportation program of the Council on Aging will be examined in some detail.

The Council's demand-response minibus system is available to people 60 years of age and older, to their spouses, and to people with physical handicaps. There is no fixed charge for rides, but riders are encouraged to make donations. Transportation service is available on a regular basis Monday through Friday and on a limited Sunday schedule. In addition, the service is available during the evenings and on weekends for special group meetings and trips. Potential riders are asked to call the office at least twenty-four hours in advance to schedule a ride with the dispatcher. A certain amount of flexibility is necessary for both the rider and dispatcher in order to reduce waiting time and increase operating efficiency. An important advantage to the Council on Aging's system is the ability to plan routes as persons request rides. Planning routes is a difficult task, but one that increases efficiency. Additionally, fixed stops are incorporated into the Council on Aging transit service. This procedure encourages group rides that increase ridership and reduce per-ride cost. Services are also available to small communities within the county one day a week. One vehicle is utilized on the county routes; it makes one trip in the morning and two trips in the afternoon. This service provides access to multipurpose shopping centers and health care facilities for the rural population.

Ridership has increased steadily since the service was initiated (55 percent increase between 1974 and 1975; 50 percent increase between 1976 and 1978). There are several reasons for this dramatic increase. One reason is that the Council has increased the number of buses in use, and as it has gained experience it has become more efficient in rendering the service. Initial use of the service was stimulated by a marketing effort that included radio and newspaper promotion. Subsequent increases can be attributed to the visibility of the buses and word-of-mouth promotion. Friends and relatives told older people not only about the buses but also about the safety, efficiency, and courtesy with which the service was conducted. Indeed, the primary goals established for the service were safety and dependability. All personnel receive training in first aid, cardiopulmonary resuscitation, and transfer techniques for handicapped individuals, as well as workshop training designed to foster sensitivity toward the specific needs of older persons. An escort service also is provided for those individuals needing assistance boarding the bus, or going from house to vehicle.

Once it has been determined that there is a need for a transportation service, there are several general factors that must be considered at the outset of planning. The size of the area to be served, and the proportion of older people in that area, will affect staff and vehicle requirements. Additional resources must be available to secure replacement of vehicles or additional vehicles if demand for the service increases. The maximum capacity of the system should be determined by the demand for the service at peak times. Ideally, a system should include back-up vehicles and at least one vehicle large enough to accommodate large groups.

Detailed knowledge of the area and the resources necessary for implementing the system will provide a basis for determining the type of transportation system best suited to the area. There are several types of transportation systems already in operation that can serve as models for those who are planning to develop a similar service. The Council on Aging determined that the demand-response minibus system described above was most appropriate for its area. Since this type of service picks people up wherever they request and delivers them to the places they wish to go, it is a personalized service and is particularly advantageous for individuals with mobility problems. The proper operation of the demand-response system depends on individuals scheduling their rides in advance. One problem inherent in this type of system is the inability to respond to unplanned rides. Every effort is made to accommodate requests on shorter notice, with trip assignments being made via two-way radio.

One alternative to the demand-response approach is the fixed-route bus system. In fixed-route systems, reservations need not be made in advance. However, the fixed route may be inconvenient, particularly for those people with mobility problems. Another alternative is the dial-a-ride system. The advantage of this system is its ability to meet the immediate demands of its riders and the capacity to offer a personalized service. The initial investment for dial-a-ride sysems is usually greater than demand-response systems because of the capital equipment necessary for implementation. Dial-a-ride systems are established to serve one person per ride. This requires more vehicles unless shared rides or group rides are incorporated into the system.

A third alternative takes the form of subsidies provided to regular public

Table 17.1: Transportation Alternatives*

Type of System	Personalized Service	Accessible to Frail People	Cost Efficient	Stigma	Reservation Necessary
demand-responsive mini-bus	A	A	B	B	C
fixed-route bus for elderly	B	C	C	B	A
dial-a-ride	A	A	B	B	A
subsidies for: bus/rail	C	C	B	A	A
taxi	B	B	B	A	A

* A = desirable condition
B = adequate condition
C = undesirable condition

transit systems in return for reduced fares for older riders. This system, of course, eliminates any stigma associated with specially provided transportation. However, several problems are inherent in this approach. While subsidizing bus or rail transportation may make their use economically feasible for the older person, the fixed route remains a problem. Taxis represent a highly individualized form of transportation, but they are also a costly alternative in terms of both the extent of the subsidy that is necessary and the amount of fuel consumed per rider.

A comparative view of the advantages and disadvantages of these systems is presented in Table 17.1. A note of caution is necessary in interpreting this matrix. Not all of these characteristics will have equal weight in determining the overall worth of a system. For example, cost alone may prohibit the implementation of a given system, while advance reservations may not always be a crucial consideration.

Transportation is both an important and integral service provided by the Council on Aging, in that it provides needed transportation to its users and facilitates the use of the Council's other services. The Council on Aging's comprehensive service delivery system contains the following programs: nutrition, information and referral, employment service, recreation, outreach, senior center operations, health screening, and legal and public benefits assistance.

For the most efficient use of a comprehensive service delivery system, it is necessary to plan the agency's activities so that they complement one another. For instance, the Council uses its transportation service to get both people and food to its congregate meal sites. In turn, congregate meal sites are used to disseminate special information about legal, income tax, medical, and other community services.

The Council on Aging attempts to coordinate its programs with services provided by other community organizations. Coordination serves a twofold purpose. One is to encourage the participation of older people in other agency service delivery systems, and the other is to develop an information-sharing procedure. Successful coordination will eliminate duplication of services and help to complement each agency's programs.

Consumer participation in planning and policy decisions has had a salutary effect on the Council on Aging's programs. The older consumer's direct involvement in planning provides immediate feedback for the agency. The Older Americans Act mandates consumer participation in the form of advisory councils, policy councils, and advocacy councils. Regardless of the form, the participatory process creates consumer acceptance and increased participation in the agency's services. Consumer involvement in planning and developing programs and services also allows the older person to become an effective spokesperson for the agency in the community.

While the transportation program is important to the services of other agencies, it is more than just a support activity. It increases the mobility of older people, and improved mobility creates opportunities to participate in personal and community activities.

18

RSVP and a Meaningful Later Life

Marjorie Jantz

People growing up in America, or even living in this society for a time, generally develop a strong desire to be productive. In fact, one is taught that productivity is the essential measure of a person's worth. In the early and middle years, this desire is usually fulfilled through one's occupation or through one's role in raising a family. However, the value our society places on productivity is not abandoned in the later years just because one is retired or because one's children are grown. Consequently, most older Americans remain highly motivated to continue living "useful" lives.

At the same time, there is a strong element of altruism in American life. Older adults have often helped friends, neighbors, and their communities throughout the history of this country. For older people, then, assisting others may be substituted successfully for earlier forms of productivity. A few examples of typical responses from older volunteer workers will serve to illustrate this point: "The help that others obtain from my work is a joy to me also"; "I'm interested in helping people and benefiting them"; "I would rather do something for others than myself." The fundamental purpose of the Retired Senior Volunteer Program (RSVP) is to provide an avenue leading to a meaningful life in retirement through significant volunteer service. The activities of RSVP are meaningful to the older volunteer precisely because they address genuine areas of need in the community.

In 1965, the Community Service Society of New York initiated a pilot program on Staten Island that involved older adults in volunteer service to their community. The particular service rendered by this pilot program was to patients of Willowbrook State School, an institution for the mentally retarded of all ages. The program was extended to serve the entire state of New York in 1969, under the administration of the New York State Office on Aging. Not only were the New York State volunteer projects successful, but the research and practical experience emanating from them laid groundwork for legislation creating a national older Americans volunteer program. Among other things, evaluators of these projects concluded that volunteer service to the community successfully replaced roles that had been lost because of advancing age and therefore enhanced the quality of life for older volunteers. However, they also concluded that strong organizational support was necessary if projects were to be successful. The most crucial areas of support were found to be a capable staff and adequate transportation for volunteers.

The Retired Senior Volunteer Program became a reality in the spring of 1971 with an appropriation from the Administration on Aging. Later that same year, responsibility for administering the program was transferred to ACTION, where an office for Older American Volunteer Programs was established. Participation in programs such as Senior Companions, Foster Grandparents, and RSVP has grown tremendously since their inception.

Anyone 60 years of age or older, retired or semiretired, is eligible to become a senior volunteer. A volunteer must be willing to serve on a regular time schedule without compensation and be willing to accept supervision. There are no education, income, or experience requirements for volunteer service, nor are there barriers relating to citizenship (or national origin), race, sex, or religious and political affiliation.[1]

There is a plethora of service positions in nonprofit organizations that senior volunteers can fill. Furthermore, many such positions throughout the country are waiting to be filled. Senior volunteers may serve in a variety of secretarial and clerical positions; assist in hospitals, nursing homes, congregate meal sites, and senior centers; help prepare educational materials; repair equipment, act as drivers, or contact people on the telephone; and provide a host of other services.

In addition to RSVP, there are two successful ACTION programs directed toward the low-income elderly: Foster Grandparents and Senior Companions. Volunteers in these programs work about a twenty-hour week and receive a stipend of $32.00 per week along with regular physical examinations, transportation to and from the volunteer job, and a meal while at work.

The Service Corps of Retired Executives (SCORE), sponsored by the Small Business Administration, also makes use of the training, skills, and experience of older adults. The volunteer retired executive assists small business owners with their problems and helps potential businesspeople assess the market and plan their business operations. SCORE volunteers are reimbursed for travel expenses.

Recognizing that older adults may live on a limited income, the Older American Volunteer Programs include some support provisions. The type and amount of assistance is established by each program and depends on conditions existing in a given community and in the sponsoring agency. In general, financial support covers some reimbursement for transportation and meals, as well as insurance benefits, and is nontaxable. Volunteer "stations" are encouraged to provide as much of the above financial assistance as possible.

Any public or private nonprofit organization or licensed proprietary health care facility may be a volunteer station. However, such an organization or facility must have the capacity to share financial responsibilities for the transportation and meals of volunteers and the ability to provide adequate in-service training and supervision.

One remaining task to be discussed is that of matching individual volunteers with the appropriate station. This is not a simple matter, since the station must be accessible to the volunteer and have need of his or her particular skills. Whatever the assignment, it cannot require more from the older volunteer than he or she is physically capable of accomplishing. This rather complex task is the responsibility of the project director or assistant director, who must take into account the ability, desires, and needs of the volunteer. At the same time, the location, quality, and needs of the volunteer station must be considered.

Sponsoring agencies may be public or private nonprofit organizations, whose charters will permit operation and administration of such a program, and must, of course, be approved by ACTION. While they will receive partial financial support from ACTION, they must be able to develop sources of nonfederal support. Examples of organizations that have sponsored RSVP programs are United Way organizations, Community Action Programs, Area Agencies on Aging, interdenominational organizations, community colleges, and senior centers.

Recent research findings indicate that many older adults serving regularly in community agencies began their volunteer activity when they were young and continued such activity into their later years.[2] The need for volunteer service is so extensive today that RSVP and similar programs can accommodate many additional older adults who have not previously been volunteers. However, many potential volunteers were so involved during earlier years in raising families and working for a living that they did not have the time or the financial security to gain experience in community service. Moreover, a large proportion of older adults have no knowledge of the many organizations providing services to the community and, as a result, do not realize the extent to which their talents and experience would benefit others. Thus, there is a considerable untapped reservoir of assistance available to agencies serving the community. It is the work of RSVP to ensure that the many skills, professional capabilities, and creativity of senior citizens are not wasted.

What makes the work of senior volunteer programs so satisfying is that, along with performing a real service for the community, the lives of the volunteers themselves are enriched. Through volunteer work people often become acquainted with resources available to the elderly in the community. For instance, one retired teacher was delighted to discover the many health services rendered by the local department of public health after she began working as a volunteer. Volunteer jobs also open up whole new areas of experience for the older person. A couple who had not had children of their own found a great deal of pleasure in working closely with elementary school children. Furthermore, volunteer service may turn an older person's attention from his own problems. Since he is actually helping to alleviate problems of others, it may become clear to him that his problems are not unique and not impossible to resolve. Occasionally, a volunteer job results in a paying job. Many employers have learned from experience that the elderly make excellent employees. Finally, an important consequence of volunteer service is that it is often the basis on which new personal relationships are developed. Many people have found new friends among their fellow volunteers, and these friendships represent an important source of support in their lives.

Notes

1. ACTION, *Retired Senior Volunteer Program Operations Handbook for Sponsors* (U.S. Government, Washington, D.C., 1978), p. 28.

2. Ibid., p. 9.

PART FIVE
Personal Dimensions of Aging

Among the theories about growing old that have emerged from social gerontological research is one known as disengagement theory, which was formulated in the late 1950s. This theory holds that, as the probability of death becomes greater, the older person will withdraw from his or her social world and, at the same time, people in that world will withdraw from the older person. According to the theory, this mutual withdrawal prepares both the older person and others for that person's impending death. It further proposes that satisfactory adjustment to old age will depend on undergoing this process sucessfully.[1] During the years since it was first introduced, disengagement theory has been tested extensively in gerontological studies. While disengagement has been found to occur under certain circumstances, gerontologists have concluded that it is not a universal process and, indeed, that successful adjustment to old age may generally be linked to the continued participation of the older person in his or her social world. An important part of such participation is that which occurs in the personal dimension considered in this section. Therefore, successful aging is likely to depend on a degree of continuity in one's personal relationships.

The quality of older people's personal relationships is determined in part by perceptions and expectations of others regarding the elderly. Crockett and Press examine the reactions of younger generations to the elderly in general as well as to specific older individuals. They address the issue of stereotypes held about old people and how stereotypical thinking may affect the interactions between old people and others. Steere concentrates on the relationships between older people and members of their families. He considers the important social question of whether the modern American family is capable of caring for its older members and what the family's responsibility is toward them.

Dailey discusses the sexuality of older people, how that is perceived by both young and old, and the ways in which continuing sexual expression contributes to the quality of personal relationships in later life. He describes the various dimensions of sexual expression and considers the effect that aging has on each of them. In the final chapter in this section, Berghorn and Schafer consider the effect of social and environmental forces on the elderly person's outlook on life. The chapter explores the extent to which feelings of personal efficacy and individual adaptation to changing circumstances contribute to the quality of life in the later years.

Notes

1. Disengagement theory was developed by Elaine Cumming and William E. Henry. For a much more thorough discussion of it, as well as other social gerontological theories, see Cary S. Kart and Barbara B. Manard, *Aging in America* (Port Washington, N.Y.: Alfred Publishing Co., 1976), Part 1.

19

Relationships Among Generations

Walter H. Crockett and Allan N. Press

American society, we are often told, is youth-oriented; it has little use for the aged. It is not hard to find evidence to support that proposition. Butler and others have pointed to the phenomenon of "age-ism," a pervasive tendency to dislike and discriminate against the elderly.[1] But we should not accept the proposition without question. Evidence can be found for positive attitudes toward the elderly as well.

The purpose of this chapter is to review and sketch out the implications of that evidence. It begins with a review of research into the attitudes that are held toward older people (with the negative considerably outweighing the positive). The second section of the chapter discusses research on the impressions that are formed of specific individuals, which shows that impressions formed of older persons are at least as positive, if not more positive, than impressions formed of young people with the same qualities. From this topic, the chapter moves to the similarities and differences in values, attitudes, and other qualities between young people and older ones. Finally, it sketches out some of the implications of research results for relationships between individuals of different generations.

Attitudes Toward Aging and Old People

The attitudes of Americans toward aging have been examined in a hundred or more different studies. It is useful to sort this research into two broad

Research reported in this chapter was supported in part by Research Grant no. 90-A-1008 from the Administration on Aging. Our thanks to Marilyn Osterkamp for assistance and comments.

groups: those that use direct measures of attitudes and those that use indirect measures. In direct measures, respondents are clearly aware that their
attitudes toward old people in general or toward the process of aging are being measured. Some of these techniques require respondents to express their
opinions on an attitude scale, agreeing or disagreeing with statements such
as "Old people tend to become rigid in thought or action" and "A person
over 70 years old has little interest left in life." Other measures ask
respondents to complete sentences. The scale developed by Golde and
Kogan includes, among other items, the following: "Most old people
fear. . .".[2] Completions of such sentences were then scored for a consistent
positive or negative stereotype of the elderly.

In still other measures, respondents may be presented with a list of personality traits and asked to check the ones that apply to old people. Or they
may be asked their opinions about aging in open-ended interviews.
Whatever the specific method, all these procedures make it clear that the investigator wants to know what respondents think about aging and the elderly. This transparency of purpose is one of the problems in this type of
research. If people are concerned at all about appearing unprejudiced toward
the elderly, as well they might be at a time when the evils of stereotyping are
often emphasized, their answers may not represent their true feelings.

There is not much evidence of a concern about bias in early work on
stereotypes and aging. Research on that topic before 1972 has been reviewed
by McTavish[3] and by Bennet and Eckman.[4] Both papers concluded that the
predominant attitude of Americans toward older people is a negative one.
To summarize these reviews of an extensive set of studies, Americans were
said to believe (1) that with age there is a general and inevitable decline in
health, sensory capacities, intelligence, sexuality, physical attractiveness,
and the like; (2) that with age people become rigid and inflexible in
thoughts, beliefs, habits, and manners; (3) that dependency increases with
age so that old people need help and assistance from others; (4) that old people cannot be expected to be responsible for their own well-being; (5) that
the elderly are depressed, fear death, and dislike their juniors; and (6) that
these negative qualities are accompanied by such unhappy personality traits
as passivity, grouchiness, despondency, and childishness. At the same time,
a few positive qualities are attributed to the elderly: wisdom, experience,
kindness, and a calm, accepting posture toward the world.

Some more recent studies have been reported that show consistently
negative beliefs about older people. Thus, Cyrus-Lutz and Gaitz reported
that psychiatrists hold a number of negative expectations toward the elderly;[5]
Wood found that there were few, if any, behaviors judged to be age-
appropriate for the elderly, suggesting that old age is a "normless"
condition;[6] Garetz found that the age of psychiatrists was inversely related

to how interesting and treatable they believed elderly clients would be;[7] and Silverman reported that people expect men to display more feminine characteristics as they pass from youth to old age.[8] In the same vein, the 1975 Harris report found evidence that Americans do not value old age as positively as younger ages, though strong negative stereotypes of the elderly were not consistently reported.[9]

On the other hand, not all of the more recent research of this type has shown a clear predominance of negative attitudes. Thorson, Whatley, and Hancock reported that their respondents gave generally favorable ratings to old people, with the degree of favorableness increasing with the raters' own age;[10] Garfinckle found that professional workers in a psychiatric clinic held generally liberal attitudes toward the elderly (except that they expected them not to talk much);[11] and Ivester and King reported generally positive attitudes toward the elderly among ninth- and twelfth-grade students.[12] In short, recent research that has used direct measures of attitudes toward the elderly has not revealed uniformly negative views of aging and of older people.

Indirect measures of attitudes toward aging and the elderly do not so obviously reveal the purpose of the research to the respondent. In one study, which used a measure that falls somewhere between the direct and indirect approaches, Rubin and Brown asked young adults to estimate how much of different types of intellectual ability would be observed in people of different ages. They obtained a curvilinear relationship between age and expected intelligence: young adults and middle-aged adults were rated most intelligent; adolescents and elderly adults were rated next most intelligent; and preadolescents, preschoolers, and infants followed in that order. The results were interpreted as reflecting a negative attitude toward the oldest age group.[13]

A more obviously indirect measure of attitudes was used by Ryan and Capadano. Respondents (college students) were asked to try to infer personality characteristics from the quality of speakers' voices. They heard recordings of people who varied in age, all reading a standard passage. Although the age of the reader was never mentioned in instructions, older women were rated as more reserved, more passive, more "out of it," and less flexible than younger women. Another sample of respondents made similar ratings from men's voices; here, only one trait varied with age—older men were rated less flexible than younger ones.[14] The negative personality qualities that were assigned to older women, and the single negative quality assigned to older men, are regularly reported to be part of the stereotype of the elderly. The fact that a speaker's voice yielded cues to the speaker's age, which then evoked stereotyped trait inferences, is indirect evidence that the respondents had negative attitudes toward the elderly.

Palmore presented still another indirect measure of attitudes. He prepared a twenty-five-item true-false test of facts and misconceptions about aging. Errors on some of the items imply a negative view of aging, while errors on other items imply a positive view. Therefore, a comparison of the proportion of positive errors to negative errors can be used as an indirect measure of the respondent's attitude toward aging. Palmore reported that a group of under-graduate students and a group of graduate students both made more negative errors than positive ones, indicating a biased view of aging and the elderly. By contrast, a group of faculty members in human development (who made relatively few total errors on the test) made about an equal pro-portion of positive and negative errors, indicating little or no bias against the elderly.[15]

Rubin and Brown also had college students communicate by telephone the rules of a simple game to people of different ages. The students' commu-nication was much more complex when they thought the listener was a middle-aged adult than when they thought the listener was either a child or an elderly person. The authors interpreted this as evidence that they "talked down" to old people as they would to a child, indicating negative expecta-tions about the elderly.[16]

We have just completed an experiment that also obtained indirect measures of attitudes. Participants were undergraduate students who were shown a set of photographs of old and young men. Each photograph had been rated by an independent group of students as to physical attrac-tiveness. The photographs of old and young had the same average degree of attractiveness and about the same amount of variability from attractive to unattractive. Students were told they would be shown a large number of pic-tures of different men, projected one at a time on a screen, and that they would later be asked to recall what they had seen. Associated with each pic-ture was a statement that described the person. One statement, for instance, was "J.W. is an experienced craftsman of furniture." Another was "R.W. is so absent-minded he misses important meetings because they slip his mind." Some of the statements described positive traits that fit the stereotype of the elderly (experienced, kind, calm, and interesting); some described negative traits that fit the stereotype of the elderly (absent-minded, depressed, rigid, and touchy); and some described positive and negative traits that do not fit the stereotype of the elderly (for instance, cheerful, optimistic, cold, and foolish).

Students were shown thirty-two such pictures — sixteen of old men and six-teen of young men — each accompanied by a statement that described one trait. Of the statements associated with pictures of both young and old, half described positive traits and half negative ones. None of the students later reported suspecting that they would be asked to compare pictures of different aged men. That was their task, however. After all thirty-two pictures had been shown, students were reminded that some were photographs of old men and some of young men. They were asked to think for a few minutes about the two groups of pictures. Then they filled out a questionnaire describing their recollections of those groups.

Among other things, the questionnaire asked for ratings of the old men and the young ones on sixteen personality traits. Twelve of those traits have been identified as part of the negative stereotype of old people, the other four as part of the positive stereotype. The results of the ratings on those sixteen traits appear in Table 19.1. As can be seen, for fifteen out of the sixteen traits, differences between ratings of pictures of young and old men were in the stereotyped direction; for twelve traits (ten negative and two positive)

Table 19.1: Scale Ratings of Pictures of Old and Young Men on Negative and Positive Personality Characteristics that are Associated with Stereotypes of the Elderly[1]

Personality Characteristic	Pictures of	
	Young People	Old People
Part of Negative Stereotype of the Elderly		
Miserly	5.90	3.99 **
Dependent	4.83	4.50
Grouchy	5.74	4.61 **
Selfish	4.90	5.26
Feels good about self*	3.66	4.40 **
Complaining	5.03	4.17 **
Touchy	4.64	3.68 **
Productive*	3.51	4.10
Stubborn	4.70	3.31 **
Meddlesome	5.87	4.61 **
Rigid	4.87	3.08 **
Active*	2.90	5.01 **
Part of Positive Stereotype of the Elderly		
Interesting	3.23	2.85
Experienced	5.28	2.39 **
Wise	5.23	2.86 **
Kind	3.70	3.46

[1] A low score indicates greater possession of each attribute.

* The reverse quality occurs in the stereotype of the elderly.

** This difference between ratings is greater than would be expected by chance one time in 100.

the ratings differed by an amount greater than would be expected by chance.

In a second part of the questionnaire, students estimated the proportion of desirable and undesirable qualities that were associated with pictures of the old men and the young ones; they also estimated the percentage of each group whose characteristics were typical for their age. As may be seen in Table 19.2, more desirable traits were remembered for young men than for old ones. Furthermore, the undesirable traits associate with pictures of old men were thought to be more typical for their age.

What does this experiment indicate? In it, students were intentionally presented with more information than they could organize and remember in the time they were allowed. In order to store the information and to respond to the questions they were asked, they must have made use of their prior expectations about the nature of old and young people. That these expectations reflected stereotyped, predominantly negative views of the elderly is clearly shown in their responses. They rated the pictured old people as possessing more stereotyped traits, especially negative ones, than the young; as showing fewer positive behaviors than the young; and as revealing more behaviors that were "typical" for their age than the young.

The research review here indicates that Americans tend to associate certain characteristics with old people and aging. Many more of those characteristics are negative than positive. One must concede that some of the characteristics—decreased sensory capability, changed appearance, decline in health—do accompany old age. But others—miserliness, grouchiness, negative self-image, touchiness, complaining, stubbornness, rigidity, inactivity, wisdom, and kindness—emphatically do not result from the aging process or characterize older people much more than young ones. It is important to examine how these attitudes affect impressions that are formed of old and young people.

Table 19.2:   Estimates of the Proportion of Pictures of Young and Old Men
              Associated with Positive or Negative Traits; Estimates of
              Typicalness of Traits for Age

	Pictures of	
	Young People	Old People
Estimated proportion of desirable traits	61.2%	54.4% *
Proportion judged typical for age	50.5%	62.4% *

*Proportions differ by an amount greater than would be expected by chance one time in 100.

Impressions of Specific Old and Young People

As we have just seen, attitudes toward aging and old people in general seem to be predominantly negative. Therefore, one would expect impressions that are formed of specific older individuals to be more negative than impressions formed of young people with the same qualities—but in this one would be wrong. A considerable number of studies have shown either that more favorable impressions are formed of a specific old person than of a young one with the same qualities, or that the impressions of specific young and old persons are equally favorable. Only one experiment has reported the opposite results. Let us look at some of this research.

Kogan and Shelton reported two related experiments. The first of these varied the age and occupation of a hypothetical person. Each perceiver read a sketch of a man who was either a steelworker, a factory manager, or a college professor and who was either 33 or 74 years old. Perceivers recorded their impressions of the man on a forty-five-item checklist. Impressions were strongly affected by the man's occupation, but not by his age. Only two of the forty-five items (energetic and alert) yielded age effects. Among the ratings for which there were no age effects were such qualities as conservative, dependent, dogmatic, grouchy, and rigid.

In the second experiment, Kogan and Shelton had people compare what they thought a young worker and an older worker would be like for each of the same three occupations (steelworker, factory manager, and college professor). Under these conditions, age effects were obtained. In one or more of the occupations, old men were judged to be more inflexible, dogmatic, demanding, strict, complaining, pessimistic, independent, and generous, and less submissive and selfish than young men. It should be made clear, though, that these stereotyped judgments were only found when perceivers knew that they were comparing individuals in the same occupations but of different age.[17]

Later research has uniformly found that more negative impressions are not formed of specific old people than of young ones. Bell and Stanfield, for example, had perceivers listen to a fifteen-minute tape-recorded discussion of ecology by a journalist who was described as either 25 or 65 years old. The older person was evaluated somewhat more positively than the younger one, although the differences were not large.[18] Weinberger and Millham reported both a study of attitudes toward old people in general and an experiment in impression formation. They first administered to students a questionnaire measuring their expectations about a representative 25-year-old and a representative 70-year-old. The questionnaire reflected age-related stereotypes. Old people were said to be less satisfied with life, to have fewer positive characteristics and more negative ones, and to be more dependent and less well adjusted. A substantial subgroup of those same students was then recruited to take part in an experiment on impression formation. They read brief autobiographies of a man who for some subjects was said to be 25 and for other subjects to be 70. The 70-year-old was judged to be more self-accepting than the 25-year-old, as well as more satisfied with life, better adjusted, more adaptable, and more appealing.[19] In the same vein, Sherman, Gold, and Sherman had participants read one of eight descriptions of a man that varied according to age (30 as against 60), whether he was active or inactive, and whether the information involved achievement-related or social activities. The older man was evaluated more positively than the younger one, whatever the other information presented.[20]

Similarly, Scheier et al. had perceivers read a bogus interview with a man either 23 or 75 years old. Half read a favorable interview (in which the man was depicted as upper-middle-class, with high ambitions, varied interests, and many friends) while the other half read an unfavorable interview (the man was lower-class, had no plans for the future, no particular interests, and few friends). Whether the interview was favorable or unfavorable, the man who was said to be age 75 was evaluated more positively than one who was described identically but was said to be 23.[21]

We have found similar results in half a dozen different experiments; one of these will be described to indicate the nature of the overall results.[22] Undergraduate students were asked to read an interview that was said to be taken from a recent survey, and then to describe their impressions of the woman who had been interviewed. For half of the perceivers, the woman was said to be age 76; for the other half, she was said to be 36. Except for the woman's age and related details, interviews were kept as nearly identical as possible. (The activities that the hypothetical woman reported were taken from the actual activities of an acquaintance of the authors who is age 76.) She reported that her husband had died of cancer eight months previously. She had three children (whose ages varied according to her own age) whom she enjoyed greatly, "but I have other interests of my own, too." Before marrying, she had worked in the bookkeeping department of a bank. She enjoyed the work, but didn't miss working when she became a housewife. Her husband had been involved in real estate and insurance. She reported that she now lives in a townhouse apartment that offers many opportunities, and that she plays bridge weekly. The 36-year-old reported going to exercise class, swimming, and playing tennis; the 76-year-old reported going to a crafts class, swimming a little, and walking. Finally, she said she has friends in church, where she teaches an adult class.

After this material had been presented in two pages of dialogue, the interviewer asked the woman what she had done yesterday. Additional variations were introduced by having different groups of perceivers read responses that described either desirable age-stereotyped behavior (working for a church or working in the garden), undesirable age-stereotyped behavior (complaining about the apartment manager or besieging a local clothing store to exchange clothing), or desirable counterstereotyped behavior (involvement in yoga meditation or codirecting a political campaign). Thus, twelve different groups of perceivers were created. After reading the interviews, perceivers spent five to ten minutes writing their impressions of the woman and then filled out a questionnaire describing aspects of their impressions.

The results showed that, whatever the behavior they read about at the end of the interview, perceivers who thought the woman was 76 reported that they would like her much better than did perceivers who thought she was 36. They also viewed her as having fewer of the stereotyped negative qualities associated with old age, and more of the positive qualities, than those who thought she was age 36. Table 19.3 presents perceivers' ratings of the woman on the same personality traits as are presented in Table 19.1. As can be seen in Table 19.3, on all but one of the negative personality

Table 19.3: Average Ratings of Impressions of a Specific Older Woman by Perceivers Who Thought She Was Either Age 36 or Age 76[1]

Personality Characteristic	Age of Woman	
	36	76
Part of the Negative Stereotype of the Elderly		
Miserly	6.17	6.88 **
Dependent	4.33	5.16 **
Grouchy	6.76	7.31 **
Selfish	6.18	7.12 **
Feels good about self*	2.61	2.03 **
Complaining	6.11	6.25
Touchy	5.81	6.18
Productive*	1.91	2.96
Meddlesome	5.95	5.96
Stubborn	5.06	5.08
Part of the Positive Stereotype of the Elderly		
Interesting	3.39	2.53 **
Experienced	3.92	3.34 **
Wise	3.84	2.91 **
Kind	2.42	2.05

[1] A low score indicates possession of the characteristic.

* The reverse quality occurs in the stereotype of the elderly.

** This difference between ratings is greater than would be expected by chance one time in 20.

characteristics, and on all four of the positive personality characteristics, the older woman was rated more favorably than the younger one. On eight of those characteristics, the difference in ratings was greater than would be expected by chance.[23]

It is clear that attitudes toward aging and old people in general are mainly negative, while impressions of specific elderly individuals are usually positive. That is, there is no evidence whatsoever that negative stereotypes of the elderly cause perceivers to pick up any negative cue that is available about an old person, and to distort positive cues, so as to form impressions that confirm the stereotype. Instead, when there was positive information available about an old individual, perceivers in these studies recognized it. They tended to form more positive impressions of an old person than of a young one with essentially the same characteristics. Why? There are at least two possible explanations: one involves a contrast effect, and the other a sympathy effect.

In all the experiments discussed above, an old person was depicted as behaving in a relatively active way, as being involved and interested in life. Very likely, such behavior contradicts people's (and especially young people's) expectations about the elderly. If you expect an old person to be inactive, passive, dependent, and complaining, then you are likely to be surprised to find one delivering a lecture on ecology or describing an interesting day's activities. You may be so impressed by the uniqueness of the old person's behavior that you lean over backward in the other direction, forming an especially favorable impression.

Evidence of this reaction was common in the experiment by Crockett, Press, and Osterkamp. Examples of illustrative comments were: "She is 76 years old but she sure has a lot of life in her"; "She's very active for her age"; "I find her very refreshing—completely opposite to the stereotype of elderly women and widows." Fully 40 percent of the perceivers who read about the 76-year-old woman commented that she was unusual for her age; none of those who read about the 36-year-old woman made a remark about her age.[24] Such comments suggest that when an old person is mentally alert, is actively involved with social affairs, or does and says things that are of interest to a young perceiver, the old person will be contrasted to what one thinks is the "typical" individual of the same age and will be evaluated even more positively than a young person acting in the same way.

An alternative explanation for the inconsistency between attitudes toward aging and impressions of old individuals is that being old is looked upon by the young as a type of stigma. People feel sympathy for the stigmatized and form especially favorable impressions of them. This explanation has been spelled out most clearly by Scheier, Carver, Schulz, Glass, and Katz. They proposed that the elderly constitute a stigmatized group, as evidenced by the negative stereotype, in much the same way as do the handicapped or minority racial groups. When a person is identified as belonging to a stigmatized group, they assert, sympathy is evoked in the perceiver. As a result of this sympathy, the perceiver rewards the stigmatized individual with more favorable ratings than are given to "normal" people.[25]

At the present time, there is no way to decide which of these explanations is more accurate. They are not mutually contradictory. However, they do carry different implications about the way relationships between the young and the old are likely to proceed. The "contrast" explanation offers some hope for positive relationships between old people and young ones. Most older people, after all, are active people. Only a minority are physically incapacitated. The rest go about their normal business in a normal way, generally indistinguishable from people ten years or more younger than they. Suppose one of these normally active old people actually has a social exchange with somebody much younger. And suppose the old person behaves (without flamboyance) as a person who keeps busy, is interested in a variety of things, is more concerned with the here and now than with the distant past, and is generally satisfied with life. According to the contrast hypothesis, the younger perceiver may form an impression favorable enough to lead to a pleasant, mutually interesting, and continuing relationship with the older person.

The "sympathy" explanation is not so optimistic. Perceivers may sympathize with members of stigmatized groups, but they also become negatively aroused upon being near them. Their first reaction is avoidance. If they can, they break off the relationship early and do not renew it. It may be that continued contact with a stigmatized individual would overcome one's initial rejection. Still, if old age operates as a stigma, avoidance would be the first response of the young toward the old, and long-term friendly relationships would be unlikely to develop.

Sources of Difference Among Age Groups

In any complex and changing society, there are forces that bring about differences among generations in values and actions. At the same time, there are processes that promote solidarity among generations. Let us first examine two types of forces that divide age groups: the differences in experiences among age cohorts and the different orientations that are implied by different age roles.

An age cohort is a group of people born in the same period of time. Being the same age, most members of the same cohort will have experienced a common set of events. Of course, not every member of an age cohort will experience or react to those events in the same way. Nevertheless, most members of any particular generation are likely to be marked in important ways by the events of their youth. What kinds of events are the significant ones? Social upheavals, for one. The Depression of the 1930s, for instance, marked the attitudes of one generation toward jobs and money. World War I affected one age group's ideas about patriotism and warfare in a different way than World War II affected a later group, and the effects of both those wars were much different from those of the Vietnam war upon a third group.

Technical innovation is also likely to produce differences among age cohorts. The radio and talking pictures did not appear until the 1920s; cross-country travel by automobile was not feasible until the 1930s; airline travel was not extensive until the 1940s; television became popular in the 1950s; and the computer age did not flourish until the 1960s. Each of these innovations had profound effects upon what people did, upon the pace and style of their lives, even upon their basic assumptions about what is valuable and what is not. In the same way, changes in morality and customs, in fashion, in tastes for music and art, in the average level of affluence, and in a variety of other aspects of society will make the experiences of young people, and, therefore, their attitudes and practices, more or less different from those of their elders.

Some of these cohort differences affect how well different age groups can perform in contemporary society. For instance, the education completed by the average American has increased over the last 60 years from less than eight grades to more than twelve. Greater education supposedly produces greater intellectual flexibility and greater ability to understand, adapt to, and control a complicated technology. The lower educational attainment of older cohorts also means that they will perform less well than younger cohorts on intelligence tests and other tasks that require reading and figuring.

Other cohort differences produce differences in values. The beliefs a person develops as a youth provide the basis for interpreting later experiences. Some of the beliefs of any individual will change, of course, as times and conditions change. But a great part of a person's beliefs are likely to remain intact over time. New times induce beliefs in young people different from those of their elders. Obviously, such differences are potential areas of conflict between members of different generations.

It should not come as news to anyone that people of different ages possess different social status. Let us now consider the effects of three such status differences: differential social power, differential stake in the social system, and differential commitment to maintaining ties with other generations.

Up to middle age or just beyond, the older person in a two-generation relationship typically has greater knowledge, a wider range of social influence, and more control over resources than the younger one. That is, social power in such relationships is asymmetrical; the older person has more of it. The older person also has more responsibility than the younger one. The relative power of people from different age groups changes, of course, as the groups age. Such changes in relative power are usually accompanied by changes—sometimes subtle, sometimes striking—in the quality of the relationship between people of different ages. In particular, consider the transition from adolescence to adulthood. Initially, the parent has almost complete power over important decisions that affect the child. Ultimately, the child is almost completely independent of the will of the parent. The shift in power almost always involves at least some conflict between parent and child. Not uncommonly, the conflict is intense; it may even persist well into the child's adulthood and the parent's old age.

Bengtson and Cutler pointed out that young people and older ones also have a different degree of commitment to the status quo. The youth is more willing than the established adult to question existing ways of doing things, to try out and advocate new ideas, to urge that existing techniques be abandoned. The adult—adapted to the system and occupying relatively important positions within it—is more likely to resist changes unless they are obviously superior to present procedures. Thus, their differential commitment to the system is likely to magnify the perception of differences between age cohorts in beliefs and values.[26]

Beyond this, members of different generations have a fundamentally different orientation toward each other.[27] The youth are interested in developing individuality, in establishing their own identity, in becoming part of their own nuclear family, in moving out of the confines of their parental home and into the larger community. Parents, on the other hand, are concerned with family continuity, with creating a set of social heirs, and with maintaining contacts with them. That concern is likely to be even greater among grandparents. While this kind of difference in orientation is often divisive, it can also have a unifying effect.

Sources of Solidarity Between Age Groups

The most obvious source of solidarity between generations is the affection and esteem that children, parents, and grandparents feel for one another. In most families, bonds of affection more than compensate for whatever differences in beliefs and values there may be. In addition, within the same family there is a continuity of values from one generation to another. More than 40 years ago, Newcomb and Svehla reported positive correlations between the attitudes toward internationalism of parents and those of their children.[28] Similarly, Hirschberg and Gilliland found significant correlations between the attitudes of parents and those of their children toward God (+.29), toward the New Deal (+.59), and toward the Depression (+.42).[29] A quarter of a century later, Flacks pointed out that the college students who were most active in the protest movement of the 1960s were children of extremely liberal parents.[30] Bengtson, in a questionnaire administered to children, their parents, and their grandparents, found that all three groups reported less disagreement among generations within their own families than among generational groups in the society at large.[31]

In other words, there is evidence that societal changes in values are assimilated at different rates into different families—conservative parents are likely to have conservative children and grandchildren, liberal parents are likely to produce liberal children and grandchildren. This continuity doubtless minimizes the conflicts among generations of the same family that would otherwise result from cohort differences in belief and values.

In any society there are many sources of solidarity that form the basis for positive ties even between unrelated persons of different generations. For example, there are innumerable customs, rituals, and other practices that persist without great change over long periods of time. They serve as a framework for agreement about the proper organization and conduct of social life, even between people who disagree about particular issues. Furthermore, members of different age groups often share interests in such things as sports, crafts, literature, and music. Older generations were direct participants in historical events that members of younger generations often enjoy knowing about. These and other factors frequently counteract the differences in belief that can produce conflict among generations.

It seems likely, furthermore, that the sources of conflict among different age cohorts can be overemphasized. The changes in level of education, in ease of transportation, and in the ease and amount of communication among different groups and nations during this century have produced a cohort of elderly individuals who are less provincial, more aware of the variety of standards and beliefs around the world, and more tolerant of diversity than any group of elderly before them. They are likely to be less moved to hostility by disagreement with the young. It is at least arguable, in addition, that these older people are less accurately described by the age-stereotypic traits than were their elderly predecessors.

Implications for Relationships Among Different Generations

Two factors are of special importance in the development of friendship between two individuals. The first is proximity; people are more apt to know and like someone they see frequently than someone they seldom see.[32] The second is similarity of beliefs; people like those who share their interests and values better than those who do not.[33] The paragraphs that follow consider briefly how these and other factors affect relationships between persons from different generations, beginning with people from the same families and then discussing unrelated individuals.

The earlier analysis of differences among age cohorts implies that the greater the age difference between two people, the more likely they are to differ in beliefs and values. Bengtson asked respondents from three generations in the same families to estimate the "gap" between each pair of generations in their own family. Respondents perceived a greater gap between grandparents and grandchildren than between members of adjacent generations.[34] Thus, even though the attitudes of parents correlate positively with those of their children, there exists a gap between generations in the same family. The greater the age difference, the wider the gap.

Does this mean that there will be greater conflict between grandchild and grandparent than between child and parent? Almost certainly not. American youth are likely to express generally positive opinions about their grandparents and be relatively critical of their parents. At least three factors contribute to this. The first is that parents, not grandparents, are responsible for their children's actions. It is they who exert power over the child. When disagreement surfaces, the parent, not the grandparent, typically takes the kind of action that provokes counteraction and may eventually escalate into open conflict.

Second, parents are in more continuous contact than grandparents with the younger generation. Differences between parent and child are more likely to arise, to become a topic for argument, and eventually to lead to hostility. Third, parents and children form a common nuclear family unit from which grandparents by definition are excluded. When conflict ends, members of the unit remain in contact. They feel remorseful. They try to make some kind of peace with each other. Commonly, neither party needs to fear a long-term estrangement from the other. Such is not the case for grandparents and grandchildren. To reprimand a grandchild or to take some other kind of action is to risk rejection and a long-term rift in the relationship. Consequently, grandparents often suppress their disapproval of grandchildren not only because they feel it is the parents' duty, not theirs, to place limits on the child, but also because they hope to maintain, for as long as possible, a close relationship with their descendants.

In short, one might expect to find greater open conflict between parent and child than between grandparent and grandchild. Despite the difference between their beliefs, one often finds reasonably close and mutually enjoyable relations between old people and young ones in the same family so long as (1) they have at least some commonality of interests and beliefs and (2) they live close enough to each other to permit relatively frequent contact.

For members of the same family, both social pressures and individual desires bring old and young people into contact with each other. But what about people of different generations who are not related by kinship? If they were simply thrown together, would it be reasonable to expect that some of them, at least, would become friends? The only study we know that has examined this question suggests that it would, indeed, be reasonable. This study was conducted by Nahemow and Lawton in a public housing project in New York City. The project contains seven fourteen-story buildings. Each floor of each building contains twelve apartments, of which three are one-bedroom units reserved for occupancy by elderly people. Residents are mostly of middle income and about equally divided between black and white. Interviews, about fifteen minutes in length, were conducted with 270 residents of three of those buildings. They were asked to name their best friends in the project, whether they lived in the same building or another one, how often they got together, and where they met. For purposes of later analysis, respondents were categorized as old, middle-aged, and young. The importance of proximity and of similarity in the kinds of friendships that were formed was obvious in the results; of all first-chosen friends, 60 percent were of the same age group, 72 percent were of the same race, and 88 percent lived in the same building. It is important to recognize that a full 40 percent of these friendships crossed age groups and that 28 percent crossed racial groups. But the effects of proximity were especially strong in regard to friendship choices that involved people of different age or race (96 percent of first-chosen friends of different age and 100 percent of first-chosen friends of different race lived in the same building).[35]

Why did proximity make so much difference? No doubt because it increased the chances that two individuals would meet. And why was proximity especially important in mixed-age or mixed-race friendships? Probably because people do not expect to have much in common with others of different age or race and, therefore, are not inclined to initiate such relationships without inadvertent contact. These ideas can be clarified by examining the importance of age similarity and of proximity to the process of getting acquainted. Because this is a chapter on relationships among age groups, not among racial groups, we will not dwell further on the effects of proximity upon interracial relations, though the principles may be much the same.

We all expect to share more interests and values with people our own age than with people older or younger than we are. And we expect to get along better with people who share our values and interests than with those who do not. Both sets of expectations are reasonable ones, as earlier parts of this chapter have made clear. And, other things being equal, these reasonable expectations make us much more likely to initiate, and to follow up on, contacts with people our own age than with older or younger ones.

Proximity of residence increases our likelihood of making friends across age lines because it diminishes the importance of individual initiative in making first contacts with other people. Whether they set out to do so or not, people who live near each other meet while waiting for the elevator, or when picking up the newspaper, or while walking down the corridor, or upon entering the building. They speak to each other when they meet. When they are together for a few minutes they chat. Eventually they are likely to discover common concerns, interests, and beliefs. Over a period of time, they become acquaintances instead of strangers, friends instead of acquaintances.

How is it possible for people of different ages to become friends when we know that age cohorts differ in so many ways? Because, as we have also seen, there are likely to be any number of similarities between people of different ages. These similarities of concerns, interests, and beliefs provide at least some basis for a friendly relationship. Not every friendship requires that the two parties agree on everything. (And a good thing, too; otherwise most of us would have exceedingly few friends.) People often maintain continuing, satisfying relationships with others with whom they disagree, sometimes deeply, on specific issues. They simply don't talk to those people about the points of disagreement; instead, they concentrate on the things they have in common. This pattern is true of most, if not all, friendships, so we should not be surprised to find the pattern occurring in friendships that cross age groups.

To summarize, one may expect to find friendly relationships between persons of different ages provided, first, that contact has been made between them and, second, that they have at least some points of similarity. Of course, not all contacts across age groups will lead eventually to friendship, any more than do all contacts between persons the same age. But there are many more possibilities for such friendships than is assumed in the stereotyped views that young people hold of the old and old people of the young. In fact, Nahemow and Lawton found that people who listed someone of a different age as their first-chosen friend reported seeing that person every bit as frequently as those who listed someone their own age as first-chosen friend.[36]

Let us consider now some of the things that operate to minimize contacts across age lines. Suppose that two people who don't know each other do meet. The meeting is likely to take place in one of three locales: at work, at or near home, or in leisure-time activities. What are the chances of meeting someone from a different age group in each of those contexts? Consider, first, the work setting. Retirement at age 65 or thereabouts is nearly universal in America today. As a result, most young people never come into contact with the elderly at work. Indeed, even when young people meet middle-aged people at work, the status differential is often too great to promote friendship. So the chances are small that at work, where most of us spend a substantial part of our lives, very many contacts will be made between individuals of widely different ages.

What about at home? There is increasing segregation of residence by age. Old people in America frequently live in retirement communities, in apartment complexes for the elderly in the center of the city, or in small towns and villages. In all such localities, younger adults are underrepresented. The age-integrated housing project studied by Nahemow and Lawton is the exception; most public housing segregates old people from young ones.[37] Elderly persons choose such settings for a variety of reasons. They offer more recreation, or a better climate, or more participation in activities, or a place to live for relatively little money. Whatever the reason for choosing age-segregated housing, that choice reduces the likelihood that neighborhood contacts will be made between old and young people, unless they are related by kinship.

If contacts across age are not made at work or at home, how about in leisure activities? Here, again, the chances are not great. For one thing, financial constraints on the elderly severely limit the range of things they can afford to do. For another, differences in interests are likely to send people of different ages to different kinds of activities. For a third, the policies of formal and informal recreational programs—at the local, regional, and federal levels—are often designed, intentionally or not, to promote age segregation. Such segregation is practiced as much by senior centers or by the projects of Area Agencies on Aging as by the Little League, by summer art programs for children, or by young adult discussion groups. Except, perhaps, for churches (which also sponsor age-graded classes and activities), there are relatively few formal or informal social activities in most American communities that cater to a clientele of mixed age.

Thus the probability is relatively low that either fate or individual choice will bring unrelated individuals of different ages into contact with each other. But what difference does it make? Why should we want people to form acquaintances and friendships across age groups? First, let's be clear that people should be free to choose their own associates, so long as their choice does no harm to someone else. Any old person who wants to avoid the young, or any young one who does not care to meet the elderly, should not be forced into such a relationship. That said, there are a number of advantages to making relationships across age groups for individuals who are open to them. The most obvious of these advantages, beyond the pleasures of friendship, is the increased breadth of experience that such relationships provide to the individuals concerned. Each person becomes aware of the other's different perspective on present and past events. In the ideal case, the older person is helped to understand better, even to sympathize with, youthful reactions that might be disliked or even scorned if they were not understood. At the same time, the younger person comes to see a continuity between present events and those of the past; comes, perhaps, to apply a more balanced viewpoint to the analysis of such events; and comes to understand and respect the older person's views. Even if they do not agree with each other, the basis is laid for a clearer understanding of one's own views and those of others.

From the point of view of society, furthermore, relationships across age groups may operate to reduce the widespread age stereotyping that was noted at the beginning of this chapter. Research into impressions of older individuals has shown that stereotyped views of the elderly are held more as tentative hypotheses, to be abandoned when they do not fit individual cases, than as inflexible expectations. At the same time, it is clear that stereotypes of the elderly are predominantly negative. Those negative expectations probably induce people to avoid relationships with the elderly, even those that might be rewarding, without really exploring their possibilities. And the fact is that most elderly individuals do not conform to the stereotype. Almost all old people differ somewhat, and most of them differ quite a lot, from the age stereotype. Then why does the stereotype persist? Probably, like most stereotypes, because people who hold it do not have enough contact with elderly people to observe that their negative expectations do not fit the facts. If we want age stereotypes to change, we need to promote contacts across age groups more than to inveigh against bigotry.

Summary

The principal points of this chapter can be summarized in five propositions.

1. It appears that Americans hold generally negative stereotypes of aging and the elderly. The extent of such age stereotyping is greater for young people than for old ones, but can probably be found to some degree among some persons of every age.

2. Age stereotypes do not serve as inflexible, impermeable expectations about all old people. In fact, impressions of specific older individuals tend to be at least as positive as impressions of young people with the same characteristics. Specific old people who are viewed positively tend to be seen as exceptions to the stereotype. It is unclear whether the relatively positive impressions of old people reflect an overreaction to the contrast between what the perceiver expected and the behavior that is observed, or sympathy for a member of a stigmatized group.

3. There are differences between different age cohorts over a wide variety

of experiences, beliefs, and values. Sometimes this leads to conflict between members of different generations. There are also continuities and similarities across generations which, if recognized, can form the basis for friendship between individuals of different ages.

4. Perhaps because they assume they will have little in common, people typically do not seek out others of a different age as much as they seek out their age peers. In addition, a wide variety of social patterns in contemporary America minimizes the chances that relationships across generations will develop. When such contact actually occurs, however, friendships across age groups are not uncommon.

5. The consequence of stereotyped expectations, combined with social patterns that inhibit a perceiver's having contact with members of the stereotyped group, is that inaccurate stereotypes persist in society over a long period of time.

Notes

1. R. N. Butler, "Age-ism: Another form of bigotry," *Gerontologist* 9 (1969), pp. 243–246.

2. P. Golde and N. Kogan, "A sentence completion procedure for assessing attitudes toward old people," *Journal of Gerontology* 14 (1959), pp. 353–363.

3. D. G. McTavish, "Perceptions of old people: A review of research methodologies and findings," *Gerontologist* 11 (1971), pp. 90–101.

4. R. Bennet and J. Eckman, "Attitudes toward aging: A critical examination of recent literature and implications for research," in C. Eisdorfer and M. P. Lawton (eds.), *The Psychology of Adult Development and Aging* (Washington, D.C.: The American Psychological Association, 1973).

5. C. Cyrus-Lutz and C. M. Gaitz, "Psychiatrists' attitudes toward the aged and aging," *Gerontologist* 12 (1972), pp. 163–167.

6. V. Wood, "Age-appropriate behavior for older people," *Gerontologist* 11 (1971), pp. 74–78.

7. F. K. Garetz, "The psychiatrist's involvement with older patients," *American Journal of Psychiatry* 132 (1975), pp. 63–65.

8. M. Silverman, "The old man and woman: Detecting stereotypes of aged men with a feminity scale," *Perceptual and Motor Skills* 44 (1977), pp. 336–338.

9. L. Harris and Associates, *The Myth and Reality of Aging in America* (Washington, D.C.: National Council on Aging, 1975).

10. J. A. Thorson, L. Whatley, and K. Hancock, "Attitudes toward the aged as a function of age and education," *Gerontologist* 14 (1974), pp. 316–318.

11. R. Garfinckle, "The reluctant therapist," *Gerontologist* 15 (1975), pp. 136–137.

12. C. Ivester and K. King, "Attitudes of adolescents toward the aged," *Gerontologist* 17 (1977), pp. 85–89.

13. K. H. Rubin and I.D.R. Brown, "Life span look at person perception and its

relation to communicative interaction," *Journal of Gerontology* 30 (1975), pp. 461–468.

14. E. B. Ryan and H. L. Capadano, "Age perceptions and evaluative reactions toward speakers," *Journal of Gerontology* 33 (1978), pp. 98–102.

15. E. Palmore, "Facts on aging: A short quiz," *Gerontologist* 17 (1977), pp. 315–320.

16. Rubin and Brown, op cit.

17. N. Kogan and F. C. Shelton, "Differential cue value of age and occupation in impression formation," *Psychological Reports* 7 (1960), pp. 203–216.

18. B. D. Bell and G. G. Stanfield, "The aging stereotype in experimental perspective," *Gerontologist* 13 (1973), pp. 341–344.

19. L. E. Weinberger and J. Millham, "A multi-dimensional, multiple method study of attitudes toward the elderly," *Journal of Gerontology* 30 (1975), pp. 343–348.

20. N. C. Sherman, J. A. Gold, and M. F. Sherman, "Attribution theory and evaluations of older men among college students, their parents, and grandparents," *Personality and Social Psychology Bulletin* 4 (1978), pp. 440–442.

21. M. F. Scheier et al., "Sympathy, self-consciousness, and reactions to the stigmatized," *Journal of Applied Social Psychology* 8 (1978), pp. 270–282.

22. W. H. Crockett, A. N. Press, and M. Osterkamp, "The effect of deviations from stereotyped expectations upon attitudes toward older persons," *Journal of Gerontology* 34 (1979), pp. 368–374.

23. This study was repeated with community residents of all ages, instead of exclusively college students. The results were not as extreme. Perceivers over the age of 40 did not form much more favorable impressions of the old woman than of the young one. Still, they did not form less favorable impressions of her, either. Instead, the age of the other woman had little or no effect upon the favorableness of impressions formed by older perceivers.

24. Crockett, Press, and Osterkamp, op. cit.

25. Scheier et al., op. cit. Similar results for handicapped others have been reported, for instance by R. Kleck, "Physical stigma and nonverbal cues emitted in face-to-face interaction," *Human Relations* 21 (1968), pp. 19–28.

26. V. L. Bengtson and N. E. Cutler, "Generations and intergenerational relations: Perspectives on age groups and social change," in R. H. Binstock and E. Shanas (eds.), *Handbook of Aging and the Social Sciences* (New York: Van Nostrand Reinhold, 1976).

27. V. L. Bengtson and J. A. Kuypers, "Generational differences and the developmental stake," *Aging and Human Development* 2 (1971), pp. 249–260.

28. T. M. Newcomb and G. Svehla, "Intra-family relations in attitudes," *Sociometry* 1 (1938), pp. 180–205.

29. G. Hirschberg and A. R. Gilliland, "Parent-child relationships in attitudes," *Journal of Abnormal and Social Psychology* 37 (1942), pp. 125–130.

30. R. Flacks, "The liberated generation: An exploration of the roots of student protest," *Journal of Social Issues* 23 (1967), pp. 52–75.

31. V. L. Bengtson, "Inter-age differences in perception and the generation gap," *Gerontologist* 11 (1971), pp. 85–90.

32. R. Athanasiou and G. A. Yoshioka, "The spatial character of friendship formation," *Environment and Behavior* 5 (1973), pp. 43–65; L. Festinger, S. Schachter, and W. Back, *Social Pressures in Informal Groups* (New York: Harper, 1950); and M. P. Lawton and B. B. Simon, "The ecology of social relationships in housing for the el-

derly," *Gerontologist* 8 (1968), pp. 108–115.

33. D. Byrne, "Interpersonal attraction as a function of affiliation need and attitude similarity," *Human Relations* 14 (1961), pp. 283–289; T. N. Newcomb, *The Acquaintance Process* (New York: Holt, Rinehart, and Winston, 1961); and R. F. Priest and J. Sawyer, "Proximity and peership: Bases of balance in interpersonal attraction," *American Journal of Sociology* 72 (1967), pp. 633–649.

34. Bengtson, op. cit.

35. L. Nahemow and M. P. Lawton, "Similarity and proximity in friendship formation," *Journal of Personality and Social Psychology* 32 (1975), pp. 205–213.

36. Ibid.

37. Ibid.

20

The Family and the Elderly

Geoffrey H. Steere

Introduction

The subject of the family life of the elderly combines two topics—the elderly and the family—about which there has been popular misunderstanding. This misunderstanding sometimes has caused people to feel anxious or even repelled by images of old age and of family life. There is a negative overgeneralization in the United States, believed by young and old alike, that produces a distorted picture of old people as uniformly poor, sick, lonely, and socially isolated—in brief, thoroughly miserable.[1] While this portrait is unrealistic in light of systematic social research,[2] it nevertheless can be disturbing. Also disturbing is a negative overgeneralization about the family, which is found often in the popular media, books, and (more rarely) in scholarly sources. The contemporary family is unfavorably contrasted with families in the past (time often unspecified), when unity, cooperation, and happiness are assumed to have characterized family life. Ideas about such matters as, for example, modern divorce, working mothers, personal geographic mobility, generation gaps, the isolation of the nuclear family, and the abandonment of the elderly are marshalled to create a distorted picture of current family decline or decay. This portrait also is unrealistic in light of social research and the perspective provided by historians of the family.[3]

There is much evidence to modify the negative portraits of uniformly miserable old people and decaying family life. Old people tend not to apply the myths of the elderly to themselves, but they do apply them to other old people. They know the myths often do not fit their own personal experience.[4] As one elderly person said, "There's nothing that I need to make my own life better. But there's so many other older people that do need help, that don't have a family and friends and neighbors like mine."[5] The self-reported experiences of old people indicate that they are considerably less distressed by inadequate income, health, and sociability, for example, than would be predicted by public expectation.[6] The morale of old people has remarkable resilience, and much of the elderly population is made up of individuals who strive to maintain middle-aged life patterns as long as possible, using their continuing (if often diminishing) abilities to cope with life's contingencies.[7]

As for the family, popular images again bear correction. It is not self-evident, for example, that divorce disrupts families more than did death in days before modern medicine. The high remarriage rate of divorced people suggests that divorce is not equivalent to disaffection with marriage and family. People today are not necessarily more geographically mobile and rootless than in the nineteenth century. Families have been nuclear (rather than extended) for several hundred years, and today's "isolated" family maintains ties with wider kin in a variety of ways (as discussed in Chapter 1 of this volume). The commitment of families to the care of their young and old remains strong. As Bane has concluded, after reviewing data relevant to the myth of the dying family, "The facts—as opposed to the myths—about marriage, child rearing, and family ties in the United States today provide convincing evidence that family commitments are likely to persist in our society. Family ties, it seems clear, are not archaic remnants of a disappearing traditionalism, but persisting manifestations of human needs for stability, continuity, and nonconditional affection."[8]

The subject of this chapter, then, is not problem-ridden oldsters whose families are examples of a decaying institution. Our focus is on elderly people continuing to adapt to and cope with life stress, in relation to other members of a resilient (if imperfect) institution to which Americans have continuing powerful allegiance—the family.

Scholarly interest in the family life of the elderly is relatively new. In 1963, a prominent article concerned with conflicting American values and the future of the American family could ignore even mentioning the elderly.[9] And in 1968, Jan Stehouwer noted that "family sociologists have hitherto shown a reluctance to deal with family relationships in the last stages of the life cycle. . . . The last stages in the development of the family have been systematically disregarded."[10] There is, however, a considerable body of recent literature on the family life of the elderly. The literature shows the characteristics of a relatively new research field: that is, studies vary widely in their sampling techniques, in the questions they ask, and in the measures they use. This means that the results often are not comparable or cumulative. Consequently, many of the generalizations we make now about the family life of the elderly will be subject to revision (especially as methodological sophistication catches up with the theoretical advances).

In this chapter, we will discuss the relationship between old people and their family-kin networks, relationships between elderly spouses, sibling relationships among old people, and relationships between the elderly and their children and grandchildren. In so doing, we will generalize from the broadest commonalities of American experience, since Chapter 13 ("The Ethnic Factor") has already traced the influences of race and ethnicity on the aged, influences that assuredly affect the family life of the elderly.[11]

The chapter closes with a discussion of changing relationships between society and the family in light of a current suggestion for social policy: i.e., deinstitutionalization of the elderly, so as to place greater responsibility for their care on family members. Families now include and will increasingly include many more old people. This is the result of the striking numerical and proportional escalation in the elderly population, from 4 percent (3 million people) in 1900 to 10 percent (20 million people) in 1974. The population of the elderly may increase even more because of biomedical research, which enables more and more people to live long or even extraordinarily long lives.[12] These trends in longevity lie behind the increasing attention given to deinstitutionalization, for the likelihood of an elderly person becoming institutionalized increases with age.[13]

But institutional care of the elderly may become ever more problematic by virtue of escalating costs and shortages of qualified institutional personnel. Consequently, thoughts are turning to the family. Families care about the welfare of their elderly members (despite myths to the contrary),[14] but society offers the family few supports for translating sentiments of filial responsibility into action. And, as Judith Treas points out,

> it is unreasonable to assume that family sentiment can ensure adequate day-to-day supervision, housekeeping, personal maintenance, or nursing of older Americans. Some families thrive on affection while others are marked by disaffection. Alienated children hardly can be expected to take on these daily ministrations, and even well-meaning kin may find that custodial care is simply too much for them. . . . However, state and federal programs might consider the wisdom of direct subsidies to families who participate in the day-to-day care of aging relatives. Families who overcome the many obstacles to home care of the aged would seem to warrant direct payments as surely as do strangers providing less personalized services. Tax breaks, special allowances, and direct reimbursements to family caretakers promise to promote those kin ties so threatened by social and demographic change.[15]

We will outline this proposition more fully and consider a number of controversial questions that the concept of deinstitutionalization raises about the relationship between the family and society in a democracy.

There are several general points about the aged and kin network that deserve attention before we consider specific categories of family relations. First, the family with third and fourth generations is more common today than ever before. This is, of course, a result of the numerical and proportional increase in the elderly population already noted. Of people 65 and over, 70 percent have grandchildren and 40 percent have great-grandchildren. But these figures minimize the number of multigenerational families: the average age when men and women become grandparents is 57 and 54 respectively (well before age 65); and they become great-grandparents at 75 and 72. Viewing these figures in another way, during the past half-century a 10-year-old white child's likelihood of having at least two living grandparents has increased from 40 percent to 75 percent, and of having at least three grandparents alive, from 10 percent to 38 percent.[16] The family, then, is now likely to include two categories of elderly people, the young old and the old old. This demographic change impinges on the family in various ways, not the least of which is that the responsibility for care of the often vulnerable very old falls on children who may themselves be relatively elderly.

Another important generalization is that old people are not physically or socially isolated from their children and relatives. Indeed, one of the best-established findings relevant to family gerontology is that "the extended kin network, defined as a social system of grandparents, adult children, and other relatives, is widespread in the United States and that help patterns among kin are common."[17] This general point was implied earlier, but it bears repeating because the social myth of "the abandoned elderly" dies slowly, and it distorts clear understanding of the family relations of later life.

While the elderly are part of an interacting family-kin network, most old people live apart from their children and relatives. Elderly people want to live independently in their own households as long as possible. Older parents want to live near their children but not with them. As Shanas so accurately noted, what older people want in relation to family members is "intimacy at a distance."[18] This attitude fits with a more generalized desire of the elderly to maintain their personal independence, reflecting the deeply held commitment of Americans to the value of self-reliance. The most gratifying family relationships for old people are those in which the elderly can minimize dependence and maximize their continued successful autonomy.[19]

As a final background generalization, we can say that the family relationships of the elderly are more voluntary than obligatory. This is really a subpoint of a larger generalization that the modern family is characterized by choice—about who to marry, how many children to have, how to conduct interpersonal relations, and so on. This freedom of choice makes family relationships relatively ambiguous. Consequently, the appropriate ways for people to relate across generations are not easy to state simply or clearly, because in a modernized society there are none of the well-understood obligatory family ties and roles characteristic of traditional societies. At one time, religious tradition, enforceable social rules, and control of resources by elders served to command for old people respect and care from their children. But the increasing capacity of younger people to determine their own lives has reduced the obligatory nature of their relationships to the older generation. Given the apparent decline of the command-obligation character of intergenerational family relations, these relationships now depend for their viability more on the willingness, imagination, and persistence of the participants.[20] Recognizing voluntarism in contemporary family relations is critically important when thinking about social policies that affect the family. With these generalizations in mind, let us consider specific categories of family relations of the elderly.

I

Parent-Child Relationships

The stereotype about families usually rejecting or abandoning their elderly members has no support in fact. There is extensive contact between elderly parents and their children and relatives. A living pattern has evolved whereby about 75 percent of elderly parents have children living within a thirty-mile travel distance, 78 percent see a child once a week, and 90 percent see a child once a month. Almost all women over 80 (98 percent) and 72 percent of men over 80 live either with a child or within ten minutes of one.[21]

Living near one another does not, of course, guarantee intimate, warm, or sharing interaction. The child's visits may be only dutiful ones "to keep tabs on mother" rather than to communicate meaningfully with her. However, generalizing about the quality of parent-child interactions is hazardous until there is more qualitative research on the topic.[22]

Irrespective of residential closeness and frequency of visits, an integrating system of help characterizes intergenerational family relations. Help usually goes from elderly parents to their married children. Parents seem to continue to give to their children in various ways as long as possible. Changes in this pattern may signal decline in parental health or finances.[23] In return, elderly parents expect from their children's families continuing affection, inclusion in some of their children's activities, and some personal services and attentions. Sussman suggests there is a pattern of "distributive justice" in cases where a declining parent requires special help from children: that is, the largest inheritance reward goes to the child who has provided the most physical care, emotional support, affection, and social interaction.[24]

These links of intergenerational reciprocity reveal the complementary needs of elderly parents and adult children. Perceptions of these links tend to differ by generation.[25] Parents interpret them as affectional relationships: parents want affection, real or imagined, and seek it in exchange with children. Children, on the other hand, perceive the links rather as services and exchanges of help: adult children must give affectionally to others (mates, children) as well as to parents, and respond to their parents' emotional needs for respect and understanding by providing specific services.

These two different views of parent-child links suggest generational "distance." As Streib notes, "The children, . . . having broken some of their emotional ties with their parents and having established new ones with their own conjugal families, do not value so highly their affectional relationships with their parents."[26] Related to the disparate valuing of affectional relationships are differences in values and standards about such issues as drinking, housekeeping, childrearing, manners, etiquette, and religious beliefs.[27] Children tend to maximize these differences between themselves and their parents, while parents do the reverse. One can imagine that such differences can be painful for elderly parents at a time in their lives when the maintenance of close emotional ties with their children may become increasingly necessary as the parents become more dependent. Elderly parents are well advised, however, not to attempt reducing the differences by changing their children's values or lifestyles through criticism or authoritarian control. The successfully adapting parent will recognize that he has lost the powers of influence and discipline formerly exerted on children and will accept compensation, preferably filial love and respect.[28] Carrying out this ideal strategy of stepping aside gracefully can, again, be painful for elderly parents. However, despite some differences between young and old in values and in interpretations of their relationship, evidence suggests that these differences do not prevent either frequent interaction between elderly parents and their adult children or gratification from their relationship.[29] As Hess and Waring point out, "despite the many real and apparent potentials for value dissonance, most families appear to have developed a 'tent of values' under which members can meet, enjoy one another's company, share a consciousness of sameness and sense of responsibility for one another."[30]

Parents, as we have seen, want to live independently as much as possible. The stereotype that elderly parents want to be dependent on their adult children—to move in with them whenever possible and/or to demand money and services from them—is an unsupportable folk belief.[31] Still, the ideal of independent living for parents can be hard to achieve under conditions of medical or economic crisis. When the elderly parents can no longer manage, they expect their children to aid them.[32] And adult children tend to be responsive to their parents' needs for help.

This developmental stage in family life, when the elderly are increasingly dependent, has been most adequately conceptualized as a phase of "filial maturity." It occurs often when children are in their 40s and 50s and "parents can no longer be looked upon as a rock of support in times of emotional trouble or economic stress but may themselves need their offspring's comfort and support."[33] Filial maturity means that the child can be depended upon by the aged parent; also, it means that the parent can be willing to accept being dependent and allow the child to become mature. This phase is characterized by variants of the strain and solidarity, give and take that occur throughout the entire range of relationships between elderly parents and their children.

Grandparents and Grandchildren

The role of grandparent has received little attention, possibly because of the great value put on child rearing within the independent nuclear family and the concomitant belief that participation in childrearing by grandparents would be detrimental.[34] Grandparents today are likely to be middle-aged: the average age at which men and women first become grandparents is 57 and 54, respectively.[35] They are often youthful, energetic job-holders, characteristics quite removed from the rocking-chair stereotype of the past. Because of the increased age of the population, the number of grandparents is large. For the same reason, grandparents are no longer necessarily the oldest members in the family, which increasingly has four generations. The younger generations see more of grandmothers than of grandfathers, since by age 65 women outnumber men 134 to 100, and at age 85 the ratio is 160 to 100.[36]

Knowledge of the attitudes that grandchildren and grandparents have about each other is sparse. Research has yielded no firm generalizations about attitudes of adult grandchildren toward their grandparents.[37] Evidence about the attitudes of grandparents toward their grandchildren is fragmentary. An attitude toward grandchildren of "glad they come, glad they go" may prevail, with stronger ties more likely to occur when grandparents and grandchildren live near one another. As grandparents get older they may prefer small children, because older grandchildren, as they become increasingly preoccupied with their peers, don't want to be bothered with their grandparents.[38] Still, in the Neugarten and Weinstein study, "the majority of grandparents expressed only comfort, satisfaction, and pleasure" in their role of grandparent.[39]

Becoming a "valued grandparent" does not come automatically with grandparenthood, notes Troll, but is a status that must be achieved through personal qualities and active practice of an "extended parental role." "As a consequence, grandmothers, who are more experienced in the details of child rearing, are more successful than grandfathers, even though mothers welcome a helper more than a substitute, and try to cut down the autonomy of the grandparent. However, the father role can't be shared, so grandfathers have to adjust to more maternal behavior."[40]

Neugarten and Weinstein identify several kinds of significance and meaning of the grandparental role. It can be a source of biological renewal ("It's through my grandchildren that I feel young again") and/or of biological continuity ("It's through these children that I see my life going on into the future"). The role can provide emotional self-fulfillment (that is, the role may be better played than was fatherhood). A small proportion of grandparents find a new role in playing the resource person (by contributing experience and/or finances to the grandchild's welfare). It may provide also vicarious accomplishment (when the grandparent sees the grandchild achieving what the grandparent or the first-generation offspring could not achieve). Finally, the grandparent role may be experienced as remote from the grandchildren's lives and have little affect on the grandparents' lives.

There appears to be a variety of styles of grandparenting.[41] The Formal Grandparent maintains a constant interest in the grandchild, but follows a carefully prescribed role that separates parenting from grandparenting and does not intrude on the former. The Fun-seeking Grandparent carries on a playful and informl relationship with the grandchild, where authority lines with either grandchild or parent are unimportant. The Surrogate Parent (usually a grandmother) assumes responsibility (at the behest of a working mother) for care of a child. The Distant Figure is the grandparent who appears in the child's life rarely (although benevolently) and is essentially remote from the grandchild. In general, the quality of the relationship between grandparent and grandchild apparently depends on factors such as the ages of the grandparents and grandchildren involved and the authority of the grandparents in the family. Grandparents over 65 are more likely to be formal and younger ones to be fun-seeking. The increased prevalence of the multiple-generation family undoubtedly will stimulate further understanding of intergenerational relationships, including transmission of values and behaviors across generations.

Husband-Wife Relationships

The long-term decline in mortality rates has meant that increasing proportions of married couples survive together as two-person families after the last child has married and left home.[42] The basic unit of family life in old age is the marital couple; among those 65 and older, over 50 percent are married couples.[43] Few couples (around 12 percent) live with their children, which is consonant with belief in "intimacy at a distance."[44]

The postparental couple is likely to have perhaps 15 years left together. The literature on married life during this period shows that there is likely to be increased companionship and emotional satisfaction, reported as somewhat comparable to the honeymoon. It should be noted, however, that couples who do not grow old together self-eliminate from researchers' data through divorce, desertion, or separation. Also, couples' interpretations of their experience may further distort information: that is, the longer a couple has remained together, the greater their investment in perceiving (and thus reporting) their relationship as worth the effort and satisfying.[45] Still, many marriages after children leave appear to mellow generally and strengthen. More specifically, strengthening means that husband and wife become closer in personality as rigid sex role expectations and behaviors are relaxed or "inappropriate" behaviors (e.g., nurturance by men, dominance by women) become more acceptable.[46] The likely pattern is that husbands adjust from the instrumental role of breadwinner to a more expressive role of household helper; and wives adjust from the role of homemaker to an even more expressive loving and understanding role.[47] Spouses at this juncture have successfully negotiated two major marital tasks of the postretirement, postparental period: shifting focus from children to each other, and incorporating the retired husband into the household.[48]

For very old couples when both are feeble, the pattern of interaction between husband and wife becomes more idiosyncratic than before. Tasks are no longer defined by sex roles, for each spouse does whatever he or she can still manage to do. The relationship at this advanced stage is highly interdependent, such that the death of one spouse means the other can no longer survive independently.[49]

A source of marital satisfaction in later years may come from a couple's simply knowing that they have survived together in an age of seemingly fragile relationships. Elderly couples may survey the disruption, separation, and divorce among younger couples and be grateful that they have successfully avoided these common pitfalls.[50] Elderly couples undoubtedly benefit from important aspects of the times into which they have survived. Postparental couples are healthier and more secure economically compared to earlier generations of elderly couples. And the changed sexual attitudes of society may have benefited elderly spouses. More open discussion of sexuality and growing recognition that there is continuing sexual responsiveness in later life may reduce guilt and raise expectations for loving sexual experience in elderly spouses.[51]

Sibling Relationships Among the Elderly

Brothers and sisters can offer each other both psychological and social support in old age. Old people today were born into large families, and most of the elderly have living brothers and sisters.[52] Ties between siblings are not as strong as those between parents and their children, but sibling relationships are the next most important source of primary relations.[53] Old people who never married are likely to keep up closer relations with siblings than those who marry and have children. When nonparents lose a spouse, they establish closer ties with siblings, but their ties are less close than those of single people.[54] Sister-sister ties, which provide mutual stimulation and companionship, appear to be stronger than between brothers and sisters (sisters usually providing emotional support for the aged brother), while brother-brother ties seem to be the weakest. This pattern is consistent with the female role of maintaining attachments that has been observed in other kinship relationships.[55]

II

The Tension Between Family and Society: Deinstitutionalizing the Elderly

The family relationships of the elderly we have reviewed in the previous pages occur in a social context. That is, the family life of old people, like all family life, does not take place in a social vacuum, but rather in an interaction between the family and outside-the-family factors. This interaction constitutes a tension in people's lives between the demands of family life and the demands of society. In a culture in which the roles and expectations of family life are both clearly understood and in close harmony with the roles and expectations in extrafamily life—as for example in the seventeenth-century Massachusetts Bay Colony[56]—the tensions will be relatively mild. But in a more complex and modernized society, such as the contemporary United States, where family and extrafamily roles and expectations are frequently ambiguous and not always in harmony with each other, tensions from conflicting demands are likely to be relatively more intense. The "rules" for managing the tensions between the family and society vary from culture to culture, and may vary over time in the history of a single culture.

We can gain some understanding of the current evolving relationship between the family and society by considering a social policy proposal for family care of the elderly. The proposal is for deinstitutionalization of the elderly: i.e., returning them from institutions into the care of their family members. The possible development of such a policy raises questions involving basic American values regarding societal regulation and privacy of American family life. Answers to these questions will be consequential not only for treatment of the elderly, but also more generally for how Americans manage the relationship between family and society.

The pressure to develop social-gerontological policy that involves the family derives from American attitudes of concern toward the elderly and from demographic trends in the twentieth century. Our attitudes regarding the aged are not unambiguous. No society can persist if its adults do not provide care for children; the social need to care for the elderly is less compelling. This discrepancy creates a problem, the solution to which is more a matter of social discretion than it is of child care. Consequently, the elderly are more vulnerable than are children in the hands of a society such as ours, in which old people typically are not seen as an asset in themselves. On the other hand, offsetting their vulnerability is the documented "affection, attention, and assistance which children routinely provide to elderly family members."[57] Given this value orientation, as well as the aging of American society—which means also the "graying" of the family—our society's need to find ways to care for the elderly is indeed compelling.

This need derives in no small part from changes in mortality and fertility rates during the twentieth century.[58] These changes have important consequences for the kin network. Survival to old age, relatively rare in the past, is quite usual now. The increase in life expectancy has reached to age 72; and there is an additional increased life expectancy of 15 years for those who live to age 65. Also, there has been continuing growth in the elderly's share in the population relative to younger age groups. Only 6.4 percent of the U.S. population was 60 or older in 1900, compared to 14.8 percent in 1975, according to the U.S. Bureau of the Census. This proportional growth has derived less from improved medical care than from the trend since 1900 toward smaller families: that is, successive generations of women gave birth to fewer children than did their mothers and grandmothers. The consequences of these shifts for intrafamily support are that "today's middle-aged adult is more likely to have a living parent than his counterpart in the past. Despite the improved survival chances of off-spring, the aging parent, having raised fewer children, will have fewer descendents to call upon for assistance than did his own parent. . . . Clearly, kin networks can offer fewer options and resources when there are fewer members of the younger generations."[59]

In addition to its growth, the elderly population has changed also in composition, presenting another dimension of the problem facing the kin network. An elderly relative is more likely to be a woman, a widow, and very old than was true even as recently as 1930. This derives from women typically outliving their husbands, because women tend to be younger than their husbands and also exhibit greater longevity than men; also, women remarry to a lesser extent than do men. Widows traditionally tend to be dependent on family supports, because they lack the economic, nursing, and housekeeping supports of a married couple living independently. Another compositional change is found in the aging of society. The survival of people born in the high-fertility years of the late nineteenth and early twentieth centuries has contributed to growth in the elderly population concentrated in those people 75 and older—the age category in which people are most likely to need assistance or institutionalization. This development contributes to what Treas calls "the demographic dilemma confronting kin networks," for as she points out, "demographic shifts have meant fewer brothers and sisters with whom to share the sometimes considerable burden of physical, financial, and emotional support of aging parents. This burden is made more poignant by the realization that some of the aged are very old. No longer are the children of these 'frail elderly' prime-age adults. The very old in greatest need of care have offspring who are the 'young old' with their declining energy, health, and finances."[60] The dilemma is unlikely to ease demographically, for the current 30 percent of the elderly (65-plus) population that is 75 and older is likely to escalate to 41 percent by the end of the year 2000.

With this brief survey of values and demography as a background, we can consider deinstitutionalization. The strategy of deinstitutionalizing the elderly has been most extensively articulated and justified in the context of family history, sociology, and demography by Sussman.[61] His proposal may be summarized as follows. Incentives to family units could be used as alternatives to institutionalization of the aged family member. Adult children or other relatives can best supply the supportive care to an elderly family member in the period of aging between independence and the need for extended total care (if that need ever occurs). While many families are willing and able to provide care to elderly kin now, others might do so if various supports were available to mitigate the stresses that such care involves. In other words, a system complementary to the institutionalization of elderly family members—one that stimulates involvement of elderly people living alone with other members of their kin network—can be developed by using and reallocating existing economic and service resources. Thus, by tapping the existing and potential roles of family structures and networks, a buffer can be built for aging members against the impositions of controlling institutions and bureaucracies. Various forms of the family (as distinguished from friends, neighbors, and acquaintances) can provide a more desirable option than institutional settings by providing requirements for survival and quality living—intimacy and human warmth. *Family* refers here not only to the immediate family (e.g., parents and children of the nuclear family of procreation), but also to people interpreted as family. This might include kin who are rather distantly related by blood or marriage (e.g., second cousin, niece, grandnephew, aunt-in-law) but who are included in the kin network.

The incentives to the family providing care could be designed contractually during a given time and involve such benefits as a direct monthly allotment of funds; specific tax write-off for expenses involved; a loan to add to or renovate a house so as to provide convenient and independent living for the old person; income tax relief for taking on the responsibility of care; availability of particular services from existing agencies (e.g., providing for daycare and homebound services) that are needed or helpful to the caretaking family; and property tax reduction proportional to dwelling use of caretakers. These incentives could relieve a family's dwindling resources and remove impediments to aiding its elderly members. By removing economic liabilities from the oldster/family linkage and offering instead a reward, modern family responsibility could be stimulated.

Sussman believes that the family's role in providing care for the elderly is inevitable, arguing that research and policy statements all point out that in the remainder of the twentieth century there will be "neither enough institutions nor trained people to staff them to meet the expanding need for health and custodial care for the growing aged population." He continues by saying:

> During the past decade federal health, welfare, and rehabilitaton agencies have implicitly followed policies of reversing the trend of providing care and treatment for the chronically ill and aged in isolated, highly bureaucratized, and impersonal institutions. Providing services in the communities of those who require them is now being advocated, and comprehensive community health facilities are but one example of implementation of such a new policy. A logical extension is to carry the service one step further, to the family.[62]

The concept of returning the elderly to the care of the family, at least in Sussman's formulation, is in many respects a thoughtful, informed, and humane policy proposal. The question arises, however, whether a deinstitutionalization policy would be good for the family. Ideally, the policy would stimulate and broaden kinship and provide warmer and less bureaucratic care for aged family members. Additionally, it is said that deinstitutionalization would further spur present momentum to reduce inefficiency and red tape in social service institutions and "return the responsibility for care to the community and ultimately to the family where it naturally resided in the past."[63]

These positive aspects could generate momentum for the policy. They have ideological appeal. Americans are likely to respond favorably (as they do to Motherhood) to notions of enhanced family relations, warm personalized care of old folks, and the honoring of historic traditions of family and community care for dependents. In addition, the assumption that deinstitutionalization is inevitable under conditons of inflation and scarcity could add further significant impetus to policy formation. There is today increasing interest in Congress concerning behaviors (e.g., teen-age pregnancy, domestic violence) within the family structure. Congressional discussion and consideration of intrafamily problems is, in itself, a change in politicians' traditional "hands-off" stance toward the family.[64] Already deinstitutionalization is said to be "the new rallying cry for service providers and policy makers."[65] Thus, while deinstitutionalization may be currently proposed by its most thoughtful advocates as an optional alternative to complement existing institutionalized care systems, there is no guarantee that it will remain a wholly voluntary option. Clearly, now is the time to ask questions about potential implications of deinstitutionalization for the family.

The family is vulnerable in the processes of change. Unlike virtually every other segment of society, it does not have organizations or representation with which to mount self-defensive systematic resistance to change initiated and supported by nonfamily organizations, associations, interest groups, and government units. While the latter have local, regional, and national organizations, treasuries, and paid lobbyists, the family has no comparable paraphernalia for promoting or defending its interests.[66] Consequently it is in the position of having to accommodate to changes initiated elsewhere,[67] including changes that may conflict with family well-being.

This point is illustrated by an example from the early 1960s, when a policy of deinstitutionalizing mental patients and returning them to their families was being heavily promoted.[68] It was supported by powerful groups, such as the National Association for Mental Health, and backed by millions of dollars in federal funds. It was assumed that the family would adapt to the returning mentally ill members (even as it was assumed in earlier decades that the family would adapt to return of family members paroled from prison). Furthermore, the family was expected to adapt to the intrusion into the home of mental health professionals concerned with the patient's recuperation (just as it was earlier expected to adapt to social workers, parole officers, and juvenile court judges). The family suffered as a result of deinstitutionalizing mental patients: it did not have the skills, resources, or preparation to handle the return of mentally ill family members. Nevertheless, the family adapted to this policy. There was no real option, because the family was and is not organized to pose and demand examination of a very basic question: Does the family have the capacity to live up to its ideological image as a haven for all its members, including those experiencing emotional disturbance or delinquency or advanced old age?

It appears that insufficient thought is given to the lot of the family during formation of policies that affect it. As Vincent points out, these sorts of questions are not raised often enough: "How will the family be affected by the return of a mentally ill member? What will double shifts do to the family? Will the regulations of ADC (Aid to Dependent Children) encourage husbands to desert the family? Will urban renewal disrupt the family and the network of extended family relationships? Would it be easier on the family to draft 45-year-old fathers for many service tasks prior to drafting 25-year-old fathers for those same tasks?"[69] Or, directly relating to deinstitutionalization policy: "Will it be used as a subtle means of enforcing family responsibility?" "What will be its impact on the affective interactions in families and on the feelings of the older person?"[70] Even if these questions were asked, no one would answer for the family, as it has no spokesperson. Consequently, those who develop policies and programs must be sensitive to the family's vulnerability and concerned for the well-being of family life. Such attitudes are reflected in Sussman's point regarding policy development of deinstitutionalization: "The task is how to more effectively involve family and kin network in long-term care of the elderly and to do this without using the power of law and without destroying the internal dynamics of the particular family unit."[71]

Are there aspects of a policy of deinstitutionalizing the elderly that could be harmful to the family? Possibly. The previous quote alludes to the potentially adverse impact on family relations of a legally enforced policy whereby family members had to care for elderly relatives. Under such conditions, existing alienation between generations would surely be increased. Very likely there would be strains in establishing multigenerational living even among those family members who voluntarily undertook it. Since old and young alike prefer living in independent households, sharing a home would be undertaken usually only as a last resort—and often at a time when the participants might be feeling at less than their best physically and emotionally. Forced multigenerational living would assuredly only intensify strain. However, household sharing can be beneficial when motivated by real affection, given adequate thought and preparation, and undertaken voluntarily.[72]

Sussman inadvertently points to another source of trouble, a values clash. He notes that incentives of economic or social benefits—inherent in the deinstitutionalization scheme—are considered by Americans to be appropriate for nonfamily units but not for the family: "these same rewards have been considered dissonant with the ideology and ethos of the family and demeaning of its values."[73] He dismisses this attitude as inappropriate, but his dismissal does not deal with the values conflict to which he points. People undoubtedly use incentives, rewards, and contracts as necessary and inherent strategies in daily family life, but they often use these strategies tacitly—without being aware of their use. Deinstitutionalization would make their use in family life obvious and the values clash clear. People who believe that these strategies are antithetical to right family living might not live well under a policy in which their use is so clearly a part. Yet, with deinstitutionalization as established policy, family members could feel constrained to cooperate, despite feeling stress and even anguish from the resulting values clash. Undoubtedly people's sensitivity to such dissonance varies. For some, receiving public supports under contract for care of an elderly relative would not be uncomfortable; for others it could be a source of mild but not prohibitive stress. One might ask which among these groups would provide elderly kin the affectionate personalized care that is both the principal gift the family can offer to the elderly and the kind of care deinstitutionalization is meant to stimulate? Is it those who accept comparatively easily an exchange-contract model of family interaction, or those who do not? There is no firm answer to this question, for the formulation of deinstitutionalization is largely untested.[74] But it is the kind of question that reveals potential competition or conflict between family values and values of society imbedded in policy.

Another possible threat to the family posed by deinstitutionalization is invasion of the family's privacy. The question of privacy goes to the heart of the persisting tension between family and society. Society has a legitimate interest in at least some aspects of family life (e.g., marriage and divorce regulation), because the family creates the new generations necessary to the survival of society. But the family needs privacy, for there its members express themselves most intimately and freely.[75] Deinstitutionalization calls attention to this relationship between family needs and society's needs. If family care of the elderly in private home settings is to be supported with public money, it is most likely that standards would be created for appropriate and effective use of such money. And from standards of accountability flow difficult questions. Who would define *appropriate* and *effective?* Who would specify standards? Who would evaluate and monitor the "right use" of public funds in homes? How would controls be carried out, and with what consequences? It would seem apparent that some forms of public inspection of private family behaviors would necessarily evolve with deinstitutionalization. To what extent would Americans be willing to tolerate public scrutiny of family behavioral interaction between generations, hitherto considered private? To what extent would families permit the intrusion into the home of professional and paraprofessional personnel concerned with reviewing care of the elderly? These questions about deinstitutionalization relate to basic values in the relationship between society and family privacy.[76]

Given complexities such as these values clashes, deinstitutionalization may come only slowly, despite pressures for rapid adoption noted earlier. Certainly time is needed to gain experience with various forms, styles, and structures of home care and public support mechanisms that clarify which ones work well under which circumstances. Ideally, this is the way to develop a genuinely viable policy—a constructive deinstitutionalization that by definition must promote equality, self-determination, and adequate resources for the eldery. Whether policy development will be guided predominantly by humane values, careful research, and field experience or by forces of political and economic expediency remains to be seen. One should watch the emerging philosophy and influence of the newly created federal Office for Families for indicators of policy development.

Families need relief from crushing burdens experienced in providing quality care for elderly members. But society, in providing such relief and thereby honoring protective social values, cannot dictate through law the conduct of family home life without violating yet other sacred American values. In whatever ways these factors may be forged into workable practice, the course of deinstitutionalization of the elderly lies on a policy frontier of competing values and priorities where the uneasy relationship between family and society is evolving.

Notes

1. See Louis Harris and Associates, *The Myth and Reality of Aging in America* (Washington, D.C.: National Council on Aging, Inc., 1975).

2. See, for example, F. J. Berghorn et al., *The Urban Elderly* (Montclair, N.J.: Allanheld, Osmun, 1978).

3. See Mary J. Bane, *Here to Stay: American Families in the Twentieth Century* (New York: Basic Books, 1976).

4. Harris, op. cit., p. 38.

5. Berghorn et al., op. cit., p. 11.

6. Ibid., p. 10.

7. Ibid., esp. Chap. 6.

8. Bane, op. cit., p. 141; see also Marvin B. Sussman, "Relationships of Adult Children with Their Parents in the United States," in *Social Structure and the Family: Generational Relations*, Ethel Shanas and Gordon F. Streib, eds. (Englewood Cliffs, N.J.: Prentice-Hall, 1965), pp. 62–92.

9. Charles W. Hobart, "Commitment, Value Conflict and the Future of the American Family," *Journal of Marriage and Family Living* 25, 4 (Nov. 1963), pp. 405–415.

10. Ethel Shanas et al., *Old People in Three Industrial Societies* (New York: Atherton Press, 1968), p. 178. See also Donald E. Gelfand, J.K. Olsen, and M. R. Black, "Two Generations of Elderly in the Changing American Family: Implications for Family Services," *The Family Coordinator* 27, 4 (Oct. 1978), p. 399.

11. See, for example, Carol E. Woehrer, "Cultural Pluralism in American Families: The Influence of Ethnicity on Social Aspects of Aging," *The Family Coordinator* 27, 4 (Oct. 1978), pp. 329–339.

12. Elaine M. Brody, "Aging and Family Personality: A Developmental View,"

Family Process 13, 1 (March 1974), pp. 23–27.

13. Of people 65 years and older who live in long-term care institutions—slightly less than 5 percent of all elderly people—those 65 to 75 compose less than 2 percent, whereas those 75 and 85 compose 7 percent, and those 85 and older constitute over 16 percent. See Sheldon S. Tobin and Morton A. Lieberman, *Last Home for the Aged* (San Francisco: Jossey-Bass Publishers, 1976), p. 211.

14. Elaine M. Brody, "The Etiquette of Filial Behavior," *Aging and Human Behavior* 1 (1970), pp. 87–94.

15. Judith Treas, "Family Support Systems for the Aged," *Gerontologist* 17, 6 (Dec. 1977), pp. 490–491.

16. Brody, "Aging and Family Personality," p. 25.

17. Ethel Shanas, "Family-Kin Networks and Aging in Cross-Cultural Perspective," *Journal of Marriage and the Family* 35, 3 (Aug. 1973), p. 505.

18. Ibid., p. 508.

19. See Berghorn et al., op. cit., p. 80.

20. See Beth B. Hess and Joan M. Waring, "Changing Patterns of Aging and Family Bonds in Later Life," *The Family Coordinator* 27, 4 (Oct. 1978), pp. 303–304.

21. Shanas et al., op. cit.

22. Hess and Waring, op. cit., p. 278.

23. Lillian E. Troll, "The Family of Later Life: A Decade Review," *Journal of Marriage and the Family* 33, 2 (May 1971), p. 267.

24. Marvin B. Sussman, "The Family Life of Old People," in *Handbook of Aging and the Social Sciences*, Robert H. Binstock and Ethel B. Shanas, eds. (New York: Van Nostrand Reinhold Co., 1976), p. 233.

25. Dean K. Black and Vern L. Bengtson, "Solidarity across Generations: Elderly Parents and their Middle-Aged Children" (Paper presented at the annual meeting of the Gerontological Society, November 1973).

26. Gordon F. Streib, "Intergenerational Relations: Perspectives of the Two Generations on the Older Parent," *Journal of Marriage and the Family* 27, 4 (Nov. 1965), p. 472.

27. Margaret Clark and Barbara G. Anderson, *Culture and Aging* (Springfield, Ill.: Charles C. Thomas, 1967), p. 279.

28. Ibid., p. 278.

29. Dean K. Black and Vern L. Bengtson, "The Measure of Solidarity: An Intergenerational Analysis" (Paper presented at the annual meeting of the American Psychological Association, 1973).

30. Hess and Waring, op. cit., p. 308.

31. Only about 4 percent of aged parents receive financial aid from their children. Fewer than 25 percent live with their children.

32. Wayne C. Seelbach, "Correlates of Aged Parents' Filial Responsibility Expectations and Realizations," *The Family Coordinator* 27, 4 (Oct. 1978), p. 342; see also Berghorn et al., op. cit., pp. 90–91.

33. Margaret Blenkner, "Social Work and Family Relationships in Later Life with Some Thoughts on Filial Maturity," in Ethel Shanas and Gordon F. Streib, eds., *Social Structure and the Family: Generational Relations* (Englewood Cliffs, N.J.: Prentice-Hall, 1965), pp. 46–59.

34. Troll, op. cit., p. 278.
35. Brody, "Aging and Family Personality," p. 25.
36. Ibid., p. 26.
37. Troll, op. cit., p. 278.
38. Ibid., p. 279.
39. Bernice L. Neugarten and Karol K. Weinstein, "The Changing American Grandparent," *Journal of Marriage and the Family* 26, 2 (May 1964), p. 200.
40. Troll, op. cit., p. 279.
41. Neugarten and Weinstein, op. cit.
42. Matilda W. Riley and Anne Foner, *Aging and Society, Volume One: An Inventory of Research Findings* (New York: Russell Sage Foundation, 1968), pp. 160, 164.
43. Gordon F. Streib, "Old Age and the Family: Facts and Forecasts," *American Behavioral Scientist* 14 (Spring 1970), p. 30.
44. Ibid., p. 30.
45. Hess and Waring, op. cit., p. 311.
46. Ibid., p. 311.
47. Troll, op. cit., p. 274.
48. Ibid., p. 273.
49. Troll, op. cit., p. 275.
50. Elizabeth Douvan, "Changes in the Family and Later Life Stages" (Paper presented at the annual meeting of the Gerontological Society, November 1978), p. 6.
51. Ibid.; see also Troll, op. cit., pp. 274–275.
52. Riley and Foner, op. cit., p. 160.
53. Ibid., pp. 544, 588; see also V. G. Cicirelli, "Relationships of Siblings to the Elderly Person's Feelings and Concerns," *Journal of Gerontology* 32, 3 (May 1977).
54. Shanas et al., op. cit., p. 166.
55. Troll, op. cit., p. 281; Cicirelli, op. cit.
56. Edmund S. Morgan, *The Puritan Family* (New York: Harper & Row, 1964).
57. Treas, op. cit., p. 486.
58. See ibid., pp. 486–487; and Gelfand et al., op. cit., pp. 396–397.
59. Treas, op. cit., p. 487.
60. Ibid., p. 488.
61. Sussman, "The Family Life of Old People," op. cit.; see especially pp. 235–241 concerning deinstitutionalizing the elderly.
62. Ibid., p. 236.
63. Ibid., p. 239.
64. *The Washington Cofo Memo* 11, 1 (Winter 1979), p. 7.
65. Sheldon S. Tobin, "The Myth of Deinstitutionalization," *Society* 15, 5 (July/August 1978), p. 73.
66. Clark E. Vincent, "Familia Spongia: The Adaptive Function," *Journal of Marriage and the Family* 28, 1 (Feb. 1966), pp. 33–34.
67. Technically speaking, this means that the family tends to be a dependent variable in the social system and in the processes of social change. See, for example, Vincent, ibid.; David F. Aberle, "Culture and Socialization," in *Psychological Anthropology*, Francis L. K. Hsu, ed. (Homewood, Ill.: Dorsey Press, 1961), pp. 381–399. This is so despite the family's documented but limited ability to effect the course of change.

See, for example, William J. Goode, *The Family* (Englewood Cliffs, N.J.: Prentice-Hall, 1964), pp. 110–114; Tamara Hareven, "Family Time and Industrial Time," *Journal of Urban History* 1 (1975), pp. 365–389. Goode argues that the strategic function of the family is found in its mediating function in the wider society. The family links the individual to the larger social structure (Goode, op. cit., p. 2). For example, the family may provide a mediating linkage between an elderly member and bureaucratic structures by helping the aged person interpret, use, and benefit from bureaucracies.

68. Vincent, op. cit., p. 34.

69. Ibid., p. 34. See also Alvin L. Schorr, *Explorations in Social Policy* (New York: Basic Books, Inc., 1968), p. 154.

70. Barbara Silverstone, "An Overview of Research on Informal Supports: Implications for Policy and Practice" (paper presented at the annual meeting of the Gerontological Society, November 1978), p. 16.

71. Marvin B. Sussman, "Family, Bureaucracy, and the Elderly Individual: An Organizational Linkage Perspective," in *Family, Bureaucracy, and the Elderly*, Ethel B. Shanas and M. B. Sussman, eds. (Durham, N.C.: Duke University Press, 1977), p. 218. It is encouraging that there has been created recently a federal Office for Families (within the Department of Health, Education and Welfare), among whose stated goals is to analyze the implications for family life of current and proposed policies. Also encouraging are the increasing numbers of studies and conferences bearing on policies and programs that affect the family. Furthermore, in several places family impact analysts are being trained. See Leo F. Hawkins, "The Impact of Policy Decisions on Families," *The Family Coordinator* 28, 2 (1979), p. 266.

72. Hess and Waring, op. cit., p. 309. For a discussion of ways to prepare and train kin for in-home caretaking, see Anna H. Zimmer and Janet S. Sainer, "Strengthening the Family as an Informal Support for Their Aged: Implications for Social Policy and Planning" (paper presented to the annual meeting of the Gerontological Society, November 1978). For discussion of the ineffectiveness of the extended family in providing long-term assistance (as distinct from acute emergency aid) to the aged, see Russell A. Ward, "Limitations of the Family as a Supportive Institution in the Lives of the Aged," *The Family Coordinator* 27, 4 (Oct. 1978), pp. 365–373.

73. Sussman, "The Family Life of Old People," p. 239.

74. Ibid. However, for preliminary research findings showing a positive inclination by respondents to programs that would provide economic assistance and services for family care of the elderly, see Sussman, "Family, Bureaucracy, and the Elderly Individual," pp. 218–219, and Sussman, *Social and Economic Supports and Family Environments for the Elderly* (Washington, D.C.: Department of Health, Education and Welfare, 1979), p. 81.

75. Bane, op. cit., p. 71.

76. There are other commitments and policies similarly challenging the boundaries between family and society. One such commitment is to sexual equality. If there should be mass adoption by women of hitherto male occupations that remove women from the home, then pressing questions would arise regarding care for children, especially young ones. Should child care increasingly be entrusted to publicly supported nonfamily units, such as day care centers? If so, to what extent will government regulation be required to carry out and monitor public programs of child rearing? How

willing will Americans be to entrust to public agencies the task of child socialization historically regarded as a sacred task of families in the privacy of their homes?

Abuse of children and the elderly raises similar questions with respect to the traditional social commitment to protect the dependent young and old. Our social values make intolerable the maltreatment in the home of helpless children and old people. But our values also make abhorrent the intrusion into family privacy of public officials for purposes of examining and controlling intergenerational relationships.

21

Sexual Expression and Aging

Dennis M. Dailey

Teaching older people about human sexual expression may be an enormous waste of time and energy. First, they often know a lot already. Time and experience can be great teachers. Secondly, they may prefer not to know, which is just as important and, frankly, a matter of civil rights. Not all old people need or want to express themselves sexually, and that choice needs to be as carefully guarded as does the option for sexual expression. Yet there are old people who do need to learn.

But teaching young people about sexuality and aging also is important, as is teaching those who will be relating to older people in some service capacity.[1] There is no easier way to engage young people in the discussion of sexual expression in older people than to remind them that they too will be old and have the opportunity to choose their own sexual futures. Unlike days gone by, many young people accept and enjoy their sexuality (at least there is more openness and less mythology), and the thought of losing it affects them profoundly. As a matter of fact it frightens them! So, what will be said here is directed at the young and those who will be working with or on behalf of older people, since they, too, are almost always younger than the elderly they work with (there are some notable exceptions, like Gray Panther Maggie Kuhn, Alex Comfort, and others).

Any discussion of human sexuality, but especially sexual expression in later life, almost always encounters three major problems: (1) the tyranny of silence, (2) the laughter curtain, and (3) the lack of a good conceptual definition of human sexuality.

The Tyranny of Silence

We live in a very sexually "uptight" society, despite the fact that there is generally a more open and accepting attitude about sex than there once was.

We have heard a lot about the so-called sexual revolution, but what is happening with respect to sexual attitudes and behavior could hardly be legitimately called a revolution. There surely are some revolts in small corners, as in certain geographic areas or on university campuses, but for the vast majority of people in America, sex still is a most difficult matter.

This inhibition lends itself to the tyranny of silence. Sexuality is still not an acceptable part of polite conversation. Jokes, yes, gossip, yes; but serious discussion of sex, which is such a pervasive part of every person's life, is generally avoided. We'll talk about almost everything else, but not sex. This is especially the case with respect to the sexual attitudes and behaviors of older people. Sex is a young person's game, and the very thought of two older people rolling around in the sack strikes most younger people dumb in their tracks. Secretly, we suspect that lots of older people do not give up sexual expression, but we have a hard time recognizing and accepting that fact. Maybe if we don't talk about sexual expression among older persons it will go away and we won't have to be bothered (or threatened) by it.

The truly unfortunate consequence of this tyranny of silence is that is produces a social milieu in which myth, distortion, and bias abound. And even worse, it isolates the older person who might have questions, concerns, and problems about sex, and creates an atmosphere not very conducive to continued growth and development. As Comfort puts it:

> There's one great problem about ageism. If you think of the other prejudices, white racists don't turn black and anti-Semites don't wake up and find they're Jewish. But we shall all get to be old. I wonder what would happen to Archie Bunker's view of immigrants if he was going to turn into a Puerto Rican on his sixty-fifth birthday. About the most unproductive prejudice is one directed against a group you're going to join.[2]

The tyranny of silence contributes significantly to ageism, which partly consists of the enormous distortions and myths that surround the sexual aspect of growing old. The tyranny of silence produces attitudes that define the older person as asexual. And those older people who maintain an interest in sex are assigned to some deviant group, like "dirty old men" or "perverted old ladies who should know better." The actual conditions surrounding the aging process need to be known if the tyranny of silence is to be broken. Again, Comfort puts it well:

> This is the most important thing to remember. You will not feel any different when you're eighty from what you do now, except for some illnesses. You may find that it's harder to get around or to be as energetic as you were. But you'll be the same person you are now. You don't find you'd suddenly become a dif-

ferent person. I remember there's a very nice account I was told about a Senator showing some party seniors around the Senate. He did all the right things. He shouted in case they were deaf, and spoke in words of one syllable in case they were doting. Well, at the end of it, he turned to an old gentleman with a white beard and said, "What used you to be?" And the man said, "I think I still am, sir."[3]

And this applies to sexual expression as well.

The Laughter Curtain

The tyranny of silence is bad enough, but what about the laughter curtain, the response produced by the discomfort and threat resulting from encounters with certain aspects of life? The laughter curtain is often lowered when the topic is sex. We get so anxious that our only response is to make jest of something that is really serious, but that we cannot treat seriously. "Old people expressing themselves sexually? What a laugh!"

Let us look at some not-so-funny examples of how the laughter curtain operates. A man in his middle 70s went to his doctor with a concern that had bothered him for some time. It was difficult for him to express his concern, in part because he was not sure of his doctor's response. Finally he said, "Say, Doc, I've noticed just lately that when I get an erection it doesn't seem the same. It doesn't get so hard as it used to. Do you think something is wrong?" The doctor chuckled nervously. He was caught off guard. Sex was the last thing he thought his patient would be asking about. His response, given with an uncomfortable laugh, was: "Oh, well, we've all got to lose it sometime." What an insensitive and erroneous answer. Here was a man who still enjoyed a reasonably active sexual life, who had a very legitimate question. But what he got was the laughter curtain. The response could just as well have been: "Well, that's not so unusual at all. As a matter of fact lots of men your age have that experience. As we age the hardness and angle of erection changes somewhat—from approximately a 90-degree to a 45-degree angle—due to stretching of the ligaments that support the erect penis. Don't worry about it." A simple, straightforward answer would have been so much more helpful. It would not have planted the seeds of sexual doubt and failure, and the suggestion that the concern was not serious or even appropriate for an older male. So the laughter curtain can separate people from potential sources of help and the possibility of emotional growth.

Another time the laughter curtain is particularly prominent is when young people are asked, say in a classroom setting, to consider the sexuality of their parents and grandparents. If you took their initial reactions (usually laughter, combined with shock) seriously you would ultimately have to ask how they all got here. A typical comment? "Well, I have two brothers and one sister, so I know they did IT (a favorite term for sexual behavior) at least four times, but not nowadays." Another comment: "Are you kidding? My mom and dad? I just can't see it." And when we talk about grandparents the room usually fills with laughter. Unfortunately, it is the kind of laughter that is injurious to older people. "The gulf between parent and child is to a large extent probably inevitable, with its roots perhaps lying in the difficulty that children have accepting their parents as sexual beings."[4] Maybe it is not so much a "generation gap" as it is the anxiety we all feel about sex that separates young people from old in terms of sexuality.

In a study entitled "Can Students View Parents as Sexual Beings?" Pocs and Godon confirmed the perspective that young people have of older people:

> The students' estimates of their parents' present coital frequency as compared to Kinsey's married sample by age categories . . . show that Kinsey's figures are usually more than twice the student estimates. If one looks at the modal age group for the study's sample (41-45 for mothers and 46-50 for fathers), the student estimate is 2.8 times per month whereas Kinsey found a frequency of about 7.0 times per month. . . .
>
> Looking at daughters' and sons' estimates of parental coital frequency and combining appropriate categories, the authors found that as many as 41% of daughters and 36% of sons estimated that parents engaged in sexual intercourse with a frequency of a few times a year to never. Combining more categories, they found that 57% of daughters and 52% of sons estimated a coital frequency of once a month or less. At the same time, over 90% of the students characterized their parents' marriage as ranging from somewhat happy to very happy, with over 80% falling within the happy to very happy range. Yet, for over half of these students, a happy marriage includes a barely active sexual life.[5]

Living with such assumptions, older people slowly learn not to be sexual and acquiesce to social pressures for conforming to the view of the elderly as nonsexual beings. Therefore, they give up a part of their life experience that by and large has been meaningful and pleasant. As they grow older, their self-perception is formed from the attitudes held by others younger than themselves.

But it is not all the fault of the young. Many people have never heard about sexuality from their parents, and for those who have, the conversation was often most uncomfortable: that nervous laughter again. As a matter of fact, many young people are very disappointed and frankly angry that their parents and elders have not given them adequate sex education as preparation for their own sexual lives. So we produce a vicious circle that has an energy of its own in our society. Older people do not talk about sex with much comfort or confidence. Thus, younger people easily assume that sex for older people is irrelevant, maybe even nonexistent. Older people, in turn, hear this message, and a self-fulfilling prophecy develops; old people begin to think of themselves in asexual terms. And we all suffer!

Human Sexuality

If we are to talk about sexuality at all, we will need an accurate and useful definition that captures the fullness and richness of this most complex human attribute, and in that context describes sexual expression as it can and often does occur among older people. When we state that we feel sexually "turned on" to a certain person, it is highly unlikely that we will be asked to define our use of the phrase. If we tell someone that we have sexual feelings, we are not likely to be quizzed about the nature of those feelings or what we mean by having sexual feelings. An enormous assumption is made that we all know what everyone is talking about when the topic is sex.

For many people sex is not a three-letter word, but rather a four-letter word. When people think about sex they usually equate it with genital functioning. In other words, sex is equated with intercourse. But *sexuality* is a nine-letter word, only three of which are *sex* as usually defined in genital terms. Surely human sexual expression is much more than genital behavior. So far as matters of definition are concerned, sexuality seems to have been relegated to that fuzzy-headed state made up of "common understanding" and generalized inexplicitness. As a general orientation, it is usually understood that sexuality refers to those instances in which a person responds in an emotionally positive way toward another person. Or it refers to a wide variety of behaviors performed in the name of sexuality. However, such a definition can be considered useful or orienting only in a grossly general and imprecise manner. Highly ephemeral feeling states and widely varying behaviors do not represent a systematic conceptual picture of the richness of sexuality as a basic human function. These highly disparate and diffuse aspects of human sexuality do not do justice to the very integrated quality of human sexuality. *Sexuality*, as it is used here, will be devided into five separate but overlapping and integrated aspects, beginning with sensuality.

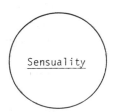

"Sensuality is the psychological and physiological enjoyment of one's own body and often, a partner's, including but not limited to the genitals; and the tension release of orgasm. Also the behaviors and partners that one perceives as potentially sensually satisfying."[6] Actually, sensuality can be seen as composed of four rather specific areas. The first is a good understanding and awareness of the physiological aspects of our sexuality. We are born with certain kinds of physiological equipment, about which many of us know very little. We don't know the names for sexual physiology, and worse, we have very little understanding of how and why it functions as it does when we are feeling sexual. This lack of understanding and awareness has a profound impact on our understanding of the elderly, since it produces much inaccuracy. The most pervasive consequence is the notion that at a certain age the physiological equipment just stops working and thus desire ends. Nothing could be further from the truth. It is true that the aging process does bring about some changes in physiology, and these are often poorly understood. These changes are experienced without good preparation, but need not be traumatic nor imply the end of one's sexual expression.

For the male there are some basic changes that might be expected to occur at some time, but before describing them we should note that Masters and Johnson found the presence of sexual activity in 70 percent of married males at the age of 70. The frequency of activity may decrease with age, but the level of satisfaction derived from the experience may be maintained. The expected changes associated with aging in males are:

1. It may take somewhat longer to achieve an erection, but the solution to this change is more direct and desired stimulation.
2. When the erection occurs it may be slightly less hard, but this does not mean that successful intercourse cannot occur.
3. It may take a slightly longer time for an ejaculation to occur. However, in the perspective of the male's partner this is likely to be seen as a positive rather than a negative effect, and it will usually bring more joy to the male, also.
4. The release of semen during ejaculation may be less forceful and the experience of orgasm may be somewhat less intense. Given the degree of pleasure that remains, this change need not be considered too important.
5. It will usually take a somewhat longer time before a second erection is possible. Again, this need not be viewed as a traumatic change.

For women there are also some expected changes, which usually occur in the context of menopause. With hormonal changes due to menopause, women can expect to experience the following:

1. The walls of the vagina are likely to become thinner, which may cause some discomfort during intercourse. Of course, gentleness on the part of the woman's partner will go a long way to alleviate this problem. Hormone creams are also useful.
2. The normal lubrication that occurs in the vagina may be less, which is likely to result in discomfort during sexual intercourse. There are products on the market today that mitigate this problem.
3. It may take some women a longer time to become aroused; but here again, patience, and taking time to enjoy the total experience, can be considered in a positive light.
4. There may be some changes in the orgasmic experience. Orgasm may be less intense, occur over a shorter period of time, and in a few cases may be experienced as uncomfortable. With respect to orgasm, there are some key issues. Women who usually have experienced orgasms should have little trouble in continuing to do so well into their 80s and 90s. Further, orgasm does not always have to be the goal for a fully satisfying sexual experience.[7]

In general, then, there are some changes accompanying aging, but none are as serious as many believe. These changes can be managed to allow older people to have physiologically satisfying sexual experiences.

The second aspect of sensuality is the satisfaction of skin hunger. Our skin is our largest sex organ, something more women know and some men are now discovering. The skin can be seen as the presenting surface in the human being. It is sensitive to touch, pressure, pain, pleasure, temperature, etc., and physiologically is one of the first aspects of another person that we encounter. All human beings are seen as having varying needs to have skin hunger satisfied. The need to touch, to be held, to make contact with another person, is a strong motivation in social behavior. The need to be touched, stroked, and held are strong desires for most people.

However, there is wide variation in individual needs that is both physiologically and socially imposed. For some, a back rub is a pleasure. For others it tickles and is irritating. Some people enjoy being touched when making social contacts; others feel assaulted. Women have more social permission to touch than men. Whatever the case may be, the satisfaction of skin hunger is one of humankind's deepest sensual needs and its presence or absence, or variation, can often define an experience as sensual or nonsensual.

For older people the satisfaction of skin hunger is very important. Holding each other, stroking each other, and feeling physiological closeness can be a fully rewarding sexual experience in and of itself. Genital contact may be far less rewarding than the satisfaction of skin hunger, which is often withheld from older people. Young people often avoid touching older people. Health

care professionals often do not touch older people in the course of their interactions. Yet being held while being comforted can be much more important than words, and a simple touch can be more affirming of one's existence
than words. Separating married couples who live in nursing homes is an unfortunate policy, since it cuts couples off from the satisfaction of skin
hunger, which may be their preferred and only sexual expression.

A third aspect of sensuality is the tension release of orgasm, the release of
sexual tension and energy via the physiological focus upon genital sexual expression. Clearly, there is some satisfaction of skin hunger in most of the
genital activity that occurs between human beings, but the physiological experience of orgasm is viewed as unique, not necessarily better. It is in the
category of tension release in orgasm that most of the materials on genital
expression fall. To look at the popular literature, one would think that genital behavior and the tension release of orgasm constitutes the bulk of human
sexuality, the result being the present "cult of the orgasm." In the perspective
taken here, the tension release of orgasm is viewed as important, but not the
sine qua non of human sexuality.

The tension release of orgasm is just as important to older people as it is to
anyone else, and the capacity to experience orgasm is also about the same.
Older people who maintain reasonably good health and who have
developed and maintained a capacity to experience orgasm are very likely to
retain their ability. Women who were nonorgasmic when young are not
likely to become orgasmic when older, although some may through masturbation. Likewise, men can usually retain the capacity to experience orgasm,
given that no health problems (such as prostatic difficulties or excessive demands to perform) interfere. It is clearly the case that men and women who
enjoyed sex and the tension release of orgasm during their younger years are
much more likely to enjoy them when they become older.

A final aspect of sensuality is somewhat harder to capture in words. It begins with the idea that the mind is the most important and powerful sex organ. In this context, one must address the importance of fantasy, memory,
and other sensory aspects of sensuality. All of the sense organs can be important to sensual reception and pleasure. Certain sights, sounds, and tastes
can be sensual. It is our sensory capacity that is central to our experience of
sensuality, yet we may very well have a highly sensual experience quite apart
from our senses in the form of fantasy and memory. Often fantasy and
memory are combined with sensory experience to make the total sexual experience full and rich. An example is masturbation, which usually involves
active use of fantasy, memory, and sensory stimulation. For the older person
who is comfortable with sexual fantasy, it continues to be an important
aspect of sensual experience. Except in the case of severe cognitive dysfunction, fantasy may be an important, or preferred, mode of sexual expression,

fully satisfying in and of itself. And remembering can be a pleasurable and rewarding sexual experience.

For some older people, desire for sexual expression may decline somewhat as they age, but total loss of sexuality usually occurs only as a result of severe health problems or by choice. For those who choose to remain sexual, the sensual aspect of sexual expression provides much variation: satisfaction of skin hunger, tension release of orgasm, fantasy, and memory.

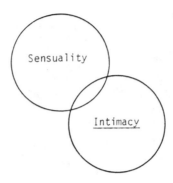

Sensuality is one aspect of human sexuality, but it does not capture the full richness of sexuality. Another aspect is intimacy. "Intimacy is the capacity for the pleasure of openness, closeness, and interdependence with another person. It is also the absence of loneliness. Also the characteristics of those with whom one chooses to be intimate."[8] Whereas sensuality tends to represent closeness in physiological terms, intimacy represents closeness in emotional and affective terms. It is characterized by the capacity of an individual to disclose inner thoughts and feelings to another in a trusting context, and likewise to be the recipient of the self-disclosure of another. Intimacy is giving and getting, in the context of basic human needs. It is in the expression of intimacy that one's sense of loving or liking another person is expressed, primarily through affection. Intimacy between persons is a highly mutual experience. It is hard to experience intimacy if another person does not accept or give it.

Oden defines intimacy in the following manner:

> Intimacy is an intensely personal relationship of sustained closeness in which the intimus sphere of each person is affectionately known and beheld by the other through congruent, empathic understanding, mutual accountability, and contextual negotiability, durable in time, subject to ecstatic intensification, emotively warm and conflict-capable, self-disclosing and distance-respecting, subject to death and yet in the form of hope reaching beyond death.

As is the case with sensuality, intimacy can take place within or outside of the context of a sexual experience. That is, one can be sexual without being intimate, and intimate without sexual expression. The male experience with a prostitute may characterize the former, while a deep friendship may characterize the latter. Oden expresses it this way:

> Much sexuality, to be sure, has the quality of intimacy. But genital orgasm can and often does occur without intimacy, and even as an offense against it. While intimacy can emerge within the framework of sexuality, intimacy is never adequately defined by sexuality. To view intimacy only as an aspect of sexuality is a peculiar misjudgment of popular modern consciousness.[9]

The obverse of what Oden says is also the case; that is, sexuality cannot be adequately defined in terms of intimacy, although many people would say that their sexuality must contain a large ingredient of intimacy for it to be a truly meaningful personal experience.

The overlap of sensuality and intimacy produces several interactions, both positive and negative, which may account for the fact that one's sensual partner may also be a close and dear friend. In the same way, the peculiar misjudgments that arise out of our contemporary sense of intimacy are what often keep people from developing intimate relationships outside of their primary bonds, i.e., because of the fear or expectation that sensual expression must naturally follow intimacy.

People search for intimacy because it is a basic human need, one of particular importance to older people. For the elderly who are married, intimacy needs are met as they always have been, and maintaining intimacy often is critical to continued fulfillment of sexual needs and desires. It is not unusual to hear about older couples who experience a deepening intimacy in their relationship and, as a consequence, rediscover or enhance their sensual experiences with each other. The statement, "Grandpa and grandma behave like a couple of young lovers," exemplifies this experience.

Intimacy also has its painful side for many older people, especially those whose partners die. With the loss of a primary intimate relationship, the older person will often give up his or her own sexual needs, and in a sense, decide to become asexual. This could be considered an unfortunate double loss. The older person who has lost an important intimacy may choose not to express his or her sexuality genitally with another person, but that does not mean that it is necessary to give up a sense of sexuality or the perception of oneself as a sexual being. Maintaining an interest in sensual needs, in terms of the satisfaction of skin hunger, through fantasy, or through memory can be a continuing vital force in the life of an older person. Many of what seem to be the most well adjusted and satisfied older people are those who maintain an awareness and image of themselves as sexual beings, even though they do not necessarily act upon that awareness.

But leaving the discussion of intimacy, there is another point necessary to our understanding of the concept. Most intimacy is seen as an occurrence between two or more persons, a social experience, but some people experience intimacy outside the usual social context, for example, with pets. It is also the case that some qualities of intimacy can be seen as an intrapersonal experience. Being "close" to one's self, having feelings of self-love and self-acceptance are also experiences of intimacy. Having self-awareness and being able to act upon that awareness can and does yield an intrapersonal intimacy of much importance to most human beings, especially those who are not part of a primary bond. Again, masturbation is a good example of sexual intrapersonal intimacy. Knowing what one prefers in sexual experience, knowing one's needs for sexual expression, and having a self-loving perspective all reflect intrapersonal intimacy.

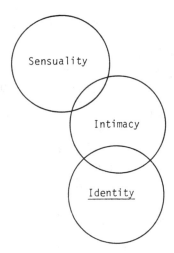

A third quality of human sexuality is identity, which is "the development of the sense of who one is sexually and how one perceives and projects a sense of maleness and femaleness."[10] At the very heart of the search for sexual identity is the more general but profound question, "Who am I?" We all spend much of our lives searching for an answer to this question. As we answer it, we build in a cumulative fashion the thing called self-concept or self-image. We develop a strong mind's eye picture of who we are, what other people see when they look at us, what others experience when they experi-ence us, and what we choose to present to others who want to know or ex-perience who we are. The search for sexual identity must be viewed in the context of our search for self-concept and self-esteem. Sexual identity is one aspect of the total person that we are and perceive ourselves to be.

As we begin to develop our sexual identity, we think of ourselves first in terms of our biological sex. If we have a penis and scrotum we are referred to as male. If we have a vulva, and later breasts, we are referred to as female. Although this is not always the case, usually the primary and secondary characteristics of our biological sex very early establish how we view our-selves and how others view us. *Gender identity* refers to this psychological state in which a person has the sense of being male or female, and our bio-logical sex and gender identity usually are in correspondence. Gender iden-tity is established early, as little children begin to see themselves in terms of being a boy or a girl.

The next level of sexual identity is somewhat more complex. *Gender role identity* refers to an individual's learning and acting upon socially accepted characteristics and behaviors that are strongly associated with a person's biological sex and gender identity. Sex role socialization begins very early also, as we receive reinforcement from our social environment. Not too long ago, the question of how a person develops the sense of being either male or female was thought to be a nearly irrelevant question, especially in terms of one's sex roles. It was assumed that boys are boys and girls are girls, and that boys will become men while girls will become women. Boys, in other words, will become masculine in their sex roles and girls will become feminine in theirs.

There is no question that the process of socialization, which we all experi-ence, has a strong influence on our gender role identity and behavior. Par-ents, family and social institutions strongly influence gender differences and thus gender role identity. Our culture has been and still remains gender spe-cific, and it is hard to escape the gender-specific influences on our identity as sexual beings. Early in life, we begin to perform masculine or feminine sex role stereotypic behavior, which reinforces sexual identity in later social rela-tionships. We still live in a world in which "little boys don't cry when they scrape their knees." Later on, males are expected to initiate and lead the way in sexual interactions; while little girls, who are still "made out of sugar and spice," later are expected to be passive in sexual interactions.

Although biological sex has obviously not changed over time, and the na-ture of gender identity has remained about the same, gender role perception and behavior have undergone some notable changes in the past few decades. There are not many instances of gender-neutral situations in our society, but there has been a steady blurring of gender roles. It is becoming increasingly difficult for many people to think in dichotomous masculine and feminine terms. In earlier times, the issue of sexual identity may have been much simpler and straightforward, although not necessarily better, than today.

Recently attention has been turned to the notion of androgyny (from the Greek *andro*, male, and *gyne*, female), the psychological state in which an individual incorporates traits, attributes, and self-perceptions that are associated with both masculine and feminine sex roles. In a sense, the individual represents the best of both. An androgynous person is one who can be both independent, industrious, and assertive, and at the same time dependent, nurturant, and tender, depending upon changing circumstances and needs. The androgynous person is more flexible in dealing with the social environment, without being constrained to behave or respond in a narrowly masculine or feminine manner. With the increase in an androgynous sex role perspective, the issue of sexual identity will likely become more complex, and in the minds of some, much more satisfying and humane.

One of the common assumptions about older people is that they are rigid and unchanging, and this assumption is also held about their gender role identity. And there is some good evidence that older people, like so many others, adhere to the rigid sex roles in both attitudes and behavior.[11] This is most apparent as one observes older people struggling with some of the contemporary changes in our society with respect to sex roles. Older people are just as sex role stereotypic as others, which should not be a surprise to anyone, given the cultural lag associated with change of almost any kind.

Yet, on the other hand, there is some suggestion that as we age we become increasingly more androgynous. That is, we become more comfortable with both the masculine and feminine qualities we possess. Block has described the development of sex role identity as a complex interaction, "a synthesis of biological and cultural forces. . .mediated by cognitive and ego functioning," which is complete only when the individual reaches the highest level of ego functioning and, through socialization, integrates traits and values that are both masculine and feminine.[12] This integration process most often occurs in the later stages of our lives and may very well account for some of the androgynous qualities of some older people. For many of the elderly the worry about adherence to rigid sex roles is no longer as important as it was in their youth and middle age. It is not unusual to see older women act on some of their masculine qualities—for example, being assertive and independent in managing their financial affairs after their husbands have died. Likewise, it is not unusual to see men expressing the nurturing and tender sides of themselves—for example, playing with and caring for their grandchildren as they may not have with their own children. Changing circumstances dictate more flexibility in dealing with the social environment, and it is clear that many older people possess sex role flexibility, which may very well contribute to a more satisfying and rewarding experience in the later stages of growth.

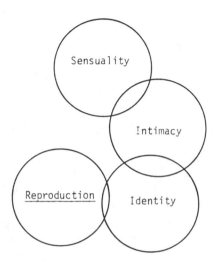

Another aspect of one's sexuality is the reproductive function. "Reproduction involves attitudes and behaviors, including self-expectations, related to producing children, and the consequences to individuals and societies as a result of these attitudes and behaviors."[13] It is a fact that certain sexual activities can and do result in the creation of new life. For some this is frightening, for others it is mysterious and miraculous, and for still others it is surprising. Our discussion of sexuality would be incomplete without considering its reproductive aspect. It is under the rubric of reproduction that one addresses such matters as male and female reproductive physiology, the role of family planning, contraception, venereal disease, abortion, sterilization, and childbirth.

For a long period in our history, sex education has generally focused upon reproductive sexuality. Young people are taught about the anatomy of the sex organs, physiological sexual functioning, conception, pregnancy, and childbirth. Factual information about the reproductive aspect of sexuality is important, but it is insufficient if isolated from the other aspects of sexuality. What is alarming is the fact that young people can know all the information well, yet the incidence of unwanted new life continues.[14] Facts divorced from attitudes represent only half a loaf. Nowhere is this more apparent than in the stories told by young people about their sex education. Morrison and Borosage quote excerpts from student reports: "The only thing my mother ever told me about was my period. No mention of the male sex organs or intercourse was ever made. When I came to college, the shock of the let's-jump-in-the-sack men really floored me. I had been brought up that my body was nothing to be ashamed of, but it wasn't to be flaunted either." Another student said, "I was one evening pulled aside by my father and told how living matter reproduces itself. Out of this explanation, I gained a rather sound understanding of cellular divisions, embryology, and fertilization. Yet there was no mention of human sexuality and its relationship to love, lust, gratification, or fulfillment."[15]

Another important aspect of reproduction in human sexuality is the deep influence it has on perspectives of human sexual functioning. This is best illustrated by what is known as "the reproductive bias." The reproductive bias holds that the only good sex is that which could conceivably result in a socially approved conception and pregnancy, and that all other sex is bad. For several centuries sex was seen only as a reproductive act. Having sex for fun or pleasure was deemed irresponsible. The result of the reproductive bias, which persists today in more subtle form, is to generate two groups of people, one sexually acceptable and one unacceptable. The former constitutes the sexual elite, and the latter, the sexually oppressed.[16] The sexual elite includes people who are married, heterosexual, healthy, young (but not too young), attractive, and rich. The sexually oppressed are those who are single, homosexual, physically disabled, mentally retarded, mentally ill, imprisoned, poor, ugly, and old.

Looking at sexuality solely from the perspective of reproduction results in a narrow and distorted picture. Yet to talk about sexuality outside the context of reproduction is equally narrow. The concern for a planned family life, alternatives to conception, and even for the larger issues of population have a central place in the definition of human sexuality. Not to be sensitive to the facts of conception, pregnancy, and childbirth as an integral aspect of human sexuality is to be irresponsible. But more important, the reproductive function and all of its related concerns need to be viewed in the context of the total picture of human sexuality.

When the issue of reproduction is raised in relation to older people, the tendency is to dismiss it as irrelevant and in fact silly. But the reproductive aspect of human sexuality is often very important to older people. Let me cite just two examples. It is very often the case that having had children is and continues to be a very positive affirmation of an older person's sexuality. In addition, since reproductive capacity for men usually exceeds that for women (due to menopause), reproduction remains an active part of a man's image of himself as a sexual being. Another example is best illustrated by the feeling that not being able to have children takes the worry out of being close. Although this may especially be the case for women, upon whose shoulders pregnancy control has fallen almost exclusively, it also applies to men. Couples who no longer need to be concerned about conception often discover a new and freer vitality in their sexual expression. Many older couples say that they did not realize how influential and controlling the reproductive aspect of their sexuality had been until pregnancy was no longer a matter of concern. This is also the case for younger couples who choose vasectomy and/or tubal ligation as alternatives for planning their family's size.

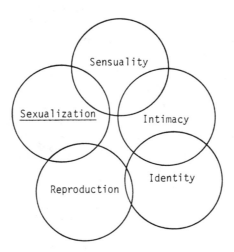

A final component of one's sexuality is sexualization, which is "the use of sexuality to influence the behavior or attitudes of others. For example, the use or withholding of intercourse in order to dominate, punish, barter with, or otherwise influence a sexual partner or others."[17] Just as communication is seldom limited to the words themselves, so it is with human sexuality, for behavior is seldom a straightforward communication. The key ideas involved in the concept of sexualization include manipulation, control, power, and influence. Probably too much of our sexual expression is accompanied by the sexualization component of human sexuality. Most of us who examine our sexuality closely will easily find elements of sexualization, past and present. The woman who uses her sexuality seductively is attempting to manipulate or influence a situation for her own purposes. Seduction becomes a form of sexual communication; unfortunately, it cannot be characterized as open or clear. Likewise, the man who interacts with women as sex objects is manipulating a situation to meet his own needs without regard for the needs of the person to whom he is relating—not an uncommon feature of our male-dominated society. And it should be made clear that sexualization is not just an adult phenomenon. We begin very early. Recall the scene in the back seat of the 1955 Chevy: "Well, if you really loved me you would."

The demanding male and the withholding female, or vice versa, are using their sexuality to control the tempo and the parameters of their relationships. Sexuality is often used to punish, and can become a weapon. An example of this is the phenomenon known as the performance demand: a partner doesn't do it well enough, quick enough, slow enough, and so on. Striking out at another person's sexual security will often be more destructive than a physical blow. It is not at all uncommon for couples who are disagreeing about finances, or vacation trips, or color of curtains, or whatever to drop subtle messages about each other's sexuality in an attempt to gain the upper hand. People's creativity and subtleness in the use of sexualization is often astounding.

It is characteristic of our sex role socialization that sexuality becomes an instrument for power and authority. The long history of male dominance as a social role has a profound influence on how men and women use their sexuality for other than meaningful sexual ends. The power/authority aspects of sexuality account for such things as sexual harassment and blackmail, which occur all too often in the world of work. Thus, it is clear that one is constantly subjected to the influence of sexualization.

Of course, the older person does not escape from the influence of sexualization. One example is the individual who uses menopause or age as an excuse to discontinue sexual activity. This is often quite unrelated to actual sexual ability. By the time people have reached their later years, they are quite aware of the enormous power that their sexuality can have in influencing others. They have usually had a good deal of practice and, in fact, sexual manipulation may have become habitual in their relationship with others. Counselors are all too familiar with the impact of sexualization in the decay and breakup of marriages late in life. It is often a subtle influence, but it is very important.

Older people are also systematically the victims of sexualization by people who are much younger. Referring to an older male who continues to have an active interest in and desire for sexual expression as a "dirty old man" is a clear example of sexualization. Suggesting that women who have a similar interest and desire "should know better" is sexualization. In many respects it is sexualization that is responsible for the sexual oppression of the elderly. It is the source of the myth that all older people are asexual.

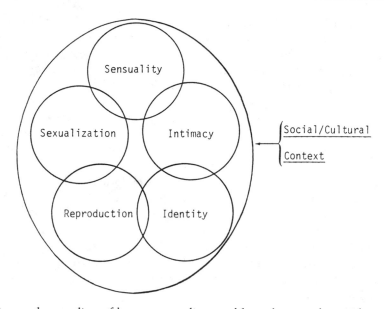

Our understanding of human sexuality would not be complete without a discussion of the wide variations that can result from the different social-cultural contexts that surround our human sexuality. Sexual attitudes, preferences, and standards vary with social-cultural influences, and we must be mindful of those influences if we are to understand any given individual in terms of his or her sexuality. Someone raised in a large urban area is likely to be somewhat different from a person whose background is rural. The black person raised in the urban ghetto is going to have some different perspectives than the white, middle-class person. Both ethnicity and socioeconomic background will influence our sexuality. In many cases age may not be the most significant factor that sets one person apart from another. But age can be a factor, and it is more often the case that older people have experienced a different social-cultural background than the one experienced by today's young people. Most older people are acting quite consistently with their history, and our judgments about the way they express their sexuality are often unfair and unreal. It must be kept in mind that today's older generation was socialized at a time when sexual norms and attitudes were very different from what they are at present.

Conclusion

We now have a complex and integrated picture of human sexuality, which goes well beyond the singular focus on genital activity. The various aspects identified here make up a more complete and richer definition of human sexuality. Although each aspect can be discussed separately, total meaning of sexuality will be fully understood only in the context of the interactive and overlapping quality of its many parts. It is a highly systemic phenomenon, and changes in one component are likely to bring changes in the others. As we increase our ability to interact intimately, we are likely to discover a more meaningful sensual experience. Likewise, conflicts over our sense of sexual identity are likely to promote sexualization. Finally, the interacting aspects of our sexuality must be viewed within the broader framework of our society and culture.

To understand the sexuality of the older person it is necessary to consider the total quality of human sexuality. In this light it is very easy to see how older people are fully sexual beings. Some older persons may be less interested in the tension release of orgasm and more interested in the satisfaction of skin hunger. But they are still experiencing the sensual aspect of their human sexuality.

Sexual expression in the older person is just as complex as that of the person who is younger. Wide individual variation in sexual expression characterizes both young and old. As myths are shattered and both young and old people stop using them to characterize each other in sexual terms, older people will more easily realize their sexual potential, and young people can look forward to a more rewarding sexual life in their later years. We all need to remember the words of Comfort: "About the most unproductive prejudice is one directed against a group you're going to join." If we want sexuality to be a part of our entire lives then we have only to set about making that happen, beginning now.

Notes

1. Defining the concept *young* is as hard as defining the concept *old*, or that vast wasteland *middle age*. For my purpose *young* will refer to anyone under 40, since I was 40 on my last birthday and feel neither youth nor age, but both.

2. Dorothy M. Easton, "Alex Comfort Speaks on Sex and Aging," *Multi-Media Resource Guide* 1, 1 (1976), p. 5.

3. Ibid., p. 7.

4. SEICUS, *Sexuality and Man* (New York: Charles Scribner and Sons, 1970), p. 22.

5. Ollie Pocs and Annette G. Godon, "Can Students View Parents as Sexual Beings?" *Family Coordination* (January 1977), p. 33.

6. Harvey L. Gochros, "A Concentration in Social Work Practice with Sex Related Problems," *Journal of Education for Social Work* 10, 2 (Spring 1974), p. 41.

7. These expected sexual changes are discussed in William H. Masters and Virginia E. Johnson, *Human Sexual Response* (Boston: Little, Brown & Co., 1966).

8. Gochros, op. cit.

9. Thomas C. Oden, "Intimacy: A Definition," in E. S. Morrison and V. Borosage (eds.), *Human Sexuality: A Contemporary Perspective*, 2d ed. (Palo Alto, Calif.: Mayfield Publishing Company, 1977), p. 468.

10. Gochros, op. cit.

11. See, for example, B. Raymond, J. Damino, and N. Kandel, "Sex Stereotyping in Values: A Comparison of Three Generations and Two Sexes," *Perceptual and Motor Skills* 39 (1974), pp. 163–166, and P. Cameron, "Masculinity/Femininity of Generations: As Self-Reported and as Stereotypically Appraised," *International Journal of Aging and Human Development* 7 (1976), pp. 143–151.

12. J. H. Block, "Conceptions of Sex Role: Some Cross-Cultural and Longitudinal Perspectives," *American Psychologist* 28, (1973), pp. 512–527.

13. Gochros, op. cit.

14. Don Byrne, "A Pregnant Pause in the Sexual Revolution," *Psychology Today* 11, 2 (July 1977), pp. 67–68.

15. Morrison and Borosage, op. cit., p. ix.

16. Harvey L. Gochros and Jean S. Gochros, *The Sexually Oppressed* (New York: Association Press, 1977).

17. Gochros, op. cit.

22

The Quality of Life and Older People

Forrest J. Berghorn and Donna E. Schafer

Introduction

There is a Harris cartoon[1] that portrays pedestrians on a city street; one is walking beneath an electronic sign that reads: Time—1:16; Temperature—58°; Quality of Life—23%. The cartoon reflects the growing public perception that conditions in the modern city are inimical to an acceptable quality of life. Air pollution, traffic jams, high crime rates, and interruptions in municiple services are just a few of the problems (albeit the more salient ones) contributing to this general malaise. Moreover, these problems now appear to be integrally related to the very technology upon which we have for so long relied to supply us with "the good life." Morrison reveals the heart of this paradox when he observes:

> For a long time the design of our technology was determined by our necessity to deal with certain external needs as efficiently as possible, dig more coal, go farther, get there faster, turn out a wider variety of goods for a larger number of people, and things like that, things we required to increase our advantage over nature. The record of achievement here is beyond all reasonable qualification; it is, of course, astounding. But our mechanical triumph may have produced a mechanical atmosphere we can't stand. So we may have reached a point where the design of our technology must take into greater account our interior needs.[2]

Nor is an escape to a more pastoral setting a guaranteed antidote for the city dweller, because the countryside has not been left undisturbed by technological development. With the rise of urban-industrial concentrations, the resources necessary for a good life were depleted in many rural areas. But perhaps the most disturbing implication of all this in the eyes of many Americans is that, like the time and temperature, the quality of life is beyond their control.

In exploring this subject, the first question to be considered is, How does one ascertain quality of life? It is, after all, a rather elusive concept. A possible approach is to settle in some manner upon a set of conditions that should theroretically contribute most to a good life. It would then be necessary to measure the degree to which these conditions are present in the life of a given individual. Conversely, a set of conditions that theoretically detract from the quality of life could in some way be determined and the extent of their presence measured. The problem with either of these approaches is that the quality of life is difficult to define a priori, since it depends on the subjective judgments of individuals. Thus the question becomes: On whose set of theoretical conditions is the determination to be made? A priori decisions generally can be avoided if the quality of life is defined by first considering the subjective judgments of individuals. It is this inductive procedure that has been used most frequently by social gerontologists to study the quality of life among older people.

The construct most often used to represent a person's subjective assessment of the quality of his or her life, and the term used predominantly in this chapter, is *life satisfaction*; but closely allied to it are the constructs of *morale* and *happiness*. In a recent article, George attempts to distinguish among these constructs. She defines life satisfaction as "an assessment of the overall conditions of existence as derived from a comparison of one's aspirations to one's actual achievements."[3] This assessment is related, then, to an individual's goals and refers to life in general. For this reason, we would not expect to find frequent and extreme fluctuation in a person's level of life satisfaction. In contrast, happiness "refers to transitory moods of gaiety or euphoria"[4] and reflects the way people feel about their immediate circumstances. Morale has been defined in several ways. Dictionary definitions tend to present this construct in the sense of esprit de corps, including such notions as discipline, confidence, and willingness to perform tasks cheerfully. Gerontologists have been inclined to conceptualize morale in a way that is more like the above definition of life satisfaction. For example, Clark and Anderson describe their measure of morale as "a bi-polar dimension indicating depression at one pole and satisfaction at the other."[5]

Recent studies have indicated that all of these constructs are interrelated and that they pertain to the same underlying phenomenon.[6] While there is no generally accepted definition of this phenomenon, for our purposes it may be defined as a more or less stable tendency to regard the world and one's relation to it in either a strongly positive or strongly negative light, or somewhere in between. We might, for example, think of the positive extreme as representing the view that life is completely fulfilling, and the negative extreme, that life is not worthwhile and is without hope. The aspect of stability must be somewhat qualified in this definition because it is not accurate to suggest that perceptions of the quality of one's life never change. While one would not expect frequent and extreme fluctuations, life satisfaction may be affected over time by the accumulation of adverse, or beneficial, events in a person's life.

The measurement of people's perceptions about the world and their relation to it is only the first step in studying life satisfaction. The next step is to identify those observable conditions that tend to be associated with relatively high or low levels of life satisfaction. Beyond this step, the objective is to determine the extent to which the relationship between condition and level of satisfaction holds for the entire population of older people. Only by meeting this objective are we able to generalize about life satisfacton. An investigator may also discover that certain conditions relate to life satisfaction only within a given subgroup of the elderly population, for instance, women. It is only through our capacity to generalize about the conditions that influence life satisfaction that we are able to develop effective strategies for improving the quality of life among older people, which is the ultimate objective.

The reason that generalizations about the quality of life (as measured by levels of life satisfaction) are possible is that subjective judgments are not formed in isolation. People develop expectations, preferences, and priorities through interaction with others. In large measure, then, their perceptions concerning their own wants, needs, and satisfactions will be conditioned by their social milieu. People living in similar social settings, therefore, will tend to share subjective judgments about their lives. At the same time, shared judgments may differ from one cultural group to another. For example, members of the same ethnic group living in one section of an American city are more likely to share subjective judgments with each other than they are with members of a different ethnic group in the same city, or with members of the same ethnic group living in a different country.[7]

Satisfaction with life, of course, is a concern for all ages, not just the elderly. Virtually everyone's life satisfaction will suffer without sufficient food, clothing, shelter, and social relations; and most studies have shown that age per se is not a significant factor in determining levels of life satisfaction.[8] Zemore and Eames compared the level of depression among young adults to that of older adults, and their findings are relevant to this discussion since depression, as they measure it, may be considered the obverse of life satisfaction. These authors reason that older people are sometimes found to be more depressed than younger people because depression is frequently measured by inventories of symptoms (e.g., sadness, pessimism, suicidal tendencies, etc.) that include somatic, or bodily, complaints (e.g., constipation, insomnia, fatigue, etc.). Somatic complaints, they argue, are likely to be the result of physiological changes that occur normally when people grow old and, therefore, should not necessarily be considered as symptoms of depression when reported by the aged. The results of the Zemore and Eames study indicate that there are differences in levels of depression between young and old when somatic complaints are included in the depression measure, but that there is no significant difference in the two age groups when they are removed from the measure.[9] These findings suggest that on the average old people are no more depressed than the young. But they also suggest that it would be a mistake to ignore differential experiences that are related to aging when attempting to generalize about life satisfaction.

Although the maintenance of life satisfaction may be problematic at any age, the way conditions supporting high life satisfaction are perceived may vary from one age to another. Most of the problems confronting people of advanced age are virtually the same as those faced by younger adults, but the context within which older people must attempt to solve their problems is different. For example, one may become ill at any age, but the way that illness is experienced is likely to differ for the aged. Many of the illnesses common to the elderly are chronic, which means that the older person frequently will have to learn to adjust to the illness rather than anticipate a cure for it. Similarly, a person can confront unemployment at any age. However, for a young adult it is likely to be viewed as a temporary setback, a circumstance to be overcome as rapidly as possible; while retirement represents permanent unemployment, a circumstance to which one must adapt. Whether one is young or old, it is not unusual to have a friend move away from one's neighborhood; but because young people as a rule are more socially active and more mobile than elderly people, it is generally easier for them to replace their loss with new friendships.

In addition, most older people live in essentially the same environments as younger people, a few exceptions being age-segregated housing such as retirement communities, nursing homes, and college dormitories. However, the way that people experience the environments in which they live is to some extent age-related. For instance, wide streets, traffic lights that change quickly, and revolving doors may represent environmental obstacles to an older person but not to a younger adult. Even in the home, some structural features that a younger person may hardly be aware of, such as stairs or high storage spaces, may constitute inconveniences or even barriers for the elderly. Therefore, an environment that enhances life satisfaction for the elderly may be quite different from one that is satisfying for younger adults.

In the United States at least, the elderly also must operate in a cultural context that distinguishes them from other age groups. Early in life, Americans are inculcated with certain social values that are not easily rejected later in life. Upon reaching late adulthood, however, they are confronted with social expectations regarding old age that directly conflict with the values learned earlier. In a sense, young Americans are taught to be dissatisfied with their lives; they are expected to seek further education, work toward more prestigious occupational positions, attempt to move their families to better neighborhoods, acquire better products, and so on. In short, they learn to value achievement, to act aggressively and competitively, and to desire improvement in all aspects of their lives. Older Americans, on the other hand, are expected to relinquish positions of authority and prestige, to be more temperate in their relations with others, and to adjust serenely to the circumstances in which they live. In other words, the socially prescribed state for older Americans is one of relative contentment, and the only thing they are expected to achieve is some degree of satisfaction. But what is likely to constitute a satisfying life for older people?

Determinants of Life Satisfaction

The well-being of the elderly has been systematically studied by social gerontologists for more than three decades, and the objective of virtually all of these studies has been to identify those factors that most strongly influence life satisfaction. As might be expected, a great many factors have the potential to affect satisfaction, and it is not possible to discuss each of them in this chapter. It is possible, however, to consider several broad categories of conditions that have been found to exert important influences on the well-being of older people. Gerontological research has indicated fairly consistently that socioeconomic status, health, certain environmental circumstances, degree of independent living, and activities are significantly related to life satisfaction. These categories will be discussed in the order just presented because, in a rough way, they represent a continuum of conditions: from those over which the older individual has little control to those over which he or she may have considerable control. And an individual's perception of the degree of control that he or she exercises over his or her own life is, in itself, an underlying dimension of life satisfaction. This point will be considered in greater detail later in the chapter.

Socioeconomic Status

There are several variables that investigators have used to represent the concept of socioeconomic status, the three principal ones being occupation, education, and income. These three are interrelated, of course, and together they determine in large measure one's general social standing and lifestyle.

We can assume that type of occupation has a greater impact on a person while he or she is working than after retirement. Still, there are some differences among retirees that are related to their previous occupations. For instance, Kimmel et al. found that the higher the previous occupational status was of retirees, the more likely it is that their retirement was voluntary. People in relatively elite occupations also tend to plan for their postretirement years more than people in lower status positions. They further found that if a person perceives that the decision to retire was under his or her control, the person is more likely to be satisfied with retirement.[10] When considering the life satisfaction of older people, however, a more fundamental concern is the effect of ceasing productive labor. A widespread perception among younger people is that, since work is equated with a person's worth, retirement is bound to reduce one's self-esteem and, therefore, satisfaction with life. However, the evidence indicates that retirement per se does not have this effect. The Cornell Study of Retirement found that "the act of retirement did not appreciably affect the percentage of people who felt satisfied or dissatisfied with life."[11] Even those people who found retired life satisfying had, previous to their retirement, anticipated that it would be worse than it actually turned out to be.[12] Among retirees in a sample of elderly urban residents, Berghorn and his associates found that only 16 percent said they would prefer still being employed. Other things being equal, employment was not related to the level of life satisfaction in this sample.[13] Retirement is, of course, a complex experience that usually includes a reduction in income, a restructuring of one's time and activity, and adjustments in one's personal relationships. However, in terms of life satisfaction, the critical question is how one adapts to such changes and not whether one is working or retired.

The influence of formal education in the lives of today's older people cannot be viewed in the same light as it might be for younger people. People who are presently classified as elderly were young adults in the 1930s and earlier. At that time, there was considerably less emphasis on formal education than there is today, and a relatively large proportion of people did not advance beyond eighth grade. A college education was considerably less common then than it has become in recent years. It is not too surprising, therefore, to discover that the effect of formal education on the life satisfaction of the elderly is comparatively minor.[14] There is some evidence that the impact of education differs by sex. Markides and Martin found that education has a greater meaning for elderly males than for females: "Men with higher education (and presumably more satisfying occupations) may retrospectively view their life as more successful and satisfying than other men with lower education. . .higher education may not be as important for older women who typically did not have an occupational career."[15] At the same time, they conclude that education's overall effect is fairly small. It is important to note, however, that the role of education in sustaining life satisfaction may be quite different for the elderly of the future. Not only are more people acquiring higher levels of education, but the relationship between education and occupational satisfaction will apply increasingly to women as it has in the past to men.

Income is generally considered to be an important variable in the level of life satisfaction, but the relationship between the two is not a simple one. Investigators have pointed out that besides the actual size of the income, one must take into account such related matters as a person's perception of its adequacy, feelings of relative deprivation, and what money represents to the individual. Obviously money is important to everyone, since it determines how well one's life may be maintained materially. Beyond providing for the necessities of life, however, what money means to the individual and how he or she uses it may differ widely. In part, this difference may be related to one's age. To begin with, a younger person may expect to increase the size of his income in the future, whether that expectation is met or not, while an elderly person generally must adjust to a rather substantial decline in income. Streib, for example, found an approximately 56 percent reduction in income upon retirement among a sample of about 2,000 people.[16] Although money may represent status, opportunity, and security for anyone, older people are likely to place more emphasis upon its security function. At the same time, the elderly appear to be generous with money. Studies suggest that when money is passed between generations within a family, the usual direction is from elderly parents to their children.[17]

While some research has suggested that the size of an elderly person's income is the most important influence on life satisfaction,[18] other investigators concluded that "perceived financial adequacy was a substantially stronger predictor of life satisfaction than were the objective indicators of socioeconomic position."[19] Liang and Fairchild agree with the importance of perceived financial adequacy, but they add that relative deprivation in reference to others and to one's former level of income is a mediating factor between objective income and perceived financial adequacy.[20] Moreover, Markides and Martin found that when other factors (health, education, and activity) are controlled for, the relation between income and life satisfaction for males is negative, though weak.[21] To illustrate the relationship among these variables, let us look in more detail at an analysis conducted by Berghorn et al., in which the association between size of income and life satisfaction is examined while controlling for income adequacy.

In this analysis, income adequacy is measured by the older person's perception of whether his or her income for the past year was insufficient, barely sufficient, or more than sufficient in meeting financial needs. Although perceived income adequacy was found to be positively related to income size, there were a number of instances in which individuals with relatively low incomes perceived them to be adequate or even more than adequate. Thus, income adequacy represents, in addition to the size of income, a person's needs, expectations, and, perhaps, money-management skills. Results of the analysis indicate that, given at least an adequate income, the relationship between income size and life satisfaction is negative. That is, for those perceiving their incomes as adequate or better, the higher the income the lower the level of life satisfaction, and vice versa. The investigators hypothesize that the most plausible explanation for this surprising finding is that older (and retired) people with incomes that are high compared to their peers have tended to experience traumatic reductions in income size relative to their middle years, while people who have been relatively poor all their adult lives do not experience marked financial discontinuity. For example, a person whose income was reduced in later life from $15,000 to $8,000 would suffer much greater discontinuity than a person whose income in later life is only $3,000, but who previously earned no more than $5,000 per year.

> Life satisfaction, it would seem, suffers most from disjunctures in one's way of life. For those who have lived most of their lives at or near the poverty level, the relative decline in income after retirement is slight compared to those who witnessed a large income precipitously drop to something approximating officially designated poverty levels. For those in the latter situation, a large redefinition of needs must be part of their adjustment process if a reduced income is to be adequate for meeting those needs.[22]

It should be understood, however, that for those whose income is not adequate, the relation between income size and life satisfaction was found to be positive. Thus, the analysis in no way suggests that the poor are better off than the more affluent. The problems associated with poverty status are well documented for all ages. Rather, it directs attention to the impact that income reduction in later life has on life satisfaction.

Health

One of the circumstances people most frequently associate with growing old is the accumulation of health problems. Although not all older people are bowed by physical ailments, a decline in physical functioning realistically must be considered part of the aging process and, therefore, it is not surprising that considerable scholarly attention has been paid to the relationship between health and life satisfaction. In almost all of those studies in which health has been included as a variable, it has been found to be significantly related to life satisfaction.[23] Indeed, in some instances, health has exerted the strongest influence.[24] As Shanas and Maddox point out, health is generally measured in one of two ways, "either in terms of the presence or absence of disease, or, alternatively, in terms of how well the older person is functioning."[25] Defining health in terms of disease or pathology is clearly more common among physicans and health care personnel. However, definitions based on level of function, "the things that an old person can do, or thinks he can do,"[26] are not necessarily inconsistent with medical evaluations.

Social gerontologists have for the most part attempted to determine the level of an older person's functioning on the basis of either self-ratings by the older person (i.e., the individual reports that his or her health is generally good, fair, or poor at the present time) or responses to specific questions concerning the individual's ability to perform daily tasks. Tissue observes that there is only partial agreement between health assessments based on medical examinations and those based on self-ratings of general health condition. He concludes that this is the case because self-ratings represent "a summary statement about the way in which numerous aspects of health, both subjective and objective, are combined within the perceptual framework of the individual respondent."[27] As an illustration, the general perception of one's health may include the way one feels, the perception of how one can expect to feel given one's age, and the perceived condition of one's peers compared to one's own condition. Generally, then, good health will tend to bolster life satisfaction and poor health detract from it, but what is meant by good or poor health is partially a subjective matter. As Palmore and Luikart note, "a person with poor objective health may still have high life satisfaction if he believes his health is relatively good, and similarly a person with good health may have low life satisfaction if he is convinced his health is relatively poor."[28]

Another measure of physical condition is the extent to which a person can successfully perform the tasks included in his or her daily routine.[29] For people who are physically fit and leading active lives, ordinary duties such as making the bed, preparing meals, and washing windows will have little bearing on the overall quality of their lives. But there are many older people whose health has declined to the point that they are no longer capable of performing even simple household tasks. Berghorn et al. asked elderly respondents whether they could accomplish a series of tasks by themselves, or whether they would need help. The tasks were making the bed, preparing a hot meal, sweeping or vacuuming, shopping for groceries, washing the windows, and shoveling snow. Results showed that as the tasks became more difficult, fewer elderly people were able to do them without help, and that fewer people over age 75 could perform each of the tasks than those 75 or younger. It is unlikely that these particular results would be affected by cohort differences. Thus, we can hypothesize that as age increases, fewer people are able to maintain themselves independently, even in their own homes. This does not mean that living successfully at home is not possible for such people, but it does mean that they will have to have some continuing source of assistance from others. At the same time, Americans tend to place a high value on independence, and for this reason a decline in physical capacity is likely to affect adversely one's feelings of self-worth and, therefore, one's level of life satisfaction. As one elderly woman commented, "The most difficult thing about life is not being able to do for yourself. I'm not able to work. I can't get out anymore. I can't drive my car, and I can't even do my housework or anything else anymore. The thing I need now to make my life better is a new body."[30] It is not surprising that her level of life satisfaction also was found to be extremely low.

Environmental Circumstances

The interaction between a person and his or her environment is an extensive and complicated subject, and one entire section in this book is devoted to it. In this chapter we will focus on two aspects of the older person's environment that have been shown to be significant determinants of life satisfaction. The first of these concerns the type of people who inhabit the older person's immediate environment. Research findings indicate that the proportion of other elderly people living close to the older person influences that person's level of life satisfaction. Although there has been some disagreement about the direction of this influence, the preponderance of evidence suggests that life satisfaction is enhanced by relatively high concentrations of older people.[31] For example, Rosow concludes:

> Several studies have definitively established that as the aged live among other old people, their friendships and interaction with neighbors increase drastically. . . . In contrast with those with few old neighbors, they have more friends, see them more often, and show a higher level of social activity. Indeed, the importance of these nearby peers is potentially so great that even a single confidant can mean the difference between an older person's stability and demoralization."[32]

Moreover, the demands the environment exerts on a person will also affect his or her level of life satisfaction. Gubrium argues that in environmental situations including a mix of young and old people, an older person is likely to face a maximum variety of social circumstances and expectations that require a wide range of behaviors. Such a person's ease in responding to one social situation may not mean similar ease in responding to others. A broad spectrum of demands and expectations can be stressful. In an environment composed almost entirely of older people, however, social situations and expectations will not be as varied. The person who can easily meet the demands of one social situation will probably be able to handle most of the demands in that environment. Similarly, an individual expects certain behaviors from himself and, at the same time, knows that others expect certain behaviors from him. Gubrium concludes that an old person's satisfaction with self and with his or her living conditions will be highest when there is congruence between self-expectations and the expectations of others.[33]

The degree of residential mobility of Americans is closely tied to stages in the life cycle. In studies of residential relocation, older people have been found to be more stable than younger people. As people grow older, then, the likelihood of their moving from a specific locale decreases, a process known as "aging-in-place." Thus, one can find concentrations of older people in older areas of inner cities, areas that have usually undergone considerable physical change. This phenomenon is not confined to the city, however. "Other processes often work in concert with aging-in-place to further accelerate the development of elderly concentrations. Many rural counties and even states report disproportionately large concentrations that would not exist if younger cohorts had not out-migrated from these locations during earlier periods."[34] In addition, elderly people in many rural areas are less well housed than those living in urban areas.[35] There obviously must be aspects of rural living that compensate for lack of services and poorer housing conditions, however, since some studies have indicated that country dwellers generally have higher life satisfaction scores than city dwellers.[36]

Since the tendency is for older people to remain in the same residence and since their most meaningful environment is the immediate one,[37] the condition of their neighborhoods has a significant impact on their life satisfaction. Responding to questions about the way they perceive their neighborhoods, the elderly indicate a concern for their personal safety and for the safety of their property. Neighborhood appearance is also important to them, especially to homeowners who have a continuing and long-term interest in their neighborhoods. Conditions of quiet and privacy are also highly valued. In addition, changes in racial and age composition are a source of anxiety for many older people. They seem particularly disturbed by the presence of teenagers, who are viewed as the principal threat to property, as well as to peace and quiet.[38] It should be noted that these perceived threats are not merely the products of suspicious minds, since many neighborhoods containing high concentrations of elderly are in physically deteriorated areas having numerous social problems. In sum, while other conditions—such as the availability of transportation and other services—may play a part in a person's assessment of his or her neighborhood, safety and attractiveness are two key elements in that assessment.[39]

As noted here and elsewhere in this volume, there are a variety of environments within which older people can and do live. Approximately 5 percent of the elderly live in nursing homes. Others live in retirement communities such as Sun City in Arizona, while still others reside in age-concentrated apartment buildings, financed either publicly or privately, that may be located nearly anywhere in the community. However, the majority of elderly people continue to live in their own homes and, in general, remain in the same neighborhoods where they spent their middle years. This last type of environment is, of course, not designed with the needs of old people in mind, while the others are to varying degrees. One would expect that problems associated with old age are likely to be taken into account in the specially designed environments. For example, environmental barriers may be reduced, special services such as health care may be available on the premises, and measures may be taken to ensure the safety of residents. At the same time, when people move from their own homes to specially created environments, whether voluntarily or involuntarily, there is a loss of control over many aspects of their lives. This loss of personal control is most apparent in institutional settings.

Independent Living

Americans value independent living. Children are expected to "grow up" and establish households that are independent of their parents. In the prime of life, Americans (particularly men) are supposed to provide for themselves and for their own families. Hsu concludes that in the United States the idea of self-reliance reaches proportions of a "militant ideal which parents inculate in their children and by which they judge the worth of any and all mankind."[40] Unfortunately, this ideal runs counter to what has been and continues to be the fundamental condition of human life, which is the dependence of each person on his or her fellow human beings, "without which we shall have no law, no custom, no art, no science, and not even language."[41] Thus, the link between independent living and life satisfaction is a precarious one, since self-reliance conflicts with the realities of human life cycles. This conflict is underscored by Clark when she observes:

> The parent must remain—or, at least, appear to remain—strong and independent. This independence is sustained at the price of ever-increasing social distance, and in many American families social relationships between generations are formal and dispassionate. Those who can sustain the semblance of complete self-reliance in this way have higher morale and self-esteem than those who cannot. They may be lonely and in need, but they are at least remaining true to their most cherished ideals.[42]

The underlying dependence that characterizes the human condition can be seen in the relationship between spouses. In almost all marriages, there is a division of labor that renders each spouse somewhat dependent on the other. However, this type of dependency is considered, both by the couple and by society, as a perfectly acceptable contractual arrangement that stigmatizes neither person. The underlying reason such an arrangement is acceptable to the couple is that their dependence is reciprocal. If one person in a relationship lacks the ability or resources to reciprocate in kind, then the exchange between them will be unequal and the dependent person is likely to define himself as a burden. Therefore, one's level of life satisfaction is not necessarily affected by dependency per se, but it certainly may be if the dependent person feels or is made to feel that he or she is a burden on friends and family. In the United States, the automobile is one of the most important supports, and symbols, of independent living; and as Carp reports, losing the use of one's own automobile means the loss of autonomy and self-sufficiency. These losses, in turn, increase the person's indebtedness to others, which can become burdensome and demeaning when reciprocation is impossible.[43]

Since growing old is generally accompanied by declining physical capabilities and economic resources, maintaining one's independence becomes increasingly difficult. Yet dependence on others need not lead to dissatisfaction with life. It is possible for the aging individual to adjust successfully to increasing dependence, although the process may not be easy. In fact, successful adjustment depends on the responses of both parties in a dependency relationship. The dependent person must come to accept the premise that all people are dependent on others to varying degrees and that such dependence does not reflect on one's self-worth. Simultaneously, the supporting person must learn to cope with the increased demands that the relationship makes on his or her personal resources. Minimizing feelings of resentment may require both parties to identify ways in which the older person can return favors, thus maintaining some reciprocity in the relationship for as long as possible.

Activity

In general, social gerontologists have concluded that there is a positive relationship between the degree of activity and the level of life satisfaction.[44] Having reviewed much of the previous research on activity, Lemon et al. express this relationship in a series of postulates: "The greater the activity, the more role support one is likely to receive. The more role support one receives, the more positive one's self-concept is likely to be. The more positive one's self-concept, the greater one's life satisfacton is likely to be."[45] Disagreements arise in the literature, however, over the type of activity most likely to promote life satisfaction. Three basic categories of activity have been analyzed by social gerontologists: formal, which includes participation in organizations such as church, social clubs, and charities; informal, which includes socializing with relatives, friends, and neighbors, traveling, and shopping; and solitary activities, including hobbies, watching television, and reading. Lemon and his associates found a modest association between informal activity with friends and life satisfaction, but no significant association between life satisfaction and other types of informal activity or any type of formal activity.[46] In contrast, Palmore and Luikart found a strong relationship between organizational (formal) activity and life satisfaction, but only a weak association between any other form of activity and well-being.[47] Fewer researchers have considered solitary activity as a separate category. Among those who have, some have found it related to life satisfaction[48] and others have not.[49] In addition, Kutner et al. add the qualification that gainful activity probably promotes higher life satisfaction than activity merely to fill free time.[50]

It is apparent from this brief review of research findings that some form of activity is an important ingredient in the maintenance of a satisfying later life. However, it is not clear from this research what type of activity is most likely to enhance life satisfaction. On the basis of evidence from their study of elderly urban residents, Berghorn et al. suggest that the specific type of activity in which an older person engages is not as important as the extent to which the activity, in whatever form, provides continuity with an older person's earlier years.[51] In that study, older people were asked to identify what they felt was the most rewarding activity in life, and then what they felt was the most rewarding activity in later life. While there was a wide range of responses to these questions, the most frequently mentioned activities appear in Table 22.1.

It can be seen that the data in Table 22.1 involve formal, informal, and gainful activities, and that responses are divided by the respondents' sex. By far the most frequently mentioned rewarding activity in earlier years is fam-

Table 22.1: Activities Perceived as Rewarding by Males and Females at Different Ages

Activity	Earlier Years Male (N=88) (percent)	Female (N=125)	Later Years Male (N=97) (percent)	Female (N=110)	% Difference Male	Female
Family Interaction	66	74	9	15	-57	-59
Hobbies	1	0	44	16	+43	+16
Church Work	17	15	32	48	+15	+33
Neighboring	6	2	10	16	+ 4	+14
Employment	10	8	0	0	-10	- 8
Association Participation	0	0	4	4	+ 4	+ 4

ily interaction, but this declines to a surprisingly low percentage in the later years for both men and women. It should also be noted that employment is the only other activity that declines in importance from the earlier to later years. Retirement is obviously the reason employment is no longer considered a rewarding activity. The reason family interaction declines in importance is more complex; however, it is sufficient here to note that the pleasure most people find in family interaction apparently derives from rather specific roles that are crucial to family formation and child-rearing.[52] Once children are grown and have left home, and after retirement, new forms of activity must be found to replace those which were so important earlier in life.

As the figures in Table 22.1 indicate, men and women tend to find different types of activities rewarding in their later years. Men identify hobbies, while women mention neighboring and church work most often. For this generation at least, the central concern of men earlier in life was providing for a family through successful activity in the labor force. For women of this generation, a major investment of their earlier lives was in the child-rearing role. Berghorn et al. suggest that hobbies represent a different form of the "instrumental" orientation of men in the workplace and in the male family role. For this sample, which included many working-class men, activities in the workplace generally involved the manipulation of objects and some degree of problem solving, both of which are inherent in many hobbies. The "expressive," or nurturant, family role of women of this generation is continued in the nurturant activity of neighboring. Similarly, women whose major role once was maintaining the family institution continue their "institution maintenance" through working for the church. "In sum, it is quite likely that activity enhances one's morale to the extent that it allows a continuation of fundamental behavior patterns and value orientations. Such continuation is dependent in large measure on the individual's ability to adjust to new circumstances brought about by the change in role structure associated with advanced age."[53]

Conclusion

Palmore and Luikart found that, after self-rated health, the variable most strongly associated with life satisfaction for people over 60 in their sample is internal control. That is, those "who believe that they tend to control their lives have greater life satisfaction than those who believe that their lives tend to be controlled by luck, fate, destiny, or powerful others."[54] As conceived here, control—much like life satisfaction—reflects the subjective assessments of individuals, and itself may be influenced by other, more objective factors. At any stage of the life cycle, control is in large measure related to successful adaptation to the changing conditions of one's world, and this is certainly true in the later years of life. There are at least two requisites for successful adaptation. One is the individual's ability to develop appropriate strategies for meeting his or her needs. The other is the extent to which society as a whole provides opportunities for meeting those needs. Such opportunities may be thought of as available resources for which all segments of the society are, to some degree, in competition. Moreover, the amount and types of resources available at any time are a consequence of larger societal, and even international, processes over which the individual has relatively little control. Let us review the "determinants" of life satisfaction discussed in the previous section from the perspective of individual control.

As suggested earlier, the elderly are less likely to have control over their socioeconomic status than the other determinants. By and large, older people exist on fixed incomes that are, in part, determined by national fiscal policy and by the health of the economy in general. Their incomes are also susceptible to the larger societal forces, such as the rate of inflation, affecting their purchasing power. While the elderly as a group are increasingly active in lobbying for what they consider to be their share of economic resources, they are competing with other segments of society who are also seeking *their* share.[55] At the same time, older people may, in a relative sense, enhance their economic circumstances by learning money management skills, familiarizing themselves with local services that reduce the cost of living, and cooperating with other people in similar financial circumstances. Still, many older people will find it necessary to adjust downward their expectations regarding their standard of living.

Older people have somewhat more control over their health and living environments than they do over socioeconomic status. The option is available to them to promote their own best possible health, whatever that may be, through exercise, appropriate nutritional habits, medical examinations, and the like. At the same time, such measures cannot assure the older individual that he or she will be able to avoid the health problems—often chronic—that generally accompany advancing age. Moreover, the older person has little contol over the quality of health care available, which is determined partially by available resources and public policy. As is the case for health, the older person has some choice concerning the environment in which he or she will live. However, this choice may be limited to some extent by an individual's declining functional capacity and/or lack of financial resources. Here again, the older person has little control over such things as national housing policies, age-related migration patterns, and neighborhood deterioration.

Continuing to live independently throughout old age is a realistic goal for most people. A majority of older people own their homes and, generally speaking, physical disabilities have to be rather severe to prevent them from remaining there. For some people to continue living at home, however, it may be necessary for them to be located close to a variety of resources (e.g., grocery and drug stores, doctor's office) or have services provided in their homes, services such as Meals on Wheels, visiting nurse care, or homemaker aid. If such public services and resources are not available, the older person will have to depend on the continuing assistance of a family member or close friend. Thus, there are a number of factors determining whether a person can live independently that are not strictly within the individual's control. At the same time, people can work out a variety of strategies for using what resources and services are available and thereby prolong their independence.

A number of studies indicate that high levels of activity are associated with high levels of life satisfaction.[56] Some elderly people find it possible to continue approximately the same pattern of activities they enjoyed in earlier years. Others, however, must adjust to changing circumstances. Declining functional capacity may curtail a person's usual pattern of activities. Limited financial resources may also preclude certain activities, such as traveling; and older people may find themselves in surroundings where opportunities for previously favored activities are not available. Yet, in spite of such circumstances, options for activity remain open to all but the most severely impaired.[57] One choice is to invest more time and energy in those activities that do remain, thus preserving some continuity with the middle years. Another is to substitute an activity that is compatible with the altered circumstances for the previously preferred one. As discussed above, it is possible to select new activities that, while different in form from the previous ones, still support the individual's underlying values. Some people may even discover new activities that are more rewarding than former ones. Because of the wide range of these options, we suggest that older people have relatively more control over their activities than they have over the other determinants of life satisfaction discussed here.

In sum, many of the conditions that affect the quality of life in American society today are the results of larger societal processes over which the individual has relatively little control. To do something about them requires a sustained national effort. Yet, as we have seen, the more immediate circumstances of daily living also bear upon the quality of one's life, and individuals have relatively more control over them. The more personal choices older people have in conducting their daily affairs, the stronger will be their sense of internal control. Since feelings of control and personal efficacy appear to be an underlying dimension of a satisfying life, public policies aimed at improving the quality of life for the elderly should offer each individual as wide a range of decision-making opportunities as possible.

Notes

1. Sidney Harris, *Saturday Review*, 1971.

2. Elting Morison, *Men, Machines, and Modern Times* (Cambridge, Mass.: The M.I.T. Press, 1968), p. 121.

3. Linda K. George, "The Happiness Syndrome: Methodological and Substantive Issues in the Study of Social-Psychological Well-Being in Adulthood," *The Gerontologist* 19 (April 1979), p. 210.

4. Ibid.

5. Margaret Clark and Barbara G. Anderson, *Culture and Aging* (Springfield, Ill.: Charles C. Thomas, 1967), p. 219.

6. See, for example, Nancy Lohmann, "Correlations of Life Satisfaction, Morale and Adjustment Measures," *Journal of Gerontology*, vol. 32, no. 1, (1977), pp. 73–75; Reed Larson, "Thirty Years of Research on the Subjective Well-Being of Older Americans," *Journal of Gerontology*, vol. 33, no. 1 (January 1978), pp. 109–125; and Cynthia Dobson et al., "Anomia, Self-Esteem, and Life Satisfaction: Interrelationships Among Three Scales of Well-Being," *Journal of Gerontology*, vol. 34, no. 4 (July 1979), pp. 569–572.

7. For an illustration of how members of the same ethnic group living in different countries may differ in their subjective judgments and how that difference affects their behavior, see Kenneth C. W. Kammeyer, *An Introducton to Population* (San Francisco: Chandler Publishing Co., 1971), pp. 104–105. See also Chapter 13 in this volume for additudinal differences among ethnic groups.

8. See, for example, Frank Clemente and William J. Sauer, "Life Satisfaction in the United States," *Social Forces*, vol. 54, no. 3 (March 1976), pp. 621–631.

9. Robert Zemore and Nancy Eames, "Psychic and Somatic Symptoms of Depression Among Young Adults, Institutionalized Aged and Non-Institutionalized Aged," *Journal of Gerontology*, vol. 34, no. 5 (1979), pp. 716–722.

10. Douglas C. Kimmel, Karl F. Price, and James W. Walker, "Retirement Choice and Retirement Satisfaction," *Journal of Gerontology*, vol. 33, no. 4 (1978), pp. 575–585.

11. Gordon F. Streib, "Retirement: Crisis or Continuities?" in *Migration, Mobility and Aging*, C. C. Osterbind, ed. (Gainesville: University of Florida, 1975), p. 25.

12. Ibid.

13. Forrest J. Berghorn et al., *The Urban Elderly* (Montclair, N.J.: Allanheld, Osman and Company, 1978), p. 78.

14. See, for example, John N. Edwards and Daniel L. Klemmack, "Correlates of Life Satisfaction: A Re-Examination," *Journal of Gerontology*, vol. 28, no. 4 (1973), pp. 497–502, and Elmer Spreitzer and Eldon E. Snyder, "Correlates of Life Satisfaction Among the Aged," *Journal of Gerontology*, vol. 29, no. 4 (1974), pp. 454–458.

15. Kyriakos S. Markides and Harry W. Martin, "A Causal Model of Life Satisfaction Among the Elderly," *Journal of Gerontology*, vol. 34, no. 1 (1979), p. 91.

16. Streib, op. cit., p. 24.

17. Marvin B. Sussman and Lee Burchinal, "Kin Family Network: Unheralded Structure in Current Conceptualizations of Family Functioning," *Marriage and Fam-*

ily 24 (1962), pp. 231–240; Eugene Litwak, "The Use of Extended Family Groups in the Achievement of Social Goals: Some Policy Implications," *Social Problems* 7 (1959-1960), pp. 177–187; and Marvin B. Sussman, "Relationships of Adult Children and Their Parents in the United States," in *Social Structure and the Family: Generational Relations*, E. Shanas and G. F. Streib, eds. (Englewood Cliffs, N.J.: Prentice-Hall, 1965).

18. Edwards and Klemmack, op. cit., p. 500.

19. Spreitzer and Snyder, op. cit., p. 458.

20. Jersey Liang and Thomas J. Fairchild, "Relative Deprivation and Perception of Financial Adequacy Among the Aged," *Journal of Gerontology*, vol. 54, no. 5 (1979), p. 754.

21. Markides and Martin, op. cit., p. 89.

22. Berghorn et al., op. cit., p. 126.

23. E.g., Ethel Shanas, "Family Responsibility and the Health of Older People," *The Gerontologist* 15 (1960), pp. 408–411; Stephen J. Cutler, "Voluntary Association Participation and Life Satisfaction: A Cautionary Research Note" *Journal of Gerontology* 28 (1973), pp. 96–100; Edwards and Klemmack, op. cit.; and Spreitzer and Snyder, op. cit.

24. E.g., Erdman Palmore and Clark Luikart, "Health and Social Factors Related to Life Satisfaction," *Journal of Health and Social Behavior* 13 (1972), pp. 185–200.

25. Ethel Shanas and George L. Maddox, "Aging, Health, and the Organization of Health Resources," in *Handbook of Aging and the Social Sciences*, E. Shanas and R. Binstock, eds. (New York: Van Nostrand Reinhold, 1976), p. 596.

26. Ibid., p. 597.

27. Thomas Tissue, "Another Look at Self-Rated Health Among the Elderly," *Journal of Gerontology* 27 (January 1972), p. 93.

28. Palmore and Luikart, op. cit., p. 192.

29. See, for example, D. P. Kent and C. Hirsch, *Needs and Use of Services Among Negro and White Aged*, Vols. 1 and 2 (University Park: Pennsylvania State University Press, 1971 and 1972); M. Powell Lawton, "The Dimensions of Morale," in *Research, Planning, and Action for the Elderly*, D. P. Kent, R. Kastenbaum, and S. Sherwood, eds. (New York: Behavioral Publications, 1972); and Berghorn et al., op. cit.

30. Berghorn et al., op. cit., p. 83.

31. See, for example, Mark Messer, "Age Groupings and The Family Status of the Elderly," *Sociology and Social Research* 52 (1968), pp. 271–279, and Berghorn et al., op. cit., pp. 104–111. For an opposing formulation, see Honshang Poorkaj, "Social-Psychological Factors and 'Successful Aging'," *Sociology and Social Research* 56 (April 1972), pp. 289–300.

32. Irving Rosow, "Old People: Their Friends and Neighbors," *American Behavioral Scientist* 14 (Spring 1970), p. 63.

33. Jaber F. Gubrium, *The Myth of the Golden Years* (Springfield, Ill.: Charles C. Thomas, 1973). For a discussion of environmental congruence theory, see Robert F. Wiseman, *Spatial Aspects of Aging* (Washington, D.C.: Association of American Geographers, 1978); and Chapters 27 and 29 of this volume.

34. Wiseman, op. cit., p. 17.

35. Raymond J. Struyk, "The Housing Situation of Elderly Americans," *The Gerontologist* 17 (April 1977), pp. 130–139.

36. See, for example, Gregory V. Donnenwerth, Rebecca F. Guy, and Melissa J. Norvell, "Life Satisfaction Among Older Persons: Rural-Urban and Racial Comparisons," *Social Science Quarterly* 59 (December 1978), pp. 578–583.

37. E.g., Wiseman, op. cit., pp. 18–21.

38. Berghorn et al., op. cit., pp. 115–120.

39. Ibid., pp. 116–120.

40. Francis L. K. Hsu, "American Core Value and National Character," in *Psychological Anthropology: Approaches to Culture and Personality*, F.L.K. Hsu, ed. (Homewood, Ill.: Dorsey, 1961), pp. 218–219.

41. Ibid.

42. Margaret Clark, "Cultural Values and Dependency in Later Life," in *Aging and Modernization*, D. O. Cowgill and L. D. Holmes, eds. (New York: Appleton-Century-Crofts, 1972), p. 273.

43. Frances M. Carp, "Retired People as Automobile Passengers," *The Gerontologist* 12 (Spring 1972), pp. 66–72.

44. See, for example, George L. Maddox, "Activity and Morale: A Longitudinal Study of Selected Elderly Subjects," *Social Forces* 42 (1963), pp. 195–204; Palmore and Luikart, op. cit.; William Sauer, "Morale of the Urban Aged: A Regression Analysis By Race," *Journal of Gerontology* 32 (1977), pp. 600–608; and Markides and Martin, op. cit. A few studies have qualified the relationship between activity and morale. For instance, Stephen J. Cutler, "Voluntary Association Participaton and Life Satisfaction: A Cautionary Research Note," *Journal of Gerontology* 28 (1973), pp. 96–100, finds no significant relationship when health and socioeconomic status are held constant.

45. Bruce W. Lemon, Vernon L. Bengtson, and James Peterson, "An Exploration of the Activity Theory of Aging: Activity Types and Life Satisfaction Among In-Movers to a Retirement Community," *Journal of Gerontology* 27 (1972), pp. 511–523.

46. Ibid.

47. Palmore and Luikart, op. cit.

48. E.g., Maddox, op. cit., and Sauer, op. cit.

49. E.g., Lemon et al., op. cit.

50. Bernard Kutner et al., *Five Hundred Over Sixty: A Community Survey on Aging* (New York: Russell Sage Foundation, 1956).

51. Berghorn et al., op. cit., pp. 72–76.

52. For a more complete discussion of the changing nature of family interaction, see ibid.; Kutner, op. cit.; Robert C. Atchley, *The Social Forces in Later Life: An Introduction to Social Gerontology* (Belmont, Calif.: Wadsworth, 1972); Gordon F. Streib, "Intergenerational Relations: Perspectives of the Two Generations on the Older Parent," *Journal of Marriage and the Family* 27 (November 1965), pp. 469–476; and Chapter 20 of this volume.

53. Berghorn et al., op. cit., p. 78.

54. Palmore and Luikart, op. cit., p. 193.

55. For more complete discussions of economic policy and political processes re-

lated to the socioeconomic status of the aged, see Chapters 11 and 12, respectively, in this volume.

56. E.g., Lemon et al., op. cit.

57. For a detailed consideration of activity alternatives, see Andrea Fontana, *The Last Frontier: The Social Meaning of Growing Old* (Beverly Hills, Calif.: Sage Publications, 1977), pp. 61–113.

PART SIX:
Creative Pursuits in Later Life

For much of the time between retirement and death, most people retain many of the personal resources they possessed during middle age. That is, they remain mentally alert and physically capable of engaging in a variety of activities. As noted previously, however, in order to remain active the aging individual sometimes has to find new forms of activity. In fact, people often discover that one of their principal concerns in the later years is how to fill their leisure time meaningfully.

To date the preponderance of programs intended to assist the elderly has aimed at meeting basic needs, such as income support, health care, and the maintenance of independence. Comparatively few programs, and those only recently, have been designed specifically to enrich the later years. There is a growing awareness, however, that providing for maintenance is only a first step in promoting a worthwhile life for older citizens. It is also becoming apparent that life enrichment programs represent a good investment, since they enable older people to share their talents and experience with other members of the society.

The selections that follow describe examples of programs intended to enrich the lives of older people. At the same time, they demonstrate the capacity of the elderly to learn new skills and, by exercising those skills, to contribute to their communities. The authors have all played important roles in the development of the programs they discuss. Cole introduces us to an extremely successful senior center that was established by combining the resources of a number of churches and synagogues and is maintained largely through the efforts of the participants themselves. Senior volunteers are organized through the center to provide other older people with services that help them remain in their own homes, as well as to offer adult education courses at the center. Duncan describes a program at one university that assists older people in attending college courses. She underscores the value of the college classroom as a vehicle for intergenerational exchange.

That life enrichment programs can benefit both the older participants and their fellow citizens is demonstrated in Neil's selection. She shows how people learn new skills in a senior arts program and in some cases become accomplished in an art form. At the same time, their accomplishments and newfound interest in the arts enhance the cultural life of their community in a variety of ways. Martin's selection reviews the life of a woman who, in her later years, became an accomplished painter, primarily of scenes from her childhood. It also describes a program designed to exhibit her paintings, not only for their esthetic worth, but also for their value as detailed documents of rural life at the turn of the century.

23
The Shepherd's Center

Elbert C. Cole

The number of senior centers in the United States has grown from only a handful in the 1950s to a few hundred in the late 1960s to thousands in the 1970s. As we enter the 1980s, the name *senior center* covers a diversity of facilities, activities, and sponsoring groups in communities all over America. The Administration on Aging has made the establishment of centers a priority, and the National Institute on Senior Centers has maintained an interest in refining goals and principles and establishing standards for the movement. Senior centers are an idea whose time has come, and some group in every community has either developed one or is in the process of doing so. The principles of organization and philosophy common to most senior centers can be obtained from the National Institute on Senior Centers in Washington, D.C.

The Shepherd's Center in Kansas City, Missouri, is a particular type of senior center. It was created in 1972 to unite the efforts and strengths of eighteen Prostestant, Catholic, and Jewish churches and synagogues through a new concept of work with older people. The center has grown from a single service in which 5 people helped 7 other people to the present nineteen major services and programs in which over 300 volunteers provide the "work force" to help over 4,000 older people. It is neither a building nor a list of activities, but rather a system of older volunteers organized in manageable teams that make arrangements with recipients to help them live their lives in the later years with sufficient security to keep them in their own homes. Life enrichment opportunities are also provided to nurture a sense of meaning and purpose in the later years.

The Shepherd's Center was developed as an experiment in providing an alternative to institutional care. Within six months of its inception, leaders of the center ceased referring to it as just an alternative to institutionaliza-

355

tion. It was their conviction that The Shepherd's Center had the promise of becoming part of a continuum of community institutions and caring systems. It was more accurate to think of the center as providing alternative lifestyles and support systems for older people. The realization that only 4.6 percent of the population over 65 lives in sheltered care raised the question of what could be done for the 95.4 percent who continue to live in the community. The question was, Could systems of service be developed, utilizing older volunteers, that would be reliable enough for people needing specific support to count on it, either for a short time or a long period?

After 7 years of operation, some ten home services have been created, each one designed to help older people remain in their own homes and continue to live as independently as possible for as long as possible. The Shepherd's Center delays entrance into sheltered care for dozens of people every year, by providing such home services as Meals on Wheels, Shoppers, Personal Security, Handyman, Friendly Visitors, Night Team, Companion Aide, and Hospice. Since older people themselves provide the services and programs, both helper and helped benefit in the process.

The Shepherd's Center Philosophy

The concept was nurtured by a small team of leaders who originally started out to build a retirement home. A consultant, realizing that the leaders had limited experience in working with the elderly, challenged them with the question of why we build institutions to house the elderly. Why don't we keep them in their own homes in the community by providing some of the same services they would receive in an institution?

The Shepherd's Center began with a staff consisting of a paid director and assistant, both retired; five board members; and a small number of volunteers. The operation was housed in the corner of a Sunday school room, with children's equipment pushed aside during the week, and the office equipment pushed aside on Sunday. Services grew one at a time. Even after 7 years of operations, The Shepherd's Center employs only a small staff: a director, a secretary, and four part-time workers, all older people. All direct service is done by volunteers 65 years of age and older, many of whom give twenty hours per week of their time. The volunteer work force also listens carefully to the concerns of the people they serve, and thereby are better able to respond to their needs.

Leaders of senior centers are often tempted to think of facilities and activities. The focus in The Shepherd's Center is on the people, specific people with specific needs to be met. As a consequence, it has become a catalyst to provide a network of services and programs of life enrichment that give older people living in the community a sense of security.

Eligibility for home services is restricted to a defined area, bounded on each side by major streets. The target area covers about fifteen square miles with a general population of 52,000 people and an over-65 population of nearly 12,000. The boundaries were imposed to ensure that the center would not dissipate its energy trying to serve more people than its volunteers could manage. It should be made clear, however, that participants in the life enrichment programs held in the churches are open to anyone, regardless of where they live. The rationale for this is that volunteers are not extending themselves in travel, and the availability of large space in the churches permits an open invitation to the larger urban area.

The Shepherd's Center currently involves twenty-five cooperating Protestant and Catholic churces and Jewish synagogues. Church properties are usually designed for peak loads on the day of worship and study, which means that most churches have unused space at other times. Making use of existing resources, both of property and of people, already available in the community makes sense. Also, utilizing churches and synagogues in this way has caused them to be perceived by the people in the community as supportive allies in the real business of living.

Organizational Structure

The Shepherd's Center was incorporated to give it a status separate from the supporting churches and synagogues. Most of the elected board members are themselves over 65, and most of them live in the community immediately served by the center. The board is responsible for ensuring that the philosophy of the center is reflected in its activities, as well as for budget planning, fund raising, and staff employment. The board, which meets monthly, is quite active and under its bylaws is self-perpetuating. It is not expected to involve itself in the daily operation of the center; however, most of the board members are themselves volunteers. The daily operation of the center is in the hands of the program council, composed of the paid staff and the coordinators of each of the nineteen major services. The council started with three people, but was enlarged with the addition of each new service. The council reviews people's needs and helps each coordinator be more effective. It is also the prime forum for the discussion of unmet community needs. The council benefits from research from the academic community and information about programs at other centers across the country, and keeps in touch with single-service providers in the larger urban area that might be useful to the participants of The Shepherd's Center. Especially in its early years, the council served as the "think tank" for the center.

Early in the process of developing each new service or program, the potential coordinator is identified and invited to give leadership in that specific area. The coordinator takes his or her place along with the other coordinators, who become a support group for the new member, assisting with their experience and information. The coordinator of a service acts as chairman or leader of a team charged with the proper management of the service. In the beginning stage, the coordinator and his or her assistants serve as a planning team and are asked to determine how the program will function and then recruit the leadership required to make the service work. Planning teams are composed of from three to thirty people, all recruited by the single coordinator to whom loyalty is developed during this planning process. On occasions, a planning team has been convened by the director of the center, but in the very early stages a coordinator is identified, placed in charge, and given the authority to plan creatively. The organizational style of The Shepherd's Center is not to proceed very far with any idea for a service unless committed leadership and volunteers are available. There seem always to be seven or eight "great" ideas waiting in the wings for leadership, and some of them have been waiting for three or four years for someone who believes enough in them to make them work. Obviously many ideas die without ever being developed, and maybe that isn't so tragic after all.

The coordinator of a new service or program and his or her planning team make appropriate progress reports to the council, the director, and other leaders of the center. When a service is well defined and ready to be made operational, the coordinator reports directly to the board of directors, which reviews the service and gives it final approval. Far from rubber stamping, the board assures itself of the appropriateness of the new service and how it relates to the goals and purposes of the center. With whatever modifications are required, the new service or program is then ready to be announced publicly to the community. The board feels strongly that premature announcements of service availability should not be made, so as to avoid false expectations and disappointments in the community. This principle has given credibility and a very high success rate to The Shepherd's Center. All services and programs have started small but have grown rapidly, probably because the center's services are known to meet the needs of older people. A few of the services have waned over the years, and when it is determined there is no longer a major need in the particular area, the service is terminated or continued only on a limited basis.

Principles of Programming

There are two major principles of programming guiding The Shepherd's Center. They developed from two central questions raised by older people in virtually every kind of economic and social situation across America. The first principle is based on the question, How can I survive in the later years of my life? The program principle is for centers to design services and programs that help older people to survive in their own homes or, if necessary, in institutional settings. Therefore, planning is oriented away from entertainment and leisure-time programs. When a center's programs address survival needs, and when the energies and abilities of older people are tapped, the result is a strong commitment by older people to the center. Some services may be needed by only a few people, such as Meals on Wheels, Handyman, or escort service, while other programs might be more generally needed, such as health programs (including inoculations, blood pressure, nutrition, and exercise classes) or educational sessions. Health enhancement programs have a high priority of importance to older persons. Other services might include job placement for those fighting inflation or boredom, or defensive driving for those desiring to increase their chances of remaining mobile. The survival principle gives the center the image of meeting real human needs that are immediately recognizable.

The second principle of program planning is based on the older persons' search for meaning and purpose in the later years. Most people in American society draw their sense of well-being from their work. A positive role for the retired has not been defined in our society, and programs that are planned without providing a meaningful role for the older person can imply that he or she is without mind or ability. Such programs, then, are self-defeating. The Shepherd's Center has an older adult education model that provides a wide choice of courses from which each person can make an on-the-spot selection according to disposition and desire on the given day. The day's curriculum is filled with courses designed to enrich life. Courses are taught by older volunteers who make use of their professional experience or knowledge gained from their hobbies. These instructors enjoy the preparation and teaching as much as the participants enjoy the classes. The day's activity has a number of by-products, such as socializing, recruitment of volunteers for worthwhile services and causes, and general information and assistance. The planning committee reflects the desires of the larger group in making sure that the "whole person" is served in the course offerings. The model includes some pure entertainment and passive enjoyment, but it also offers mind-stretching opportunities. Psychological and spiritual courses with suggestions for a vital lifestyle for daily living are popular.

Leaders in The Shepherd's Center have also developed life enrichment groups, which are really mental health courses. The term *life enrichment* is used because older people tend to associate the words *mental health* with mental illness or insanity. In these life enrichment groups, participants deal with life issues as presented by a professional leader. Much of their work involves small group interaction. The objectives of the courses are to develop new attitudes and healthy self-images, and to provide assistance in dealing with many of life's everyday problems. Older adults really have few opportunities to "talk through" what is happening to them or to reflect on life during their later years with other people in their age group. The same organizational style used for planning home services is used in developing programs in the life enrichment area. This dual focus on survival and meaning conveys to older people an image of the center as representing something essential, a resource center that responds to their needs and enlists them in meeting those needs.

Future Directions and Summary

Most older people continue to be as creative and capable as they were in younger years, but what they have to contribute is largely lost to a society that has not learned to appreciate their capabilities. (Benjamin Franklin at 81 helped write the Constitution of the United States, but if he were living today, he probably would not be invited to the Constitutional Convention.) Those senior centers that tap the knowledge, ability, and energy of older people can provide programs and services that will help not only older adults, but also the entire community.

Given the enormous costs of maintaining the Social Security system, the disproportionate dollars required for the health care of older adults, and the general competition for tax-supported services, attention needs to be given to the question of how older people can continue to make a contribution to the welfare of the whole society. Although a case can be made for older people having earned the right to preferred treatment, perhaps that often-quoted line, "Ask not what your country can do for you—ask what you can do for your country" has fresh implications for older adults. Continuing to be useful, having something significant to do with one's life, and providing a service to someone else that otherwise would not be performed might take some of the fear out of growing old. Antiques increase in value, and maybe some day in our society people will, too. Senior centers have a serious task to perform—for today's elderly, making potholders and playing bingo are not enough.

24

The Classroom—A Setting for Intergenerational Exchange

Beulah Duncan

One of the unfortunate features of contemporary life is the age segregation that permeates our society. This separation is at least partially responsible for the perpetuation of myths about older people and for the fear of growing old that exists among younger generations. The educational system is one of the most rigidly age-segregated of our social institutions, and one of the most pernicious myths about the elderly is that they are no longer capable of assimilating new knowledge and/or are no longer willing to do so. In popular terms, this myth is conveyed by the half-serious aphorism, "You can't teach an old dog new tricks."

One of the most logical places to bring together old and young people, and thereby help dispel such myths and fears through intergenerational exchange, is the classroom. This chapter reports on one effort to develop a program of intergenerational interaction in the university classroom. It is a "senior scholars" program developed by the Division of Continuing Education at the University of Kansas. The program was initiated by a directive from the state Board of Regents that any resident of Kansas 65 or older could audit classes on a space-available basis without paying fees. Auditors do not receive university credit, although they may participate in the class as fully as traditional students if they choose to do so.

The first step in implementing the program was enlisting the cooperation of the Adult Life Resource Center (part of the Division of Continuing Education) and the university's Office of Admissions and Records. The former arranged for promotional work in the community, advised students, obtained permission from instructors for senior scholars to audit their classes, and kept records of classes that senior scholars had attended. The latter supplied enrollment materials, coordinated enrollment with appropriate university departments, and awarded certificates to senior scholars with the completion of each course.

Community civic and church groups were quite willing to publicize the senior scholars program. Some of the procedures used to inform people of the program could be undertaken in any community. Articles were published in all newsletters that were likely to be read by potential students (e.g., the American Association of Retired Persons and the American Association of Retired Teachers) and in church bulletins. Speakers were available to discuss the program at civic club meetings, and public service radio announcements were aired. In the early stages, the best publicity was found to result from stories, with pictures, in the local newspaper. Once the program was under way, the most successful publicity came from endorsements by participants to their peers.

A more difficult problem than publicity, one requiring close and sustained coordination between the university and the community, was the provision of regular transportation to and from class for those who needed it. Many potential senior scholars had stopped driving their own cars, and even those who had not found parking to be a serious problem. Moreover, walking from one's home or from a parking lot presented a formidable problem for many senior scholars, particularly in winter weather. In this particular case, the solution to the transportation problem was to enlist the cooperation of an established county bus service for older people. The buses now provide door-to-door service from home to classroom and back. While this is an excellent example of a community and university working together, other communities may approach this problem in different ways. The use of taxis or public transportation with a rate subsidy, volunteer drivers, or car pools are possible approaches.

Advisors to senior scholars should be familiar with both university schedules and the academic backgrounds of older students. Care should be taken to avoid placing senior scholars in classes with prerequisites beyond their academic preparation. This necessitates fairly close communication with individual instructors. Since many potential students feel more comfortable about enrolling in a class if they can attend it with a friend, the advisor should attempt to accommodate multiple placements. In general, the advisor's major task is to match the student's interests with appropriate courses. In the University of Kansas program, for example, a garden club member has been particularly pleased with a class in urban botany; a retired engineer found a course in solar energy challenging; and a couple planning a trip to Italy enjoyed a class in the history of architecture. As these examples illustrate, advisors are likely to find that the interests of senior scholars are as varied as the interests of traditional students.

The initial response to the program was relatively small and generally confined to people who had previous experience with higher education. At least at the beginning of a senior scholars program, it is quite likely that a major portion of the response will come from people with such previous experience and, in general, from people of higher socioeconomic status. For others, the prospect of attending university courses for the first time is somewhat intimidating. To reach this latter group, it takes an added effort and a considerable amount of sensitivity to the personal challenge represented by enrollment in university courses.

While a senior scholars program may not be attractive for all older adults, it promises rewarding experiences for those who are able to take advantage of it. Besides being presented with new concepts and new material, the senior scholar may gain renewed confidence in his or her ability to learn. Moreover, the intellectually challenging environment of the classroom is likely to stimulate older students to carry on intellectual activities in other contexts of their lives. They also have the opportunity to come in contact with the concerns and viewpoints of younger people. But the benefits of this program are not confined to senior scholars. The majority of college-age students have little interaction with older people, except perhaps with their grandparents. It is a worthwhile experience for younger people to see representatives of older generations engaged in learning for its own sake, rather than for some sort of material reward. On many occasions, senior scholars can make valuable contributions to the class as resource people. For instance, a retired physician who had practiced medicine before the era of "miracle drugs" provided an interesting perspective in a public health class. Several senior scholars, having lived through the Great Depression, were able to share their personal experiences in an economics class. A woman who had lived in Germany during the Hitler regime contributed valuable insights to a history class covering that period. As a final example, older students have regularly participated in a gerontology class, bringing obvious expertise to the subject matter.

These are but a few examples of the older student's potential for contributing to the classroom experience. In return, participants in a senior scholars program receive the satisfaction that accompanies the extension of their education and the opportunity of exchanging ideas with their peers and with younger people.

25

Creativity and Self-Expression in Later Life

Mary Laning Neil

The aged in America today constitute a new leisure class. A large proportion of Americans are living many years beyond their retirement age, and during this period they are essentially free from gainful work and familial responsibilities. Not only are the elderly the most rapidly expanding segment of our population, but on the average they are younger physically and more diverse in experience than their forebears.[1] Thus each is confronted with a question that is relatively new to the aged in American society: How does one fill the hours of free time? As C. Wright Mills noted, human behavior may be understood as adaptation to changing conditions;[2] and conditions have changed for the elderly. It is often necessary for the retired person to establish a new social identity by creating new roles through leisure activities. The focus of this selection is on the manner in which society can help provide the older adult with creative avenues of self-expression.

The Older Americans Act of 1965 provided the money necessary for developing new programs aimed at addressing a broad range of needs among the elderly. Among other provisions, it earmarked funds for community facilities, such as multipurpose senior centers and congregate meal sites, in which a wide variety of services and programs could be made available to older people. Such facilities constitute the setting for providing cultural and recreational opportunities.[3] During the same year that the Older Americans Act was passed, Congress also created the National Endowment for the Arts. Funds appropriated for the National Endownment during its first year ($2.5 million) represented a small beginning. By 1978, however, the yearly appropriation had grown to over $123 million.[4] The creation of the National Endowment fostered the rapid growth of community arts councils across the country. In the past decade, the number of state and local arts councils increased from less than 100 to more than 1,800.[5]

The simultaneous development of federally supported facilities for older adults and community arts councils has provided a framework within which older Americans can use their leisure time creatively. The arts and leisure have always had a close association. Traditionally, artistic activity has been sponsored by people who had both the leisure and financial resources to be patrons or collectors of art. The rapid growth of community arts councils, however, clearly indicates the increasing breadth of support that the arts enjoy in American society. Participation in the arts is no longer confined to those traditionally associated with the arts establishment. According to a Harris poll in 1976, over 60 percent of respondents felt that the arts were necessary in sustaining the quality of life.[6] Or, as Robert Henri observed, "Art, when really understood, is the province of every human being. It is simply a question of doing things, anything, well. It is not an outside, extra thing."[7]

The arts and aging project discussed here represents one effort to provide older people with opportunities for meaningful leisure activities in the arts as both participants and audience members. A large part of the financial support for this project was supplied by the state's arts commission and the National Endowment for the Arts. A full-time coordinator and three part-time artists in residence were employed in this one-year project. Classes and workshops were offered, free of charge, at twenty-one congregate meal sites, as well as at a county home for the aged and a community college. Instruction was provided in painting, drawing, acting, and creative writing. Additional acitivities included a discussion series in the humanities,[8] special tours, and exhibits.

In addition to the regularly scheduled classes, over 350 people went on tours to the opera, the symphony, the ballet, and area stage productions. Fifty-six participants in the painting and drawing classes exhibited their work in libraries, banks, schools, and community centers. Five students, from an acting class of 16, were selected as performers for a local theater group. These classes and activities were designed to acquaint older people with various art media through personal instruction by an artist of recognized ability. By making performances and exhibits accessible to participants, the project also helped to develop an appreciation for the performing and visual arts. A further consequence was to increase the awareness among arts administrators that older people constitute an important source of new audiences.

The project reached over 800 older adults, about 25 percent of the target population. This proportion is considerably larger than that found among older people nationally; one study reported that only 11 percent of those 60 and over are audience/participants in the visual and performing arts. A related and interesting finding is that only 4 percent of arts administrators were actively seeking the older adult audience.[9] The participants in the arts and aging project ranged in age from 55 to 98, and from the highly mobile to the wheelchair bound. They represented a broad socioeconomic spectrum, including retired truckdrivers, business executives, farm wives, and teachers. Less than 10 percent had held jobs in any way related to the arts. A few were draftsmen, printers, music teachers, and the like. But for a large majority of the participants, the project represented the first direct contact with some form of the arts that they had ever experienced.[10] The project staff were surprised to discover that most of the participants, though lifelong residents of the community, had never attended a local museum or theater production.

It is difficult to measure the results of arts programming for the elderly. By its very nature, creativity is intangible and subjective. But, although it is not possible to conclude with certainty that participation in the arts and aging project caused specific changes in the behavior or attitudes of participants, project staff believe they observed marked increases in the self-esteem of participants. One drawing student, for example, remarked, "The class has made me feel that I'm not so useless and a little confident in myself." Two other students discontinued therapy sessions for depression at the county mental health center. They indicated they had found new outlets for self-expression in their acting class.

Any situation that offers the opportunity to learn new skills carries the potential for enhancing one's self-worth and personal efficacy. Few of us, whatever our age, possess the special talents to become recognized artists, actors, or writers, but regardless of the extent of one's talent, creative activity entails autonomous effort. Learning to paint, write, or perform, even at an elementary level, cannot help but enhance one's feelings of competency. While participants in the classes attained various levels of skill, each student had the tangible satisfaction of seeing his or her own progress as it was reflected in successive class exercises and assignments. As students mastered more difficult painting techniques, felt more at ease in performing, or attempted more complex compositions, their willingness to experiment with their work increased along with their self-confidence.

The particular motivation for enrolling in a class, as well as the principal source of satisfaction derived from the experience, varied, of course, among the participants. For some, the ability to share new knowledge and skills with friends and family was most satisfying. Others expressed pleasure at creating a work of art that could be left to children or grandchildren as a lasting expression of themselves. Still others derived satisfaction from their first exhibit and sale of artwork. Regardless of the specific source of satisfaction, these responses reflect a common desire for recognition. The elderly are hardly unique in their desire for approval from others, yet it is not always a simple matter for an older, retired person to find a satisfactory channel for his or her efforts and abilities. For at least some older people, creative activity may provide a continuing avenue for achievement and recognition. It is also important to note that participants would not have taken pleasure in sharing their work with others if they had not derived satisfaction themselves from their own accomplishments. Had they considered their creative activities trivial, simply a way to fill time, it is unlikely that they would have sought recognition from others for their work. Time-consuming, but personally meaningless, activities offer little reward for one's effort, and therefore do little to enhance feelings of self-worth.

While learning a skill is generally a satisfying experience, the learning process can at first be frustrating until a person has evidence of improvement. In general, the older students were highly motivated and, therefore, made progress. Moreover, students did not seem to be embarrassed in their initial efforts at creative work. That the students were not at the outset self-conscious may be attributable in part to the type of setting in which the classes occurred. They were scheduled at facilities already serving the elderly.[11] Congregate meal sites, senior centers, and retirement complexes represent meeting places with which potential participants are familiar and in which they feel at ease. Moreover, they will already have established personal relationships at these places that provide mutual support and encouragement. Such environments, then, reduce the sense of risk involved in trying a new activity. Finally, since participants were learning artistic skills together, and most for the first time, the classes themselves added a further dimension to the fellowship and social interaction already occurring at a given facility.

Another factor that may have reduced the anxiety people sometimes feel when learning a new skill was the rapport that soon developed between the artist-instructors and the older adult students. Participants were not intimidated by the instruction they received from the much younger, but artistically more experienced, instructors. Artist-instructors were respected by their students for their expertise, and the trust that developed contributed to the students' progress. For the artist-instructors, in turn, it was a valuable experience to have close contact with older people who are attempting new activities, learning new skills, and achieving new levels of competence. Indeed, one of the more salutary long-term consequences of the project was the mutual regard that students and instructors developed for each other.

Artist-instructors were encouraged to maintain journals of their personal impressions. The artist in residence in acting and creative writing commented, "Their memories stretch back to their grandparents, which makes a time span of 150 years. We've discussed that their generation has experienced the technological boom in all its force—from horse and buggy to man on the moon." By learning about participants' experiences and backgrounds, this instructor was able to help them record, in prose and poetry, events from the past. Personalized instruction, although carried out in a group setting, enabled the artist-instructor to tailor his or her instruction to individual skill levels and to take into account possible physical disabilities of elderly students. For example, one instructor cut and sized canvas board to fit the hands of a student with severe arthritis. Another instructor taught a visually impaired student to paint with the aid of a magnifying glass. In the acting class, the instructor utilized theater games and exercises to stimulate the older students in imagination and in physical movement.

The culmination of the arts and aging project was a senior arts festival held in one of the community's parks. Approximately 80 older adults, many of whom were participants in the project, exhibited their artwork or gave theatrical and musical performances. The event drew over 3,700 visitors. For people of all ages, it was a celebration of the arts and vivid proof of the contributions the elderly can offer the community.

An important outcome of the project was the formation of the Senior Arts Council of Greater Kansas City. Composed of interested citizens and area artists of all ages, the council works to provide older adults with expanding opportunities in the arts as artists, teachers, and performers. Among other activities, it promotes intergenerational exchanges in the arts through exhibits, oral histories, and group discussions, and informs civic groups about the creative activities of older adults.

Accessibility is a major consideration in attempting to involve the aged in artistic activity. There are several ways to help older people participate in the arts: (1) by introducing providers (artists, arts administrators, performers, teachers) into the older person's environment; (2) by encouraging arts groups and institutions to actively seek the older adult audience; and (3) by involving the older adult in the community's schools and civic groups as contributing artists, students, performers, or teachers. All of these methods were used in the project described here, thus creating opportunities in the arts for older people by using existing cultural and educational institutions. Given the simultaneous development of programs for the elderly and the proliferation of community arts councils during the last decade, organizational structures exist for cooperative programs to increase the participation of older people in the arts. Developing closer ties between community arts groups and agencies serving the elderly would provide older people with more opportunities for creativity and self-expression. Such developments would not only benefit the elderly, but would encourage the sharing of their experiences with the larger community in which we are all participants.

Notes

1. Matilda White Riley, Anne Foner, and associates, *Aging and Society: An Inventory of Research Findings* (New York: The Russell Sage Foundation, 1968), p. 38.

2. Steven J. Miller, *Older People and Their Social World: The Subculture of Aging* (Philadelphia: F. A. Davis, 1965), pp. 79–92.

3. M. P. Lawton and T. Byerts, "Community Planning for the Elderly" (U.S. Department of Housing and Urban Development, Washington, D.C., 1973), pp. 12–13; United States Codes Administration, Older Americans Act Amendments of 1967, 42 U.S.C.A., SS 3021, p. 650; SS 3035, p. 668; SS 3041, p. 673; and SS 3045, p. 689.

4. Jill Wechsler, "Washington Report: The Arts and Congress," *American Artists* 41 (January 1977), p. 40.; and *The Budget of the United States*, FY 1980 (Office of the President).

5. Betty Chamberlain, "Matters of State and Local Coordination," *American Artist* 41 (February 1977), p. 12.

6. Louis Harris and Associates, "Americans Respond to the Arts Movement," *Washington Post*, December 16, 1976, Section A, p. 211.

7. Robert Henri, *The Arts Spirit* (New York: J. B. Lippincott, 1939).

8. Materials in history, literature, and philosophy were provided for the discussion series by the Senior Center Humanities Program of the National Council on Aging, through a grant from the National Endowment for the Humanities.

9. Alton C. Johnson and E. Arthur Prieve, "Older Americans: The Unrealized Audience for the Arts," Center for Arts Administration, Graduate School of Business, University of Wisconsin, Madison, Wisconsin.

10. For a discussion of the effects of previous social and occupational roles on the leisure pursuits of the elderly, see Andrea Fontana, *The Last Frontier: The Social Meaning of Growing Old* (Beverly Hills, Calif: Sage Publications, 1977).

11. It was found that facilities not regularly programmed for senior adult activities, or facilities in which groups of older people met only once a week, were less likely to provide a climate of continuing participation in the project classes and workshops.

26

A Creative Life:
The Later Years of Daisy Cook

Edeen Martin

It is often assumed that achievement and recognition by society is no longer possible for a person of advanced age. Daisy Cook is a striking example of the fallacy of this assumption. Mrs. Cook began a new career in painting at the age of 61 and, before her death at 76, achieved considerable stature as a naive artist. Although she demonstrated exceptional talent, she is not unique among older people in having applied herself to a new career in later life.

Daisy Cook belongs to a small but distinguished group of American painters who, in the quiet moments of later years, paused to reflect upon their childhood and youth and brought these memories to life on canvas. (Anna Mary "Grandma" Moses of New York State and "Aunt Clara" McDonald Williamson of central Texas are earlier and more broadly recognized members of this group.) These painters are, in general, part of a nonacademic tradition; that is, they were not trained in formal techniques and style. Like her predecessors, Daisy documented a rural past—one that changed dramatically in her own lifetime. Perhaps it is the awareness of change, coupled with a remarkable memory of the past, that is the special gift of such artists.

Daisy painted pictures from memories of her childhood on a southwestern Missouri farm at the turn of the century. Her paintings show, in detail, the daily activities and special occasions of rural life. Daisy was adamant about

Details on Mrs. Cook's life were drawn from personal interviews with Daisy and her husband Warren. The interviews, conducted by Edeen Martin and Linna Funk Place, were done in connection with the Mid-America Arts Alliance Traveling Exhibition, "Daisy Cook Remembers."

painting only what she herself had experienced. She captured tasks that were an ordinary part of the rhythm of daily life, such as cleaning lamp chimneys, and made them somehow special.

Most of Daisy Cook's works are genre paintings. They constitute invaluable records of a way of life for which detailed documents often do not exist. Many of the customs, beliefs, and practices that make up community life were transmitted orally from one generation to the next rather than through the written word. In essence, paintings like Daisy Cook's are visual manifestations of the oral tradition. Her works provide a setting for many objects that we may now only see in museums or antique shops. Through her paintings we learn how these objects were used in daily life and something of their value to the people who used them. Buildings, agricultural practices, foodways, and local festivities all combine in her work to provide us with a richer understanding of the past. She was above all a storyteller, and a very gifted one.

Daisy attended a state teachers' college in Missouri in the late 1920s. She had been interested in drawing and painting when she was a little girl, but since she belonged to a large farm family, she could not afford to spend time or money on anything besides obtaining her teaching credentials. She spent many years as a teacher while raising five children and running a dairy farm in southern Missouri. Then in the mid-1950s her husband, who worked for the federal government, was transferred to a town in Texas. Since her credentials did not qualify her to teach there and the last of her children had gone away to school, she was suddenly left with time on her hands. She enrolled in a YMCA painting class and in addition to her class assignments began painting scenes from memory. Her instructor suggested that his classes could do little to enhance her individual style and counselled her to continue working on her own.

Having won several amateur competitions in Arlington, Texas, Daisy was encouraged to continue painting when she and her husband moved back to southern Missouri in 1967. She also began showing her work at annual Ozark crafts festivals. Daisy's paintings drew the attention not only of older adults who had shared the experiences she recorded, but also of younger art enthusiasts. She had brought to life the way things were done in a bygone era. Pictures like "The Spinning Wheel" and "The Creek Baptism" document activities that have become extinct in today's world. On the other hand, scenes depicted in "The Farm Sale" and "Ice Skating" give a sense of continuity, representing activities that have changed very little as a result of modernization. People from all parts of the United States purchased her paintings. Toward the end of her life she regretted selling them, since to her the paintings represented the story of her childhood and those that had been purchased seemed like missing chapters in the story.

Mid-America Arts Alliance, with a special grant from the National Endowment for the Humanities, sent forty of Daisy Cook's paintings on a tour through five midwestern states in 1978 and 1979. In addition to the traveling exhibit, workshops for schoolchildren, historical societies, and older adult groups were conducted in each of the twenty-four participating communities. These workshops focused on the wealth of information available through the study of material culture and helped communities investigate various ways of preserving their heritage. For example, a high school in one community videotaped interviews with older adults, and another community's newspaper ran a series of articles based on interviews with older residents.

The exhibit, "Daisy Cook Remembers," had two major purposes. The first was to show a collection of paintings by an accomplished regional artist, and the second was to examine her paintings as detailed and sensitive documents of rural life at the turn of the century. This combination made the exhibit an excellent vehicle for involving in the visual arts groups not normally served by museums and galleries. A film showing Daisy discussing her paintings and her childhood was made to accompany the exhibit.

Daisy Cook's artistic career spanned only the last 15 years of her life, years characterized by unusual achievement. The events of her first 60 years were relatively ordinary; yet Daisy recognized a richness and value in her whole life, and that recognition is handed down to us in the form of her paintings. The way she chose to share her life serves as a model for other older adults who look to the arts, or some other avenue of self-expression, to fill their new-found leisure time creatively.

PART SEVEN
Environmental Aspects
of Aging

The remaining chapters explore the spaces and places that constitute the environment within which older Americans live. Although the environment includes various dimensions, this section is concerned primarily with its manmade aspects. As will be seen, one should not consider the environment as simply a backdrop for human activities. It is, rather, a constant force working upon the individual, and a force with which the individual is in continuous interaction. People are capable of modifying the character of their surroundings, but the interaction between person and enviroment may vary according to the resources that person possesses, and such resources are known to correspond to one's place in the life cycle. Indeed, there is compelling evidence that as people grow old they become more susceptible to the constraints of their environments. If, for instance, one's health has declined significantly in the later years, then certain features of the environment may become barriers to physical mobility. In like manner, a marked decline in income following retirement may restrict one's choice of residence.

The elderly live in a wide variety of environments. Most, however, reside in community settings that have not been created with their specific needs in mind. Furthermore, many older Americans live in the same neighborhoods where they spent their middle years, but the character of these neighborhoods may have changed over time. Wiseman discusses the nature of this community environment. He analyzes its stressful aspects and considers strategies for reducing environmental stress on the elderly. Longino describes several examples of communities specifically designed for older people. He compares various types of retirement communities and examines the process by which people choose to move to such settings. He also evaluates the relative benefits of living in various types of retirement communities.

Campbell's chapter begins by examining the ways in which the "micro," or housing, environment affects the behavior of old people. This examination includes the physical design of both institutions and private households. Campbell also explains the relationship between design features and feelings of personal competence and control over one's life. Edwards focuses on the nursing home environment. While only about 5 percent of the aged population lives in nursing homes, the condition of those who do has commanded public attention and widespread concern, for they are among America's most dependent and vulnerable elderly. Edwards' emphasis is on the social environment in the nursing home. He is especially concerned with the way homes may be organized and managed to provide the best possible care for their residents.

27

Community Environments for the Elderly

Robert F. Wiseman

Every living organism exists within an environment and has a set of relationships with that environment. The set of interactions that exist between people and their environments has been the subject of much research from a variety of disciplinary perspectives, but the elderly have received little specific attention. This is unfortunate for several reasons. First, several studies have shown that the environment directly influences the well-being of older people.[1] For example, mortality rates increase when older individuals move from their homes to institutions, or even from one institution to another.[2] Second, although it is generally accepted that older people are more sensitive to environmental influences than most other age groups, attempts to improve the lives of older people are often made without informed consideration of environmental aspects. For example, it is common to find nursing homes located along heavily traveled highways in the remote portions of the suburban environment. It does not take much imagination to realize that feelings of boredom and isolation can accompany life in such a setting. Similarly, congregate housing facilities provided expressly for low-income older Americans are often found in downtown urban renewal areas. These areas often lack other residents and the resources needed to sustain and enrich life—e.g., grocery stores, churches, beauty shops, and parks.

Furthermore, the sensitivity of the older individual to environmental influences provides the researcher with an ideal opportunity to learn more about general relationships between individual and environment. Although much is now known about microenvironmental relationships, allowing us to design better homes for older people, there is a notable paucity of information about the older individual's environmental interactions outside the home. At any one time, only 4 to 5 percent of the elderly population resides in an institutional setting. Thus, a major portion of life in old age is spent in a more typical community environment.

The purpose of this chapter is to discuss the ways in which the community environment is perceived and the general relationships between older people and that environment. We begin with a consideration of what is meant by the term *environment*, focusing on environmental content and spatial context. This is followed by a brief discussion of a major research model of environmental interaction. Then gerontological theories are reviewed that focus on the aging individual within his or her environment. Attention is also given to the aging of the community environment itself. Finally, directions for future study are indicated in the context of strategies that exist for enhancing relationships between the older person and the community environment.

The Community Environment

In its most general form, the environment can be defined as everything that lies beyond the individual. The community environment can be delimited to include everything beyond the individual and the home. A functional definition of *community environment* can be obtained by considering environmental content, which consists of several interrelated dimensions: physical, social, and cultural. Each dimension can be disaggregated into its constituent elements; thus, the physcial dimension may be reduced to those elements which constitute the natural environment and the built environment—whether a single housing unit, a neighborhood, or an entire city.

Research produces definitions and studies of the environment that often focus primarily on a single dimension. For example, Gubrium articulates a socioenvironmental theory of aging that stresses the sociological dimension of the environment.[3] He suggests that older people who possess little "behavior flexibility," that is, have low personal resources, are most sensitive to the environment, especially its social norms. These older people, living in an environment with a wide range of social situations and norms, might feel dissatisfied with themselves when what is expected of them by significant others is more than they can achieve, or is incongruent with what they might expect of themselves. Such people might be happier in an age-homogeneous environment where their personal resources more closely match those of other older people. Although studies such as this provide significant insights into a specific set of environmental relationsips, their focus on one dimension of the environment makes it difficult to integrate our knowledge and to produce a balanced picture of later life experiences with the environment.

Each dimension of the environment is composed of discrete elements that have varying importance for the individual. The built environment, for example, consists of streets, sidewalks, homes, and other buildings. However, only some of these elements have relevance for any given individual. In addition, entire sets of elements affect our lives differently at different times. Streets and thoroughfares facilitate movement within the environment for motorists but often impede pedestrians. Similarly, the meaning of such sets of elements in our lives may vary according to our age. The highly individualistic nature of our relationship to the environment compounds the difficulty of clearly understanding the role that the environment plays in the lives of older people.

Another way of understanding what is meant by environment is to describe where it is located. It is difficult, if not impossible, to identify where self ends and one's environment begins.[4] Since the concern of this chapter is with the community environment this problem can be skirted, but it reemerges when we attempt to distinguish between the home and other portions of the community environment. Indeed, boundary problems arise whenever general conceptualizations of environmental spaces are developed. A geographical conceptualization of the environment is shown in Figure 27.1. Several zones, or spaces, are identified at different distances from the home environment. The first is "surveillance spaces," which lie beyond the home but generally within the neighborhood. Such spaces are often just beyond the windows of the home or within the view of an individual's frequently traveled routes and stopping points. Our relationship with such spaces is not obvious, and research has not revealed how important they are in our lives. For some people, especially older people with low mobility, strong emotional attachments to these spaces may exist. The loss of a tree, the closing of a store, the blocking of a view by the construction of a building next door may constitute a sharply felt reduction in their environment. A "neighborhood zone" extends beyond the surveillance spaces and contains elements such as people and stores that provide opportunities for socializing and obtaining the necessities of life. The larger environment of the city or town contains a broader range of environmental elements, such as places of employment and opportunities for recreation and entertainment. "Beyond spaces" might include places where we vacation, where we have lived before, or the communities where relatives and friends live.

The concepts of environmental content (dimensions, elements, and specific phenomena) and location (spaces, places, and zones) can be integrated through an interactionist perspective. In this perspective, interaction consists of direct transactions between the individual and specific phenomena in the environment. For example, the most obvious interaction occurs when an individual moves from one space to another. Viewed in this

Figure 27.1: Environmental Spaces

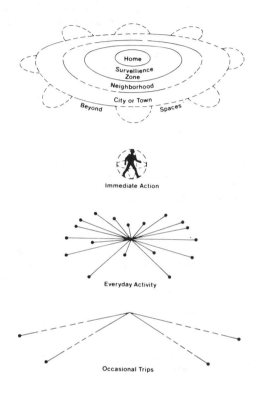

Source: From Graham D. Rowles, <u>Prisoners of Space?</u>
          <u>Exploring the Geographical Experience of</u>
          <u>Older People,</u> Boulder, Colorado, Westview
          Press, 1978, pp. 165, 172.

way, the environment becomes a setting in which individual behavior occurs. By examining the behavior of different age groups, or the same people
at different ages, in the same environmental setting, we can determine how
aging influences environmental relationships. By observing behavior in different environmental settings, the role and nature of environment can be
ascertained.

Several forms of interaction with the environment can be identified.[5] One
is action, or physical movement, which has already been mentioned. Action
can be spatially immediate, in that it occurs within our home or
neighborhood, or it can occur in the city portions of the environment, as

well as in periodic trips to other communities. Because it is an obvious manifestation of environmental interaction, many studies focus upon the frequency of movement expressed in daily or weekly individual activity patterns. Such studies consistently show more restricted patterns of environmental interaction for older people than younger cohorts. Not only is the geographic extent of older people's activity smaller, but the content of their environmental experience is also reduced.[6] The significance of this restriction in the lives of older people is indicated in the results of a nationwide survey. In all but church or synagogue, elderly people reported lower levels of activity. Thirty percent had not been to a restaurant within the past year. Seventy percent and more had not participated in entertainment such as going to a movie, library, concert, or even a park. Ten percent had not even gone shopping.

Other forms of environmental interaction, because they are less obvious, have been given less research attention. Visual interaction in the surveillance zone is a good example. Another example is fantasy experience. This is an indirect environmental interaction that can be displaced in both time and space. When we reflect on a former experience or project ourselves into an anticipated experience, we are interacting with the environment. Research has not ascertained the significance of these types of environmental interactions, but it is thought that they may be particularly important to the lives of older people. For example, it has been suggested that as one's mobility declines, action with the immediate environment is replaced with more vicarious and indirect types of interaction.

From the interactionist perspective, then, the environment is viewed as a setting for behavior that presents opportunities for and obstacles to obtaining the necessities and amenities of life. The content of one's environment may be rich or sparse in opportunities and obstacles. Thus, interaction patterns are strongly influenced by environmental content. They are also influenced by the locational context. We interact most frequently with our immediate environment, because availing ourselves of opportunities at greater distances involves a variety of costs, e.g., costs for transportation, physical exertion costs, and the cost of time spent in traveling.

This is not to say that the environmental content and context absolutely determine interaction patterns. Individual needs, preferences, and especially resources are also very important. Even if an environment contains the opportunity for necessary or desired activities, only people who have sufficient financial, social, and other appropriate resources can undertake those activities. Moreover, in a setting deficient in or devoid of opportunities, an individual with high mobility resources can undertake the activity elsewhere. It is primarily changes in individual resource levels associated with the process of aging that make the relationships between the environment and the aging person uniquely important to the quality of later life. This can best be shown by reviewing several theoretical statements about aging and the environment.

The Aging Individual and the Environment

This discussion relies heavily on the work of environmental psychologists and others who focus on the microenvironment, i.e., that portion of the environment extending from the individual to the limits of what is considered to be the boundary of the home. Although many of the concepts and findings from these studies can be transferred to other levels of environmental study, it is dangerous to engage in wholesale transfer for several reasons. First, we use and interact with different parts of the environment in different ways. Although one might argue that going to the refrigerator and the grocery store are similar activities because they share a common purpose, the physical capability needed to undertake these activities is very different. Obviously the frequency of these interactions would also differ considerably. Second, microenvironmental findings generally are based on studies of only a very small proportion of the elderly, mostly those found in institutional or public housing settings. Despite these problems theoretical statements derived from microenvironmental studies provide considerable insight into environmental relationships of older people at the community scale.

Pastalan articulates an "age loss continuum": "as a person continues to age beyond his sixth or seventh decade of life, a number of crucial age-related losses occur and accumulate until ultimately the person will lose all semblances of autonomous being and will depend entirely on others to sustain his very life."[7] In this view, old age is a time when one is likely to lose a spouse or friends and have one's income and social roles reduced, as well as suffer health declines. Although the exact age at which an individual may experience such losses is highly variable, the last stage of life is characterized for most people as a period of cumulative loss, considerable deprivation, and a diminution of resources that requires major personal adjustment. By applying the developmental aspects of Pastalan's statements to the present discussion, we can depict a hypothetical model of environmental interaction over the course of life, such as that shown in Figure 27.2. For example, during early childhood, environmental interaction is extremely limited but might be expected to expand rapidly into the early years of school attendance. A period of modest increase might be followed by rapid growth of mobility with the acquisition of a driver's license, additional income from employment, or a change in residence to attend college. The last years of life are characterized by a constriction in activity patterns because of the losses which characterize old age.

Figure 27.2: Age-Loss Continuum Across the Life Span

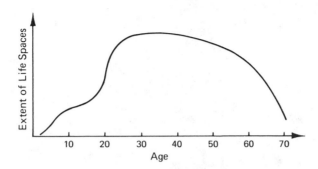

This depiction is logically appealing and to some extent empirically substantiated. However, it assumes that the environment remains fairly constant over the span of life. Furthermore, it suggests that the processes of growth and decline are more symmetrical than seems to be the case. However, Pastalan's perspective has been widely shared among gerontologists. A derivative can be seen in the "environmental docility hypothesis."[8] This hypothesis states that as an individual ages, competence (individual resources) declines and the environment becomes more difficult for the older person. Numerous studies have supported this hypothesis by demonstrating that environmental interaction declines with advanced age and is positively related to resource levels.

This somewhat negative view of the relationship between older individuals and the environment, as conveyed in the term *docility* and the frequently cited concept of environmental stress, has been recently modified by Lawton.[9] He further develops the notion that resource level strongly influences environment interaction. In doing so, he acknowledges the highly variable nature of resource (competence) levels among elderly individuals and indicates that the environment can have positive as well as negative influences (press) in the lives of older people. A graphic depiction of this theory is presented in Figure 27.3. Lawton's theory postulates that behavioral adaptation to one's environmental setting can vary between negative and positive depending on the interplay of individual competence and environmental press. The theory allows for inclusion of the total range of environmental influences, all types of individual resources, and many types of behavior.

A hypothetical example helps to clarify some of the terms and relationships depicted in Figure 27.3. Assume that an individual at position a has a given level of competence and resides in an environment with a given level

Figure 27.3: An Ecological Model of Aging

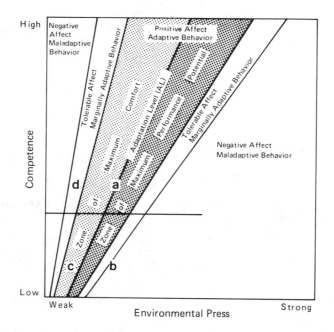

Source: After M. Powell Lawton and Lucille Nahemow,
          "Ecology and the Aging Process," in The
          Psychology of Adult Development and Aging,
          edited by Carl Eisdorfer and M. Powell Lawton
          (Washington, D.C.: American Psychological
          Association, 1973): 661. Reprinted by
          permission.

of press. If the individual experiences a stroke, there is a subsequent loss of competence (position b), and the individual's competence level is too low for positive adaptive behavior in the same environmental setting. The individual might cope with this problem by reducing the level of press, perhaps moving to an environment that provides limited care (position c). At this point, the level of environmental press is well below the individual's level of competence. The individual can easily cope with the environment and probably enjoys an environment-competence situation that might be termed "maximum comfort." However, if this individual recovers fully from all effects of the stroke and regains his or her original level of competence, environmental press in the new residence is probably too low. That is, the environment no longer is challenging enough to keep the person's abilities from atrophying, and maladaptive behavior may result (position d). Now another change of environment might be warranted, one which results in a healthier balance between competence and press, (position a).

Lawton identifies some problems inherent in this formulation. For example, neither press nor competence is a one-dimensional concept. It is impossible to measure the multidimensional environment described earlier with a single value. Similarly, the various resources that make up individual competence are difficult to synthesize into a single indicator, and it is likely that strong endowment in one resource might substitute for deficiencies in another. Despite these and other problems, the theory is useful in that it recognizes that older individuals vary in terms of competence level, that environmental influences can be positive as well as negative, and that different environmental settings contain different amounts and types of press.

Kahana takes a more prescriptive view and develops the notion of environment-individual congruence.[10] She views older people as having highly individualistic sets of needs and preferences that should be matched to effect congruence with the salient characteristics of specific environments. She identifies several dimensions along which the matching should occur. For example, on the social dimension, the individual's preference for change or stability should be matched with the age heterogeneity or homogeneity of the neighborhood or housing environment. The notion of congruence is similar to Lawton's zone of adaptability, i.e., when press equals competence.

These theories call attention to the fact that the process of aging induces change within the individual, which in turn necessitates changes in the set of relationships that exist between the individual and the environment. Consider again the loss of mobility that occurs when one loses the ability to drive a car, a common experience in old age. If the environment remains constant, the individual must adapt to this change. As we have seen, for many people this adaptation involves a constriction in activity patterns and more limited environmental interaction. Others, however, may employ a more active coping strategy by shifting to other modes of transportation, changing the mix of activities undertaken within the environment, or changing the environmental setting through relocation.

The Aging Environment

Gerontological theory as exemplified above focuses primarily on changes that occur in the individual due to the passage of time. These changes generally result in a diminution of individual resources needed to conduct environmental transactions. But what of the other side of the individual-environment relationship? Over time, the content and spatial structure of the community environment changes (friends die or move away, and old stores close as newer shopping centers are developed). Let us briefly consider the aging of an urban community environment.

Beyond a consideration of the home environment, the choice of a residential location is often made with considerable attention to the content of the neighborhood and the spatial relationship of the neighborhood to the broader city or town environment. It is reasonable to assume that because a choice is involved in selecting location, a reasonable amount of individual-environment congruence exists. A problem arises, however, because older people are residentially very stable compared to younger age groups. In fact, one-third of those over 64 have been living at the same address for more than a quarter of a century.[11] This indicates that many elderly people selected a location within the environment at an earlier stage in life, when they were still employed and rearing families. With the passage of time and the transition from one life cycle stage to another, clearly their needs and preferences have changed, thus engendering environmental incongruence. For example, the importance attached to environmental elements such as schools and a social situation appropriate to rearing children, which may have weighed heavily in residential choice earlier in life, is reduced or eliminated in later life.

Even in the rare case in which the set of individual needs and preferences remains essentially unchanged, the passage of time results in perceived and often very real declines in most environmental dimensions. The built environment decays. The social fabric of the neighborhood changes such that many older people residing in inner-city locations now find themselves in environments with unstable populations and high crime rates. Shopping and entertainment opportunities once plentiful in older neighborhoods relocate to newer parts of the community. The downtown portion of most urban environments, once the hub of employment, shopping, and recreation, is drained of its resources by suburban development. The decentralization of shopping opportunities in recent decades is a dramatic example of environmental changes to which the older person must respond by changing activity patterns. Unfortunately, many aging people are suffering from mobility reduction at a time when the environment demands greater mobility for merely sustaining life. Over time, then, both the content and spatial structure of the environment change and often begin to exceed the older person's competence level.

Programs and Alternatives for Enhancing Environmental Congruence

Implicit throughout this chapter and explicit in most gerontological studies is the picture of the older person confronted with ever-increasing environmental incongruence that ultimately threatens the person's very existence. Whether this incongruence derives from changes in the aging individual's level of resources or in the environment or both, the resulting problems are numerous. There appear to be three general strategies that might be employed to improve the relationship between the older individual and his or her environment. These are: (1) increasing the person's level of resources; (2) improving the individual's environment; and (3) facilitating environmental interaction.

Improving the individual's resource level appears to be the most difficult strategy, but it is an area that warrants greater attention than it has received in the past. Health is a fundamental resource, and one that has received considerable attention. Medicare, Medicaid, advances in medicine and medical practice, as well as increased emphasis on geriatric research, are resulting in significant health improvements for today's elderly population. The congregate meals program, and health screening and educational activities often attached to this program, are also making contributions. Other important resources, however, are being attended to less well. Income remains a problem in old age despite Social Security and Supplemental Security Insurance payments. The development of Individual Retirement Accounts[12] is one means of ensuring adequate financial resources in old age. Social, psychological, and educational resources for dealing with everyday problems also warrant more consideration. It would be preferable to anticipate declines in resources and prevent them when possible rather than treat them in remedial fashion at a later date. Greater attention could still be paid to preventive health care. Preretirement counseling and planning could be made more widely accessible, as could counseling following the losses that attend later life. Clearly, much more can be done in pursuing this strategy.

Changing the individual's environmental setting is another strategy that has been employed with some degree of success. The most obvious example of this strategy is the relocation of elderly people to more healthful environments. Older people whose resource levels are high often can achieve a better level of environmental congruence by relocating. For many whose resources — particularly financial ones — are extremely low, voluntary relocation may be impossible. Some assistance is available to these people, primarily through federal programs that provide publicly owned or subsidized housing. Congregate housing arrangements are also a response by both public and private sectors to the older person's declining resource base and need for a more congruent environment. We appear to be slowly moving toward the provision of a wide range of residential options for older people that include increasingly lower levels of environmental stress and greater amounts of care and personal assistance. However, in all of these developments it appears that greater attention can be paid to the neighborhood and broader environmental context in which such housing is developed.

Most older people, however, do not want to relocate in order to achieve better environmental congruence. Indeed, it appears that they will tolerate and adapt to very high levels of environmental stress rather than relocate. After years of living in one setting, many people are willing to relocate only after very heavy resource decline and the experience of several significant losses, such as income loss coupled with loss of spouse and precipitous health decline.

When relocation is not feasible, then the most reasonable strategy is to improve the present environment. Unfortunately, in the past neighborhood improvement and renewal have often meant the removal of the elderly. This is less true today in regard to publicly funded neighborhood improvement programs, but it is increasingly the case in neighborhoods that are "coming back" through redevelopment by the private sector.[13] Forced relocation of older people is obviously a less desirable means of improving environmental congruence, but improving the neighborhood environments of older people is posing serious difficulties. Much that is relevant to the environments of older people falls outside of governmental control. Could we, even if we chose to do so, control the social structure of a neighborhood? How much of an incentive and subsidy would have to be provided to private entrepreneurs to reestablish shopping, entertainment, and other activities within those parts of the environment vacated earlier by the same entrepreneurs for financial reasons? One interesting alternative is to provide mobile services to neighborhoods containing older people. The growth of the Meals on Wheels program might encourage further developments of this sort. In an admittedly limited way, it would certainly be possible to reestablish activity opportunities in neighborhoods by converting large vans or trucks into mini–shopping malls or entertainment and recreation centers.

The third strategy, facilitating environmental interactions, is also being employed. A wide variety of transportation programs has been developed to enhance the mobility of older persons. Many of these programs are described in Chapter 17 of this volume. But what of the other, less direct, forms of environmental interaction? Today, communication is increasingly taking the place of transportation. Telephoning a friend substitutes for a face-to-face visit. Clearly, the quality of life would be diminished for all of us without telephones, television, books, and newspapers, but these media are probably more important to the elderly than they are to younger adults. People working with mass media are becoming more aware of their potential use in service to the elderly. The program "Over Easy" is just one example of the role that television can play. Audio and visual environmental transactions through such communication devices may be less preferable than direct action, but they do enormously expand the mix and frequency of interaction.

An even less direct, and less studied, form of environmental transaction is fantasy experience. So little is known about this form of transaction that it is impossible to identify its role and importance in life. What are the cues in the immediate environment that trigger fantasy experiences with environments in other times and places? What thoughts interrupt the nightly weather report when an older person hears that it is snowing in an important "beyond space," her daughter's community? For some older people this highly indirect but very personal form of environmental transaction may be extremely important. Could it be facilitated? Should it be? What is being suggested here is not that society anesthetize the older person into a state of euphoria through a supersaturation of vicarious experience. Rather, it is hoped that more thought would be given to making the totality of environmental experience commensurate with the individual's needs and resources. Just as we are now attempting to provide the older individual with a range of housing and living environments to match changing needs and abilities in later life, we should also be developing a wide range of environmental experiences.

Before this can be accomplished, a considerable amount of research and experimentation must be undertaken. The environmental concepts presented here must be further refined and considered in the light of alternative paradigms.[14] Salient dimensions of the environment must be identified and their importance to our lives assessed. The differential significance of elements that make up environmental dimensions should be more clearly understood for all stages of life. The content, structure, and use of different spaces in the environment must be better understood. Similarly, there is a clear need to investigate all forms of environmental interaction. Studies along these lines will reveal much about the complex relationships between the community environment and the aging person. More importantly, such knowledge can lead to direct improvements in those relationships, and, therefore, in the quality of later life.

Notes

1. See, for example, M. Powell Lawton and Jacob Cohen, "Environment and the Well-Being of Inner-City Residents," *Environment and Behavior* 6, 2 (1974), pp. 195–211.

2. Sheldon S. Tobin and Morton A. Lieberman, *Last Home for the Aged* (San Francisco: Jossey-Bass, 1975).

3. Jaber F. Gubrium, *The Myth of the Golden Years: A Socio-Environmental Theory of Aging* (Springfield, Ill.: Charles C. Thomas, 1973).

4. Gregory Bateson, *Steps to an Ecology of Mind* (New York: Ballantine Books, 1972).

5. Graham P. Rowles, *Prisoners of Space? Exploring the Geographical Experiences of Older People* (Boulder, Colo: Westview Press, 1978).

6. Perry Hanson, "The Activity Patterns of Elderly Households," *Geografiska Annaler* 59, Series B., no. 2 (1978), p. 109–124.

7. Leon A. Pastalan, "Research in Environment and Aging: An Alternative to Theory," in Paul G. Windley, Thomas O. Byerts, and F. Gene Ernst (eds.), *Theory Development in Environment and Aging* (Washington, D.C.: Gerontological Society, 1975), pp. 219–230.

8. M. Powell Lawton and Bonnie Simon, "The Ecology of Social Relationships in Housing for the Elderly," *Gerontologist* 8, 2 (1978), pp. 108–115.

9. M. Powell Lawton, "Competence, Environmental Press, and the Adaptation of Older People," in Paul G. Windley, Thomas O. Byerts, and F. Gene Ernst (eds.), *Theory Development in Environment and Aging* (Washington, D.C.: Gerontological Society, 1975), pp. 18–83.

10. Eva Kahana, "A Congruence Model of Person-Environment Interaction," in Paul G. Windley, Thomas O. Byerts, and F. Gene Ernst (eds.), *Theory Development in Environment and Aging* (Washington, D.C.: Gerontological Society, 1975), pp. 181–214.

11. Department of Housing and Urban Development, *Annual Housing Survey: 1973 Housing Characteristics of Older Americans in the United States* (Washington, D.C.: Government Printing Office, 1979), p. 14.

12. Robert F. Wiseman and Timothy Peterson, "Elderly Migration and Independence Maintenance," *East Lakes Geographer*, Vol. 14, (Fall 1979), pp. 6–16.

13. Howard J. Sumaka, "Displacement in Revitalizing Neighborhoods: A Review and Research Strategy," in *Occasional Papers in Housing and Community Affairs*, Vol. 2 (Washington, D.C.: Department of Housing and Urban Development, 1978), pp. 134–167.

14. Amos Rapoport, "An Approach to the Construction of Man-Environment Theory," in W. F. E. Preiser (ed.), *EDRA Proceedings II* (Stroudsburg, Pa.: Dowden, Hutchinson & Ross, 1973), pp. 124–135.

28
Retirement Communities

Charles F. Longino, Jr.

The term *retirement community* tends to conjure up the image of active, wealthy elders living in a country club setting. This may be one type of living environment for retired people, but it is only one of many. The idea is actually a good deal broader.

Community is a vague concept. Abstractly defined, it is a relatively stable context for autonomous living, a living environment.[1] It is most often applied to stationary settings, thus excluding nomadic settlements. (The nomads would disagree.) It is generally used for groups with residential boundaries, thus excluding intellectual, political, or religious "communities" that may be scattered geographically.[2] All social systems, including communities, maintain some kind of boundaries; people know if they are members. Stationary residential communities maintain explicit jurisdictional boundaries.

While the boundaries of retirement communities are sometimes civic and political in nature, they are more often like those of ethnic neighborhoods or condominium complexes rather than of municipalities. Retirement communities are defined more clearly by their membership than by their geographical boundaries.[3] A retirement community is any living environment to which most of its residents have moved since they retired. This does not mean that none of the residents are employed. In fact, Long and Hansen found that nearly an eighth of "retired" household heads who had moved from one state to another were still working to some extent.[4] On the other hand, some retirement community residents have never been employed outside the home. Nonetheless, nearly all who have worked have also retired from full-time employment at least once. The above definition excludes communities of retirement-age people who have "aged in place." Retirement communities are settings to which retired people move. Retirement and relocation are the essential elements of the definition. The largest are like small towns with several thousand residents, and have a complex institutional structure that meets a variety of the residents' personal and household needs. The smallest ones are groupings of a few households of retired people who identify themselves as members of a living environment, a small neighborhood or apartment house.

Housing is easier to define than community. It is limited to the property owned, leased, rented, or borrowed by someone for whose household it provides a dwelling place. Housing is found both in communities of varying size and cohesion and on land outside the spatial boundaries of any officially recognized community. However, both the house and the community represent living environments. The dwelling is an element of the community environment.[5] Simultaneously, it is a living environment in its own right and has the most personal impact upon the individual. The community is the location for institutions, organizations, and individuals that provide goods and services to members of the household unit, goods and services that cannot be provided efficiently or effectively from within the dwelling. It is this dynamic relationship between the microenvironment (the dwelling unit), and the larger community that has been of enduring interest to environmental gerontologists and provides for them the special subject matter of retirement community research.[6]

Three Types of Retirement Communities

The major dimension along which retirement communities can be differentiated is the degree to which they are consciously planned for retired people. Some communities, for example, deliberately limit eligibility for membership to persons who have reached a certain chronological age. These are retirement communities de jure, for they are designed as such. Others place no age restrictions upon new residents but overwhelmingly attract people who are retired. These are not designed as retirement communities, but in them a series of organizations and services arise that cater to older people. These are de facto retirement communities.[7]

A minimum age limit for housing eligibility is but one element of planned retirement communities. By consciously limiting residence to those of retirement age, it is possible to design both community and dwelling environments that take into account the more common needs arising from physiological aging. Transportation, shopping and medical services, and social and recreational opportunities can be built into the living environment. Thus, the most planned communities would be those that meet the greatest range of resident needs most fully.

Planned communities may be separated into two subtypes: subsidized and nonsubsidized. The subsidized planned community, in its most common form, is congregate housing provided by various programs of the United States Department of Housing and Urban Development (HUD). According to Carp, HUD has housed approximately 600,000 older people since 1956.[8] This type of housing has been well described in a number of works.[9] There is also a variety of nonsubsidized planned communities for older people, ranging along a continuum from housing provision alone to life-care communities, which attempt to provide a full range of services, including medical care. The cost of residence, of course, increases with the level of services.[10]

In 1975, the Social Security Administration funded an ambitious comparative study of midwestern retirement communities. This three-year project involved ethnographic field work and extensive interview surveys in eight retirement communities. Both de facto and de jure, subsidized and nonsubsidized planned communities were studied by a team of social scientists representing the disciplines of sociology, anthropology, psychology, and economics.[11] Three communities were chosen from the files of this project for use as examples of the theoretical and research material presented in this chapter. In the following paragraphs these communities are briefly described, with emphasis on their physical setting, development, and ambiance.

A De Facto Retirement Community: The Ozark Lakes Country

There are several places in the United States that have begun to attract the retired in large numbers since World War II. One of these is the Ozark region connecting the states of Missouri, Arkansas, and Oklahoma. The major influx has been into Arkansas, but migration into the southwestern Missouri counties is also typical of the area. These mountainous counties, like most of rural America, recorded a population drain each decade in this century until after World War II, when a series of dams were built that created miles of fishing lakes nestled among the wooded peaks. The lakes provide outdoor recreation that attracts summer tourists. Local residents, and some entrepreneurs from the outside, quickly capitalized on the natural environment and the hillbilly mystique of the area. The result was the rapid development of a major tourist and resort industry.

Tourism exposed the sleepy mountain communities to the outside world, and particularly to middle-class vacationers from midwestern metropolitan areas. Retired people began trickling into these counties at an increasing rate. The existing towns expanded to accommodate the migrants, many of whom had sold homes in the suburbs of midwestern cities and paid cash for smaller homes in the Ozarks. New communities sprang up in scenic spots, and this land development boom contributed further to the economic growth of the area. The median resident age of the old mountain towns climbed as the proportion of retired migrants exceeded that of native-born residents. There was some resentment of the outsiders at first, but the newcomers brought many needed resources to the community. By the mid-1970s, older migrants had come to represent the dominant force in most of the area churches, civic and community organizations, and neighborhoods. The towns in the Ozark lakes country had become retirement communities, de facto.

The Ozark communities are not age restricted. Young families do move there, attracted by the economic expansion in the area. It is clear, however, that community institutions cater to the old. This may not be so evident to the casual visitor, but an adult community center doing a booming business, the number of bridge clubs, a public library whose management and clientele are mostly retired, a new cardiac unit in the local hospital, and an expanded trust department in a local bank are examples of institutional adjustments to a shifting age structure. Otherwise, the round of community life would strike an outsider as similar to other small communities in resort areas. The predominance of older people in the population is hardly apparent to the casual observer, especially during the summer tourist season.

A Subsidized Planned Retirement Community: Horizon Heights

Horizon Heights is part of a network of public housing facilities in a midwestern city with a population of 170,000. The public housing network consists of nineteen buildings with 2,000 individual units. Seven of these buildings are specified for elderly tenants and twelve for low-income families. They were initially funded by the United States Department of Housing and Urban Development under a 40-year bond, and the department subsidizes their operation and maintenance.

Constructed in 1969, Horizon Heights is located in a deteriorated neighborhood approximately five blocks from the central business district of the city. In 1970, the racial composition of the census tract where Horizon Heights is located was 43 percent black, and 16 percent of the households were classified as having incomes below the poverty level. Most Horizon Heights residents have lived in the city all their lives; many once lived in the immediate neighborhood.

This subsidized planned community is housed in a sixteen-story poured concrete building. There are eighteen apartments on each of the fifteen residential floors. An additional area contains thirty-three garden apartments, built primarily with exterior brick construction. The surroundings of the project resemble a city park, with walks connecting the garden apartments to one another and to the high-rise building. Residents give personal touches to the apartments by adorning their yards with bird baths, rose trellises, and flower and vegetable gardens. The high-rise building faces a busy city street. Three hundred people live in Horizon Heights.

The tenants of this subsidized community pay only 25 percent of their adjusted income for rent. A number of formal services and activities are provided to residents by the Horizon Heights staff as well as by groups from outside the community. There are social activities, voluntary service groups, religious and educational programs. The most prominent service to residents is the meal program provided by the Administration on Aging. Weekday noon meals are made available, and about 115 residents attend daily. Staff members refer residents to several publicly and privately funded service agencies designed to help people with financial, physiological, and psychological problems. Resident-staff commmunication difficulties, however, hamper the dissemination of information about community services, and the system looks better on paper than in reality. The overall impression of Horizon Heights is one of social vitality, reflected in a high frequency of social exchanges and the alertness of residents to the ebb and flow of daily activity.

The physical layout of Horizon Heights contributes to one's impressions of the community. The stark, modernistic building appears stately and imposing. Wall decorations and house plants are few, and vinyl upholstered chairs contribute to the starkness. There is a paucity of adornment in the public spaces. The black and white color scheme encourages a feeling of detachment and coldness. However, the institutional atmosphere is balanced by the heavy use made of the lobby and other common space, and the warm, friendly sounds of laughter and small talk as residents visit. The building seems to conspire against an insistent community.

The staff is a pervasive presence. The message is quickly received in Horizon Heights that residents had better toe the mark. As one walks through the front doors a sign reads "Wipe your feet." On the television set a note says "Do not adjust." "Please" and "thank you" are conspicuously absent in these messages. Residents are quick to complain that they are patronized like children. Staff members are easy to identify. They walk faster than the residents and have an air of authority. They are friendly and reasonably approachable, but busy.

The ambiance of Horizon Heights is paradoxical. It is institutional, run by a busy staff. Keeping the rules enforced and everything in order makes their work manageable. In all institutions, from universities to prisons, in a sense the rules and routines exist to meet staff rather than client needs. One senses this in Horizon Heights. Simultaneously, there is an equally strong feeling of vitality, of cheerful community involvement, tempered by realism and tenacity. There is a toughness about these residents. They are the survivors, mostly women born between 1890 and 1910. They are also survivors in another sense. The tempo, warmth, and interaction of genuine community

survives amidst the signs, locks, and polished tile floors. The institutional
character of Horizon Heights does not escape comment, but the residents
tend to view it as a problem to be lived with, to be ignored when possible,
and to be overcome. "It might have been hard to adjust to this place,"
asserted one resident thoughtfully, "but I didn't let it be." The lady with the
two tall grocery bags in her arms turned as she entered the elevator. "The
first hundred years are the hardest," she said and smiled as the door closed.

A Nonsubsidized Planned Retirement Community: Carefree Village

Carefree Village was the child of post–World War II Protestant expansion
in the suburbs. It was launched as a church-related project, but as it grew it
became less and less dependent upon church support. Since 1961 its
management organization has established over forty life-care retirement
communities in seventeen states. Carefree Village, with over 3,000 residents,
is the largest and is considered the prototype.

The village is located in a suburban community near a midwestern
metropolitan center. Single and two-bedroom units, incorporated into
apartments and cottage-style houses, dominate village housing. All wings of
the apartment complexes are interconnected by enclosed passageways protected from outside heat or cold. In the middle of the village stands a health
center serving the housebound. Doctors', dentists', psychologists', and
chaplains' offices are located nearby. A short distance away, and unobtrusively located, is the skilled nursing facility for bedfast residents. Throughout
the village, there are a number of activity settings including dining room and
cafeterias; swimming pool; bowling alley; gift, plant, craft, barber and beauty
shops; a bank; chapel; ice cream parlor; and a cavernous community
auditorium. Carefree Village as a whole, then, is a sprawling suburban set-
tlement of houses, apartments, cottages, public buildings, recreation areas,
and health care operations. It is an upper-middle-class planned community,
populated by retired people and managed for a profit by a large service
organization.

There is no doubt that Carefree Village sells itself as a specialized provider
of supportive services, and of health care in particular. "Life care" is the
name of the package; it includes freedom from maintenance worries,
ultimate health care, and a wide range of formal services. The Human Services Division responsible for these services is staffed by a dentist, physician,
optometrist, audiologist, social worker, and several chaplains. Visiting
nurses check on people and administer medications. Meals are brought to
people who are unable to prepare their own, and housekeeping services are
available for brief periods twice a month. Villagers confined to wheelchairs
are pushed to meals or other places by young staff members hired for that
task. Buildings and lawns are maintained by the village, and a visible secu-

rity force, wearing distinctive uniforms, is always on patrol. Residents moving into Carefree Village have to acclimate themselves to this new service-oriented environment.

The initial impression that one gets from Carefree Village is of genteel affluence. There is a sense of newness. The residents dress as if on their way to club or church meetings. The architecture and landscaping are reminiscent of southern California. It is relatively easy to identify the professional staff: they are young and immaculately groomed in conservative clothes and they speak very softly and deliberately. The entire feeling of Carefree Village is one of enclosure. It is an indoor environment in which the climate is controlled year round and everyone speaks in low tones.

There are several levels of physical access to health care and other services, defined by residential location. People living in the outlying cottages tend to be younger and healthier than those in the apartment complexes. Those with apartments nearer the Health Center are older and most needful of health care access. The nursing home, at the center of the village, is only used for residents who can no longer be maintained in their apartments even with outpatient and home-delivered health care. As disability increases, residents are gradually moved from one level of care to the next, until eventually they are cared for in the nursing facility. This process is designed to prolong independent living and reduce costs for institutionalization.

Unless death arrives unexpectedly, there comes a time when an inevitable decision about institutionalization must be made. In a community of 3,000 older people, this is a recurring event. The resident, his or her physician, the administration, and family members when possible are involved in this decision. After the patient is transferred to the nursing home, a padlock is placed on the door of his or her apartment and, if there are relatives, they will come and claim personal belongings. The unit is then sold to another buyer. The final institutionalization is usually brief. Life care has been completed.

Age and Relocation

If retired people never moved, there would be no retirement communities as defined in this chapter. In order to assess the potential for retirement community development, therefore, it is important to review what is known about the patterns of migration of the elderly and the characteristics of aged migrants. Older people are less likely to move than the general U.S. population. In 1970, slightly over half (53 percent) the total population over age 5 reported living at the same address 5 years earlier. For people age 65 and older, the figure was 72 percent. The fact that over one-quarter of the people age 65 and above had moved in this 5-year period strikes many as surprisingly high, for two reasons. First, occupational opportunity, a major migration motivator for the general population, is less salient for the older population. Second, older households have fewer dependents, so there are more households per thousand among the elderly than among the general population.

Not only does the absolute amount of residential movement differ for older people, but they are somewhat more likely to move shorter distances.[12] In 1970, over one-fifth (21 percent) of movers of all ages were interstate migrants, as compared with one-sixth (16 percent) of older movers. While a majority (58 percent) of all movers relocate within the same county, the percentage for older people approaches two-thirds (65 percent). In this regard, it is instructive to treat age as a continuous, rather than a categorical, variable and to compare mobility rates for successive age cohorts.[13] Seen in this way, there is a middle-age plateau at which the rates of residential relocation do not change much from one decade to the next. In the 65-to-70 age cohort, there is a jump in the interstate migration rate, especially for men. This is the time when older people are most inclined to make long-distance moves. On the other hand, local moves gradually decline during the middle and later years, increasing (especially for women) only after age 75. If these trends are reflected in retirement community residential populations, we would expect the communities more attractive to interstate migrants to have different distributions of resident characteristics than those attracting mostly local movers.

What can be learned from the Census about the distributional patterns of older people? Where do they move? A recent study reports the distributional patterns of two categories of older movers, those who moved across state lines and those who moved within their states. Only people who were age 60 and over in 1970 were studied.[14] The interstate flows were quite channelized.[15] That is, half the interstate migrants were moving into the seven states most popular with elderly migrants. Nearly one-quarter of all older interstate migrants (23.5 percent), by the end of the 1965–70 migration period, had moved to Florida, and almost one-tenth (9.5 percent) to California. The state ranking third in receiving older interstate migrants was Arizona (4.4 percent) and close behind was New Jersey (4.1 percent). Then came Washington, Texas, and Oregon, each attracting between 3 and 4 percent. This study examined not only the destinations of the migrants, but their origins as well.[16] Only three states drew their older migrants from a large number of noncontiguous states. These national migration centers are Florida, California, and Arizona. Their major recruitment areas, however, are different. It is as though a Great Divide stretching in a line south from Lake Michigan created two drainage systems, eastward to Florida and westward to Arizona and California.

Several regional migration centers also were identified, attracting older migrants disproportionately from surrounding states. They were the Olympic Peninsula in Washington State, the Ozarks region in Missouri and Arkansas, and the southern coastal counties of New Jersey. All of these areas also have strong tourist industries.

It would be easy to conclude that the Sunbelt has a monopoly on de facto retirement communities, as defined in the previous section. When in-migrants to the Sunbelt states of all ages are compared with those over age 60, disproportionate migration by the elderly is indeed apparent: 56 percent of all in-migrants came from outside the area, while 70 percent of older in-migrants did.[17] Sunbelt migration, however, is neither that simple nor that uniform. A state-by-state analysis shows wide variation in the attractiveness of individual states in the area to migrants from the Snowbelt. Half the states in this warmer area received a majority of their elderly migrants from other Sunbelt states. At the same time, migration rates of the aged to many states simply reflect general patterns. Only in nine of the fifteen states were proportions of older migrants higher than those of all migrants from the Snowbelt. Furthermore, only four of the top ten receiving states for elderly migrants are located in the Sunbelt, and nearly one-third (32 percent) of the older Snowbelt migrants came from Sunbelt states. Thus, although aged migrants were more attracted to the Sunbelt than were general migrants, migration of the elderly is not simply a Sunbelt phenomenon.[18]

Most intrastate movement is within and between Standard Metropolitan Statistical Areas (SMSAs). (An SMSA includes a central city of 50,000 or more, the county in which it is located, and any surrounding heavily suburban counties.) Two-thirds of the older intrastate movers between 1965 and 1970 were making this type of move. Another one-quarter moved from one location to another outside of SMSAs. Most people, therefore, moved within the same general type of environment in which they had been living. Very small proportions moved from small towns or rural areas to SMSAs (2.6 percent) or from SMSAs to areas outside of SMSAs (4.2 percent). There are higher rates of relocation among SMSA than among non-SMSA residents; it is a phenomenon of city life. This holds for young and old alike. But for the few who move to a different type of environment, more go to the country than to the city.[19]

While it is true that the volume of intrastate, but interlocational, moves is relatively small, interesting variations appear when these types of moves are examined state by state.[20] Certain states are experiencing a greater-than-average migration of people over age 60 from non-SMSA locations to the central cities and suburbs of SMSAs. These include Kansas, Oklahoma, Colorado, Minnesota, Virginia, and Kentucky, which are primarily rural states. Rural locations attract a disproportionate number of older intrastate movers in Connecticut, Michigan, New Jersey, and Missouri. Each of these states has well-known rural recreational areas. The Connecticut and New Jersey coasts, the Michigan north woods, and the Ozark area of southwestern Missouri may account for these findings. These are also likely locations for de facto retirement communities.

Relocation to Retirement Communities

Where do retirement community residents come from? Carp estimates that subsidized, planned communities house only about 3 percent of older persons and nonsubsidized planned communities house even fewer.[21] De facto retirement communities house more, but it is impossible to estimate how many more.

Retirement communities have different fields of recruitment, like colleges and universities. Some recruit locally and others recruit from a larger area. This may be demonstrated by comparing the three example retirement communities previously described (see Table 28.1).

Subsidized planned communites tend to recruit from the local area. Horizon Heights is typical, drawing four-fifths of its residents from the same county. Nonsubsidized planned communities vary in their recruitment range depending upon the size, sophistication, and vitality of their sales staff and upon the availability of local residents who fit their market profile. As a rule, more restrictive entrance requirments increase the market area. For nonsubsidized planned communities offering extensive service packages at substantial cost, like Carefree Village, local recruitment may not be sufficient to sustain growth or maintain necessary residence levels. Therefore, the more complex and complete the service levels in planned communities of this type, the larger the proportion of interstate migrants one could expect

Table 28.1: Residential Relocation by Retirement Community

Percent of Residents Who Moved From:	Horizon Heights	Carefree Village	Ozark Lakes Country
Same County	81	48	5
Different County	7	28	31
Different State	12	24	64
Total	100	100	100

to find among the residents. De facto retirement communities in attractive outdoor recreational settings, such as the Ozark lakes country, could be expected to attract high proportions of interstate migrants. It is not surprising, therefore, to see that a majority of the older Ozark residents are from out of state.

For a further explanation of why different patterns of residential relocation are found in the different types of retirement communities, we now turn our attention to the question of which older people are likely to move. It would be easy to conclude that movers and stayers are pretty much alike, if they are over age 60. Because the characteristics of movers are so varied, they tend to look very much like nonmovers when taken as a group.[22] The major differences between nonmovers and movers generally have to do with household composition and marital status. Nonmovers are more likely to be living independently with their spouses. Biggar's study found that migrants, those who move across county or state lines, were younger, while local movers were often widowed. Two-thirds (67 percent) of the migrants were living independently, while only 56 percent of the local movers lived in independent households. Furthermore, local movers had consistently lower levels of socioeconomic status than either nonmovers or migrants. In other words, local movers are poorer, on the whole, than migrants.

Most of the household heads who were interstate migrants and who said that retirement was their reason for moving had income from pensions. Because of income from sources other than earnings, the retired migrants had total household incomes equal to the average for all households (including younger people) moving between states.[23] In other words, migrants, on the whole, are richer than local movers.

These findings suggest that local movers tend to be selected from among the more dependent older population. One might infer from these national profiles that retirement communities attracting people from farther away (migrants) are likely to be different in their resident profile than communities attracting mostly local movers. This inference can be examined in the three example communities. Horizon Heights, the subsidized planned community, draws its residents primarily from the local area. Eighty-one percent moved from the same county. Most of the residents in Horizon Heights are over age 70; the mean age is 78. Over four-fifths (83 percent) are female and less than one-fifth (18 percent) have a living spouse. Three-fifths (59 percent) are black. The median household income for Horizon Heights residents in 1976 was $2,608. Only half (48 percent) rated themseles as in good health. In the aggregate, Horizon Heights residents resemble the national profile of older local movers.

As seen in Table 28.1, Carefree Village, the nonsubsidized planned community, attracts about half its residents from the migrant and half from the local mover categories. In this community, the residents are similar to those in Horizon Heights in terms of age, sex, and marital status. The mean age is 76 and nearly three-quarters (72 percent) are women. Two-fifths are married. They are quite different, however, in socioeconomic status and health. They are all white, and the median household income of $7,700 in 1976 was triple that of Horizon Heights. Nearly two-thirds (64 percent) rate their health as good.

The Ozark lakes country attracts mostly migrants; only 5 percent had moved from within the county. The characteristics of its retired residents are an exaggeration of the national migrant profile. Ozark retired migrants are relatively young, with a mean age of 68. Most of them (86 percent) are married, while only 56 percent of all interstate migrants over age 60 in 1970 were married. Virtually all (99 percent) are white. The median household income for all interstate migrants who gave retirement as their reason for moving was $11,899 in 1976,[24] a figure that is comparable to the general population of the three towns making up the Ozark area sample. Almost three-fourths of the Ozark residents rated their health as good. The inference that distance of move in retirement community recruitment is related to community resident profiles is clearly demonstrated with the example communities. But this raises broader issues, such as, How general is the pattern in which people with similar characteristics move to the same community? And if it is widespread, why does it happen? Answers to these questions depend on the reasons why people move in the first place.

The decision to move has been a theoretical puzzle since 1885, when Ravenstein set down his "laws of migration." He felt that some people moved for essentially negative reasons, attempting to escape heavy taxes, unattractive climate, or uncongenial social surroundings. These were among the factors he said "pushed" some people out of their original residence in search of another. But, Ravenstein continued, more people were attracted to new locations by the desire to better themselves. That is, the "pull" factors in the migration decision outweigh the "push" factors for most people.[25] Lee added to this formulation the idea that there are intervening obstacles that may prevent a move, even if the motivation is there.[26] Just wanting to move is no guarantee that the move will take place. It may be too costly, too risky, or the idea may not be congenial to other household members.

For voluntary moves, at least, it is probably safe to assume that people do not move when they are perfectly satisfied with their present location.[27] How unsatisfied they have to become before they reach a decision to move (and the particular factors contributing to a high level of dissatisfaction) are hotly disputed by migration theorists.[28] There is a growing consensus, however, that the decision process is multistaged.[29]

The only multistaged decision model developed for studying residential relocation of retirement-age people was recently proposed by Wiseman.[30] In this model, the decision process begins with a triggering mechanism. It may center on dissatisfaction with one's current location for a variety of reasons, or on the attractiveness of an alternative location. That is, the decision process may be triggered by "pushes", such as critical life events or unhappiness with the old neigborhood, or by "pulls" from friends and family members in other places, as well as perceived opportunities for a more pleasant life in a new location.

The second set of factors in Wiseman's model includes facilitating or inhibiting mechanisms. These may be divided into three categories: resources, past experience, and community ties. One's personal characterisitics and past relocation experience would influence the decision. If one has seldom moved as an adult, there may be considerable resistance to a retirement move.[31] If the decision is not to move, Wiseman predicts that this will be followed by adjustments that reduce dissatisfaction with the present situation, like repairing the house or reasoning that moving was a foolish idea in the first place.

If the decision is in favor of moving, a secondary decision follows — selecting the new location. Several locations may be considered before one is selected. The move itself contains two inseparable elements: distance and destination. Knowledge about potential destinations is the key to selection. Such knowledge is a necessary, but in itself insufficient, motivation for moving. Knowledge, of course, is influenced by the location of family members and friends and one's own earlier travel and migration experience.

Why People Move to Retirement Communities

Triggering Mechanisms

People in Horizon Heights, Carefree Village, and the Ozarks came to these communities for a variety reasons. It must be remembered that each community is different in both its attractions and its built-in inhibiting features. The selection from among potential migrants is based on these characteristics and increases the homogeneity of the resident population. Horizon Heights, for example, offers services and safety. Cost of residence is not prohibitive if one is poor, but the financial screening of applicants would discourage or prohibit the admission of a new resident who is too wealthy. Carefree Village advertises its life-care plan, emphasizing health care in particular. The cost of residence would be an obstacle to the poor applicant. The Ozark lakes country offers a beautiful natural setting, but does not have many of the specialized services of Carefree Village. The potential migrant who is in his or her 70s might consider this location too risky.

People in all of the communities were asked for the single most important reason for their move. Their answers were placed in the categories seen in Table 28.2. There is indeed a congruence between personal needs and community selection. The financial advantage of subsidized housing is not overlooked by Horizon Heights residents. Over half the Carefree Village residents listed health needs as the major reason for their selecting this life-care commuity. Finally, there is a congruence between the outstanding natural beauty of the Ozarks and the motivation for moving there.

People in the three communities were asked, "How did you come to be living here?" Their answers were taken down word for word and analyzed for evidence of what Wiseman called positive and negative triggering mechanisms in the relocation decision process. There were more "push" responses among Horizon Heights residents; "push" and "pull" responses were about even among Carefree Village residents, with the edge perhaps given to the "push" responses. Among the Ozark immigrants, the "pull" responses were overwhelming.

We have seen that the Ozarks attract people from farther away than the two types of planned communities; the people that move there are also younger, most are married, and they are in better physical and financial health than those who moved to the two planned communities. Their

Table 28.2: Most Important Reason for Relocating in the Retirement Community

Reasons	Horizon Heights	Carefree Village	Ozark Lakes Country
Financial	23	2	5
Health Needs	4	51	2
Physical Incapacity; Manageable Environment	4	2	1
Security	8	8	0
Services	14	19	13
To Leave Old Neighborhood	25	2	2
Role Loss	6	3	1
Social Needs	16	13	21
Natural Environment	0	1	54
Total Percent	100%	101%*	99%*

*Rounding error

reasons for moving are also positive. Planned communities, on the other hand, specialize in providing services and meeting special needs of older people. They make their advantages to residents known, and as a result they tend to attract people who, due to critical events in their lives or unhappy neighborhood situations, feel they must move. Old people who are poor are also more likely to find themselves in critical or unhappy life situations, and this is reflected in a higher "push" level in their explanation of the move to Horizon Heights.

Selective Recruitment

The process producing the individual-environment congruence we find in the example communities includes more actors than one. The individual makes the decision to move and selects the community. This view from the perspective of the individual is called "self-selection" in migration studies. However, the process also involves the recruitment effort by the community itself. From the perspective of the community, the process is seen as "selective recruitment." Selective recruitment as it affects the general population is indirect. Communities recruit labor-force participants by recruiting employers. The type of employer then determines the characteristics of the labor-force migrants who move to town. In the case of migration to retirement communities, however, selective recruitment is more direct. In Horizon Heights there is a waiting list. Not much open recruiting goes on by the Housing Authority, which manages the community. Rather, social service agencies, particularly those who have as clients people with low incomes, refer clients with pressing housing problems to Horizon Heights.

In Carefree Village there is a large sales force that aggressively recruits new residents, using skillful newspaper, radio, and television campaigns. Unlike Horizon Heights, the selectivity process filters into the community those who can afford the entrance fee and monthly maintenance payments. In the Ozarks, land developers acquire and use large mailing lists of people nearing retirement age. These mailings proclaim the pleasures of picturesque mountain life.

Thus retirement communities, with varying degrees of success, selectively search for new residents, just as persons self-selectively search for destinations that will meet their perceived needs. When asked who first talked with them about the retirement community they chose, over one-third of the Horizon Heights residents said that community social service providers told them about Horizon Heights. Almost one-third of Carefree Village residents said that community sales representatives first talked with them about the village. In the Ozarks, over one-fifth said that developers and realtors first approached them. Selective recruitment, then, cannot be ignored when considering the migration decision process of older people. In addition to people who are involved in official recruitment efforts, there are many informal recruiters in retirement communites, and their efforts also facilitate self-selection on the part of their friends or family members considering a move.

Network Recruitment

Once retired people begin moving into an area they like, they tell retired family members and friends about their new community. This leads to visits and sometimes to being joined by migrating friends. Knowing someone ahead of time is a major factor facilitating adjustment to the new environment.[32]

Residents of the three example communities were asked if they had known anyone living in the community before they had moved there themselves. In each community, about half the residents had known someone before they moved. Whether the residents had moved from the same county or from out of state, the proportion remained about half. How many people had they known? The average is five in Horizon Heights and seven each in Carefree Village and the Ozarks. Most residents chracterized these prior acquaintances as friends. Nearly all the Ozark and Carefree Village residents had visited their communities at least a couple of times before moving. Network recruitment, like selective recruitment, is a part of the filtering process of persons and locations resulting in a general similarity of migrant backgrounds within respective communities. Network recruitment, however, has the greater long-range impact on an area because it initiates and maintains migration streams from one location to another.

The Final Decision To Move

When the issue of retirement community moves is discussed, a speculation which nearly always arises is how many residents are "put there" by their children. Carefree Village, Horizon Heights, and Ozark lakes country residents were asked a battery of questions about who participated in the final decision. Of those who received help in making the decision, that help came mostly from spouses. Children tended to play a relatively minor role. Fewer than one-quarter of the residents, in most settings, turned to children for help with the relocation decision. It was surprising to learn that about half the people acknowledged help from no one. When others did participate in the decision, they primarily did so by giving advice. Practically no one felt coerced by others. Who actually made the final decision, then? A handful of women said their husbands decided. Otherwise, couples said they made the decision jointly, and the unmarried said they made the final decision alone. In Horizon Heights, some residents had been displaced by urban renewal projects and had relocated in public housing as a result. They admitted that the final decision was not entirely theirs. Are retirement community residents placed there by their children? A few probably are, but the number is almost negligible by comparison to the vast majority who make the final decision themselves or with their spouses. Most do not even involve their children in the decision at all.

Person-Environment Interaction: Support Systems

The process by which retirement communities recruit new members and retired people choose to migrate to new residential locations should result in compatability between the person and his or her new living environment.[33] The details of how living environments, including retirement communities, meet the needs of their inhabitants is not clearly understood. Before the process can be examined in the context of the example communities, it is necessary to define some terms and discuss some concepts.

Support Systems Theory

Lopata was the earliest sociologist to consistently and repeatedly apply the concept of support systems from the perspective of persons rather than organizations.[34] She defined a support system as "a set of interactions containing patterned giving and receiving of actions or objects which either or both the giver or receiver define as necessary or helpful in maintaining a style of life."[35] Lopata's early work on social roles and the considerable theoretical heritage from her father, Florien Znaniecki, is evident in the centrality of social interaction to her definition.

A support system may be visualized with a person and his or her needs at the center, with interaction links radiating from the person outward to the resources (persons and groups) that meet those needs. Resources often overlap. One resource may meet several needs or several resources may focus upon the same need. Thus, support may be diffuse or specific. When one resource provides support in several areas, it may be described as diffuse. Diffuse support can be expected when obligations are felt toward the person, regardless of particular needs. Spouses and primary relatives are often diffuse resources in support systems. These resources are sometimes referred to as informal[36] or natural,[37] as opposed to organizational resources such as social service agencies. Specific resources offer support in a narrow range of specialized needs such as income maintenance, health care, or services such as transportation or housekeeping. The support systems of most residents may differ in shape from one retirement community to another since the range of resources available within the different communities and the ease of access to them may vary.

Support systems have a dynamic character. Persons build their support systems over time, adding and deleting resources as needs change. There is also a time dimension in the frequency, volume, and importance of the support flowing from particular resources to the supported person. Some resources dispense support regularly and others sporadically.

Family members are vital in the support systems of most people. This is due not only to the diffuseness of their support, but to the fact that they often serve as scouts for additional specialized (often organizational) resources. When family members are absent or reduced in number, as in the case of the orphaned, the widowed, or the never married, resource deficits exist that may or may not be compensated for by other people in the individual's support system.

Are not support and independence mutually exclusive? Perhaps not. At this point Lopata's definition of support system as giving and receiving of actions or objects becomes relevant. Independence is an illusion created by reciprocally balanced support linkages. When receiving and giving of support are balanced by prevailing exchange standards, feelings of dependency are neutralized.[38] When support flows in one direction only, however, a dependency relationship exists. Such an unbalanced condition, if mutually defined as such, produces feelings of dependency in the receiver and may produce feelings of imposition, unfairness, and exploitation in the giver. Self-sufficiency, in this context, does not mean the absence of support, but the ability to reciprocate support in some meaningful way. The standards that define a fair exchange may be built into the system or negotiated. In either case, exchanges of support are built on social contracts between parties.

The need for support increases with age. Health declines, necessitating increased health support—but more importantly, affecting social interaction, especially when speech and hearing impairment are present. Social contact becomes more difficult to maintain and even personal services become more problematical. The increasing need for support may upset the balance in the reciprocal relationship between the person and the source of support and cause feelings of independence and autonomy to shift to feelings of dependency. A number of strategies may help redefine the support linkages so they may be perceived as balanced, thereby saving self-respect.

What do the support systems of retirement community residents look like? How many resources live or work in the same retirement community? What do they do for the residents? Do residents in planned communities have more resource deficits than people in the Ozarks? Comparisons of the three retirement communities will help answer these questions.

Retirement Communities and Support Systems

Residents of Horizon Heights, Carefree Village, and the Ozark lakes country were asked to list every person who meant a great deal to them, everyone currently important in their lives. When each resident had completed his or her list and checked it over to make sure no one had been left out, these resources, and the types of support they gave, were discussed. Resources not appearing on the primary list were sometimes mentioned during the discussion. These were added as secondary resources.

When the support systems are compared, it becomes clear that people in both planned and unplanned communities are similar in one important way. The average number of resources in the support systems of Ozark inmigrants (between eight and ten) is not very different from that of the people in the planned communities. The reason for this similarity is found in the balance between primary resources and secondary resources. Ozark inmigrants, on the whole, have more primary resources than do Carefree Village residents. Horizon Heights residents have the fewest. People living in the planned communities, however, have the greatest average number of secondary resources, although there are more in Carefree Village than in Horizon Heights. Furthermore, the average number of resources who live or work in the community with the respondents is highest in Carefree Village and lowest in the Ozark lakes country, although the number of resources living outside is similar for residents of all three living environments.

Instrumental support involves particular kinds of help (such as housekeeping, transportation, or shopping) on a more or less regular basis for the retirement community resident. In all three communities, about half of the primary resources in the support systems of the residents provide no instrumental support. Most of them probably live too far away to help on a regular basis. Some secondary resources provide no instrumental support either, but not nearly as many. As a consequence, the average number of resources providing instrumental support for residents of Horizon Heights and Carefree Village is larger than that for Ozark residents.

One of the serious threats to the support systems of older people is the loss of primary resources. Parents, uncles, and aunts die, then older siblings and one's spouse, then friends and more distant relatives, and finally, perhaps even younger siblings and older children. This results in increased resource deficits at the very time when increasing support is needed. The family is a fertile recruiting ground for primary resources. If a person starts with fewer family members, as does one with no siblings or one who never married or married but had no children, the loss of additional primary resources can be painful, reducing options and increasing demands, which may strain remaining resources. As this happens, there is likely to be a search for new resources, especially those that can provide balance linkages and stave off dependency.

Support Systems and Self-Selection to Retirement Communities

It is at this point that support systems theory intersects with migration decision theory. Resource deficits, in the face of rising support needs, can be a powerful triggering mechanism in the decision to move. Both subsidized and nonsubsidized planned communities are service-enriched living environments, designed in accordance with the particular needs of older people. It should not be surprising, therefore, that more of the people who move to these environments are local rather than long-distance movers, feel "pushed" rather than "pulled," and emphasize in their reasons for moving those very areas of support that are the strengths of the planned community. Nor should it be surprising that the retirement-age people who are attracted to planned communities tend to have characteristics that imply greater need and vulnerability. Such people, on the whole, are older, more often widowed, and less healthy than the retired people who move to unplanned, de facto retirement communities like the Ozark lakes country. For those who move to subsidized retirement communities such as Horizon Heights, one can add that they are also much poorer. The fit between living environment and individual needs would seem, then, to be reasonably good in retirement communities. People with a greater need for instrumental support tend to be attracted to communities built to meet that need, and support indeed seems to flow from within the community to the people who move there.

Relative Benefits of Planned Retirement Community Residence

The foregoing section would seem to imply that residents of planned retirement communities are better off than they would be in other environments. But we cannot be certain that this is the case. For one thing, almost all voluntary movers, including those to retirement communities, feel better off in their new surroundings than at their former address. For another, while developers and managers of retirement communities claim a special benefit, one could hardly expect them to say otherwise. Finally, retirement communities are specialized and do not attract a cross-section of the general population of older people, as we have seen.

The study of midwestern retirement communities that provided the example communities for this chapter compared retirement community residents with subgroups of a national sample of older people.[39] These subgroups had characteristics similar to those of the retirement community residents; each of the subgroups was matched to one of the retirement community samples. In this way, the study controlled for the effect of self-selection into the retirement communities.[40] The results of this study provide a basis for assessing the relative benefits of moving to different retirement communities.

The Nonsubsidized Planned Community

Carefree Village provides a living environment with measurable benefits to residents in the areas of medical care, freedom from fear of crime, and social supportiveness. When asked whether they had a problem getting enough medical care, nearly nine-tenths of Carefree Village residents answered that they did not. Their counterparts in the general population were somewhat more likely to say that sufficient medical care was a problem for them. One would expect people attracted to life-care communities to feel this way. Access to health care, after all, is the community's major attraction.

As compared with their counterparts in the general population, Carefree Village residents benefit even more from a second environmental feature. Uniformed security guards are very visible on the grounds, and the suburban location places the village in a low crime area. These factors contribute to the substantial difference between residents and their counterparts in their perception of crime as a personal problem. Nine-tenths of the residents said that it was not. Only half of their counterparts from the national sample made that claim.

When their social support problems were compared, Carefree Village residents, again, were clearly better off. They were less likely than their counterparts to say they were troubled with loneliness, lack of friends, feeling unneeded, or being bored. While it is clear from these comparisons that residents of the nonsubsidized planned community are better off, as a whole, than their counterparts in the general population, it must be recalled that residents pay for these advantages. It is not inexpensive to live in Carefree Village.

The Subsidized Planned Community

Beneficial living environments, happily, are not reserved for the affluent only. Even though medical care is much less extensive in Horizon Heights than in Carefree Village, over four-fifths of Horizon Heights residents said getting sufficient medical care was not a problem for them. Their counterparts in the general population were more troubled by insufficient medical care.

As in Carefree Village, a greater difference between community residents and their counterparts was seen in response to the question, "Is fear of crime a very serious problem for you personally?" Over three-fourths of the people in Horizon Heights said that it was not a problem. Only two-fifths of their counterparts said the same. Many residents had moved from high crime areas into Horizon Heights, whose security guards and exclusively elderly occupants made them feel safe. Social support seems less problematic in Horizon Heights as well. While one-quarter of the residents said that loneliness was a problem for them, it was a problem for over half of their counterparts. Community residents were also more likely than their counterparts to feel that they had enough friends and enough to do to keep busy. Perhaps more basic, less than one-tenth felt that poor housing was a problem for them personally. Over one-quarter of their counterparts did. Public housing for the elderly is clearly beneficial to the people it attracts when compared to other people with the same background characteristics.

The only study that has been made of the same people both before and after they entered planned living environments was conducted by Carp.[41] She compared nonmovers with movers to subsidized public housing communities, and not only measured the initial adjustment to the move after a year, but conducted a final interview with the movers after 8 years.[42] Her findings of positive benefits reinforce those reported for Horizon Heights. Carp reported that satisfaction with housing and living environment increased after the move and was higher for retirement community residents even after 8 years. She concludes that "the factors which predict short-term adjustment in elderly-designed public housing tend to predict long-range adjustment, implying that the new environment will benefit the same people in the long run as in the short run."[43]

At this point, the question of relative benefit seems adequately answered for planned communities, at least those with well-developed service packages. It remains to be assessed for unplanned, de facto communities like the Ozark settlements, and for planned communities that offer very low levels of services, such as hotels catering to single room occupants and some Florida condominiums. One would expect that residents of such unplanned, or at least unserviced, communities would become increasingly burdened with health and service needs over time. The absence of built-in services makes them problematic environments for the very old. A secondary move away from such communities, triggered by such "push" factors as inadequate supports of many kinds, is predictable. There is already some evidence to support this prediction.[44] The counterflows of people age 60 and over from Florida to New York and Ohio in the 1970 census were heavily laden with widows, the poor, and the very old. Many were returning to their state of birth, and significant numbers relocated in the households of children and siblings.

Positive Outcomes of Age Homogeneity

Retirement community research has been dominated by two theoretical issues during the past generation. One concerns the social outcome of age homogeneity in community settings; the other centers on the relationship between the aging individual and his or her living environment. Sociologists have been more interested in the former and environmental psychologists in the latter.

Rose suggested that there was developing in America a subculture of the aging.[45] Where the growth of this subculture has proceeded furthest, Rose saw the emergence of "aging group consciousness," the replacement of negative stereotypes of aging by group pride. Thus, participation in the aged subculture should mean for the older person an increase in interaction with other elders, changes in values and attitudes (particularly an increase in activism and aggressiveness), and increased morale or feelings of self-worth. As Rose saw it, not all people participate in the aged subculture, nor is its normative content clearly defined. Yet he expected an aged subculture to emerge when the following conditions intersect: (1) "The members of the group have a positive affinity for each other on some basis (e.g., gains to be had from each other, long-standing friendships, common background and interests, common problems and concerns). . . ." (2)"The members are excluded from interaction with other groups in the population to some significant extent."[46]

Irving Rosow, a decade later, argued that being old is a status-losing proposition.[47] One should not be surprised, therefore, that people in their later years do not embrace that identity easily, and that socialization to old age is an ambiguous experience since it has few clearly defined roles. The rewards, increased status and positive models associated with earlier socialization, are mostly absent. Rosow argues that the situation can be different, however. "The critical factor . . . is the insulation of the elderly from other age groups and their increased association with age peers. This represents two essential conditions: (1) the reduction of content and weakening of ties with younger people and (2) the concentration of socially similar older persons within a local setting, preferably residential."[48]

Both Rose and Rosow expect enhanced morale to result from the development of a positive age-based identity for the elderly (though Rose talks in terms of the aged subculture, and Rosow in terms of socialization to clearly defined roles). Both authors look to social similarity and age segregation as essential preconditions for developing a positive age-based identity.

While the issue is still debated, our research has suggested that the subculture hypothesis is probably correct if modified. Again residents of several types of retirement communities were compared with samples of the general older population that had been matched to the retirement community samples on background characteristics. Residents were less likely to feel useful as community members and to have no higher rates of social participation than did their matched counterparts. Yet they had significantly fewer problems of loneliness and social isolation and more positive self-regard, and they exhibited evidence of gerontophilia (a pride in and desire to associate with their age group).[49] The picture of retirement community residents that emerges in our example communities is not one of activism or aggressiveness, as Rose predicted. The residents seem to represent a retreatist rather than an activist style. The type of retreatism, however, is different for those who were attracted to the service-enriched living environments of public housing and life-care communities than it is for those attracted to the small resort towns in the Ozarks.

Understanding the major motivations for relocation, along with the differences in background characteristics of the residents, helps us to see the retreatist dynamics involved. Retirees moving to the Ozark settings tend to be younger, richer couples who are retreating on an extended vacation. They have earned it and are enjoying themselves. They don't feel an especially strong need to be socially active or useful community members, yet their morale is high. Theirs is what Parsons called a "consumatory" phase of life.[50]

Those who seek out age-segregated settings, however, tend to be older, more often widowed, and, in public housing, poorer. They are seeking shelter from the gathering storm of late-life troubles, seeking a more manageable environment, more tailored and accessible services, and the warm companionship of those like themselves. Subcultural indicators are higher in these environments. But it is also a retreat, a haven.

And it appears that residents of all the communities find what they are looking for. Their levels of social activity may not be especially high, but expectations may not be either, and the social contacts they do have are more likely to be confined to other elders or younger people whose business it is to serve them. In this context, a type of gerontophilia does develop, though not so combative as Rose had expected. Respondents saw older people in general as getting enough respect from younger people; they also perceived them as being useful members of their communities. The implication is clear: older people are seen as deserving the respect they get. It probably also means that residents of these communities feel no lack of respect themselves. Thus an aged subculture in retirement community settings develops in nonpunitive environments where there is less pressure to perform but where retirement-age people can still feel good about themselves.

Summary

A retirement community is any living environment to which most residents have moved since they retired. Planned communities may be subsidized, like public housing sites for the elderly, or nonsubsidized, like the growing variety of private communities. The range of supportive services built into these living environments varies greatly. In addition to planned communities, there are de facto retirement communities resulting from concentrated migration into popular retirement settings.

Subsidized planned communities tend to attract from the local area residents who are seeking to escape from a negative environmental situation, many being dependent and vulnerable. Planned nonsubsidized communities filter out the poor. Their residents are more apt than public housing residents to give positive reasons for their relocation choice. But like the subsidized communities, they tend to attract the widowed and the very old. De facto retirement communities, which do not offer especially rich service environments, attract younger and wealthier retirees from greater distances. This "fit" between individual needs and living environments results from three interrelated migration processes: self-selection, selective recruitment, and network recruitment. Apparently very few retirement community residents move there involuntarily. Support systems theory helps to explain the particular appeal of planned retirement communities, whose service-enriched environments provide support for residents caught in a bind between declining resources and rising support needs.

Are people in planned communities really better off for having moved there? A definitive answer to this deceptively simple question is methodologically difficult. The best recent studies, however, suggest that residents of service-enriched living environments benefit measurably from them.

Notes

1. R. L. Warren, "Toward a Non-utopian Normative Model of the Community," *American Sociological Review* 35 (1970), pp. 219–228, and F. M. Carp, "Living Environments of Older People," in *Handbook of Aging and the Social Sciences*, edited by R. H. Binstock and E. Shanas (New York: Van Nostrand Reinhold Company, 1976).

2. R. L. Warren, *The Community in America*, 2d ed. (Chicago: Rand McNally, 1972).

3. I. Webber and C. C. Osterbind, "Types of Retirement Villages," in *Retirement Villages*, edited by E. W. Burgess (Ann Arbor: University of Michigan Press, 1961).

4. L. H. Long and K. A. Hansen, "Reasons for Interstate Migration," *Current Population Reports*, P-23 81, U.S. Bureau of the Census (1979), pp. 1–32. The question about employment in the Annual Housing Surveys in 1974 and in 1976 referred to the week immediately preceding each survey.

5. F. M. Carp, op. cit.

6. See F. M. Carp, *A Future for the Aged* (Austin: University of Texas Press, 1966); M. P. Lawton, L. Nahemow, and J. Teaff, "Environmental Characteristics and the Wellbeing of Elderly Tenants in Federally-Assisted Housing," *Journal of Gerontology* 30 (1975), pp. 601–607; M. P. Lawton and J. Cohen, "The Generality of Housing Impact on the Wellbeing of Older People," *Journal of Gerontology* 29 (1975), pp. 194–204.

7. S. M. Golant, "Locational-Environmental Perspectives on Old-Age-Segregated Residential Areas in the United States," in *Geography and the Urban Environment*, Vol. 3, edited by R. J. Johnson and D. T. Herbert (London: John Wiley & Sons, 1980).

8. F. M. Carp, "Living Environments of Older People," pp. 245–246.

9. See W. Donahue, "Impact of Living Arrangements on Ego Development in the Elderly," and F. M. Carp, "Effects of Impoverished Housing on the Lives of Older People," both in *Patterns of Living and Housing of Middle-Aged and Older People*, edited by F. M. Carp (Washington, D.C.: GPO, 1966); A. Lipman, "Public Housing and Attitudinal Adjustment in Old Age," *Journal of Geriatric Psychiatry* 2 (1968), pp. 88–101; and M. P. Lawton and J. Cohen, "The Generality of Housing Impact on the Well-being of Older People," *Journal of Gerontology* 29 (1975), pp. 194–204.

10. See M. B. Hamovitch, "Social and Psychological Factors in Adjustment in a Retirement Community," in *The Retirement Process*, edited by F. M. Carp (Washington, D.C.: GPO, 1968), and G. L. Bultena and V. Wood, "The American Retirement Community: Bane or Blessing?" *Journal of Gerontology* 24 (1969), pp. 209–217.

11. Drs. Warren A. Peterson and Charles F. Longino, Jr., the project's principal and coprincipal investigators, are both sociologists and social gerontologists. Sociologists David B. Oliver, Jill S. Quadagno, David R. Dickens, Michael G. Lacy, and Linda Phelps worked on various phases of the project. Psychologist Thomas Blank and economist Mark Evans contributed their expertise. Anthropologist Robert C. Smith, with the assistance of Ruth G. Kuhar, conducted the ethnographic community studies.

12. S. M. Golant, "Spatial Context of Residential Moves by Elderly Persons," *International Journal of Aging and Human Development* 8 (1977), pp. 279–289.

13. R. F. Wiseman and C. C. Roseman, "A Typology of Elderly Migration Based on the Decision-Making Process," *Economic Geography* (1979), pp. 324–337.

14. For a concise summary of this and other studies of migration of the aged, see G. K. Bowles, "Aged Migration: Research Summary," *Research on Aging* 2 (1980), in press.

15. R. F. Wiseman, "National Patterns of Elderly Concentration and Migration," in *The Locational and Environmental Context of the Elderly Population*, edited by S. M. Golant (New York: Halsted Press, 1979).

16. C. B. Flynn, "General vs. Aged Interstate Migration 1965–70," *Research on Aging* 2 (1980), in press.

17. J. C. Biggar, "The Sunning of America: Migration to the Sunbelt," *Population Bulletin* 32 (1979), pp. 1–43, and "Reassessing Sunbelt Migration," *Research on Aging* 2 (1980), in press.

18. J. C. Biggar and C. F. Longino, Jr., "Reassessing Sunbelt Migration: New Evidence" (paper presented at the Thirty-Second Annual Scientific Meeting of the Gerontological Society, November 1979).

19. C. F. Longino, Jr., "Intrastate Migration of the Elderly," in C. B. Flynn, J. C. Biggar, C. F. Longino, Jr., and R. F. Wiseman, *Aged Migration in the United States, 1965–70: Final Report* (Washington, D.C.: National Institute on Aging, 1979), Appendix D.

20. C. F. Longino, Jr., "Residential Relocation of Older People: Metropolitan and Nonmetropolitan, 1965–70," *Research on Aging* 2 (1980), in press.

21. F. M. Carp, "Living Environments of Older People," p. 248.

22. J. C. Biggar, "Who Moved Among the Elderly, 1965 to 1970: A Comparison of Types of Older Movers," *Research on Aging* 2 (1980), in press.

23. L. H. Long and K. A. Hansen, op cit. Long and Hansen analyzed the 1974 to

1976 Annual Housing Survey data that were collected by the Census Bureau for HUD. They were surprised that the household income of retired interstate migrants was so high.

24. Ibid., p. 20.

25. E. G. Ravenstein, "The Laws of Migration," *Journal of the Royal Statistical Society* 48 (1885), pp. 165–227.

26. E. S. Lee, "A Theory of Migration," *Demography* 3 (1966), pp. 47–57.

27. H. A. Simon, *Models of Man* (New York: John Wiley & Sons, 1957).

28. P. A. Morrison, "Chronic Movers and the Future Redistribution of Population: A Longitudinal Analysis," *Rand*, P-4440 (1970); and J. Wolpert, "Behavioral Aspects of the Decision to Migrate," *Papers: Regional Science Association* 15 (1965), pp. 159–169, and "Migration as an Adjustment to Environmental Stress," *Journal of Social Issues* 22 (1966), pp. 92–102.

29. P. H. Rossi, *Why Families Move* (Glencoe, Ill.: The Free Press, 1955); P. A. Morrison, "Unresolved Questions About Population Distribution Policy: An Agenda for Further Research," *Rand*, P-4630 (1971); and L. A. Brown and E. G. Moore, "The Intra-Urban Migration Process: A Perspective," *Geografiska Annaler* 15 (1970), pp. 368–381.

30. R. F. Wiseman, "Elderly Migration," *Spatial Aspects of Aging*, Resource Paper 78-4 (Washington, D.C.: Association of American Geographers, 1979), and "Why Do Old People Move: Theoretical Issues," *Research on Aging* 2 (1980), in press.

31. R. McGinnia, "A Stochastic Model of Social Mobility," *American Sociological Review* 33 (1968), pp. 712–722, and P. A. Morrison, "Duration of Residence and Prospective Migration: The Evaluation of a Stochastic Model," *Demography* 4 (1967), pp. 553–561.

32. E. Kahana and B. Kahana, "Support Networks of Long Distance Movers: the Cultural and Geographical Transition" (paper presented at the Thirty-Second Annual Scientific Meeting of the Gerontological Society, November 1979).

33. F. M. Carp, "Person-Situation Congruence in Engagement," *Gerontologist* 8 (1968), pp. 184–188.

34. H. Z. Lopata, *Widowhood in an American City* (Cambridge, Mass.: Schenkman, 1973), "Support Systems of Elderly Urbanites: Chicago of the 1970s," *Gerontologist* 15 (1975), pp. 35–41, and *Women as Widows: Support Systems* (New York: Elsevier North Holland, 1978).

35. This definition is taken from a 1975 unpublished report of Lopata's urban widows projects.

36. See E. Litwak, "Family and Primary Group Options" (paper presented at the Twenty-Ninth Annual Scientific Meeting of the Gerontological Society, November 1976), and J. O'Brien, "Joint Symposium: A Spectrum of Community Support Options for the Elderly" (paper presented at the Twenty-Ninth Annual Scientific Meeting of the Gerontological Society, November 1976).

37. A. H. Zimmer, S. Gross-Andrew, and D. Frankfather, "Incentives to Families Caring for Disabled Elderly: Research and Demonstration Project to Strengthen the Natural Supports System" (paper presented at the Thirtieth Annual Scientific Meeting of the Gerontological Society, November 1977).

38. J. J. Dowd, "Aging as Exchange: A Preface to Theory," *Journal of Gerontology* 30 (1975), pp. 584–594.

39. When the Social Security Administration funded our Comparative Study of Midwestern Retirement Communities in 1975, its focal interest was a comparative evaluation of retirement community costs and benefits. We needed to norm the study's noneconomic data on a recent national survey, and the survey conducted by Louis Harris and Associates in 1974 for the National Council on Aging was chosen. Many of its questions were replicated in our interview schedule.

40. Standardization procedures evolved (after other methods were tried) into a system of shadow sampling. Shadow samples were drawn from the Harris survey sample in the following manner: (1) A matrix of five or six background variables was created for each community. Each cell in the community matrix represented one particular combination of the background variables of age, gender, marital status, education, and income. Race was also used in the public housing samples where there was racial diversity. (2) Cases in the national sample that conformed to the combination of characteristics in each cell were selected randomly and in the same proportion as in the retirement community sample. The result of this matching technique is that for every widowed black woman over age 75 with an elementary school education living on less than $2,000 a year in Horizon Heights, a person with the same profile of characteristics was drawn from the general population sample and placed in the Horizon Heights shadow sample. The process was repeated for every other combination of the background variables. Shadow samples were drawn to be as large as possible consistent with preserving the correct proportions of respondents with the specified background characteristics. In this way, our study deals with the problem of the unrepresentativeness of retirement community populations and attempts to control for the effect of selective recruitment—at least as far as it relates to background variables.

41. F. M. Carp, A Future for the Aged (Austin: University of Texas Press, 1966), and "Effects of Impoverished Housing."

42. F. M. Carp, "Short-term and Long-term Prediction of Adjustment to a New Environment," Journal of Gerontology 29 (1974), pp. 444–453.

43. F. M. Carp, "Living Environments of Older People," p. 248.

44. C. F. Longino, Jr., "Going Home: Aged Return Migration in the United States, 1965–70," Journal of Gerontology 34 (1979), pp. 736–745.

45. A. M. Rose, "The Subculture of the Aging: A Topic of Sociological Research," Gerontologist 2 (1962), pp. 123–127, and "The Subculture of the Aging: A Framework for Research in Social Gerontology," in Older People and Their Social World: The Subculture of the Aging, edited by A. M. Rose and W. A. Peterson (Philadelphia: F. A. Davis Company, 1965).

46. A. M. Rose, "The Subculture of the Aging," p. 3.

47. I. Rosow, Socialization to Old Age (Berkeley: University of California Press, 1974).

48. Ibid., pp. 154, 156.

49. K. A. McClelland, C. F. Longino, Jr., and W. A. Peterson, "The Aged Subculture Hypothesis: Social Integration, Gerontophilia and Self-Regard" (paper presented at the Thirty-Second Annual Scientific Meeting of the Gerontological Society, November 1979).

50. T. Parsons, "Old Age as a Consumatory Phase of Life," Gerontologist 3 (1963), pp. 53–54.

29

Microenvironments of the Elderly

David E. Campbell

A comedian once told the story about a wife who was entertaining her lover in her bedroom when, unexpectedly, the husband came home early. Quickly, her lover hid in the closet as the husband approached the room. The husband, suspicious, searched the bedroom and finally opened the closet door, exposing the unclad lover. Furiously the husband demanded, "What are you doing here?" The trembling lover thought a moment and finally said, "Well, everyone's got to be somewhere!"

Indeed, the lover was quite right. We all have to be somewhere. And where we are can have profound effects on our activities. Behavioral scientists have only recently begun to pay close attention to this commonsense notion. On the pages that follow, we will examine what is currently known about how the environment is related to human activities. The discussion will be largely confined to environmental influences on the lives of older people. But first, the general context of environmental psychology as applied to the aged will be described.

Psychologists are engaged in the scientific study of human behavior and experience. They typically focus their research on the ways in which our behavior can be explained by our past learning, physiological processes, personality predispositions, mental capacities, and physical abilities. When features of the environment are acknowledged as causes of behavior, the explanatory effort generally is limited to the social environment (peer influence, social reinforcement, group processes, and so on) or to the typically contrived stimuli associated with the study of perception (e.g., momentary light displays). Characteristics of the physical environment per se have generally been neglected in the research enterprise. In the early 1960s, this led to a problem for psychologists. At that time, environmental designers realized that their architectural plans were guided mainly by considerations of aesthetics and engineering principles. What was missing from their plans was specific knowledge of human needs. Despite the early advice of Frank Lloyd Wright that form must follow function, the human element had unfortunately been left out of architectural planning. In fact, photographs of new designs submitted in competition for awards rarely even included human occupants. The result of this misplaced attention was buildings that did not work well in terms of their occupants' needs. Many buildings were simply not used as the designers had intended. Outdoor sitting spaces went unused; narrow lobbies became gathering places for socializing; areas intended for storage lay empty — all for reasons that were unclear.

The architects decided that they needed to know more about the people for whom they were designing so they could better accommodate user needs and preferences in their plans. They approached psychologists and sociologists and asked for design guidelines. This seemed a reasonable request. However, behavioral scientists had not been attending to influences of the physical environment on people. They knew essentially nothing about the influence of the built environment on occupants. At best, they had a set of research methods that could be brought to bear upon the problem. As a result of that contact with designers in the early 1960s, a small group of social psychologists and sociologists left their current academic areas and began to collaborate with designers in environmental design research. In time, this new area of research attracted behavioral scientists from related disciplines such as geography and anthropology.

Most environmental design research has dealt with people in institutional settings (students, workers, prisoners, hospital patients), while some has involved housing needs of residents and some has dealt with two extreme age groups, children and the aged.[1] Studies dealing with the very young and the very old can be particularly informative because these two groups may be relatively restricted in the degree to which they can control or change their environments. Hence, the impact of the environment should be relatively greater upon them. Existing environment-behavior relationships should be most clear and identifiable for those who have relatively high susceptibility to environmental influences. It should be clear from this argument that the aged are a particularly suitable group for environmental psychologists to study. While the number of environmental studies of the aged is not large (as the remainder of this chapter will show), sufficient work has been completed to allow some preliminary statements regarding optimal environments for the elderly. Further, several theoretical models have been advanced that serve to organize existing data and guide future research efforts. An ecological theory of environmental competence and cognitive control will be described in the final sections of this chapter. But first, we will concern ourselves with the experimental efforts to measure the influences of the environment on older persons.

Experimental Manipulation of the Environment

It is a fundamental belief among scientists that if you want to understand how two phenomena are related, you must change one (under carefully controlled circumstances) and see if the other changes as a consequence. For example, if you believe that the degree of life satisfaction for a group of older persons is influenced by the amount of privacy available to them, then you first measure their life satisfaction, perhaps by means of standardized interview questions. You then provide more (or less) privacy and, after a suitable time, you again assess satisfaction to see if it has increased (or decreased). Of course, it is important to ensure that the amount of privacy is the only thing that changes during the experimental period. We know that in the real world this is rarely the case. At the very least, your sample of elderly persons is getting older during the experimental period. For this reason, an additional group of similar persons is also studied for comparison purposes. This "control group" is given the same life satisfaction interview but does not experience any change in privacy level. Your research analysis would take the form of determining whether the changes in satisfaction level were greater for the experimental group (which experienced the manipulation of privacy) than for the control group. Such experimental studies of environments for older persons are rare, but some have been attempted.

Robert Sommer, a psychologist, was asked by a physician at a state psychiatric hospital in Canada to visit the female geriatrics ward and observe the patients' behavior.[2] The center of ward social life for these patients was the day room. Yet they generally sat around in this room staring into space or taking brief naps, and only rarely engaging in mutual conversation. Recently the ward had been redecorated with new curtains, a new tile floor, a television set, brightly colored chairs, and window air conditioners. Despite the improved environment, the patients appeared to experience no more zest for life than before. (Ironically, the ward had won an improvement award based on before-and-after photographs.) Sommer sat in the day room and observed. He saw up to 50 women in the room but rarely more than one or two brief conversations at a time. He also noticed the chair arrangement. The chairs paralleling walls were placed in back-to-back rows in the center of the room and around floor-to-ceiling columns facing outward. Such an arrangement is often called "sociofugal" because it repels conversation between seated persons. Sommer suggested that conversation among patients might be increased by rearranging the furniture into a "sociopetal" arrangement, with small numbers of chairs arranged in conversational groupings. He suggested the removal of three old couches and the addition of several tables around which the chairs could be placed.

This rearrangement was made in the context of an experiment. Prior to the changes, baseline observations were made of the frequency of conversational interactions in the day room. After two weeks, the furniture was rearranged. Two more weeks were allowed for the patients to get accustomed to their new surroundings (during which time several of them strenuously objected to the change in the established order of the ward). Finally, another set of observations was made to record the frequency of conversation. The results appear in Table 29.1. As the before-and-after comparisons show, both the brief and the more sustained conversations increased markedly. Unfortunately for the experiment, furniture rearrangement was not the only change that occurred. The physician was impressed with the new arrangement and sent in the occupational therapist to set up a crafts program at the tables. Therefore, the change to a more sociopetal arrangement was confounded with a change in attention from the therapist. Nevertheless, the findings from this experiment are important since they raise the possibility that the women originally conversed at a low rate not because of internal (psychological) factors, but because of characteristics of their physical milieu.

Sommer tried to examine only one feature of the environment—furniture arrangement. This is in keeping with the reductionistic philosophy of science that one can best understand systems by studying their most elementary parts. Other researchers feel that the progress of science will advance faster if we deal with whole environmental systems, comparing intact environmental "packages" that may differ in many ways. An example is provided by the work of Lawton, Liebowitz, and Charon.[3] They wished to find out whether the remodeling of a section of a drab geriatrics ward to make it appear more livable would result in improved patient behavior. The rooms chosen for remodeling had an institutional appearance; the bedspreads, window shades, and gray walls all lacked pattern and design. Originally, the two

Table 29.1: Frequency of Verbal Interaction before and after Furniture Rearrangement in Female Geriatrics Ward

	Brief Interactions	Sustained Interactions
Before	47	36
After	73	61

rooms housed nine patients. These rooms were divided into six small individual rooms (for privacy), each opening onto a small common social space containing a table and chairs (for social interaction). The researchers attempted to enhance the patients' personal identity by the addition of a mirror, dresser, and shelf space for each person's personal belongings. Visual enrichment was provided through bright and contrasting colors in drapes, walls, and the floor. The patients' visual experience also was enriched by textures, lighting, and by adding a planter, pictures, and a bird in a cage.

The original intention was to move the nine patients into other rooms during the remodeling and then move six of them back. Unfortunately, the remodeling took eight months to complete. During this period, six of the patients died, one became ill, and one became "behaviorally unsuited" for the new area—so only one of the original patients could be moved back. The solution to this dilemma was to match the former patients with new ones who were similar in health and general competence. The data from this study consisted of before-and-after observations of patient behavior. Unlike the Sommer study, however, a wide variety of data was involved, including number of staff in the area, staff-patient interactions, patient-patient interactions, self-maintenance, active interests such as reading or watching an activity, and excursions out of the experimental area.

Examination of the results proved rather discouraging to the researchers. After the remodeling, incidents of patient-patient interaction decreased, even though a specific area had been provided to encourage an increase in such interaction. Similarly, patient-staff interaction decreased. Apparently this was because the patients were now observable by staff from the corridor; only a half-wall separated the new patient area from the corridor. Before, the staff members actually had to poke their heads in the doorway to monitor their patients. The data on excursions showed that patients exhibited increased mobility following the remodeling. This was coincident with more social contact with patients outside the new area. This need not be attributed to the remodeling, however, since the new patients may have been merely going back to see old friends. Self-maintenance actually decreased despite the provision of private rooms. Incidents of active interest doubled, but this appeared to be due to the fact that the recreation therapist chose to spend more time in the ward after remodeling.

As the Sommer and Lawton studies show, experimental modifications of the environment are difficult to conduct. Yet they are the most powerful research techniques available for identifying causal relationships between environmental surroundings and the behavior of older people. Only rarely does a researcher have the opportunity to actually create a change in living environments of the elderly and then assess the impact of the modification. However, "natural experiments" occur whenever new facilities are created for the elderly, such as nursing homes, congregate housing, and senior citizens' community centers. Much could be learned by careful evaluation of each of these natural experiments. The growing literature on evaluation research[4] indicates that researchers will exploit such opportunities with greater frequency in the future. Meanwhile, our assessments of environment-behavior relationships involving the elderly will have to rely on inferences from nonmanipulational studies. These are dealt with in the next section.

Nonmanipulational Research Involving the Elderly

A fair number of studies dealing with environments of older people are based on nonexperimental data collected by the researchers. While observations may be made or interviews conducted, the researcher does not actually create or modify the environmental conditions. Such research is often termed *correlational* because the analysis involves correlations between aspects of the environment and characteristics of the inhabitants. For example, if you were studying the relationship between crowding and social behavior, you would measure both degree of crowding and amount of social behavior for a variety of people, covering a wide range on both variables. You would then determine, perhaps by calculating a correlation coefficient, the degree to which the two variables are related. One hypothesis might be that the two variables are positively correlated, meaning that individuals living in crowded conditions would engage in much social behavior and those in uncrowded conditions would engage in little social behavior. The studies that follow in this section generally involve this form of analysis, even though the variables may not be thoroughly defined and correlation coefficients may not be reported here.

The first study concerns the public behavior of older people in congregate housing.[5] The general tack taken in this research was to watch the elderly in order to learn their needs. In this case, Lawton and his coworkers systematically observed the activities of older persons in twelve different high-rise apartment complexes designed specifically for elderly residents. Each housing site was studied by a trained observer who made complete tours through all indoor and outdoor common spaces. During each tour, a record was made of the number of people seen, their locations, and their activities. The results of the observations showed that use of common spaces depended on the availability of off-site resources. For example, use of common spaces was low for housing located near a boardwalk or a downtown mall. Available data on resident health showed that common space occupancy and mean health status were negatively correlated ($r = -0.60$). It appeared that poorer health made the on-site spaces more important.[6] In the high-rise apartments, the only people in the halls were those going to some specific place. This provided an interesting contrast with observations from nursing homes, where the halls are often highly populated with visitors and residents conversing in chairs. Lawton's data singled out the lobby as the most important area of housing for the elderly. Lobby occupancy was particularly high in sites that had hotel-style lobbies, with comfortable seating from which resident traffic could easily be watched. By contrast, the peripheral sitting rooms in these same buildings had only about one-fifth as many occupants. The general activity spaces (e.g., recreation rooms) tended to be most used in housing with minimal lobbies. The most populated activity room had a bank of windows overlooking the main entrance and the street. Apparently these older people had a strong desire to view, and discuss, the activities of others. They may not have wanted to be very active physically, but they could enjoy activities vicariously through watching other people. Observations of outdoor spaces reflected this same theme. The highest occupancy was in an outdoor sitting area characterized by protection from two sides of the building, choice of a ninety-degree or a street-oriented conversational grouping, staff monitoring of the residents from the windows, and a boundary divider that helped to separate the building grounds from the public sidewalk. In contrast, there was low outdoor occupancy in another housing site where the only seats were regularly spaced, fixed, flat concrete benches with no backs. There was nothing to look at, no conversational grouping possible, and physical discomfort from using the benches.

Lawton's approach was to learn the needs of the elderly by observing them. A more direct approach is to simply ask them about their needs. Older people representing 174 households in Fort Collins, Colorado, were interviewed by Tucker and her associates.[7] The residents were asked about their daily activities and about the degree to which their home environment accommodated their activities. Most owned their own homes, so they represented a different type of elderly population from those living in the housing for the elderly observed by Lawton. Given that these people were living in their own homes, it is not surprising that most were highly satisfied with their surroundings. Those who were dissatisfied generally wanted more space. This conflicts with the belief that the elderly need small, compact living units (but agrees with the conclusions of Blonsky,[8] who found that the elderly preferred to remain in deteriorated, three-story walk-up apartment buildings rather than move to the new high-rise in their neighborhood, because the rooms in the new building were too small). Tucker's interviews highlighted the variability of environmental preferences among the elderly. While meals were usually eaten in the kitchen, approximately one-third of the respondents preferred to eat in a separate dining area. While most wanted a compact, one-person kitchen, many needed more space for canning and for a helper during after-meal clean-up. Overnight company stayed in 83 percent of the homes during the year. Space for such guests was rated very important by about half the residents. In the case of four-room houses, 90 percent of the respondents desired two bedrooms. The second bedroom could be used for guests, an ill person, work space, or storage. At the same time, near consensus was reached on some topics. For example, there was high agreement concerning stairs; all but one person wished to avoid them. Almost all respondents felt that housing for the elderly should involve only one floor. They also agreed that the bath area required at least two safety features, handrails on the wall and a nonskid surface on the floor of the tub or shower.

The concern of older people for bathroom safety deserves a digression here for emphasis. In 1972, the Department of Housing and Urban Development estimated that 275,000 people were injured annually in the United States while using bathtubs and showers. The bathroom is clearly one of the most hazardous areas of the house. This is understandable, given the hard surfaces and the fact that many activities occur upon wet, soapy surfaces. The hazards are multiplied for elderly people, who suffer a number of age-related impairments such as visual impairment, tactile loss, and loss of equilibrium and balance. Kira[9] has studied the adequacy of bathroom design. He concluded that it is perhaps the most important private place in the house, yet it is unquestionably the most badly designed. Based on the study of human physical dimensions and laboratory tests, Kira has recommended several ways of making bathroom facilities more appropriate to older people. These include a washbasin height of 34 to 36 inches with lever water controls (easier to manipulate with arthritic hands), and a nonslip bottom to the tub with a grab bar at the entry (for getting in and out) and bars at the side (for getting up and down). The shower should include a storage shelf, a place to sit while bathing, and a detachable, hand-held nozzle (rather than a permanently wall-mounted nozzle). The elderly are best served by a "high-rise" toilet next to a wall (so that support bars can be conveniently mounted) and with paper to the side (not to the rear). Actually, most of these special requirements for the aged are not so special. As Kira notes, they would be equally suitable and useful for the younger population.

The approach used by Tucker of asking the elderly about their environmental needs took a slightly different form in a study by Hartman, Horovitz, and Herman.[10] The study was done in San Francisco when the redevelopment agency was acquiring hotels and evicting the elderly residents so that new office buildings could be built. The residents were given almost no help in relocating in a city that had virtually no vacant low-rent units. The people involved sought legal help. In later court proceedings, the judge ruled that these people must be provided with low-cost housing. The redevelopers decided to provide the housing, which was financed by the city's hotel tax, but let the residents help design and manage it. The initial problem was to find out the housing needs of these single, elderly people. Certainly the architects did not know their needs. None of the architects had experienced old age, and none even knew of a practicing low-income elderly architect.

At this point, Hartman's research team was called in. Hartman quickly found that door-to-door interviewing of the elderly people (who, after all, were being displaced by the redevelopers) generally produced suspicion and therefore inadequate interviews. His solution was to go to organizations that provided free lunches (e.g., the Salvation Army), where many of these people ate. He encouraged them to remain after lunch to view slides of various living environments. The slide presentation took the form of showing contrasting designs (e.g., high-rise vs. low-rise, modern vs. traditional design). The residents were asked which they preferred and why. The resulting findings provided a number of design guidelines for low-income elderly in inner-city areas. It was clear that the residents did not want to duplicate their current old hotels, comfortable and homey as they might be. Over 80 percent preferred modern-looking structures on the grounds that they were cleaner, more prestigious, and had more amenities. Opinion was equally divided as to low-rise versus high-rise structures. A clear majority wanted some commercial use of the ground floor, but they also wanted to avoid bars, liquor stores, and massage parlors, which might attract undesirable and dangerous persons to the premises. Building entries that suggested prestige and aesthetic appreciation were preferred, but the main concern was safety. Wealthier elderly might find a landscaped courtyard entry quite attractive. However, these low-income residents rejected it as "a lovely place for a mugger to hide." They preferred an entrance providing quick, secure passage from the street. Hartman found that 75 percent of the residents wanted a lobby. They worried that it might attract outsiders and noted the lack of privacy for persons coming and going. Nevertheless, in corroboration of Lawton's observations, they clearly desired a hotel-like lobby for leisure space. For security reasons, almost everyone wanted the mailboxes placed within the lobby rather than outside the front door.

Hartman reached two major conclusions about the environmental needs of these people. First, the elderly are very conscious of territory. They want clear distinctions between individual space, communal space for building residents, and public space for outsiders. Second, the elderly are very concerned about personal safety, and they weren't referring to grab bars in the bathroom. They see themselves as vulnerable to violence and theft by other persons. Given the realities of big-city crime statistics, they have good reason for concern.

A novel approach to identifying the environmental needs of the elderly has been taken by Pastalan at the University of Michigan.[11] According to

Pastalan, if you want to learn how the elderly respond to the environment, you should simulate their sensory capacities and learn firsthand how they experience the environment. To do this, he uses what he calls the empathic model to simulate age-related sensory loss. He notes, for example, that as a person ages, changes in the lens of the eye cause a loss of visual acuity. This occurs because of gradual stiffening and opacification of the lens, preventing the projection of a sharply focused image on the retina of the eye. To simulate this impairment, Pastalan uses specially prepared spectacles with coated lenses. Similarly, hearing loss is mimicked with earplugs, loss of the tactile sense is simulated with a gluelike fixative smeared on the fingertips, and cotton is placed in the nostrils for decreased smell. Once the various implements of the empathic model are in place, the individual finds the world much changed. Signs become hard to read, glare makes vision difficult, and conversation is difficult to separate from background noise. Since 1970, Pastalan has used his devices in training people who must work with the elderly. Architects, housing sponsors, administrators, social service agency staffs, and others have gained a clearer idea of how the world is perceived by older people through Pastalan's work. One outcome of this training may be better design of environments for older people. Sensory loss can be offset to some extent by providing redundant cues from the environment. For example, housing for the elderly can include a specific color to code each floor and a large numeral to indicate the floor level, perhaps on the elevator door. Different functional spaces can be indicated not only by color differences but by differences in texture of wall and floor materials.

Pastalan's work highlights the need to perceive the physical environment of the elderly accurately. Other correlational studies have dealt with needs concerning the social environment. Just what sort of social environment do the elderly prefer? Do they want the security of living in a homogeneous group of older persons, or would they rather have the vitality and enrichment provided by having persons of all age groups around?

Many of our interests, concerns, and attitudes are related to age and our particular stage in the life cycle. Persons of similar age will tend to have similar interests. Rosow, however, posed a question that required people to consider separately the factors of interests and age of neighbors.[12] In interviews with 1,200 aged people, he asked, "If you had to make a choice, who would you pick for neighbors—younger people that you had a lot in common with or retired people that you had little in common with?" The results revealed that 62 percent chose similar younger people, 27 percent chose different older people, and 11 percent expressed no preference. Given the growing tendency for the elderly to live in age-segregated surroundings, we can conjecture that the desire for a social environment of like-minded people is a strong motivation for this age group. Given Rosow's results, it appears that the current popularity of retirement communities has at its heart the general tendency for humans to seek the company of others who share their interests and concerns.

The extent to which older people engage in a variety of social activities, given a congenial social environment, depends on the distance that must be traversed to reach the social activities. The activities of older people seem to be inhibited by distance to a greater degree than the activities of younger adults. Interviews of 2,457 residents of low-rent public housing have shown the elderly to be somewhat less mobile in high-rise buildings than in low-rise buildings.[13] Perhaps the vertical distance from upper floors to off-site areas constitutes a greater psychological barrier to mobility than the horizontal distances involved in low-rise arrangements. Lawton and Simon reported on interviews with residents of five housing projects.[14] They found that proximity was of great importance in the creation of each project's social structure. The apartment house floor became the central locus of interaction for each individual. This tendency for social interaction to be strongly influenced by spatial factors has been shown across age levels. But given the restricted mobility of many older persons, spatial factors gain particular prominence.

The correlational studies discussed thus far have indicated needs for security, territory, safety, and social outlets. Environmental features such as distance and number of floors have been linked with these needs. But the results of such studies may amount to only so many irrelevant facts unless we can apply them to the problem of creating better environments for older people. Efforts have been made to translate the research results into design guidelines for the benefit of environmental designers and managers of housing for the aged. While a list of all the design "do's and don't's" would be too long for this chapter, a few references will be discussed that can lead the interested reader to a usable set of design guidelines.

Lawton[15] has provided a number of suggestions for housing the institutionalized elderly to best accommodate their needs. We have already discussed his findings on the importance of lobbies. They provide a desired social space near a used building entrance for sitting and watching. Halls that provide visual monotony encourage disorientation, especially where every doorway looks alike, where each floor looks alike, and the building has mirror-image wings or wraparound hallways. Ceiling lighting reflecting on over-polished floors causes glare that can add to the problem of negotiating halls. It is more desirable to arrange the building space in smaller units using color-coding and other features suggested by Pastalan. The importance of outdoor sitting spaces has also been discussed. The Lawton references review some of the desirable features of outdoor seating, such as a view of major traffic, security, overlooking windows from which staff can check on the area, and protection from the weather. Further design suggestions are provided by Schwartz under the following categories: need for familiarity, ease of manipulation, safety, clarity, sensory signals and cues, supportive and prosthetic systems, comfort, ease of mobility, and sensory stimulation. He notes that "design concepts, construction, and modifications, when effectively implemented . . . constitute the kind of prosthetic environment which compensates the elderly in large measure for their losses, and helps them maintain functional competence to a significant degree."[16] However, he cautions that "a very fine line often exists between the supportive, compensating, prosthetic environment and environmental inputs which either subtly or blatantly tend to preempt the functional capacities of the aged individual and, therefore, to infantilize such persons. . . . Any environment which tends to infantilize the older person will subvert his sense of self-worth and self-esteem."[17] We will return to this point in a later section of this chapter.

A number of relatively molecular environmental details have been covered by the Massachusetts State Housing Board in a publication on standards of design for the elderly.[18] The authors note, for example, that lever-type door knobs should be used in place of round knobs. An electrical outlet should be available for a night light between the bedroom and the bathroom (a number of fatal falls occur at night when the elderly are attempting to visit the bathroom). Storage areas should not be located over the stove or refrigerator and, in fact, no shelf should be placed higher than six feet. Architects will probably find especially useful the design criteria provided by Zeisel, Epp, and Demos.[19] They suggest, for example, that maximum uninterrupted wall lengths should be provided in living rooms and bedrooms to accommodate a variety of alternative arrangements for the large pieces of furniture that older people bring with them from their homes. The accumulated mementos and keepsakes of a lifetime can be important to the morale of the elderly. To accommodate them, adequate storage and display space should be provided, such as deep window sills upon which objects can be placed. Security needs must be acknowledged. For example, visitors at the front door should not be able to see into the rest of the apartment. Windows to the world are given high importance. Residents should be able to see outside from the eating area. They should also be able to see outside when seated in the living room or lying in bed.

Theoretical Developments

The provision of design guidelines based on behavioral criteria is a reasonable goal for environmental researchers. However, a few of these scientists are responding to an additional set of motivations. They are engaged in theory development, sifting through the bits of evidence and facts from previous research to provide an organized explanation of behavior-environment transactions that will not only bring coherence to prior research but will provide guidance for future studies. These theoretical concerns will make up the remainder of this chapter.

Environmental Competence and Cognitive Control

The task of reviewing the relevant concepts and theoretical developments could quickly become unwieldy. It will serve our needs and add coherence to the rest of this chapter if a general model linking the physical environment to important outcome variables for older people is provided at the outset. By means of this framework, the various theoretical considerations can be organized and shown to fit, in various ways, a general explanation that identifies environmental competence and cognitive control as central elements. The reader should refer to Figure 29.1 in conjunction with the following discussion.

Consider two different living environments for older people. The first includes such features as ramps (instead of stairs) with handrails. It has storage areas placed at midlevel rather than near the floor or the ceiling. The entrance to the dwelling is clearly marked with easy-to-read signs and unique coloring. Within the residence, lights are mounted on the walls where bulbs can be changed safely. A wall-mounted thermostat allows the individual to personally control the local temperature. Where rugs are used, the pile is thin so that a wheelchair can be moved over them with a minimum of effort. Contrast the environment just described with a second environment including stairs, low and high storage areas, a lack of orienting cues, ceiling lights, centrally controlled institutional heating, and thick-pile rugs. Environmental features such as these could influence the behavior of an aged resident in important ways.

The first environment could be labelled a competence-enhancing or negotiable environment. It is called negotiable because it assists the individual in pursuing personal goals such as home maintenance, self-grooming, and recreation with a maximum of independence. The individual can enter all areas of the residence unassisted. Individual goals can be pursued with confidence and a sense of security. For example, the bulb in a wall-mounted light fixture can be changed safely. An older person may be able to stand on a chair to change a ceiling light, but not with confidence of safety. Similarly, a person may feel secure in waiting for an elevator under the watchful eyes of passersby or office staff. However, to wait for the elevator in an out-of-sight location involves far less security. The negotiable environment allows an older person to pursue goals with ease and comfort. The second environment described above could be called a non-negotiable or incompetence-enhancing environment. The actual degree of negotiability achieved would be influenced by pressures from other persons regarding appropriate behav-

Figure 29.1: Theoretical Model Relating Environmental Features to Important Outcome Variables.

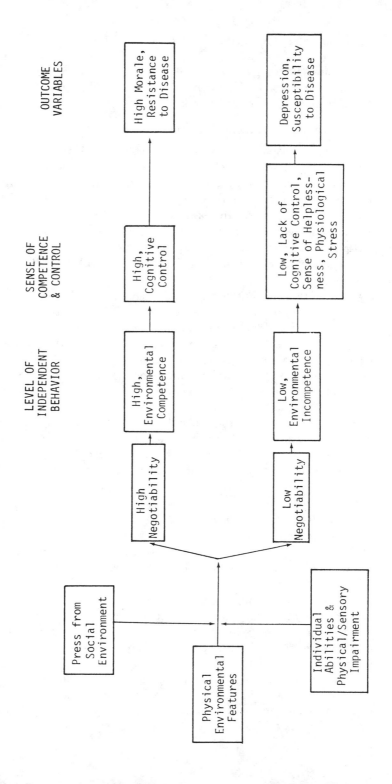

ior and by the individual's current physical and sensory capabilities.

With reference to Figure 29.1, we can make two sets of predictions about environments differing in negotiability. First, the behavioral performance of the elderly resident can be expected to differ under the two environmental conditions. High negotiability should encourage relatively high levels of independent behavior, defined as the degree to which a person can engage in personally desired activities without the direct assistance of others. Highly independent behavior with regard to the environment may be termed environmental competence. Its converse under conditions of low environmental negotiability may be called environmental incompetence. One's sense of competence and control over important events in one's life is at least partially derived from knowledge of the outcomes of one's efforts. If personal goals can be reached with a high degree of independence, then this should lead to a self-perception of competence and control. This has been called cognitive control; it is a subjective state that may or may not conform to accurate judgments of one's actual control over environmental events. The converse of this subjective state is a lack of control that is closely allied to a sense of helplessness in influencing one's condition. Symptoms of physiological stress are predicted in association with this state. Over a period of time, high levels of cognitive control are expected to lead to high morale and satisfaction with one's state in life. The literature on psychosomatic medicine would also lead us to expect relatively high levels of resistance to disease and physiological deterioration. Conversely, a sense of helplessness and low cognitive control over time should result in low morale and depression. Similarly, physiological stress should eventually result in heightened susceptibility to disease and an increased rate of physiological deterioration.

Little will be said here about how the concepts in this theoretical model should be operationalized (measured). Probably the most challenging measurement problem is posed by the concept of environmental negotiability. The environment in question might be subjected to a negotiability survey such as that used by Norris-Baker and Willems' research team in Houston.[20] In this survey, the residents rated all items in the living environment as to whether each could be properly used without assistance from another person. In addition to this independence measure, one could add indices of mobility (number of environmental locations that can be entered alone) and environmental diversity (variety of different types of settings that can be entered alone).

Two variations of the proposed model will be considered. First, several authors have argued that the environment can be made *too* safe and easy to use—encouraging a feeling of incompetence (recall the caution made by Schwartz about an environment that infantilizes). Figure 29.2 illustrates how the relationship between environmental negotiability and the sense of

Figure 29.2: The Curvilinear Relationship between Environmental
              Negotiability and Sense of Competence.

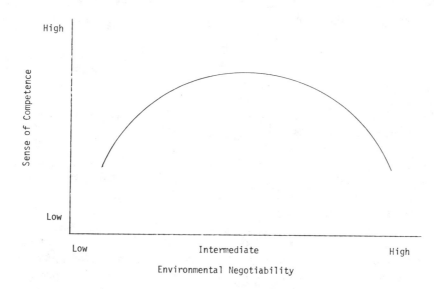

Environmental Negotiability

competence can be curvilinear. For example, it has been suggested that bathrooms for the elderly should include water controls that can be manipulated with arthritic hands, flush handles requiring little pressure, toilet paper to the side rather than to the rear of the toilet, and so on. In fact, a toilet has even been placed on the market that "wipes" (with warm water), dries (with warm air), and flushes automatically while the resident merely hangs on to the many grab bars. But this may foster a sense of incompetence. Probably the optimum degree of environmental negotiability changes with age for any given individual.

In the second variation on the proposed model, we recognize the importance of differences between present and desired environmental characteristics. A given older person's sense of cognitive control may be only moderately influenced by the degree of independence and negotiability allowed by the current environment. On the other hand, the size of the *difference* between present and desired negotiability may be of considerable importance. Hence, the model might be made more accurate by adding a discrepancy term. In Figure 29.1, the terms for high and low negotiability could be replaced by terms for high and low *discrepancy* between desired and present environmental negotiability. Such an amendment to the model could result in an improved accounting of individuals' different responses to the environment. Consider several older persons, each in the same low-negotiability environment. Given similar levels of physical and sensory impairment, these individuals would be expected to display uniformly low levels of behavioral independence. However, they could differ in the degree to which this lack of independence led to helplessness or depression. If degree of discrepancy between desired and actual negotiability is important, then the amended model would allow us to predict the different responses of these individuals to the same environment.

Territory and Privacy

We would expect that older people are most competent when on their own territory. Carp found strong evidence of territoriality shown by the residents of Victoria Plaza, a nine-story public housing apartment building in San Antonio, Texas.[21] The ground floor of the building housed a county community center, but the tenants were quite aggressive toward any outsider who dared to use this facility, which they saw as their "living room," despite the best efforts of the administrators to discourage such behavior. In two related studies, Patterson examined the marking or personalization of territories by elderly homeowners.[22] This marking took the form of fences, *Keep Out* signs, chimney initials, and so on. Subsequent interviews with these people revealed that fear of crime was inversely (negatively) correlated with the degree of territorial marking. This is in agreement with the proposed model only to the extent that territoriality indicates high negotiability and that fear of crime is associated with a sense of helplessness.

Privacy is related to territory in that one tends to have greater privacy on one's personal territory. Unfortunately, the institutionalized elderly often have little or no privacy. Watson describes inspection tours in which the visitors were free to peer into the patients' rooms as if gazing at so many interesting animals.[23] In such institutions, privacy is apparently sacrificed for greater ease of nursing activities, including surveillance of patients. Lack of privacy forms the basis of a criticism of the otherwise desirable lobby sitting area. Carp, Hartman, and Lawton have each reported that older people resent having to run the gauntlet of lobby sitters, "virulent gossipers" all, when leaving or entering the building. In this situation, what encourages a sense of cognitive control in the watcher results in an unwanted lack of privacy in the person watched. Given the choice, older people will often act in ways that maximize their privacy. Where multiple-bed rooms are used, residents will often cooperate so that only one person at a time uses the room during the day.[24] Referring to the proposed model, a person should be least constrained, and consequently achieve greatest control, in situations in which there is a high degree of privacy. High morale is one predicted outcome of such situations. Support for this hypothesis is provided by interviews with older persons from three nursing homes reported by Kahana.[25] The extent to which an older person had the desired level of privacy turned out to be one of the best predictors of morale in all three homes.

Current notions regarding privacy have gone beyond the commonsense idea of being alone. Privacy has come to be regarded as the degree of personal control over one's solitude, intimacy, and anonymity. Altman's definition of privacy as control of access of self to others has been generally accepted by researchers in this area.[26] Under this definition, privacy is closely allied to the notion of environmental control and negotiability. Altman has suggested that we might best serve human needs by creating "responsive environments," environments that can be altered to suit one's present needs, e.g., for privacy or togetherness. He warns, though, that people must be trained to make appropriate use of such flexible and adaptable environments.

Environmental Relocation

Negative effects following the change in residence of wild animals have long been known. Zookeepers will quickly attest to the high death rate of animals newly acquired by zoos. Considerable attention has been directed in recent years to whether similar negative effects follow the residential relocation of the aged. Seligman reports the results of a fire in a geriatric ward.[27] No one was injured in the fire, but the patients had to be moved out of the ward for several weeks while repairs were made. Within a month of the move, five of the forty patients had died; three more died in the next two months. This 20 percent death rate was strikingly higher than the 7.5 percent death rate of the preceding three months. It was suggested that stress from being moved accounted for the increased death rate.

The role of cognitive factors in such mortality rates was suggested in a study by Ferrare.[28] Female applicants to a Cleveland, Ohio, nursing home were classified as being admitted by choice or not by choice. Within ten weeks of admittance, a dramatic differential death rate was found: all but one of those there by choice were still alive, but all except one who were admitted involuntarily had died. It is not clear from this study whether the two patient groups were equal in health and other factors prior to admittance, so the data must be seen as suggestive, not conclusive. However, other studies of environmental relocation are available that include greater experimental control. For example, Lawton and Cohen compared 574 rehoused older persons with 324 controls (people who experienced no change in residence).[29] Their statistical analysis allowed them to control for a number of variables such as differences in initial health prior to the move. After one year, the rehoused group was rated significantly worse on functional health, defined as frequency and vigor of performing various tasks. In another study, the trauma of forced relocation was examined for residents of nursing homes in New York that were forced to close because they could not comply with the local fire or health codes.[30] Overall, the death rate for relocated persons did not differ from that of controls after one year. However, additional analysis revealed that relocation was associated with an elevated death rate for the more vulnerable patients, i.e., those diagnosed as having severe brain syndrome or severely impaired motor performance. In reference to the proposed model, individuals with physical and sensory impairment are predicted to suffer most from environmental factors that decrease competence.

It is possible that people's reactions to relocation can be modified by increasing their familiarity with the new place and their control over the move. Pastalan reported a study in which one group of relocated elderly were prepared with photographic slides of the new facility and visits by its staff.[31] Another group received more extensive preparation, including weekly visits to the new facility. The two groups were matched in age, sex, and health. One year following the move, the death rate was 52 percent for those in the first group and 27 percent for those in the second group. These results were interpreted as support for the notion that the harmful effects of relocation can be ameliorated by preparation. Relocation need not always be associated with increased mortality rates. Carp reports that eight years after moving to Victoria Plaza, a public housing apartment building for the elderly, 26 percent of the relocated group were dead or in the hospital to die as compared with 37 percent of the control group.[32] It should be noted that the relocated tenants had actively sought the move and were in relatively good health prior to it.

Schulz and Brenner, after reviewing the studies on relocation of the aged, developed a theoretical model to integrate the various relocation effects.[33] According to their model, the greater the choice given the individual in the relocation process, the less negative the effects of relocation. Thus, voluntary relocatees should fare better than involuntary relocatees. Since control subsumes predictability, the more predictable a new environment is, the less negative the effects of relocation. The response to relocation is mediated by differences in environmental controllability (negotiability) between the old and new environments, such that decreases in control should have negative effects, and vice versa. The Schulz and Brenner model agrees well with the model proposed here. Their review provides tentative support for the two models.

A similar theoretical perspective has been proposed by Schooler.[34] His model postulates stress as a major variable in explaining the impact of relocation. He argues that "the anticipation of residential relocation frequently initiates a decline in health or morale that is reinforced or accelerated by an actual move."[35] In view of our emphasis upon cognitive control, Schooler's quote of Lieberman is particularly interesting. In summarizing his four studies, Lieberman concludes, "facilitative environments were those characterized by relatively high degrees of autonomy fostering, personalization of the patients, and community integration. . . . facilitative environments placed the locus of control much more in the hands of the patients, differentiated among them, and permitted them a modicum of privacy."[36] In terms of our proposed model, relocation, especially when involuntary, can place the older person in a strange environment of low negotiability. The resulting sense of helplessness and increased susceptibility to disease culminating in elevated mortality rates would be predicted by the model and appears to be generally congruent with the available research to date.

Crowding and Density

Crowding and density in environments for the elderly have received little attention. However, work with other age groups suggests that these variables may enter into our model at the level of environmental features. Density, as defined by number of persons per unit of space, is characteristic of each person's environment. Rodin and Baum have suggested that in settings where density is high (and hence privacy is low), the individual's perceived sense of control over environmental events will tend to be low.[37] Depending upon the architectural arrangements of a residential space, the impact of high density may be high, resulting in the resident's inability to regulate social experience, or the impact may be low. Sherrod and Cohen have suggested several ways in which architectural arrangements can be manipulated to enhance the perception of cognitive control and decrease the impact of high density.[38] The sense of control can be increased by provision of private places or by designing apartment buildings so that fewer apartments share a common entrance and hallway. Environmental features that help the individual to construct a clearer "cognitive map" of the area (as with redundant cueing) should enhance cognitive control. Features that encourage a sense of safety and security (e.g., windows overlooking outdoor seating areas) should serve the same function. The authors also suggest that when environmental features accommodate one's behavioral goals (when environmental negotiability is high), cognitive control should be enhanced. They propose that control can be increased by allowing people to have a say in changes that are to be made to their environments. This concept of user participation in design has received widespread endorsement in the literature, although examples of its successful implementation have been few. In general, the efforts made to relate density to the concept of cognitive control through characteristics of the environment appear to support our proposed model.

Environmental Forces and Individual Competence

Some of the ideas expressed by the proposed model can be found in other theoretical models that relate environmental forces to the competence of older people. For example, Lawton[39] used the concept of environmental press to describe how environmental characteristics and individual competencies interact to determine a person's resulting feelings and behavior. Lawton's model is represented by Figure 27.3 in Chapter 27 of this volume.

In this model, *press* refers to the degree to which environmental forces (be they other people or architectural features) encourage or inhibit goal-directed activities on the part of the individual. It may be seen that environments that are too high or too low in degree of press are associated with negative outcomes. How a given individual will respond to any particular level of environmental press depends on the person's own competence level. This aspect of Figure 27.3 will be clearer if we consider the effects of different levels of press for an individual who operates at a single level of competence. This would be indicated by drawing a horizontal line across the graph corresponding to the person's competence level. The results, shown in Figure 29.3, suggest that the individual responds best to intermediate levels of press. The dip at the apex of this curve indicates that moderate amounts of environmental change are desirable. A slight change toward lessened press results in maximum comfort while slightly increased

Figure 29.3: Environmental Press and Individual Response for a Single Level of Competence.

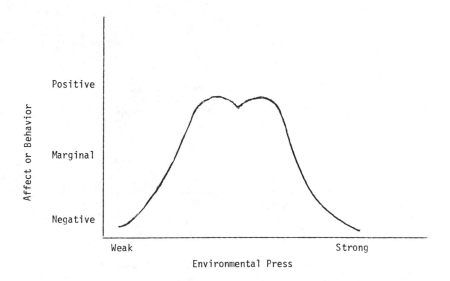

press tends to motivate the individual toward maximal behavioral performance.

The concept of environmental press appears also in the congruence model developed by Kahana.[40] She places particular emphasis on the degree of congruence (lack of disparity) between environmental press and individual needs (see page 434). High congruence is expected to lead to positive outcomes for the individual. Kahana cautions, however, that complete congruence between an individual's needs and the environment may be harmful. There may be an optimal amount of incongruence. Hence, the congruence-outcome relationship may take the form indicated by Figure 29.3.

What happens when a person becomes significantly less environmentally competent, whether because of modification of the environment, relocation, changes in abilities, or changes in the social environment? We might expect the person to attempt to regain the lost control. This is indicated in the first part of the diagram shown in Figure 29.4, adapted from the work of Wortman and Brehm.[41] If the initial reaction successfully restores environmental competence, positive outcomes are predicted. If, on the other hand, the reaction is unsuccessful, the individual is predicted to stop trying and exhibit a state of helplessness. As Figure 29.4 shows, the details of the individual's responses to a loss of environmental competence depend on the person's competence at the outset. The highly competent person will make a strong effort to restore control. Following failure to cause change, this individual would

Figure 29.4:   Dynamics of Motivation to Exert Control

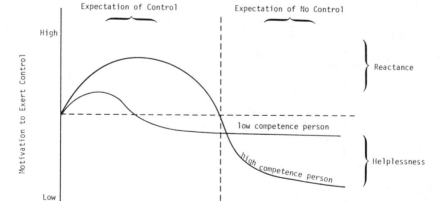

Source: Adapted from C. W. Wortman and J. W. Brehm. "Responses to
          Uncontrollable Outcomes: An Integration of Reactance Theory
          and the Learned Helplessness Model." In L. Berkowitz, ed.,
          Advances in Experimental Social Psychology, Vol. 8. New York:
          Academic Press, 1975. Reprinted by permission.

exhibit a contrasting response and develop even more marked symptoms of helplessness than the low-competence person.

Cognitive Control

The hypothesized relationship between loss of cognitive control and mortality is currently a focus of debate among researchers. The debate is necessarily prolonged because much of the evidence has the weaknesses of correlational research, yet clear-cut experimental studies would be unethical. Seligman has reviewed some of the correlational evidence involving humans.[42] He cites some of the early work of Cannon, which gave credence to the phenomenon called "voodoo death." Numerous incidents have been documented in which apparently healthy individuals have been "hexed," believed that they would die as a result, and shortly thereafter died. Researchers at the University of Rochester reported that among women who had precancerous cells in the cervix, those who had recently experienced a significant loss in their lives (and apparently responded with feelings of hopelessness) were over twice as likely to develop cervical cancer as those who did not experience such a loss.

Relatively few studies deal specifically with cognitive control in the aged. An investigator recently checked 800 newspaper obituaries to determine individuals' dates of death as compared with their birth dates. The hypothesis was that if dying persons could willfully control the general timing of their deaths and if it were important to them to live through an approaching birthdate, then the death rate should be depressed during the months prior to the birth date and elevated during the months following. Figure 29.5 shows that this indeed was the case. In another study, Langer and Rodin arranged for one group of nursing home residents to be given increased choice and personal responsibility for events in their lives.[43] They were given small plants to care for, allowed to decide whether and when to attend movies, and generally encouraged to take responsibility for such factors as their self-care, room arrangement, and visiting. The comparison group was given relatively less control and responsibility. At the end of the three weeks, the re-

Figure 29.5: Dates of Death in Relation to 800 Individuals' Dates of Birth

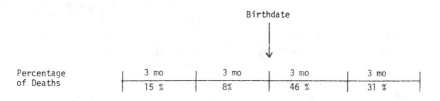

sponsibility group reported higher morale and appeared more alert thar comparison group. The patients were followed for two years. At the en that period, a significant difference in health had developed between the groups, favoring the responsibility group. Further, twice as many resid in the comparison group had died than was the case for the responsib group.[44] This study suffers from the defect that each group consisted of tients from only one floor of the nursing home, and opportunity for resp sibility may not have been the only difference between the treatment of tients on the two floors. Nevertheless, the results of these two studies suggestive and deserve attempts at replication.

Summary

The foregoing discussion and literature review has presented what is esse tially a psychological interpretation of environment-behavior relationship the lives of older people.[45] Most of the comments have dealt with living e vironments, particularly residences and institutions for the aged; howeve the principles derived could be applied as well to working environments an public settings. To recapitulate, the study of environments for the elderly is relatively recent development among researchers involved in the scientifi study of human behavior and experience. True experimental manipulation of the environment have been rare and have tended not to produce clear-cu conclusions. Most of the research in this area has been correlational ir nature. These correlational approaches have frequently taken the form of asking older people about their environmental needs and preferences. Based upon such studies, sets of guidelines have been developed for environmental designers and administrators who must make decisions about the arrange- ment and use of spaces for older people. A more recent development in envi- ronmental research has been the creation of concepts and theoretical models to organize previous findings and to allow predictions for future studies to test. A model was proposed that posits environmental competence and cognitive control as central constructs. A review of other models pro- posed by Lawton, Kahana, Schooler, Rodin, and others revealed a con- siderable degree of theoretical convergence in the literature.

The preceding discussion has emphasized the potential impact of the phys- ical environment on older people. It may have appeared at times that the author considers the environment to be the most potent influence upon be- havior. Such an emphasis has not been intentional. Clearly the environ- ment is just one factor that has impact on our lives, and other factors—past learning, personality styles, reinforcement, physiological processes, and in- terpersonal influences, to name just a few—may very well account for the greater share of variance in the behavior and experience of older people.

While it is far too soon to pass judgment upon this fledgling area of interest, we can assert that, sometimes and in some ways, characteristics of the environment do have profound effects on the lives of all people, and particularly older people. It remains for further research to specify the details of this assertion so that the design guidelines of the future will be more useful and the theories of the future will be more accurate.

Notes

1. Rhonda P. Ross and David E. Campbell, "A Review of the EDRA Proceedings," in *New Directions in Environmental Design Research*, edited by W. E. Rogers and W. H. Ittelson (Washington, D.C.: Environmental Design Research Association, 1978).

2. Robert Sommer, "Small Group Ecology in Institutions for the Elderly," in *Spatial Behavior of Older People*, edited by L. A. Pastalan and D. H. Carson (Ann Arbor: University of Michigan, 1970).

3. M. P. Lawton, B. Liebowitz, and H. Charon, "Physical Structure and the Behavior of Senile Patients Following Ward Remodeling," *Aging and Human Development* 1 (1970), pp. 231–239.

4. David E. Campbell, "Evaluation Research in Man-Environment Systems," *JSAS Catalogue of Selected Documents in Psychology* 6 (1976), p. 129; David E. Campbell, "Evaluation of the Built Environment: Lessons from Program Evaluation," in *The Behavioral Basis of Design, Book I*, edited by L. M. Ward et al. (Stroudsburg, Pa.: Dowden, Hutchinson & Ross, 1976); and A. Friedmann, C. Zimring, and E. Zube, editors, *Environmental Design Evaluation* (New York: Plenum, 1978).

5. M. P. Lawton, "Public Behavior of Older People in Congregate Housing," in *EDRA Two: Proceedings of the 2nd Annual Environmental Design Research Association Conference*, edited by J. Archea and C. Eastman (Pittsburgh: Carnegie-Mellon University, 1970).

6. I assume that many readers are familiar with the interpretation of the correlation coefficient. For those who are not, it is an index of the association between two variables (phenomena that can take on different values of some attribute). The coefficient can have values from -1.00 to $+1.00$. Values near zero indicate little or no relationship. Values near $+1.00$ or -1.00 indicate very strong relationships. An example of a positive correlation was given at the beginning of this section. A negative correlation would be anticipated if we hypothesized that high levels of crowding would be associated with low levels of social behavior, and vice versa. Further details on correlation coefficients can be obtained from any elementary statistics text.

7. S. M. Tucker, M. E. Combs, and A. M. Woolrich, "Independent Housing for the Elderly: The Human Element in Design," *The Gerontologist* 15 (1975), pp. 73–76.

8. L. E. Blonsky, "The Desire of Elderly Nonresidents to Live in a Senior Citizen Apartment Building," *The Gerontologist* 15 (1975), pp. 88–91.

9. Alexander Kira, *The Bathroom* (New York: Viking, 1976).

10. C. Hartman, J. Horovitz, and R. Herman, "Designing with the Elderly," *The Gerontologist* 16 (1976), pp. 303–311.

11. L. A. Pastalan, "Privacy as an Expression of Human Territoriality," in *Spatial Behavior of Older People*, edited by L. A. Pastalan and D. H. Carson (Ann Arbor: University of Michigan, 1970).

12. I. Rostow, "Discussion of Amos Rapoport's Paper 'Community and Urban Design'," in *Environmental Research and Aging*, edited by T. O. Byerts (Washington, D.C.: Gerontological Society, 1974).

13. M. P. Lawton, L. Nahemow, and J. Teaff, "Housing Characteristics and the Well-Being of Elderly Tenants in Federally-Assisted Housing," *Journal of Gerontology* 30 (1975), pp. 601–607.

14. M. P. Lawton and B. Simon, "The Ecology of Social Relationships in Housing for the Elderly," *The Gerontologist* 8 (1968), pp. 108–115.

15. M. P. Lawton, "The Human Being and the Institutional Building," in *Designing for Human Behavior*, edited by J. Lang et al. (Stroudsburg, Pa.: Dowden, Hutchinson & Ross, 1974), and M. P. Lawton, *Planning and Managing Housing for the Elderly* (New York: Wiley, 1975).

16. A. N. Schwartz, "Planning Micro-Environments for the Aged," in *Aging: Scientific Perspectives and Social Issues*, edited by D. S. Woodruff and J. E. Birren (New York: Van Nostrand Reinhold, 1975), p. 289.

17. Ibid., p. 291.

18. Massachusetts State Housing Board, *Standards of Design: Housing for the Elderly* (Boston, 1954).

19. J. Zeisel, G. Epp, and S. Demos, *Low Rise Housing for Older People: Behavioral Criteria for Design*, U. S. Department of Housing and Urban Development, Office of Policy Development and Research (Washington, D.C.: U.S. Government Printing Office, 1977).

20. C. Norris-Baker and E. P. Willems, "Environmental Negotiability as a Direct Measurement of Behavior-Environment Relationships: Some Implications for Theory and Practice," in *Environmental Design: Research, Theory, and Application*, edited by A. D. Seidel and S. Danford (Washington, D.C.: Environmental Design Research Association, 1979).

21. F. M. Carp, "The Elderly and Levels of Adaptation to Changed Surroundings," in *Spatial Behavior of Older People*, edited by L. A. Pastalan and D. H. Carson (Ann Arbor: University of Michigan, 1970).

22. A. H. Patterson, "Territorial Behavior and Fear of Crime in the Elderly," *Environmental Psychology and Nonverbal Behavior* 2 (1978), pp. 131–144; L. M. Pollack and A.H. Patterson, "Territoriality and Fear of Crime in Elderly and Non-Elderly Homeowners" (paper presented at the annual meeting of the American Psychological Association, Toronto, 1978).

23. W. H. Watson, "Institutional Structures of Aging and Dying," in *Environmental Research and Aging*, edited by T. O. Byerts (Washington, D.C.: Gerontological Society, 1974).

24. M. P. Lawton, "Ecology and Aging," in *Spatial Behavior of Older People*, edited by L. A. Pastalan and D. H. Carson (Ann Arbor: University of Michigan, 1970).

25. E. Kahana, "A Congruence Model of Person-Environment Interaction," in *Theory Development in Environment and Aging*, edited by P. G. Windley, T. O. Byerts,

and F. G. Ernst (Washington, D.C.: Gerontological Society, 1975).

26. I. Altman, *The Environment and Social Behavior* (Monterey, Calif.: Brooks/Cole, 1975).

27. M.E.P. Seligman, *Helplessness: On Depression, Development, and Death* (San Francisco: Freeman, 1975).

28. N. A. Ferrare, "Institutionalization and Attitude Change in an Aged Population: A Field Study and Dissidence Theory" (Ph.D. dissertation, Western Reserve University, 1962); N. A. Ferrare, "Freedom of Choice," *Social Work* 8 (1963), pp. 104–106.

29. M. P. Lawton and J. Cohen, "The Generality of Housing Impact on the Well-Being of Older People," *Journal of Gerontology* 29 (1974), pp. 194–204.

30. A. E. Goldfarb, S. P. Shahinian, and H. T. Burr, "Death Rate of Relocated Nursing Home Residents," in *Research Planning and Action for the Elderly*, edited by D. P. Kent, R. Kastenbaum, and S. Sherwood (New York: Behavioral Publications, 1972).

31. L. A. Pastalan, "Research in Environment and Aging: An Alternative to Theory," in *Theory Development in Environment and Aging*, edited by P. G. Windley, T. O. Byerts, and F. G. Ernst (Washington, D.C.: Gerontological Society, 1975).

32. F. M. Carp, "Impact of Improved Living Environment on Health and Life Expectancy," *The Gerontologist* 13 (1977), pp. 242–249.

33. R. Schulz and G. Brenner, "Relocation of the Aged: A Review and Theoretical Analysis," *Journal of Gerontology* 32 (1977), pp. 323–333.

34. K. K. Schooler, "Environmental Change and the Elderly," in *Human Behavior and Environment: Advances in Theory and Research*, vol. 1, edited by I. Altman and J. F. Wohlwill (New York: Plenum, 1976), and K. K. Schooler, "Response of the Elderly to Environment: A Stress-Theoretical Perspective," in *Theory Development in Environment and Aging*, edited by P. G. Windley, T. O. Byerts, and F. G. Ernst (Washington, D.C.: Gerontological Society, 1975).

35. Schooler, "Environmental Change," p. 283.

36. M. A. Lieberman, "Relocation Research and Social Policy," *The Gerontologist* 14 (1974), p. 500.

37. J. Rodin and A. Baum, "Crowding and Helplessness: Potential Consequences of Density and Loss of Control," in *Human Response to Crowding*, edited by A. Baum and Y. M. Epstein (Hillsdale, N.J.: Lawrence Erlbaum, 1978).

38. D. R. Sherrod and D. Cohen, "Density, Personal Control, and Design," in *Humanscape: Environments for People*, edited by S. Kaplan and R. Kaplan (North Scituate, Mass.: Duxbury, 1978).

39. M. P. Lawton, "Competence, Environmental Press and the Adaptation of Older People," in *Theory Development in Environment and Aging*, edited by P. G. Windley, T. O. Byerts, and F. G. Ernst (Washington, D.C.: Gerontological Society, 1975), and M. P. Lawton and L. Nahemow, "Ecology and the Aging Process," in *The Psychology of Adult Development and Aging*, edited by C. Eisdorfer and M. P. Lawton (Washington, D.C.: American Psychological Association, 1973).

40. Kahana, "A Congruence Model."

41. C. B. Wortman and J. W. Brehm, "Responses to Uncontrollable Outcomes: An

Integration of Reactance Theory and the Learned Helplessness Model," in *Advances in Experimental Social Psychology*, vol. 8. edited by L. Berkowitz (New York: Academic Press, 1975).

42. Seligman, *Helplessness*.

43. E. J. Langer and J. Rodin, "The Effects of Choice and Enhanced Personal Responsibility for the Aged," *Journal of Personality and Social Psychology* 34 (1976), pp. 191–198.

44. J. Rodin and E. J. Langer, "Long-Term Effects of a Control-Relevant Intervention with the Institutionalized Aged," *Journal of Personality and Social Psychology* 35 (1977), pp. 897–902.

45. For a more extensive review, see M. P. Lawton, "The Impact of the Environment on Aging and Behavior," in *Handbook of the Psychology of Aging*, edited by J. E. Birren and K. W. Schaie (New York: Van Nostrand Reinhold, 1977).

30

The Nursing Home Environment

K. Anthony Edwards

By the year 2000, more than 30 million Americans will be considered elderly. Scientific crystal ball gazers predict that medical technology will keep pace with the increase in multiple chronic ailments generated by this extended life span. Many elderly, however, will continue to need some type of long-term care. Hospitals alone are insufficient, and rehabilitation centers provide facilities only for people in transition from medical institutions to independent home support systems. Thus, nursing homes will still be needed to provide continuous care for dependent elderly who do not have alternatives.

Much has been written about the deplorable conditions existing in many nursing homes. Indeed, much has been said about the problems of the nursing home industry in general. Most nursing homes are run for profit, often at the psychological, medical, and financial expense of the patient. Staff turnover is greater than in most businesses, and many owners attempt to run these "homes" more like fast food outlets or hospitals than residences.

While it is necessary to bring these larger problems to the attention of the public, it is also important to provide specific recommendations for improving the daily lives of people now living in nursing homes. But before discussing some specific steps that can be taken to improve the quality of care and thus enhance the everyday lives of residents, let us consider what life would be like in an ideal nursing *home*—one in which you and I might like to live.

This chapter is based on the work of the Living Environments Group under the direction of Todd R. Risley at the University of Kansas.

Oak Knolls

Oak Knolls rests at the edge of the city. It has beautifully tailored lawns and trees, bubbling brooks, and fern-lined ponds where swans glide and dabble. It has skilled care, intermediate care, and personal care. But what is most unusual about Oak Knolls is that it has an attached retirement center.

Upon entering the building, one is at once impressed by its large lobby. To the left of the main entrance is the three-story nursing home. In the basement are laundry equipment, a kitchen, and other needed areas such as storage space for belongings not in use at present by the elderly resident, and living spaces. Personal-care residents are housed on the main floor; intermediate- and skilled-care patients are located on the second and third floors. Each floor has its own staff, and staff on each floor are assigned to zones of responsibility.

To the right of the main entrance are shops and parlors available to both nursing home and retirement center residents, but used mainly by those living in the retirement section. The shops are filled with curios and gimcracks of all kinds made by residents of both sections, and people come from miles around to buy. Residents then receive the money to put aside for purchases of more materials with which to make more items for sale, and to buy items and services from others. In other words, a small-scale economy is blossoming. And the parlors—Martin's Hair Stylists, Jacque's Haberdashery, Emily's Boutique—are all run by residents. Administrative offices are tucked unobtrusively away in a hall behind a wall. There is a well-kept residents' dining room, and antique furnishings.

Outside are cottages for those who wish to reside away from the main building for greater privacy. Most do not want the added separation; some feel it is too isolated, and others prefer to be closer to those who can assist in a possible emergency.

Residents and patients are given numerous opportunities for an active life. One has taken responsbility for the care of plant life for the entire home. Another has recently organized a group to stage a three-act play. A third cares for the aquariums in the facility. Others tend the shops and parlors. Those with less desire to be enterpreneurs spend a great deal of time making things such as ceramic pots, ashtrays, and icons to be sold in the gift shops.

When residents enter the home for the first time, they are greeted by a hostess, informed of the shops in the building, and told of the activities that are available. There are movies, group meetings, bingo games, dancing, arts and crafts, and educational workshops and classes. Residents are encouraged to, and do, participate in the residents' council, advisory committees, and advocate groups.

Staff are carefully scheduled. Supervisors always know where staff are and who they are assisting. At intervals the supervisor drops in unannounced and "checklists" the staff member's performance, much as a pilot checks his equipment before flying, to ensure that all procedures are being properly followed. A nurse informs the staff member about correct and incorrect medical procedures. When inappropriate performances are noted, a correct routine is modeled and the staff member is guided through it. All this is done quietly, with the goal of positive feedback to maximize work performance.

Patients and residents are unobtrusively, but closely, watched for visual, auditory, and other sensory changes. For instance, residents noticed to be consuming large amounts of sugar with their meals, indicated by large numbers of empty sugar packets left by their plates, are examined for diabetes and cancer. Residents showing sudden weight gains are examined for metabolic shifts and given food servings lower in calories. Residents' attendance and participation in activities is observed. Medical examinations are routinely given and vital signs examined by physicians specializing in geriatric disorders, but with the bedside manner of the once-beloved general practitioner. Although such observations take time, they are done in a manner that seems casual, as a part of the everyday routine, not mechanically. Monitoring is done carefully because the staff care about the whole patient. They are skilled in both observing and treating the patient or resident humanely. Patients and residents know their physicians, nurses, and aides on a first-name basis, and because the staff are knowledgeable and skillful, the emphasis in this nursing home is not on *nursing* but on *home*. The arrangement resembles that of a family, both to those involved and to observers from outside the setting.

Oak Knolls, as far as this author knows, does not exist. Its organization and management are idealized. Like most facilities, it has appropriate physical accoutrements—these are required by law. It also has dietary and physical therapy consultants and an in-service program for staff training. It has good housekeeping, which is watched closely by relatives and state inspectors. It has good medical and dietary care—also closely watched by relatives and authorities. What it has that other facilities, those we are accustomed to visiting, do not have are (1) training for and supervision of quality care, and (2) ample free access to activities for residents and patients.

Although Oak Knolls is idealized and thus difficult to imagine existing, it is not difficult to describe facilities of poor quality. These are the ones my grandfather had in mind when he said, "If anyone ever tries to put me in one of those places, I'll put a shotgun to my head!" And they are the facilities amply detailed in Mendelsohn's *Tender Loving Greed*.[1]

Many nursing homes, however, are administered by well-intentioned people who, if given appropriate technologies, would certainly use them. Trained in management theories appropriate to products and not people, and schooled in accounting principles focused on fiscal rather than staff management, administrators face a variety of complex problems. Furthermore, the medical model based on acute patients has failed to provide guidelines for the chronic patients found in nursing homes. Several reasons for shifting the direction of organization and management in nursing home administration, and some strategies for doing this, have been described by the author in an earlier publication.[2] Therefore, this chapter will focus on procedures for improving nursing home environments (and other institutional care facilities) that are based on the results of research conducted in representative facilities.

Nursing Homes

The number of nursing homes in this country has grown at a rapid rate in the past two decades.[3] Like fast food stores, they often have provided a source of quick profit for a few people who have a major interest in money and little, if any, interest in elderly people.[4] This rapid expansion and development of facilities took place before nursing home conditions could be examined and guidelines for appropriate policy established. In view of the important role that nursing homes will play in the lives of many older people, it is becoming increasingly important that reasonable guidelines be established for their development and maintenance.

Of the total U.S. population, about 1 percent is institutionalized.[5] As age increases, however, there is an increase in the proportion of institutionalized people. What is more, there are variations in individual characteristics of nursing home residents. Five percent of those age 65 or older are residents of various types of institutions, including nursing homes and mental institutions, and about one-fifth of those age 85 or more are institutionalized.

The nursing home population in 1974 consisted of 1.1 million people, nearly 90 percent of whom were over 64 years of age. Nearly three-fourths of these were females, and females predominated at all age levels. Of all residents, only 12 percent were currently married, but only about 20 percent had never been married. As residents' ages increase, female-to-male ratios increase, and the percentage of those who had never married declines.

In the 1980s, there will probably be more older people (over 65) and very old people (over 85) in American society, which means that multiple chronic conditions also will increase. In other words, there will be a greater demand for health care because there will be more elderly people. At the same time, health care costs will become a greater burden to society because of the increased number of nonworking elderly.[6] As the population of elderly increases, and the expense of the support for retired elderly rises, the tax burden on the young increases also. One report notes the possibility that three persons will be needed to support two by the year 2031 if 55 years of age were established for retirement, as some Canadian pension plans already allow.[7] In 1974, approximately $90 billion was spent for personal health care in the United States. Of this amount, nearly 30 percent was spent for older people. The per capita health care cost for an older person was $1,218, nearly three times as much as the $420 spent for younger adults. Benefits from government programs accounted for three-fifths of the health expenditure for older persons, compared with three-tenths for adults under age 65.[8]

Not only is it costly to support people who are receiving assistance, but some evidence has indicated that only about one-third of those who may be eligible for assistance under formal programs are receiving it. Of these 3 to 7 million disabled people, 0.8 to 1.4 million may be receiving no long-term care at all, but they would be if they could be identified.[9] To what extent can hospitals assume some of the burden for this projected increase in the health needs of older people? Hospital care is costly and, although they are well equipped for acute care, hospitals are poorly equipped for chronic care. Moreover, the framework for care of the elderly in hospitals is based on the medical model, which views the patient in terms of his or her medical problem and essentially ignores individual behavioral patterns.[10]

Quality of Nursing Home Care

It has been difficult in the past to define what constitutes quality care in nursing homes. One problem has been the inappropriate assumption that nursing homes are hospitals. Certainly the quality of care should be defined in terms of care-giving procedures and their outcomes. Many nursing homes provide the services needed when a person's condition is too severe to keep him or her at home. Many meet individual needs for environmental support and are essential to those for whom there are no other alternatives available.[11] Thus far no known alternative to nursing home care for some has been developed.[12] It seems appropriate therefore to conclude that present nursing homes are needed, and may be needed for a long time to come.

Another problem facing nursing homes is the adverse publicity they have received, which leads to a basic distrust of the entire industry. Improved care and humane treatment of the elderly, which should not be too difficult to achieve, would probably go a long way in countering such adverse publicity. More efficient and effective treatment, which could be achieved by more effective training of staff, not only would enhance the public image of nursing homes, but also would reduce the cost of care.[13] At the present time, however, nursing homes are viewed by Americans in an unfavorable light.[14]

Nursing home entrepreneurs have attempted to meet the need for less costly care by increasing the number of available beds in individual nursing homes, but in general they have not tried to institute more effective organization and management techniques. If they wish to improve their image, they should be looking carefully at alternative approaches to care within their homes.

One nursing home resident recently described her life in the following way:

> Almost a year has passed. Is this it? There seems to be nothing else I can do. I've become less rebellious. Maybe there is a need to calm down and be tamed. It takes so much energy to penetrate and be heard. I feel choked; I can't express myself, and I could contribute so much. As long as this is my home, I want to feel a part of it in some way.[15]

This description seems to represent the feelings of many nursing home residents, particularly those whose mental faculties have not been impaired. The woman reports being treated like a child; and in fact such treatment is the rule rather than the exception. Patients have varying degrees of impairment and it is essential that they are not all treated alike. While nursing homes are necessary in our society, we cannot continue to tolerate facilities that do not allow residents to live out their later years with dignity, the loss of which may even reduce their chances for survival. We must work at making nursing homes into places where each resident participates fully in the community of the home. The question that must be answered now is how to improve nursing homes so that the quality of life for the elderly (and others living in these environments) is maximized.

The Structure and Function of the Nursing Home

Nursing home staff are often divided into the following departments: administration (bookkeeping, payroll, etc.); housekeeping; dietary services; nursing; social/rehabilitation; and, perhaps, in-service (staff training). Each has its own department head who is directly responsible to the nursing home administrator. In general, concern for nursing home problems seems to center principally around nursing care, housekeeping, and administration, while little attention is given to social/rehabilitation or staff training. In other words, the activities of daily living for residents tend to receive little attention. While problems of nursing, diet, housekeeping, and administration have been essentially "solved" by experts in each of these fields (generally with the help of skilled consultants and a push from bad press and angry relatives), the behavioral problems of residents and staff remain. These problems are addressed in the remainder of this chapter.

The subsections that follow will examine nursing homes on the departmental level. The departments are viewed from two perspectives: (1) a case example of the way department heads perceive the purpose, goals, and primary problems of their departments;[16] and (2) a discussion of the conclusions and recommendations of one research team,[17] of which the author was a member, regarding the operation of departments in several nursing homes.

Administration

Administration involves the management of bookkeeping, hiring and terminating staff, scheduling work times, and monitoring the ongoing activities of staff to ensure the continuation of operations. The administrator represents an interface between the public and the nursing home system. His or her job is to keep the system operating smoothly, effectively, and humanely for the good of the patients; to maintain an income level sufficient to pay for the operation; and to ensure that the consumers of the "goods" (i.e., patient care and quality of life) are satisfied with the products. Table 30.1 describes the purposes, goals, and three primary problems of administration as viewed by one administrator of a nursing home.

This administrator has determined that her department must coordinate activities and delegate responsibilities so that health care and a stimulating home environment are provided. In order to achieve her mission she has set four goals. Staff-administration communication and systematic monitoring

Table 30.1: Purpose, Goals, and Problems of an Administrator

Purpose To coordinate activities and delegate responsibilities to departments so that the facility offers good health care, and a supportive stimulating home environment.

Goals 1) to provide good systems to facilitate intra- and inter-departmental communications.

2) to develop procedures and tools of monitoring quality of care and job performance.

3) to give residents as much decision-making power and as active a role in the home as possible.

4) to create an atmosphere of cooperation and team effort to include not only staff but patients and their families as well.

Problems 1) turnover, 2) interdepartmental communications and relations, and 3) measures of quality.

---

of quality of care are necessary ingredients in a well-run nursing home. Patients sharing responsibility in an atmosphere of cooperation and team effort are appropriate target outcomes. But are these realistic goals? This author thinks so. However, the impediments to achieving these results, according to the administrator, are staff turnover; lack of interdepartmental communications; problematic relations with patients' relatives; and lack of evaluative measures of care quality.

Good monitoring requires that the administrator know the location of any staff member at any time and what he or she is, or should be, doing. Knowing where staff are, what they are supposed to be doing, and when it should be done is a major difficulty in any organization. The master schedule board shown in Figure 30.1 was placed by the research team in a nursing home to help nursing staff to monitor patients and aides.[18] With the use of this tool, each department becomes responsibile for updating the board, and each department head can more easily check on staff as they perform their tasks. The way this board is organized, department staff become more visible. Thus, they can be monitored by supervisors, consultants, or by relatives and advocates. In addition, the board can be used to examine each resident's daily schedule at a glance.

Of course, crises regularly occur and can stop a system such as this from

Figure 30.1: A Master Schedule Board

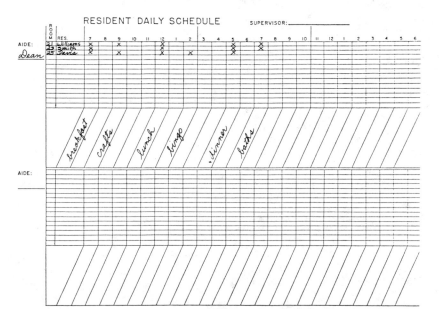

working. Some problems can be readily resolved by requiring work orders to be filled immediately. Work routines should not become compartmentalized, and department members should be cross-trained to fill in when necessary.

From our team's research in nursing homes and in other settings, it appears that the purposes of this administrator can indeed be accomplished with a smoothly running, efficient organization. Effective training programs can enhance the humane treatment of patients. Development of subsystems for the transfer of information, measures of quality care and job performance, and monitoring strategies will upgrade staff performances. Resident councils, with power to implement change, can aid the administrator in reaching these goals. Staff turnover can be decreased by careful screening, overstaffing, intensive training, and incremental pay increases as skill levels are improved. Interdepartmental communications and relations can be boosted by suggestion boxes and publicly displayed answers to staff and residents' comments. Quality can be measured by questionnaires addressed to staff, relatives of residents, and residents themselves.

Housekeeping

One of the most visible departments in a nursing home is housekeeping. The housekeeping staff are primarily responsible for maintaining cleanliness of the facility, and housekeeping aides are rarely in direct contact with residents. Still, the nursing home is the resident's living space, so housekeepers cannot be permitted to disengage from those with whom the organization is primarily concerned. Housekeepers should be required to learn skills necessary to maintain constructive interactions with patients. One way is to train all aides in all departments to help residents develop independence in daily living (eating, dressing, etc.). An example of checklists used to develop such independence among nursing home patients is shown in Figure 30.2. With this type of checklist, aides can be supervised directly and provided training necessary for interactions that promote independence among patients.

The housekeeper of one nursing home stated the purposes, goals, and primary problems of her department as shown in Table 30.2. The primary goal in her department had already been addressed by our research group in another nursing home. The system we devised included the removal of insects. Because housekeeping duties were uncoordinated, the home was not being kept sufficiently clean. Patients' relatives brought this to the attention of the administrator, who assigned housekeeping staff to begin systematically cleaning rooms, starting at one end of a three-wing building. Cleaning progressed from this wing across the nursing station and out to the end of the adjacent wing. The housekeepers then returned to the center and worked north to the end of the wing. Two rooms were scheduled for complete

Figure 30.2: A Sample Checklist: Developing Independence

Developing Independence

Training: Observe one entire visit, scoring items each time an opportunity
for patient self-help arises.

Score: +, 0, or NA   Criterion: + or NA for all items

Did the helper:							
	Observer:						
	Date:						
	Type of Situation:						
1. Politely ask patient to help himself before giving any physical assistance?							
2. Allow time for patient to try the task before assisting?							
3. Refrain from nagging (not ask more than once before helping)?							
4. Give only the help needed (a light touch, help in getting started)?							
5. Focus full attention on the patient?							
6. Enthusiastically praise all efforts (even small ones)?							
7. Vary the kind of praise given (use different expressions, sometimes touch the patient, smile and look at the patient)?							
COMMENTS: (Please date)	Feedback Received (initials)						

cleaning daily in addition to all other housekeeping duties. Each room was across the hall from the other. Since there were about thirty pairs of spaces, including linen closets and other storage areas (and excepting the kitchen), the entire procedure could be started again on about the same day each month. This resulted in a thorough cleaning of each patient's room once monthly and the virtual elimination of bugs.

Checklists like the one shown in Figure 30.2 were used to train aides in the housekeeping process. Although this particular checklist is not involved with cleaning, it does exemplify a set of steps that virtually anyone should be able to follow. The basic design for checklists applies to nearly all routines; only the content varies. Thus, housekeeping aides could be trained to systematically clean rooms while a supervisor occasionally watched them per-

Table 30.2: Purposes, Goals, and Problems of a Head Housekeeper

---

Purposes To keep the facility clean and sanitary for the residents; to see
that the work assigned to staff is done in the right way and in the
right order; and to maintain the laundry, housekeeping, and janitorial
services within the home.

Goals 1) to keep the home clean and safe for residents, employees, and
visitors.

2) to keep the laundry clean and repaired.

Problems 1) staff and own attendance, 2) interference from other departments,
and 3) not being informed of deaths and admissions to the hospital
(sic).

---

forming the steps and later examined the results. Checklists can be used not
only for training but also for maintaining adequate performances by the
aides. The head housekeeper's purposes were met, to a large extent, by this
method.

In summary, the research done in this and other nursing homes, as well as
at other sites by our research team, suggests that the problems noted by the
head of the housekeeping department of this nursing home might be easily
solved. Also, it is likely that absenteeism of staff would be reduced if there
were clearer job descriptions.

Dietary Services

Most visitors to a nursing home look first at the dining room. Thus, the
dietary department is also one of the most visible in the facility. Dietary staff
prepare the meals, serve the residents in the dining room or in their rooms,
clean the dining room and kitchen after meals, and begin preparing the next
meal or snack. The director of dietary services at one facility perceived her
role as shown in Table 30.3. Although she has stated appropriate goals, a
worthy purpose, and three very real problems, she has neglected to mention
one goal most critical to the care of nursing home patients: opportunities for
socializing.[19]

Results of the research team's studies indicated the importance of making
the meal setting more pleasant and indicated that aides and other staff
might be encouraging dependence at mealtimes. In another study, family-
style meal service at small tables seating four to six was compared with
institutional-style meal service at larger tables. Individual residents in-

Table 30.3: Purposes, Goals, and Problems of a Dietary Services Director

---

Purposes To fix and serve three nourishing and attractive meals each day,
     and to treat patients with dignity.

Goals 1) to meet each patient's personal food needs and amounts within
     their own special diet.

     2) to keep the budget down.

     3) to work together as a team.

Problems 1) keeping the eggs warm on the breakfast trays, 2) communications
     between nursing and the kitchen, and 3) repair of loose tile blocks on
     the kitchen floor, and provision of a runner on the floor in front of
     the sink that isn't slick.

---

teracted more than twice as often when dining family style, and the conversations were more evenly distributed among all residents. Residents seemed to recall better what had been eaten when served family style, although this was not experimentally confirmed. Food consumption seemed to be unaffected.[20]

In some preliminary work at one nursing home, dining room aides were observed while performing their tasks. Often, pressed to complete more "urgent" work, they failed to appear in the dining room. When present, however, nearly all their time was spent assisting in some way. Close observation revealed that assistance was usually total; that is, residents were rarely encouraged to finish feeding themselves once an aide had begun assisting. A better program would be one in which the aide is trained to patrol the dining room systematically, assisting only to the extent that help is needed. This can also be an occasion for providing social support to encourage the development of residents' independence and sociability. A set of easily understood written instructions describing each step in assistance at meals was developed as a part of a program to encourage residents to feed themselves (see Figure 30.2).[21] Initial observations indicated that many residents may need little more than some verbal encouragement. In a short time, many residents thought incapable of feeding themselves eventually did so. Residents' and relatives' evaluations of a videotaped sequence of mealtime routines indicated that a trained aide performed much better than an untrained aide in terms of efficiency, effectiveness, and humaneness of feeding assistance.

Nursing Care

Although we tend to think nursing care is always provided by licensed nurses, this is only partly true. Most nursing care in nursing homes is provided by geriatric aides who assist nurses in the medical care of patients. Much of their time is spent assisting residents with activities of daily living (dressing, bathing, transporting), as well as caring for medical needs by giving tests for blood sugar and acid levels in urine samples. Nurses dispense medications and treat lesions (e.g., bedsores). The director of nursing care in one nursing home perceived her role as described in Table 30.4.

Incontinence (uncontrolled bowel and/or bladder movements) appears to be a pervasive problem among nursing home residents. One study examined the frequency of incontinence encountered at 254 institutions in Utah, Massachusetts, and Virginia. The median proportion of incontinent patients per facility was reported at 19 percent, and the proportion of incontinent patients for all facilities combined was 30 percent.[22] One national survey indicated that 50 percent of all residents of nursing homes are incontinent.[23]

The so-called "senile" patient is not only incontinent but also nonambulatory, confused, dehydrated, and inactive.[24] Such patients are usually left in their own rooms without opportunities to experience the wider environment. Given the extent of the problem, how is it possible for a nursing department to guarantee consistent quality nursing care of each resident

Table 30.4: Purposes, Goals, and Problems of a Director of Nursing Services

---

Purposes To guarantee consistent quality, the best possible nursing care of each resident 24 hours every day; to have harmony among staff of all shifts; and to develop good working ties between nursing care and social behaviors.

Goals 1) to provide consistent quality care 24 hours.

2) to foster good intradepartmental working relationships in order to achieve total individualized care.

3) to develop an atmosphere among nursing staff which a) fosters pride, b) strengthens desire, and c) promotes learning.

Problems 1) continuity of good nursing care, right kind of help, and communication; 2) strained intradepartmental relationships, and 3) need pan flushes, and better quality in dispensing medications.

---

twenty-four hours every day? Our research group attempted to show how this problem might be approached by developing a system to integrate activities that were previously fragmented. In one of our studies, sixteen nonambulatory patients—one-fourth of whom were measurably dehydrated and inactive 75 percent of their waking hours, and all of whom were incontinent—were systematically visited once each hour by a trained assistant.[25] The assistant provided a set of services for severely impaired patients with the aid of a "comfort cart" loaded with diapers and linens, juices, and recreational equipment. Training of staff followed a prescribed sequence, and records were systematically kept on a checklist. When the procedures were followed, dehydration was eliminated, incontinence reduced by half, and engagement with the environment measurably increased. Nearly all individuals showed some improvement on all measures. While the "comfort cart" is busy with the more serious problems that require brief but skilled nursing care, a personal-care cart could be routinely making rounds visiting patients with less severe but more time-consuming problems. The second cart thus systematically patrols the same zone assisting with baths and showers, shaving, shampooing, nail care, grooming, changing clothes, and the like.

Social/Rehabilitation Activities

Last on our list of departments, and one usually receiving the least attention, is social/rehabilitation. Generally called "activities therapy," the social/rehabilitation department plans and conducts activities for residents intended to add to the quality of their lives. One director of social/rehabilitation in one nursing home described her purposes, goals, and problems as shown in Table 30.5. While this person's goals are certainly appropriate, they have not as yet been attained in many nursing homes. Achieving them is not a simple matter; for one thing, physical disabilities must be taken into account in any activities therapy.[26] Despite the difficulties, our research group was able to develop some effective methods for increasing levels of activity among patients.

In our early work we found that nursing home residents spent most of the day without engaging the environment.[27] In one series of studies, a method was found for increasing levels of participation for patients seated in geriatric chairs during much of the day.[28] When recreational equipment was placed on the tray of the "gerry chair,"[29] participation regularly increased, but this occurred only when residents were prompted orally or physically. In another study, designed to reduce inactivity and nonparticipation in the residents' lounge area, games and materials were displayed and made available for use.[30] When materials were given to residents, participation was high, but when the equipment was merely available, there was little increase in participation.

Table 30.5: Purposes, Goals, and Problems of a Social/Rehabilitation Director

<u>Purposes</u> To keep residents as mentally alert and active in their remaining years as possible; to offer them friendship; to help whenever they need me; and to serve as their contact with the family when they cannot do so.

<u>Goals</u> 1) to bring to the residents fun and stimulation through constructive activities.

2) to bring in as much of the outside community to the residents as possible so they won't have to feel they have nothing left and are shut off from the rest of the world.

<u>Problems</u> 1) more cooperation between departments is needed because there is a lack of communication sometimes with problems or changes in residents; 2) messages aren't always delivered to the activities department, especially from volunteers; and 3) appointments or programs (are often) set up without first discussing it with the activities department.

Effective methods of nursing home care are being developed, as we have seen. Beyond health and rehabilitation, however, nursing homes will have to concentrate on ways of providing a total ecology of the residents' living space.[31] That is, health and rehabilitation procedures will not be effective unless individuals are allowed to participate as fully as possible in the life of what is, after all, their home. In the next section, a training program for aides and nurses is described that could further effective and humane nursing home organization and management.

Formal Training Courses

In the spring of 1978, the research group was authorized to teach a state-approved course for training geriatric aides. The course offered both university credit and state certification. Its format followed Keller's[32] design, which permits students to work at their own pace through small units. The students were assisted by proctors who had earlier mastered a respective unit. Unit mastery was required, and students moved to the successive units only after they demonstrated knowledge of the current one. Several variations of Keller's plan were employed. One was the inclusion of a one-hour lecture and demonstration each week. Another, necessary to nearly all community-based educational programs, was a "hands-on" practicum. Here, students were required to practice the routines with fellow students and then to work under supervision of nursing staff with patients in their facility. The academic portion was supervised by a university faculty member, and the practicum by a registered nurse. Both supervisors participated in every portion of the course. Taught in this way, a course can provide the ingredients for a trained staff working efficiently and humanely with geriatric patients. Without supervision, however, the training is of little consequence. Since licensed nursing staff are the logical supervisors of geriatric (i.e., nursing) aides, we will focus on them in our discussion of supervision.

Supervision

Nurses, like many people placed in supervisory positions, tend to take the easy way out when the staff they are supervising fail to get the job done — they do it themselves. However, nurses are paid for highly skilled work and are required to perform a number of tasks that others cannot legally provide; nursing homes obviously cannot afford to allow nurses to undertake mundane tasks. There are supervisory skills nurses can learn that will help them avoid such tasks. A nurse may occasionally observe an aide performing a task, checklist the performance on the task, and provide the aide with constructive feedback. This simple procedure will allow the nurse more time to meet professional responsibilities.

In general, evaluations of aides should be scheduled frequently, perhaps once each week, until mastery is demonstrated. If mastery is not reached after several observations, further instructional sessions should be scheduled. Once mastery is demonstrated, the aide can be certified on that routine, but still should be observed occasionally. Evaluations should not be conducted covertly, but they do not have to be announced in advance. Feedback should be provided to the aide as soon as possible after the evaluation. He or she may choose to request additional evaluations.

In addition to the regular chain of command in a nursing home, it is useful to enlist the services of an external monitor. Such a person does not supervise anyone or intervene in the supervisory process. Rather, he or she observes the various daily activities of the home and makes regular reports to the administrator.

Conclusion

As many nursing homes add more buildings, more residents, and more beds, it becomes increasingly easy for a staff member to get lost in the crowd. If jobs are assigned on an "as needed" basis, it is difficult to evaluate the performance of individual employees. And when individual performances cannot be evaluated adequately, it is impossible to evaluate the performances of supervisors and, ultimately, of the administrator. Gains or losses in patient care and rehabilitation are difficult to measure accurately. Because gains or losses generally occur only over a long interval, they often are not taken into account in evaluation procedures. But without systematic evaluation, the staff is unable to learn better ways of caring for nursing home residents. Such evaluation should be attempted, since it is perhaps the best mechanism for preventing ineffective or even inhumane, though often inadvertent, practices within the nursing home.

Another desirable goal for nursing home staff is to promote more independence among residents. To achieve this goal, some modification is necessary in the organization and management of nursing homes. In particular, licensed nurses should be trained to act as supervisors of nursing home aides, and consultants should be enlisted to monitor the activities of the home. As a result of such organizational changes, those who work most closely with the residents would be able to receive adequate training in techniques that engender self-care among residents. For those who are capable of caring for themselves, at least partially, adjunctive programs such as day care and homemaker services could then be developed. Such programs will go a long way in reducing the dependence of many older people on total nursing home care. Perhaps Oak Knolls may one day be a reality.

Notes

1. M. A. Mendelsohn, *Tender Loving Greed* (New York: Random House, 1975).

2. Todd R. Risley and K. Anthony Edwards, "Behavioral Technology for Nursing Home Care: Toward a System of Nursing Home Organization and Management" (paper presented at the Nova Behavioral Conference on Aging, Port St. Lucie, Fl., May 1978).

3. U. S. Department of Commerce, *The Future of Long-Term Care in the United States — The Report of the Task Force*, DHEW Publication No. 00-16874 (Washington, D.C.: National Conference on Social Welfare, 1977).

4. Mendelsohn, op. cit.

5. Figures in this paragraph and the next are taken from Health Resources Administration, *Health: United States, 1975*, DHEW Publication No. (HRA) 76-1232 (Rockville, Md.: U. S. Department of Health, Education and Welfare, 1976).

6. Health Resources Administration, *Working With Older People: A Guide to Practice. I: The Practitioner and the Elderly*, DHEW Publication No. (HRA) 74-3116 (Washington, D.C.: U. S. Government Printing Office, 1974).

7. "Pension Plans Have Shaky Future," *Futurist* 11 (1977), pp. 251–253.

8. *Facts About Older Americans, 1976*, DHEW Publication No. (OHD) 77-20006 (Washington, D.C.: U. S. Government Printing Office, 1977).

9. A. M. Rivlin, *Long-Term Care for the Elderly and Disabled* (Washington, D.C.: U. S. Congressional Budget Office, 1977).

10. B. B. Manard, R. E. Woehle, and J. W. Heilman, *Better Homes for the Old* (Lex-

ington, Mass.: D. C. Heath, 1977).

11. E. V. Beverley, "Confronting the Challenge of Dependency in Old Age," *Geriatrics* 31 (1976), pp. 112–119.

12. Rivlin, op. cit.

13. Risley and Edwards, op. cit.

14. "How the Nation Looks at Nursing Homes," *American Health Care Journal* 3 (1977), pp. 57–60.

15. E. Z. Hughes, "Angry in Retirement," *Human Behavior* 3 (1974), pp. 56–59.

16. The nursing home in which department heads candidly gave their descriptions of departmental purposes, goals, and problems is a county home named Valleyview that houses 61 patients. It provides intermediate care and personal care. The care provided is far better than average, but the problems are typical. The administrator at Valleyview, Kathy Smith, has provided a great deal of assistance in much of the work reported in this and other papers.

17. The Living Environments Group, c/o Todd Risley, 313 Bristol Terrace, Lawrence, KS, 66044, stocks a wide range of important research papers on a variety of settings involving living environments such as day care centers for infants and toddlers, extended day care programs, institutions for the profoundly mentally retarded, and nursing homes. These and other materials are available on request.

18. It should be noted that schedule boards and their installation are not without problems. Staff have often objected to such visibility and, in this particular instance, the board was acceptable only in the nurses' lounge, away from public scrutiny.

19. A summary of this work was recently published in K. Anthony Edwards, "Dining Experiences in the Institutionalized Setting," *Nursing Homes* 28 (1979), pp. 6–17.

20. T. R. Risley, P. Gottula, and K. A. Edwards, "Social Interaction During Family- and Institutional-Style Meal Service in a Nursing Home" (paper presented at the Nova Behavioral Conference on Aging, Port St. Lucie, Fl., May 1978).

21. See Edwards, op. cit., and Risley and Edwards, op. cit.

22. Manard et al., op. cit.

23. Office of Nursing Home Affairs, *How to Select a Nursing Home* (Rockville, Md.: U. S. Department of Health, Education and Welfare, Public Health Service, 1976).

24. See K. Anthony Edwards, "Restoring Functional Behavior in 'Senile' Elderly," in J. Ferguson and C. B. Taylor, eds., *Comprehensive Handbook of Behavioral Medicine. Vol. 3: Extended Applications and Issues* (Jamaica, N.Y.: SP Medical and Scientific Books, in press).

25. P. F. Spangler, K. A. Edwards, and T. R. Risley, "Behavioral Care of Non-Ambulatory Geriatric Patients" (paper presented at the annual meeting of the Association for the Advancement of Behavior Therapy, Atlanta, Ga., December 1977).

26. The most frequent primary diagnoses at the last medical examination, for all ages of nursing home residents, are hardening of the arteries (22.5 percent), senility/old age/ill-defined conditions (13.6 percent), stroke (10.5 percent), and mental disorders (9.6 percent). With increase in age, hardening of the arteries and senility/old age/ill-defined conditions increase, while mental disorders decline. Most nursing home residents can read newspapers with glasses, although many have difficulty even with them, and about 3 percent are blind. With increased age, the incidence of visual difficulty increases. Difficulties with hearing are similar, but difficulties with speech

occur less often with older residents (85 plus) than with those who are younger (Health Resources Administration, *Health: United States, 1975*).

27. L. E. McClannahan and T. R. Risley, "Design of Living Environments for Nursing Home Residents: Increasing Participation in Recreation Activities," *Journal of Applied Behavior Analysis* 8 (1975), pp. 261–268.

28. L. E. McClannahan and T. R. Risley, "Activities and Materials for Severely Disabled Geriatric Patients," *Nursing Homes* 24 (1975), pp. 10–13.

29. "Gerry chairs" are similar in construction to a child's high chair.

30. McClannahan and Risley, "Design of Living Environments."

31. See T. R. Risley, "The Ecology of Applied Behavior Analysis," in A. Rogers-Warren and S. Warren, eds., *Ecological Perspectives in Behavior Analysis* (Baltimore, Md.: University Park Press, 1977), pp. 149–163; R. Sommer, *Personal Space: The Behavioral Basis of Design* (Englewood Cliffs, N.J.: Prentice-Hall, 1969); R. Sommer, *Tight Spaces: Hard Architecture and How to Humanize It* (Englewood Cliffs, N.J.: Prentice-Hall, 1974); and O. Lindsley, "Geriatric Behavioral Prosthetics," in R. Kastenbaum, ed., *New Thoughts on Old Age* (New York: Springer, 1964).

32. F. S. Keller and J. G. Sherman, *The Keller Plan Handbook* (Menlo Park, Calif.: W. A. Benjamin, 1974).

Bibliography

Abbott, M. H.; Abbey, H.; Bolling, D. R.; and Murphy, E. A. "The Familial Component in Longevity—A Study of Offspring of Nonagenarians: III Intrafamilial Studies." *American Journal of Medical Genetics* 2 (1978):105–120.

Abbott, M. H.; Murphy, E. A.; Bolling, D. R.; and Abbey, H. "The Familial Component in Longevity—A Study of Offspring of Nonagenarians: II Preliminary Analysis of the Completed Study." *Johns Hopkins Medical Journal* 134 (1974): 1–16.

Aberle, David F. "Culture and Socialization." In Francis L. K. Hsu (ed.), *Psychological Anthropology*. Homewood, Ill.: Dorsey Press, 1961.

Abramson, P. "Generational Change and the Decline of Party Identification in America: 1952–1974." *American Political Science Review* 70 (June 1976):469–478.

Adams, G. M., and deVries, H. A. "Physiological Effects of an Exercise Training Regimen Upon Women Aged 52 to 79." *Journal of Gerontology* 28 (1973):50–55.

Adler, M. "History of the Gerontological Society." *Journal of Gerontology* 13 (1958):94–100.

Agger, R.; Goldstein, M.; and Pearl, S. "Political Cynicism: Measurement and Meaning." *Journal of Politics* 23 (August 1961):477–506.

Aldrich, C. Knight. "Some Dynamics of Anticipatory Grief." In Bernard Schoenberg et al. (eds.), *Anticipatory Grief*. New York: Columbia University Press, 1974.

Altman, I. *The Environment and Social Behavior*. Monterey, Calif.: Brooks/Cole Publishing Co., 1975.

Alvirez, David, and Bean, Frank. "The Mexican-American Family." In Charles H. Mindel and Robert W. Habenstein (eds.), *Ethnic Families in America: Patterns and Variations*. New York: Elsevier, 1976.

Anderson, Barbara G. "The Process of Deculturation—Its Dynamics Among United States Aged." *Anthropological Quarterly* 45 (1972):209–216.

Anderson, J. E. *Public Policy-Making*. New York: Praeger Publishers, 1975.

Anderson, W. A., and Anderson, N. "The Politics of Age Exclusion: The Adults Only Movement in Arizona." *The Gerontologist* 18 (1978):6–12.

Andrew, W. *Cellular Changes With Age*. Springfield, Ill.: Charles C. Thomas, 1952.

Andrus Gerontology Center. "Social and Cultural Contexts of Aging." University of

Southern California, Community Survey Report, 1977.

Annett, M. "The Classification of Instances of Four Common Class Concepts by Children and Adults." *British Journal of Educational Psychology* 29 (1959):223–236.

Arenberg, D. "A Longitudinal Study of Problem Solving in Adults." *Journal of Gerontology* 29 (1974):650–658.

———. "Concept Problem Solving in Young and Old Adults." *Journal of Gerontology* 23 (1968):279–282.

Arth, Malcolm. "Ideals and Behavior: A Comment on Ibo Respect Patterns." *The Gerontologist* 8 (1968):242–244.

Astrand, I.; Astrand, P. O.; Hallback, I.; and Kilbom, A. "Reduction in Maximal Oxygen Uptake with Age." *Journal of Applied Physiology* 35 (1973):649–654.

Atchley, Robert C. *The Sociology of Retirement.* New York: Halsted Press, 1976.

Athanasiou, R., and Yoshioka, G. A. "The Spatial Character of Friendship Formation." *Environment and Behavior* 5 (1973):43–65.

Balazs, E. A. "Intercellular Matrix of Connective Tissue." In Caleb B. Finch and Leonard Hayflick (eds.), *Handbook of the Biology of Aging.* New York: Van Nostrand Reinhold Co., 1977.

Ball, Robert M. "Income Security After Retirement." *Social Policy, Social Ethics, and the Aging Society.* Chicago: Committee on Human Development, University of Chicago, 1976.

Baltes, P. B. "Longitudinal and Cross-sectional Sequences in the Study of Age and Generation Effects." *Human Development* 11 (1968):145–171.

Bane, Mary Jo. *Here to Stay: American Families in the Twentieth Century.* New York: Basic Books, 1976.

Bascue, L. O., and Lawrence, R. E. "A Study of Subjective Time and Death Anxiety in the Elderly." *Omega* Vol. 8, No. 1 (1977):81–90.

Bateson, Gregory. *Steps to an Ecology of Mind.* New York: Ballantine Books, 1972.

Batson, C. Daniel. "Experimentation in Psychology of Religion: An Impossible Dream." *Journal for the Scientific Study of Religion* Vol. 16, No. 4 (1977):413–418.

Bayley, N., and Oden, M. H. "The Maintenance of Intellectual Ability in Gifted Adults." *Journal of Gerontology* 10 (1955):91–107.

Bell, Bill, ed. *Contemporary Social Gerontology: Significant Developments in the Field of Aging.* Springfield, Ill.: Charles C. Thomas, 1976.

Bell, Bill, and Stanfield, G. G. "The Aging Stereotype in Experimental Perspective." *The Gerontologist* 13 (1973):341–344.

Bell, Daniel. "Ethnicity and Social Change." In Nathan Glazer and Daniel P. Moynihan (eds.), *Ethnicity: Theory and Experience.* Cambridge, Mass.: Harvard University Press, 1975.

Bender, A. D. "The Effect of Increasing Age on the Distribution of Peripheral Blood Flow in Man." *Journal of American Geriatric Society* 13 (1965):192–198.

Benet, S. *Abkhasians — The Long-Lived People of the Caucasus.* New York: Holt, Rinehart & Winston, 1974.

———. *How to Live to Be 100.* New York: Dial Press, 1976.

Bengtson, Vern L. "Ethnicity and Aging: Problems and Issues in Current Social Science Inquiry." In Donald E. Gelfand and A. J. Kutzik (eds.), *Ethnicity and Aging.* New York: Springer Publishing Co., 1979.

_____ . "Inter-age Differences in Perception and the Generation Gap." *The Gerontologist* 11 (1971):85–90.

Bengtson, Vern I.., and Cutler, N. E. "Generations and Intergenerational Relations: Perspectives on Age Groups and Social Change." In R. H. Binstock and E. Shanas (eds.), *Handbook of Aging and the Social Sciences.* New York: Van Nostrand Reinhold Co., 1976.

Bengtson, Vern L., and Kuypers, J. A. "Generational Differences and the Developmental Stake." *Aging and Human Development* 2 (1971):249–260.

Bengtson, Vern L.; Cuellar, Jose B.; and Ragan, Pauline K. "Stratum Contrasts and Similarities in Attitudes Toward Death." *Journal of Gerontology* Vol. 32, No. 1 (January 1977):76–88.

Bennet, R., and Eckman, J. "Attitudes Toward Aging: A Critical Examination of Recent Literature and Implications for Research." In C. Eisdorfer and M. P. Lawton (eds.), *The Psychology of Adult Development and Aging.* Washington, D.C.: American Psychological Association, 1973.

Berghorn, F. J.; Schafer, D. E.; Steere, G. H.; and Wiseman, R. F. *The Urban Elderly: A Study of Life Satisfaction.* Montclair, N.J.: Allanheld, Osmun & Co., 1978.

Bermant, Chaim. *Diary of an Old Man.* New York: Holt, Rinehart & Winston, 1966.

Bestinger, L.; Schachter, S.; and Back, W. *Social Pressures in Informal Groups.* New York: Harper & Row, 1960.

Beverley, E. V. "Confronting the Challenge of Dependency in Old Age." *Geriatrics* 31 (1976):112–119.

Bielby, D. D., and Papalia, D. E. "Moral Development and Egocentrism: Their Development and Interrelationship Across the Life-span." *International Journal of Aging and Human Development* 6 (1975):293–308.

Biggar, J. C. "The Sunning of America: Migration to the Sunbelt." *Population Bulletin* 32 (1979):1–43.

_____ . "Reassessing Sunbelt Migration." *Research on Aging* 2 (1980), in press.

_____ . "Who Moved Among the Elderly, 1965 to 1970: A Comparison of Types of Older Movers." *Research on Aging* 1 (1979), in press.

Biggar, J. C., and Longino, C. F., Jr. "Reassessing Sunbelt Migration: New Evidence." Paper presented at the Thirty-Second Annual Scientific Meeting of the Gerontological Society, November 1979.

Binstock, R. H. "Federal Policy Toward the Aging—Its Inadequacies and Its Politics." *National Journal Reports* 10 (1978):1838–1845.

Binstock, R. H., and Shanas, E., eds. *Handbook of Aging and the Social Sciences.* New York: Van Nostrand Reinhold Co., 1976.

Birren, James. "Increments and Decrements in the Intellectual Status of the Aged." *Psychiatric Research Reports* 23 (1968):207–214.

Birren, James, ed. *Handbook of Aging and the Individual: Psychological and Biological Aspects.* Chicago: University of Chicago Press, 1959.

Birren, James, and Morrison, D. F. "Analysis of the WAIS Subtests in Relation to Age and Education." *Journal of Gerontology* 16 (1961):363–369.

Black, Dean K. "Solidarity Across Generations: Elderly Parents and Their Middle-Aged Children." Paper presented at the Annual Meeting of the Gerontological Society, November 1973.

Black, Dean K., and Bengtson, Vern L. "The Measure of Solidarity: An Intergenerational Analysis." Paper presented at the Annual Meeting of the American Psychological Association, 1973.

Blenkner, Margaret. "Social Work and Family Relationships in Later Life with Some Thoughts on Filial Maturity." In Ethel Shanas and Gordon F. Streib (eds.) *Social Structure and the Family: Generational Relations*. Englewood Cliffs, N.J.: Prentice-Hall, 1965.

Block, J. H. "Conceptions of Sex Role: Some Cross-Cultural and Longitudinal Perspectives." *American Psychologist* 28 (1973):512–527.

Blonsky, L. E. "The Desire of Elderly Nonresidents to Live in a Senior Citizen Apartment Building." *The Gerontologist* 15 (1975):88–91.

Boren, H. G.; Kory, R. C.; and Syner, J. C. "The Veterans Administration–Army Cooperative Study of Pulmonary Function: II The Lung Volume and its Subdivisions in Normal Men." *American Journal of Medicine* 41 (1966):96–114.

Borzilleri, Thomas C. "The Need for a Separate Consumer Price Index for Older Persons." *The Gerontologist* 18 (1978):230–236.

Bowles, G. K. "Aged Migration: Research Summary." *Research on Aging* 2 (1980), in press.

Brandfonbrener, M.; Landowne, M.; and Shock, N. W. "Changes in Cardiac Output with Age." *Circulation* 12 (1955):557–566.

Brant, Charles S., ed. *Jim Whitewolf: The Life of a Kiowa Apache Indian*. New York: Dover Publications, 1969.

Breen, L. Z. "The Aging Individual." In C. Tibbitts (ed.), *Handbook of Social Gerontology*. Chicago: University of Chicago Press, 1960.

Brinley, J. F.; Jovick, T. J.; and McLaughlin, L. M. "Age, Reasoning, and Memory in Adults." *Journal of Gerontology* 29 (1974):182–189.

Brody, E. "The Etiquette of Filial Behavior." *Aging and Human Behavior* 1 (1970):87–94.

Brody, H. "Organization of the Cerebral Cortex: III A Study of Aging in the Human Cerebral Cortex." *Journal of Comparative Neurology* 102 (1955): 511–556.

Brody, H., and Vijayashankar, N. "Anatomical Changes in the Nervous System." In Caleb B. Finch and Leonard Hayflick (eds.), *Handbook of the Biology of Aging*. New York: Van Nostrand Reinhold Co., 1977.

Bromley, D. B. "Some Effects of Age on the Quality of Intellectual Output." *Journal of Gerontology* 12 (1957):318–323.

Brotman, Herman B. "Income and Poverty in the Older Population in 1975." *The Gerontologist* Vol. 17, No. 1 (February 1977):22–26.

Bultena, G. L., and Wood, V. "The American Retirement Community: Bane or Blessing?" *Journal of Gerontology* 24 (1969):209–217.

Burgess, Ernest W. *Aging in Western Societies*. Chicago: University of Chicago Press, 1960.

Burgess, Ernest W.; Tibbetts, C.; Havighurst, R. J.; and Cavan, R. W. "Social Adjustment in Old Age: A Planning Report." New York: Social Science Research Council, 1946.

Burns, R. B. "Age and Mental Ability: Re-testing with Thirty-Three Years Interval." *British Journal of Educational Psychology* 36 (1966):116.

Butler, Robert N. "Age-ism: Another Form of Bigotry." *The Gerontologist* 9 (1969): 243–246.

_____ . *Why Survive? Being Old in America.* New York: Harper & Row, 1975.

Butler, Robert N., and Lewis, Myrna I. *Aging and Mental Health.* 2d ed. St. Louis: C. V. Mosby Co., 1977.

Byrne, Don. "Interpersonal Attraction as a Function of Affiliation Need and Attitude Similarity." *Human Relations* 14 (1961):283–289.

_____ . "A Pregnant Pause in the Sexual Revolution." *Psychology Today* Vol. 11, No. 2 (July 1977):67–68.

Campbell, Angus. "Politics Through the Life Cycle." *The Gerontologist* 11 (1971): 112–117.

Campbell, David E. "Evaluation Research in Man-Environment Systems." *JSAS Catalogue of Selected Documents in Psychology* 6 (1976).

_____ . "Evaluation of the Built Environment: Lessons from Program Evaluation." In L. M. Ward, S. Coren, A. Gruft, and J. B. Collins (eds.), *The Behavioral Basis of Design, Book I.* Stroudsburg, Pa.: Dowden, Hutchinson and Ross, 1976.

Cantor, Marjorie. "Effect of Ethnicity on Life Styles of the Inner-City Elderly." In M. Powell Lawton, Robert J. Newcomer, and Thomas O. Byerts (eds.), *Community Planning for an Aging Society.* Stroudsburg, Pa.: Dowden, Hutchinson and Ross, 1976.

Carlie, M. K. "The Politics of Age: Interest Group or Social Movement?" *The Gerontologist* 9 (1969):259–263.

Carp, F. M. *A Future for the Aged.* Austin: University of Texas Press, 1966.

_____ . "Effects of Living and Housing of Middle-Aged and Older People." In F. M. Carp (ed.), *Patterns of Living and Housing of Middle-Aged and Older People.* Washington, D.C.: U.S. Government Printing Office, 1966.

_____ . "The Elderly and Levels of Adaptation to Changed Surroundings." In L. A. Pastalan and D. H. Carson (eds.), *Spatial Behavior of Older People.* Ann Arbor: University of Michigan Press, 1970.

_____ . "Impact of Improved Living Environment on Health and Life Expectancy." *The Gerontologist* 17 (1977):242–249.

_____ . "Living Environments of Older People." In R. H. Binstock and E. Shanas (eds.), *Handbook of Aging and the Social Sciences.* New York: Van Nostrand Reinhold Co., 1976.

_____ . "Person-Situation Congruence in Engagement." *The Gerontologist* 8 (1968): 184–188.

_____ . "Short-Term and Long-Term Prediction of Adjustment to a New Environment." *Journal of Gerontology* 29 (1974):444–453.

Carpenter, W. L. "The Relationship Between Age and Information Processing Capacity of Adults." *Industrial Gerontology* 8 (1971):55–57.

Cattell, R. B. *Abilities: Their Structure, Growth, and Action.* Boston: Houghton Mifflin Co., 1971.

Center for Public Management. *Curriculum Research Findings and Training Intervention Strategies for Strengthening the Capacities of Area Agencies on Aging.* A final report submitted to the AoA, 1976.

Chatfield, Walter F. "Economic and Sociological Factors Influencing Life Satisfaction of the Aged." *Journal of Gerontology* Vol. 32, No. 5 (September 1977):593–599.

Chevan, Albert, and Korson, J. Henry. "The Widowed Who Live Alone: An Examination of Social and Demographic Factors." *Social Forces* 51 (1972):45–53.

Cicirelli, V. G. "Relationships of Siblings to the Elderly Person's Feelings and Concerns." *Journal of Gerontology* 25 (1970):317–322.

Clark, M. "An Anthropological View of Retirement." In Francis Carp (ed.), *Retirement*. New York: Behavioral Publications, 1972.

———. "The Anthropology of Aging, A New Area for Studies of Culture and Personality." *The Gerontologist* 7 (1967):55–64.

———. "Cultural Values and Dependency in Later Life." In Donald O. Cowgill and Lowell D. Holmes (eds.), *Aging and Modernization*. New York: Appleton-Century-Crofts, 1972.

Clark, M., and Anderson, Barbara G. *Culture and Aging: An Anthropological Study of Older Americans*. Springfield, Ill.: Charles C. Thomas, 1967.

Clark, M. and Mendelson, Monique. "Mexican-American Aged in San Francisco: A Case Description." *The Gerontologist* 9 (1969):90–95.

Cobb, R. W., and Elder, C. D. *Participation in American Politics*. Baltimore, Md.: Johns Hopkins University Press, 1975.

Coles, Robert. *The Old Ones of New Mexico*. New York: Doubleday & Co., 1975.

Comalli, P. E.; Wapner, S.; and Werner, H. "Perception of Verticality in Middle and Old Age." *Journal of Psychology* 47 (1959):259–266.

Comfort, A. *Aging, The Biology of Senescence*. London: Routledge & Kegan Paul, 1964.

———. *The Biology of Senescence*. New York: Elsevier, 1979.

Committee on Human Development. *Social Policy, Social Ethics, and the Aging Society*. Chicago: Committee on Human Development, University of Chicago, 1976.

Converse, P. E., et al. "Continuity and Change in American Politics: Parties and Issues in the 1968 Election." *American Political Science Review* 63 (December 1969): 1101–1105.

Cowgill, Donald O., and Holmes, Lowell D., eds. *Aging and Modernization*. New York: Appleton-Century-Crofts, 1972.

Crockett, W. H.; Press, A. N.; and Osterkamp, L. "The Effect of Deviations From Stereotyped Expectations Upon Attitudes Toward Older Persons." *Journal of Gerontology* 34 (1979):368–374.

Crouch, Ben. "Age and Institutional Support: Perception of Older Mexican-Americans." *Journal of Gerontology* 27 (1972):524–529.

Cuellar, Jose. "El Senior Citizens Club: The Older Mexican-American in the Voluntary Association." in B. Myerhoff and A. Simić (eds.), *Life's Career – Aging: Cultural Variations on Growing Old*. Beverly Hills, Calif.: Sage Publications, 1978.

Cutler, N. "Aging and Generations in Politics: The Conflict of Explanations and Inference." In A. R. Wilcox (ed.), *Public Opinion and Political Attitudes*. New York: John Wiley & Sons, 1974.

———. "A Foundation for Research in 'Political Gerontology.'" *American Political Science Review* 71 (September 1977):1011–1025.

Cutler, N., and Bengtson, V. "Age and Political Alienation: Maturation, Generation, and Period Effects." *Annals of the American Academy of Political and Social Sciences* 415 (September 1974):160–175.

Cyrus-Lutz, C., and Gaitz, C. M. "Psychiatrists' Attitudes Toward the Aged and Aging." *The Gerontologist* 12 (1972):163–167.

Dahl, R. *Pluralist Democracy in the United States.* Chicago: Rand McNally & Co., 1967.

Davies, C.T.M. "The Oxygen Transport System in Relation to Age." *Clinical Science* 42 (1972):1–13.

Davies, D. *The Centenarians of the Andes.* London: Barrie and Jenkins, 1975.

Davis, Dolores. "Guide for Minority Aging Program at the Institute of Gerontology, University of Michigan: Student Perception Approach." Ph. D. dissertation, School of Education, University of Michigan, Ann Arbor, 1974.

Dawson, R. E. *Public Opinion and Contemporary Disarray.* New York: Harper & Row, 1973.

Degueker, J.; Remans, J.; Franssen, R.; and Waes, J. "Aging Patterns of Trabecular and Cortical Bone and Their Relationships." *Calcium Tissue Research* 7 (1971):23–30.

Dehn, M. M., and Bruce, R. A. "Longitudinal Variations in Maximal Oxygen Intake with Age and Activity." *Journal of Applied Physiology* 33 (1972):805–807.

Demkovich, L. E. "Senior Citizens Groups Put Past Differences Aside in the Hope of Improving the Plight of the Elderly." *National Journal Reports* 10 (1978):1726–1727.

Denney, D. R., and Denney, N. W. "The Use of Classification for Problem Solving: A Comparison of Middle and Old Age." *Developmental Psychology* 9 (1973):275–278.

Denney, D. R.; Denney, N. W.; and Ziobrowski, M. J. "Alterations in the Information-processing Strategies of Young Children Following Observations of Adult Models." *Developmental Psychology* 8 (1973):202–208.

Denney, N. W. "Classification Abilities in the Elderly." *Journal of Gerontology* 29 (1974):309–314.

_____ . "Classification Criteria in Middle and Old Age." *Developmental Psychology* 10 (1974):901–906.

_____ . "Evidence for Developmental Change in Categorization Criteria for Children and Adults." *Human Development* 17 (1974):41–53.

Denney, N. W., and Acito, M. "Classification Training in Two- and Three-Year-Old Children." *Journal of Experimental Child Psychology* 17 (1974):37–48.

Denney, N. W., and Cornelius, S. "Class Inclusion and Multiple Classification in Middle Age and Old Age." *Developmental Psychology* 11 (1975):521–522.

Denney, N. W., and Denney, D. R. "Modeling Effects on the Questioning Strategies of the Elderly." *Developmental Psychology* 10 (1974):400–404.

Denney, N. W., and Lennon, M. L. "Classification: A Comparison of Middle and Old Age." *Developmental Psychology* 7 (1972):210–213.

Dennis, W., and Mallinger, B. "Animism and Related Tendencies in Senescence." *Journal of Gerontology* 4 (1949):218–221.

Doherty, N.; Segal, J.; and Hicks, B. "Alternatives to Institutionalization for the Aged: Viability and Cost Effectiveness." *Aged Care and Services Review* 1 (1978):3–16.

Donahue, W. "Development and Current Status of University Instruction in Social Gerontology." In R. E. Kushner and M. E. Bunch (eds.), *Graduate Education in Aging Within the Social Sciences.* Ann Arbor: Division of Gerontology, University of Michigan, 1967.

_____ . "Impact of Living Arrangements on Ego Development in the Elderly." In F.

M. Carp (ed.), *Patterns of Living and Housing of Middle-Aged and Older People.* Washington, D.C.: U.S. Government Printing Office, 1966.

———— . "Training in Social Gerontology." *Geriatrics* 15 (1960):801–809.

Douvan, Elizabeth. "Changes in the Family and Later Life." Unpublished ms., Survey Research Center, University of Michigan, Ann Arbor.

Dowd, James J. "Aging as Exchange: A Preface to Theory." *Journal of Gerontology* 30 (1975):584–594.

Dowd, James J., and Bengtson, Vern L. "Aging in Minority Populations: An Examination of the Double Jeopardy Hypothesis." *Journal of Gerontology* 33 (1978):427–436.

Droppelt, J. E., and Wallace, W. L. "Standardization of the Wechsler Adult Intelligence Scale for Older Persons." *Journal of Abnormal and Social Psychology* 51 (1955):312–330.

Dubois, H. "Water and Electrolyte Content of Human Skeletal Muscle: Variation with Age." *Review of French Studies of Clinical Biology* 17 (1972):503–513.

Easton, Dorothy M. "Alex Comfort Speaks on Sex and Aging." *Multi-Media Resource Guide* Vol. 1, No. 1 (1976).

Edwards, K. Anthony. "Dining Experiences in the Institutionalized Setting." *Nursing Homes* 28 (1979):6–17.

Eisdorfer, C., and Wilkie, F. "Intellectual Changes with Advancing Age." In L. F. Garvick, C. Eisdorfer, and J. E. Blum (eds.), *Intellectual Functioning in Adults.* New York: Springer Publishing Co., 1973.

Eisdorfer, C.; Busse, E. W.; and Cohen, L. D. "The WAIS Performance of an Aged Sample: The Relationship Between Verbal and Performance I.Q.'s." *Journal of Gerontology* 14 (1959):197–201.

Eisenstadt, S. N. "Transformation of Social, Political, and Cultural Orders in Modernization." In S. N. Eisenstadt (ed.), *Comparative Perspectives on Social Change.* Boston: Little, Brown & Co., 1968.

Ellison, David L. "Alienation and the Will to Live." *Journal of Gerontology* 24 (1969): 361–367.

Erikson, Erik H. *Childhood and Society.* 2d ed. New York: W. W. Norton & Co., 1963.

Erikson, R., and Luttberg, N. *American Public Opinion: Its Origins, Content and Impact.* New York: John Wiley & Sons, 1973.

Etzioni, Amitai. "'Alternatives' to Nursing Homes." *Human Behavior* 3 (1974):10–12.

Eveleth, P. B., and Tanner, J. M. *Worldwide Variation in Human Growth.* International Biological Programme, vol. 8. New York: Cambridge University Press, 1976.

Everitt, A. B. "Food Intake, Growth and the Aging of Collagen in Rat Tail Tendon." *Gerontologia* 17 (1971):98–104.

Fandetti, Donald V., and Gelfand, Donald E. "Care of the Aged: Attitudes of White Ethnic Families." *The Gerontologist* 16 (1976):544–549.

Ferrari, N. A. "Freedom of Choice." *Social Work* 8 (1963):104–106.

———— . "Institutionalization and Attitude Change in an Aged Population: A Field Study and Dissidence Theory." Ph.D. dissertation, Western Reserve University, 1962.

Flacks, R. "The Liberated Generation: An Exploration of the Roots of Student Protest." *Journal of Social Issues* 23 (1967):52–75.

Flavell, J. H. "Cognitive Changes in Adulthood." In L. B. Goulet and P. B. Baltes (eds.), *Life-span Developmental Psychology: Research and Theory*. New York: Academic Press, 1970.

———. *The Developmental Psychology of Jean Piaget*. New York: Van Nostrand Reinhold Co., 1963.

Foulds, G. A., and Raven, J. C. "Neural Changes in Mental Abilities of Adults as Age Advances." *Journal of Mental Science* 94 (1948):133–142.

Franke, H. W., and Wilcok, R. C. "A Syllabus and Annotated Bibliography on the Economics of an Aging Population." Ann Arbor: Division of Gerontology, University of Michigan, 1959.

Freeman, J. L. *The Political Process: Executive-Bureau-Legislative Committee Relations*. New York: Doubleday & Co., 1955.

Friedberger, E.; Brock, G.; and Furstenheim, A. "Zur Normalantikorperkurve des Menschen Durch Die Verschiedenen Lebensalter und Ihre Bedentung fur die Erklarung der Hautteste." *Z Immunitatforsch* 64 (1929):294–319.

Friedmann, A.; Zabe, E.; Zimring, C., eds. *Environmental Design Evaluation*. New York: Plenum Publishing Corp., 1978.

Friend, C. M., and Zubek, J. P. "The Effects of Age on Critical Thinking Ability." *Journal of Gerontology* 13 (1958):407–413.

Frubel-Osipora, S. I. *The Basis of Gerontology*. New York: Academic Press, 1969.

Fuller, Edward. "Aging Among South African Bantu." In Donald O. Cowgill and Lowell D. Holmes (eds.), *Aging and Modernization*. New York: Appleton-Century-Crofts, 1972.

Futuhata, T., and Eguchi, M. "The Change of the Agglutinin Titer with Age." *Proceedings of the Japanese Academy* 31 (1955):555–557.

Gallop, P. M.; Paz, M. A.; Pereyera, B.; and Blumenfeld, O. O. "The Maturation of Connective Tissue Proteins." *Israel Journal of Chemistry* 12 (1974):305–317.

Garetz, F. K. "The Psychiatrist's Involvement with Older Patients." *American Journal of Psychiatry* 132 (1975):63–65.

Garfinckle, R. "The Reluctant Therapist." *The Gerontologist* 15 (1975):136–137.

Gelfand, Donald E., and Black, M. R. "Two Generations of Elderly in the Changing American Family: Implications for Family Services." *Family Coordinator* 27 (1978):395–403.

Gibson, Robert M.; Mueller, Marjorie S.; and Fisher, Charles R. "Age Differences in Health Care Spending: Fiscal Year 1976." *Social Security Bulletin* Vol. 40, No. 8 (August 1977):3–14.

Gilmour, R., and Lamb, R. *Political Alienation in Contemporary America*. New York: St. Martin's Press, 1975.

Glaser, Barney A. "The Social Loss of Aged Dying Patients." *The Gerontologist* Vol. 6, No. 2 (June 1966):77–80.

Glazer, Nathan. "Introduction." In Nathan Glazer and Daniel P. Moynihan (eds.), *Ethnicity: Theory and Experience*. Cambridge, Mass.: Harvard University Press, 1975.

Glazer, Nathan, and Moynihan, Daniel P. *Beyond the Melting Pot.* Cambridge, Mass.: M.I.T. Press, 1963.

Glenn, N. D. "Aging and Conservatism." *Annals of the American Academy of Political and Social Sciences* 415 (September 1974):176–186.

Glueck, C. J.; Gartside, P. S.; Fallat, R. W.; Sielski, J.; and Steiner, P. M. "Longevity Syndromes: Familial Hypobeta and Familial Hyperalphalipoproteinemia." *Journal of Laboratory Clinical Medicine* 88 (1976):941–957.

Glueck, C. J.; Gartside, P. S.; Steiner, P. M.; Miller, M.; Todhunte, T.; Haaf, J.; and Pucke, M. "Hyperalphalipoproteinemia and Hypobetalipoproteinemia in Octogenarian Kindreds." *Atherosclerosis* 27 (1977):387–406.

Gochros, Harvey L. "A Concentration in Social Work Practice with Sex Related Problems." *Journal of Education for Social Work* Vol. 10, No. 2 (Spring 1974):40–46.

Gochros, Harvey L., and Gochros, Jean S. *The Sexually Oppressed.* New York: Association Press, 1977.

Golant, S. M. "Spatial Context of Residential Moves by Elderly Persons." *International Journal of Aging and Human Development* 8 (1977):279–289.

Golde, P., and Kogan, N. "A Sentence Completion Procedure for Assessing Attitudes Toward Old People." *Journal of Gerontology* 14 (1959): 355–363.

Goldfarb, A. E.; Shaninian, S. P.; and Burr, H. T. "Death Rate of Relocated Nursing Home Residents." In D. P. Kent, R. Kastenbaum, and S. Sherwood (eds.), *Research Planning and Action for the Elderly.* New York: Behavioral Publications, 1972.

Goode, William J. *The Family.* Englewood Cliffs, N.J.: Prentice-Hall, 1964.

Gouldner, Alvin W. "Reciprocity and Autonomy in Functional Theory." In Llewellyn Gross (ed.), *Symposium on Sociological Theory.* New York: Harper & Row, 1957.

_____ . "The Norm of Reciprocity: A Preliminary Statement." *American Sociological Review* Vol. 25, No. 2 (April 1960):161–178.

Grad, Susan. *Income of the Population Age 60 and Older, 1971.* Washington, D. C.: U.S. Department of Health, Education, and Welfare, Social Security Administration, Office of Research and Statistics, 1977.

Greeley, Andrew. "An Alternative Perspective for Studying American Ethnicity." In A. Greeley (ed.), *Ethnicity in the United States: A Preliminary Reconnaissance.* New York: John Wiley & Sons, 1974.

Greenberg, L. J., and Yunis, E. J. "Histocompability Determinants, Immune Responsiveness and Aging in Man." *Federation Proceedings* 37 (1978).

Gubrium, Jaber F. *The Myth of the Golden Years: A Socio-Environmental Theory of Aging.* Springfield, Ill.: Charles C. Thomas, 1973.

Gubrium, Jaber F., ed. *Late Life: Communities and Environmental Policy.* Springfield, Ill.: Charles C. Thomas, 1974.

Gutman, Herbert. "Work, Culture and Society in Industrializing America." *American Historical Review* 78 (1973):531–587.

Guttman, E. "Muscle." In Caleb B. Finch and Leonard Hayflick (eds.), *Handbook of the Biology of Aging.* New York: Van Nostrand Reinhold Co., 1977.

Guttman, E., and Hanzlikova, V. "Motor Unit in Old Age." *Nature* 209 (1966): 921–922.

Hall, D. A. *Aging of Connective Tissue.* New York: Academic Press, 1976.

Hamovitch, M. B. "Social and Psychological Factors in Adjustment in a Retirement Community." In F. M. Carp (ed.), *The Retirement Process*. Washington, D.C.: U.S. Government Printing Office, 1968.

Hansen, H. J. "Studies of Pathology of the Lumbosacral Disc in Female Cattle." *Acta Orthopaed Scandia* 25 (1956):161–182.

Hanson, Perry, "The Activity Patterns of the Elderly Householder." *Geografiska Annaler* Vol. 59, Series B, No. 2 (1978):109–124.

Hardcastle, David A. "Work and Welfare: A Policy and Practice Model." *Journal of Social Welfare* Vol. 2, No. 3 (Winter 1975):63–75.

Hareven, Tamara. "Family Time and Industrial Time." *Journal of Urban History* 1 (1975):365–389.

Harris, Louis, and Associates. *The Myth and Reality of Aging in America*. Washington, D.C.: National Council on Aging, 1975.

Hart, C.W.M., and Pilling, A. R. *The Tiwi of North Australia*. New York: Holt, Rinehart & Winston, 1960

Hartman, C.; Horovitz, J.; and Herman, R. "Designing with the Elderly." *The Gerontologist* 16 (1976):303–311.

Hauser, Philip M. "Aging and World-Wide Population Change." In R. H. Binstock and E. Shanas (eds.), *Handbook of Aging and the Social Sciences*. New York: Van Nostrand Reinhold Co., 1976.

Havighurst, Robert J. "The Future Aged: The Use of Time and Money." *The Gerontologist* Vol. 15, No. 1 (February 1975):10–14.

Hawkins, Leo F. "The Impact of Policy Decisions on Families." *The Family Coordinator* 22 (1979):264–271.

Heglin, H. J. "Problem Solving Set in Different Age Groups." *Journal of Gerontology* 11 (July 1956):310–316.

Heilbroner, Robert L. *The Making of Economic Society*. Englewood Cliffs, N.J.: Prentice-Hall, 1972.

Helfman, P., and Bada, J. "Aspartic Acid Racemization in Dentine as a Measure of Aging." *Nature* 262 (1975):279–281.

Heller, L. T., and Whitehorn, W. V. "Age-Associated Alterations in Myocardial Contractile Properties." *American Journal of Physiology* 222 (1972):1613–1619.

Hess, Beth B., and Waring, Joan M. "Changing Patterns of Aging and Family Bonds in Later Life." *Family Coordinator* 27 (1978):303–314.

Hickey, T., and Davies, C. T. "The White House Conference on Aging: An Exercise in Policy Formulation." *Aging and Human Development* 3 (1972):233–238.

Hirschberg, G., and Gilliland, A. R. "Parent-Child Relationships in Attitudes." *Journal of Abnormal and Social Psychology* 37 (1942):125–130.

Hobart, Charles W. "Commitment, Value Conflict and the Future of the American Family." *Journal of Marriage and Family Living* 25 (1963):405–415.

Holloway, H., and George, J. *Public Opinion: Coalitions, Elites, and Masses*. New York: St. Martin's Press, 1979.

Holmes, Lowell D. "The Role and Status of the Aged in a Changing Samoa." In Donald D. Cowgill and Lowell D. Holmes (eds.), *Aging and Modernization*. New York: Appleton-Century-Crofts, 1972.

Holtzman, A. "Analysis of Old Age Politics in the United States." In C. B. Vedder (ed.), *Gerontology: A Book of Readings*. Springfield, Ill.: Charles C. Thomas, 1963.

Homans, George C. "Social Behavior as Exchange." *American Journal of Sociology* Vol. 63, No. 6 (May 1958):597–606.

Horn, J. L. "Organization of Data on Life-Span Development of Human Abilities." In L. B. Goulet and P. B. Baltes (eds.), *Life-Span Developmental Psychology: Research and Theory*. New York: Academic Press, 1970.

Horn, J. L., and Cattell, R. B. "Age Differences in Fluid and Crystallized Intelligence." *Acta Psychologica* 26 (1967):107–129.

Hout, M., and Knoke, D. "Change in Voting Turnout, 1952–1972." *Public Opinion Quarterly* 39 (Spring 1975):52–68.

"How the Nation Looks at Nursing Homes." *American Health Care Journal* 3 (1977): 57–60.

Hoyt, Danny R., and Babchuk, Nicholas. "Ethnicity and the Voluntary Associations of the Aged." Paper presented at the Society for the Study of Social Problems meetings, September 1978.

Hruza, Z. "Aging of Cells and Molecules." *Handbuch der Allberg Pathology* 4 (1972): 83–108.

Hsu, Francis L. K. "American Core Value and National Character." In F.L.K. Hsu (ed.), *Psychological Anthropology: Approaches to Culture and Personality*. Homewood, Ill.: Dorsey Press, 1961.

————— . "Incentives to Work in Primitive Communities." *American Sociological Review* Vol. 8, No. 6 (December 1943):638–642.

Huang, Lucy Jen. "The Chinese American Family." In Charles H. Mindel and Robert W. Habenstein (eds.), *Ethnic Families in America: Patterns and Variations*. New York: Elsevier, 1976.

Hudson, Robert B. "Client Politics and Federalism: The Case of the Older Americans Act." Paper presented at the American Political Science Association meetings, 1973.

————— . "Rational Planning and Organizational Imperatives: Prospects for Area Planning in Aging." *Annals of the American Academy of Political and Social Sciences* 415 (September 1974):41–54.

Hughes, E. Z. "Angry in Retirement." *Human Behavior* 3 (1974):56–59.

Inhelder, B., and Piaget, J. *The Early Growth of Logic in the Child*. New York: Harper & Row, 1964.

Ippolito, D.; Walker, T.; and Kolson, K. *Public Opinion and Responsible Democracy*. Englewood Cliffs, N.J.: Prentice-Hall, 1976.

Ivester, C., and King, K. "Attitudes of Adolescents Toward the Aged." *The Gerontologist* 17 (1977):85–89.

Jackson, D. S. *Aging, Advances in Biology of Skin*. Vol. 6. New York: Pergamon Press, 1965.

Jackson, Hobart. "National Caucus on the Black Aged: A Progress Report." *Aging and Human Development* 2 (August 1971):226–231.

————— . "Origin of the National Caucus on the Black Aged." An address to the National Caucus on the Black Aged, Indianapolis, Indiana, June 17, 1972.

Jackson, Jacquelyne Johnson. "Aged Negroes: Their Cultural Departures From Statistical Stereotypes and Rural-Urban Differences." *The Gerontologist* 10 (1970):140–145.

_____ . "Present Training Programs." Symposia of the Twenty-Fifth Annual Scientific Meeting of the Gerontological Society, San Juan, Puerto Rico, December 21, 1972.

_____ . "Aged Blacks: A Potpourri in the Direction of the Reduction of Inequities." In Beth B. Hess (ed.), *Growing Old in America*. New Brunswick, N.J.: Transaction Books, 1976.

James, Muriel, and Jongeward, Dorothy. *Born To Win*. Menlo Park, Calif.: Addison-Wesley Publishing Co., 1971.

Jaros, D. *Socialization to Politics*. New York: Praeger Publishers, 1973.

Jarvik, L. F., and Blum, J. E. "Cognitive Declines as Predictors of Mortality in Twin Pairs: A Twenty-Year Longitudinal Study of Aging." In E. Palmore and F. Jeffers (eds.), *Prediction of Lifespan*. Lexington, Mass.: D. C. Heath & Co., 1971.

"Life for the Elderly in 1975—Many Are Hungry and Afraid." *U.S. News and World Report* 78 (February 10, 1975):48–51.

Lipman, A. "Public Housing and Attitudinal Adjustment in Old Age." *Journal of Geriatric Psychiatry* 2 (1968):88–101.

Lipset, S. M., and Raab, E. "The Election and the National Mood." *Commentary* 55 (January 1973):43–50.

Litwak, E. "Family and Primary Group Options." Paper presented at the Twenty-Ninth Annual Scientific Meeting of the Gerontological Society, November 1976.

Long, L. H., and Hansen, K. A. "Reasons for Interstate Migration." *Current Population Reports* P-2381 (1979):1–32.

Longino, C. F., Jr. "Going Home: Aged Return Migration in the United States, 1965–70." *Journal of Gerontology* Vol. 34, No. 5 (1979):736–745.

_____ . "Intrastate Migration of the Elderly." In C. B. Flynn, J. C. Biggar, C. F. Longino, Jr., and R. F. Wiseman (eds.), *Aged Migration in the United States, 1965–70: Final Report*. Washington, D.C.: National Institute on Aging, 1979.

_____ . "Movement To, From and Within Metropolitan and Non-Metropolitan Settings, 1965–70." *Research on Aging* 2 (1980), in press.

Looft, W. R., and Charles, D. C. "Egocentrism and Social Interaction in Young and Old Adults." *International Journal of Aging and Human Development* 2 (1971):21–28.

Lopata, Helena Z. *Polish Americans: Status Competition in an Ethnic Community*. Englewood Cliffs, N.J.: Prentice-Hall, 1976.

_____ . *Widowhood in an American City*. Cambridge, Mass.: Schenkman Publishing Co., 1973.

Lowi, T. J. "American Business, Public Policy, Case-Studies, and Political Theory." *World Politics* 16 (1964):677–715.

Lowry, C. H.; Hastings, B. A.; Hull, T. Z.; and Brown, A. N. "Histochemical Changes Associated with Aging." *Biological Chemistry* 143 (1942):271–280.

Makinodan, T. "Immunity and Aging." In Caleb B. Finch and Leonard Hayflick (eds.), *Handbook of the Biology of Aging*. New York: Van Nostrand Reinhold, 1977.

Manard, B. B.; Woehle, R. E.; and Heilman, J. W. *Better Homes for the Old*. Lexington Mass.: D. C. Heath & Co., 1977.

Maslow, Abraham. *Motivation and Personality*. New York: Harper & Row, 1970.

Mason, J. Barry, and Bearden, William D. "Profiling the Shopping Behavior of the Elderly Consumers." *The Gerontologist* Vol. 18, No. 5 (October 1978):454–461.

Massachusetts State Housing Board. *Standards of Design: Housing for the Elderly.* Boston, Mass., 1954.

Maugh, T. H. "Any Horse Trader Could Have Told You." *Science* 205 (1979):574.

Mazess, R. B., and Forman, S. H. "Longevity and Age Exaggeration in Vilcabamba, Ecuador." *Journal of Gerontology* 34 (1979):94–98.

McCay, C. M., and Crowell, M. F. "Prolonging the Lifespan." *Science Monthly* 39 (1934):405–414.

McClannahan, L. E. "Design of Living Environments for Nursing Home Residents." Ph.D. dissertation, Department of Human Develoment, University of Kansas, 1973.

McClannahan, L. E., and Risley, T. R. "Design of Living Environments for Nursing Home Residents: Increasing Participation in Recreation Activities." *Journal of Applied Behavior Analysis* 8 (1975):261–268.

McClelland, K. A.; Longino, C. F., Jr.; and Peterson, W. A. "The Aged Subculture Hypothesis: Social Integration, Gerontophilia and Self-Regard." Paper presented at the Thirty-Second Annual Scientific Meeting of the Gerontological Society, November 1979.

McGinnis, R. "A Stochastic Model of Social Mobility." *American Sociological Review* 33 (1968):712–722.

McKeown, F. *Pathology of the Aged.* London: Butterworth & Co., 1965.

McTavish, D. G. "Perceptions of Old People: A Review of Research Methodologies and Findings." *The Gerontologist* Vol. 11, No. 4, part 2, (1971):90–101.

Mendelsohn, M. A. *Tender Loving Greed.* New York: Random House, 1975.

Messer, Mark. "Race Differences in Selected Attitudinal Dimensions of the Elderly." *The Gerontologist* 8 (1968):245–249.

Milbrath, L. W., and Goel, M. L. *Political Participation.* 2d ed. Chicago: Rand McNally & Co., 1967.

Mindel, Charles H., and Habenstein, Robert W., eds. *Ethnic Families in America: Patterns and Variations.* New York: Elsevier, 1976.

Moore, Joan. "Situational Factors Affecting Minority Aging." *The Gerontologist* 11 (1971):88–93.

Morgan, A. B. "Differences in Logical Reasoning Associated with Age and Higher Education." *Psychological Reports* 2 (1956):235–240.

Morgan, Edmund S. *The Puritan Family.* New York: Harper & Row, 1964.

Morgan, Kathryn. "Caddy Buffers: Legends of a Middle-Class Negro Family in Philadelphia." *Keystone Folklore Quarterly* 11 (1966):67–88.

Morrison, P. A. "Chronic Movers and the Future Redistribution of Population: A Longitudinal Analysis." Rand, P-4440 (1970).

_____ . "Duration of Residence and Prospective Migration: The Evaluation of a Stochastic Model." *Demography* 4 (1967):553–561.

_____ . "Unresolved Questions about Population Distribution Policy: An Agenda for Further Research." Rand, P-4630 (1971).

Mosher, F. A., and Hornsby, J. R. "On Asking Questions." in J. S. Bruner, R. R. Olver, and P. M. Greenfield et al. (eds.), *Studies in Cognitive Growth.* New York: John Wiley & Sons, 1966.

Mozersky, D. J.; Sumner, D. S.; Hokanson, D. E.; and Strandness, D. E.

"Transcutaneous Measurement of the Elastic Properties of the Human Femoral Artery." *Circulation* 46 (1972):948–955.

Muiesan, G.; Sorbini, C. A.; and Grassi, V. "Respiratory Function in the Aged." *Bulletin of Physio-Pathology Respiration* 7 (1971):973–1007.

Murray, Janet. "Activities and Expenditures of Preretirees." *Social Security Bulletin* Vol. 38, No. 8 (August 1975):5–21.

Myerhoff, Barbara G. "Aging and the Aged in Other Cultures: An Anthropological Perspective." In E. E. Bauwens (ed.), *The Anthropology of Health*. St. Louis: C. V. Mosby Co., 1978.

———. *Number Our Days*. New York: E. P. Dutton & Co., 1978.

———. "A Symbol Perfected in Death: Continuity and Ritual in the Life of an Elderly Jew." In Barbara G. Myerhoff and Andrei Simić (eds.), *Life's Career — Aging: Cultural Variations on Growing Old*. Beverly Hills, Calif.: Sage Publications, 1978.

Myerhoff, Barbara G., and Simić, Andrei. *Life's Career — Aging: Cultural Variations on Growing Old*. Beverly Hills, Calif.: Sage Publications, 1978.

Nagy, Maria H. "The Child's View of Death." In Herman Feifel (ed.), *The Meaning of Death*. New York: McGraw-Hill Book Co., 1959.

Nahemow, L., and Lawton, M. P. "Similarity and Proximity in Friendship Formation." *Journal of Personality and Social Psychology* 32 (1975):205–213.

Nahemow, Nina, and Adams, Bert N. "Old Age Among the Baganda: Continuity and Change." In Jaber F. Gubrium (ed.), *Late Life: Communities and Environmental Policy*. Springfield, Ill.: Charles C. Thomas, 1974.

National Caucus on the Black Aged. *Golden Page* Vol. I–III, No. 2 (1979).

Nesselroade, J. R.; Schaie, K. W.; and Baltes, P. B. "Ontogenetic and Generational Components of Structural and Quantitative Change in Adult Behavior." *Journal of Gerontology* 27 (1972):222–228.

Neugarten, Bernice L. "Age Groups in American Society and the Rise of the Young-Old." *Annals of the American Academy of Political and Social Sciences* 415 (1974):187–198.

———. "The Awareness of Middle Age." In Bernice L. Neugarten (ed.), *Middle Age and Aging*. Chicago: University of Chicago Press, 1968.

Neugarten, Bernice L., and Weinstein, Karol T. "The Changing American Grandparent." *Journal of Marriage and the Family* 26 (1964):199–204.

Newcomb, T. N. *The Acquaintance Process*. New York: Holt, Rinehart, & Winston, 1961.

Newcomb, T. N., and Svehla, G. "Intra-Family Relations in Attitudes." *Sociometry* 1 (1938):180–205.

Newquist, Deborah, and Torres-Gil, Fernando. "Transportation and the Older Mexican-American: Sex Differences in Mobility Patterns and Problems." Andrus Gerontology Center, University of Southern California, Report of the USC Social and Cultural Contexts of Aging Research Project, n.d. (late 1970s).

Nie, N., et al. *The Changing American Voter*. Cambridge, Mass.: Harvard University Press, 1976

Norris-Baker, C., and Willems, E. P. "Environmental Negotiability as a Direct Measurment of Behavior-Environment Relationships: Some Implications for

Theory and Practice." In A. D. Seidel and S. Danford (eds.), *Environmental Design: Research, Theory, and Application.* Washington, D.C.: Environmental Design Research Association, 1979.

Novak, Michael. "Probing the New Ethnicity." In Joseph Ryan (ed.), *White Ethnics: Their Life in Working Class America.* Englewood Cliffs, N.J.: Prentice-Hall, 1974.

———. *The Rise of the Unmeltable Ethnics.* New York: Macmillan, 1972.

"Now the Revolt of the Old." *Time,* October 10, 1977, p. 18.

Oden, Thomas C. "Intimacy: A Definition." In E. S. Morrison and V. Borosage (eds.), *Human Sexuality: A Contemporary Perspective.* 2d ed. Palo Alto, Calif.: Mayfield Publishing Co., 1977.

Olson, M., Jr. *The Logic of Collective Action.* Cambridge, Mass.: Harvard University Press, 1965.

Osness, W. H. "Aging Now and in the Future: A Physiological Perspective." *Journal of Social Welfare* Vol. 5, No. 1 (1978):15–23.

———. "Cardiac Rehabilitation Through Exercise for Older Americans." *Gerontology Review* Vol. 1, No. 5 (1978):1–2.

Owens, W. A. "Age and Mental Abilities: A Longitudinal Study." *Genetic Psychological Monographs* 48 (1953):3–54.

———. "Age and Mental Ability: A Second Adult Follow-Up." *Journal of Educational Psychology* 57 (1966):311–325.

Palmore, E. "Facts on Aging: A Short Quiz." *The Gerontologist* 17 (1977):315–320.

———. "The Future Status of the Aged." *The Gerontologist* Vol. 17, No. 1 (February 1977):23.

———. *The Honorable Elders.* Durham, N.C.: Duke University Press, 1975.

Palmore, E., and Kivett, V. "Change in Life Satisfaction: A Longitudinal Study of Persons Aged 46–70." *Journal of Gerontology* 32 (1977):311–316.

Palmore, E., and Luikart, L. "Health and Social Factors Related to Life Satisfaction." *Journal of Health and Social Behavior* 13 (1972):185–200.

Papalia, D. E. "The Status of Several Conservation Abilities Across the Life-Span." *Human Development* 15 (1972):229–243.

Papalia, D. E.; Kennedy, E.; and Sheehan, N. "Conservation of Space in Noninstitutionalized Old People." *Journal of Psychology* 84 (1973):75–79.

Papalia, D. E.; Salverson, S. M.; and True, M. "An Evaluation of Quantity Conservation Performance During Old Age." *Aging and Human Development* 4 (1973): 103–109.

Parsons, Talcott. "Some Theoretical Considerations on the Nature and Trends of Change of Ethnicity." In Nathan Glazer and Daniel P. Moynihan (eds.), *Ethnicity: Theory and Experience.* Cambridge, Mass.: Harvard University Press, 1975.

Pastalan, L. A. "Privacy as an Expression of Human Territoriality." In L. A. Pastalan and D. H. Carson (eds.), *Spatial Behavior of Older People.* Ann Arbor: University of Michigan Press, 1970.

———. "Research in Environment and Aging: An Alternative to Theory." In P. G. Windley, T. O. Byerts, and F. G. Ernst (eds.), *Theory Development in Environment and Aging.* Washington, D.C.: Gerontological Society, 1975.

Pati, C., and Jacobs, R. C. "Mandatory Retirement at 70: Separating Substance from Politics." *The Personnel Administrator* 24 (February 1979):19–25.

Patterson, A. H. "Territorial Behavior and Fear of Crime in the Elderly." *Environmental Psychology and Nonverbal Behavior* 2 (1978):131–144.

Patterson, A. H., and Pollack, L. M. "Territoriality and Fear of Crime in Elderly and Non-Elderly Homeowners." Paper presented at the Annual Meeting of the American Psychological Association, Toronto, 1978.

Pattison, E. Mansell. "The Living-Dying Process." In Charles A. Garfield (ed.), *Psychosocial Care of the Dying Patient.* New York: McGraw-Hill Book Co., 1978.

Pearl, R., and Pearl, R. D. *The Ancestry of the Long-Lived.* Baltimore, Md.: Johns Hopkins University Press, 1934.

"Pension Plans Have Shaky Future." *Futurist* 11 (1977):251–253.

Peters, George R. "Interagency Relations and the Aging Network: A Study of the State Unit on Aging and the Area Agencies on Aging in Kansas." Paper presented at the Annual Meeting of the Gerontological Society, 1976.

Pfeiffer, Busse, and Pfeiffer, Eric, (eds.) *Behavior and Adaptation in Late Life.* 2d ed. Boston: Little, Brown & Co., 1977.

Plonk, Martha A., and Pulley, Mary Ann. "Financial Management Practices of Retired Couples." *The Gerontologist* Vol. 17, No. 3 (June 1977):256–561.

Pocs, Ollie, and Godon, Annette G. "Can Students View Parents as Sexual Beings?" *Family Coordinator* 25 (January 1977):31–36.

Pollack, O. "Social Adjustment in Old Age." New York: Social Sciences Research Council, 1948.

Pratt, H. J. "Old Age Associations in National Politics." *Annals of the American Academy of Political and Social Sciences* 415 (1974):106–119.

Press, Irwin, and McCool, Mike. "Social Structure and Status of the Aged: Toward Some Valid Cross-Cultural Generalizations." *Aging and Human Development* 3 (1972):297–306.

Price, John A. "North American Indian Families." In Charles H. Mindel and Robert W. Habenstein (eds.), *Ethnic Families in America: Patterns and Variations.* New York: Elsevier, 1976.

Priest, R. F., and Sawyer, J. "Proximity and Peership: Bases of Balance in Interpersonal Attraction." *American Journal of Sociology* 72 (1967):633–649.

Puner, Morton. *To the Good Long Life: What We Know About Growing Old.* New York: Universe Books, 1974.

Ragan, P., and Davis, W. J. "The Diversity of Older Voters." *Society* 15 (1978).

Rapoport, Amos. "An Approach to the Construction of Man-Environment Theory." In W.F.E. Preseir (ed.), *EDRA Proceedings II.* Stroudsburg, Pa.: Dowden, Hutchinson and Ross, 1973.

Ravenstein, E. G. "The Laws of Migration." *Journal of the Royal Statistical Society* 48 (1885):167–227.

Redford, S. *Democracy in the Administrative State.* New York: Oxford University Press, 1969.

Rhudick, P. J., and Gordon, C. "The Age Center of New England Study." In L. F. Jarvick, C. Eisdorfer, and J. E. Blum (eds.), *Intellectual Functioning in Adults.* New York: Springer Publishing Co., 1973.

Riegel, K. F. "Ergebnisse und Probleme Der Psychologischen Alternsforschung." Parts I and II. *Vita Humana* 1 (1958):52–64, 204–243.

Riegel, K. F., and Riegel, R. M. "Development, Drop, and Death." *Developmental Psychology* 6 (1972):306–319.

Riley, Matilda W., and Foner, Anne, and Associates. *Aging and Society: An Inventory of Research Findings.* New York: Russell Sage Foundation, 1968.

Rimoldi, J.G.A., and Woude, K.W.V. "Aging and Problem Solving." *Industrial Gerontology* 8 (1971):68–69.

Risely, T. R. "The Ecology of Applied Behavior Analysis." In A. Rogers-Warren and S. Warren (eds.), *Ecological Perspectives in Behavior Analysis.* Baltimore, Md.: University Park Press, 1977.

Risely, T. R.; Gottula, P.; and Edwards, K. A. "Social Interaction During Family and Institutional Style Meal Service in a Nursing Home." Paper presented at the Nova Behavioral Conference on Aging, Port St. Lucie, Fla., May 1978.

Rivlin, A. M. *Long-Term Care for the Elderly and Disabled.* Washington, D.C.: Congress of the U.S., Congressional Budget Office, 1977.

Roberts, S. "Greying of the Budget Puts U.S. in Bind." *Kansas City Times.* December 30, 1978.

Robertson, A. Haeworth. "Issues in the 1978 Budget." *Brookings, The Brookings Bulletin* Vol. 14, No. 1–2 (1977):3.

———. "OASDI: Fiscal Basis and Long Range Cost Projections." *Social Security Bulletin* Vol. 40, No. 1 (January 1977):20–21.

Robins, S. P.; Shimokomaki, M.; and Bailey, A. J. "The Chemistry of the Collagen Cross-Links. Age-Related Changes in the Reducible Components of Intact Bovine Collagen Fibers." *Biochemistry Journal* 131 (1973):771–780.

Rockstein, M., and Brandt, K. "Changes in Phosphorous Metabolism of the Gastroenemius Muscle in Aging White Rats." *Proceedings of the Society of Experimental Medicine* 107 (1961):377–380.

Rodin, J., and Baum, A. "Crowding and Helplessness: Potential Consequences of Density and Loss of Control." In A. Baum and Y. M. Epstein (eds.), *Human Response to Crowding.* Hillsdale, N.J.: Lawrence Erlbaum, 1978.

Rodin, J., and Langer, E. "Long-term Effects of a Control-Relevant Intervention With the Institutionalized Aged." *Journal of Personality and Social Psychology* 35 (1977):897–902.

Rones, Phillip L. "Jobs With Agencies on Aging." *Occupational Outlook Quarterly* (Fall 1976):31–33.

Rose, A. M. "The Subculture of the Aging: A Framework for Research in Social Gerontology." In A. M. Rose and W. A. Peterson (eds.), *Older People and Their Social World.* Philadelphia, Pa.: F. A. Davis Co., 1965.

———. "The Subculture of the Aging: A Topic of Sociological Research." *The Gerontologist* 2 (1962):123–127.

Rosenfeld, Anne H. *New Views on Older Lives, A Sample of NIMH Sponsored Research and Service Programs.* Rockville, Md.: National Institute of Mental Health, 1978.

Rosow, I. "Discussion of Amos Rapoport's Paper 'Community and Urban Design.'" In T. O. Byerts (ed.), *Environmental Research and Aging.* Washington, D.C.: Gerontological Society, 1974.

———. *Socialization to Old Age.* Berkeley: University of California Press, 1974.

Ross, Rhonda, P. and Campbell, David E. "A Review of the EDRA Proceedings." In

W. E. Rogers and W. H. Ittelson (eds.), *New Directions in Environmental Design Research*. Washington, D.C.: Environmental Design Research Association, 1978.

Rossi, P. H. *Why Families Move*. New York: Free Press, 1955.

Rowles, Graham D. *Prisoners of Space? Exploring the Geographical Experiences of Older People*. Boulder, Colo.: Westview Press, 1978.

Rubin, K. "Extinction of Conservation: A Life-Span Investigation." *Developmental Psychology* 12 (1976):51–56.

_____. "The Relationship Between Spatial and Communicative Egocentrism in Children and Young and Old Adults." *Journal of Genetic Psychology* 125 (1974): 295–301.

Rubin, K., and Brown, I.D.R. "Life Span Look at Person Perception and Its Relation to Communicative Interaction." *Journal of Gerontology* 30 (1975):461–468.

Rubin, K.; Attewell, P.; Tierney, M.; and Tumolo, P. "The Development of Spatial Egocentrism and Conservation Across the Life-Span." *Developmental Psychology* 9 (1973):432.

Rubinstein, L. J. *Structure and Function of Muscle*. Vol. 2. New York: Academic Press, 1960.

Ryan, E. B., and Capadano, H. L. "Age Perceptions and Evaluative Reactions Toward Speakers." *Journal of Gerontology* 33 (1978):98–102.

Sanders, S.; Laurendeau, M.; and Bergeron, J. "Aging and the Concept of Space: The Conservation of Surfaces." *Journal of Gerontology* 21 (1966):281–285.

Schafer, Donna E., and Wiseman, Robert. "Racial Differences in the Support Networks of Older People." Paper presented at the Thirty-First Annual Meeting of the Gerontological Society, Dallas, 1978.

Schaie, K. W. "A General Model for the Study of Developmental Problems." *Psychological Bulletin* 64 (1965):92–107.

Schaie, K. W.; and Labouvie-Vief, G. F. "Generational Versus Ontogenetic Components of Change in Adult Cognitive Behavior: A Fourteen-Year Cross-Sequential Study." *Developmental Psychology* 10 (1974):305–320.

Schaie, K. W., and Strother, C. R. "A Cross-Sectional Study of Age Changes in Cognitive Behavior." *Psychological Bulletin* 70 (1968):671–680.

Schaie, K. W.; Labouvie-Vief, G. F.; and Buech, B. V. "Generational and Cohort-Specific Differences in Adult Cognitive Functioning: A Fourteen-Year Study of Independent Samples." *Developmental Pscychology* 9 (1973):151–166.

Scheier, M. F.; Carver, C. S.; Schulz, R.; Glass, D. C.; and Katz, I. "Sympathy, Self-Consciousness, and Reactions to the Stigmatized." *Journal of Applied Social Psychology* 8 (1978):270–282.

Schooler, K. K. "Environmental Change and the Elderly." In I. Altman and J. F. Wohlwill (eds.), *Human Behavior and Environment: Advances in Theory and Research*. Vol. 1. New York: Plenum Publishing Corp., 1976.

_____. "Response of the Elderly to Environment: A Stress-Theoretical Perspective." In P. G. Windley, T. O. Byerts, and F. G. Ernst (eds.), *Theory Development in Environment and Aging*. Washington, D.C.: Gerontological Society, 1975.

Schubert, M., and Hamerman, D. *A Primer on Connective Tissue Biochemistry*. Philadelphia, Pa.: Lea & Febiger, 1968.

Schulz, Richard. *The Psychology of Death, Dying, and Bereavement*. Reading, Mass.:

Addison-Wesley Publishing Co., 1978.

Schulz, Richard, and Brenner, G. "Relocation of the Aged: A Review and Theoretical Analysis." *Journal of Gerontology* 32 (1977):323–333.

Schwartz, A. N. "Multi-Purpose Day Centers: A Needed Alternative." *Nursing Homes* 27 (1978):20–24.

———. "Planning Micro-Environments for the Aged." in D. S. Woodruff and J. E. Birren (eds.), *Aging: Scientific Perspectives and Social Issues.* New York: Van Nostrand Reinhold Co., 1975.

Seagull, L. *Youth and Change in American Politics.* New York: New Viewpoints, 1977.

Sedlin, E. D.; Villanueva, A. R.; and Frost, H. M. "Age Variations in the Specific Surface of Howship's Lacunae as an Index of Human Bone Resorption." *Anatomy Record* 146 (1963):201–207.

Seelbach, Wayne C. "Correlates of Aged Parents' Filial Responsibility Expectations and Realizations." *Family Coordinator* 27 (1978):341–350.

SEICUS. *Sexuality and Man.* New York: Charles Scribner's Sons, 1970.

Seligman, M.E.P. *Helplessness: On Depression, Development, and Death.* San Francisco: W. H. Freeman and Co., 1975.

Selzer, S. C., and Denney, N. W. "Conservation Abilities Among Middle-Aged and Elderly Adults." Paper presented at the biennial meeting of the Society for Research in Child Development, New Orleans, March 1977.

Semmens, M. "The Pulmonary Artery in the Normal Aged Lung." *British Journal of Diseases of the Chest* 64 (1972):65–72.

Shaffer, William. "Partisan Loyalty and the Perceptions of Party, Candidates, and Issues." *Western Political Quarterly* 25 (September 1972):424–434.

Shanas, Ethel. "Family-Kin Networks and Aging in Cross-Cultural Perspective." *Journal of Marriage and the Family* 35 (August 1973):505–511.

Shanas, Ethel, et al. *Old People in Three Industrial Societies.* New York: Atherton Press, 1968.

Shelton, Austin J. "The Aged and Eldership Among the Igbo." In Donald O. Cowgill and Lowell D. Holmes (eds.), *Aging and Modernization.* New York: Appleton-Century-Crofts, 1972.

Sheppard, Harold L., and Rix, Sara E. *The Graying of Working America: The Coming Crisis in Reitrement Age Policy.* New York: Free Press, 1977.

Sherman, N. C.; Gold, J. A.; and Sherman, M. F. "Attribution Theory and Evaluations of Older Men Among College Students, Their Parents, and Grandparents." *Personality and Social Psychology Bulletin* 4 (1978):440–442.

Sherman, S. R. "Leisure Activities in Retirement Housing." *Journal of Gerontology* 2? (1974):325–335.

Sherrod, D. R., and Cohen, D. "Density, Personal Control, and Design." In S Kaplan and R. Kaplan (eds.), *Humanscape: Environments for People.* N. Scituate Mass.: Duxbury Press, 1978.

Shneidman, Edwin S. *Deaths of Man.* Baltimore, Md.: Penguin Books, 1974.

Shortman, K., and Palmer, J. "The Requirement for Macrophages in the In Vitro Immune Response." *Cellular Immunology* 2 (1971):399–410.

Siemka, Howard J. "Displacement in Revitalizing Neighborhoods: A Review and Research Strategy." In *Occasional Papers in Housing and Community Affairs.* Vol. ? Washington, D.C.: U.S. Department of Housing and Urban Development, 197?

Silberberg, R., and Silberberg, M. "Male Sex Hormones and Osteoarthrosis in Mice." *Journal of Bone Joint Surgery* 43A (1961):243–248.

Silverman, M. "The Old Man and Woman: Detecting Stereotypes of Aged Men with a Femininity Scale." *Perceptual and Motor Skills* 44 (1977):336–338.

Simić, Andrei. "Aging in the United States and Yugoslavia: Contrasting Models of Intergenerational Relationships." *Anthropological Quarterly* 50 (1977):53–64.

Simmons, Leo. "Aging in Preindustrial Societies." In C. Tibbitts (ed.), *Handbook of Social Gerontology*. Chicago: University of Chicago Press, 1960.

_____ . *The Role of the Aged in Primitive Society*. New Haven, Conn.: Yale University Press, 1945.

Simon, H. A. *Models of Man*. New York: John Wiley & Sons, 1957.

Smith, D. K. "The Einstellung Effect in Relation to the Variables of Age and Training." Ph.D. dissertation, Rutgers–The State University. *Dissertation Abstracts* 27B (1967):4115.

Smith, Stanley H. "The Older Rural Negro." In E. Grant Youmans (ed.), *Older Rural Americans*. Lexington: University of Kentucky Press, 1967.

Sommer, Robert. *Personal Space: The Behavioral Basis of Design*. Englewood Cliffs, N.J.: Prentice-Hall, 1969.

_____ . "Small Group Ecology in Institutions for the Elderly." In L. A. Pastalan and D. H. Carson (eds.), *Spatial Behavior of Older People*. Ann Arbor: University of Michigan Press, 1970.

_____ . *Tight Spaces: Hard Architecture and How to Humanize It*. Englewood Cliffs, N.J.: Prentice-Hall, 1974.

Spangler, P. F.; Edwards, K. A.; and Risely, T. R. "Behavioral Care of Non-Ambulatory Geriatric Patients." Paper presented at the meeting of the Association for the Advancement of Behavior Therapy, Atlanta, Ga., December 1977.

Stanford, R. L. "Services for the Elderly: A Catch-22." *National Journal Reports* 10 (October 1978):1718–1721.

Staples, Robert. "The Black American Family." In Charles H. Mindel and Robert W. Habenstein (eds.), *Ethnic Families in America: Patterns and Variations*. New York: Elsevier, 1976.

_____ . "The Mexican-American Family: Its Modification Over Time and Space." *Phylon* 32 (1971):171–192.

Steinberg, Raymond M. *A Study of Funding Regulations, Program Agreements and Monitoring Procedures Affecting the Implementation of Title III of the Older Americans Act*. A final report submitted to the AoA, 1976.

Steinmetz, Suzanne K. "Battered Parents." *Society* 15 (1978):54–55.

Stevens, Robert B., ed. *Statutory History of the United States: Income Security*. New York: Chelsea House Publishers, 1970.

Storck, P. A.; Looft, W. R.; and Hooper, F. H. "Interrelationships Among Piagetian Tasks and Traditional Measures of Cognitive Abilities in Mature and Aged Adults." *Journal of Gerontology* 27 (1972):462–465.

Streib, Gordon F. "Intergenerational Relations: Perspectives on the Two Generations of the Older Parent." *Journal of Marriage and the Family* 27 (1965):469–476.

_____ . "Old Age and the Family: Facts and Forecasts." *American Behavioral Scientist* 14 (1970):25–39.

———— . "Social Stratification and Aging." In R. H. Binstock and E. Shanas (eds.), *Handbook of Aging and the Social Sciences.* New York: Van Nostrand Reinhold Co., 1976.

Strother, C. R.; Schaie, K. W.; and Horst, P. "The Relationship Between Advanced Age and Mental Abilities." *Journal of Abnormal and Social Psychology* 55 (1957): 166–170.

Sundquist, J. *Dynamics of the Party System.* Washington, D.C.: Brookings Institution, 1973.

Sussman, Marvin B. "The Family Life of Old People." In R. H. Binstock and E. Shanas (eds.), *Handbook of Aging and the Social Sciences.* New York: Van Nostrand Reinhold Co., 1976.

———— . "Relationships of Adult Children with Their Parents in the U.S." In Ethel Shanas and Gordon F. Streib (eds.), *Social Structure and the Family: Generational Relations.* Englewood Cliffs, N.J.: Prentice-Hall, 1965.

Swash, M., and Fox, K. P. "The Effect of Age on Human Skeletal Muscle. Studies of the Morphology and Innervation of Muscle Spindles." *Journal of Neurological Science* 16 (1972):417–432.

Tanner, J. M. *Fetus Into Man.* Cambridge, Mass.: Harvard University Press, 1978.

———— . *Growth at Adolescence.* Oxford, England: Blackwell, 1962.

Tanner, J. M.; Whitehouse, R. H.; and Takaishi, M. "Standards from Birth to Maturity for Height, Weight, Height Velocity and Weight Velocity; British Children, 1965." *Archives of Disease in Childhood* 41 (1966):454–71; 613–35.

Thorson, J. A.; Whatley, L.; and Hancock, K. "Attitudes Toward the Aged as a Function of Age and Education." *The Gerontologist* 14 (1974):316–318.

Tibbitts, Clark. *Handbook of Social Gerontology: Societal Aspects of Aging.* Chicago: University of Chicago Press, 1960.

Tobin, Sheldon S., and Lieberman, Morton A. *Last Home for the Aged.* San Francisco: Jossey-Bass, 1976.

Tomlinson-Keasey, C. "Formal Operations in Females from Eleven to Fifty-Six Years of Age." *Developmental Psychology* 6 (1972):364.

Treas, Judith. "Family Support Systems for the Aged: Some Social and Demographic Considerations." *The Gerontologist* 17 (1977):486–491.

Troll, Lillian E. "The Family of Later Life: A Decade Review." *Journal of Marriage and the Family* 33 (1971):263–290.

Trotter, M.; Broman, G. E.; and Peterson, R. R. "Densities of Bones of White and Negro Skeletons." *Journal of Bone Joint Surgery* 42A (1960):50–58.

Tucek, S., and Gutmann, E. "Choline Acetyltransferase Activity in Muscles of Old Rats." *Experimental Neurology* 38 (1973):349–360.

Tucker, S. M.; Combs, M. E.; and Woolrich, A. M. "Independent Housing for the Elderly: The Human Element in Design." *The Gerontologist* 15 (1975):73–76.

U.S., Congress, Senate, Special Committee on Aging. *Hearings: Training Needs in Gerontology.* Part 1. 93d Cong., 1st sess., 19 June 1973. "Letter from Wayne Vasey, Institute of Gerontology U.M. WSU, Ann Arbor, Michigan."

U.S., Department of Commerce. *The Future of Long-Term Care in the United States— The Report of the Task Force.* DHEW Publication No. (HRP) 00–168741. Washington, D.C.: National Conference on Social Welfare, 1977.

U.S., Department of Commerce. *Statistical Abstracts of the United States, 1977*; *98th Annual Edition*. Washington, D.C.: Bureau of the Census, 1977.

U.S., Department of Health, Education, and Welfare. *AoA Occasional Papers in Gerontology, No. 3, Employment Issues in Agencies on Aging*. DHEW Publication No. (OHD) 79-20079. Washington, D.C.: U.S. Government Printing Office, 1979.

U.S., Department of Health, Education, and Welfare. *Facts About Older Americans, 1976*. DHEW Publication No. (OHD) 77-20006. Washington, D.C.: U.S. Government Printing Office, 1977.

U.S., Department of Health, Education, and Welfare. *Older Americans Act as Amended*. Washington, D.C.: U.S. Government Printing Office, March 1976.

U.S., Department of Health, Education, and Welfare, Health Resources Administration. *Health: United States, 1975*. DHEW Publication No. (HRA) 76-1232. Washington, D.C.: U.S. Government Printing Office, 1976.

U.S., Department of Health, Education , and Welfare, Health Resources Administration. *Working with Older People: A Guide to Practice. I: The Practitioner and the Elderly*. DHEW Publication No. (HRA) 74-3116. Washington, D.C.: U.S. Government Printing Office, 1974.

U.S., Department of Health, Education, and Welfare, Office of Nursing Home Affairs. *How to Select a Nursing Home*. Washington, D.C.: Public Health Service, 1976.

U.S., Department of Housing and Urban Development.*Annual Housing Survey: 1973 Housing Characteristics of Older Americans in the United States*. Washington, D.C.: U.S. Government Printing Office, 1979.

Vincent, Clark E. "Familia Spongia: The Adaptive Function." *Journal of Marriage and the Family* 28 (1966):29-36.

Wagman, I., and Leese, H. "Conduction Velocity of Ulnar Nerves in Human Subjects of Different Ages and Sizes." *Journal of Neurophysiology* 15 (1952):235-244.

Ward, Russell A. "Limitations of the Family as a Supportive Institution in the Lives of the Aged." *Family Coordinator* 27 (1978):365-373.

Warren, R. L. *The Community in America*. 2d ed. Chicago: Rand McNally & Co., 1972.

_____ . "Toward a Non-Utopian Normative Model of the Community." *American Sociological Review* 35 (1970):219-228.

Wass, Hannelore, and Scott, Martha. "Aging Without Death?" *The Gerontologist* Vol. 17, No. 4 (August 1977):377-380.

Watson, W. H. "Institutional Structures of Aging and Dying." In T. O. Byerts (ed.), *Environmental Research and Aging*. Washington, D.C.: Gerontological Society, 1974.

Webber, I., and Osterbind, C. C. "Types of Retirement Villages." In E. W. Burgess (ed.), *Retirement Villages*. Ann Arbor: University of Michigan Press, 1961.

Wechsler, D. *The Measurement and Appraisal of Adult Intelligence*. Baltimore, Md.: Williams & Wilkins Co., 1958.

Weed, Perry L. *The White Ethnic Movement and Ethnic Politics*. New York: Praeger Publishers, 1973.

Weibel, E. R. "Morphometrics of the Lung." In *Handbook of Physiology-Respiration*. Washington, D.C.: American Physiological Society, 1964.

Weinberger, L. E., and Millham, J. "A Multi-Dimensional, Multiple Method Study of Attitudes Toward the Elderly." *Journal of Gerontology* 30 (1975):343–348.

Weisman, Avery D., and Kastenbaum, Robert. *The Psychological Autopsy: A Study of the Terminal Phase of Life.* Community Mental Health Monograph, no. 4. New York: Behavioral Publications, 1968.

Wellin, Edward, and Boyer, Eunice. "Adjustments of Black and White Elderly to the Same Adaptive Niche." *Anthropological Quarterly* 52 (1979):49–60.

Wetherick, N. E. "Changing an Established Concept: A Comparison of the Ability of Young, Middle-Aged and Old Subjects." *Gerontologia* 11 (1965):82–95.

———. "A Comparison of the Problem-Solving Ability of Young, Middle-Aged and Old Subjects." *Gerontologia* 9 (1964):164–178.

Whithead, J. M. *Psychiatric Disorders in Old Age.* Qylesbury, England: Harvey Miller and Metcalf, 1974.

Wilson, R. S. "Concordance in Physical Growth for Monozygotic and Dizygotic Twins." *Annals of Human Biology* 3 (1976):1–10.

Wiseman, R. F. *Spatial Aspects of Aging,* resource paper 78-4. Washington, D.C.: Association of American Geographers, 1979.

———. "National Patterns of Elderly Concentration and Migration." In S. M. Golant (ed.), *The Locational and Environmental Context of the Elderly Population.* New York: Halsted Press, 1979.

———. "Why Do Old People Move: Theoretical Issues." *Research on Aging* 2 (1980), in press.

Wiseman, R. F., and Peterson, Timothy. "Elderly Migration and Independence Maintenance." *East Lakes Geographer* 14 (1979):6–16.

Wiseman, R. F., and Roseman, C. C. "A Typology of Elderly Migration Based on the Decision-Making Process." *Economic Geography* 55 (1979):324–337.

Woehrer, Carol E. "Cultural Pluralism in American Families: The Influence of Ethnicity on Social Aspects of Aging." *Family Coordinator* 27 (1978):329–339.

Wolpert, J. "Behavioral Aspects of the Decision to Migrate." *Papers: Regional Science Association* 15 (1965):159–169.

———. "Migration as an Adjustment to Environmental Stress." *Journal of Social Issues* 22 (1966):92–102.

Wood, V. "Age-Appropriate Behavior for Older People." *The Gerontologist* 11 (1971):74–78.

Woodson, Robert. "Hospice Care in Terminal Illness." In Charles A. Garfield (ed.), *Stress and Survival: The Emotional Realities of Life-Threatening Illness.* St. Louis: C. V. Mosby Co., 1979.

Work in America: Report of a Special Task Force to the Secretary of Health, Education and Welfare. Cambridge, Mass.: M.I.T. Press, 1973.

Wortman, C. B., and Brehm, J. W. "Responses to Uncontrollable Outcomes: An Integration of Reactance Theory and the Learned Helplessness Model." in L. Berkowitz (ed.), *Advances in Experimental Social Psychology,* vol. 8. New York: Academic Press, 1975.

Wu, Frances. "Mandarin-Speaking Aged Chinese in the Los Angeles Area." *The Gerontologist* 15 (1975):271–275.

Wyshak, G. "Fertility and Longevity in Twins, Sibs and Parents of Twins." *Social Biology.* 25 (1979).

Yanagisako, Sylvia Junko. "Two Processes of Change in Japanese-American Kinship." *Journal of Anthropological Research* 31 (1975):196–224.

Youmans, E. Grant, ed. *Older Rural Americans.* Lexington: University of Kentucky Press, 1967.

Young, M. L. "Age and Sex Differences in Problem Solving." *Journal of Gerontology* 26 (1971):330–336.

_____ . "Problem-Solving Performance in Two Age Groups." *Journal of Gerontology* 21 (1966):505–509.

Zeisel, J.; Epp, G.; and Demos, S. *Low Rise Housing for Older People: Behavioral Criteria for Design.* Washington, D.C.: Department of Housing and Urban Development, Office of Policy Development and Research, 1977.

Zimmer, A. H., and Sainer, Janet S. "Strengthening the Family as an Informal Support for the Aged: Implications for Social Policy and Planning." Paper presented to the Annual Meeting of the Gerontological Society, November 1978.

Zimmer, A. H.; Gross-Andrew, S.; and Frankfather, D. "Incentives to Families Caring for Disabled Elderly: Research and Demonstration Project to Strengthen the Natural Supports System." Paper presented to the Thirtieth Annual Meeting of the Gerontological Society, November 1977.

Index